Christiar

Christian Faith

Dogmatics in Outline

B. A. Gerrish

WJK WESTMINSTER JOHN KNOX PRESS LOUISVILLE • KENTUCKY

First edition
Published by Westminster John Knox Press
Louisville, Kentucky

15 16 17 18 19 20 21 22 23 24—10 9 8 7 6 5 4 3 2 1

Book design by Drew Stevens
Cover design by Allison Taylor

Library of Congress Cataloging-in-Publication Data

Gerrish, B. A. (Brian Albert), 1931–
Christian faith : dogmatics in outline / B.A. Gerrish. -- First edition.
pages cm
Includes bibliographical references and index.
ISBN 978-0-664-25698-2 (alk. paper)
1. Theology, Doctrinal. 2. Dogma. I. Title.
BT75.3.G47 2015
230--dc23

2014049526

♾ The paper used in this publication meets the minimum requirements of the American National Standard for Information Sciences—Permanence of Paper for Printed Library Materials, ANSI Z39.48-1992.

To my students at the Divinity School
of the University of Chicago
who worked with me through Dogmatics I–III,
1965–1996

Test everything: hold fast what is good.
—The Apostle Paul

Contents

Preface

During my thirty-one years at the University of Chicago, I regularly taught both the history of Christian thought and what I persisted in calling "dogmatics." In the yearlong dogmatics sequence, the class worked through the whole of Calvin's *Institutes* and Schleiermacher's *The Christian Faith,* with only a few minor omissions, on the way to putting together individual constructive statements on the entire range of Christian doctrines. My original plan was to keep busy in retirement by preparing my store of lecture manuscripts and scattered notes for separate publications in historical theology and dogmatic theology, perhaps also for a weightier study of Schleiermacher than I attempted in my little book *A Prince of the Church: Schleiermacher and the Beginnings of Modern Theology*. (I paid my dues to my other favorite theologian in *Grace and Gratitude: The Eucharistic Theology of John Calvin.*) For two reasons, besides the brevity of human life, I decided to condense and combine the materials in a single project based on the blueprint I sketched in *Saving and Secular Faith: An Invitation to Systematic Theology.*

First, although a volume or two on the entire history of Christian thought and a separate study of Schleiermacher might have had some pedagogical value, I could not persuade myself that I had anything fresh to contribute. Besides the contributions of others, I myself had already written widely on the periods for which I could best claim to have furthered the state of the literature: the Reformation and modern Protestantism (with special attention to the relationship between them). In addition to books on Luther, Calvin, and nineteenth-century Reformed theology, I had published the specialized articles on Reformation theology and modern religious thought later collected in *The Old Protestantism and the New, Continuing the Reformation,* and *Thinking with the Church*. For the earlier periods, by contrast, I had not too much but too little to show. My lectures on patristic and medieval thought came from independent reading of primary sources, but only here and there had I been able to say anything fresh about Fathers and schoolmen, and the gaps in my reading would have been embarrassingly obvious.

Second, and more important, to combine my historical and dogmatic interests reflects my understanding of the task of dogmatics, which I take to be *critical transmission* of the Christian heritage. Dogmatic theologians are not like freelance philosophers who, though they may find their inspiration in the history of their discipline, are always able, in principle at least, to begin de novo. One might better compare dogmaticians to relay runners, except that in dogmatics the baton not only changes hands but also may itself be changed—if real dogmatic theology is being done, not *uncritical* transmission. The dogmatic theologian asks what sense may still be made, in our day, of the historic tradition or traditions of the churches; and that, obviously, presupposes a working knowledge of the traditions as well as the present. This is one reason why I retain the name "dogmatics": it expresses the intention to interpret and assess Christian faith as it has been articulated in the dogmas—the authorized beliefs—of the churches and in the thinking of the church theologians who shaped them. But more on this in the introduction.

It may be that to speak of "dogmas" risks compromising the place of dogmatic theology among the various fields of academic study if, as frequently happens, the word is taken to imply that the church claims privileged access to authoritative truths not available for assessment by common human reason and experience. But that is not the understanding of dogma I shall be working with here; and dogmatics, like any other discipline, must naturally be defined from the inside—without undue concern for whatever misunderstandings of its scope and method may come from the outside. The point of dogmatic theology is to *test* the authorized beliefs of the churches, not merely to *propagate* them. Perhaps it remains a drawback of the word "dogma," and therefore of "dogmatics," that—even when their use implies no esoteric pretensions—their cognate is the adjective "dogmatic," which suggests truculence and intransigence. Though the dictionaries do assign to "dogmatic" the meaning simply of being related to dogma, the primary sense is "given to asserting or imposing personal opinions, arrogant, intolerantly authoritative." (I quote from *The Oxford Dictionary and Thesaurus,* American edition, 1996.) If the aim of the dogmatic theologian is to promote understanding, critical reflection, and conversation, a dogmatic attitude in *that* sense is not likely to help, though it may well recruit disciples. But it is excluded in principle from the following chapters.

I take it that, next to showing how the present has arisen out of the past, the task of an outline of dogmatics is to sum up the main options of the present with as impartial a hand as one can, even if, in an outline, a full account and appraisal of them is hardly possible. Clearly, however, one is not doing dogmatics unless a case is argued for the trajectory judged most likely to be fruitful in the future. There is no need to deny that where circumstance has placed the dogmatic theologian in the present is bound to influence the case made. For myself, I admit that some of my initial preferences are suggested by my location in the Reformed or Calvinist tradition, for example, the choice to assign a regulative role to the concepts of covenant and election or to conclude with the Calvinist watchword—in its way, a perfect summary of dogmatics—that the end of the world is the manifestation of God's glory. Still it is Christian, not Reformed, dogmatics that I am attempting to do; whether a Reformed perspective, as one among others, can help to further the larger task is not to be presupposed but judged by the criteria to which the discipline of dogmatics must answer. This, too, is more fully discussed in the introduction.

I should perhaps add that others, whether approvingly or scornfully, have called me a "liberal," whereas I have always considered myself an "evangelical" in the old, Reformation sense: one who holds that "the real treasure of the church is the sacred gospel of the glory and grace of God" (as Luther said in his Ninety-five Theses). But the word *evangelical* has come to mean something other than it meant to the Protestant Reformers: nowadays, it usually identifies a party within Protestantism. Party badges such as "liberal," "conservative," "evangelical," "postliberal," and "postmodern" may have some limited use in theological typology. But over time they tend to become more misleading than helpful; adopted as substitutes for careful distinctions, they may even come to serve the abuses of complacency and disparagement of others. They are avoided in the pages that follow. But I see no reason to abandon "evangelical" in the Reformation sense.

Another prefatory word should be offered on the style I have striven for. Dogmatics, as I understand it, is not preaching. It should not emulate the rhetoric of the pulpit, even if, as I believe, it should be tested in the pulpit. (Many of the themes treated here have their homiletic counterparts in the collection of my sermons ably edited by Mary Stimming, *The Pilgrim Road*.) Neither do the aims of dogmatics fit the style appropriate to history or philosophy. Good history is an art as well as a science: it is a story told with narrative verve and color. Philosophy of religion is also an art, only with different rules: it is the art of laying out detailed, painstaking arguments. An outline of dogmatics must often sacrifice color and detail to usefulness. It is intended to open up reflection and conversation, not to beguile the reader or to provide full and definitive arguments on every question that may arise. I am painfully aware that each topic touched on in this book could be, and already has been, the subject of a book to itself—or of many books. But I have stuck to the concept of an outline, and I cannot think of a better ideal for a dogmatic outline than the style John Calvin adopted for exegesis in his commentaries: "perspicuous brevity" (although he knew well that brevity, in itself, runs the risk of obscurity). Hence I have begun each chapter with a thesis that is intended to sum up the essence of the explication that follows; and the explication itself also aims at perspicuous brevity as far as the limits of an outline and the subject matter of the item under discussion will permit. Readers will judge for themselves how well I have succeeded. From the thesis they will gain a sense of where a chapter is headed, and they will no doubt refer back to it after going through the chapter to which it belongs. To display the connection between one thesis and another, I have brought them all together in the appendix.

Naturally, I hope that my outline makes a contribution to the disciplines of historical theology and dogmatic theology. But the ideal of perspicuous brevity persuaded me to keep the needs of students and Christian educators in mind and to leave the chapters that follow uncluttered by the surfeit of distracting footnotes or endnotes that the academy looks for. Occasionally, a substantive footnote is needed, and the reader expects to be told the source of quotations and allusions made. However, instead of detailed footnotes for every work cited, I have used abbreviated references parenthetically within the text, wherever feasible, and in the bibliography for each chapter I have included literature cited in the chapter itself simply by authors' names (with or without dates or book titles). I also decided to begin each section of the bibliography with the readings from Calvin and Schleiermacher that guided my classes through the yearlong dogmatics sequence at the University of Chicago Divinity School. My references for foreign-language authors, including Calvin and Schleiermacher, are (where possible) to readily available English translations, but they have been checked against the originals.

It is self-evident that as texts to accompany a class in a systematic discipline it is better to take one or two whole works rather than gathering numerous selections. My case for the two guides I have chosen was to juxtapose a classical and a modern dogmatic system (though I dare say my predilections had something to do with it). I was myself initially surprised to discover how readily, though not perfectly, the respective frameworks of Calvin's *Institutes* and Schleiermacher's *The Christian Faith* lend themselves to thematic comparison. Of course there was, and is, no intention to exclude other theological resources (also noted in the bibliography). But the reader may find, as we did, that the comparison of Calvin and Schleiermacher can initiate a lively and fruitful conversation, wherever the conversation may lead next. I hope that this volume may alert readers to the host of insights still to be learned from these two great doctors of the church, who have both suffered from ill-informed criticisms. With this in mind, I let Calvin and Schleiermacher figure prominently in the historical observations with which, as a rule, the chapters in parts I and II begin, after the review of scriptural foundations but before moving on to the constructive proposals epitomized in my theses. The constructive proposals could, I suppose, be read without the historical preambles, or the historical sketches without the constructive conclusions. But it will be obvious that to my mind they belong together.

The book is dedicated to my former students, who have contributed more to it, perhaps, than they realize. Some of them have never given up inquiring when it would be published. I am grateful to them for their patience and continued interest. I also owe a debt of gratitude to three friends and colleagues (a Catholic, a Lutheran, and a Presbyterian) who commented on my manuscript: John O'Malley, Matthew Becker, and George Stroup. It goes without saying that none of them will agree with all my theological opinions, even now that I have made changes in response to their questions and criticisms. In addition, I am indebted to my scientist son-in-law, Timothy Starn, who cast a critical eye on my account of the relationship between theology and science, and to my wife, Dawn DeVries, for her unfailing support in some difficult times.

Abbreviations

ACW — *Ancient Christian Writers: The Works of the Fathers in Translation.* Ed. Johannes Quasten et al. Westminster, MD: Newman, 1946–.

ANF — Ante-Nicene Fathers. Ed. Alexander Roberts and James Donaldson. Rev. ed. A. Cleveland Coxe. 10 vols. Reprint, Grand Rapids: Eerdmans, 1950–57.

BC — *The Book of Concord: The Confessions of the Evangelical Lutheran Church.* Trans. and ed. Theodore G. Tappert et al. Philadelphia: Fortress, 1959.

CC — *Creeds of Christendom.* Ed. Philip Schaff. 3 vols. (1877). Reprint, Grand Rapids: Baker, 1966.

CD — Karl Barth, *Church Dogmatics*. Trans. and ed. G. W. Bromiley et al. 4 vols. in 13, plus index volume. Edinburgh: T. & T. Clark, 1936–77. Cited by volume/part, section (§), and (as needed) subsection, followed in parentheses by page numbers. In the main body of a chapter, cited by volume/part and page number only.

CF — Friedrich Schleiermacher, *The Christian Faith.* Ed. H. R. Mackintosh and J. S. Stewart. Trans. Mackintosh et al. Edinburgh: T. & T. Clark (1928). Reprint, 1999. Cited by section (§) and (where needed) subsection, followed in parentheses by page numbers. I have abbreviated Schleiermacher's addendum (*Zusatz*) to a section as "ps.," following "postscript" in the English version. In the main body of a chapter, usually cited by page number only. I have occasionally made slight alterations to the English translation.

CG — Friedrich Schleiermacher, *Der christliche Glaube nach den Grundsätzen der evangelischen Kirche im Zusammenhange dargestellt.* 2nd ed. Berlin: Reimer, 1830–31. Critical edition in Schleiermacher, *Kritische Gesamtausgabe.* I,13/1–2. Ed. Rolf Schäfer. 2 vols. Berlin: de Gruyter, 2003.

CO — *Ioannis Calvini opera quae supersunt omnia*. Ed. Wilhelm Baum, Eduard Cunitz, and Eduard Reuss. 59 vols. *Corpus Reformatorum,* vols. 29–87. Brunswick: C. A. Schwetschke & Son (M. Bruhn), 1863–1900. Cited by volume and column (or page).

Comm. — John Calvin's biblical commentaries. Cited by biblical text. My quotations from the commentaries follow the complete English versions of the Calvin Translation Society (Edinburgh, 1844–56). Reprinted as *Calvin's Commentaries.* 22 vols. Grand Rapids: Baker, 1981.

CT — *The Church Teaches: Documents of the Church in English Translation.* Trans. John F. Clarkson et al. St. Louis: Herder, 1955.

DS — Henry Denzinger. *The Sources of Catholic Dogma.* Trans. of Denzinger's *Enchiridion symbolorum*, 30th ed., by Roy J. Deferrari. St. Louis: Herder, 1957.

DV — *The Documents of Vatican II.* Ed. Walter M. Abbott. New York: Herder, 1966.

FC — *The Fathers of the Church.* Ed. R. J. Deferrari. Washington, D.C.: Catholic University Press, 1947–.

GD — Karl Barth, *The Göttingen Dogmatics: Instruction in the Christian Religion*. Vol. 1. Ed. Hannelotte Reiffen. Trans. of Barth, *Unterricht in der christlichen Religion* (3 vols., *Karl Barth: Gesamtausgabe*, vols. 17, 20, 38), vol. 1, §§1–18, by Geoffrey W. Bromiley. Grand Rapids: Eerdmans, 1991.

Institutes — John Calvin, *Institutio Christianae religionis.* Cited in the definitive 1559 edition by book, chapter, and (where needed) section, followed in parentheses by the corresponding pages in the standard English translation: *Institutes of the Christian Religion.* Ed. John T. McNeill. Trans. Ford Lewis Battles. 2 vols. LCC 20–21. London: SCM; Philadelphia: Westminster, 1960. In the main body of a chapter, usually cited only by volume and page in the English version. I have occasionally made slight alterations to the English translation or cited the translation by Henry Beveridge, 2 vols. Reprint, Grand Rapids: Eerdmans, 1957 (noted as Beveridge). The Latin is available in OS 3–5.

JR — *Journal of Religion.*

KJV — King James Version of the Holy Bible (Authorised Version), 1611, 1769.

LCC — Library of Christian Classics. Ed. John Baillie et al. 26 vols. London: SCM; Philadelphia: Westminster, 1953–66.

LW — Luther's Works (American Edition). Ed. Jaroslav Pelikan and Helmut T. Lehmann. 55 vols. St. Louis: Concordia; Philadelphia: Fortress, 1955–86.

LWZ — *The Latin Works and Correspondence of Huldreich Zwingli.* Trans. and ed. Samuel Macauley Jackson et al. 3 vols. Vol. 1, New York: Putnam's Sons, 1912. Vols. 2–3, Philadelphia: Heidelberg, 1922–29.

MPL — J. P. Migne, ed. *Patrologiae cursus completus, Series Latina.* 221 vols. Paris, 1844–1900.

NOAB — *The New Oxford Annotated Bible, with the Apocryphal / Deuterocanonical Books: New Revised Standard Version*. Ed. Bruce M. Metzger and Roland E. Murphy. New York: Oxford University Press, 1991.

NPNF[1]	*Nicene and Post-Nicene Fathers,* First Series. Ed. Philip Schaff. 14 vols. (1886–90). Reprint, Peabody, MA: Hendrickson, 1994.
NPNF[2]	*Nicene and Post-Nicene Fathers,* Second Series. Ed. Philip Schaff and Henry Wace. 14 vols. (1890). Reprint, Peabody, MA: Hendrickson, 1994.
NRSV	New Revised Standard Version of the Bible.
OS	*Joannis Calvini opera selecta.* Ed. Peter Barth, Wilhelm Niesel, and Doris Scheuner. 5 vols. Munich: Chr. Kaiser, 1926–52.
RSV	Revised Standard Version of the Bible.
ST	Thomas Aquinas, *Summa theologiae* (or *Summa theologica*). Cited by part, question, article, and (where needed) objection (obj.) or reply (ad.), followed in parentheses by volume and page numbers in the American edition: *Summa Theologica* (First Complete American Edition). 3 vols. Trans. Fathers of the English Dominican Province. New York: Benziger, 1947. In the main body of a chapter usually cited by volume and page only.
SWC	*Selected Works of John Calvin: Tracts and Letters.* Trans. Henry Beveridge et al. 7 vols. Reprint, Grand Rapids: Baker, 1983. The letters (trans. David Constable and Marcus Robert Gilchrist) are in vols. 4–7.
SWZ	*Ulrich Zwingli (1484–1531): Selected Works* [1901]. Ed. Samuel Macauley Jackson. Trans. Lawrence A. McLouth, Henry Preble, and George W. Gilmour. Reprint, Philadelphia: University of Pennsylvania Press, 1972.
TT	*Calvin's Tracts and Treatises.* Trans. Henry Beveridge. 3 vols. Edinburgh, 1844–51. Included in SWC, vols. 1–3.
WA	*D. Martin Luthers Werke: Kritische Gesamtausgabe* (Weimarer Ausgabe), 1883–.
ZSW	*Huldreich Zwinglis sämtliche Werke.* Ed. Emil Egli et al. Corpus Reformatorum 88–101. 14 vols. Berlin: Schwetschke, 1905–56. The early volumes were reprinted and the series resumed in 1984 by Theologischer Verlag, Zurich.

INTRODUCTION
Dogmatics as a Field of Inquiry

1. Subject Matter of Dogmatics

Christian dogmatics, as a part of Christian theology, has for its subject matter the distinctively Christian way of having faith, in which elemental faith is confirmed, specified, and represented as filial trust in God the Father of Jesus Christ.

The Greek word *theologia* ("theology") is older than Christianity, but it is not to be found in the Greek New Testament.[1] The second-century Apologists, sometimes regarded as the first Christian theologians, took more readily to the term *philosophia* ("philosophy"), which does occur once in the New Testament—in the pejorative sense of "sophistry" (Col. 2:8). Justin Martyr (ca. 100–ca. 165) continued to wear his philosopher's cloak after he embraced Christianity: he thought of himself as a Christian philosopher. But "theology" became the accepted term for Christian reflection and discourse on God, and the number of Christian "theologians" was taken to include the biblical writers themselves, preeminently the author of the Fourth Gospel. By drawing attention to the theological motives of the individual authors or compilers of the New Testament books, modern biblical scholarship—in particular, redaction criticism of the Gospels—confirms the justice of finding the church's first theologians already in the Scriptures. Old Testament scholars have made a similar case for the individual sources of the Pentateuch. Gerhard von Rad identified J (the so-called Yahwist source) as the first major Hebrew theologian.

In the Old and New Testaments theological reflection remained unsystematic—even in Paul's Letter to the Romans, in which a limited pattern of sorts becomes visible. A more orderly and extensive presentation of Christian theology appeared in the third century in Origen of Alexandria's (ca. 185–ca. 254) *On First Principles.* However, "theology" as the name for a comprehensive science of matters that relate to God established itself only with the growth of the medieval universities, in which theology took its place as one discipline among others—and supposedly their "queen." Even then other names were used, such as *sacra pagina* ("the sacred page," i.e., interpretation of Scripture) and *doctrina fidei* ("the doctrine of faith").

1. In some manuscripts, the author of the Revelation to John is called "John the *theologos*" (KJV "St. John the Divine").

I. From Sacred Doctrine to the Science of Faith

Thomas Aquinas (1225–74), the most eminent of the medieval schoolmen, distinguished the theology that pertains to sacred doctrine from the theology that is part of philosophy. The science of sacred doctrine is called "theology," he explains, because its concern is with God and with other things only insofar as they relate to God; and it differs from philosophical theology in that it views everything under the single aspect of revelation. Why, then, did Thomas proceed in his summary of sacred doctrine, the *Summa theologiae* (or *Summa theologica*), to offer five rational proofs for the existence of God, which surely belong to the domain of philosophy? We may let his procedure pose for us the general question, Where should *any* system of theology begin, including our own?

1. Sacred Doctrine and What Everyone Calls "God"

Thomas decided to launch his *Summa theologiae* not with the articles of faith, but with what he called a "preamble" to the articles of faith: a demonstration that God exists. "For faith presupposes natural knowledge, even as grace presupposes nature, and perfection supposes something that can be perfected" (*ST* 1:12). Thomas's "five ways" infer the existence of God from God's effects, which are open to sense experience. Why he chose to present the proofs before dealing with the proper concern of sacred doctrine—the revealed knowledge of God—has been debated. The objection has been made that his proofs start Thomas off on the wrong foot, because they are at odds with Blaise Pascal's (1623–62) famous *Memorial*, the record of his religious experience of 23 November 1654, found in the lining of his coat after his death: "God of Abraham, God of Isaac, God of Jacob, not of the philosophers and the learned . . . God of Jesus Christ." Why speak in sacred theology about God as first mover, first efficient cause, a necessary being, and so on? I offer a suggestion that cannot pretend to lay the problem to rest but will contribute to the direction in which I propose to take the dogmatic project.

The proofs might better be understood not as intruding an alternative to the biblical God, but rather as seeking to get back to a more elemental idea of God presupposed by biblical faith. The idea is generally recognizable, for each of the proofs, though couched in philosophical language, concludes with some such assertion as: "And this is what everyone calls 'God.'" For example, everyone understands that by "God" we mean a "being having of itself its own necessity, and not receiving it from another." In this general idea of God Thomas does not have the full Christian belief in God; it is *not yet* the distinctively Christian God he is describing. Rather, he has offered a provisional and generally accessible notion of God such as one must suppose to underlie Christian faith in the God of revelation. He thinks that "to know that God exists in a general and confused way is implanted in us by nature." The proofs of God's existence, whether or not they succeed as proofs, serve to articulate this natural knowledge for those who have the aptitude to follow them. But they do not give us the full Christian idea of God. For "to know that someone is approaching is not the same as to know that Peter is approaching, even though it is Peter who is approaching" (*ST* 1:12).

There is no need, for our purposes, to distinguish Thomas's five ways any further, or to assess their cogency as philosophical arguments. Our interest is in the initial methodological move they may be said to propose for the project of sacred doctrine or Christian dogmatics. It needs to be shown next that the principle, "Faith presupposes natural knowledge, even as grace presupposes nature," underlies, in effect if not in name, the choice of a starting point in the Protestant dogmatic works of John Calvin (1509–64) and Friedrich Schleiermacher (1768–1834): the definitive edition of Calvin's *Institutes of the Christian Religion* (1559) and the second, revised edition of Schleiermacher's *The Christian Faith* (1830–31). We will then be in a position to see how the Thomist principle might be retrieved and adapted to launch our own dogmatic project.

2. *The Sum of Piety and the Innate Sense of God*

Calvin's theme is the knowledge of God. But it is a knowledge that engages the heart. Where there is no religion or piety, we cannot say that God is known. Accordingly, the 1559 *Institutes* begins with what we might describe as an introduction, partly borrowed from the Roman philosopher Cicero (106–43 BCE), on the concept of piety—or on religion, the outward expression of the pious disposition. Calvin argues that a sense of divinity, or awareness of God, is *engraved* on every human heart; it is what distinguishes humans from mere animals. Even idolatry attests its presence, as does the panic fear that calls on God in a life-threatening crisis. Calvin can also employ a metaphor from farming to describe this sense of divinity: it is the *seed* of religion. In a world overflowing with inestimable divine riches, the seed ought to grow naturally into genuine piety. But it doesn't. It is either suppressed or corrupted. The *sparks* (another metaphor!) are put out, or else the sense of divinity issues in idolatry, denial of God's concern for the world, craven terror instead of reverence, or superstition.

What is the theological point of this introduction to Calvin's *Institutes*? We will not ask, for now, about the content of his natural religion, or about whatever persuasiveness it may have, if any, for philosophers and historians of religion. The question is what function he assigns to it as the first move in his theological project. It may appear that the sole purpose of Calvin's natural history of religion (if we may call it such) is to establish the guilt of all humanity in sin, because scarcely one person in a hundred cultivates the seed, and in none at all does it naturally mature or bear fruit. Calvin takes a Ciceronian natural theology and puts it to a Pauline use. Paul wrote: "What can be known about God is plain to them [humans, who suppress the truth]. . . . So they are without excuse" (Rom. 1:19–20). The door is firmly closed against any natural ascent to sound knowledge of God, and another door is opened to God's self-revelation. Is there, then, no parallel in Calvin's prolegomena to the Thomist principle that faith presupposes natural knowledge?

It is essential to Calvin's case to insist that the sense of divinity cannot be eradicated; if it ever were, the accusation of human guilt would disappear with it. But there is more. When he turns to the necessity for the added light of God's Word, he compares Scripture to the provision of spectacles for the elderly or for anyone else whose vision is clouded. The Word focuses the otherwise confused knowledge of God in our minds and clearly shows us the true God. I will need to return later (in chap. 9) to the hint that one may think of revelation not as items of supernaturally conveyed information but as divinely improved vision. For now, the point is that the sense of divinity is self-evidently the condition for the possibility of the revelation that brings it to a focus. Faith does presuppose a natural awareness of God, an awareness that gives Calvin his point of departure because it meets one of his principles of good order: that one must always begin with what is better known and not too far removed from common sense. Paul exemplified the principle when he began his address to the Athenians not with Scripture but with nature—with the God who made the world. They were already convinced that there is a deity, but their confused opinion and perverted religion needed to be corrected (Comm. Acts 14:15; 17:24).

The sense of divinity is not evoked at the conclusion to a rational proof of God's existence, a proof on which the knowledge of revelation could, without further ado, be securely built. The interposition of sin requires revelation to be not merely an addition (though that is how Calvin can speak of it), but a corrective (as his simile of the corrective lenses implies). This, to be sure, is not Calvin's only line of thought about revelation; the ambiguity in his presentation is one reason for scholarly disagreement about it. Sometimes he describes humans before the gift of revelation as "blind"; and glasses, one hardly needs to point out, are not prescribed for blindness but for poor vision. Still, in the simile of the spectacles there is a possible line of theological argument that Calvin himself did not fully or consistently exploit. Some of his readers are glad he didn't. Karl Barth (1886–1968) remarked that "Calvin at the end of the discussion in the first chapters of the *Institutes* was perspicacious enough to raise the whole question again, to oppose the Christian knowledge of God dialectically to natural knowledge, and to proceed as though there were only the former." In Barth's eyes, the very title of Calvin's work, *Institutio Christianae religionis*—"instruction in the Christian *religion*"—was not above suspicion.

Calvin might seem to have given comfort to those who want theology to be about human religiousness. But Calvin himself was exonerated by Barth, who borrowed Calvin's title for his own Göttingen lectures on dogmatics. The adversary was not Calvin, but Friedrich Schleiermacher and his friends.[2]

3. *Piety and the Science of Christian Faith*

In Schleiermacher's *The Christian Faith*, as in Calvin's *Institutes*, attention is focused first of all on "piety." Before turning directly to explication of Christian doctrines, he proposes what he calls a "placement" of Christianity among the various forms of the religious consciousness. This requires him, first, to state the essence of piety, then to indicate the distinctive nature of Christianity. He maintains that the essence of *piety* is the feeling of absolute dependence: "the consciousness of being absolutely dependent, or, which is the same thing, of being in relation with God" (*CF* 12). The equivalence of "being absolutely dependent" and "being in relation with God" gives him what he takes to be

2. Karl Barth, *GD* 8–10, 92, 182. Calvin's theological masterpiece is usually referred to as his *Institutes* (as though the word were plural), which obscures the meaning of the Latin *institutio* (singular), "instruction." I come back to Barth's critique of Schleiermacher's conception of dogmatics in chap. 3.

the original signification of the word *God*. God is the "whence" of our existence implicit in our consciousness of absolute dependence, a consciousness accessible, he thinks, to anyone who is capable of a little introspection.

But Schleiermacher's dogmatic treatise is not about the feeling of absolute dependence; his subject matter is the Christian way of having faith, which includes the feeling as one element but is much more. The pious self-consciousness, though in itself constant as the feeling of absolute dependence, is variously present in actual religious communities by reason of its combination with other defining characteristics. What Schleiermacher means is reasonably clear when he defines the essence of *Christianity* in the thesis that introduces §11: "*Christianity is a monotheistic faith, belonging to the teleological type of religion* [i.e., a religion directed to moral ends], *and is essentially distinguished from other such faiths by the fact that in it everything is related to the redemption accomplished by Jesus of Nazareth*" (*CF* 52). The feeling of absolute dependence is present in every religion or faith, but to define the essence of Christian faith requires specifying the differentiae Schleiermacher indicates.

In this way, Schleiermacher invites his readers—future ministers of the gospel, for whom *The Christian Faith* was written—to look within, where being religious ("pious") will disclose itself as a universal phenomenon of human consciousness, including their own; and he holds that the feeling of absolute dependence, once they verify it in themselves, becomes in reflection the elemental idea of God as the source of the feeling. Though he begins there, this is *not yet* what he wants to say about the distinctively Christian idea of God. If one speaks of the feeling of absolute dependence in a system of Christian dogmatics, it can only be by *abstraction* from Christian faith. Christians have religion entirely in their relationship with Christ (*CF* 131–32, 161–62). Only in the order of presentation does Schleiermacher put the feeling of absolute dependence first, to locate Christian faith on a larger map for the sake of unfolding its distinctive nature.

Some have objected that his point of departure misconstrues Christian faith at the outset by imposing on it a generic concept of religion, viewing Christianity as one religion among others. Emil Brunner (1889–1966), for example, denied that Christianity is one of the world's religions, since Christian faith stands on the unique revelation of God in Christ. The objection seems to overlook Schleiermacher's express assertion that the introduction to *The Christian Faith* takes up the concept of religion as an *abstraction* from Christian faith, although verifiable simply by introspection. Accordingly, a more proper line of criticism would need to demonstrate that Christians do not, in fact, have a feeling of absolute dependence on God. Other critics of Schleiermacher have charged the exact opposite: that his "feeling of absolute dependence" was not merely Christian but Calvinist. In that case, we would have to say that he did not impose a generic concept of religion on Christianity but imposed his Christianity, and even his Calvinism, on his generic concept of religion. That, however, is a question we can leave to the history-of- religions department. My intention is not to defend Schleiermacher's starting point but to explore the formal principle on which Thomas and Calvin would agree with him: that the dogmatic theologian should look for a starting point, whatever it may be, in an elemental concept that may serve the explication of distinctively Christian faith.

There is no necessity here to trace the steps by which Schleiermacher arrived at his definition of the distinctively Christian way of having faith or to compare his approach and terms in detail with what we have found in Thomas and Calvin. Our concern is with the methodological procedure that required him to begin *The Christian Faith*, as Calvin began his *Institutes*, with an analysis of piety or being religious. There are obvious differences from Calvin, even more obvious differences from Thomas Aquinas. Yet each of them began from an elemental and supposedly accessible point of departure: what everyone calls "God" (Thomas), an indisputably universal human awareness of God (Calvin), or a readily verified feeling of absolute dependence that can only be construed as being in relation with God (Schleiermacher). Is it possible for us to adopt the formal methodological principle they shared—without being obliged to accept the content any one of them assigned to his starting point?

II. Elemental Faith, Religious Faith, Christian Faith

Christian dogmatics may take more than one suitable form. Practitioners of the discipline must specify their own approach, defend it as best they can, and show why they decline to follow other options. In the end, their endeavor can be justified only by their execution of it—piece by piece and as a whole. But where are they to begin? Obviously, they must state at the outset what they are talking about, the subject matter of dogmatics, and they should do so in a manner that is in principle open and accessible to critical scrutiny. The following paragraphs are not simply a neutral description of Christian dogmatics (in all its variations, past and present, that would hardly be possible), but they are not an arbitrary prescription either. In form, if not in content, they follow a classical option. The intention is to modify and extend the trajectory we have traced from Thomas, through Calvin, to Schleiermacher. In the way in which they launch their respective dogmatic projects, Calvin and Schleiermacher both provide models exemplifying (in effect) the Thomist principle that grace presupposes nature. But in place of Calvin's "sense of divinity" and Schleiermacher's "feeling of absolute dependence," our own point of departure will be what I call "elemental faith."

1. Elemental Faith

The subject matter of theological studies, and therefore of dogmatic theology, is the distinctively Christian way of having faith, conveyed in Scripture in the primary language of symbols, metaphors, similes, and allegories; stories, including myths, legends, biographies, parables, folktales, and fables (such as the Tale of the Trees in Judg. 9:8–15); personal letters and erotic lyrics; legal codes, ritual prescriptions, liturgies; hymns, prayers, poetry, confessions of faith; prophecies, visions, apocalypses; proverbs; and the distinctively Christian literary genre of "Gospel." Christian *faith* begins from the revelation of God in Jesus Christ, and at the operational level—knowing when and how to use it—the primary language works to express, communicate, and nurture faith in Christ within the believing community. But Christian *dogmatics*, as critical reflection on the primary language and the church dogmas in which it is articulated, begins with concepts and assertions that are generally recognized, or can readily be shown, as at least significant; and by "generally" I mean, borrowing one of Calvin's expressions (*Institutes*, 1:59), common to strangers as well as the household of God. If we say, then, that the subject matter of dogmatics is the Christian way of having faith, the natural point of departure will be for us to state, at the outset, what we mean by "faith," thinking back from the concrete utterances of discourse within the Christian community until the basic term *faith* can be assigned a public meaning. Such a concept can properly be called an "abstraction" from Christian faith—*not yet* an adequate account of how Christians have faith.

The English words *faith* and *belief* encompass a range of meanings. Usually, they are not sharply differentiated, and it is commonly assumed that faith is *belief without proof.* The assumption is not necessarily hostile. Thomas Aquinas points out that if there were proof for what is proposed to us for our belief, our minds would be *obliged* to yield assent and there would be no merit in believing, which can only be an act of free will. If we ask what, according to Thomas, are the things we ought to believe, and why we ought to believe them, his answer is twofold: that we must give explicit assent to the main articles of faith set forth in the creeds by authority of the church, and that we must be ready to accept, by implicit faith, whatever else is contained in Scripture or may be proposed for our belief by those whose business it is to instruct us. Thomas thought that there is a *motive* to believe even without sufficient *reason*. Thomist faith was belief that rested not on proof but on the authority of the church, to which the Christian ought to submit. This, however, was the understanding of faith that was scorned by the freethinkers of the Enlightenment. For them, the wise always proportion their belief to the evidence, and they will be especially cautious when the purported evidence comes to them secondhand from ecclesiastical authority, which is likely to be tainted with clerical self-interest. From this enlightened principle springs the customary opposition between faith and reason.

There is, however, one kind of faith that is justified not by demonstration but by the recognition that we cannot do without it. I mean the elemental faith that underlies all human activity: confidence in the intelligibility of the world we experience and of our own existence in it. We encounter our environment as order, not (impossibly!) as chaos. Without this confidence, not only religion but also the entire enterprise of science and learning and, quite simply, living and being human would collapse. As a rule, it is tacitly presupposed rather than explicitly affirmed; and many of those who do affirm it might not wish to acknowledge its status as faith. In its very essence it is a confidence that can only be exhibited or elicited, not proved; and it has the further characteristic that its validity cannot be *dis*proved either, since every argument against it presupposes what it intends to disprove—the rational structure of experience. The correlate of this elemental faith is the order, meaning, or reasonableness—in short, the *logos*—that the experienced world actually has, and the Christian theologian will add that there we have the elemental concept of God. But elemental faith, so understood, is not peculiarly Christian, or even peculiarly religious. Much less is it contrary to reason. It is the faith on which the exercise of reason, tacitly or explicitly, always rests. And its opposite is neither unbelief nor heresy, but the despair of nihilism and meaninglessness.

The concept of elemental faith will occupy us further when we come to the supposed conflict between science and religion and the nature of estrangement and reconciliation. In their elemental faith, the natural scientist and the theologian start from common ground. But elemental faith, though in thought it appears inevitable, in everyday existence is constantly threatened, and the gospel is addressed precisely to the predicament of elemental faith under siege. Two observations should be added at this stage that will play their part in shaping these later discussions.

First, the fact that elemental faith is always latent but seldom made the object of reflection suggests that a distinction might usefully be made between faith itself and the belief in which it comes to expression. There is at least the hint of a difference in English between "faith" and "belief." It seems natural to say I have *faith in* someone (rather than "belief in") and to affirm my *belief that* something is the case (rather than "faith that"). At any rate, it makes good sense to think of elemental faith as our way of being in the world—experiencing our environment as order, accessible to reason—and to regard the belief that the world is ordered as bringing this faith to reflection and articulation.

Second, the order perceived by elemental faith is in part moral. Insofar as our environment is not only natural but also social, we construe it as laying moral obligations on us that call for obedience. Our species habitually assumes, or implies, or asserts that there are things we ought to do as fellow humans, and things we ought not to do. It does not follow that we agree on which things are which. There may be universal moral principles; that is open to argument. But there is no denying that one characteristic of our species is that we construe our environment not only as order but also as *moral* order. *Ought* is written into our human discourse and structures our existence. And while there is little to be said for the argument that we must first establish the existence of God if we are to affirm the existence of moral order, the theologian will argue that the *fact* of moral order adds something essential to the elemental concept of God.

2. *Religious Faith*

Christian faith *confirms* elemental faith in an orderly environment and *specifies* it; that is, it spells out the nature of the perceived order in ways that go beyond the common faith of humanity and may conflict with alternative accounts of world order. There is no necessity to assert further of elemental faith that it is the essence of religion or piety. My intention is not to offer a theory of religion but only to propose a suitable point of departure for our account of Christian faith. It is important to recognize, however, that the utterances of Christian faith, like those of every religion, can seldom be construed as plain, literal assertions. Whatever may be the common essence of religion (if there is a common essence), it will be generally agreed that the most basic *language* of religion consists in imagery and story.

There are, of course, many uses of what we conveniently abridge as "religious language." But the difficulty in them all is that they presuppose the possibility of applying to God predicates taken from discourse about finite entities.

For this reason, both Thomas and Schleiermacher prefaced their treatment of Christian doctrines with sections on theological language, and Calvin rolled out his principle of accommodation whenever needed. Christian theologians have always recognized what Calvin perceived as a certain "impropriety" in language about God, since nothing can be said of the divine majesty except by images taken from created things.[3] But whereas Calvin was not greatly troubled by the problem, Thomas confronted it with his notion of analogy, and Schleiermacher held that it is the task of dogmatics to move, as far as possible, beyond the primary, figurative language—not to replace it, but to guide us in our use of it.[4]

Since the middle of the last century, the nature of religious language has been a major topic in the philosophy of religion. The philosophers ask whether religious metaphors can be cognitive, whether anything literal or nonsymbolic can be predicated of God, and so on. The opposition between realist and nonrealist interpretations of religious language is not strictly a dogmatic question. It is not impossible that religious language is illusory (misconstruing a merely natural referent) or wholly subjective (lacking any outward referent at all). But dogmatics seeks to take Christian faith as it is, and it will hardly be denied that Christians generally assume that their talk of God has a real referent, not reducible to merely natural objects such as the phenomena of nature itself. But they are willing to grant that religious language is fundamentally metaphorical. Detailed theories of the religious use of metaphor, analogy, and symbol may be left to the philosophers of religion. But no responsible dogmatics will fail to acknowledge at the outset that religious language is, in Thomas's aphorism, "a mean between pure equivocation and simple univocation" (*ST* 64). Without either adopting or rejecting Thomas's theory of analogy, I will borrow his aphorism as a procedural guide in interpreting Christian doctrines, taking it for granted that the metaphors in which they are conveyed are intended to be informative, but being willing to ask where they may fall short. This is by no means to belittle the task of entering in detail into the current philosophical discussions of religious language. It is a task that belongs to Christian theology, but not to dogmatics. Theology is a field-encompassing field, as my next chapter attempts to make clear, and in the interests of specialization the duties of the whole field are not assigned to every part.

3. Christian Faith

If we take "metaphor" in its dictionary sense, "the application of a name or descriptive term or phrase to an object or action to which it is imaginatively but not literally applicable," we may use "represent" as the corresponding verb. Christian faith not only confirms and specifies elemental faith but also

3. Calvin, Comm. Heb. 1:3. The view that biblical language is accommodated to our limited human capacities (see, e.g., *Institutes* 2.16.2–3 [1:504–6], on God's "wrath") is rooted in the hermeneutics of Origen of Alexandria.

4. In *CF* §16.1, 3 (78–81) Schleiermacher's concern is to contrast the "descriptively didactic" language of dogmatics with the poetic and rhetorical expressions of the primary religious utterances (cf. §§17.2 [84]; 28.1 [118]). For him, too, this includes the problem of God-talk. See, for example, §50.1 (195) on the divine attributes and §109.3 (500–501) on justification by faith.

represents it as "filial trust in God 'the Father of Jesus Christ.'" In the New Testament, the identity of the Christian God is conveyed by this expression, with minor variations of wording. In 2 Corinthians, Ephesians, and 1 Peter, doxologies to "the God and Father of our Lord Jesus Christ" follow prominently after the initial greetings (2 Cor. 1:3; Eph. 1:3; 1 Pet. 1:3). Elsewhere, Paul writes variously of "the God and Father of our Lord Jesus Christ" (Rom. 15:6), "the God and Father of the Lord Jesus" (2 Cor. 11:31), and "God, the Father of our Lord Jesus Christ" (Col. 1:3). Paul also writes of "God *our* Father and the Lord Jesus Christ."[5] But it is only because God was first "the Father of Jesus Christ" that he became *our* Father (Rom. 8:29).

The metaphor of divine fatherhood, which likens Christian faith to filial trust, is not chosen at random for the pivotal representation of the Christian God. It is grounded in the Gospel reports of the words and deeds of Jesus. We need to exercise caution toward the criticism that the image of God as Father has been used, or abused, as an instrument of male domination and should be superseded. The evidence of a patriarchal bias in the Judeo-Christian tradition is persuasive.[6] But it remains true that the original form of the Christian revelation was given in the relationship of Jesus with his heavenly Father, and it is by this relationship that the meaning of divine fatherhood must be understood. Hence my first thesis is not about God simply as Father, but about God "the Father of Jesus Christ." It does not follow that this is the only appropriate metaphor for the Christian God. All that follows is that our first task is to understand it in its historical particularity, not making our own experience of fatherhood the measure of God. As Calvin says, "properly speaking, [God] is indeed the only true Father; . . . this name is only as it were by way of concession applied to men" (Comm. Heb. 12:9).

5. My emphasis. See Rom. 1:7; 1 Cor. 1:3; 2 Cor. 1:2; Gal. 1:3; Phil. 1:2; Phlm. 3. Cf. "Jesus Christ and God the Father" (Gal. 1:1), "our God and Father" (Gal. 1:4). The christological significance of these descriptions of God is taken up in chap. 11 below.

6. For this reason, I follow the current practice of avoiding exclusively masculine pronouns for God or believers in God, but not when citing or discussing other sources, including English translations of the Bible.

2. Definition of Dogmatics

Christian dogmatics is distinguished from every other part of Christian theology as the theoretical, critical, and systematic discipline that seeks to establish the unity, and to test the adequacy, of the beliefs and dogmas in which Christian faith is expressed.

The subject matter of dogmatics, as part of Christian theology, is determined by reference to the concept of faith. But a *definition* of dogmatics can be given only by finding its place among the several theological fields and subfields. The problem of classification that the definition of dogmatics thus poses is no older than the end of the eighteenth century, when Christian theology began to splinter into relatively independent studies. But the seeds of the problem go back further and are already present, at least in part, in Scripture. One can point to the New Testament for the distinction between doctrine and exhortation, for instance, which contains in germ the distinction between dogmatic and moral theology. And as soon as the Christian theologian moves beyond the task of interpreting individual books and particular passages of Scripture, we have the beginnings of biblical theology—a theology that takes the canon of Scripture as a whole for its frame of reference and seeks to understand the Bible's "message."

I. The Unity and Fragmentation of Christian Theology

A comparison of Calvin's *Institutes* with Schleiermacher's *The Christian Faith* shows how different in scope Reformation theology and a modern dogmatics could be. The *Institutes* is properly called a "system," in which every part is to be understood in relation to the whole. But although we may also call it, by license, a "dogmatics," it is not strictly a work of dogmatic theology in the modern sense. During the eighteenth century, the demands of scholarly specialization led to the increasing independence of disciplines within a theological curriculum and to the creation of new ones. Dogmatics became one discipline among many, and much that Calvin included in his *Institutes* was transferred to other fields.

1. The Unity of Theology

Until the twelfth century, the material of theological study was largely biblical exegesis, as pursued in the monastic schools. A shift was brought about by the *Four Books of Sentences* of Peter Lombard (ca. 1100–1160), which became the theological textbook of the universities. A collection of thematically arranged opinions (*sententiae*) from the Fathers and masters, it was influenced by the dialectical method of Peter Abelard's (1079–1142) *Sic et Non*, which proceeded by juxtaposing seemingly contradictory pronouncements from various ecclesiastical authorities. The dialectical method shaped in turn the great theological *summae* of high scholasticism, which eventually superseded Lombard's *Sentences* as the favored textbooks in the universities. The schoolmen continued to write biblical commentaries, as well as commentaries on the *Sentences*, but the *summa* displaced exegesis as the crown of theological studies. The aim was to compile an exhaustive list of the theological questions generated by biblical study and to move from the apparent clash of authorities to a correct presentation of the church's teaching in its entire range.

With the Protestant Reformation, partly under the impulse of Renaissance scholarship, the focus of theological interest swung back again from scholastic theology to biblical exegesis. In his open letter *To the Christian Nobility*, Martin Luther (1483–1546) conceded to the study of the Fathers and Lombard's *Sentences* only a propaedeutic value in the early stages of a student's theological education; advanced study was then to concentrate on Scripture. Impatience with what he held to be the fruitless quibbling of late medieval scholasticism also led Luther to a shift in the scope and style of theology. He narrowed the scope of theology to humanity as guilty and lost and God the Justifier or Savior, insisting that "whatever is asked and discussed in theology outside this subject, is error and poison." And in a memorable epigram he wrote: "It is living—no, rather it is dying and being damned that make a theologian, not understanding, reading, or speculating."[1]

Calvin shared Luther's concern for the practical anchorage of theology in Christian experience and even made utility into something like a test of sound theology: "The theologian's task is not to divert the ears with chatter, but to strengthen consciences by teaching things true, sure, and profitable" (*Institutes*, 1:164). The title page of the first edition of the *Institutes* (1536) described the book as a *pietatis summa*, adding that it was "very well worth reading by all persons zealous for piety." Even as the work grew from the original six chapters to the eighty chapters of the definitive edition, Calvin maintained the practical concern for piety. But the intended readership changed. For the original version, he had in mind a catechetical handbook "by which those who are touched with any zeal for religion might be shaped to true godliness [*pietatem*]." But the 1539 edition was more like a theological textbook: "a summary of religion in all its parts" for students of theology.[2] And there he differed from Luther. Whereas Luther was an occasional writer, in his *Institutes* Calvin aimed at a comprehensive and orderly presentation of the Christian religion—not, however, in competition with Bible study.

In the new edition, Calvin thought of his work as a companion to biblical studies for ministerial candidates. The student of Scripture needs a simple

1. Martin Luther, *To the Christian Nobility of the German Nation* (1520), LW 44:204–5; *Exposition of Psalm 51* (1532/38), LW 12:311; *Operationes in Psalmos* (1519–21), WA 5:63 (my trans.).
2. The 1539 preface is found in the older Beveridge translation, 1:21.

introduction that will teach "both what he ought principally to look for in Scripture, and also to what end [*scopum*] he ought to refer whatever is contained in it." The revised *Institutes* now took the form of a series of seventeen theological commonplaces like the *Loci communes* (1521) of Philip Melanchthon (1497–1560), that is, explanations of recurring biblical concepts such as law, faith, prayer, and so on. Calvin's plan was to spare readers of his commentaries the tedium of long doctrinal digressions, frequently repeated, by referring them to his textbook of commonplaces. He stressed the order in which he had arranged his "summary of religion in all its parts," but he evidently became dissatisfied with it. In 1559 he replaced it in the definitive *Institutes* with a logical design that transformed a compilation of relatively independent topics into a systematic theology. We will need to return to it in the next chapter, since it raises questions of dogmatic method. In the 1559 preface Calvin wrote: "I was never satisfied until the work had been arranged in the order now set forth." But the *purpose* of the third main edition remained the same: to serve theological students as a guide to Scripture and a companion to his commentaries.

Given his understanding of the proper use of his *Institutes*, it naturally followed that Calvin kept the interpretation of Scripture foremost in mind. The task and method of the dogmatician, as he understood them, were not so very different from the task and method of the biblical commentator, and much of the *Institutes* was devoted to exegesis, or perhaps one should say to exegesis and "proof-texting." But along with biblical exegesis Calvin included, besides polemical digressions, matters we would be inclined to assign to Christian ethics, pastoral theology, church polity, and even church history. In the fourth book, for instance, he gave an outline history of the papacy (chap. 7). What we are calling "dogmatic theology" thus coincided in part with biblical theology, and it remained virtually undifferentiated from historical theology and practical theology as well.

2. The Fragmentation of Theology

By the beginning of the nineteenth century, as learning became increasingly specialized, Christian theology had splintered into several independent fields and subfields, and scholars in the historical disciplines began to assert the strictly scientific claims of their subject against the churchly and confessional enterprise of the dogmaticians. The appearance of so-called theological encyclopedias—the genre to which Schleiermacher's *Brief Outline on the Study of Theology* belongs (1811; 2nd ed. 1830)—was intended to recapture the lost unity of theological studies, not by disregarding the fields of specialization but by showing the relationship between them—a unity of order rather than indiscriminate inclusiveness. In practice, however, the encyclopedias confirmed the fragmentation by establishing a fourfold division of the Protestant theological curriculum into biblical studies, church history, systematic theology (including apologetics, dogmatics, and theological ethics), and the practical arts of ministry. Roman Catholic education for the priesthood followed a variant division into fundamental, historical, systematic, and practical theology, biblical exegesis being included with church history in historical theology.

For the systematic theologians, the problem was not only how to recover a sense of theological study as a single enterprise but, still more, how to differentiate their field from the other three while defending its scholarly credentials against the historians, who were inclined to locate dogmatics in the practical field, under the arts of ministry. In the United States, the problem was exacerbated by the transference of theological studies from the university to the seminary, where systematic theology had to defend its relevance to the practice of ministry rather than the seriousness of its academic claims. The universities, by and large, became increasingly inclined to ignore religion, to marginalize it in seminary-like divinity schools, or to encourage explicitly nontheological ways of studying it.

In his *Brief Outline*, Schleiermacher proposed his own independent path through the complex world of theological studies. He held theology to be a "positive science" like law and medicine, that is, an assemblage of sciences, or fragments of sciences, that have their natural home in the faculty of philosophy (or, as we say, "arts and sciences") but are brought together to educate practitioners for a learned profession. Medicine, for example, brings together information from anatomy, physiology, pharmacology, and so on, for the training of physicians. Similarly, for the sake of preparing clergy for church leadership, the study of theology assembles disciplines that apart from this practical goal would scatter to whatever departments of the arts and sciences they came from: philology, literature, history, and so on. And Schleiermacher thought that, to maintain the academic integrity of their work, those who teach in the professional schools (as we call them) should either hold joint appointments in the arts and sciences faculty or be required to give occasional lectures there.

It follows that the scientific status of dogmatics for Schleiermacher cannot be settled simply from its place in the theological curriculum or from its institutional location in a divinity school: it depends more properly on its theoretical location in the system of sciences. There are admittedly some tensions in Schleiermacher's pertinent utterances on the place of dogmatics, and his organization of the sciences is couched in language that can mislead because it differs at points from ours. But it is plain that he saw no opposition between historical and dogmatic theology, and there is no justification for the judgment of Ernst Troeltsch (1865–1923) and others that he turned dogmatics over to practical theology. On the contrary, he regarded dogmatics precisely as a historical science.

Briefly, he proposed a threefold division of theology into philosophical, historical, and practical theology, and classified dogmatics, along with exegetical theology and church history, as part of *historical* theology: it belongs to the scientific treatment of a historical phenomenon, the life of a Christian community. He could also describe dogmatics as *empirical*, because its concern is with real facts of experience that constitute a particular way of believing or being religious. And he expressly warned against letting commitment to the church prejudice either the theologian's research or his presentation of it. Of course, it remains entirely possible that his practice did not come up to his principles, as D. F. Strauss (1808–74) argued concerning Schleiermacher's lectures on the life of Jesus, in which Strauss uncovered a devout Pietist masquerading as a historian. But it is the principles that concern us here. By reason of its subject matter, which is a historical community, historical theology belongs to the modern study of history; dogmatics differs from the other two branches of historical theology, exegetical theology and church history, as knowledge of the *present* condition of the community, more particularly of its thinking and believing side. Schleiermacher did not represent dogmatics as the science of supernaturally revealed truths; he held it to be a strictly human science that deals with a fundamental aspect of human experience. Although it is combined with other disciplines to make up a theological education, in itself it is a humanistic rather than a professional discipline.

It is easy to understand why Schleiermacher was inclined to speak of *Glaubenslehre* rather than *Dogmatik*—the science of faith rather than the science of dogma. In his view, set out in *The Christian Faith,* genuine dogmatic propositions arise out of disciplined reflection on the immediate utterances of Christian faith (*CF* 81), that is, on the primary religious language. It is the task of the dogmatic theologian to establish the coherence of these utterances with one another and to determine how far they are adequately represented in the language of a particular Christian church at a particular time (83, 88). Where the church's language is shown to be inadequate to the faith it purports to represent, it needs to be revised or replaced (see, e.g., 270, 281, 390). Hence Schleiermacher spoke of the dogmatician's assignment as *the development of doctrine,* not mere preservation and transmission of it (113–15).

II. The Place of Dogmatic Theology

In our own time, there is no consensus either about theological study as a whole or about its several parts. Disagreement over the concept of a "biblical theology" continues, and one of the fields—practical theology—is in the midst of a radical transformation. The prevailing use of the term *theology* to designate just *one* of the theological fields, rather than the curriculum as a whole, obscures what was once assumed to be the theological character of them all. These days, Bible, church history, and the practical field may all be pursued in conscious or unconscious exclusion of "theological" questions, that is, questions that should be turned over to systematic or constructive theology. The Bible scholar and the church historian are willing to talk about Paul's or Luther's theology of justification by faith, say, but a curt veto may rule out as illegitimate a student's question about the meaning of justification by faith today: "That's a theological question."[3] In the ever-burgeoning practical field, by contrast, which was once supposed to be simply the application of theological concepts to clerical practice, theological questions are often disregarded rather than vetoed. The skills required for the work of the priesthood or ministry may appear less dependent on theology than on current educational theory, popular psychology, and the principles of good business administration. The attempt to rethink the practical field more broadly as reflection on Christian praxis may establish a new,

3. There are also those who think that Bible study gives all the theology the student needs, so that a separate theology field is at best superfluous, at worst an intrusion of alien ideas into biblical theology. Obviously, I disagree.

two-way connection with systematic theology that goes beyond the application of ready-made theological ideas to practical tasks.

1. *The Defining Characteristics of Dogmatics*

Generalizations about theology at the present time are hazardous. But our sole need is to be clear about the task before us—what it is, and what it is not. And for this purpose we may take our bearings from the fourfold division of theological study into Bible, church history, systematic theology, and practical theology without either endorsing it or entering further into current debates about it. Dogmatics is not the whole of Christian theology but a part of it—a part that could perhaps be at home in the humanities as well as in a seminary curriculum for prospective ministers. At any rate, it aims to be a serious scholarly enterprise ("scientific"), not merely edifying, although its presence in a theological curriculum assumes that it does contribute to the work of the priest or minister of the gospel.

Three characteristics distinguish dogmatics from the other main fields of theological education. (1) As a *theoretical* discipline, in the primary sense of the word *theoretical*, it is "concerned with knowledge but not with its practical application"[4]—knowledge of Christian faith and of the beliefs and dogmas in which it is conveyed. It is of course possible to conceive of Christian ethics and practical theology as theories about action, and in this sense as also theoretical. And Schleiermacher actually classified Christian doctrine (*Glaubenslehre*) and Christian ethics (*Sittenlehre*) as coordinate branches of a single descriptive dogmatics. He proposed to do theological ethics in the indicative rather than the imperative mood: it describes the patterns of behavior that flow from life in Christ (as does Paul's ethic of love in 1 Cor. 13, which tells what love does, not what it ought to do). Other variant definitions of the theological fields and subfields may suggest further complications for taking "theoretical" as a distinguishing mark of dogmatics. But what I intend should be sufficiently clear: dogmatics is about knowledge of Christian faith.

I take dogmatics to be (2) a *critical* discipline that tests the adequacy of the beliefs and dogmas (authorized doctrines) in which the Christian way of having faith is formalized. Its assignment does not end with factual knowledge about what Christians believe or have believed. That belongs rather to the two fields that we are accustomed to classify as "historical": Bible and church history. The dogmatic theologian moves on to appraise the beliefs and dogmas in which the church and its theologians have embodied Christian faith and, where necessary, ventures to make a case for alternative language.[5] Dogmatics is about the development of doctrine in Schleiermacher's sense: development not simply as a historical observation (that Christian doctrine *has* developed), but as recognition of a critical and constructive task (that Christian doctrine *needs* to be developed). Like the church itself, the church's teaching is *semper reformanda*,

4. *The Oxford Dictionary and Thesaurus*, American Edition, 1996.

5. In my historical studies of Christian doctrine, I have proposed "historical theology" as an intermediate, critical step between the history of doctrine and constructive or systematic theology. Here, as should be evident, I have in mind a "constructive criticism" that does not merely expose defects but suggests corrections and improvements.

always to be reformed. The task of dogmatic theology is misconstrued when it is thought to be simply a matter of learning and accepting whatever the church teaches. That would be indoctrination, not dogmatics.

In the Protestant theological curriculum, apologetics, dogmatics, and theological ethics have commonly been grouped together as the three subdivisions of systematic theology. But, as a further distinguishing mark, I define dogmatics itself as (3) a *systematic* discipline. Once again Schleiermacher provides the model. The English title of *The Christian Faith* is an abbreviated translation of the German, which would be fully translated as "Christian Faith Presented Systematically [*im Zusammenhange*] according to the Principles of the Evangelical Church." We might render the German as "presented in the way it all hangs together [*zusammenhängt*]." Dogmatic theology cannot be adequately done in pieces, since the meaning of each part is conditioned by its relation to every other part, that is, by its place in the whole. So, for example, the role of predestination in Calvin's theology cannot be understood if it is torn out of its context and treated as an isolated doctrine unconnected with anything else—much less if one calls it "Calvin's central dogma," although he does not get to it until near the end of book 3.

By marking the lines that distinguish dogmatics from other branches of Christian theology, we have a working definition of our task as *the theoretical, critical, and systematic discipline that seeks to establish the unity, and to test the adequacy, of the beliefs and dogmas in which Christian faith is expressed.* To sum up: Dogmatic theology seeks both understanding of Christian faith and, where needed, reformation of the doctrines in which it is conveyed. What it seeks to understand is in particular the unity or logical coherence of Christian beliefs, and what it seeks to reform, as needed, are the inherited formulations of the Christian way of believing. Unlike *apologetic* theology, it aims at comprehension, not justification, of belief. Unlike *historical* (including biblical) theology, it is critical as well as descriptive and is logically, not chronologically, ordered. Unlike *practical* theology, its immediate goal is understanding, not action. Unlike *moral* theology, or Christian ethics, it studies the beliefs that inform Christian behavior, not Christian behavior itself.

2. *The Dogmatic Theologian in the Church and the Academy*

The formal definition still leaves room for different *kinds* of dogmatics, as will become clear later. Moreover, nothing like a total isolation of dogmatics is either desirable or possible. In a church's theological curriculum the several parts of Christian theology are coordinate and at times overlap. This too will become clear in due course. Least of all is it my intention to set a *No Trespassing* sign over dogmatic theology. The demands and advantages of specialization are beyond question, and sometimes confusion results from disregarding the boundaries. But there is no reason why a church theologian should not venture into another field than her specialization, provided that the rules of the other field are respected and the need for conversation with its leading representatives is acknowledged. In the twentieth century, biblical exegesis and historical theology were influenced by the excursuses in Barth's *Church Dogmatics*, as was the field of systematic theology by the work of New Testament scholar Rudolf

Bultmann (1884–1976). The definition of dogmatics marks out the court; it does not decide who plays.

But must the players at least be believers? If so, what becomes of the claim of dogmatics to be also a humanistic discipline with one foot in the arts and sciences division of a university?

Barth was not concerned to find a place for Christian theology amid the various sciences of the academy; on the contrary, he thought the attempt to do so was likely to misrepresent the distinctive character of dogmatic theology. He saw the church as the proper home of dogmatics, which is possible and meaningful only in the church, and prayer as the attitude without which there can be no dogmatic work (*CD* I/1:xiii, xv, 7–10, 17, 23, 275–87). Schleiermacher's view was more ambiguous. His division of the sciences appeared to secure for dogmatics a home in the humanities: it deals in facts that are assigned, in his system of sciences, to the modern study of history. Yet he asserted, "Dogmatics is only for Christians" (*CF* 60); indeed, the dogmatic method "only exists in the interests of preaching" (88).[6] The fundamental fact that dogmatics studies is "the *inner* fact of Christian piety which it postulates" (121; my emphasis). Hence he placed on the title page of *The Christian Faith* the Anselmian mottoes: "I believe in order to understand (*credo ut intelligam*)," and, "Anyone who has not experienced will not understand."[7]

Plainly, Schleiermacher assumed that dogmatics, whatever its scientific classification, could be done only from the inside, and this may seem to justify its marginalization in the university, or its total exclusion. But a distinction should be drawn between the understanding required of the teacher and the understanding of the pupil. It is one thing to insist that the dogmatic theologian needs to be *expertus* ("experienced") in order to give an adequate presentation of the Christian way of believing, quite another to infer that nobody else will understand what is taught unless she or he, too, has experienced it. And we can hardly demand of our theologians a more ascetic standard of detachment than we expect of their colleagues in other departments of the humanities. The best humanistic scholarship arises out of a powerful and infectious sense of the abiding value of some tradition of learning. The same is surely permitted to the teaching of dogmatics as a humanistic discipline. (I have suggested elsewhere a parallel with the evangelistic zeal of the scholars who taught me, when a schoolboy, to love the Greek and Latin classics.) For our present purpose, however, the institutional place of dogmatics—in the church, or in the academy, or both—is less important than its place among the various fields of Christian theology.

6. When Schleiermacher says in the same section (*CF* §19.1 [89]) that a dogmatic presentation must be *apologetisch*, he does not mean that it is, after all, directed to an unbelieving world outside; he means that, unlike the historian, the dogmatic theologian must be willing to take a stand for the dogmatic formulas he himself accepts or proposes. See also *CF* §28.3 (122).

7. I take it that this differentiates dogmatics from philosophy of religion, which is a part of philosophy, not of theology. Nowadays, the term *philosophical theology* is sometimes used synonymously with *philosophy of religion*, but it would be better to treat it rather as a more appropriate alternative for *apologetics*, that is, a theology that uses philosophical resources to explore the speculative implications of Christian faith.

3. Method of Dogmatics

Christian dogmatics tests "the proper doctrine of faith" (redemption) and the theistic doctrine of faith presupposed therein (creation) both by Christian tradition, which interprets the Apostolic witness to Jesus Christ, and by present-day thought and experience, insofar as they call for reinterpreting the tradition.

If the subject matter of Christian dogmatics is the Christian way of having faith, and if its task is not merely descriptive but critical of the beliefs and dogmas in which faith is articulated, what are the sources and norms with which dogmatics works? It might seem that we have the most important alternatives in our two main models. Calvin, it is said, appealed to Scripture alone, and Schleiermacher based everything on religious experience. But such a simplistic antithesis, though frequently repeated, will not do. Calvin often appealed to experience, even, interestingly enough, when trying to establish the unique authority of Scripture: "I speak of nothing other than what each believer experiences within himself—though my words fall far beneath a just explanation of the matter" (*Institutes*, 1:80–81). Schleiermacher, for his part, understood exegetical theology and dogmatic theology to be distinct disciplines. But he thought that the dogmaticians must be willing to await fresh insights from the independent labors of the exegetes (*CF* 92, 650–51). And despite his separation of exegetical and dogmatic theology, *The Christian Faith* has a respectable index of New Testament references (and, though I would not make too much of it, the index to the English translation has no entry at all for "experience"). The agenda for this chapter requires us to ask, first, about the nature and role of *biblical authority* in our two principal guides.

No adequate discussion of biblical authority can fail to take account of such closely related topics as revelation, inspiration, tradition, dogma, creeds and confessions, the canon of Scripture—and, of course, hermeneutics (the procedures for ascertaining the original sense of a text and its sense for readers today). A detailed treatment of these topics cannot be given here. But they will have a modest place within the framework of what I take to be a fundamental division between classical and modern Protestant theology. The Reformation called for reappraisal and correction of the inherited tradition. So also did modern Protestant theology, and it still does. Since the eighteenth century, however, the most urgent need for change has been found not in corruption of the tradition by the infidelity of the church, but rather in the estrangement of the church's tradition from the mental habits of the modern world. The problem is no longer "Scripture and tradition" but *tradition* (including Scripture) *and the modern world.* Present-day understandings of the world and humanity are bound to have a formative influence on the task of dogmatics. We must ask, second, how this apparently alien norm is to be determined and related to the domestic norm of the church's own tradition.

A further question for dogmatic method is how the material is to be ordered. The conventional sequence of topics follows, with variations, a quasi-historical order. After a preamble on biblical authority, it typically begins with God and God's eternal plan, moves through creation and providence, the fall, redemption by Christ, the establishment of the church and its sacraments, and ends with the so-called last things. The arrangement of the dogmatic system is not a trivial matter. It has a significant influence on the interpretation of the individual topics, and the supposedly historical order is subject to serious difficulties that present-day dogmatics must seek to overcome. The third theme in the present chapter, then, is *the shape of Christian dogmatics.*

I. Biblical Authority in Calvin and Schleiermacher

The nature of biblical authority cannot be reduced to the question of plenary inspiration and infallibility, on which there has been endless discussion. Other questions come quickly to mind. Is its inspiration the only, or even the main, reason why the dogmatic theologian takes Scripture as authoritative? Is Scripture the sole norm of doctrine (*sola scriptura*)? Is everything in the Bible equally authoritative, or should we look for a canon within the canon? Calvin's answers to these questions are misrepresented if the excursus on biblical authority in book 1 of the *Institutes* (1:74–96) is taken for all he has to say on the subject. The excursus can be properly understood only when read together with his later discussion (book 4) on the authority of the church (2:1149–79) and with his actual use of Scripture—in his commentaries as well as in the *Institutes*. Nor can Schleiermacher's thoughts on biblical authority be inferred from his statement in the introduction to *The Christian Faith* that dogmatics appeals to the New Testament Scriptures only "in default"—that is, in the absence of pertinent confessions of faith (*CF* 112). Not until part 2 does he offer his account of biblical authority and the ministry of the Word, and in some respects his account is not the opposite of Calvin's, but a reinforcement of it.

1. Christ as the "Target" of Scripture

Some have said that Luther's Christ-centered view of Scripture was lost in Calvin's "biblicism," in which authority is ascribed to the letter of Scripture as such, so that simply quoting a biblical text or two is sufficient proof of right doctrine. Biblicism, in this sense, is not difficult to find in Calvin (nor, for that matter, in Luther). It is underscored by Calvin's fondness for describing the Scriptures as "dictated," the human authors being amanuenses of the Holy Spirit. If inspiration means word-by-word dictation, taken literally, we must admit that it is discredited by modern biblical scholarship, which has taught us the way many books of the Bible have come down to us: by a long process of collecting and editing sources, so that the author of the final text is an editor or redactor rather than an amanuensis. But I doubt that Calvin meant "dictation" to be more than a metaphor to convey his reverence for Scripture as containing the Word of God—a reverence that did not prevent him from noting, in his commentaries, errors and discrepancies in the text. Moreover, he could affirm as plainly as Luther that the authority of Scripture rests not only on the supposedly miraculous manner of its production but also on its priceless *content*, which is Christ.

Calvin tells us how to use Scripture correctly in a striking passage he added in 1543 to his very first statement of evangelical faith, his preface to the French translation of the New Testament by his cousin Pierre Robert Olivétan (first published in 1535). What we are to seek in the whole of Scripture is truly to know Jesus Christ: "our minds ought to come to a halt at the point where we learn in Scripture to know Jesus Christ and him alone."[1] In his commentary on the Fourth Gospel, Calvin points to the christocentric principle, as we may call it, in Scripture itself. Jesus is reported as saying in answer to "the Jews" (as John tendentiously calls them): "You search the scriptures, because you think that in them you have eternal life; and it is they that bear witness to me" (John 5:39 RSV). Calvin discovers here two different ways of reading the Bible. The wrong way is to seek life in the letter; the right way is to look for Christ in Scripture, who alone gives life to the letter. We should read the Scriptures with the express design of finding Christ in them. "Anyone who turns away from this target, however much he wearies himself with learning his whole life long, will never arrive at knowledge of the truth." Scripture has a mark, a target (*scopus*), at which we should aim. Calvin makes the same point in a sermon on Ephesians 4:20–24. Many have turned Scripture over, page by page, and can give a good account of it, but their aim is not directed at our Lord Jesus Christ, and without Jesus Christ we have nothing (Calvin 1973: 423).

The idea that the Bible has a "target" is linked with Calvin's characteristic emphasis on the activity of the Holy Spirit. The Spirit not only inspired the human authors of Scripture and now persuades the reader that Scripture is the Word of God; the Spirit also transforms the letter of the text into the life-giving presence of Christ. What Calvin says of the law summarizes his understanding of the "letter" in general: cut off from the grace of Christ, it merely sounds in the ears. "But if through the Spirit it is efficaciously sealed [*efficaciter imprimitur*] upon hearts, if it proffers [*exhibet*] Christ, it is the word of life" (*Institutes*, 1:95 alt.). It is remarkable that Calvin uses here key terms from his sacramental vocabulary (as I have indicated by modifying the language of the standard English translation). Through the action of the Spirit, the Word does what the sacraments do, which by the power of the Spirit efficaciously present what they represent. We will need to return to Word and sacraments as the Spirit's instruments (chaps. 18 and 19). We must also return to Calvin's thoughts on biblical authority in the context of the Spirit's activity in the church (chap. 17). His treatment of biblical authority remains incomplete until book 4 of the *Institutes*, where it is related to the power of the church to explain the articles of faith.

1. *Calvin: Commentaries*, trans. Joseph Haroutunian and Louise Pettibone Smith, LCC 23 (Philadelphia: Westminster, 1958), 70.

Calvin holds that the voice of the church has precedence over the individual's right to private interpretation of Scripture, in which the heart of Protestantism is often (erroneously) thought to consist.

2. *The Apostolic Witness to Christ*

Schleiermacher places "Holy Scripture" not in the introduction to *The Christian Faith* but under ecclesiology. Together with the ministry of the Word, Scripture is the first of the essential and invariable features of the church. In this location, it is not presented as a storehouse of proofs for right doctrine—it is witness to Christ, indeed, the means by which Christ makes on us today the same personal impression he made on the first disciples. The ground of faith for us is essentially what it was for them. As their faith sprang from Christ's preaching of himself, so our faith springs from the preaching of Christ by the Apostles and many others.[2] And "[i]nsofar as the New Testament writings are such a preaching come down to us, faith springs from them too" (*CF* 593). This by no means requires prior acceptance of the doctrine that the writings had their origin in a special divine revelation or inspiration.[3] Schleiermacher rejects the custom of identifying Scripture with revelation—the original divine revelation is Christ. The authority of Scripture is not the foundation of faith in Christ; quite the reverse, it is by virtue of faith in Christ that a special authority is ascribed to Scripture. The nature of biblical authority is explained accordingly.

The New Testament Scriptures provide the *norm* for all succeeding interpretations of Christian faith,[4] and in the ministry of the Word everything must be traceable to apprehending Christ from Scripture. Why? Because the New Testament contains "the presentations given in preaching by the immediate disciples of Christ" (*CF* 595). In a footnote, Schleiermacher points to John 15:27, where Jesus promises the disciples that the Spirit of truth will testify to him and that "[y]ou also are to testify because you have been with me from the beginning." Schleiermacher thinks there is no need to confine the action of the Spirit strictly to the inner circle of the Apostles. With Peter's statement in Acts 1:21–22 as his warrant, he speaks rather of the "apostolic class," which includes the wider circle of those who accompanied the Twelve (599). An individual book of the New Testament might come from this circle even if not in fact written by the author to whom it is attributed. Nor is it required that every later presentation must be simply lifted verbatim from the books of the New Testament. But "nothing can be regarded as a pure product of the Christian Spirit except so far as it can be shown to be in harmony with the original products" (596). Indeed, if we ask what is Schleiermacher's final authority, it can only be "the self-proclamation of Christ," which gave rise to the faith and preaching of the first disciples. "For

2. Where the reference is only to the Twelve, or to one of them, I capitalize "Apostles," "Apostle," and "Apostolic" (as in thesis 3). My lowercase expression "apostolic ministry" (as in thesis 16) recognizes the broader use of *apostolos* in the New Testament.

3. Schleiermacher rules out the suggestion that "in virtue of their divine inspiration the sacred books demand a hermeneutical and critical treatment different from one guided by the rules which obtain elsewhere" (*CF* §130.2 [600]). His own view of inspiration turns around his heterodox understanding of the Holy Spirit (see n. 7 in chap. 20 below).

4. Schleiermacher says "*the* norm," and in what follows I have tried to interpret his intricate thoughts on dogmatic method by a provisional distinction among *norm, criterion, source, limit,* and *codeterminant.*

there is only *one* spring from which all Christian doctrine is derived, namely, the self-proclamation of Christ" (92).

The understanding of the scriptural norm as vested in the Apostolic witness to Christ limits the range of what can be judged strictly canonical. Like Luther, Schleiermacher concedes (1) that not all the books included in the New Testament are "equally fitted, by content and form, to vindicate their place in the Canon" (*CF* 605). Moreover, he insists (2) that authority does not extend to thoughts that are merely incidental to Scripture's main theme (596). And in a postscript to his discussion of Holy Scripture, he adds (3) that despite the historical connection between them, the Old Testament writings do not "*share the normative dignity or the inspiration of the New*" (608). What Christians have been accustomed to call "the Old Testament" is better regarded as containing the Scriptures of another religion (60–62, 115). Calvin would not agree, since he contended that the one covenant of grace held the two Testaments together, whereas Schleiermacher saw in Judaism a different religion, a religion of law. Be that as it may, in our own time it has become the rule in the academy to speak of "the Hebrew Scriptures" rather than "the Old Testament," and many scholars now guard the field against trespassing by Christian theologians.

The New Testament writings provide Schleiermacher with his dogmatic norm, but he has other *criteria* of a sound dogmatic proposition. In the introduction to *The Christian Faith* he asserts that dogmatic propositions have a twofold "value," ecclesial and scientific (*CF* 83). The ecclesial value (in a marginal note he says that this might be called the proper value) is the success with which a proposition articulates the religious affections and their reference to Christ as Redeemer. The scientific value lies (1) in the definiteness of the concepts by which the proposition explains the primary religious language, and (2) in its systematic harmony with other dogmatic propositions. Schleiermacher's entire conception of the nature and method of dogmatics is compressed into this statement of the twofold value of its propositions. But there is more.

He wrote his dogmatics with the union of the two evangelical churches of Germany in mind, and *The Christian Faith*—especially part 2—is replete with citations from the Lutheran and Reformed confessions. Because the scriptural norm can determine only whether a proposition is Christian, an explicitly evangelical dogmatics is bound to include the Protestant confessions among its *sources*. But, like all ecclesiastical doctrines, the confessions remain subject to the scriptural norm (*CF* 113, 618–19). In addition, Schleiermacher determines whether, on particular points, the confessions are adequate expressions of evangelical faith. And how does he do that? Partly by appealing directly to the devout self-consciousness of his readers. In this sense, one might say that Christian experience (not religious experience!) is also a source for Schleiermacher's dogmatics. Unlike Calvin, who appeals to experience for confirmation, Schleiermacher can claim that his explanations of Christian doctrines actually describe Christian experience. In his account of redemption by Christ, for instance, he can say: "This exposition is based entirely on the inner experience [of the Christian]; its only purpose is to describe and elucidate that experience" (428).

A fuller account of the marks of appropriate doctrine in *The Christian Faith* would need to consider the typology of heresies that Schleiermacher deduces from his definition of the essence of Christianity. While the development of doctrine is bound (by definition) to be heterodox—as a recommended modification of inherited language—he sets up the heresies as the *limit* within which heterodoxy must be confined (*CF* 95–101, 110–11, 606). But I must move on, lastly, to a point of theological method that is succinctly stated in his *Brief Outline on the Study of Theology* (§167): "the development of doctrine is determined by the whole state of science and especially by prevailing philosophical views." Science and philosophy are not put forward in *The Christian Faith* as an actual norm, independent of the scriptural norm, and what Schleiermacher says there about philosophy is mainly given in careful qualifications: in particular, that philosophy can provide the form of dogmatic propositions but not the content (see, e.g., *CF* 81–83, 92–93, 118–19, 122, 126). We might convey his point by speaking of science (including philosophy) as *codeterminant* of his dogmatic propositions.

I will not conclude by commenting in detail on this remarkably careful and comprehensive summary of the guidelines that determine the work of the dogmatic theologian. But in everything that follows it will be apparent that I have learned from Schleiermacher as well as from Calvin.

II. Tradition and the Modern World

For Calvin, the aim of Scripture was knowledge of Jesus Christ; for Schleiermacher, the norm of sound doctrine was the Apostolic witness to Christ. There was agreement between them on the decisive point: Scripture is to be read with Christ as its center, and in this, mainly, lies its authority in the church. Their agreement does not exclude differences, and it is certainly not without its problems. In particular, their focus on the biblical Christ highlights all the difficulties about the Christ of faith and the Jesus of history that have been so much a matter of controversy in modern times. We will consider them in due course (chap. 11). But the agreement also raises more immediate questions about how we should use the many other things the Bible appears to contain *besides* the Apostolic witness to Christ—most obviously, questions about the use, or disuse, of the Old Testament. Schleiermacher's view may seem drastic. Calvin held that the Law and the Prophets, too, point to Christ. But if, as he liked to say, the Sun of Righteousness has arisen, even Calvin could hardly assign to the Old Testament equal authority with the New *as a dogmatic norm*. Still, the historical bond between the Testaments calls for more systematic attention to the Hebrew Scriptures than Schleiermacher allowed for. I recognize the wisdom of his case for giving exegetical theology its due as a separate discipline, coordinate with dogmatics. But my usual procedure for dealing with each dogmatic theme will be to begin by attending to both the Old Testament and the New as the primary *sources* for understanding Christian faith, while affirming the unique *authority* of the Apostolic testimony to Christ. But is Scripture the sole dogmatic norm?

1. *Scripture and Tradition*

From the time of the Protestant Reformation, the discussion of dogmatic norms in the Western churches has focused on the relation of Scripture to tradition.

The alternatives have frequently come to expression in polarized formulas that seem to demand a choice: either *sola scriptura* (Scripture only) or Scripture plus tradition. The Reformation was a call for the church to amend its life and theology by returning to the earliest Christian sources. But the Roman Catholic Church based its claim to authority partly on its possession of unwritten traditions, and it reserved for itself the sole right to interpret Scripture—which it did partly by means of allegorical interpretations. With its companion principles *scriptura sui ipsius interpres* (the Bible its own interpreter) and *sola historica sententia* (only the historical or literal sense), *sola scriptura* was intended to exclude what the Protestants held to be the evasions of the papal church. But if the three hermeneutical principles of the Protestants were justified—as a demand to give the Word of God free course in the church—so also was the Roman Catholic riposte: the Bible comes to us only as transmitted through the historical life of the church, and it remains in this sense the church's book. Without tradition, there would be no Scripture.

On the other hand, the Roman Catholic formula that calls for receiving the written books and unwritten traditions with equal devotion and reverence is also open to objection.[5] In its own way it too detaches Scripture from tradition. The interpretation of the Tridentine formula has been a subject of debate, but the prevailing view is that it treats Scripture and tradition mainly as distinct and supplementary norms. A third alternative, which neither rejects tradition nor makes it an independent norm, is Calvin's understanding of tradition as nothing other than a "handing down" (*tradere*) of the Word of God. He did not isolate Scripture from the church's tradition but could still insist on the absolute precedence of Scripture, so that it is always possible and needful to judge tradition by the Word, "from which it will become clear what is the genuine tradition of the church and what on the other hand is either inconsistent with it or does not belong to it" (Calvin 1996: 66). And Calvin had not the slightest doubt that the interpretation of the Word cannot be left to each person's individual insight or fancy but requires the collective judgment of a "synod of true bishops" (*Institutes*, 2:1176).

We may hold Scripture and tradition together, then, by taking as our primary norm *Christian tradition, which interprets the Apostolic witness to Jesus Christ*. Historical study of Christian beginnings requires us to understand the New Testament Scriptures as the product of ecclesial tradition. The circumstances of the earliest Christian communities shaped the Gospels, and the gradual determination of the New Testament canon was itself a process in the life of the church. The canon fixed a gospel tradition that was at first oral and from the beginning had the distinctive character of witness to the event of Jesus Christ. The witness of the New Testament is distinguished from all subsequent witness for precisely the reason the church gave in determining the canon: because of the unique authority of those who stood closest to the original event, this being the criterion of "Apostolicity." Scripture is thus a part of tradition *and a uniquely authoritative part*. It cannot be cut off from tradition, and yet it must always have free course to judge all subsequent witness to Christ, which can never be more than interpretation

5. *Canons and Decrees of the Council of Trent*, sess. 4; DS 244. Cf. Vatican II's *Dei verbum*, art. 9; DV 117. See further O'Malley 2013: 97–98.

of the primary witness. This remains axiomatic for the centuries of subsequent tradition, even after the emergence of a plurality of distinct traditions. Though each serves as normative for the life of the particular church in which it belongs, all have been, and still are, accountable to the authority of the Apostolic witness to Christ. With this conclusion, however, the question of dogmatic method is not exhausted. The history of tradition itself shows the continual admission of a secondary determinant from outside the tradition of the church, whether it was regarded as a welcome resource or as the occasion for heresy.

2. Tradition and the Present

The entire postcanonical tradition of the church has been marked, on its theological side, by a series of attempts to come to terms with secular knowledge. Hence in affirming tradition one is already affirming the legitimacy of borrowing a second norm from outside Scripture. Even within the New Testament itself the process of bringing together the Word of God and extracanonical thought-forms has already begun (notably, in the Fourth Gospel), and from this undeniable fact the dogmatic theologian may draw justification for the continuing search after appropriate language, wherever it may be found, in which to convey the meaning of Christian faith. Several models come immediately to mind: the role of Platonism or Neoplatonism in Augustine (354–430), Aristotelianism in Thomas, and so on, down to the role of existentialism in Bultmann, Whiteheadian metaphysics in process theology, and Paul Tillich's (1886–1965) method of correlation. It remains difficult, however, to describe in advance the kinds of resources that may be available and their exact relation to the primary norm of tradition.

We may call the secondary norm by which to test the adequacy of Christian doctrines *present-day thought and experience, insofar as they call for reinterpreting the tradition*. This language is intentionally broad—at the risk of vagueness. It does not restrict conceptual borrowing to the construction of grand philosophical syntheses between Christian faith and worldly wisdom. Rather, in the chapters that follow I will invoke ad hoc the secondary norm wherever common thought and experience—that is, thought and experience that do not arise exclusively from the Christian community—may require, or seem to require, revision of inherited Christian doctrines. Most important at the present time are (1) findings of the natural and social sciences that appear to conflict with traditional Christian views of the world and humanity, and (2) the experience of racial discrimination, poverty, and masculine bias that gave rise to black, liberation, and feminist theologies in the second half of the twentieth century. For example, the majority of Christian theologians now grant that the scientific worldview requires rethinking the doctrine of creation, and feminist theologians have argued for rethinking the doctrine of sin.

My intention in framing the norms as I have is to make the primary norm answerable to the authority of the Apostolic witness and to limit use of the secondary norm to its role in reinterpreting the tradition. The conception of the nature and method of dogmatics that I have outlined, partly in agreement with Schleiermacher, was subjected to sharp criticism during the twentieth century. The criticism often paid little or no attention to what Schleiermacher actually said about Scripture and the preaching of the Word. In an address titled "The Word in Theology from Schleiermacher to Ritschl," Karl Barth retrieved from Schleiermacher's discussion of the ministry of the Word only the description of preaching as "self-communication" (1962: 202; cf. *CD* I/1:62). He did not mention that Schleiermacher immediately goes on to insist that no true Christian can wish to commend himself, "but rather Christ alone and whatever of Christ lives in him," and that this is strictly subject to the scriptural norm, "so that one can only act as the recollecting and developing organ of Scripture" (*CF* 612–13). Schleiermacher believed that all good preaching is testimony (69). "Self-communication" says no more than Paul wrote to the Thessalonians: "we are determined to share with you not only the gospel of God but also our own selves" (1 Thess. 2:8).

This is not to deny a difference between Barth and Schleiermacher and certainly not to underestimate the force of Barth's single-minded insistence that the Word of God comes new every morning, so that one can never be its master but must simply listen (Barth 1962: 200). To be sure, the difference may not be as total as is commonly assumed. Like Schleiermacher, Barth held dogmatics to be a critical discipline, undertaken for the sake of preaching; and like Schleiermacher, he spoke of the biblical witness to the revelation in Christ as the norm by which dogmatic criticism is carried out. Further, although Barth rejected the view of dogmatics as the science of faith, he did not reduce it to biblical exegesis. "[D]ogmatics as such does not ask what the apostles and prophets said but what we must say on the basis of the apostles and prophets" (*CD* I/1:52; cf. I/2:820–21). Nor did he confuse dogmatics with the actual event in which the Word of God is heard; the dogmatic theologian can only deal with a Word remembered and expected again (I/1:249). If it would be unjust to infer that Barth's dogmatic method was, after all, anthropocentric—starting with the remembering theologian—might it also be unjust to infer that Schleiermacher's science of faith was anthropocentric because he focused on the believing Christian? Barth said he could see no way from Schleiermacher to "the word of the apostles" (1982: 271–72). I do not doubt that Schleiermacher would agree. His thought moved in exactly the opposite direction, *from* the word of the Apostles *to* the formation of his dogmatic propositions.

Nevertheless, Barth contended that the *sole* concern of dogmatics is to test the church's proclamation with the Word, meaning, in the final analysis, the Bible as witness to revelation— that is, as the "concrete form" of the Word of God. Other criteria, or supposed criteria, are simply irrelevant to the dogmatic theologian's task. That, certainly, is one clear difference from Schleiermacher's method—and from my own proposal of a secondary dogmatic norm. We will speak of it further in connection with the individual Christian doctrines. For now, it remains to address the third topic of this chapter: how to organize the dogmatic material.

III. The Shape of Christian Dogmatics

The shape that Schleiermacher gave to his dogmatic masterwork parallels, broadly speaking, the shape of Calvin's *Institutes*, whether consciously or not.

Both of them, we may say, present two-part systems that deal, in turn, with the doctrines of creation and redemption, and both of them begin with lengthy introductions (though Calvin does not *call* his *Institutes* 1.1–4 [1:35–51] an "introduction"). There are, to be sure, *some* differences between them on what is assigned to each part. Most obviously, Calvin locates the doctrine of the Trinity in the first book of the *Institutes*, under "The Knowledge of God the Creator" (1:120–59), whereas Schleiermacher postpones it to the very end of *The Christian Faith*, part 2, after "The Divine Attributes which relate to Redemption," as his "Conclusion" (*CF* 738–51). Moreover, there are instructive differences in the respective grounds they have for the sequence of the two parts. While they agree in presenting first creation and then redemption, Calvin assumes, and Schleiermacher denies, that the relationship between creation and redemption is temporal.

1. *Two Stages in the Knowledge of God*

The arrangement of the 1559 *Institutes* was evidently something to which Calvin gave special attention. He wrote that he was not satisfied "until the work had been arranged in the order now set forth" (*Institutes*, 1:3). His meaning has been debated, and it is pointed out that his arrangement conforms (roughly) to the sequence of the Apostles' Creed. But he is certainly referring, partly if not wholly, to his distinction between "Knowledge of God the Creator" and "Knowledge of God the Redeemer," which appears for the first time in the 1559 edition. At several points he takes pains to remind the reader of the distinction, indicating how it shapes the progress of his exposition. Hence his reminder in book 1, chapter 6, that he is not yet dealing with "the proper doctrine of faith" (70)—"faith" in the fully Christian sense, which pertains to God as Redeemer in Christ. In the same chapter, he uses the expression "the proper doctrine of faith and repentance" (72); and in the French version of 1560, he speaks of "full faith" (*pleine foi*).

With full faith, or the proper doctrine of faith (the doctrine of redemption), he contrasts "the primal and simple knowledge to which the very order of nature would have led us if Adam had remained upright" (*Institutes*, 1:40): knowledge of God simply as Creator. Calvin wants to postpone "redemption faith" and to speak first about "creation faith," as I shall call them: "First in order came that kind of knowledge by which one is permitted to grasp who that God is who founded and governs the universe. Then that other inner knowledge was added, which alone quickens dead souls, whereby God is known . . . also in the person of the Mediator as the Redeemer" (70–71). We may ask: What kind of order is that? In another passage, it is the order in which God *shows* himself (40; cf. 179–80). But that is not the order in which God is *known*, since the consequence of Adam's fall is that redemption must come before a sound knowledge of God the Creator can be acquired (340–41). Although the invisible Deity is made manifest in the workmanship of the universe, without revelation we lack the eyes to see him clearly (68). (Recall the simile of the spectacles given to the elect to improve their defective vision.) Evidently, Calvin is not tracing the experience of the individual, but the supposed history of the human race. He begins where the creed begins, with "God the Father Almighty, Maker of heaven and earth."

Calvin was not entirely successful in keeping the two kinds of knowledge distinct or in explaining the relationship between them. He gave a dogmatic reason for asserting the priority of the knowledge of redemption over the knowledge of creation: a fallen humanity cannot perceive the hand of the true God in the fabric of the universe until God adds his Word in Scripture. Yet the order he adopted reversed the priority, setting creation before redemption. Why? Because, presumably, his thinking was constrained by the church's story of the creation, fall, and redemption of humanity. No such constraint determined Schleiermacher's arrangement.

2. *Two Kinds of Dogmatic Proposition*

Schleiermacher, too, deals with creation and preservation first, then redemption, but his reason is different. The distinction he makes between the doctrines of creation and redemption is not *temporal* but *logical*—not, that is, about successive stages in a divine drama but about two kinds of dogmatic proposition that are required to explicate Christian faith. (1) As the science or doctrine of Christian faith, dogmatics is about the Christian way of having faith, in which everything is related to the redemption accomplished by Jesus of Nazareth. Faith in the Redeemer is the proper subject matter of Christian dogmatics; it constitutes the second, main part of *The Christian Faith.* But (2) Christian faith in the redemption brought about by Jesus Christ presupposes certain things about the way Christians see the world and its relation to God. In the first part of *The Christian Faith,* these presuppositions are the subject matter of the doctrines of creation and preservation, laid out in propositions that are "*presupposed by and contained in every Christian religious affection.*" Thus there are propositions *asserted* by the distinctively Christian awareness of the grace of Christ and propositions *presupposed* by it. But why set the presuppositions first, before the doctrine or doctrines of redemption? Schleiermacher's answer is that if they were placed last, as logically they could be, they would be only a feeble appendix to the properly Christian theme of redemption. The temptation would be to cut them short, and that would be a mistake because they have acquired a special significance as the field on which the modern conflict between theology and natural science is being fought out (Schleiermacher 1981: 60).

The distinction between the two types of proposition may perhaps strike the reader as gratuitous, but it is crucial for what Schleiermacher makes of the Christian doctrines of creation and the fall. He would attribute the "creationism" of the present day to a misunderstanding of Christian faith. For what Christian faith presupposes is not a world brought into existence by God at a past moment of time, but a world whose course is absolutely reliable because in *every* moment of time it is wholly dependent on a Creator God and can therefore be the stage or theater of redemption (*CF* 722, 735). Similarly, Christian faith presupposes not the creation and fall of humanity as historical events, but the possibility for humans to be conscious of God in *all* events, and its frustration by sin. In general agreement with Schleiermacher, my third thesis affirms that the doctrine of creation is about a *theistic* understanding of the world, God, and humanity presupposed by Christian faith in redemption. And this is the subject of part I of my outline.

3. Creation Faith and Redemption Faith

The twenty-one chapters of the outline are structured by two main organizing principles. The first is intended as a development of the *two-part system* found, with variations, in Calvin and Schleiermacher. The outline is accordingly divided into two parts, preceded by an introduction and followed by a conclusion. The theme throughout is faith, and the movement of thought is from the abstract notion of an *elemental* faith that determines human existence as such (the introduction); through the *theistic* faith in a Creator God ("creation faith") that is presupposed by faith in Christ but has much in common with the other two "Abrahamic faiths," Judaism and Islam (part I); to, finally, the distinctively *Christian* faith in redemption by Jesus Christ ("redemption faith") that is most properly the theme of Christian dogmatics (part II). In this way, the distinctiveness of Christian faith is affirmed without closing off the possibility of interpreting it in connection with other modes of faith—a concern that has grown enormously in our time.

The order of presentation is not experiential—as though a person first had elemental faith, then came to faith in the order of creation, and finally ascended to faith in Christ. Nor does it lay down three steps in a linear argument. My introduction does not provide a foundation for believing in Christ, and part I is not an independent natural theology designed to make an outsider receptive to the credibility of Christian faith. Dogmatics aims at understanding; rational justification falls within the province of apologetics. To be sure, insofar as dogmatics seeks an understanding of Christian faith that is consonant with the present state of pertinent knowledge in the natural and social sciences, its presentation should serve the interests of apologetics. But the admonition one sometimes hears that mediation between biblical faith and modern thinking is capitulation to alien ideas misses the point: the modern mind is not just the enemy out there, but the believer—sometimes the perplexed believer—in the pews, or even in the pulpit.

The second organizing principle lies in the determination to present faith throughout—elemental, theistic, and distinctively Christian—as a *two-sided concept*, both cognitive and moral: both a way of seeing, looking at, or knowing the world and the hearing of an imperative in one's being in the world. Each side of faith has its corresponding affective states: feeling at home in the world, for example, and despondence or rage at the corrupt condition of humanity. But in itself faith is cognitive and moral: it experiences our environment as a secure order, and it construes the order as the medium of a moral imperative. Conversely, the absence or diminution of faith is not mere unbelief but the experience of *dis*order and insensitivity, or even resistance, to moral obligations. A corresponding two-sidedness will be affirmed in, for instance, the Christian doctrine of estrangement as at once mistrust and defiance (chap. 7) and the doctrine of redemption as restoration of both the confidence and the obedience of faith (chaps. 12–13). In this way we can avoid the one-sided representation of estrangement in terms of hostility to God (it is also loss of confidence in God) and one-sided representation of the gospel as addressed to the removal of guilt (it is also about trust in God's purposes and commitment to God's rule).

PART 1: CREATION
Theism as the Presupposition of Christian Faith

4. The World as Creation

Faith in God "the Father of Jesus Christ" presupposes that the world is neither an accident nor a mechanism, but a moral order experienced as both support and demand; and this is what is meant by representing the world as "creation."

Creation, as popularly understood, is the act or series of acts by which God brought the universe into being. Most Christians assume that the first two chapters of the Old Testament are about creation in this sense. But many have assumed further that the two creation narratives in Genesis (Gen. 1:1–2:4a; 2:4b–25) are not to be understood literally even if they *represent* actual events. Until early modern times, it was common for theologians to think that the seven "days" of the first narrative, and the single day of the second, should not be taken for twenty-four-hour time spans and that the task of exegesis was to look *through* created things to the symbolic meanings the Creator assigned to them. Some have argued, however, that Protestant insistence on the literal sense of Scripture had two unintended consequences: it nurtured scientific inquiry into nature for its own sake, but it also "opened up for the first time in the history of biblical interpretation the real possibility that parts of the Bible could be false" (Harrison 1998: 268).

In our own day, the possibility of conflict between scientific and religious accounts of the way the world began is seen most obviously in the controversy over creationism. Advocates of creationism maintain that the earth is about six thousand years old, or no more than ten thousand years, and that the appearance of different species of animal life must be attributed to direct divine intervention, not to evolution through natural selection. They commend their views not as religious beliefs but as scientific conclusions; hence, in their opinion, their "creation science" has every right to be taught in schools as an alternative to Darwinism. In the main, the scientific arguments for creationism have consisted simply in exposing the alleged shortcomings of evolutionary theory. More recently, the proponents of intelligent design set aside creationist dating of the creation, and they do not deny the evidence that evolution has occurred. But they focus on the "irreducible complexity" of many living organisms, which, they argue, defies explanation of the origin of species by blind law alone.

My own agenda will not center on the creationism debate, though I do not entirely neglect it. I take the dogmatic locus of "creation" to refer not to the beginning of the world but (1) to the *kind* of world presupposed by Christian faith (the theme of the present chapter) and (2) to the distinctively theistic understanding of the *relationship* between the continuing course of the world and the creative activity of God (the theme of the following chapter). Chapter 6 then turns to the place of humanity in creation: to women and men as made in the image and likeness of the Creator.

I. Creation as the Establishing of Order

Creation is the first theme in our Bibles, and Christian theologies of creation are expected to include interpretation of the first two chapters of Genesis, understood as narratives—whether literal or symbolic—of events in the primeval past. But the Hebrew word for "create" (*bārā'*) is not used in the Old Testament exclusively of the original creation; it is also applied to God's creative activity in history and in the future (e.g., Isa. 43:1, 15; 65:17–18). Old Testament scholars have argued that although the creation stories in Genesis come first in our Bibles, the theme of God's action in the beginning is a relatively late feature of Hebrew religious thought, an inference from Israel's encounter with God in history. Creation in Genesis is about the dependence of the whole world on the God of the covenant: it exhibits the way the world *is,* or is perceived to be by faith, in the form of a story about how it *began;* and this is what is intended by calling the two creation stories *myths.* In our popular usage, "myth" has come to mean a falsehood, especially a deliberate falsehood. But that is not the way the historians of religion use it. Taken as primitive science, the creation stories are false; taken as myth, they may very well be true. The truth, or truth claim, of the creation myths lies in their reference to the way the world always is, in every moment.[1]

Dogmatic theology does not need to look behind the Hebrew creation stories for the Near Eastern mythologies they drew from. Our interest is in the function of the stories in the faith of Israel, insofar as that tells us something about the presuppositions of faith in Christ. Together with the Psalms and the Wisdom literature, the Genesis accounts testify that belief in creation is belief in a divine *order,* of which humanity is a part. It does not follow, however, that *dis*order is taken lightly or disposed of once and for all. The Old Testament gives evidence of the belief that the victory of order over chaos at the creation of the world was not total or final: chaos remains a continual threat (e.g., Job 3:8; 7:12).

Genesis 1 has been intractable to Christian theology not because of the distribution of God's labor over six "days"—since even before the rise of modern science the days were not always taken literally—but because creation is represented as the imposition of order on chaos. For this invites the question, Where did the chaos come from? The question is especially pointed if the opening

1. Karl Barth preferred the term *saga* rather than *myth* because, in his view, the truth of saga "is identical with the historical picture which is presented by it" (*CD* III/1:86 [§41.1]). He defined "saga" as "an intuitive and poetic picture of a pre-historical reality of history which is enacted once and for all within the confines of time and space" (81; cf. I/1:327–29 [§8.2]). It should also be noted that Barth did not allow dogmatics in general, or the doctrine of creation in particular, to be formed by concern for harmony with natural science (I/1:72 [§3]; III/1:x [preface]). For the reasons given, I differ with Barth on both these points.

verses are translated, as many scholars contend they should be (and as a note in the NRSV points out): "When God began to create the heavens and the earth, the earth was a formless void, and darkness covered the face of the deep, while the spirit of God swept over the face of the waters." Chaos appears as a second principle alongside the creative Spirit of God, though by no means its equal. To rule out gnostic dualism and the philosophical concept of an eternal matter, Christian theologians formulated the doctrine of *creatio ex nihilo* ("creation from nothing"), and they have sometimes justified it from the Apocrypha: "look at the heaven and the earth and see everything that is in them, and recognize that God did not make them out of things that existed" (2 Macc. 7:28; cf. Rom. 4:17). But whether or not the author (or redactor) of Genesis 1 understood the formless void to have been created by God, he clearly took creation to be the establishment of order.

II. Creation Faith

Faith, Calvin says, "has its own peculiar way of assigning the whole credit for Creation to God. . . . For unless we pass on to his providence . . . we do not yet properly grasp what it means to say: 'God is Creator'" (*Institutes*, 1:197). Not that he questions the reference of Genesis 1 to an original creation. But, as always, his concern is for piety, and this means that it is essential not to make God a momentary Creator who finished his work once and for all. The accent shifts from what God once did to what God does always—a *creatio continua* ("continuous creation"), though Calvin does not use the term. A similar understanding of what we are calling "creation faith" appears in the Heidelberg Catechism, and Schleiermacher's thoughts incline him in the same direction.

1. Calvin

Calvin's remarks on creation in book 1 of the *Institutes* (chap. 14) seem, at first glance, to be wholly conventional. He assumes that the world is not yet six thousand years old, and he values the biblical story of creation because it excludes pagan errors on the subject: Moses gave the *true* account of the way the world began to prevent believers from being led astray by heathen fabrications. However, it is quickly apparent that Calvin is less interested in the story of beginnings as such than in its usefulness to present piety. He states expressly: "it is not my purpose to recount the creation of the universe" (*Institutes*, 1:180). We are not to take the Mosaic narrative as a scientific account of how things began. For Calvin, it is a mirror in which the living likeness of God shines and moves us to pious gratitude. Like spectacles, it enables us to discern the true God. The distribution of the work of creation over six days is intended to aid our contemplation of God's goodness; and in the very sequence of events we ought to recognize God's fatherly love to humankind, since he did not create Adam until he had first made the earth ready for him, filling it with good things. We should respond with thankfulness.

In his commentary on Genesis, Calvin points out that the creation story is aimed at the limited capacities of the uneducated, so that anyone who wants to learn astronomy, or any other abstruse discipline, must go elsewhere (Comm. Gen. 1:6). By the two "great lights" in Genesis 1:16, for example, Moses meant the sun and the moon, whereas the astronomers prove that Saturn is in fact greater than the moon. To be sure, astronomy is both enjoyable and useful: it unfolds the marvelous wisdom of God. But Moses wrote for ordinary folk, and to them the moon is bigger because it *looks* bigger. We are not to worry about an apparent discrepancy with science, but rather should be aroused to gratitude for the light. "For since the Lord stretches forth, as it were, his hand to us in causing us to enjoy the brightness of the sun and moon, how great would be our ingratitude were we to close our eyes against our own experience?" (on Gen. 1:16).

Calvin does not doubt that the first chapter of Genesis ("The First Book of Moses") is about the actual beginning of the universe. But in the *Institutes*, as in his commentary on Genesis, he points the readers' attention away from past history to present experience: "Moses, accommodating himself to the rudeness of the common folk, mentions in the history of the Creation no other works of God than those which show themselves to our own eyes" (*Institutes*, 1:162). Calvin would not have approved of the attempts made by later Calvinists to override the principle of accommodation and deduce a "Christian physics" from the Bible. He acknowledged the authority of the scientists in their own domain. There is, of course, the much-quoted rhetorical question that used to be attributed to him concerning Psalm 93:1: "The LORD . . . has established the world; it shall never be moved" (cf. Ps. 96:10). Calvin supposedly asked: "Who will venture to place the authority of Copernicus above that of the Holy Spirit?" Though dutifully transmitted by historians of science, no exact reference for the question is ever provided, and the Calvin scholars have searched for it in the *Opera omnia* without success. It seems that the "quotation" is spurious, and in any case it is out of keeping with Calvin's express intention to distinguish between theological and scientific discourse.[2] Creation faith is one thing; natural science is something else.

2. *The Heidelberg Catechism*

Reformed theology after Calvin did not always follow his tendency to elide the distinction between creation and providence. Johannes Wollebius (1586–1629), for example, wrote in his widely used *Compendium of Christian Theology* (1618): "Creation is the act by which God made the world and all that is in it. . . . The record of creation is in Genesis 1 and 2." But a different approach to the doctrine of creation appears in one of the classical Reformed confessions. In the Heidelberg Catechism (1563), the first article of the Apostles' Creed is interpreted "existentially" (as we would say), that is, as a statement about the believer's self-understanding. The answer to the question (q. 26), "What do you believe when you say, 'I believe in God the Father Almighty, Maker of heaven and earth'?" affirms: "I trust in him so completely that I have no doubt that

2. In a sermon on 1 Cor. 10:19–24 (CO 49:677), Calvin did make a scornful remark about those who say that it is the earth, not the sun, that moves. But he did not refute them from the Bible. If they "pervert[ed] the order of nature," he probably meant that they contradicted the dominant scientific opinion.

he will provide me with all things necessary for body and soul." Creation and providence here run together, and the profit of acknowledging them is that we may have patience in adversity, gratitude in prosperity, and confidence for the future (q. 28, apparently echoing Calvin, *Institutes*, 1:219).

3. *Schleiermacher*

Schleiermacher takes the reflections of Calvin and the Heidelberg Catechism a step further. By his time, it had become a commonplace to classify as "mythology" prescientific accounts of the beginning of spatial and temporal existence. In *The Christian Faith* he turns away from creation in the beginning to what we may call the *creature-consciousness* of Christians in every time: the consciousness of being absolutely dependent on a source outside themselves. Hence there can be, for Schleiermacher, no real distinction between "creation" and "preservation" (*Erhaltung*, his preferred term for "providence"). He retains the traditional distinction because he finds it convenient to deal separately with what absolute dependence excludes (under "creation") and what is its positive content (under "preservation"). In his view, the problem with the idea of creation as an event lying in the remote past is that it cannot possibly represent anything given in the religious consciousness of the present. If we reply that it is after all an item of faith, that could only mean "faith" in the improper sense of assent to revealed information about things that lie outside our experience. This is not to say that the question of origins is uninteresting, but simply that it arises out of curiosity, not piety, and can be turned over to the cosmological speculations of the natural scientists. But if that disposes of the imagined conflict between science and the traditional doctrine of creation, there remains the supposed conflict between science and the doctrine of providence or preservation.

The first part of Schleiermacher's *The Christian Faith* contains a pioneering venture into theological naturalism. He admits that the common tendency of believers is to picture God's universal sustaining activity as interrupted from time to time by a supernatural act of divine intervention, that is, by a miracle. They fear that natural science, by reducing the entire course of nature to regular, undeviating patterns ("laws"), constitutes a threat to the devout expectation that an omnipotent God can and does interrupt the course of nature when and where he chooses. Indeed, it is chiefly to just such extraordinary acts of divine interference that they look for evidence of God's providence. Piety thus seems to have a vested interest in opposing the advance of scientific research; and the better the scientists understand the working of the natural order, the less devout they are likely to be.

Schleiermacher contends for the exact opposite: the interests of piety coincide with the interests of science. The intrusion of an element of unpredictable irregularity into the course of events would undermine not only scientific research but piety as well. A divine intervention in the created order would be needed only if the order were defective to begin with. "If such an interference be postulated as one of the privileges of the Supreme Being, it would first have to be assumed that there is something not ordained by Him which could offer Him resistance and thus invade Him and His work" (*CF* 179). And for piety that is unthinkable. Rightly interpreted, the heart of piety, according to Schleiermacher, is the feeling of absolute dependence that the regularity of nature actually arouses in us. The conviction that everything is grounded in nature's causal nexus coincides completely with devout confidence in the absolute dependence of all finite being on God.

For Schleiermacher, then, it is the regular course of nature that fits it to be the theater of redemption (*CF* 735). "[B]y creation all things are disposed with a view to the revelation of God in the flesh. . . . [T]he whole disposition of Nature would have been different from the beginning had it not been that, after sin, redemption through Christ was determined on for the human race" (723). He refers to Colossians 1:16, which reads in the NRSV "[F]or in him [Christ] all things in heaven and on earth were created . . . all things have been created through him and for him." This was Schleiermacher's creation faith. In place of a course of events frequently interrupted by unpredictable divine interventions he sets the undeviating movement of nature and history toward its divinely ordained goal in the incarnation. Obviously, this raises questions concerning Christian beliefs about sin, the fall, evil, and the renewal of creation (Gen. 3; Rom. 8:18–25), all of which appear to presuppose interruptions in the passage of events. We will need to come back to them. For now, we simply take note of Schleiermacher's attempt to reinterpret the doctrine of providence or preservation in terms of the natural causality investigated by science.

III. Creation and Christian Faith

Creationism, whatever its merits and defects in detail, has unnecessarily heightened the so-called warfare of science and religion. To affirm creation faith, there is no need to defend the creation stories of Genesis as literal, or even symbolic, accounts of how the universe came to be. The doctrine of creation is not about the origin of the world; it seeks to answer the question, What sort of world is presupposed by faith in God "the Father of Jesus Christ"?

1. Creation Faith and Cosmic Order

The "proper doctrine of faith," or "full faith" (as Calvin calls it), affirms that in Christ is revealed the creative *Logos*—the Word, Reason, or Wisdom of God—by which all things were made (Prov. 8:29–30; Sir. 1:9–10; Wis. 7:22; John 1:3; cf. Col. 1:15–17; Heb. 1:2). Presupposed, therefore, is that the world is accessible to human reason because it is in fact a work of Reason. It is true that the Bible and Christian tradition talk of creation mainly in the past tense, as a finished series of events in prehistoric time. But it is by no means playing fast and loose with tradition if we take the language to be more about the way things *are* than the way they *started* or even if we resign the question of beginnings entirely to the domain of the scientific cosmologists. Christian theologians from Augustine on have treated creation and providence (or preservation) as a unity. Dogmatic theology is bound to be more interested in what the theologians have generally subsumed under the heading of "providence."

It is, of course, Schleiermacher's language that suggests the formula "presupposed by" faith in God the Father of Jesus Christ. (The first part of *The Christian*

Faith is headed: "The Development of that Religious Self-Consciousness which is always both presupposed by and contained in every Christian Religious Affection.") But my own point of departure for speaking of the world as created is elemental faith, not the feeling of absolute dependence. At the bottom of all human investigation, and indeed of every human endeavor, is the perception of our environment as intelligible—and the assumption that even beyond our immediate perception the world as a whole *must be* intelligible. The "world as a whole" is not an object of experience but of thought. We cannot experience it but can only think it, and the thought of it as an ordered whole is a condition of our persistent inquiry into it. The thought finds continual confirmation in experience as the quest for understanding the world and our place in it meets with success; its tenacity is attested in that *lack* of success does not cause us to abandon it.

So far from being in conflict with natural science, the creation faith of Christians presupposes what the scientific enterprise presupposes: that observed events around us follow consistent patterns—that the world is ordered and therefore open in principle to our efforts to understand it and deal with it. The unpredictable behavior of subatomic particles does not cancel the recognition that there could be no science without the confidence that what is discovered on Monday will hold good on Tuesday or that what is discovered in Göttingen will be true in Cambridge or Chicago. Working scientists do not like the words *faith* and *belief*, which they take to be religious and alien to objective inquiry. They may insist that their confidence in the regularity and predictability of nature is just a working assumption. It has worked nicely for a very long time and probably will continue to do so; if it does not work tomorrow morning, there will be reason to worry about it then, not now. But such an account of scientific research does not adequately differentiate between a hypothesis and the underlying faith that drives the inquiry and generates the hypothesis. If a hypothesis is not confirmed by observation and experiment, the researcher goes back to the drawing board, as we say, and begins again—convinced that there *must be* an explanation of the data. The scientific enterprise does not founder when a particular project founders. In this respect, the scientist's faith is not unlike religious faith. "In fact," as one philosopher observes, "we may say that the belief of the scientist is one kind of religious belief—a kind, moreover, which is not incompatible with what is called Christian belief, for it is a part of it."[3]

2. *The Alternatives: Order as Subjective, Accidental, or Mechanical*

Confidence in cosmic order, though it certainly gives rise to belief without proof, is not blind assent to somebody else's say-so. In all of us it arises as an inevitable conviction out of our own actual commerce with the world of sense, and all further commerce with the world of sense depends in turn on preserving the conviction. But even at the abstract level of elemental faith, different

3. R. M. Hare, "The Simple Believer," in *Religion and Morality: A Collection of Essays*, ed. Gene Outka and John P. Reeder Jr. (Garden City, NY: Anchor/Doubleday, 1973), 405. Cf. Albert Einstein: "Certain it is that a conviction, akin to religious feeling, of the rationality or intelligibility of the world lies behind all scientific work of a higher order" (1954: 262).

accounts of the perception of order are possible, and they serve to define more exactly the creation faith presupposed by faith in Christ.

Against the British empiricists, Immanuel Kant (1724–1804) argued that the mind is not passive in the acquisition of knowledge but imposes order on the data of perception. Since there is no access to "things in themselves" except through the activity of the mind, we have no means to determine whether the order perceived is anything more than *subjective,* reflecting not the external world but the structure of consciousness. Kant's argument has had no more than partial and limited success either in natural science or in Christian theology. The sciences have generally been pursued on a realist assumption—that the order grasped by the mind is really there. It can hardly be doubted that a realist assumption holds good also for the religious faith of nearly all who have it (if not all who merely talk about it). But neither science nor theology has held a naive realism. Both have acknowledged a *critical* realism that allows for the role of the mind in shaping reports of a reality independent of our knowing it. In this respect, the myths and metaphors of religion are counterparts to the "models" constructed in the natural sciences (Barbour 1974).

A second view is that the world order, though objectively real, is *accidental*—a fortuitous rearrangement of atoms, as the ancient Greek atomists proposed. Such a view certainly runs into conflict with the creation faith of Christians, which goes beyond a bare elemental faith by setting cosmic order in the context of a divine purpose. Perhaps it conflicts even with elemental faith itself. For while it is not inconceivable that order might have arisen by chance out of disorder, the belief that it in fact did so might prove incapable of sustaining thought and disciplined inquiry. What came from disorder may as well return to disorder, and there would be no reason to anticipate continuation of intelligible order from one day to the next. Elemental faith, as abiding confidence in order, would be undercut. Hence the exclusion of chance or accident, except as a limited factor of contingency within a stable and reliable order, is perhaps given with the notion of elemental faith. In any case, the confidence of creation faith clearly differs from the notion that order is an accidental and transient phenomenon.

A third view is that world order is *mechanical,* and we may judge that this, too, is certainly inimical to creation faith and possibly to elemental faith as well. The comparison of the world to a mechanism was fostered by seventeenth-century physics and was once regarded as the most convincing proof for the existence of a God who designed and constructed it. But the analogy was problematic to theology for two reasons. It invited the conceptions (1) of an absentee deity, who made the mechanism and then left it to run on its own,[4] and (2) of a deterministic world order, which left very little room, if any, for free and responsible human activity. Hence my fourth thesis states that Christian faith *presupposes that the world is neither an accident nor a mechanism, but a* moral *order.* It is not merely a network of law-governed physical events but also (at least in our tiny corner) a network of personal relationships that make moral claims on us.

4. For Isaac Newton, a mechanical philosophy of nature was not incompatible with divine omnipresence. But for others, such as Voltaire, the image of the clockmaker implied an absentee God.

One might wish to include the notion of "moral order" in elemental faith, as I suggested in chapter 1. Arguably, both faith in cosmic order and belief that the order is moral have the status of what A. J. Balfour (1848–1930) called "inevitable beliefs." It is interesting that Calvin could write in his commentary on the Fourth Gospel, "The *light* which still dwells in corrupt [human] nature consists chiefly of two parts; for, first, all men naturally possess some seed of religion; and, secondly, the distinction between good and evil is engraven on their consciences" (on John 1:5). Schleiermacher, too, although he was famously unwilling to acknowledge a moral element in the essence of religion or piety, says of conscience exactly what he says of the feeling of absolute dependence: it is an original revelation of God (*CF* 10–11, 17–18, 342). In the present context, however, our question is whether the distinctively Christian way of believing *presupposes* faith in a moral order. That it does is hardly likely to be questioned. And this has the important consequence that creation faith encounters the world order not only as a source of security, confidence, or support, but also as an ever-present and sometimes disquieting claim or demand.

For dogmatics, the problem is that elemental faith, although it appears on reflection to be a matter of inevitable belief, in actual experience continually fails and slips away from us. If everyone all the time perceived the environment as ordered and therefore meaningful, and if everyone all the time construed the environment as a secure moral order, there would be no need to talk of *redemption* faith. The gospel, I will argue, is addressed to an elemental confidence in the depths of the human self, but it is a confidence assailed by doubt and tired by life's contradictions. It fluctuates and sometimes is overwhelmed; it needs reassurance and healing. Hence the Redeemer is presented not merely as a teacher but as a physician (Matt. 9:12; Mark 2:17; Luke 5:31). But before turning to redemption faith in part II, we must consider what it means to speak of God as "Creator" and humans as "created in God's image."

5. God as Creator

Faith in God "the Father of Jesus Christ" presupposes that the creative principle of cosmic order is not only inconceivably powerful and mysterious, but also the source of goodness and justice, like authentic parental care; and this is what is meant by representing the creative principle as "Creator" and "Father Almighty."

In the previous chapter I presented "the world as creation" simply as descriptive of the cosmic order presupposed by Christian faith. But "creation" implies that the order is not just there: it is "made," ascribed to a Creator or Maker. The particular way in which creation faith pictures the relation of the world to God is commonly tagged "theist." The term *theism* does not belong to the primary religious language of Christian faith but rather to theological and philosophical accounts of it. It made its appearance in the seventeenth century and came to distinguish a third option for understanding the relationship between the world and God. Against *deism*, the view that God made the world but remains aloof from it, theism affirms that the God who made, or makes, the world is continually engaged with it. Against *pantheism*, the view that God and the world are one, theism insists on the ontological distinction between Creator and creatures. The three types of belief in God have been subjects of debate in the philosophy of religion. But I begin the present chapter by looking at the primary language of the particular instance of theism presupposed by faith in Christ: the so-called ethical monotheism of the Hebrew Scriptures.

I. The God of Israel

The books of the Old Testament were composed and edited over several centuries, and a uniform theology is not to be expected between one book and another, or even within a single book. Differences must be noted. But, for all the variations in Hebrew religion, the main features of a distinctive picture of the Deity do emerge, capable of being compared with pictures of the God or gods of other religions. The God of Israel is "Yahweh" (for the Hebrew Tetragrammaton *YHWH*). In the words of the Shema (Deut. 6:4), "Hear, O Israel: the LORD [*Yahweh*] is our God, the LORD [*Yahweh*] alone." The English versions, following the Septuagint's *kyrios*, regularly translate *Yahweh* as "the LORD" (capitalized). But this tends to obscure the historical particularity of the divine name first revealed to Moses (Exod. 3:13–15; 6:2–3; but see Gen. 4:26). For this reason,

I regularly prefer "Yahweh" to "LORD," except in direct quotations from the NRSV.[1]

Exclusive worship of Yahweh as the God of Israel probably came before the conviction that he is not just peerless but the only God there is, and for a time henotheism continued alongside strict monotheism. The psalmist can imagine Yahweh taking his place in the council of the gods, and yet he is confident that the other gods will perish like mortals. Yahweh presides as judge over the whole earth, "for all the nations belong to [him]" (Ps. 82:1, 6–8; cf. 95:3). In the prayer of King David, declaration of the greatness of Yahweh, made known in the redemption of Israel, passes over into the affirmation, "There is no God besides you" (2 Sam. 7:22; cf. Deut. 3:24; 4:35, 39; Ps. 77:13; Isa. 45:5, 21–22). Insofar as it was assumed that his favor was strictly for Israel, or even for a faithful remnant only (e.g., Isa. 10:22; Joel 2:32), particularism survived the recognition that Yahweh was the one and only God. But it was also widely believed that other nations would share in the blessings Yahweh had bestowed, or would bestow, on his own people (see chap. 14, on election).

1. *God as Creator, Ruler, Savior*

To begin with, Yahweh is *Creator,* maker of heaven and earth. "It is he who made the earth by his power, who established the world by his wisdom, and by his understanding stretched out the heavens" (Jer. 10:12). And he preserves what he has made—the hosts of heaven and all that is on the earth and in the seas: "to all of them you give life" (Neh. 9:6; RSV has "thou preservest all of them"). The fixed order of nature is attributed to him, not to the fertility god Baal (Jer. 31:35–36; Ps. 148:5–6). It is he who feeds the animals (Ps. 147:9), and he is the source of earth's abundance even if his own people fail to realize it (Hos. 2:8). His sovereignty over nature should be plain when he *withholds* his blessings and sends famine, drought, and pestilence instead (Amos 4:6–13). Yahweh's majesty is manifested in thunder and lightning, in the plagues that fell on the Egyptians, and in their drowning in the Red Sea. He turns rivers into a desert, and a desert into pools of water (Pss. 29:3–9; 107:33–35). The awesome power of the Creator reduces Job to silence (Job 38:1–40:5; cf. 36:24–37:24).

Sovereign over nature, Yahweh is sovereign also over history: the Creator is supreme *Ruler.* "For dominion belongs to the LORD, and he rules over the nations" (Ps. 22:28). In a world overshadowed by the conflicts of the great powers—Egypt, Assyria, Babylon, and Persia—the Hebrew prophets announce that the course of international events is securely under Yahweh's control, whose purpose is to chastise his people and in due time to destroy their enemies. Assyria is unknowingly the rod of his anger against his faithless people (Isa. 10:5–7); Nebuchadnezzar, Chaldean king of Babylon, is his servant (Jer. 27:6; see also Dan. 4:1–37; 5:21); Cyrus, king of Persia, is his anointed (Isa. 45:1), of whom he says, "He is my shepherd, and he shall carry out all my purpose" (Isa. 44:28). The sacking of Jerusalem and the captivity of her children are punishment for

1. There is no consensus either on the source of the name "Yahweh" or on its meaning; see the commentaries on Exod. 3:13–15. In the following pages, I do not multiply texts unnecessarily for common features of the OT picture of God; references can easily be added. I remind the reader of n. 6 in chap. 1 above, on the use of masculine pronouns for God.

her transgressions (e.g., Lam. 1:5), but Yahweh stirs up the spirit of Cyrus to let the exiles return and rebuild the temple (Ezek. 1:1–4). The prophetic vision of history is different from the later apocalyptic drama, in which God, for a time, turns the present world over to the power of evil. True, the hand of Yahweh in history is not obvious. He is a God who hides himself (Isa. 45:15). Yet all history moves at his behest and ministers to his purposes—even the suffering of his chosen people. Yahweh does not forget Zion: the furnace of affliction is the refinement of Israel (Isa. 48:10; 49:14–16).

The God of Israel is not only Creator and Ruler; he is Israel's *Savior* or *Redeemer,* who brought his people out of Egypt and gave them the land of Canaan (Josh. 24:2–18; Judg. 6:8–9; 1 Sam. 12:9–15; Neh. 9:6–37) and who promises to bring them back from the Babylonian captivity (Jer. 23:7–8). Recollection of Yahweh's glorious deeds on behalf of his faithless and ungrateful people is a constant theme in the Psalter (Pss. 78, 105, 106, 135, 136; cf. Deut. 26:4–9), and in Deuteronomy it furnishes the premise, many times repeated, of Moses' call to the people to observe the commandments (Deut. 4:32–40; 5:6; 6:20–25; 11:2–8; 15:15; 16:12; etc.).

To speak of Yahweh as Savior or Redeemer means, above all, that he saves and redeems his chosen *people,* delivering them from subservience to other nations, rescuing them from their enemies, forgiving their sins (Pss. 106:10; 130:7–8). As the prophet Jeremiah says, "Truly in the LORD our God is the salvation of Israel" (Jer. 3:23). But Yahweh is also the Savior of the *individual* Israelite who asks to share in the blessings of the people (Ps. 106:4–5) or who turns to him in the day of trouble (Pss. 70, 130). The Psalter is full of individual pleas for divine aid or thanks for aid given. Yahweh is invoked as "my salvation" (Pss. 27:1; 38:22; etc.; cf. Isa. 12:2), or "God of my salvation" (Pss. 25:5; 88:1; cf. Mic. 7:7; Heb. 3:18), who delivers the psalmist from his enemies and oppressors, forgives his sins, heals his diseases, and snatches him from the jaws of death (Pss. 18 [/ / 2 Sam. 22], 86, 102, 103, 130).

2. *Attributes of God: Justice, Love, and Goodness*

In Christian theology, the character of God as Creator, Ruler, and Savior has traditionally been summed up in the doctrine of the divine attributes. Occasionally, the Old Testament brings several attributes together and even seems to rank them in importance, as the situation requires. Calvin (*Institutes,* 1:97–98) found summaries of what he called the divine "virtues" in Exodus 34:6–7, Psalm 145, and Jeremiah 9:24. My own limited intention is not to furnish a comprehensive list but to lift up attributes characteristic of the faith of Israel in comparison with other ancient religions. Three stand out: *justice* (or righteousness), *steadfast love,* and *goodness.* At the risk of oversimplifying the historical and linguistic data, some brief remarks on each of these three attributes will have to suffice for the present purpose, which is to sketch the relationship presupposed by Christian faith between the world and the Creator.

The sovereignty of Yahweh is his moral governance over Israel and all the peoples of the earth, that is, his *justice* or *righteousness* (*ṣedeq, ṣedaqah*), the attribute by which he deals with all "according to their ways, according to the fruit of their doings" (Jer. 17:10; cf. 1 Sam. 26:23; Ps. 5:4–6, 12). He delights in justice, and all his ways are just (Deut. 32:4; Pss. 11:7; 37:28; 145:17; Isa. 61:8; Jer. 9:24). The psalmist praises Yahweh, "who executes justice for the oppressed; who gives food to the hungry . . . sets the prisoners free . . . opens the eyes of the blind . . . lifts up those who are bowed down . . . loves the righteous . . . watches over the strangers . . . upholds the orphan and the widow" (Ps. 147:7–9). His justice is bound up with the justice he requires of his people; his character is reflected in the duties of the good king, who "delivers the needy when they call, the poor and those who have no helper" (Ps. 72:1–4, 12–14; cf. Jer. 23:5–6). But when the people first demanded, "Give us a king to govern us," Samuel had warned them against the ways of kings (1 Sam. 8:4–18), and the history of Israel became a story of forgetfulness and rebellion that brought down Yahweh's retribution on his people and their leaders. In 2 Chronicles the kings of Judah and Israel are divided into those who did what was right in the eyes of Yahweh and those who did evil. The outward fortunes of the two kingdoms are interpreted accordingly. Bad kings bring divine retribution at the hands of their enemies, and good kings are rewarded with divine intervention against armies much more powerful than theirs.

Yahweh's retribution is said to be the work of his anger. He is a God of vengeance (Ps. 94:1; cf. Deut. 32:35; Ezek. 25:14–17), a jealous God (Exod. 20:5; 34:14; Deut. 4:24; 5:9; 6:15; Josh. 24:19; Nah. 1:2). But "wrath" is not to be taken simply as personal pique and set aside as an outmoded religious fancy, as Schleiermacher thought (*CF* 350). Often enough, it is indeed anger at Israel's paying to other deities what Yahweh claims exclusively for himself (Num. 25:3; Deut. 31:16–20; 32:16–22; Judg. 10:6–8; Jer. 25:6; etc.). He will not share his glory with another (Isa. 42:8; 48:11), and there are certainly cultic sins that deserve his curse (see, e.g., Mal. 1:6–14; 3:8–9). But wrath is also, and preeminently, a *moral* term (e.g., Exod. 22:21–24). A moral interpretation of Yahweh's demands lies at the heart of the protest made by the eighth-century prophets and Jeremiah against any temptation to equate faithfulness to God with the performance of rituals (Isa. 1:10–17; Jer. 6:20; 11:15; Hos. 6:6; Amos 5:21–25; Mic. 6:6–8). The objects of Yahweh's anger are dishonesty and failure to care for the needy. It is no use repeating, "This is the temple of the LORD, the temple of the LORD, the temple of the LORD" if you continue to oppress the alien, the fatherless, and the widow or if you steal, murder, commit adultery, swear falsely, and go after other gods (Jer. 7:1–11; 22:3, 13–17; cf. Ezek. 18:5–18; 22:6–12, 25–29). Many of the offenses that provoke Yahweh are the characteristic sins of those in power—the shepherds who feed themselves and not the sheep (Jer. 10:21; 23:1–4; 25:34–38; 50:6; Ezek. 34:1–10; 45:9). The postexilic prophets, too, despite their paramount concern for the temple and the priestly cult, could warn that the wrath of God is directed against social sins (Mal. 2:13–16; 3:5; Zech. 7:8–12; 8:14–17; 10:2–3; 11:4–5). Even in the midst of its detailed ritual prescriptions, Leviticus—postexilic in its final form—lays down the moral duties the Israelite owes to parents, siblings, neighbors, resident aliens, the poor, the hired hand, and the elderly, because the character of Yahweh demands it. "You shall be holy, for I the LORD your God am holy. . . . [Y]ou shall love your neighbor as yourself: I am the LORD" (Lev. 19:2, 18; cf. 25:17).

Some interpreters argue that the eighth-century prophets and Jeremiah did not mean to renounce ritual and the temple cult, only to insist that ritual without justice is futile. They were saying, with Samuel, that "to obey is *better* than sacrifice," or, with the later proverb, that "to do righteousness and justice is *more* acceptable to the LORD" (1 Sam. 15:22; Prov. 21:3; emphasis mine). But Amos and Jeremiah do seem to say that the sacrificial cult was not ordained by Yahweh, or at least that the relationship between Yahweh and his people was better during their years of wandering, when there was no sacrificial cult (Amos 5:21–25; Jer. 7:22–23; cf. Ps. 40:6–8, quoted in Heb. 10:5–7). Elsewhere, it is thanksgiving and contrition that are said to be, like justice and obedience, the sacrifices acceptable to God (Pss. 50:13–14; 51:16–17; 69:30–31).

The prologue to the Code of Hammurabi, the Amorite king of Babylon (ca. 1792–1750 BCE), anticipated the Hebrew idea of God insofar as it represented the sun god, Shamash, as god of justice commissioning the king to cause justice to prevail in the land. But the elevation of justice or righteousness as the prime attribute of the one and only God differentiates Hebrew religious thought from the beliefs of other Middle Eastern religions (see, for instance, the commentaries on the reason why Yahweh caused the great flood, Gen. 6:5). More striking is the gulf between Yahweh and the Olympian gods of ancient Greece. The Homeric deities acted to assert their place at the head of a hierarchical order that had little to do with maintaining "justice" in any sense that a Hebrew would have recognized, and their behavior was not inhibited by tedious moral standards. As Herodotus observed, divinity was entirely a matter of envy.[2] The Olympian gods had their favorites and could be won over by gifts. But Yahweh "is not partial and takes no bribe, [he] executes justice for the orphan and the widow" (Deut. 10:17–18). The psalmist pictures him rebuking the other gods in the divine council because they do *not* judge justly or "maintain the right of the lowly and the destitute" (Ps. 82:2–4). If there is a "preferential option for the poor" in the Hebrew Bible, it only asserts their rights; it does not compromise the strict impartiality of God's justice, as though he tilted the scales in their favor (Exod. 23:3; Lev. 19:15; Deut. 1:17; 16:19–20).

Alongside Yahweh's justice, the Hebrew Scriptures tell of his *love*. Justice and love belong together: "Righteousness and justice are the foundation of your throne; steadfast love and faithfulness go before you" (Ps. 89:14; cf. 33:5; 116:5; Jer. 9:24). The single word regularly translated as "steadfast love" in the NRSV is the Hebrew *ḥesed*. (The KJV usually has "mercy" or "lovingkindness.") Psalms 89 and 136 are songs of praise for Yahweh's *ḥesed* and make its special sense clear as *covenant* love—faithfulness to the promises made to his servant David. "Steadfast love" and "faithfulness" are often used synonymously in tandem (Exod. 34:6–7 [// Num. 14:18]; Pss. 86:15; 89:14; etc.). The glory of Yahweh is that he remains faithful to the covenant even when his people are faithless.

Hosea views Israel's sin precisely as a breach of the covenant bond established by a God of steadfast love. The story of the prophet's marriage to Gomer, "a wife of whoredom," whether or not it is a narrative of actual events, serves as an allegory of Yahweh's *marital* love for his unfaithful people (Hos. 2:19–20; cf. Ezek. 16 and 23). Hosea also adapted the language of *parental* love to Israel's deliverance from servitude: "When Israel was a child, I loved him, and out of

2. Herodotus, *Histories* 1.32. Zeus is a partial exception, e.g., he is sometimes said to care about honesty in the marketplace. But we know him best for his sexual escapades.

Egypt I called my son. . . . [I]t was I who taught Ephraim to walk. I took them up in my arms" (Hos. 11:1–4). God's love, like God's justice, calls for an answering disposition in his people, who must reflect the nature of their God: "hold fast to love and justice, and wait continually for your God" (Hos. 12:6; cf. 10:12). Similarly, Micah insists that there is no doubt about what Yahweh expects of his people: "He has told you, O mortal, what is good; and what does the LORD require of you but to do justice, and to love kindness [*ḥesed*], and to walk humbly with your God" (Mic. 6:8).

Justice, then, is not the last word about Yahweh's nature. He is "slow to anger and abounding in steadfast love. . . . [H]e does not deal with us according to our sins, nor repay us according to our iniquities" (Ps. 103:8, 10; cf. Neh. 9:17, 31; Pss. 30:5; 78:38; 85:2–10; 86:5; Dan. 9:9, 18; Joel 2:13; Mic. 7:18; Jonah 4:2). "Although he causes grief, he will have compassion according to the abundance of his steadfast love; for he does not willingly afflict or grieve anyone" (Lam. 3:31–33). There are, to be sure, passages in which Yahweh's compassion is made contingent on the obedience or repentance of his people (Lev. 26:14–45; Amos 5:14–15); and there are others in which "his wrath is quickly kindled" (Ps. 2:12) and he kills without pity, retreating into a cloud that no prayer can penetrate (Lam. 3:43–44). But sometimes—even in the same passage—the message is that Yahweh's compassion takes precedence over his anger, which is "but for a moment" (Ps. 30:5; cf. 103:8–9), and that he forgives simply because he is God ("for my own sake," Isa. 43:25).

Still, *ḥesed* has its limits. All the nations are summoned to praise Yahweh for his steadfast love (Ps. 117); it is attested by the work of creation (136:4–9), fills the earth (33:5; 119:64), and extends to the heavens (36:5). And yet, as Yahweh's covenant love it is most properly his love for the chosen people, and even for them it does not rule out divine retribution for their wickedness. Hosea testifies that the covenant bond has been broken (Hos. 8:1): the third child born to him and Gomer is to be named *Lo-ammi*, "Not-my-people." True, the prophet immediately holds out the prospect of Israel's restoration as "children of the living God" (1:8–9; see also 2:7, 23). In general, however, *ḥesed* is doubly restricted: it is love for the covenant people, and it is conditional on their keeping the covenant (Ps. 103:17–18).

The *goodness* (*ṭôb*) of Yahweh may be seen as a more comprehensive divine attribute than his steadfast love. The best proof of his goodness is, to be sure, his love to Israel (Ezra 3:11; Pss. 106:1; 107:1–2; 135:3–4; Hos. 3:5; Zech. 9:16–17). Yet the psalmist can say: "The LORD is good to all, and his compassion is over all that he has made" (Ps. 145:9). For their favorite image of God as "the fountain of good," the Protestant reformers Luther, Zwingli, and Calvin could appeal to the Psalter, in which the goodness of God is a recurring theme (see Pss. 23:6; 25:7–8; 27:13; 31:19; 34:8; 68:10; 69:16; 100:5; 103:5; 118:29; 119:68; 136:1). Ulrich (Huldrych) Zwingli (1484–1531) read the story of creation in Genesis 1 as a testimony to the goodness of God. He noted that a striking feature of the story is the repetition of the formula, "And God saw that it was good." It appears in the work of days three to six, twice in day three (vv. 10 and 12), and with a minor difference of wording in day one. (Its absence from the report of the second day may be evidence of an earlier version.) As a summing up of the entire six-day work of creation, the formula appears again, slightly modified, in verse 31: "God saw everything that he had made, and indeed, it was very good." On the seventh day he rested (2:1–3). From the goodness of the creation Zwingli inferred the goodness of the Creator,[3] and he discovered in the creation story a happy link with Plato (428/427–348/347 BCE). In answer to the question why the Artificer made the world, Plato (in the person of Timaeus) says: "He is good; what he made is good; no good person is ever grudging with anything good."[4]

Of course, Yahweh has other attributes, but if we take his goodness to include his covenant love, without being reducible to it, we can sum up by saying that in the Hebrew Scriptures God is characterized by two attributes in particular: justice and goodness. They qualify but do not negate his power and his mystery. The immense *power* of Yahweh is attested by Second Isaiah (the presumed author of Isa. 40–55), whose God created the stars by the greatness of his strength (40:26), makes a wilderness into a pool of water (41:18), "brings princes to naught, and makes the rulers of the earth as nothing" (40:23). But Second Isaiah can only represent the transcendent power of God as located at the top of the same scale, so to say, on which human power is situated: "he sits above the circle of the earth, and its inhabitants are like grasshoppers" (40:22; cf. Pss. 7:17; 9:2; Dan. 9:4). Yahweh has in overwhelming measure the kind of power that a strong man has. The *mystery* of God, on the other hand, breaks the anthropomorphic mold—it is sheer ineffability.

Yahweh reveals himself precisely as mystery. Even his giving of his name (Exod. 3:14) leaves the mystery intact, however the name is interpreted: "I am what I am," "I will be what I will be," or perhaps "I cause to be whatever I cause to be." The personal name of Israel's God asserts his otherness, and in the synagogues it became the practice not even to utter it, *Adonai* ("Lord") or *Elohim* ("God") being pronounced instead. The awesome mystery of Yahweh could also be conveyed by the symbolism of, for example, Isaiah's vision of the holy God in the temple (Isa. 6). Even there, however, God is still presented in terms of elevation or magnification rather than ineffability, and the overwhelming sense of God's sheer otherness is bound up with the prophet's consciousness of sin. This is something different from the radical Platonic aphorism of Philo, "Not only is God not of human form [*anthrōpomorphos*]: God is without any properties at all [*apoios*]."[5] Still, the idea of God's "holiness" clearly sets God apart as what Rudolf Otto (1869–1937) taught us to call the *mysterium tremendum* (see the editorial note in *Institutes*, 1:38–39).

II. The Living God

The Hebrew understanding of God took shape in the context of Israel's history, interpreted in terms of election, covenant, and redemption. Hence a good deal must be postponed to part II below. For the present, our concern is to

3. Ulrich Zwingli, *Commentary on True and False Religion* (1525), *ZSW* 3:645, 650–51, 668; *LWZ* 3:64, 70–71, 91.

4. Ulrich Zwingli, *Sermon on Providence* (1530), *ZSW* 6/3:71–72, 106–7; *LWZ* 2:131, 151–52. The Plato reference is to *Timaeus*, 29d–e. Cf. Calvin, *Institutes* 1.5.6 (1:59). Similarly, Thomas wrote that God "intends only to communicate His perfection, which is His goodness" (*ST* 1, q. 44, art. 4 [1:232]; see also q. 6, art. 3 [1:29]).

5. Philo Judaeus (ca. 30 BCE–ca. CE 40), *Nomōn hierōn allegoriai* (Allegories of Sacred Laws), 1.13 (trans. mine).

determine the basic concept of deity presupposed by Christian faith in God "the Father of Jesus Christ," that is, to characterize the general relation of God to the world, the Creator to the creatures (including humankind), not yet the particular relation of humanity to God the Redeemer in Christ. This will also be the place to comment on the supposed conflict of theism with the natural sciences.

1. *The God of Israel in the New Testament*

The classification of the God of Israel as "theist" is self-evident. Yahweh continually interacts with the world but is never confused with it. He acts on the world from above, and in this he is closer to the God of deism than to the God of pantheism. If, then, in addition to Yahweh's transcendence we speak of his immanence, it does not denote an uninterrupted cosmic force that dissolves divine causality in natural causality but rather the continuity of divine interaction with nature and history. No lengthy argument is needed to certify that this is the Deity presupposed by Christian believers.

We can go further and say that the attributes of justice, goodness, and steadfast love, by which the ethical monotheism of the Old Testament characterizes God's relation to the world of humankind, are carried over into the New. For example, when he reproves the scribes and Pharisees, Jesus sanctions the prophetic witness to the *justice* (or righteousness) that a just God requires: "You tithe the mint, dill, and cummin, and have neglected the weightier matters of the law: justice [*krisin*] and mercy and faithfulness [NRSV 'faith']" (Matt. 23:23, echoing Mic. 6:8; cf. Mark 12:28–34; Luke 11:42). And he is reported praying to God as "Righteous Father" (John 17:25; cf. "Holy Father" in v. 11). As for the *goodness* of God, Zwingli finds confirmation of his belief that God is "the fountain and spring of all good" in Jesus' answer to the rich young man: "There is only one who is good" (Matt. 19:17; cf. Mark 10:18; Luke 18:19). And Jesus exhorts his disciples to love as their heavenly Father loves, for "he makes his sun to rise on the evil and on the good, and sends rain on the righteous and on the unrighteous" (Matt. 5:45). The substance of the Hebrew term for God's *steadfast love* is partly carried over into the Greek word *charis* ("grace"), to which I return in chapters 9 and 12. God's justice, goodness, and love do not negate the mystery of God in the New Testament. For example, 1 Timothy bears witness to the God who gives life to all things: "It is he alone who has immortality and dwells in unapproachable light, whom no one has ever seen or can see" (1 Tim. 6:16).

According to some, what was distinctive about the teaching of Jesus was his naming God "Father." This is not strictly true. We can leave it to the New Testament scholars to explain why in Luke, and especially in Mark, Jesus is reported speaking of God as Father much less frequently than in Matthew. Perhaps the predilection for the divine name "Father" in the First Gospel should be partly credited to Matthew. In any case, God was already likened to a father in the Hebrew Scriptures—both as the one who created Israel or humankind (Deut. 32:6–7; Isa. 45:11–12; 64:8; Mal. 2:10) and as a caring parent (Exod. 4:22–23; Deut. 1:31; 8:5; 14:1; 2 Sam. 7:14–15; Pss. 68:5; 89:26; 103:13; Isa. 63:16; Jer. 3:14, 19; 31:9, 20; Hos. 1:10; 11:1–4; Mal. 1:6; 3:17). What was new about Jesus'

teaching on the fatherhood of God was the remarkable way in which he called God "*my* father," especially in Matthew and John; and on this there will more to say later (chap. 11).

There are, of course, difficulties in the Hebraic way of speaking about God. I have in mind not only the occasional unpleasant stories that could not be included in the church lectionary but even more the central theme of Israel's history. Yahweh's leading his people out of bondage and into the promised land was accompanied by his command for total destruction of the cities and peoples that stood in the way, including the wholesale massacre of women and children—hard to harmonize with either justice or goodness (Deut. 2:34; Josh. 6:17, 21; 8:2, 24–29; 10:38–40; 11:10–15, 20; etc.; cf. the story of Agag in 1 Sam. 15:17–33). Moreover, the correlation of sin and retribution—so that where suffering is observed, sin is inferred as its cause—is already questioned in the Hebrew Scriptures themselves. On this, too, there will be more to say later (chap. 8). Our immediate task is to consider how far, if at all, biblical faith in the Creator God needs reinterpretation in the light of present-day thought (our secondary dogmatic norm). Theism, or the understanding of God as Creator, is the context in which the most persistent questions about religion and natural science arise, just as the doctrine of God the Redeemer in Christ raises the most persistent questions about God and historical science.

2. *God the Creator and Natural Science*

Talk of "the problem of science and religion," as usually understood, has proved misleading for at least two reasons. First, it has given rise to the misconception that religion can be judged simply as bogus science, a superannuated rival to modern natural science.[6] The debate over creationism may have lent plausibility to the misconception. But religion is a complex form of human activity, and several academic disciplines ("sciences") study it as an academic field of inquiry. Besides the philosophy of religion, the psychology of religion, and the sociology of religion, Christian theology is one such discipline—or may be, depending on how its task and method are defined. The so-called history of religions, or "science of religion" (*Religionswissenschaft*), is another; it is often promoted as more properly scientific than theology, which is perceived as compromised by supernaturalism, unverifiable revelation claims, and tacit apologetic motives—a perception that does scant justice to the varieties of Christian theology. Schleiermacher, for example, held his theological method to be empirical, and he dealt with sin and redemption as facts of experience (Schleiermacher 1981: 45). The "empirical theology" movement in American religious thought of the twentieth century traced its lineage, in part, back to him.

We would do well to speak not of a conflict between religion and science, only of better or worse accounts of religion, some of which purport to be scientific. It would be an improvement to rephrase the problem as "*theology* and *natural* science," and even this oversimplifies the fact that just as there are

6. Many writers on science and religion hold that the misconception fails to distinguish the *how* explanations of science (in terms of structure, causes, and natural processes) from the *why* explanations sought by religion (in terms of purpose and meaning). See, e.g., Gilkey 1985: 66–80.

varieties of Christian theology, so also there are more natural sciences than one, and they may not all have the same relation to theology. Since the late twentieth century, physicists have been, on the whole, more amenable to theological perspectives than biologists. One eminent physicist goes so far as to say: "It may seem bizarre, but in my opinion science offers a surer path to God than religion" (Davies 1983: ix).

Second, the expression "science and religion" has been taken as disjunctive, calling for a choice: either science or religion. The metaphor of a continual "warfare" places the scientists on one side and the theologians on the other. It owes its currency largely to A. D. White's old but still influential two-volume history (1896). Against the earlier study by Draper (1874), White designated as his subject the warfare of science and *dogmatic theology*, not the warfare of science and religion. This could have been an improvement. But White's history did not do justice to the fact that innovations in the natural sciences can divide both the scientific and the theological community. Indeed, the champions of scientific progress have often come from the theological community, or at least from believers. As Nancy Frankenberry remarks, the titans of the Scientific Revolution (she names Galileo, Kepler, Bacon, Pascal, and Newton) were "all devout believers to a man" (Frankenberry 2008: ix). And the scientists she reviews closer to our own time include such unconventional believers as Albert Einstein (1879–1955), who believed in Spinoza's God, and such agnostics as Stephen Jay Gould (1941–2002), who appealed for a "concordat between the magisteria of science and religion."

Recent studies in the history of science have shown that the relationship between natural science and theology has never been reducible to conflict or warfare—nor to happy harmony. The reception of Darwin's evolutionary theory is a case in point: some theologians rejected it, but others (including the advocates of so-called theistic evolution) welcomed it for the added light it shed on the ways of God. It has been pointed out that "[c]ontrary to common assumptions, no church in Darwin's era officially rejected evolution and his adversaries tended to include more scientists than religious authorities" (Phipps 2002: 88–89). And, of course, there have always been times when theology and natural science have simply gone their separate ways, not least because natural scientists and theologians are not always competent in the other field. Lack of competence in theology and religious studies, however, has not always deterred the cultured despisers of religion from offering opinions on the subject, and it is tempting to rebuke the advocates of the so-called new atheism for their "religious illiteracy" (Haught 2008: 63).

I have set aside, as a misinterpretation of the literary genre of Genesis 1–2, the supposed competition between religion and natural science on the question of origins. Whether the Big Bang theory is correct is up to the scientific cosmologists to settle by generally accepted scientific arguments. Religion, if it minds its limitations, cannot offer any shortcuts without being caught trespassing. On the other hand, it does not follow that because natural scientists do not need the "God hypothesis" to get on with their work, therefore there is no God. What surely follows is that God cannot be an item in the chain of causes and effects in nature that the natural scientists investigate. It cannot even be said that God is the *First* Cause, if that is taken to mean the first efficient cause in a temporal sequence of causes; that would still be a cause among causes even if it served as their apex. This, admittedly, is the way Thomas Aquinas spoke explicitly in the second of his five ways to prove the existence of God, and implicitly in the first. But his fifth way hints at another conception of divine causality: it is taken from God's governance of the world, in which God appears as an intelligent being "by whom all natural things are directed to their end" (*ST* 1:14). If we can take this as a judgment about the world as a whole rather than each individual entity within it, then God's activity is not an item in the causal nexus of nature but a teleological principle that directs the total course of nature to its end—a view of God and nature that points toward Schleiermacher.

Almost two hundred years ago, Schleiermacher predicted that, quite apart from the Mosaic creation stories, theologians would eventually have to do without the very concept of creation as usually understood and that the concept of a miracle also would not be able to continue in its traditional form. Otherwise, the theologian would become an object of ridicule. Christianity would be identified with barbarism, and science with unbelief (Schleiermacher 1981: 60–61). What made this prediction possible and necessary for Schleiermacher was his idea of divine causality as coextensive with natural causality but different in kind (*CF* 200–202). He ruled out supernaturalism, or divine interventionism, as subversive of science and religion alike. The activity of God cannot be construed in terms of intervention. A world open to religion is not one in which God freely *interrupts* the regular course of things but one in which God freely *ordains* the regular course of things and *steers* it toward its appointed goal. Because the omnipotence of God grounds the entire temporal system of nature, divine and natural causality cannot be confused. Schleiermacher concludes that God must be a cause in a unique, nontemporal and nonspatial way. And how, exactly, is that? He admitted that we can only have recourse to analogies. We are to think, for example, of our own self (*das Ich*), which is the enduring ground of the changing mental phenomena of our existence (206).

Schleiermacher and others, such as Johann Gottfried von Herder (1744–1803), were attempting to rethink the relation of God to the world in the light of the natural science of their day. Of course, they wrote before Charles Darwin's (1809–82) theory of the role that chance plays in the origin of species. But the emergence of a new species does not negate the laws of nature—it presupposes them. It was a contemporary of Darwin, the Augustinian friar Gregor Mendel (1822–84), who discovered laws of heredity without which Darwin's theory of inherited characteristics fell short. Antagonism between Darwinism and dogmatic theology arises when the theologian imagines that biological change is not brought about according to divinely established laws but by the Creator's interruption of them. As John Polkinghorne says, "mainstream theology has never thought of God in terms of an important but invisible actor on the stage of the world but rather as the Author and Producer of the cosmic play" (1998: 18).

We will return more than once in the following chapters to the nature of God's relation to the world, including humanity: when we come to speak of free will, God and evil, acts of God (including special revelation), and the miracles attributed to Jesus. The present chapter is intended to present the biblical understanding of the Creator God, but to show that the activity of the Creator need not be taken to imply the divine interventionism that occasions the supposed conflict of religion and natural science. Before moving on to humanity as created, we should address the opinion that if the Creator is thought of as a *person*, interventionism is inevitable. Albert Einstein put his finger on the problem: "The main source of the present-day conflicts between the spheres of religion and of science lies in [the] concept of a personal God" (Einstein 1954: 47).

3. *God the Creator as Person*

There is no need to argue the obvious: the Hebrew Scriptures picture Yahweh anthropomorphically, in human form. Not, to be sure, exclusively. Impersonal images of God are also employed: he is a fountain, a devouring fire, a lamp or light, a dwelling place, a hiding place, a refuge, a rock, a shield, and so on. He is also compared to animals: lion, leopard, bear, eagle, a mother hen. But the dominant images of Yahweh are personal: he is king, judge, warrior, shepherd, father, husband, gardener, and so on. He is pictured "walking in the garden at the time of the evening breeze" (Gen. 3:8), coming down to inspect the tower of Babel (11:5) or to see if the rumors about Sodom and Gomorrah are true (18:21). Sometimes, he must be awakened from sleep (Ps. 44:23), and sometimes he wakes up "like a warrior shouting because of wine" (78:65). Various parts of Yahweh's body are mentioned, as also is his dwelling place. And, like humans, he gets angry and changes his mind.

The conventional image of God in Christian art still looks like Daniel's Ancient of Days, his clothing white as snow and the hair of his head like pure wool (Dan. 7:9). At the operational linguistic level, the symbolic meaning of anthropomorphic images is readily grasped. God hides his face because he is displeased; his outstretched arm is his sovereign power; and so on. Occasionally, Scripture itself warns against too easy a comparison of divine and human states of mind. Yahweh is not a man that he should repent (1 Sam. 15:29; but see v. 35!) or that he cannot restrain his anger (Hos. 11:9). But these words of caution do not move us out of anthropomorphic language for God; they only qualify it. If we take "anthropomorphism" in its dictionary sense ("the attribution of a human form *or personality* to a god, animal, or thing"), it covers God's displeasure or anger as well as the hiding of his face.

Calvin tells us that talk of God as angry or changing his mind, like all other descriptions of God in human terms, is accommodated to our limited capacity to understand. God represents himself (*se figuret*) not as he is in himself, but as he is perceived by us (*Institutes*, 1:227, 504–6). That said, Calvin does not hesitate to make free use of accommodated language: his God wills and talks like a human. Faith is "knowledge of God's will toward us, perceived from his Word" (549). In Scripture, God "opens his own most hallowed lips" (70); Scripture "has flowed to us from the very mouth of God" (80). What occasionally makes Calvin pause to offer correction is the mistaken supposition that God has human emotions or an actual body. God's nature is spiritual, and for this reason he is incomprehensible (121; cf. 559). We should not ask what he is (*quid sit Deus*) but what he is like (*qualis*); his attributes show him as he is to us (*qualis erga nos*), not as he is in himself (*non quis sit apud se*; 41, 97). However, anthropomorphic statements about God, though tempered to our feeble grasp, are not said falsely (505). Calvin has, in general, no problem with the biblical picture of a personal God who acts as one agent or cause among others in nature and history (e.g., 310–11), and that is where the possibility of conflict with scientific explanation arises.

That the relation of the believer to God is *personal* is the consistent testimony of Christian experience as well as the normative practice and teaching of Jesus. But just as consistent throughout the church's history has been the recognition that God is not *a person* just like us. Various accounts of the experience of God as person have been proposed. (1) Polkinghorne's analogy—God as Author and Producer of the cosmic drama, not an actor on the stage—does not, as such, question the concept of God as person but relocates it (so to say) off stage. (2) Schleiermacher thought that anthropomorphism, though inevitable, should not be transformed into a metaphysical concept of divine personality. In his view, we cannot in fact form any real conception of the highest being. The "attributes" we ascribe to God do not refer to particular characteristics of God in himself but rather to the divine causality, of which we are conscious in the feeling of absolute dependence. Schleiermacher's principle that divine and natural causality are coextensive meant that, in his view, "we have no formula for the being of God in Himself [*an sich*] as distinct from the being of God in the world" (*CF* 198, 748). But his analogy for God's relation to the world—the self as the enduring ground of a person's own changing mental activity—foreshadows a third option: (3) Charles Hartshorne's (1897–2000) "neoclassical theism," in which God is related to the world as a human person is related to the living cells of his or her own body. In this sense, God is the whole of things, and the whole is personal (Hartshorne 1936). For all their differences, these three options have in common the refusal to take literally naive talk of God as a supremely powerful person acting among a crowd of less powerful persons on the cosmic stage, repeatedly interrupting and redirecting the way the world goes—the picture of God that Einstein found so problematic.

Others have explained (4) that the relationship of the believer to God is personal because the believer, not God, is a person (an explanation already implied in Schleiermacher's admission that anthropomorphism is inevitable). John Hick appropriates the Kantian distinction between *phenomena*, things as they appear to us, and *noumena*, things as they are in themselves (*an sich*), and maintains that "the divine Reality is not directly known *an sich*. But when human beings relate themselves to it in the mode of I-Thou encounter they experience it as personal. Indeed in the context of that relationship it *is* personal, not It but He or She" (Hick 1989: 245). Of course, a margin of agnosticism around talk about God is by no means without precedent in the theological tradition long before Kant, as Calvin's talk about the incomprehensibility of God in himself attests.[7] When Paul Tillich spoke of "the God above the God of theism," he was drawing, in particular, on the tradition of the medieval mystics.

A further proposal is (5) that "God" does not name a personal *Creator*, but rather the *creativity* discoverable in the world by observation and analysis. For Henry Nelson Wieman (1884–1975), God-talk was not about a Supreme Being endowed with consciousness: it referred to "the creative event" in which

7. Cf. Thomas Aquinas: "We cannot know the essence of God in this life, as He really is in Himself" (*ST* 1, q. 13, a. 2, ad 3 [1:62]).

human good is unpredictably enlarged and enriched. The creative event is suprahuman only "in the sense that it creates the good of the world in a way that man cannot do" (Wieman 1995: 76). In his recent study *In the Beginning . . . Creativity*, Gordon Kaufman offers further reflections on his notion of God as "serendipitous creativity." Modern evolutionary thinking is irreconcilable, he contends, with the traditional idea of God's purposive activity in the world. But there are "*trajectories* or *directional movements* that emerge spontaneously in the course of evolutionary and historical developments," and one such trajectory has led to the development of human life. In contrast to the questionable idea of a Creator, Kaufman finds the idea of creativity entirely plausible—the coming to be of something new or novel in the evolutionary process (Kaufman 2004: 42, 46, 55, 74).

I cannot enter as fully as I would like into these five proposals for interpreting personal language about the Creator God. They may suffice to show that Christian theologians are by no means under necessity to take as literal truth the way naive piety speaks of a personal God as one agent among others. But I must conclude on a positive note by drawing out the systematic connection of the present chapter with the findings of previous chapters. Our primary dogmatic task requires us to give an account of the language current in the, or a, Christian community, but the hermeneutical rule we borrowed from Thomas, that religious language is "a mean between pure equivocation and simple univocation," must be followed here—as everywhere else. If we ask not "Is the Creator a person?" but "Is there something about experience of the Creator God that invites personal language?" our answer lies in what we have determined concerning the world as creation. To admit, with the theological tradition, that God is incomprehensible cannot mean that there is nothing at all we can say about God. True, no serious account of Christian faith will fail to grant that a penumbra of mystery surrounds all that Christian faith affirms or presupposes about knowledge of God. But it must at least be possible to *identify* God, and this we do when we say that the concept of God the Creator corresponds to creation faith in the world as moral order. To call the God of theism "the Creator" means that God is *the creative principle of cosmic order.*[8]

All we can say further will be said in harmony (1) with our description of "the world as creation" in chapter 4, (2) with the picture of the God of Israel sketched in the present chapter, and (3) with our recognition of the metaphorical or analogical nature of language about God. Hence thesis 5 affirms that the creative principle of the world order is *not only inconceivably powerful and mysterious, but also the source of goodness and justice,* and this invites comparison with *authentic parental care.* The comparison is made by an analogy of relation (*analogia relationis*): the relation of the Creator to the creation is like the relation of parents to the nurture and moral development of their children. In this way, the mystery of the Creator *in se*—so much a part of the theological tradition—is acknowledged. But other kinds of analogy are not excluded, in particular the

8. To call God "the creative ground" has much to commend it: "ground" suggests the underlying basis of things. But ground-talk inevitably suggests inert *passivity,* so that "creative ground" is an oxymoron. "Cause" in present-day usage just as inescapably implies *efficient* causality. "Principle," though a common term in science and philosophy, is perhaps a bit esoteric, but I use it in one of its dictionary senses for "fundamental source."

analogy of being (*analogia entis*) that likens the being of God to the being of the human self in relation to its own bodily activities.[9]

In conclusion, the Scriptures nowhere assert, in as many words, the existence of a personal God; they speak rather of the living God. The expression no doubt arose from the contrast of the God of Israel with the lifeless idols of the pagans (Jer. 10:5, 10; cf. Pss. 115:4–7; 135:15–18; Isa. 44:9–20; Heb. 2:18–19; etc.), and this connection is carried over into the New Testament when Paul says to the Thessalonians, "you turned to God from idols, to serve a living and true God" (1 Thess. 1:9; cf. Acts 14:15). Yahweh is the true God, the living God (Jer. 10:10; cf. 17:13). God's true people are "children of the living God" (Hos. 1:10, quoted in Rom. 9:26). It is for the living God that the psalmist thirsts (Ps. 42:2; cf. 84:2). In answer to Jesus' question "Who do you say I am?" the confession of Peter at Caesarea Philippi was, "You are the Messiah, the Son of the living God" (Matt. 16:16; cf. the NRSV note on John 6:69). Jesus himself speaks of God as "the living Father" (John 6:57). And the Letter to the Hebrews draws attention to the Deity as mysterium tremendum with the reminder, "It is a fearful thing to fall into the hands of the living God" (Heb. 10:31).

9. Barth, as is well known, dismissed the *analogia entis* as "the invention of Antichrist" (*CD* I/1:xiii). He did use an *analogia relationis*—differently than I do—to refer to "the relationship *within the being of God* on the one side and between the being of God and that of man on the other" (III/2:220 [§45.1]; italics mine). But I cannot pursue the difficult problem of analogy here.

6. Humanity as Created

Faith in God "the Father of Jesus Christ" presupposes that humanity is uniquely endowed with the capacity to respond freely to the Creator not only with awe or dread, but also with thankful confidence and willing obedience; and this is what is meant by representing humans as God's "children," created in the image and likeness of God.

A sense of the littleness of humanity in the cosmos was not foreign to the ancient Hebrews. The psalmist contemplated the starry night and asked, "what are human beings that you are mindful of them, mortals that you care for them?" (Ps. 8:4). But humility passed quickly over into celebration of humans as God's deputies in charge of the earth; their special privilege made them only a little lower than God or the angels (*'ĕlōhîm:* see the NRSV note on v. 5). In the modern world, it is different. The status of humanity has been steadily diminished. After the initial shock at the dislocation of their home from the supposed cosmic center, the chilling vastness of the universe left humans lost in their remote corner of nature. The coordinates of the cosmic map vanished, and in Pascal's reflections the question became: "What is a man in the Infinite? . . . The eternal silence of these infinite spaces frightens me."[1] And there was more to come. Humans had to suffer the indignity of being told that on their tiny speck of a planet they share a common ancestry with the apes. Darwin's opinion that the difference in mental capacity between humans and chimpanzees is one of degree only, not of kind, has not won general assent; but the biological kinship is no longer doubted. And there have been several attempts to uncover the allegedly delusional roots of humankind's persistent belief in a God who cares about them. It is ironic, then, that in recent years the vastness and complexity of the universe have given rise to a new argument for the unique dignity of humankind.

The ancient Stoics believed that the gods assigned to humans a special place in the world,[2] and this fitted well with the naive anthropocentrism of the Christian doctrine of creation. The church's theologians found evidence of design everywhere in nature and assumed that humans were the intended beneficiaries of it. By the eighteenth century, confidence in the status of humanity as the high point of creation wavered. The skeptical arguments of David Hume's (1711–76) *Dialogues concerning Natural Religion* (1779) led many, probably

1. Blaise Pascal, *Pensées*, nos. 72, 206; trans. W. F. Trotter, Modern Library (New York: Random House, 1941), 22, 75.
2. Seneca, *De beneficiis* 2.29.3, 6; 6.23.3–7.

most, theologians to admit that the argument from (or to) design is flawed. Remarkably, however, something like it has reappeared among philosophically minded scientists who speak of "the anthropic principle." The principle admits of more than one formulation. Generally, its advocates argue that only a finely tuned universe and the passage of many billions of years could account for the emergence of life as we know it, and this is the universe we have. The minutest deviation from the cosmological constants in our universe would have made human life impossible.

Not everyone is willing to infer that the universe must therefore have been designed for the appearance of a species capable of observing it. The anthropic principle is not an established scientific theory. Neither is the alternative, many-universes theory, which is sometimes thought to improve the odds that the appearance of life would eventually have happened by mere chance. For all we know, it may be that different physical laws obtain in other universes than ours. More pertinent to a scientific understanding of humanity consistent with theistic faith is the shift from a deterministic worldview to the acknowledgment of contingency in the new physics. We will come back to it. But first we need to outline the way humanity has been understood in Christian tradition.

I. Humanity in the Bible

No book in the Bible presents a systematic doctrine of humanity (a "theological anthropology," as we say), and it would be an impossible task to bring all the pertinent material together in a brief outline. Even if it could be done, we would not then have a normative dogmatic statement. Hebrew religion is not revelation; at most, it is the form of revelation in the Old Testament. But the dogmatic theologian will note a characteristic emphasis in Old Testament utterances about human nature; it is carried over into the New Testament, where, however, it is inextricably bound up with the theme of redemption through Christ and must await fuller attention in part II of our outline. Our theme for now is the view of humanity *presupposed* by faith in Christ.

1. *Human Nature*

If we bring the familiar Platonic dualism of body and soul to the Old Testament utterances about human nature, the characteristic emphasis of the Hebrew vocabulary is immediately plain: the Hebrews held a unitary conception of human nature. Whereas Plato spoke of the soul as an essence separable from the body, they understood the entire person as "flesh" (Heb. *bāśār*). "Flesh" and "soul" are occasionally distinguished (e.g., in Isa. 10:18, where the NRSV translates *bāśār* as "body"), but they do not belong on two different ontological levels. Similarly, the word translated "soul" (*nepeš*) refers not to something a man or woman *has* but to what they *are*—living beings (as in Gen. 2:7), not as such distinguished from animals. Hebrew use of other anthropological terms is not entirely consistent. As functions of the living human being, "heart" (*lēb*) and "spirit" (*rûaḥ*) are not clearly differentiated. And Hebrew lacks a distinct word for much that we ourselves would assign to activities of the "will."

The various aspects of the living whole were not thought of as parts, much less as separable parts. All the terms in Hebrew "psychology" (if we dare so call it) were probably pictured as having physical sites, located at various places on a single scale of bodily existence. There was no belief in an immortal soul that survives bodily dissolution. Finitude and death were seen as facts of nature. It is true that this perception of the natural limits of humanity appears to be contradicted in Genesis 2–3, where death is treated not as natural but as the punishment of sin (Gen. 2:17; 3:3–4). Even there the message is ambiguous: 3:19 represents Adam's return to the ground as his natural end (cf. 2:7). Exegetical problems also beset the attempt to understand the divine "image" in Adam and Eve, which, in a sense, is the very antithesis of their creatureliness.

2. *The Image of God*

Possible borrowings from Babylonian mythology will not tell us what the making of humankind meant to the Priestly writer of Genesis 1:26–27. In view of the importance that Adam's creation in the image (*ṣelem*) and likeness (*dĕmût*) of God acquired in Christian theology, it is surprising that it reappears in the Old Testament only twice. Genesis 5:1–3 tells us that Adam, who was made in the likeness of God, fathered a son, Seth, in *his* likeness and image. Genesis 9:6 warns: "Whoever sheds the blood of a human, by a human shall that person's blood be shed; for in his own image God created humankind." These two passages shed little light on the meaning of the divine image. But the second clearly implies that the image, whatever it is, was not lost through Adam's "fall."

Two passages in the Apocrypha may be added to the canonical three. The Wisdom of Solomon, written in Greek, betrays its Hellenistic context by connecting the image with immortality—albeit as a gift for the righteous, not as a natural attribute of the soul (Wis. 2:23). The seventeenth chapter of Ecclesiasticus (The Wisdom of Jesus, Son of Sirach) contains a passage that might almost be considered a more traditionally Hebraic commentary on humanity's creation in the image of God (Sir. 17:1–14). The finitude of human beings is balanced by their dominion over beasts and birds. They were created with eyes and ears, by which they saw the majesty of God and heard his voice. God gave them knowledge of good and evil, the law of life, and his eternal covenant.

Only twice do we find allusions in the New Testament to the idea of a created image that was not lost by the fall. (1) Paul says in 1 Corinthians 11:7 that in meetings for prayer and prophecy a man ought not to have his head veiled because man, not woman, is the image and reflection of God (*eikōn kai doxa theou*), whereas woman is the reflection of man. In his commentary on this verse, Calvin insists that both sexes were created in the image of God: the "image" of which Paul is speaking here pertains only to the *social* order of male and female in marriage (cf. *Institutes*, 1:190). The NOAB simply notes that 1 Corinthians 11:7 "[r]eflects Gen. 2.21–23, not 1.26–27." (2) James says (Jas. 3:9) that with the tongue "we bless the Lord and Father, and with it we curse those who are made in the likeness of God [*kath' homoiōsin theou*]." Neither of these two passages tells us what exactly the created image of God in humanity denotes, and it is a quite different line of thought when the New Testament speaks of

God's Son as the unique image of God (2 Cor. 4:4; Col. 1:15; cf. Heb. 1:3) and the image to which the Christian is to be conformed (Rom. 8:29; 1 Cor. 15:49; 2 Cor. 3:18).[3]

To sum up the biblical data: Genesis 1:26 stands virtually alone, since verse 27 merely reports that God did what verse 26 says he determined to do and expressly affirms that male and female were alike created in the image of God. (Genesis 2:21–22 does not mention the dual creation of man and woman in God's image but reports that, subsequently to Adam's creation, God made woman from one of Adam's ribs.) Not surprisingly, theological discussion of the image of God in humanity often makes little pretense to being exegesis. But interpretation of this unique text sometimes proceeds by drawing inferences from other things said about Adam and Eve in the context or by connecting the thought of a created image in everyone with the thought of the unique image of God in Christ, imparted to some by redemption. One may fairly argue that interpretation along these lines can be done without violence to the meaning of the image in Genesis 1:26, which it intends only to supplement from other scriptural passages. On the other hand, it is an unjustifiable imposition on the text to discover in it a connection with the doctrine of the Trinity, either because a human being is a trinity of memory, intelligence, and will (Augustine) or because the relation of male and female in humanity is analogous to the Trinitarian relations in God (Barth, *CD* III/1:191–206).

II. Humanity in Christian Theology

The history of the ways in which Christian theologians have understood creation in the image and likeness of God is of cardinal importance to a Christian estimate of humanity. It is a complicated history in which the views of individual theologians are not always clear or consistent. Obviously, I cannot trace it here. It must suffice to comment, as usual, on the contributions of Calvin and Schleiermacher. Particularly interesting is one strand in the understanding of humanity that Calvin infers from the image of God in Adam. But Schleiermacher finds insuperable obstacles to beginning with the story of Adam and Eve, and he allows no dogmatic weight to the concept of the image of God.

1. Calvin on the Mirror of God's Goodness

The way Calvin begins his discussion of human nature is not very promising (in the light of the biblical sources). "[T]hat man consists of a soul and a body," he says, "ought to be beyond controversy" (*Institutes*, 1:184). By "the soul" he understands an immortal but created essence; it is the nobler part of human nature, imprisoned in the body. "[T]here lies hidden in man something separate from the body," and at death it leaves the "tabernacle of the flesh" (185). The soul dwells in the body "as in a house" (192). Calvin provides arguments, both

3. The "image of [the] creator" in Col. 3:10 makes the Creator God, rather than Christ, the pattern of renewal. See also Eph. 4:24, where it is the "new self" (*ton kainon anthrōpon*) that is "created according to [the likeness of] God."

empirical and scriptural, for this dualistic understanding of a human being. His most persuasive appeal is to 2 Corinthians 5:1–10, where Paul seemed to move beyond a unitary conception of a human being; and Calvin reads Romans 7:24 in much the same way (353, 716). Unlike Plato, however, Paul did not think of a disembodied existence after death but rather of being "further clothed" (2 Cor. 5:4; cf. 1 Cor. 15:44 on the "spiritual body"); and unlike Calvin, he did not think of the soul as immortal by nature.

Calvin introduces the concept of the divine image in a surprisingly offhand manner, as further proof of what he has been saying about the soul (*Institutes*, 1:186). As is his custom, he criticizes erroneous or inadequate interpretations and works his way to a formal definition. A theological tradition going back to Irenaeus (ca. 130–ca. 200) distinguished the image from the likeness. Irenaeus held that the *image* refers to Adam's equipment with reason and free will, the *likeness* to a growing godliness initiated in him by the Holy Spirit but interrupted by sin. This is one of the views Calvin rejects (though he does not name Irenaeus as its source). He explains that the phrase "image and likeness" is an example of Hebrew repetition (we would say "Hebrew parallelism"), in which one thing is indicated twice by the use of two virtually synonymous expressions. In presenting his own view of the image, Calvin aims to be comprehensive: the image includes "whatever has to do with spiritual and eternal life" (190). But he has two particular criteria for a sound interpretation. First, the creation of humans in the image of God is "a tacit antithesis . . . which raises man above all other creatures" (188). Hence, to determine what the image means, we must note the difference between humans and animals. Second, we know what was comprehended in the created image—before the fall—by considering its restoration in Christ, the second Adam, who is "the most perfect image of God" (190).

There are ambiguities in Calvin's conclusions about the image—in particular, about its condition since Adam's fall. But from his definition (*Institutes*, 1:188) this much is clear: he did not find the image in Adam's gifted powers as such, but rather in their unimpaired use and ordering (their *integritas*), and he held that the image is absent or vitiated where there is no acknowledgment to the Creator for the unique gifts bestowed on humanity. Sometimes Calvin speaks of the image as *engraved* on Adam. But his definition fits better with another metaphor he uses: the image is like a *reflection* in a mirror. All of God's creatures are mirrors of God's glory; humans are distinguished by their ability to reflect the glory of God in a conscious response. The brute beasts owe their existence to God, but they do not know it. "[W]e differ nothing from the brute creation, if we understand not that the world has been created by God. To what end have men been endued with understanding and reason, except that they might *acknowledge* their Creator?" (Comm. Heb. 11:3; emphasis mine). In this way, Calvin defines humanity (over against the animals) by the uniquely human image of God and takes "image" in a special sense: not the possession of a soul, which he describes as the "seat" of the image (i.e., the mirror), and not the possession of reason either, but reflection of the bountiful Creator in the act of thanksgiving, which defines, for Calvin, the attitude of *pietas* to God. It is here—in the link between the image and thankfulness—that his contribution is most interesting.

2. *Schleiermacher on Original Perfection*

Schleiermacher's treatment of the "original perfection" of the world and humanity, though relatively brief (*CF* 233–56), is the gateway to understanding his interpretation of sin and redemption in part 2 of *The Christian Faith.* In the dogmatic tradition that he inherited, "original perfection" was ascribed to the creation understood in a temporal sense as an event, or series of events, in primeval time; the original perfection of humans was assumed to mean the created state from which the first humans fell in the paradise of Eden. Schleiermacher, by contrast, prefaces his discussion with the assertion that the term "original" (*ursprünglich*) does not refer to an actual, onetime state of the world and humankind but rather to the constitution of finite existence antecedent to all temporal development (234–35). His inquiry is not about the blessed state that Adam and Eve forfeited; it is about the inalienable humanity of every man and every woman. And he is giving an account of human nature mainly, he says, in relation to God; that is, in relation to the presence of the God-consciousness in human self-consciousness (237)—a crucial limitation of his task, which by no means purports to give an exhaustive study of humanity.

Where does that leave the story of Adam and Eve? Schleiermacher's answer comes from his understanding of the dogmatic task as *Glaubenslehre* ("doctrine of faith"). Abundant faith experience attests the ways in which human life develops from original perfection (in his sense); but how the first man and woman developed could be a question only of history, not of faith.

Historical statements are not faith propositions (not *Glaubenssätze*); faith is not historical knowledge (*CF* 248). This is perhaps an echo of Luther's rejection of *fides historica* ("historical faith"); in any case, it is a fundamental principle in what Schleiermacher will later say about the person and work of Christ. He points out that even if we were to take the Genesis narrative as history, it would only establish the *uniqueness* of the first humans and would therefore contribute little or nothing to a properly dogmatic concept of our common human nature. And, as a matter of fact, the narrative lacks precisely the features that would qualify it as "history" in the modern sense. It can only be understood as symbolic (320). "[A]ll attempts to form a historical picture of the first beginnings of human existence are bound to fail, because, as we have no experience of an absolute beginning, we have no analogy by which we could make the absolute beginning of rational consciousness intelligible" (250). As for the expression "image of God," it illustrates the principle that biblical expressions "can seldom be adopted in the terminology of Dogmatics without more ado" (253; cf. 79). Besides, the vitality of the God-consciousness, as a being of God in us, seems to be something *more* than likeness to God (252)—an observation that again points (implicitly) to Schleiermacher's understanding of the person of Christ.

In the introduction to *The Christian Faith,* he has already shown that the God-consciousness—the feeling of absolute dependence—is an essential element in human self-consciousness, actualized in conjunction with what he calls "the sensible self-consciousness," that is, by interaction with the natural and social environments (*CF* 12–26). He now adds that, along with the disposition to God-consciousness, the physical, mental, and social conditions for its actualization must also be present in the original perfection of humanity. (The corresponding original perfection of the world is that it offers an abundance of stimuli for actualization of the consciousness of God [238].) In his concluding remarks to §60, the systematic link with part 2 of *The Christian Faith* becomes transparently clear. He is talking about the conditions for the occurrence of redemption,[4] that is, about all that the redemption faith of Christians presupposes concerning the human species. Though he does speak of human nature, and even of spirit becoming soul in the body, his interest is strictly in a capacity (*Vermögen*), in human existence (*Dasein*), and in the conditions (*Bedingungen*) for the God-consciousness. The English translators tilt his language misleadingly toward substantialism by rendering the German terms as "faculty," "nature," and "basis," respectively.

Schleiermacher maintains that his thesis (*CF* §60) includes "all the conditions necessary for the continuous existence of the God-consciousness in every human individual, and also [the social condition] for its communication from one to the other" (247; cf. 245). He adds expressly that in the social condition, which is the consciousness of humankind as a class or species,[5] he includes the condition for the communication of the God-consciousness from the Redeemer to the redeemed (247). It is the social, collective, or corporate perspective that will dominate part 2 of *The Christian Faith*: in particular, the treatment of sin, redemption through Christ, and election. The very last sentence of part 1 reaffirms the christological bearing of the original perfection of human nature. Like Calvin, Schleiermacher contends that "if we are to see everything that can develop out of such original perfection all together in a single human instance, it is not to be sought in Adam, in whom it must again have been lost, but in Christ, in whom it has brought gain to all" (256).

III. Children of the Living God

In the older works of systematic theology, the Christian understanding of humanity took the form of questions about *human nature*. It was asked whether men and women have souls; and, the presumption being that they do, how they came by them (by biological propagation or by individual acts of divine creation), how their souls are related to their bodies, and whether Scripture (notably 1 Thess. 5:23 and Heb. 4:12) adds "spirit" to body and soul as a third part of human nature. The traditional mode of thought about humanity was mainly essentialist or substantialist: the soul was an entity, a thing, and possessing it was said to be the big difference of humankind from chimpanzees. One drawback with this approach was that it gave rise to another round in the so-called conflict of religion with the natural sciences—this time, the sciences of anatomy, physiology, and psychology. It would have been better to grant that human nature is a scientific question, not a dogmatic one. A theological anatomy might prove to be just as vulnerable to scientific criticism as a theological cosmogony. Moreover, the dualism of René Descartes (1596–1650) has gone out

4. This fitness (*Angemessenheit*) has nothing to do with the semi-Pelagian notion of preparation for grace. It belongs to the idea of human nature included in the divine decree for the redemption of humankind (*CF* §61.4–5 [253–54]).

5. The German has *Gattungsbewußtsein*, not *Rassebewußtsein* ("racism").

of favor in philosophy, especially since Gilbert Ryle argued, in his classic *Concept of Mind* (1949), that Cartesian dualism rests on logical confusion: it takes the grammatical similarity of discourse about mental activities and discourse about bodily activities to mean that the mind must be an entity like the body (but see Goetz and Taliaferro 2011).

I certainly do not intend to cut off conversation between theological and scientific or philosophical accounts of human being. But my constructive agenda in this chapter requires me, first, to phrase the question of humanity as a question about the presuppositions of Christian faith. For this purpose, a better idiom is the talk of the existentialist theologians about *possibilities of human existence* rather than the constitutional nature of humans. Second, I will take account of just one present-day topic of conversation between theological anthropology and natural science.

1. A Possibility of Human Existence

The rejection of dualism in recent thought about humankind invites retrieval of the Hebrew unitary idea of a human being. Calvin was more under the influence of Plato than of Moses when he judged it beyond question that a human consists of *body and soul* and that the soul is a created essence separate from the body. He expressly commended Plato's conception of the soul but declared that he was content to leave the psychological details to the *philosophi* (*Institutes*, 1:192–94)—shall we say "the scientists"? Very different was Barth's approach. To be sure, like Calvin (and Schleiermacher), he held that "true man, the true nature behind our corrupted nature, is . . . revealed in the person of Jesus, and in His nature we recognise our own, and that of every man" (*CD* III/2:43). But, unlike Calvin, he rejected the dualistic misconception of human nature as the coexistence of two substances. The true man, Jesus, is not a union of two parts or substances but "one whole man, embodied soul and besouled body" (326–27). Body and soul are "two moments of the indivisibly one human nature." And "spirit" is not a third part of human nature but "the immediate action of God Himself, which grounds, constitutes and maintains man as soul of his body . . . unifies him and holds him together as soul and body" (393).

A closer look at Barth's understanding of body and soul, or his defense of it against both monistic materialism and monistic spiritualism, is not possible here. (It is embedded in a volume that runs in the English translation to some 650 pages.) I cite him here to illustrate the turn away from anthropological dualism—a turn that many, probably most, Christian theologians these days share with him, myself included. The next task is to state our own thoughts on *the image of God* in humanity.

If calling humans "flesh" suggests their kinship with animals, to say that Adam and Eve were made in the image and likeness of God sets them apart from the rest of creation, including other animals, and attributes to them a kinship with God. The dogmatic theologian will be unwilling to reduce the kinship to physical resemblance, although some Old Testament scholars think this is suggested by the parallel use of "likeness" and "image" for Seth's resemblance to his father, Adam (Gen. 5:3). There remain two principal alternatives if we ask what singles out Adam and Eve in the creation narratives of Genesis. One alternative is that the sequence of phrases in Genesis 1:26 identifies the image with the gift of *dominion over the rest of creation,* and this finds an apocryphal echo in Ecclesiasticus (Sir. 17:3–4; cf. Ps. 8:6–8). The idea of human dominion over the world of nature has become a bone of contention in the current discussion of the environmental crisis. The discussion falls mainly to the field of theological ethics, but I come back to it in the discussion of sin and evil.

A second alternative finds the distinctiveness of humankind in that, whereas the rest of creation is brought into existence by the Word of God, in both of the creation accounts in Genesis, Adam (that is, "man") is *addressed by* the Word of God (Gen. 1:28–30; 2:15–17). A rich exegetical tradition encourages us to look for more in the text, whether for historical exegesis or for theological construction. But the second alternative may serve as our point of departure. It leads us to locate the image—and thus the defining characteristic of humanity presupposed by Christian faith—in a relation, not, or not only, in a faculty such as the gift of reason. This too has its echo in Ecclesiasticus: "their ears heard the glory of his voice" (Sir. 17:13).

In his debate with Barth on natural theology, now almost forgotten but still instructive, Emil Brunner proposed that the image in Genesis should be understood precisely as the possibility of being addressed (*Ansprechbarkeit*), by which he meant a "capacity for words" (*Wortfähigkeit*) and what we might translate as "response-ability" (*Verantwortlichkeit*). He identified the purely formal capacity for words as the point of contact for the Word of God but argued that the Word itself creates the ability to hear it *in faith*. However, he went on to include in the point of contact "everything connected with the 'natural' knowledge of God."[6] Perhaps that muddies the water. But I too am unwilling to reduce the point of contact to the human capacity for words. In the *Church Dogmatics* Barth also came to speak, in the plural, of "natural points of contact for the covenant of grace" (*CD* III/2:371).

The Genesis texts tell us not simply that Adam had a capacity for words, and not simply that God spoke to him, but also that *what* God said was in the form of both a gift and a demand. The twofold *gift* was the assignment of a unique place for Adam in the natural order (Gen. 1:26–30) and the provision of a companion to share his humanity with him (2:18–24). The notion of cohumanity appealed strongly to Barth, Brunner, and other theologians influenced by the I-Thou philosophy of Ferdinand Ebner (1882–1931) and Martin Buber (1878–1965), for all of whom a person was not an individual substance but was constituted a person by encounter with an "other." Hence Barth said that humanity was created for "covenant-partnership with God" but also "as a being . . . with others" (*CD* III/2:243). The *demand* is also twofold: it includes the directive to exercise the special status conveyed by the gift (Gen. 1:28; 2:15) and the prohibition of the forbidden fruit (2:17). We may add a third: the gift of a helper as Adam's partner, since the gift carried responsibility with it (2:23–24). Once again, we find a useful hint in Ecclesiasticus: "And he gave commandment to each of them concerning the neighbor" (Sir. 17:14). Here the "other" confronts a human not as a gift but as a demand.

6. Brunner, in Brunner and Barth 1946: 23, 25, 31–33. See also Brunner 1946–62, 2:55–61.

There cannot be any question of simply taking the Genesis accounts as a dogmatic norm. If, out of deference to its established place in Christian theology, we appropriate the language of "image and likeness," it will have to be tested by our dogmatic norms like everything else in the primary religious language. We will need to interpret it in harmony with our previous conclusions, especially with the concept of elemental faith in chapter 1 and the theme of God as Creator in chapter 5. This I have attempted to do in my sixth thesis. I will come back to elemental faith later, since I take it to be the cardinal point of contact with the gospel (chap. 12). The verbal correspondence between thesis 5 (God as Creator) and thesis 6 (humanity as created) is, I assume, obvious. I have continued the parental metaphor: humans are "children of the living God." (The expression comes from Hos. 1:10, but the metaphor is ubiquitous in Scripture.) I need only underscore one or two further items in thesis 6, although they are probably obvious enough from all that has been said so far.

The thesis is about humanity, not the first human couple. It says nothing of an immortal soul, or any other "part" of human nature, but describes a possibility of human existence; and it takes the distinctively human consciousness as given, however humans came by it—by a special act of creation, a gradual process of evolution, or a sudden mutation. Christian faith presupposes the capacity to respond to the Creator as a unique endowment—as far as we know—of humans. (Angels and extraterrestrial beings need not detain us.) The capacity does not make humans the center of the universe, but it does attribute to them a special role in the universe as the point at which the creation becomes conscious of the Creator. With Schleiermacher, we want to "avoid the appearance of representing man as the central-point of all finite existence" (*CF* 237). And it would of course be a misunderstanding to suppose that having the unique capacity to respond means that everyone actually does, or even can, respond to the Creator in the manner described in my thesis. As Augustine points out in the parallel case of love, the capacity to love does not mean that everyone loves.[7] The human capacity to respond to the Creator may be inhibited. What goes awry with human existence is the subject of the next chapter (on estrangement). But first a comment on *free will*, since my thesis states that the image is the capacity to respond *freely*. Freedom has often been identified as the essence of being human. It has also, however, been found problematic for the belief that God is in control.

2. Free Will

The theistic idea of God presupposed by Christian faith affirms that the Creator is continually engaged with the creatures. But just *how* divine and creaturely activity are connected has been a major question in the dogmatic tradition and the subject of a lively debate in recent theological literature. In Reformed dogmatics, it comes under the heading of the divine concurrence (*concursus divinus*), or God's cooperation with secondary causes—part 2 of the doctrine of providence (Heppe 1950: 258–61; Barth, *CD* III/3:58–238). The question has many facets. It touches on the daily experience of every devout person

7. Augustine, *On the Predestination of the Saints* (428 or 429), NPNF[1] 5:503.

who wonders if praying to God can change God's mind or who agonizes over the evil and suffering in a God-governed world. It is also a problem for the philosophers and theologians who reflect on the underlying conceptual questions. Christian faith presupposes a Creator who is still actively involved in the course of the creation. But if the object of divine causality is *the world,* how can the divine activity be construed without either surrendering belief in providential concern for each *individual* creature in every moment or else relapsing into the old idea of irregular divine interventions, which has proved so vulnerable to the scientific concept of the laws of nature?

The dilemma could have been posed in the preceding chapter, on God as Creator. But it becomes especially urgent when we ask about the Creator's relation to creatures that are believed to be free agents, not wholly determined by inflexible divine control. Calvin pictured God as "the ruler and governor of all things, who in accordance with his wisdom has from the farthest limit of eternity decreed what he was going to do, and now by his might carries out what he has decreed" (*Institutes,* 1:207; cf. 210, 227). He supported his understanding of divine activity from Scripture and Augustine, and he dismissed the charge that he was advocating the Stoic dogma of fate. But it must be admitted that his language was close to Seneca's (ca. 4 BCE–CE 65), who asserted that the gods never repent of their original plan (*primi consilii*).[8]

Critics of the Augustinian-Calvinist tradition infer that divine power, in this view, must be coercive, overriding human freedom—the power of a tyrant or an impersonal force. But the inference is mistaken. Calvin was an advocate of what present-day philosophers call "compatibilism," the view that human activity can exhibit both necessity and self-determination at the same time. And to illustrate the way the Father draws us to Christ (John 6:44), Augustine likened it to holding out a green twig to a sheep, or offering candy to a child. We are not drawn against our will—the mind is drawn by love or delight. Augustinian grace is irresistible (or, more correctly, invincible), but it achieves its end by winsome attraction, not by force.[9] This, of course, is said specifically of the call to salvation. But it surely implies an understanding of divine action in general. Even so, the church's theologians have debated whether Adam *really* sinned freely if the fall was ordained by God and whether Judas *had to* betray Jesus if Jesus was "handed over . . . according to the definite plan and foreknowledge of God" (Acts 2:23). The debate has turned in part on subtle distinctions between different kinds of necessity. We cannot follow it any further. (For Calvin's views, see *Institutes,* 1:210, 230; 2:955–57.) I only want to point to the interesting fact that theological and philosophical criticisms of the old divine determinism seem to fit well with the idea of an open universe in recent physics.

Schleiermacher approved of Calvin's assertion that God foresees the future because he decreed it, though he thought it would be better to say with John

8. Seneca, *De beneficiis* 6.23.1. Seneca and Calvin both spoke of the divine "plan" (*consilium*) and the divine "decrees" (*decreta*).

9. Augustine, *Homilies on the Gospel of John,* NPNF[1] 7:169–70. Process theologians who take from Alfred North Whitehead the notion of "the lure of God" should recognize here something not unlike it. William James found a noncoercive compatibilist analogy in the interaction between a master chess player and a novice (*The Will to Believe and Other Essays in Popular Philosophy* [New York: Longmans, Green, 1897], 181–82).

Scotus Erigena (ca. 810–ca. 877) that God *sees* rather than *foresees* (*CF* 220). Calvinist predestinarianism harmonized, in Schleiermacher's thinking, with the determinism of Isaac Newton's (1642–1727) laws of mechanics and the necessitarian philosophy of Baruch Spinoza (1632–77). A century after Schleiermacher, Einstein was instrumental in overthrowing Newtonian science, but he remained committed to the worldview of Spinoza. His unflinching necessitarianism led him to deny free will as an illusion, and he greeted the new quantum mechanics with the famous remark, "God does not play at dice." But a radical change in theoretical physics cast doubt on determinism and suggested a change of partner for theological accommodation to science.

What provoked Einstein's remark was Werner Heisenberg's (1901–76) uncertainty (or indeterminacy) principle, which states that it is impossible to determine exactly both the position and the velocity of a subatomic particle at the same time. Hence the future cannot be predicted with certainty. Various implications of the principle have been alleged. The uncertainties in quantum theory could be attributed merely to the limitations of our minds: the future may be causally determined even if we cannot predict it. But the uncertainty principle has generally been held to point to a real contingency in the world around us. Paul Davies concludes that "quantum theory undermines determinism" (Davies 1983: 143). Recent work in chaos theory can be understood to point in the same direction—not to a sheerly random or chaotic universe, but to a universe in which order and contingency belong together. Polkinghorne suggests that "chaos theory should encourage belief in a more subtle and supple physical reality than the clockwork world of Newton" (1998: 42).

The surrender of a strict determinism still leaves unanswered the question *how* divine activity and human activity are connected. The most persuasive answer at the present time comes, I think, from process theology, rooted in the philosophy of Alfred North Whitehead (1861–1947) and developed by Hartshorne and others. Whitehead pointed out that the new physics no longer imagines nature as composed of solid particles moving about in space; matter is energy, and the objects of daily observation are clusters of events or "actual occasions." The illusion of self-contained entities gives way to the recognition that "the environment enters into the nature of each thing." Accordingly, what we call "causation" is more properly "mutual immanence," not one thing bumping into another like two billiard balls. "[E]ach happening is a factor in the nature of every other happening" (Whitehead 1938: 188, 225–26).

On the foundation of the new physics, Whitehead built the philosophy of organism in his daunting magnum opus, *Process and Reality* (1929, 1978). There he describes nature as a moving, developing, living complex of events mutually forming and being formed by one another. Each finite entity or actual occasion is thereby related to God, who is himself identified as an actual entity (Whitehead 1978: 18–19, 87–88). Like all such entities, God both affects the world and is affected by it. He *acts on the world* by presenting to each entity the possibilities open to it. But every entity is endowed with a measure of self-determination, and in humans the power of self-determination is such that God does not dictate which possibilities they will choose. Freedom of choice leaves the future open. Strictly speaking, then, God "does not create the world, he saves it; or, more accurately, he is the poet of the world, with tender patience leading it by his vision of truth, beauty, and goodness" (345–46). Moreover, *the world acts on God*. "Each actuality in the temporal world has its reception into God's nature." This, indeed, is how God saves. "He saves the world as it passes into the immediacy of his own life." Hence it is not the world only that is subject to change and growth: God also develops as he takes into his own life whatever can be saved in the experience of finite entities, and this is their immortality. "What is done in the world is transformed into a reality in heaven, and the reality in heaven passes back into the world. . . . In this sense, God is the great companion—the fellow-sufferer who understands" (346, 348, 349, 351).

Process and Reality is a venture in metaphysics: it isn't science, though it builds on science; and it isn't religion, though it makes use of religious language. Whitehead cautions us explicitly that in speaking of God's "tender care" and "infinite patience" he is employing images (346). Still, his metaphysical ideas have become influential in contemporary theology. To be sure, his thought is not immune to theological objections. He states explicitly, for instance, that his God is not the ultimate metaphysical principle—creativity is. The world and God are both "in the grip of the ultimate metaphysical ground, the creative advance into novelty" (349). Whitehead's importance is not that he spoke the last word but that he has inspired a theological movement marked by variations as well as a fundamental affinity.

On our present question, process theologians insist that free will is inconceivable without contingency. The future cannot be ineluctably predetermined: in creating humans, God creates cocreators—self-creating creatures. This conclusion agrees with so-called open theism, which argues on biblical grounds, without the appeal to Whiteheadian metaphysics, that the future is "open" even to God. Since the future does not exist, it makes no sense to suppose that it is known by anyone, including God. There will be more to say later on the subject of free will because most theological talk about freedom occurs in the context of the Christian understanding of sin and the call of the gospel. For now, I need only conclude by pointing out that the use of the word *freely* in my sixth thesis does not depend on settling the current debate about process theology and open theism. Augustine and Calvin, rightly interpreted, could also give their assent to it. But I have indicated my belief that the contribution of process theology may prove to be the best way forward on the problem of God's activity and human freedom.

PART II: REDEMPTION
The Distinctive Affirmations of Christian Faith

Division 1: Christ and the Christian

Humanity's plight of sin

Augustine – pride

Calvin – unfaithfulness

Schleiermacher – God-forgetfulness

Kierkegaard – anxiety (occasion for sin) → despair that shrinks from freedom

7. Estrangement

Estrangement from the Creator may, as mistrust, be guiltless; but as defiance to the Creator it is sin, which arises from inborn egocentrism and the collective pressures of society, infects a person's entire existence with self-interest, and makes the self powerless to achieve the purpose of its creation without redemption.

Christian faith is redemption faith: faith in God the Redeemer in Christ. Under the rubric *Creation,* part I has outlined some *presuppositions* of Christian faith concerning the world, God, and humanity and brought them into relation with present-day secular views of humanity and the environment. Part II, *Redemption*, turns to the distinctive *affirmations* of Christian faith about the Redeemer and new life through him. Obviously, "redemption" implies something from which humanity is redeemed, and this has traditionally been presented, before the doctrines of Christ's work and person, as "man in the state of sin." But it has generally been held that the question, What is sin? can be fully answered only from the perspective of redemption. Hence, in harmony with his consistently christological approach, Karl Barth changed the traditional dogmatic order and dealt with sin in the context of the divine work of reconciliation in Jesus Christ, not as a separate dogmatic locus that comes before reconciliation (*CD* IV/1:359). But there can be no objection to treating the sin of humanity, as well as the original perfection of humanity, before Christology if, with Calvin and Schleiermacher, we recognize that the measure of both is the person of the Redeemer. The *conviction* of sin, as Christian faith understands it, arises from confrontation with the Christ who is proclaimed in the gospel. But this experiential sequence need not determine dogmatic order. The christological reference may govern the *account* of sin either by the order adopted, as in Barth, or by conscious and explicit anticipation, as in Calvin (*Institutes*, 1:189, 248; Comm. Gal. 2:21) and Schleiermacher (*CF* 270, 279). We can more readily retain the link with our two principal guides if we take the second option.

It is precisely the connection of sin with the words and work of Jesus Christ that raises doubts about the one-sided concept of sin in the Western theological tradition. The identification of sin with active resistance to the will of God is an unwarranted narrowing of all that comes between God and fallen humanity in Scripture generally, and particularly in the message of Jesus. There seem, then, to be two choices for dogmatic theology: either to enlarge the concept of sin or else, as in my thesis 7, to acknowledge that sin is not the whole of alienation or estrangement from God.

I. Estrangement as Rebellion and Pride

The understanding of sin in Western theology was shaped by Augustine, who is credited with coining the expression *peccatum originale* ("original sin"). But it had its roots in Scripture—or, at least, in the way he read Scripture—and he claimed that Cyprian and the consensus of the church supported him.[1] We must first take note of a twofold conception of sin in the Bible, then of Augustine's theological reflections on the sin of Adam and Calvin's revision of them. We will turn next to some attempts to modify the dominant Augustinian view of sin or to replace it, before I bring together, in a final section, the conclusions summed up in thesis 7.

1. *Prophetic and Priestly Conceptions of Sin*

The Hebrew Scriptures occasionally list the things that Yahweh reproves. (Besides the Ten Commandments in Exod. 20:3–17 and Deut. 5:7–21, the curses in Deut. 27:15–25, and Job's protestation in Job 31:5–40, see Ps. 15; Prov 6:16–19; Ezek. 18:5–8.) Naturally, the lists reflect the character of the God of Israel: offenses against Yahweh include, above all, disregard of the social obligations his justice enjoins. A variety of Hebrew words convey aspects of the nature of sin; some assign special importance to *peša'*, a favorite term in the prophetic indictment of Yahweh's wayward people. Norman Snaith pointed to the use of *peša'* in Amos, Hosea, Micah, and Isaiah; and he argued, following H. Wheeler Robinson, that it is inadequately rendered in our English versions as "transgression." More correctly, it means "rebellion." The corresponding verb is in fact used in the historical books of the Old Testament for a political revolt.[2] The image of a people in revolt against their God is also conveyed by other Hebrew words, particularly words from the root *mrd*. What, then, is the remedy for sin so understood? The prophetic remedy is repentance. The prophets call (passim) for the people to repent and return to the God of the covenant.

In contrast to the *prophetic* understanding of sin as rebellion, the *priestly* writers think of many things that disrupt the relation between Yahweh and his people as like a stain or contamination that requires cleansing by rituals. Along with such Old Testament scholars as Snaith, an earlier generation of biblical theologians sharply contrasted the personal (or prophetic) and the impersonal (or priestly) views of sin in the Hebrew Scriptures; they judged the impersonal view to belong to the category of taboo and for this reason to be of less permanent significance. Millar Burrows wrote: "In the New Testament the impersonal conception of sin has dropped out entirely, and with it the traditional conceptions and practices related to it."[3] But scholarly interpretation of priestly religion arose in part from theological commitments brought to the sources, not discovered in them. A more recent Old Testament scholar remarks that classical Protestantism in particular "has had a profound aversion to cult, regarding

1. Augustine, *On the Merits and Forgiveness of Sins, and on the Baptism of Infants* (412), NPNF[1] 5:72–74.
2. Norman H. Snaith, *The Distinctive Ideas of the Old Testament* (London: Epworth, 1944), 64.
3. Millar Burrows, *An Outline of Biblical Theology* (Philadelphia: Westminster, 1946), 165.

cultic activity as primitive, magical, and manipulative, thus valuing from the Old Testament only the prophetic-ethical traditions" (Brueggemann 1997: 651).

Lists of sins appear also in the New Testament: two or three times in the Synoptic Gospels (Mark 7:21–22 [// Matt. 15:19]; Luke 18:11), more frequently in Paul (Rom. 1:28–31; 13:13; 1 Cor. 5:9–11; 6:9–10; 2 Cor. 12:20–21; Gal. 5:19–21; Col. 3:5–8), and elsewhere (Eph. 5:3–5; 1 Tim. 1:9–11; 6:3–5; 2 Tim. 3:2–4; Titus 3:3; 1 Pet. 4:3; Rev. 21:8; 22:15).[4] The perpetrators of these sins can be called "God-haters" (Rom. 1:30; cf. 5:10; 8:7) or "godless" (1 Tim. 1:9), but the sins named are nearly all such as we would classify as moral transgressions; even idolatry is twice equated with "greed" (Eph. 5:5; Col. 3:5). Sinners can also be described as "lawless and disobedient" (1 Tim. 1:9), and in one place sin is apparently *defined* as "lawlessness" (1 John 3:4). Jesus' reverence for the law (Matt. 5:17–20; cf. Luke 16:17) led him to oppose the Pharisaic "tradition of the elders" with the commandment of God (Mark 7:8); but he could also rebuke the Pharisees for their insistence on rigid adherence to the letter of the law (Mark 2:23–3:6) or for being obsessed with lesser injunctions (Matt. 23:23–24; Luke 11:42). His quotation from Hosea 6:6, "I desire mercy, not sacrifice" (Matt. 9:13; 12:7), and his admonition that "there is nothing outside a person that by going in can defile" (Mark 7:14, 18–20) are commonly taken as evidence that Jesus' understanding of sin belonged entirely to the prophetic tradition, not the priestly tradition of ritual cleansing. It must be pointed out, however, that when the first generation of Christians spoke of Jesus and the significance of his redemptive work, they freely availed themselves of the priestly language of cult, sacrifice, and expiation, and this we must take up later (chap. 10).

Besides providing lists of sins, Paul has more to say than Jesus about the *nature* of sin. It is life according to the "flesh" (*sarx*). The corresponding Pauline adjectives (*sarkikos, sarkinos*) were nearly always translated in the KJV with the English word "carnal," which in our usage most often suggests sexual activity or lust. But "flesh" in Pauline usage means—more broadly—"*the whole sphere of that which is earthly or 'natural'*" (Bultmann 1951–55, 1:234). The NRSV can translate *sarkikos* with "material" (Rom. 15:27; 1 Cor. 9:11), "earthly" (2 Cor. 1:12), or "merely human" (2 Cor. 10:4), and to live in the flesh is translated "live as human beings" (2 Cor. 10:3); it is worldly, mundane existence. Hence, along with licentiousness, drunkenness, and so on, Paul includes among the works of the flesh "enmities, strife, jealousy, anger, quarrels, dissension, factions, envy" (Gal. 5:19–21); and he can admonish the Corinthians: "you are still of the flesh. For as long as there is jealousy and quarreling among you, are you not of the flesh, and behaving according to human inclinations?" (1 Cor. 3:3).

In Romans 1–2, Paul depicts the besetting sins of both Gentiles and Jews, and he concludes in chapter 3 that "all, both Jews and Greeks, are under the

4. Where more or less identical parallels exist in the Synoptics, I usually cite Mark only, thought by most NT scholars to be the earliest of the Gospels, supplemented by Matthew and Luke with a presumed collection of Jesus' sayings (Q). I also follow the widely, though not unanimously, held opinion that Ephesians, 2 Thessalonians, and the so-called Pastoral Letters are pseudonymous—written by unknown authors in Paul's name to interpret and urge the Apostle's teaching in new situations. This is not to deny them their place in the canon, merely to acknowledge that they should not be taken as primary sources for the theology of Paul. Opinion is divided over the authenticity of Colossians; I take it to be Pauline. The Letter to the Hebrews does not bear Paul's name, and the traditional attribution to him (followed by the KJV) has been abandoned by common consent.

power of sin, as it is written, 'There is no one who is righteous, not even one'" (3:9–10, echoing Ps. 14:3). Despite the plain evidence of God's power and divinity in the creation, the Gentiles "did not honor him as God or give thanks to him. . . . Claiming to be wise, they became fools." They turned to idols, and "God gave them up to degrading passions" (Rom. 1:21–23). As for his own people, the Jews, Paul attributes to them the same offenses that the Gentiles committed (2:1–3, 22–23). Presumably, the accusation does not apply to all Jews all the time, any more than all the Gentiles always disregard the law "written on their hearts" (2:14–16). In any case, it differs from Jesus' charge in Matthew 23 that the scribes and Pharisees were "hypocrites." Jesus did accuse them of not practicing what they preach (Matt. 23:3). Their hypocrisy, however, was not that they failed to keep the rules but that in keeping them they were putting on a self-serving act (Matt. 6:2, 5, 16; 23:5–7).[5] But it is entirely in line with Jesus' parable of the Pharisee and the Tax Collector (Luke 18:9–14) when Paul aims some of his keenest arrows at hyperreligious and censorious individuals whose strict adherence to the law breeds self-satisfaction and "boasting" (Rom. 2:17, 23). And what does he see as the remedy for boasting? It is the gospel, which is "the power of God for salvation to everyone who has faith, to the Jew first and also to the Greek" (1:16). The gospel message of a way of salvation "apart from law" (3:21) leaves no room for boasting (3:27)—unless for boasting of the Lord (1 Cor. 1:31; 2 Cor. 10:17, alluding to Jer. 9:23–24; see also Gal. 6:14).

Paul's thoughts on the nature of sin move, broadly speaking, within the bounds of the personal or prophetic conception. There are, to be sure, characteristic emphases. He can think of sin as a fearful power that holds sinners in bondage or even, through the law, kills them (Rom. 7:11–25). And like the Jesus of the Gospels (Mark 3:23, 26; 4:15; 8:33; Luke 10:18; 13:16; 22:31; cf. Mark 1:13), he can speak of evil as a person: the devil or Satan. When he does so, it is Satan as tempter or obstructionist, or the cunning of Satan, not the lethal power of sin, that he has chiefly in mind (1 Cor. 5:5; 7:5; 2 Cor. 2:11; 11:14; 12:7; 1 Thess. 2:18; cf. 2 Cor. 11:3). New, in comparison with the Old Testament, are Paul's thoughts on the *origin* of sin in the disobedience of Adam and Eve.

2. *The Sin of Adam*

The story of Adam and Eve in Genesis 3 is not taken up anywhere else in the Old Testament. By Paul's day, however, it had become a story of the fall of humankind and its consequences (Wis. 2:23–24; Sir. 25:24; cf., a little later, 2 Esd. 4:30). Allusions to the sin of Adam and Eve in the New Testament are rare and not very enlightening. First Timothy argues that a woman must learn from men in silence because it was Eve, not Adam, who "was deceived and became a transgressor" (1 Tim. 2:11–14). In 2 Corinthians Paul too mentions only that it was Eve whom the serpent deceived by its cunning (2 Cor. 11:3). But the two passages in which he contrasts Adam and Christ are of major theological importance. In 1 Corinthians 15, where he is explaining the resurrection of the dead, he states that "as all die in Adam, so all will be made alive in Christ" (1

5. In Classical Greek *hypokritēs* meant "actor," one who plays a role. See also Matt. 7:5; 15:7–9; 22:18; Luke 12:56; 13:15.

Cor. 15:22). We will need to look closely at this passage in our final chapter. Here it is the second passage, Romans 5:12–21, that concerns us: it was the main biblical source on which Augustine rested his doctrine of original sin.

Paul's contrast between Adam and Christ in Romans 5 is summed up in verse 19: "For just as by the one man's disobedience the many were made sinners, so by the one man's obedience the many will be made righteous." From Adam to Moses—that is, until the giving of the law—death, which is the penalty for sin, exercised dominion even over those whose sin was not a willful transgression like Adam's act of disobedience. Why, then, did death reign if, as Paul says, "sin is not reckoned when there is no law" (v. 13; cf. John 15:22)? Augustine read verse 12 in Latin and concluded that death spread to all because all *sinned* in Adam (*in quo omnes peccaverunt*). But how can everyone have sinned in Adam? Augustine's answer was that all sinned "in Adam's loins." On this interpretation he based his doctrine of original, or hereditary, sin—his doctrine that sin is transmitted from Adam by "carnal generation." Further support came from Psalm 51:5 ("I was born guilty, a sinner when my mother conceived me") and from the association of sin with the inordinate passion that accompanies sexual intercourse. The case was clinched by appeal to the church's practice of infant baptism, which presupposes, according to Augustine, that infants inherit original sin before they are capable of actual sins.[6] His argument was flawed,  not least because of his misinterpretation of Romans 5:12. In Paul's Greek, the text does not say that death spread from Adam "*in whom* all sinned," but "death spread to all *because* [*eph' hō*] all have sinned." If theological insight is to be retrieved from Augustine's doctrine, it lies in his metaphor of original sin as a sickness or disease (passim), since most diseases are communicated by association and infection but not by sexual activity (venereal disease excepted).

But what, in Augustine's view, was the nature of Adam's fall that brought about the ruin of humanity? The question is crucial because he assumed that the first sin shows the essence of sin. He had a number of ways of putting it, but they all say much the same thing: sin is concupiscence, turning from the Creator to earthly things, turning from God to self; it is self-love, pride, disobedience, the will to be one's own master. The priority goes to *pride*: from Ecclesiasticus (Sir. 10:13) Augustine learned that pride is the beginning of sin.[7] The fall of the bad angels and the first humans was the origin of two cities, one of them constituted by *self-love*: "two cities have been formed by two loves: the earthly by the love of self, even to contempt of God; the heavenly by the love of God, even to the contempt of self. The former, in a word, glories in itself, the latter in the Lord."[8]

6. Augustine, *Merits and Forgiveness*, 18–24, 36, 40–41; *On Marriage and Concupiscence* (419), NPNF[1] 5:274–75. He developed his argument for original sin in an extensive work against the Pelagian Julian of Eclanum that remained unfinished at his death; there he states that all were present "seminally" in Adam's loins (MPL 45:1442).

7. Augustine, *The Literal Meaning of Genesis* (415), *ACW* 42:138, 146–48, 164; *The City of God* (413–27), NPNF[1] 2:271–77. Concupiscence is not strictly reducible to sexual desire, but "for practical purposes [Augustine] identifies concupiscence with it" (Kelly 1977: 365).

8. Augustine, *City of God*, 282–83; cf. 226. The "cities" are to be understood "mystically" (284). He does not, or not usually, equate them with observable communities. Hence, in both the Roman Empire and the Catholic Church the two cities are mingled together (21, 205, 391, 431); this becomes important later, when we speak of church, ministry, and sacraments. Note further that Augustine affirms

Like Augustine, Calvin found the nature of sin in the sin of Adam. As we would expect, he saw the fall as the exact counterpart to the image of God in humanity: by the image Adam reflected the bounty of God, and by the fall "he shamefully spurned God's great bounty, which had been lavished upon him" (*Institutes*, 1:245). The fall was a fall from thankfulness (cf. Rom. 1:21). In at least two respects Calvin modified Augustine's account. First, he tried to get behind pride to the cause of pride: "Unfaithfulness . . . was the root of the Fall. But thereafter ambition and pride, together with ungratefulness, arose" (ibid.; cf. 55). Calvin saw the essence of unfaithfulness and disobedience in not heeding the Word of God: Adam was unwilling to believe the Word (he was *verbo incredulus*). Both sin and the gospel alike, as Bernard of Clairvaux (1090–1153) rightly teaches, get in through the ears (246). Second, though he used the language of "hereditary corruption," Calvin denied that the corruption of the whole human race could have proceeded from Adam by natural procreation. His explanation of original sin may strike us as no great improvement on Augustine's: he was content to say simply that by the appointment of God what Adam lost he lost for all humanity (249–50; Comm. John 3:6). But dissatisfaction with Calvin's explanation should not let us overlook that in his mind, as in Augustine's and Paul's, sin and redemption have an inescapably social or collective aspect: they are about *humanity*, the human race. "For," as Paul says, "as all die in Adam, so all will be made alive in Christ."

II. Forgetfulness, Social Sin, and Anxiety

Augustine's view of Adam's sin as an act of pride, and its transmission to others by natural procreation, has exercised a fateful influence on Christian theology in the West. (Eastern Orthodoxy has been more inclined to the opinion of Augustine's Pelagian adversaries that we can incur guilt only by *imitation* of Adam's sin.) But Augustine's view has also evoked dissent that goes well beyond Calvin's slender modifications, and dissent has been furthered by the recognition that "Adam" does not name an individual in prehistoric time but stands for humanity in every time. Schleiermacher approved of Augustine's view of sin as a turning away from the Creator, but on the transmission of sin he broke relatively new ground. And Søren Kierkegaard (1813–55) gave the discussion another fresh direction by his searching psychological reflections on anxiety and the sickness of despair.

1. *God-forgetfulness and Sin as Social*

Schleiermacher suggested that the plight of humanity in sin could be called *God-forgetfulness* (*CF* 54). Plainly, this is the obverse of his definition of religion as God-consciousness. He could have pointed out, though he didn't, that forgetting God is one of the ways in which the sin of the chosen people is frequently stated in the Old Testament. But his notion of God-forgetfulness was

a proper self-love that is strictly subordinate to love of God and neighbor (476; *On Christian Doctrine* [396–426/427], NPNF[1] 2:528–30).

more abstract than the sin of the Israelites, who failed to remember the covenant and the commandments. Hosea traced the cause of forgetfulness to Yahweh's *blessings*: "When I fed them, they were satisfied; they were satisfied, and their heart was proud; therefore they forgot me" (Hos. 13:6; cf. Deut. 32:15). Echoing Paul's language in Galatians 5:17, Schleiermacher traced the cause of forgetfulness to the constitution of every human being as flesh and spirit: sin is "a positive antagonism of the flesh against the spirit" that impedes consciousness of God (271).[9]

Schleiermacher understood *the flesh* in the Pauline manner, as whatever belongs to the merely earthly sphere—not sensuality but "world-consciousness," as Barth rightly says (*CD* III/3:324). But by "spirit" (capitalized in the NRSV of Gal. 5:17 as "the Spirit") he meant, in this context, the consciousness of God, which must struggle against preoccupation with mundane existence. This "sensible self-consciousness," as he called it, has the advantage over the God-consciousness that in all of us it develops first (*CF* 19–20, 273–75). The consciousness of sin arises as we recognize our responsibility for arresting the development of the God-consciousness, and this recognition (Schleiermacher cites Rom. 7:25 and 8:2) comes from the consciousness of redemption (*CF* 272, 278–79). Talk of development does not mean that the consciousness of sin is merely recognition that much still lies ahead of us in the natural growth of our consciousness of God. "[T]his view, in nullifying as it does not only the reality of sin but also the need of redemption, leaves so little room anywhere for the peculiar work of a Redeemer that it can scarcely be regarded as a Christian view at all" (278; see also 54–55, 274, 336–37). We are not to imagine an unbroken development in the power of the God-consciousness (343).

As for the notion of *original sin*, Schleiermacher rejected the belief that it refers to a state into which the human race, as a consequence of Adam's sin, fell from a previous state of original righteousness. We have to surrender the belief that "original perfection" and "original sin" denote successive moments in the story of humanity: they always coexist in humanity as possibilities grounded in the self-same features of human nature (*CF* 299, 301, 303–4). But it is entirely right to say, "*We are conscious of sin partly as having its source in ourselves, partly as having its source outside our own being*" (§69 [279]). And it is just here that Schleiermacher maintained the historical continuity of doctrine, not dismissing the church's dogma of original sin but making adjustments to it (281). Each of us is born into a world that has been determined by the sins of the entire previous generation; it is in this sense that sin has a source beyond ourselves. If we think of original sin as the work of successive generations, not as the one-time deed of an individual in prehistoric times, then the source beyond ourselves is collective. Original sin (German *Erbsünde*, "inherited sin") is about the network of human relationships that makes sin *social*—in all the sin of each, and in each the sin of all. "[O]nly in this corporate character, indeed, can [sin] be properly

9. Schleiermacher has been faulted for saying that there is no sin where there is no consciousness of sin (*CF* §68.2 [277]). Perhaps he had in mind something like the Pauline distinction between "sin" generally and "transgression" as a willful kind of sin (Rom. 5:14). In any case, he obviously did not mean to say that sin is purely subjective—without source or ground. The "germ" of sin is everything that arrests the development of the consciousness of God, whether acknowledged as sin or not (§66 [271–73]).

and fully understood" (287–88). Later, Schleiermacher will be saying the same about redemption: it too can be understood only in its corporate character—as implied in Paul's comparison of Adam and Christ in Romans 5.

2. *Finitude and Anxiety as the Occasion for Sin*

The influence of Kierkegaard on the Christian understanding of sin is evident in the work of Reinhold Niebuhr (1892–1971) and Paul Tillich. Kierkegaard identified anxiety as the occasion, though not the inevitable cause, of sin. The structure of our existence opens up the possibility of becoming genuinely human by the exercise of freedom. But Kierkegaard held that the prospect of freedom unnerves us, makes us anxious. Anxiety is the possibility given with freedom. It is not sinful to feel anxiety: sin is the despair that shrinks from freedom.

In the first volume of his masterly study *The Nature and Destiny of Man* (chaps. 7–8), Niebuhr commends Kierkegaard's analysis of anxiety and sin but does not simply reproduce it. He agrees that the precondition of sin lies in the ambiguity of human existence between finiteness and freedom and that the resulting anxiety is not itself sin—it is the occasion of sin. But he finds in anxiety both the basis of human creativity and the occasion of two distinct kinds of sin. A man may try either to deny his finiteness or to escape from his freedom; that is, he may fall either into the sin of pride or into the sin of sensuality. Sexual passion is not the only form of sensuality, but, like extravagant living and drunkenness, it shows the two-sidedness of sensuality as the attempt either to aggrandize the ego or to escape from it—ultimately, into unconsciousness. Niebuhr describes a man's sensuality, a little vaguely, as "seeking to hide his freedom and . . . losing himself in some aspect of the world's vitalities" (Niebuhr 1941: 191). But he takes *pride*, not sensuality, to be the primary definition of sin in both the Bible and classical Christian theology; and he exposes the sin of pride not only in the life of the individual but also in the collective behavior of nations and churches—an important anticipation of his social and political use of the doctrine of justification by faith (see chap. 12 below).

Niebuhr discovers three types of pride. The *pride of power* may rest on a strong sense of security; but it may also arise from a lack of security and the consequent grasp for more power. The *pride of intellect* imagines that finite knowledge, gained from a particular perspective, is final and ultimate knowledge. The vehemence with which an adversary is accused of error betrays a desperate effort to hide the limitations of one's own position. The *pride of virtue* mistakes its standards for God's standards. It is "the pretension of finite man that his highly conditioned virtue is the final righteousness and that his very relative moral standards are absolute" (Niebuhr 1941: 212). Moral pride has been responsible for "our most serious cruelties, injustices and defamations against our fellowmen"; and it generates the spiritual pride that makes religion not a self-evident good, but "merely a final battleground between God and man's self-esteem" (213).

Deeply immersed in existentialist philosophy and depth psychology, *Tillich* gives a profound analysis of anxiety in his remarkable little book *The Courage to Be* (1952).[10] Like Ernst Troeltsch before him, he suggests that the dominant reli-

10. In a fuller presentation of Tillich's thoughts on anxiety and sin, *The Courage to Be* would need to be read in conjunction with the third part of his systematic theology. See Tillich 1951–63, 2:44–59.

gious question changes from one historical period to the next: the ancient world was haunted by the anxiety of fate and death, the Middle Ages (including the Reformation) by the anxiety of guilt and condemnation, and the modern world by the anxiety of emptiness and meaninglessness. Existential anxiety is not neurotic anxiety: "In all three forms anxiety is existential in the sense that it belongs to existence as such" (38). Moreover, the three forms, though normally under the dominance of one of them, are immanent in one another. And every form of the religious question is rooted in the experience of finite freedom. "Anxiety is finitude, experienced as one's own finitude" (33).

The influential studies by Niebuhr and Tillich have undoubtedly shed new light on traditional Christian understandings of sin. But they have also been subjected to sharp criticisms. From the perspective of feminist theology, a groundbreaking article by Valerie Saiving, published in 1960, suggested that Niebuhr and Swedish theologian Anders Nygren (1890–1978) represented sin in terms that had more to do with men's experience than women's. The suggestion was taken up in the Yale dissertation of Judith Plaskow (published 1980), an acute critical reading of Niebuhr and Tillich on sin. Plaskow points out that in the Western world the lives of women have been largely determined by the passive role assigned to them by men. "A woman does not define and create her own identity, but is defined by her husband and children" (24). The particular sin of women, illustrated by Doris Lessing's character Martha Quest, may be their acceptance of society's view of them to the detriment of finite freedom; it is not glorification of the self but failing to take the responsibility to become a self. Plaskow concludes that Niebuhr should have looked more closely at the sin of sensuality along with the masculine sin of pride. But she commends Tillich for his thoughts on what he called "uncreative weakness."

III. Estrangement and Faith

Traditionally, the Christian understanding of sin has been presented through the story of Adam and Eve. But the story has always been employed not only for historical explanation of the presence of sin in the world but also for analysis of the nature of sin: it is assumed that in describing the sin of Adam and Eve one is analyzing the sin of every man and every woman. For this reason, traditional interpretations of Genesis 3 have an importance that goes beyond the question of historical veracity. Just as the doctrine of humanity as created is strictly about a possibility of human existence, the doctrine of original sin is about another possibility, and the gospel is addressed to persons in whom the second possibility has become actual. Christian faith holds that the first possibility is therefore attainable only by way of redemption.

1. The Vocabulary of Sin

Much of what is needed for a constructive view of sin can be approached through critical reappraisal of some key terms in the discussion. If we retain the language of (1) *the fall*, it can only be about humanity, not about the first human pair. Sin is present, the fall happens, whenever a person "falls short" of the glory of God (Rom. 3:23)—that is, fails to reflect the radiance of God, in whose image humankind is created. But the failure does not count as sin when it lacks the character of a conscious transgression (5:13–14), a deliberate turning away from the first possibility—to live in gratitude and obedience to the Creator. The presupposition of sin is recognition of this unique human possibility; where the recognition is lacking, where (in Pauline terms) there is no law, guilt is also lacking. If we focus on the dawning of this recognition in the individual—either for the first time or for each time—it is not inappropriate to represent it as a fall from innocence, a fall in which the weakness or neglect of life toward God is acknowledged as one's own fault.

The most comprehensive term for the failure to reflect the glory of God is (2) *estrangement*. The term *estrangement* is not biblical, but the idea of estrangement as the consequence of sin obviously is (Isa. 59:2; 2 Thess. 1:9; cf. Gen. 3:24; Lev. 13:46); it is the condition presupposed by the word of reconciliation (Rom. 5:10; 2 Cor. 5:18–20). Dogmatics needs to distinguish the *state* of being a sinner from sin as *act*. The distinction between "original sin" and "actual sin" in the older dogmatics could be taken to meet this need, provided that it is freed from spurious questions about why and how all humankind are condemned on account of the sin of Adam and Eve.[11] But we will speak rather of estrangement as the state of the sinner and will follow the Westminster Shorter Catechism (1648) in defining the act of sin as "any want of conformity unto, or transgression of, the law of God" (q. 14; cf. 1 John 3:4). Act and state are then related reciprocally:

acts of sin give rise to estrangement, and estrangement produces acts of sin.

Perhaps the commonest idea of sin in Christian literature is (3) the *self-love* that goes with the first humans' pride, ambition, and temptation to become like gods (Gen. 3:5). But Christians infer the precise nature of sin not just from the story of the fall but also, and decisively, from the proclamation of redemption. The message of Jesus came as a summons to self-denial (Mark 8:34), and Paul's gospel announced the crucifixion of the old self (Rom. 6:6; Gal. 2:19–20; 5:24). It follows from the remedy that those who have identified the sickness of sin with *amor sui* (love of self) are not mistaken: the root of sin is egocentrism. The source of this condition is in part the natural perception of early childhood that the entire environment is there to meet the child's needs. We might say that sin (rather than religion, as the Freudians say) is infantile regression. In this sense, we can agree with the traditional doctrine that we are *born* sinners. We need not dismiss even Calvin's gloomy observation that the entire nature of infants is a kind of "seed-bed of sin" (*Institutes*, 1:217 [Beveridge]). But are not infants also seedbeds of *grace*?

The infection of personal existence by love of self is not necessarily cured by religion; it may, on the contrary, vanquish even my religion if what I seek from religion is what I have been unable to secure for myself by any other means. The gain of godliness is then the success it brings me here and the bliss it promises hereafter. Instead of being conformity to the Creator's design, piety becomes a means of using God for the sake of my own advancement. The old Calvinistic dogma of (4) *total depravity* teaches precisely that the infection of sin

11. In "Holy Willie's Prayer" Robert Burns ridiculed the conventional view by having Willie confess: "I, wha deserv'd most just damnation, / For broken laws / Sax thousand years ere my creation."

runs through the whole of an individual's personal existence, not even excluding the relationship with God.[12] It does not assert that the unredeemed person is utterly bad. Calvin was too good a classical humanist not to admire human achievements in art, science, philosophy, and civic virtue. But, in agreement with Augustine, he considered them vitiated by a thankless pride that does not receive them as gifts of the Spirit: "Let us be ashamed of such ingratitude, into which not even the pagan poets fell, for they confessed that the gods had invented philosophy, laws, and all useful arts" (*Institutes*, 1:274). Total depravity means that no aspect of human existence escapes the perversion of sin, not even the exercise of reason (as the schoolmen were inclined to suppose). In a striking image, Calvin suggests that the good gifts remaining in humans since the fall are spoiled like good wine turned sour in a bad barrel (Comm. John 3:6).

"Blind self-love is innate in all mortals" (Calvin, *Institutes*, 1:343). But self-love is not simply innate: it is constantly fed by the interaction of one self with other selves, the other being perceived as both a threat to one's own ego and the material for its fulfillment. Sin is always (5) *social sin*. The collective pressures of society, open to daily observation, have encouraged modern attempts to reinterpret original sin precisely as solidarity in sin. Augustine's harsh verdict that humankind is a single damnable lump (a *massa perditionis*) can then be retrieved as the recognition that each of us is not merely an individual sinner but inextricably entangled in a network of sinful (that is, self-serving) relationships, to which we make ourselves captive and for which we share responsibility. In Emil Brunner's vivid simile, we are "like the individual strawberry plants which, underneath the surface, are tied up with one another in a texture of roots."[13]

The theme of solidarity in sin, strongly affirmed by Schleiermacher and Albrecht Ritschl (1822–89), became a cornerstone in Walter Rauschenbusch's (1861–1918) theology of the social gospel. Any attempt to correlate sin and redemption needs to avoid the individualistic perspective that often misrepresents both of these doctrines. Of course, individual responsibility is not to be dissolved in collective guilt: I am not absolved by pointing my finger at the corruption that ensnares me. That is why Jeremiah and Ezekiel protested against the proverb, "The parents have eaten sour grapes, and the children's teeth are set on edge." Only the individual who sins will die (Jer. 31:27–30; Ezek. 18:2–4; 33:1–20; cf. Deut. 24:16; 2 Sam. 24:17; Job 21:19). The obverse truth is that a person's righteousness saves only that person, no one else (Ezek. 14:12–20). To hold collective and individual responsibility together is not always easy, but it is nonetheless essential to a proper understanding of sin and redemption.

A final expression that calls for comment is (6) *bondage* or *servitude*. We have already noted the problem of free will in the Augustinian and Calvinist traditions, and we will need to return to it in connection with the discussion of conversion, where it becomes the question whether a person is equally free to accept or to reject the call of the gospel. Here I need only say that, in my opinion, Luther confused two issues that ought initially to be distinguished.

12. Unlike Calvin, the Westminster Confession (1647) has lent its authority to an intensive, not solely extensive, view of human depravity (6.4).

13. Emil Brunner, *The Scandal of Christianity* (London: SCM, 1951), 65. A powerful dramatic portrayal of social solidarity in wrongdoing is J. B. Priestley's play *An Inspector Calls.*

He tried to support his profound insight into the bondage of the sinful will by adopting John Wycliffe's (ca. 1325–84) assertion that "to purpose anything either evil or good is in no one's control, but . . . everything happens by absolute necessity." That was to mix a moral or psychological necessity with metaphysical necessity. The metaphysical issue cannot be ignored (as we have seen), but it is *another* issue, different from the plight of the will turned in upon itself in self-love. As Bernard put it in a homely illustration, it is not as easy to climb out of a pit as it is to fall into one. Or, as Brunner says: "the sinner is in principle capable of avoiding every particular sin. But what he cannot do is this: he cannot *not* be a sinner" (1946–62, 2:111).

2. *Two Types of Faithlessness*

It is no doubt true that in the Old Testament the emphasis falls on sin as rebellion. But due account must be taken of the historical context. In the story of Israel, sin is naturally viewed as a rebellious people's spurning the covenant. The gospel of Jesus, on the other hand, did not come only as judgment on the sin of going after other gods. It was also—and foremost—addressed as good news to persons who were burdened by hardship and pain. Jesus could certainly denounce the presumptuous sins of the self-righteous. But, according to the Gospels, he understood his ministry to be the fulfillment of the prophecy of Isaiah: the Spirit had anointed him to bring good news to the poor, to proclaim release to the captives and recovery of sight to the blind (Luke 4:16–22; see Isa. 61:1–3). Matthew testifies that Jesus fulfilled another passage from Isaiah: "He will not wrangle or cry aloud. . . . He will not break a bruised reed or quench a smoldering wick until he brings justice to victory" (Matt. 12:17–21; Isa. 42:1–4; cf. Ps. 147:3). Remarkably, this was not the angry messiah John the Baptist anticipated (Luke 3:7–9; in Matt. 3:7–12 the angry words are addressed to the Pharisees and the Sadducees, not to the crowd generally). Jesus' mission was to the lost (Matt. 10:6; 15:24; 18:11; Luke 19:10; but see Luke 12:49), and the series of parables in Luke 15 suggests that there are more ways than one of being lost. The prodigal son was lost willfully, but the sheep wandered off aimlessly, and the coin went uselessly out of circulation.

The nature of estrangement is understood not simply from the sin of Adam, nor from Paul's controversy with the Pharisees, but mainly from the gospel: the malady is known in the cure, and what we need is disclosed in what we are given. In terms of our concept of faith, there are at least two kinds of faithlessness: *mistrust* as well as *defiance*. Alongside the word of judgment that shatters the defiant ego, there are the words of gentle rebuke to those of little faith (Mark 4:40; Matt. 6:30; 8:26; 14:31; 16:8; Luke 8:25; 12:28; 17:5) and words of compassion to the weary, who carry heavy burdens (Matt. 11:28). The message comes as reassurance to the mistrustful, and it calls the defiant to account. As such, it stirs the two-sidedness of elemental faith in an intelligible world that makes moral sense to us. Elemental faith is seen on reflection to belong to the class of inevitable beliefs, but in actual experience it sometimes slips away. The gospel is a reaffirmation of something in the depths of every human being so that it is heard not as heteronomous, or imposed from without, but as corresponding to the law of our being: it resonates within. This, to be sure, is not *all* the gospel is and does! More belongs to the doctrines of redemption, to which the present chapter is only a prelude.

For now, thesis 7 sums up my critical comments on the vocabulary of sin and is structured by the recognition that there are more ways than one of lacking or losing faith. Estrangement from God may be grounded in willful rebellion, but it may also be a lack of trust that has more to do with depletion of the self than with self-assertion. Of course, this does not exhaust the varieties of estrangement, and there is no need to suppose that these two are wholly exclusive. *Mistrust* may be blameworthy if it refuses the reassurance of grace and reflects the pathological self-preoccupation of the victim. *Defiance*, when it comes to itself, discovers that not guilt but the Father's compassion has the last word (Luke 15:17, 20). But mistrust and defiance will serve as ideal types for the dogmatic presentation of what it means to live by faith. My seventh thesis is ordered accordingly, and it seeks also to take account of my observations on the sources, extent, and debilitating effect of sin. We will see, in particular, that estrangement and reconciliation are mutually defining also in this: both are essentially social concepts.

8. God and Evil

Estrangement from the Creator cannot be separated from the way in which the creation is perceived but is precisely being at odds with the world order, either through anxiety about the course of the world (in particular, about natural evil) or through abuse of its resources and inhabitants for self-centered ends (which is social evil); and the magnitude of evil in the world raises the question of theodicy, which faith answers with commitment to the healing work of God in Jesus Christ.

Schleiermacher speaks out of his experience among the Moravian Pietists when he says that "in the consciousness of a person in the grip of conversion, every sense of human intermediation vanishes, and Christ is realized as immediately present in all His redeeming and atoning activity, prophetic, priestly, and kingly" (*CF* 492). His testimony must be taken, however, along with his thoughts on the individual's relation to the church and the world. He repeatedly insists on the communal setting in which the Word of Christ lays hold on the individual (e.g., 477–78). More will need to be said on the connection between the individual and the community when we turn to the doctrine of the church. But Schleiermacher grasped, in addition, the point that became pivotal in the theology of Albrecht Ritschl: sin and redemption are about the individual's relation not to God or Christ only, but also to *the world.* As Ritschl says, justification by faith is not simply removal of the penalties for sin—it entails a change of attitude to the world on the part of those who previously were sinners (Ritschl 1966: 30; see also 168, 418–19, 498).

The changed attitude of believers to the world will be taken up in chapter 12, on reconciliation. The present chapter is an appendage to the doctrine of estrangement: it concerns the way the world is perceived by the two kinds of faithlessness named in my seventh thesis: mistrust and defiance. And in this context we will ask how belief in a good and just Creator can be harmonized with the existence of evil—the problem of *theodicy,* usually dealt with in traditional dogmatics under the doctrine of providence and more fully in apologetics, philosophical theology, and the philosophy of religion. By "evils" (plural) is meant things and events that inhibit human well-being or cause human suffering. They are usually classified as either *natural,* if no human agency is involved, or *social,* if brought about by human agency. The two kinds of evil are not always wholly distinct: some natural disasters, for example, are the result of human mismanagement of nature. But as a working distinction the contrast between natural (or physical) and social (or moral) evils is indispensable.[1]

Our agenda, then, calls first for analysis of the connection between estrangement and the two kinds of evil, natural and social. Next some account, however brief, must be given of biblical and theological answers to the problem of theodicy, to which the existence of evil gives rise. But evil is not just an obstinate intellectual puzzle, never finally and definitively answered. I conclude, therefore, with observations on evil as an experiential problem for the life of faith. It will be obvious that the themes divided under these three headings overlap; I deal with them separately for the sake of orderly presentation.

I. Estrangement and Evil

Mistrust becomes *anxiety* in the face of natural evils that shake a person's confidence in an intelligible world order; and defiance to the moral character of the world order issues in *abuse* of its resources and inhabitants. Anxiety is a hurt experienced by the victim; abuse of the creation is a hurt inflicted by others. The abuse of persons can, of course, also be considered from the viewpoint of the victim. But it will be convenient to speak first of anxiety mainly, though not exclusively, with respect to natural evils; then of abuse of the world and its inhabitants.

1. Natural Evil, Anxiety, and Sin

There is a kind of anxiety that arises from the possibility of freedom over nature: an individual may shrink from the call of "dreadful freedom." But there is also an anxiety that arises from being crushed by nature. In Scripture, natural evil is a frequent theme. The biblical writers generally had little difficulty fitting natural evils into their worldview. Storms, floods, earthquakes, sickness, and famine were ascribed to the God who caused evil as well as good (1 Kgs. 17:20; Isa. 45:7; Amos 3:6). When they were not simply tokens of the Creator's awesome power (Job 37:1–7; Pss. 29:3–9; 104:31–32), they could be subsumed under the fundamental principle of retribution for sin (e.g., Amos 4:6). Even historical catastrophes that overwhelmed the chosen people could be viewed not simply as social evils—brought about by human agency—but also as the work of Yahweh for punishment of the nation's infidelity (Mic. 2:3; Jer. 4:6). But the evils that afflicted Job drew from him the cry of many sufferers, Why me? "For [God] crushes me with a tempest, and multiplies my wounds without cause. . . . [H]e destroys both the blameless and the wicked. When disaster brings sudden death, he mocks at the calamity of the innocent" (Job 9:17, 22–23).

1. To avoid the implication that anything created could, as such, be judged bad, some accounts recognize "metaphysical evil" as a further category: that is, the limitations imposed by finitude—"mere imperfection," as Leibniz says (Leibniz 1985: 136). Barth achieves the same goal with his distinction between "the shadow side of creation" and the enemy of Creator and creature that he calls "nothingness" (*das Nichtige*: *CD* III/3:295–96 [§50.1]), and by Schleiermacher with his distinction between nature itself and the sinful perception of nature.

Calvin kept close to the biblical account of the nature of evil, but he laid a distinctive emphasis on the psychological impact evil makes on a person's life. As we have seen, he held creation and providence tightly together: "For unless we pass on to his providence . . . we do not yet properly grasp what it means to say: 'God is Creator'" (*Institutes*, 1:197). Yet he read the created order and the continuing passage of events very differently. On the one hand, God discloses himself in the beautiful workmanship of the universe. Those who study astronomy, medicine, and other natural sciences delve more deeply into the divine wisdom; but even the uneducated, who simply use their eyes, have no excuse for not knowing the Artificer (52–53, 197). On the other hand, the course of daily events is different. To be sure, seemingly fortuitous happenings are directed by God's ever-present hand executing his eternal decrees (198–99, 201, 207–8, 218). But the hand of providence is not always evident: God's judgments are *hidden*, his plans *secret*. "[T]he order, reason, end, and necessity of those things which happen for the most part lie hidden in God's purpose" (208).

Calvin vividly portrayed the plight of anyone who tries to make sense of daily perils without the guidance of the Word. His examples of daily perils embraced—without explicit distinction—both natural disasters (storms, shipwreck, famine, drought, disease, etc.) and human wrongs (robbery, murder, etc.). Because the causes of events are sometimes, indeed usually, hidden, the thought insinuates itself that there is in fact no order or pattern in human affairs—only blind fortune. Accidents that threaten life or limb can paralyze us with fright; the apparent chaos of events can even drive a person to suicide. To the objection that he was listing bad things that rarely happen, Calvin replied that they *do* happen and *can* happen to us. Only the light of divine providence frees us from extreme anxiety and dread (211, 214, 223, 224). In this respect, Calvin's language anticipates the analysis of precarious human existence in the existentialist writers of our own time.

Schleiermacher defined "evils" broadly as "causes of hindrance to life," but he meant, more particularly, "hindrance to spiritual life." Unlike Calvin, he expressly distinguished between natural evil and social evil, and he traced them both to sin. *Natural* evils are hindrances to human life that are independent of human action. From the viewpoint of the original perfection of the world and humanity, nothing affecting bodily existence—not even death, or the disease and debility that precede it—would be construed as a hindrance to the life of the human species, since it would not exclude consciousness of God. But when the flesh dominates, every obstruction to bodily life is viewed as evil. It is sin, therefore, the dominance of the flesh, that makes the world appear to be a place of evil (*CF* 315–16). Natural perils to our bodily existence are "evils" because that is how the sinner perceives them; objectively considered, in themselves they are incentives to the development of the spirit (319).[2]

Social evils are hindrances to human life brought about by human acts that issue from sin. Such an act could not, in itself, hinder the spiritual life of others,

2. The interest of dogmatics is strictly in the subjective viewpoint. Hence Schleiermacher's later statement (*CF* §78 [322]) that his position calls neither for passive endurance of evil nor for the endeavor to do away with evil in itself. Any activity directed against one's suffering, and not rather against one's sin, would not be motivated by the Christian religious consciousness, but by the lower (sensible) region of life (§78.2 [324]; cf. §71.4 [290–91]).

only their sensible life. But it will become a hindrance to their spiritual life if the dominance of their consciousness of God has given way to the sensible consciousness (the "flesh"). Here, too, as in the case of natural evils, evil arises only with sin. Sin and evil are strictly phenomena of human consciousness. What in one person (the perpetrator) issues from sin becomes evil for the consciousness of another (the victim). Schleiermacher preferred to speak of "social" rather than "moral" evil to avoid any suggestion that the moral term *badness* can, as such, be subsumed under the concept of "evil." Good and bad are alike to be placed under the idea of absolute dependence on God. Only the victim's consciousness of sin causes a morally bad act to become evil, that is, to inhibit the God-consciousness (*CF* 184, 316).

Like everything else, according to Schleiermacher, we must trace the connection between sin and evil to the divine causality. In this sense we can properly say that evil is the "punishment" of sin; indeed, that God is "the Author of sin" (*CF* 317, 325). But we are not to think of the punishment of sin apart from the universal world order and to imagine that God singles out individual sins for individual punishment (318–19): *"on no account must the evils affecting the individual be referred to his sin as their cause"* (320). It is a dangerous error to suppose that for the individual "the measure of his sin is the measure of the evil that befalls him" (321). Schleiermacher refers to John 9:3, where Jesus explicitly rejects the dogma that *natural* evil—in this case, blindness—can be explained as due to the victim's own sin. As for *social* evils, it is an essential Christian belief that penal suffering may fall on one who is free from the common guilt (322).

Clearly, Schleiermacher's approach to the problem of natural evil is different from Calvin's. Up to a point, they supplement each other. Calvin describes the fearful anxiety generated by natural disaster and daily accidents, whenever the Word of God is absent. Schleiermacher wants us to think about the sin that generates the perception of natural evil whenever the consciousness of God recedes. Neither of them represents human existence, even after redemption, as trouble free—as though, in Schleiermacher's words, "the guiding hope would be merely that a joyous emergence of the God-consciousness might possibly take place once we had become prosperous and happy" (*CF* 318). We will come back to their thoughts on theodicy (section II below). But we turn next to the problem that arises from the ability of the human species not to be crushed by nature, but to control nature and its inhabitants: the problem not of anxiety, but of *abuse* or *exploitation.* And here we must take into account the social evils of "oppression and antagonism" that Schleiermacher has already touched on (317).

2. *Abuse of Nature and Persons*

Ritschl's insistence on the connection between justification and the believer's attitude to the world is in principle well taken, but what he made of it was limited by the thought of his day. He appealed to Luther, whose first thesis in *The Freedom of a Christian* (1520) was that "a Christian is a perfectly free lord of all, subject to none" (Ritschl 1966: 498; LW 31:344). He faulted Luther because "[i]n all his later writings he limits the freedom which flows from justification to its negative sense of freedom from the law and from sin," neglecting "positive world-dominating freedom" (181). But "positive world-dominating freedom" is not exactly what Luther meant by "a spiritual dominion" that turns evil and suffering to good if only we believe (LW 31:355, citing Rom. 8:28 and 2 Cor. 12:9). Ritschl's problem arose from the nineteenth-century antithesis of nature and spirit: "the contradiction in which man finds himself, as both a part of the world of nature and a spiritual personality claiming to dominate nature" (1966: 199). In our own day, the notion of humankind's privilege of "domination" sounds too much like the exploitation of nature and persons, in which we are inclined to locate sin rather than the blessing of religion. It is precisely a sense of the human community as "a part of the world of nature" that strikes us as needful.

The problem is not only that humans now have the ability to destroy life on the planet in a single nuclear war. Quite apart from such a total cataclysm, the long-term ability of the planet to sustain human existence is in question. The earth must meet the demands of a growing world population, and uncontrolled *exploitation of nature* further diminishes finite resources either directly or indirectly. Deforestation, unregulated fishing of the oceans, and the pollution created by industrial waste are well-documented threats to the human environment, as also is the global warming caused mainly by carbon dioxide and other greenhouse gases from human inventions and activities. But it is difficult to persuade commercial interests to look beyond short-term financial gain or even to acknowledge that the prophetic voices of doom are not exaggerating or imagining the crisis.

Historian Lynn White Jr. initiated a fresh round of discussion with his widely read essay, "The Historical Roots of Our Ecological Crisis" (1967), in which he argued that Christianity bears a burden of guilt for the crisis. Christianity removed an obstacle to the scientific investigation of nature by destroying pagan animism, but more important: "Especially in its Western form, Christianity is the most anthropocentric religion the world has seen" (in Barbour 1973: 25). According to White, the human-centered arrogance of orthodox Christians toward nature shaped the mentality that drives the scientific and technological enterprises. "What we do about ecology depends on our ideas of the man-nature relationship. More science and more technology are not going to get us out of the present ecologic crisis until we find a new religion, or rethink our old one" (28). White recommends the attitude to nature of Francis of Assisi (1182–1226), whose panpsychism was clearly heretical.

It is hard to deny that White has a point. The dominion granted to Adam and the divine injunction to subdue the earth (Gen. 1:26, 28) set humans above nature; they are not admonished to see themselves as part of nature. In his reply to his critics, White reports that the most common charge was that he had misunderstood the nature of human dominion, which is not arbitrary rule but stewardship (in Barbour 1973: 60). The criticism may well come from a sounder Christian interpretation of the place of humans in the created order, but it hardly addresses White's historical thesis: the medieval perception of nature, in his view, was not about stewardship. Perhaps it was not White but our forebears who misunderstood the nature of Adam's dominion. Certainly, much more needs to be said about biblical thoughts on the place of humanity in nature. There is the psalmist's wistful petition, for instance, "I am a stranger in the earth: hide not thy commandments from me" (Ps. 119:19 KJV). But since

Christian faith no longer shapes the cultural outlook as it did in the Middle Ages, it is unlikely that either a new religion or a corrected old one will get us out of the ecological crisis. At best, the creation faith of Christians will play a modest part, and so must Christian perception of the self-interest that infects public policy. A candid appeal to sinful self-interest may have a better chance of success than holding up the worthy ideal of stewardship. But at this point dogmatics passes the torch to Christian ethics.

It is another question whether Christian anthropocentrism necessarily leads to exploitation of the environment. In Calvin it led to thankfulness and was strictly subordinate to the mission of humanity to declare the glory of God, who created humans and put them in the world to this end (Geneva Catechism). For him, a theocentric faith trumped an anthropocentric cosmology. But it has proved difficult for Christians, as for everyone else, to make the mental adjustment demanded by the Copernican and post-Copernican redrawing of the cosmic map. G. W. Leibniz (1646–1716) judged the old maxim that everything is made solely for humankind "somewhat discredited": he saw no reason to suppose that the happiness of rational creatures is God's whole or final aim (Leibniz 1985: 189). Yet even Schleiermacher, who warned against "representing man as the central-point of all finite existence" (*CF* 237), nevertheless asserted that the whole disposition of nature was designed with a view to the redemption of humankind by Christ (723). Similarly, Karl Barth's perceptive comments on "man in the cosmos" still left room for the improbable assertion that "man . . . is the partner in the covenant of grace which is the whole basis and aim of creation" (*CD* III/2:14). Troeltsch, by contrast, was persuaded that neither religious sensibility nor Christian theology could escape the consequences of the Copernican revolution: anthropocentrism must yield to the recognition that the entire human epic, from beginning to end, will be like breath on cold window panes, which disappears the next moment (1991: 58).

Triumph over nature may be one of the ways humans hide from themselves the prospect that the roles must eventually be reversed. As the Durants said, "Generations of men establish a growing mastery over the earth, but they are destined to become fossils in its soil."[3] That is certainly a thought that can intensify anxiety at the course of the world. What is at stake in overcoming anthropocentrism, however, is not only a painful acknowledgment of human finitude, but also the need to think again about the relation of humanity to other life-forms on planet Earth. Does the biblical representation of humanity as set above the rest of creation warrant the assumption that animal and plant life can be treated merely as instrumental to human happiness or pleasure? Or, to put it anthropomorphically, is it not the clear teaching of Genesis 1 that everything—including plants and animals—is made for the Creator's delight, not just for Adam's convenience? "God saw everything that he had made, and indeed, it was very good" (Gen. 1:31).

Questions have long been raised about the morality of blood sports, vivisection, the use of animals in genetic engineering, and eating animal flesh. *Ahimsa* in the Indian religions and Albert Schweitzer's (1875–1965) "reverence for life"

3. Will and Ariel Durant, *The Lessons of History* (New York: Simon & Schuster, 1968), 14–15.

have been much discussed.[4] But a comprehensive study of animal rights is relatively new. It now has its own journal and institutional home in the Oxford Centre for Animal Ethics. The "animal theologians" have stirred lively controversy and unseemly ridicule—even from the side of ecological theologians. Important dogmatic issues are involved. The debate has shed fresh light on, for example, the Pauline inclusion of all creation in the hope of redemption (Rom. 8:18–25). But the discussion on animal rights has been carried on chiefly in the field of Christian ethics.

Exploitation of nature and its resources is at least indirectly an ethical issue: it is tacit denial of the need for moral limits to consumption of the environment. *Exploitation of persons*, the earth's inhabitants, is a more direct and explicitly moral issue. As we have seen, social or moral evils are fundamental to the biblical understanding of sin, and Yahweh's condemnation of them is fundamental to the distinctively Hebrew portrayal of God. It is perhaps not difficult to justify the existence of a modicum of social evil as part of the Creator's design. Leibniz, who gave currency to the term *theodicy*, asserted that "a little acid, sharpness or bitterness is often more pleasing than sugar; shadows enhance colours; and even a dissonance in the right place gives relief to harmony. . . . And is it not most often necessary that a little evil render the good more discernible, that is to say, greater?" (1985: 130). But we must surely ask, Why is there so much evil in the world if a little evil would do?

History and observation provide endless examples of massive exploitation of persons. In our own American history, it is slavery that comes first to mind. In Europe, the last century witnessed a crime of such magnitude that it is sometimes said to have made an end to traditional belief in an all-powerful deity who intends the well-being of humans. Nazi Germany (1933–45) was responsible for the horrific death of an estimated six million Jews. The immense number of the victims sent to the gas chambers is hard to grasp, and yet the total number of the victims of Nazi inhumanity would be greatly increased if it took account of the killing of Gypsies (Roma), the handicapped, communists, male homosexuals, Jehovah's Witnesses, Germans of African parentage, non-Jewish Poles, and Soviet prisoners of war. The purpose of all the killing was to establish the purity of the "superior" Aryan race in Germany.

Postwar debate about the meaning of the Holocaust, or Shoah, has sharply divided Jewish thinkers. Some have maintained its continuity with other catastrophes in Jewish history, such as the destruction of the northern kingdom (722/721 BCE) and the southern kingdom (587/586 BCE) and the sacking of Jerusalem by the Romans (70 CE).[5] For them, it remained possible to draw on the old theme of a God who punishes the sins of his chosen people by hiding his face. Like the ancient Hebrews, the Jewish people had brought destruction on themselves by their unfaithfulness. But for others the enormity of the systematic program of genocide called for abandonment of the belief in a chosen people—and abandonment of traditional belief in God (Rubenstein 1966; cf.

4. See, e.g., Barth's critique (*CD* III/4, esp. 324–26, 349–50 [§55.1]) and the response of Andrew Linzey (1995: 9–12).

5. The book of Esther purports to tell of a failed plot to exterminate Jews in the Persian empire of Ahasuerus (Xerxes I). Had such a plot been carried out, it would have invited comparison with the Holocaust.

the novels of Elie Wiesel). And there we have already made the transition to theodicy: the attempt to vindicate the divine justice. Whether or not we agree with those who insist on the monstrous uniqueness of the Holocaust, the problem of theodicy has preoccupied Christian thinkers from the beginning. Why is there so much evil in a world supposedly made and governed by a good and just Creator?

II. God and Evil

By common consent, the problem of God and evil is the most serious challenge to Christian faith. But it is by no means a problem thrown at believers from the outside. On the contrary, it is a frequent theme within the Christian tradition and goes back to Scripture itself: two entire books of the Hebrew Scriptures, Job and Habakkuk, are devoted to it. The problem often arises from a sense of the *inequality* in God's dealings with humanity. Job complains, "Why do the wicked live on, reach old age, and grow mighty in power?" (Job 21:7; cf. 12:6). The psalmist admits, "my feet had almost stumbled; my steps had nearly slipped. For I was envious of the arrogant, I saw the prosperity of the wicked" (Ps. 73:2–3; cf. Pss. 10, 37, 49). Jeremiah expostulates with Yahweh, "Why does the way of the guilty prosper?" (Jer. 12:1). The prophet Habakkuk is bewildered: "Your eyes are too pure to behold evil, and you cannot look on wrongdoing; why do you look on the treacherous, and are silent when the wicked swallow those more righteous than they?" (Hab. 1:13). In Malachi, the disgruntled priests demand to know, "Where is the God of justice?" and the whole nation protests that there is no profit in serving God, since it is evildoers who flourish (Mal. 2:17; 3:14–15).

Clearly the problem of evil is squarely confronted in Scripture, whether or not it is definitively solved. And the other great religions, too, have wrestled with the persistence of pain and suffering in the world. The conclusions drawn from the existence of evil are not always negative. One agnostic philosopher of the last century, C. E. M. Joad, reported that in the aftermath of war, the seriousness with which sin and evil are faced in Christianity led him back to faith and to the candid confessions of sin in the Anglican Book of Common Prayer. But the path he took was unusual. Generally, the appalling evidence of sin and suffering has led to doubt or total unbelief. It has also led to attempted solutions to the problem of God and evil.

1. Biblical Solutions

The Old Testament does not offer one definitive answer to the question, Why is there evil in a world created and governed by a just and good God? (1) The narrative of the fall in Genesis 3 has lent prominence to the dualistic image of *an evil power* that works against God. Although the identification of the serpent with Satan is not warranted by the text, the image of Satan or the devil elsewhere in Scripture is an important reminder that *evil* is not merely a collective term for things and events that obstruct human well-being but names a threatening reality that can well be called (metaphorically) *demonic*. However, though there are indeed evil powers, they do not usurp the sovereignty of Yahweh or relieve him of the final responsibility for evil. He alone is God, and beside him there is no other. The Satan ("Adversary" or "Accuser") who makes his appearance in the prologue to Job and in Zechariah 3:1–2 acts strictly at Yahweh's behest. Theological scruples apparently led the Chronicler to attribute to Satan the incitement of David to commit the sin of counting the people (1 Chr. 21:1), whereas in 2 Samuel 24:1 the incitement came from Yahweh. The Chronicler's reserve is not shared by others, who admit that it is Yahweh who sends an evil or lying spirit (Judg. 9:23; 1 Sam. 16:14–16, 23; 1 Kgs. 22:23; cf. 2 Sam. 17:14); who both kills and makes alive, wounds and heals (Deut. 32:39; cf. 1 Sam. 2:6); who forms light and creates darkness, makes weal and creates woe (Isa. 45:7; cf. Amos 3:6; Mic. 1:12). When his wife urges him to curse God and die, Job retorts: "Shall we receive the good at the hand of God, and not receive the bad?" (Job 2:10).

If it is God who causes suffering, the question is, To what end? Sometimes the explanation is (2) that suffering is for the sake of *parental discipline* of God's children. "Know then in your heart that as a parent disciplines a child so the LORD your God disciplines you" (Deut. 8:5). Though painful, discipline is to be welcomed, "for the LORD reproves the one he loves, as a father the son in whom he delights" (Prov. 3:11–12; cf. Ps. 94:12; Heb. 12:7).

Pervasive in the Old Testament is the belief (3) that suffering is to be explained as *punishment for sin*, so that "no harm happens to the righteous, but the wicked are filled with trouble. . . . Misfortune pursues sinners, but prosperity rewards the righteous" (Prov. 12:21; 13:21; cf. Sir. 39:22–31). The dogma of just retribution is a pillar of Deuteronomist piety. The future prospect for the chosen people turns on their obedience or disobedience to Yahweh's commandments: if they disobey, horrendous curses (detailed in Deut. 28) will be the punishment for their sin (cf. Lev. 26:14–39). But this is no solution to the problem of evil; it does not even face the problem. If the psalmist can say, "I have been young, and now am old, yet I have not seen the righteous forsaken or their children begging bread" (Ps. 37:25), he must speak out of very limited experience. The Teacher came to exactly the opposite observation: "In my vain life I have seen everything: there are righteous people who perish in their righteousness, and there are wicked people who prolong their life in their evildoing. . . . [T]he same fate [death] comes to all" (Eccl. 7:15; 9:2).

The notion of (4) *inherited guilt*—that children may suffer the punishment due to the sins of their parents—accentuates rather than solves the problem (e.g., Deut. 5:9), as does the notion of (5) *vicarious suffering* (Isa. 53:4–11) in the absence of a clear explanation of how such suffering can be redemptive. Another explanation of evil is (6) that recompense, though inevitable, is sometimes by *justice delayed*. The prosperity of the wicked is only for a time (Pss. 37:1–2, 9–10; 73:16–20; 92:7; 94:23; Hab. 2:2–3; Mal. 3:18–4:1). Yahweh laughs at them, "for he sees that their day is coming," and the word to the righteous is, Wait! (Ps. 37:13, 34; cf. Hab. 2:3; 3:16). But this interpretation of events, too, defies the evidence; and where there is no belief in an afterlife, the hope for an eventual balancing of the books is futile.

The book of Job is irresistibly fascinating precisely because Job scorns the customary explanations of suffering but offers no comforting alternative. His friends—"worthless physicians," "miserable comforters"—lay out the conventional wisdom for him: suffering is good discipline (Job 5:17; 33:14–18); sometimes a man suffers for the sins of his children (8:4); by adversity God opens the ear of the sufferer (36:15); the exulting of the wicked is short (20:4–29). But the main argument of the friends is that suffering is punishment for sin (4:7–8; 8:1–22); therefore, Job must have sinned (4:17–21; 11:1–6). A list of sins is provided to help him discover his guilt (22:6–11). Job does not dissent from the general principle that no human being can be strictly pure before his Maker, but he cannot think that his plight is to be explained by alleged harboring of some unconfessed transgression (4:17; 13:26; 31:5–40): "until I die, I will not put away my integrity from me" (27:5). Infuriated by his friends' verdict that, by justifying himself rather than God, he added presumption to his sins (32:1–2; 34:37), Job wants to argue his case before God himself, perhaps through an advocate after his own death.[6]

When Yahweh finally speaks, he does not say what Job wanted to hear. His first address awes Job to silent recognition of his insignificance: "See, I am of small account . . . I lay my hand on my mouth" (Job 40:4). The second address rebukes him for trying to justify himself, putting God in the wrong (40:8). Job can only respond, "I despise myself, and repent in dust and ashes" (42:6). Utter humility, not the arrogance of self-justification, is the right attitude before Yahweh, and it provides Job with the only vindication he can hope for. It is generally agreed that the epilogue (42:7–17), in which Yahweh rewards Job with "twice as much as he had before," did not belong to the original story. But verse 7 is not inappropriate as the conclusion to the book, which is not strictly a theodicy at all: it determines the right response to the failure of theodicy. The last word, it seems, is Yahweh's vindication not of Job's claim to innocence but of his surrender of any claim whatever on God. Job's resignation, not the pious lectures of his friends, is the true religion of Yahwism. To Eliphaz Yahweh says: "My wrath is kindled against you and your two friends; for you have not spoken of me what is right, as my servant Job has" (v. 7).

2. *Christian Theodicy*

There is an extensive and ever-growing literature on Christian theodicy, both past and present. No more can be attempted here than to draw attention to a few high points, in particular the influential contributions of John Hick and David Ray Griffin. Hick's *Evil and the God of Love*, first published in 1966, set the terms for much of the discussion in the last third of the twentieth century. Taking up the contrast in the ancient church between Western and Eastern estimates of humanity, he developed it into two types of theodicy. The Augustinian type pictures humans as created perfect, but falling into sin and misery by a wrong use of their original freedom. The blame for the existence of life's

6. In 19:25–26, Job looks confidently for a redeemer or vindicator ("I know that my Redeemer [*gō'ēl*] lives," etc.), who may be identical with the "umpire" of 9:33 and the heavenly "witness" of 16:19–22. Cf. the "mediator" in 33:23–25, who provides a ransom for the afflicted. One of the heavenly beings who stand in God's presence is probably meant (1:6; 2:1; 15:8). But the interpretation of 19:25–26 is notoriously difficult. In particular, it is uncertain whether Job expects his vindication to be during his lifetime ("in my flesh") or afterward ("without my flesh"). See the alternative translations in the NRSV and the note in NOAB.

evils accordingly rests with humans. Augustine's view has dominated Western theology, Protestant as well as Roman Catholic, down to the present time. But there was another, earlier view in the theology of the Greek fathers—the "minority report," as Hick called it—with Irenaeus (ca. 130–ca. 200) as its leading representative.

An Irenaean type of theodicy sees the perfection of humanity not in the beginning but in the eschatological future. It rests in part on a distinction (linguistically untenable) between "image" and "likeness" in Genesis 1:26. By their creation in the image of God humans were created as immature children; likeness to God can come to them only over time, as the result of moral development and growth. "And instead of the Augustinian view of life's trials as a divine punishment for Adam's sin, Irenaeus sees our world of mingled good and evil as a divinely appointed environment for man's development towards the perfection that represents the fulfilment of God's good purpose for him" (Hick 2010: 215). In continuity with the Irenaean tradition, Hick proposed his own "vale of soul-making" theodicy, in which coping with evils is understood as essential to the formation of character and a deepening relationship with God. (He borrowed the expression "vale of soul-making" from the poet John Keats.) His main biblical warrants were from Paul on spiritual growth into the likeness of the Lord (Rom. 8:29; 2 Cor. 3:18) and from Jesus, Paul, and the Letter to the Hebrews on the way of suffering (Luke 9:22; Rom. 5:3–4; Heb. 2:10; 12:3; etc.).

My summary represents only the main line in Hick's contrast between two types of theodicy, and I cannot follow him here in detail as he traces their historical progress from the patristic period to the present. But I should at least comment on what he says about Calvin and Schleiermacher. He is critical of Calvin and constructs his own "theodicy for today" in continuity with Schleiermacher. He could perhaps have found something interesting in Calvin's attempt to sort out the liability for evil by distinguishing the intentions of the three agents—God, Satan, and the Chaldeans—in the raid on Job's flock and shepherds (Job 1:17). God intended to exercise his servant's patience; Satan, to drive him to despair; the Chaldeans, to acquire illicit gain (*Institutes*, 1:310–11, where Calvin also notes differences in the *modus agendi* of the three agents). But Hick's concern is to point out that Calvin's approach, along with Augustine's, fails because predestination undermines the attribution of blame for evil to the misuse of human freedom. Adam was created with freedom of choice (*electio*). But since he fell by God's decree (see *Institutes*, 1:195–96, 469; 2:951, 955–57), the responsibility for evil seems to be God's, not his.

Plainly, this raises again the question of the nature of free will. Since Adam's fall the will has remained free, according to Calvin, insofar as it produces voluntary acts that flow from the agent's own nature: freedom is freedom from external coercion, no longer freedom to choose between options. Hence Calvin thought it best to avoid altogether the term *liberum arbitrium*, which properly means "free choice" (*Institutes*, 1:195, 262–66). Hick wanted to allow more to free will: "For personal life is essentially free and self-directing. It cannot be perfected by divine fiat, but only through the uncompelled responses and willing co-operation of human individuals in their actions and reactions in the world in which God has placed them" (2010: 255; see also 59–69, 117–26, 274–75). Calvin would reply that the divine fiat is realized precisely in uncompelled human responses. But I agree that, as I concluded in chapter 6, a strict divine determinism, in which everything is inflexibly foreordained from eternity, allows too little to the concept of free will.

There is a good deal of Augustine and Calvin in Schleiermacher, including their determinism, which harmonized well with the modern philosophy he found in Spinoza. He appeared to assert what Calvin denied: that God is the author of evil (*Institutes*, 1:310). But he arrived at this conclusion by way of his very different understanding of sin as the source of evil. God does not *create* sin (*CF* 331, 335); for the sake of redemption, God *ordains* sin, which for Schleiermacher can only mean that God causes the impotence of the God-consciousness to appear in our consciousness as something for which we bear responsibility (336, 340, 366). Like everything else, the existence of sin must be due to the divine causality. But we can speak of the consciousness of sin only as an abstraction from the consciousness of redemption (325–26, 328, 336–38, 346, 351). There is but one divine decree: the decree to redeem humanity through Christ (501). "*But as we never have a consciousness of grace without a consciousness of sin, we must also assert that the existence of sin alongside of grace is ordained for us by God*" (326; cf. 270). And finally: "*What has been said concerning the divine causality with regard to sin holds good also with regard to evil, in virtue of its connexion with sin*" (338). By this circuitous route, Schleiermacher arrives at the conclusion that God is indeed the author of evil—but only as the author of redemption (339, 341).[7]

Hick classifies Schleiermacher's account of evil with the Irenaean type because, as we have seen, Schleiermacher replaced talk of the fall and its punishment with a developmental understanding of the God-consciousness in its interaction with an environment that contains evil as well as good. This enabled him to view evil as instrumental: "In his teaching that sin and evil are ordained by God as the preconditions of redemption Schleiermacher has sponsored the thesis that evil ultimately serves the good purpose of God" (Hick 2010: 231). Hick agrees. The difficulty is, of course, as he acknowledges, that there is so much evil in the world, and some of it is so monstrous or apparently senseless—even demonic—that we cannot *see* how it serves God's good purpose (288–89, 327–31). Hick's response is twofold. (1) To justify our description of the world as an environment in which good and evil are essential to the development of personal life, we are not required to show how each particular event contributes to this end (375). Still, even the mystery of dysteleological suffering—random and unjust—does in fact "contribute to the character of the world as a place in which true human goodness can occur and in which loving sympathy and compassionate self-sacrifice can take place" (333–36). (2) The fulfillment of God's purpose is only *begun* in this life. Christian hope for an afterlife leads us to affirm that "there will in the final accounting be no personal life that is unperfected and no suffering that has not eventually become a phase in the fulfilment of God's good purpose" (340). Still, Hick's honesty leaves the reader with the question of Ivan Karamazov to his brother, the devout Alyosha: whether *he* would create a world that would make men happy in the end, if it required torturing to death just one little child. Alyosha's subdued answer is

7. Barth objects that sin is real not only in our consciousness of God, but first and foremost for God himself. It is God's adversary, vanquished in Jesus Christ (*CD* III/3:329 [§50.3]).

no.[8] Hick reformulates Ivan's question: whether there can be "a future good so great as to render acceptable, in retrospect, the whole human experience, with all its wickedness and suffering as well as all its sanctity and happiness" (386). He answers with a tentative "perhaps."

A decade after the original publication of Hick's *Evil and the God of Love*, another major work on theodicy appeared, written from the standpoint of process thought: Griffin's *God, Power, and Evil* (1976). Hick had criticized Augustine's and Calvin's "free-will defense," which sought to blame the existence of evil on Adam's wrong use of his free will and thereby to exonerate God. Their predestinarianism simply failed to allow an adequate understanding of human freedom. Griffin, in turn, objects to Hick's theodicy, which he classifies as "the hybrid free-will defense," because it still assumes that the Deity is all-powerful. According to Hick, God could have created a world without sin and evil but chose instead, by an act of self-limitation, to create a better world of persons free to love God or not, and therefore free to sin. In this way, the belief of traditional theism in the sovereignty of God remains unquestioned (Griffin 2004: 186–87). But that is exactly the view of God's omnipotence that process theism rejects.

Griffin argues that because the exercise of divine power is persuasive, not coercive (as supposedly in traditional theism),[9] God *cannot* in fact control human decisions (2004: 4–5, 280). "According to process thought, the reason is metaphysical, not moral. God does not refrain from controlling the creatures simply because it is better for God to use persuasion, but because it is necessarily the case that God cannot completely control the creatures" (276). In Whiteheadian terms, all actual entities share with God the power of self-determination: "creative power is inherent throughout the realm of actuality" (281). God does not have a monopoly on power (268); his power is not absolute but, as Hartshorne says, "absolutely maximal" (273). Griffin concludes: "[I]f we deny that God can exert coercive efficient causation, then the problem of evil largely falls away" (6). But problems remain, I think, for both Griffin and Hick.

Anyone looking for purely rational arguments is bound to judge it a weakness in Hick's case that he postpones the final justification of God to an afterlife. His theodicy, intended to defend faith, thus rests on faith. Griffin's case rests on a metaphysical system that is by no means uncontested by the philosophers; and even if it is taken to be sound, it seems only to relocate the problem of divine responsibility for evil, not to solve it. For Griffin concedes that, although God cannot control the occurrence of evil in the world, he could have "ceased stimulating novelty prior to the advent of life" (Griffin 2004: 308).[10] The question is "whether the positive values that are possible in our world are valuable enough to be worth the risk of the negative experiences" (309). But that is precisely the problem of theodicy.

8. Fyodor Dostoevsky, *The Brothers Karamazov*, trans. Constance Garnett (1912; repr., New York: Barnes & Noble, 2004), 227.

9. I have indicated above (chap. 6) that the process theologians' one-sided characterization of so-called traditional theism, often accompanied by heady rhetoric about the "tyrant God," is not well founded.

10. For process thought, God is not "Creator" of the world but the metaphysical principle that moves the world to ever greater creation of value.

The critique of "omnipotence" by process theists has been sharply criticized in turn for advocating the concept of a finite God. But their insistence that human freedom must entail a real contingency of events, and that God cannot act independently of the laws of nature, is well taken. It does not follow that the problem of theodicy is solved, but at least that the *first* response to an instance of social evil should be to expose the human decisions that caused it. And the *first* response to natural evil should not be "Why did God do that?" but "What are the natural causes that brought it about?" They are bound to conform to the same laws of nature that sustain life. We may rule out such frivolous conundrums as, "Can an omnipotent God tie a knot he cannot untie?" and should look for God's omnipotence in God's ceaseless activity in every circumstance, not simply introducing God as the inflexible cause that brought it about. And it is a remarkable fact of religious experience that, to put it in Schleiermacher's terms, a consciousness of God is not excluded from any negative situation, however bleak or devastating. Not always and for all, but always for some. And this leads us to further examination of the nature of Christian faith.

III. Evil and Faithfulness

The way in which estrangement is connected with evils, natural and social, is summarized in my eighth thesis, and I have now reviewed some of the solutions that have been proposed to the resulting problem of theodicy. Important though they are, the studies by Hick and Griffin represent only a small fragment of the pertinent literature, and I cannot pretend to have given a thorough account even of Hick and Griffin. More may be delegated to other theological and philosophical disciplines. But dogmatic theology cannot leave the subject there. The problem of evil in a world attributed to a good and just Creator is not merely an inconclusive, never-ending academic exercise. It is a disturbing, sometimes devastating challenge to the Christian way of having faith, which it is the task of dogmatics to explicate. Faith in search of understanding naturally turns to theodicy for further light. Insights gained in the academic debates may well aid the interpretation of Christian faith, and they need not be partisan insights from just one standpoint. But philosophical and theological debates on the existence of evil in the world treat Christian faith, for the most part, as an *explanation* of the way the world goes and test its plausibility alongside other explanations. Faith, however, has its own distinctive logic—not immune to philosophical scrutiny, but first of all attested in Scripture and Christian experience. Dogmatic theology needs to take account of faith as *victory* and faith as *faithfulness*.

1. *Faith as Victory*

It cannot be expected of dogmatics to affirm the principle of Leibniz that ours is "the best of all possible worlds." Voltaire's ridicule of the principle in *Candide* (1759) did scant justice to an acute philosophical mind, but we must agree with Schleiermacher that the doctrine of the best world "did not arise as a statement about the religious consciousness but as a product of speculation." As far as dogmatics is concerned, "we must stop at the affirmation that the world is *good,* and can make no use of the formula that it is *the best*" (*CF* 241). Calvin admitted that if God had made a human being who either could not or would not sin, that would have been a more excellent nature. But he insisted that God was under no obligation to create such a being (*Institutes*, 1:196). The obligation, we may say, lies on us: to deal with the world and humanity only as they are.

Speculation about the possibility of a better world is at best out of place in dogmatics, at worst misleading—especially if, as often happens, it is assumed that the best of all possible worlds must be the one that affords the most comfort and pleasure for humans. Christian faith starts with the acknowledgment that this is the only world we have, and it seeks to gain a practical understanding sufficient for dealing with it, not to provide a detailed explanation of it. Faith as "world-*dominating*" does not ring true anymore if it is supposed to legitimate exploitation of the world's natural resources. But we can appropriate the Johannine description of faith as *victory* over the world, if "the world" means, or includes, the threat of evil. "[T]his is the victory that conquers the world, our faith. Who is it that conquers the world but the one who believes that Jesus is the Son of God?" (1 John 5:4–5). Plainly, this points faith to the revelation in Jesus Christ.

The nature of Christian faith is reflected in Jesus' reply to his disciples when they see the man born blind. They ask: "Rabbi, who sinned, this man or his parents, that he was born blind?" (John 9:2). Evil, they suppose, demands an explanation, and the explanation has to fit the dogma that evil is the consequence of sin. On some occasions, Jesus did imply that sin and suffering could be connected (Mark 2:5; John 5:14); on others, he cautioned against too simple a cause-and-effect connection (Luke 13:1–5). This time, he rejects the disciples' question as misguided: asked for an explanation, he answers with an assignment. Neither the blind man himself nor his parents sinned, but God's works are to be revealed in him. "We must work the works of him who sent me while it is day; night is coming when no man can work" (v. 4). Here the work of God is not the infliction of suffering but the healing of it, and it is work to which the Jesus of the Gospels summons his disciples along with himself. He greets the victory of the Seventy over "demons" with the declaration, "I watched Satan fall from heaven like a flash of lightning" (Luke 10:18). My thesis 8 concludes, then, that faith answers the question of theodicy *with commitment to the healing work of God in Jesus Christ*. Not really an answer, but replacement of the question with an imperative!

2. *Faith as Faithfulness*

The final lesson of the book of Job was unconditional faithfulness in the face of an inscrutable Deity. Habakkuk reached the same conclusion: "The righteous live by their faithfulness" (Hab. 2:4; see NRSV note). The prophet watched and waited for the destruction of the Chaldeans (2:1–5; 3:16), but in the end his faithfulness was unconditional—come what might. "Though the fig tree does not blossom, and no fruit is on the vines; though the produce of the olive fails, and the fields yield no food; though the flock is cut off from the fold and there is no herd in the stalls, yet I will rejoice in the Lord; I will exult in the God of my salvation" (3:17–18). Equally emphatic was the *But if not* of Shadrach, Meshach, and Abednego when threatened with the furnace of blazing fire. They answered King Nebuchadnezzar that their God would deliver them. "*But if not*, be it known to you, O king, that we will not serve your gods and we will not worship the golden statue that you have set up" (Dan. 3:18; emphasis mine).

In the philosophical debates of the mid-twentieth century, what we may call the peculiar *But-if-not* character of faith was often discussed, and it was widely held that it betrayed the meaninglessness of faith utterances (Flew and MacIntyre 1955). If the believer who says, "God loves me," will not allow anything to count against it, then she could not be making a factual assertion. The language of faith, unless it is in principle open to verification or falsification, has no factual meaning. Even when the criterion of verifiability was found to be too narrow as a test of meaning, the question remained: What is the use of supposedly factual assertions if nothing is permitted to count against them or if the believer who asserts them really expects nothing different than the unbeliever who does not? Aren't they simply pointless?

One much-discussed answer, proposed by the philosopher R. B. Braithwaite, was to interpret religious statements as fundamentally ethical: they express commitment to a way of life. Hence the Christian assertion that "God is love [*agapē*]" announces an "intention to follow an agapeistic way of life" (Braithwaite 1955: 18). Included in the language of religion are "stories" that the believer need not believe to be true but which serve to reinforce the commitment to a way of life. Braithwaite offered his account of Christian language as himself a Christian, and it will be obvious from all I have said that a strongly ethical interpretation of religion appeals to me. However, Braithwaite's proposal about the status of religious stories is not strictly an interpretation of Christian faith but a suggested correction of it. It may work as an unconventional faith for sophisticated believers but not for ordinary believers who are persuaded that the work to which they are summoned is *God's* work and consequently rests on a whole nest of convictions about the way the world is. If we ask *why* faith is so tenacious, the answer carries us into one particular story, to which chapters 7 and 8 are strictly preambles. That faith is belief without proof does not mean (as is commonly assumed) that faith is without evidence. Its evidence is the story of redemption, which led the church to justify Adam's sin as the "happy fault" (*felix culpa*) that merited so great a Redeemer.

9. The Covenant (I): Revelation

Although no event can be either more or less the effect of divine activity than any other event, God the Creator, the Father Almighty, is made known in the covenant of grace: that is, in a particular story that includes the call of Israel, the gift of the law, and the manifestation of the gospel in Jesus Christ; and this is what is meant by "special revelation" and "the mighty acts of God."

The Christian story of redemption means in particular the "gospel history" (*historia evangelica,* as Calvin liked to say): the narrative of the life, death, and resurrection of the Redeemer. But the birth of the Redeemer was in "the fullness of time" (Gal. 4:4), and from the earliest beginnings of the church he was hailed by his followers as Israel's long-awaited Messiah. Hence the exhortation with which Peter ended his address on the day of Pentecost: "Therefore let the entire house of Israel know with certainty that God has made him both Lord and Messiah, this Jesus whom you crucified" (Acts 2:36). Neither Jesus' own teaching nor the teaching of others about him can be understood without the antecedent history, and in this sense the Christian story of redemption continues, or includes, the story of Yahweh and Israel. Although actual historical events lie behind the story, it is not history as a present-day historian understands history—it is a confession of faith in narrative form. Even when the actual events can be established with some degree of confidence, there may be more than one way of construing them. It was not "the entire house of Israel" that was persuaded by Peter's exhortation; on the contrary, there are alternative Jewish readings of the rise of Christianity and its relation to the faith of Israel. And other religious groups besides Christianity have claimed to be the true Israel, including the Qumran community that became known to us from the Dead Sea Scrolls. It is not the task of dogmatics to decide between one story and another, only to explicate the story current in the church.

In the twentieth century, the term *Heilsgeschichte* ("salvation history") was widely used in biblical and dogmatic theology to describe the biblical attachment of redemption to a particular historical trajectory. The term was a scholarly construct, and its meaning and viability were contested. In the Hebrew Scriptures the traditions of the individual tribes were linked in a single narrative by the metaphor of a *covenant,* which was carried over into the New Testament and came to play a central role in classical Reformed theology. It has not been as prominent in the systematic theology of other Protestant traditions, and its role in Reformed dogmatics diminished over time, except in systems consciously modeled on Reformed orthodoxy. But it was strongly reaffirmed by Karl Barth in the last century. Following Gottlob Schrenk, he named Zwingli as the one who first introduced the covenant concept, in defense of infant baptism. Barth commented: "The scheme was not altogether satisfactory as a basis for infant baptism, but in its actual content it stood for something which cannot be surrendered, the character of the covenant as the true light which lighteth every man (Jn.1:9) and for which, therefore, every man is claimed" (*CD* IV/1:57).

The note of universalism to which Barth drew attention was characteristic of covenant theology (see Heppe 1950: 371–72), which is also sometimes said to counterbalance the Reformed preoccupation with election and predestination by shifting attention from the eternal decrees to the interaction of God and humanity in history. That may well be so. But covenant and election belong logically together: both refer to God's decision to choose one people over all others. The problem of universalism and particularism will be deferred to chapter 14, in which election is the first item in the doctrine of *the church*. The present chapter explores the concept of the *covenant of grace* in Scripture and in covenant theology and then draws out its implications for understanding some other key dogmatic concepts in the doctrine of redemption: law and gospel, faith and revelation, and the "mighty acts of God" in history.

I. The Covenant of Grace

The Authorised (King James) Version of the Bible translated the title of Jesus in Hebrews 9:15 as "the mediator of the new *testament*" (NRSV "new covenant"). Linguistically, the translation was not incorrect: the Greek word for "covenant" (*diathēkē*) is also the word for "will" in the sense of our expression "last will and testament" (Heb. 9:15–22; Gal. 3:15–18). But it invites the inference that Jesus' office as Mediator pertains only to the New Testament, and that is the view that the covenant theologians worked against. For them, there was a single covenant of grace that bound the Old and New Testaments together. Schleiermacher thought otherwise, and at no point was his departure from the Calvinist tradition more evident.

1. Covenant in Scripture

Many covenants are recorded in the Old Testament (cf. Rom. 9:4; Gal. 4:21–27), and they are of more than one kind. The Hebrew word *bĕrît* was used for an agreement between two individuals (Gen. 21:25–32; 31:44–54; 1 Sam. 18:3; 23:18; 2 Sam. 3:112; 1 Kgs. 20:34), between king and people (1 Chr. 11:3), and between the priest of Yahweh and the military commanders (2 Kgs. 11:4). The same word was used also for agreements to which God was a party. Old Testament scholars have shown that Yahweh's covenants with Israel reflected the pattern of the suzerainty treaties in the ancient Middle East, best known to us from Hittite sources. A suzerainty treaty asserted the rights of a supreme ruler, named in a preface, over a vassal state—usually a state defeated in war. Although the agreement bound the suzerain, even if only tacitly, to protect the vassal, it was not a deal between equals (not a "parity covenant") but the imposition of a superior on an inferior, and a major part of the agreement was a list of the suzerain's demands (the "stipulations").

The covenant of Yahweh with Abraham places the emphasis entirely on Yahweh's commitment: his promise to give Abraham the land and to make of him a great nation and a blessing to every nation (Gen. 12:1–3; 15:18–21; 17:1–22). In this sense, the Abrahamic covenant is a covenant of pure grace, an everlasting covenant dependent solely on the faithfulness and steadfast love of Yahweh; and the same holds good for the later covenant with David (Pss. 89:3–4, 19–37; 132:11–12; cf. 2 Sam. 7:8–17; 1 Chr. 17:7–14), which can be viewed as a supplement to the covenant with Abraham, Isaac, and Jacob. The Mosaic covenant at Sinai, on the other hand, conforms more closely to the suzerainty pattern. The preface to the Ten Commandments names Yahweh and states the basis of his claim (Exod. 20:2; Deut. 5:6), and the emphasis then falls on his particular demands. Though initiated by divine grace, the continuance of the Mosaic covenant is conditional on the people's obedience (Deut. 30:15–20)—albeit, unlike the stipulations in the suzerainty treaties, the demands made are in large part ethical, summed up in the second table of the law (Exod. 20:12–17; Deut. 5:16–21). More will need to be said later (in chaps. 12 and 14) about the concept of *grace* as the unconditional love of God.

In Jeremiah, Yahweh announces a new covenant with his people, who have broken the covenant he made with their ancestors when he brought them out of Egypt (Jer. 31:31–34). Yahweh will write the law on their hearts, not on tablets of stone. "I will put my law within them, and I will write it on their hearts; and I will be their God, and they shall be my people. No longer shall they teach one another, or say to each other, 'Know the LORD,' for they shall all know me, from the least of them to the greatest, says the LORD; for I will forgive their iniquity, and remember their sin no more." The formula, "I will be their God, and they shall be my people," is associated elsewhere with the covenant concept (Exod. 6:7; Lev. 26:12; Jer. 32:38–40), and in Ezekiel Yahweh promises to give his exiled people a new heart and a new spirit, "so that they may follow my statutes and keep my ordinances" (Ezek. 11:19–20; 36:26–27). But the express promise of a new covenant is unique to Jeremiah in the Old Testament. In the New Testament, we find that the first generation of Christians believed it was fulfilled in Jesus Christ.

The Greek word for "covenant" (*diathēkē*) occurs relatively infrequently in the New Testament, but it appears in key passages. (1) The Letter to the Hebrews expressly proclaims Jesus as "the mediator of a better covenant" (8:6; cf. 7:22; 9:15; 12:24) in fulfillment of Jeremiah 31:31–34 (quoted in full, Heb. 8:8–12; cf. 10:16–17). The law could only foreshadow the reality that was to come (10:1). Hence the new covenant, which is eternal (13:20), supersedes the old, Mosaic covenant. "In speaking of 'a new covenant' [God] has made the first one obsolete. And what is obsolete and growing old will soon disappear" (8:13). Nevertheless, the ancient heroes of faith, who saw the heavenly homeland only from afar, will eventually arrive there with us (11:13–16, 39–40). (2) In 2 Corinthians 3 Paul agrees. He asserts that God has "made us competent to be ministers of a new covenant [*diakonous kainēs diathēkēs*], not of letter but of spirit; for the letter kills, but the Spirit gives life" (v. 6). The Mosaic covenant, written in stone, was the ministry of condemnation; the new covenant is the ministry of justification. The glory of the old fades in the light of the new; indeed, it is "set aside" (vv. 7, 13).

Yet this is by no means a judgment on the Old Testament. (3) In the third chapter of Galatians, Paul reaches back behind the Mosaic covenant to the covenant with Abraham and insists that "the law, which came four hundred thirty years later, does not annul a covenant previously ratified by God, so as to nullify the promise" (v. 17). When the Scripture says that the promises were made to Abraham and his seed or offspring (*sperma*), the singular "offspring" (not "offsprings"!) means Christ (v. 16): in him the blessing of Abraham comes to Gentiles who receive the promise by faith (v. 14). Paul concludes that "those who believe are the descendants of Abraham," whose faith was counted as righteousness (vv. 6–9; cf. Gen. 15:6). But the promise to Abraham is not what he means by the "old covenant," which is rather the covenant made at Sinai and now set aside (cf. 2 Cor. 3:14). (4) In the Letter to the Romans, Paul reiterates the point and furnishes it with an illustration. Abraham is the father of those who are justified by faith (Rom. 4:16–17, 23–25; cf. Gen. 15:6; 17:5); as children of the promise, they are to think of themselves, with due humility, as wild shoots grafted onto an olive tree (Rom. 9:8; 11:17–24; cf. Eph. 2:11–22).

Most important is (5) Paul's account of the institution of the Lord's Supper, the central rite of Christian worship (1 Cor. 11:23–25). According to Paul's account—which he presents as the handing on of a tradition—when Jesus gave the cup to his disciples, he said: "This cup is the new covenant in my blood" (v. 25). The parallel evidence of the Synoptic Gospels is divided. The word "new" is not in all the manuscripts of Mark 14:24 or Matthew 26:28, and in some manuscripts the whole of Luke 22:20 is missing. It is perhaps more likely that a scribe might insert "new" rather than delete it. But the liturgical traditions of the churches are unanimous in taking it as original. Whenever the Eucharist is celebrated, the recital of the words of institution confirms the Christian belief that in Christ the promised new covenant was established. That this means "new" in contrast to the Mosaic covenant seems clear from the expression "the new covenant *in my blood*," which echoes Exodus 24:8: "Moses took the blood and dashed it on the people, and said, 'See the blood of the covenant that the LORD has made with you.'"

2. *Covenant Theology*

Here, then, is the biblical testimony by which the covenant, or federal, theologians of the seventeenth century, notably Johannes Coccejus (1603–69), sought to order their dogmatic systems. Behind the old covenant made at Sinai lay the still older covenant with the patriarchs, and, as an unconditional divine promise, it can never be broken—however much the chosen people may be unfaithful to it. The "new" covenant of grace is a renewal, or reaffirmation, of the promise to Abraham, now extended to the Gentiles. Fundamental to the thinking of the covenant theologians was the unity of the two Testaments as different "administrations" or "dispensations" of the one covenant of grace. They spoke of the covenant of *grace* as the second covenant, instituted after the failure of the first, the covenant of *works* God made with Adam when God promised life to him and his posterity on condition of perfect obedience (cf.

Hos. 6:7; Westminster Confession 7). They spoke also of the eternal covenant of *redemption,* the pact by which the Son of God accepted his Father's commission to become the means of human salvation (see Heppe 1950: 375–82).

There is no need for us to incorporate the covenant of works in our own dogmatics, though it could be taken as a picture of everyone's relation to God apart from redemption, not as a literal statement about Adam and Eve as historical individuals. And there is certainly no need for a separate discussion of the covenant of redemption. A conference between God the Father and the Son of God may serve the devout imagination, but it can hardly be transferred to dogmatics. Our interest is in the covenant of grace that is taken to unite the Old and New Testaments; and on that we can refer to Calvin, who in this respect anticipated the covenant theologians of the seventeenth century.

In successive chapters of the *Institutes* (2.10–11), Calvin sets out what he sees as the similarities and the differences between the Old Testament and the New. His presentation is intricate because he does not want to leave out anything pertinent that he found in Scripture, including Paul's whimsical exegesis of the Old Testament in Galatians and the elaborate comparison between the two covenants in the Letter to the Hebrews. In essence, however, his twofold argument is plain, summed up in his own words: "The covenant made with all the patriarchs is so much like ours in substance and reality that the two are actually one and the same. Yet they differ in the mode of dispensation" (*Institutes,* 1:429). (1) The "substance and reality" of the covenant is the grace of Christ, and the Jews "were partakers in the same grace with us. For they attained that in Christ" (366). Calvin points to the passage in the Fourth Gospel where "Abraham is said [by Jesus himself] to have seen Christ's day and to have rejoiced" (424; John 8:56), and he can ask forthrightly, "Who, then, dares to separate the Jews from Christ?" (431). But (2) even Abraham's vision was clouded, and the preaching of the prophets was "both obscure, like something far off, and . . . embodied in types" (455). The entire *ceremonial* law (as distinct from the *moral* law) consisted in "shadows and figures" designed to guide the ancients, as one guides a child, to Christ. The ceremonies were efficacious in their time as means of the grace of Christ, but since his coming they have been abrogated (349–50, 364–66; 2:1301). The clouds are now dispersed; Christ the Sun of Righteousness has arisen (1:446, 455; 2:987, 1154; cf. Mal. 4:2).

Clearly, the connection Calvin saw between the two Testaments was, first of all, *christological.* That Christ is the Mediator of the one covenant of grace is demanded, he believed, by the unconditional necessity for atonement. "[S]ince God cannot without the Mediator be propitious to the human race, under the law Christ was always set before the holy fathers as the end to which they should direct their faith" (*Institutes,* 1:344–45). The sins of the fathers were "remitted through Christ" (Comm. Heb. 9:15). But one could equally well say that for Calvin the connection between the Old and New Testaments was *ecclesiological.* He assumed that in speaking of the holy fathers of old he was speaking of the church before the appearance of Christ (343–49). Luther described the Old Testament as "the swaddling cloths" in which Christ lies (LW 35:236); Calvin found there "the very swaddling clothes" of *the church* (*Institutes,* 2:1037). There are plainly issues here that we must place on our agenda when we come to the person of Christ and the nature of the church. For now, I want to keep our focus on the concept of the covenant of grace and its implications for dogmatic theology.

II. The Covenant as Revelation

My interest in retrieving the idea of the one covenant of grace by no means obliges me to perpetuate every detail in covenant theology. But besides giving *covenant* the attention due to every key biblical term, I affirm it as a dogmatic category for the reason conveyed by my ninth thesis: the Creator is *made known in a particular story that includes the call of Israel, the gift of the law, and the manifestation of the gospel in Jesus Christ.* I take this to be what was essential in the account that Calvin gave of the covenant of grace. Some have objected that he had no real sense of redemption as a historical event, because what mattered to him was the unchanging Word of God in the Old Testament and the New. It is true that Calvin was concerned to affirm the constancy of the word of grace, and for that we will not fault him. But he perceived all history moving to and from the event of Christ, and he had a profound sense of the "diversity of times" to which God has accommodated the *form* of his Word. Hence Calvin readily appropriated Paul's metaphor of the childhood stage of God's people before the advent of Christ. Indeed, he thought that even the redemptive word of Christ himself exhibited development, since at first he admonished his disciples and the Canaanite woman that his mission was only to the lost sheep of Israel (Matt. 10:6; 15:24; cf. Mark 7:27; Luke 15:24). The call of the Gentiles came later (*Institutes*, 1:461–64).

Others have objected that Calvin erred in failing to see any real difference between a covenant of grace and a covenant of law. Unlike Schleiermacher at a later time, he perceived a fundamental harmony between the Testaments. I have pointed out that even for Calvin the Old Testament could not have equal authority with the New as a dogmatic norm. But to those who thought that only the New Testament was needed, he replied: "it does not therefore follow that we ought not to be edified by the law and the prophets." He neglected to mention that some parts of the Old Testament do not make for edifying reading; he was more concerned to show, with a reference to 1 Peter 1:12, that Christians are now in a better position to enjoy the doctrine of the prophets than those who heard it spoken (Calvin 1973: 216; cf. *Institutes*, 1:455–56). That, to be sure, is not a sound principle for historical-critical exegesis of the Old Testament; it is a statement of how the Old Testament may function for the Christian faith that supplies the data of dogmatics. But did he fail to recognize the possibility of a harmful influence of Old Testament religion on Christian faith? Did he, as his Lutheran critics have sometimes said, confuse law and gospel?

1. *Law and Gospel*

There is a decided contrast between Calvin and Schleiermacher on the gospel and the moral law, and it stands out in their respective statements about the Old Testament. Schleiermacher acknowledged the historical connection of Christianity with Judaism, and on occasion he could find a use for Old Testament terms in his dogmatics (*CF* 60–62, 115, 438–41). But he insisted on the fundamental difference between the two Testaments as the sacred Scriptures of two different religions. He held that "a strong inclination to the use of Old Testament texts in expressing pious feeling is almost invariably accompanied by a legalistic style of thought or a slavish worship of the letter," and that the "effort to find our Christian faith in the Old Testament has injured our practice of the exegetical art" (609–10; cf. 660). These are telling observations, and they need to be taken seriously. But so also does Calvin's disapproval of "those who always erroneously compare the law with the gospel by contrasting the merit of works with the free imputation of righteousness" (*Institutes*, 1:426).

The nature of God's law is misinterpreted, in Calvin's view, when seen only in the context of Paul's struggle against the legalism of false religion. There is indeed a contrast between the merit of works and the free imputation of righteousness. "But the gospel did not so supplant the entire law as to bring forward a different way of salvation. . . . [W]here the whole law is concerned, the gospel differs from it only in clarity of manifestation" (*Institutes*, 1:426–27; cf. 459). Calvin appeals to Paul's argument that the giving of the law did not annul the covenant with Abraham (Gal. 3:17). He appeals also to 2 Timothy, which explicitly contrasts the eternal *giving* of grace in Christ, before time began, with the *manifestation* of grace through the historical appearance of Christ. This shows, according to Calvin, that "the fathers under the Law" were able to share in the grace of Christ before its manifestation in Christ, who was "the same yesterday as today" (Comm. 2 Tim. 1:9–10, alluding to Heb. 13:8). He makes the same point in commenting on the Letter to Titus: God was always a kindly father, but he *demonstrated* his goodness and love when Christ was manifested, becoming man and revealing himself in the gospel (Comm. Titus 3:4).

Calvin's understanding of "law" and "gospel" turns on his recognition that in Scripture both terms are understood in a narrower and a broader sense (see, e.g., *Institutes*, 1:351, 424–27, 456–57). We do not need to follow the details. His main point is that whereas the exigencies of polemic sometimes led Paul to a narrow view of law as contrary to the gospel, David (the supposed author of the Psalms) took it in its broader sense to mean "the whole doctrine of the law," that is, "the whole covenant by which God had adopted the descendants of Abraham to be his peculiar people." In this sense the law *includes* the gospel (Comm. Ps. 19:8). When David declares that he took such sweet delight in God's law, "he comprehends the whole doctrine of the Law, the chief part of which is the covenant of salvation" (Comm. Ps. 119:103). It is interesting that Jewish usage of the word *torah*—"instruction" or "teaching"—also allows narrower and broader meanings. It can refer to the revelation at Mount Sinai, or the Pentateuch as a whole, or the entire body of divine teachings. Calvin also anticipated the description of Jewish religion in recent Old Testament scholarship as "*covenantal* nomism." He saw that Paul's narrow use of the word "law" was peculiar to his situation (*Institutes*, 1:456). Elsewhere in Scripture, law is "graced [*vestita*] with the covenant of free adoption" (351). When the Fourth Gospel states that "the law indeed was given through Moses; grace and truth came through Jesus Christ" (1:17), the contrast between Moses and Christ cannot mean that grace was absent from the Mosaic revelation; it means that the grace of Christ was already present in the law. "[F]or *Christ* is the soul which gives life to that which would otherwise have been dead under *the law*" (Comm. John 1:17).

It is not possible to discuss here how well Calvin understood the attitude of Jesus to the law, which itself is a complicated subject. In any case, discussion of Calvin's view has focused on his difference from Luther and the Lutherans; and one might well say that on this issue Schleiermacher could sound more Lutheran than Reformed, although he fully agreed with neither. Luther distinguished two uses of the law: (1) a civil or political use to restrain sin and preserve public order, and (2) a theological or spiritual use to expose and condemn sin. He held that the second was "the chief and proper use"; its effect was depicted in the terror that accompanied the giving of the law on Mount Sinai. In its second use, law must come before gospel, but its ultimate purpose is not to terrify us but to drive us to Christ. Those who are in Christ do not need the law to make them do what they do spontaneously. But insofar as the flesh remains active even in the "saints," the second use uncovers and hammers their lingering sinfulness. This is why the law was given on Mount Sinai to a people already "washed, righteous, purified, and chaste."[1] Sometimes Luther also said that the law, especially the Ten Commandments, shows Christians *what* to do, hence not to dream up works for themselves, such as running off on pilgrimages.[2] In the 1535 edition of his *Loci communes,* Philip Melanchthon developed this side of Luther's thinking into (3) a third use of the law, which was endorsed by the Lutheran Formula of Concord (1577). In the "solid declaration," article VI, the formula states that Christians "should daily exercise themselves in the law of the Lord. . . . For the law is a mirror in which the will of God and what is pleasing to him is correctly portrayed" (*BC* 564). The "epitome" describes the third use, more exactly, as "a definite rule according to which [the regenerate] should pattern and regulate their entire life" (479–80). But, in agreement with Luther, the formula states (commenting on 2 Tim. 3:16) that "to reprove is the real function of the law" (566), and this may seem to invite collapsing the third use into the second (as some Lutherans recommend).

Calvin accepts the civil and theological uses of the moral law but reverses Luther's order. (1) The law convicts everyone of sin, as a *mirror* shows the blemishes on a person's face; it alarms the wicked but sends the children of God to God's mercy in Christ (*Institutes,* 1:354–58). This is Luther's second, theological use. (2) The law maintains social order with the threat of punishment; it is a *bridle* to restrain sin—Luther's first, civil use. Though not for the innocent (1 Tim. 1:9), like a guardian the law is useful even for the children of God before they are called (358–60; Gal. 3:24). Finally (3) in the regenerate the law serves as both a *light* to their path (Ps. 119:105), instructing them more thoroughly in the Lord's will, and a *goad* to their obedience; for "the law is to the flesh like a whip to an idle and balky ass." The harmony of law and gospel, in Calvin's view, is evident in Psalm 119, where David "lays hold not only of the precepts, but the accompanying promise of grace, which alone sweetens what is bitter" (360–61).

1. Martin Luther, *Lectures on Galatians* (1535), LW 26:274–76, 308–18; 27:96–97. In his introductory statement of Paul's "argument," Luther pointed to Rom. 3:20, "through the law comes the knowledge of sin" (26:6).

2. See, for example, Luther's *Treatise on Good Works* (1520), LW 44:15–114: "we have to learn to recognize good works from the commandments of God" (23).

In adopting the third use of the law, Calvin was in effect identifying with the trajectory from Luther, through Melanchthon, to the later Formula of Concord. But, unlike the Lutherans, he found in the third use the *proper* use of the moral law—its use for the regenerate—and this follows from the giving of the law to God's chosen people on Mount Sinai. The first use (Luther's second use) is *accidental*: the law brings death only "because our corruption provokes and draws upon us its curse" (Comm. Rom. 7:10–11; cf. *Institutes*, 1:356; Comm. 2 Cor. 3:7).

No extensive evidence is required to verify that Schleiermacher's perception of law, like Luther's, was largely negative. Indeed, he seemed to edge closer than Luther to antinomianism. His attitude to Judaism and the Old Testament rested in part on his aversion to legalism (*CF* 609). Under the law the prevailing religious temper was fear (729), and he thought Christian ethics would do better "if it drop[ped] the imperative mood altogether" (524)—that is, if it followed Paul, who tells us what love does and not what it ought to do (1 Cor. 13). In Schleiermacher's view, there is no place for law in the Christian life: love does more than law can do, and in Christ we have a far more perfect means of recognizing where we fall short (523). Conversion arises "out of the vision of the perfection of Christ" (484). If, with the theological tradition, we speak of Christ's "active obedience," it does not mean his perfect fulfillment of the divine law but rather his perfect fulfillment of his Father's will that sent him on his mission (455–56; cf. John 4:34; 5:19, 30; 6:38). All of this appears to dismantle Calvin's perception of the identity of the two Testaments, as also does Schleiermacher's refusal to speak of "the church" in the Old Testament (693–94). Yet he managed to preserve a fundamental insight of Calvin's covenant theology. It was not the saving love of God but the temporal manifestation of God's love that began with the appearance of Christ, so that "from the beginning there has never been any source of salvation for men, or any ground of divine favour towards men, other than Christ" (695; see also 388; cf. Calvin, *Institutes*, 1:130; 2:1153).

Although they may seem remote today, the sixteenth-century arguments over the uses of the moral law generate enduring, and rather different, images of the Christian. Luther showed the Christian fleeing from the law to Christ; Calvin showed the Christian gladly accepting the law as the will of his Father. These are images we will carry with us to chapters 12 and 13 on the meaning of Christian existence. My conclusion, for the moment, is that Schleiermacher's aversion to legalism does serve as an acute warning, not least to Calvinists, but that it betrayed him into a distorted perception of Jewish piety. By subsuming law under the covenant of grace, Calvin gave a sounder interpretation of the Old Testament than Schleiermacher could. If we are to do justice to Jesus' own saying, "Salvation is from the Jews" (John 4:22), we will do well to retrieve the concept of the one covenant of grace. The story in which the grace of God is revealed begins with the call of Israel; and the law, properly understood, is God's gift to God's people.

2. Faith and Revelation

The meaning of grace was *revealed* to the Hebrews in their historical experience. "The people who survived the sword found grace [*ḥēn*] in the wilderness" (Jer. 31:2), and Yahweh promised that the story of escape from Egyptian bondage would be continued in the return from the dispersion. "[I]t shall no longer be said, 'As the LORD lives who brought the people of Israel up out of the land of Egypt,' but 'As the LORD lives who brought the people of Israel up out of the land of the north and out of all the lands where he had driven them'" (16:14–15; also 23:7–8). If this continuing story reveals the meaning of grace, what is "revelation"?

As a theological term, "revelation" (Latin *revelatio*, "unveiling") means *disclosure* of what was formerly unknown, or imperfectly known, in contrast to all that has been, or could be, *discovered* by human inquiry. It is also used to denote *what* is revealed (the *revelatum*). Various means of revelation are attested in the Bible. To Job's complaint that God does not answer him, Elihu replies that God "speaks" in several ways: by dreams or visions, by the infliction of pain, through an angel or a mediator (Job 33:14–25). The Letter to the Hebrews states that "God spoke to our ancestors in many and various ways by the prophets" (Heb. 1:1). Other means of ascertaining God's will may strike us as primitive, such as divination by consulting the Urim and Thummim.[3] And when Yahweh did not answer him by dreams, or Urim, or prophets, Saul had recourse to a medium, who brought up Samuel from the dead—although Saul himself had expelled mediums and wizards from the land and necromancy was expressly forbidden in the law (1 Sam. 28:3–19; Deut. 18:10–11; Lev. 19:31; 20:6, 27). Elsewhere in 1 Samuel, Yahweh's will is conveyed by a "sign"—not necessarily a miracle in itself, but the predicted occurrence of a natural event (10:1–9; 12:16–18; 14:6–15).

Calvin did not invent the metaphor of revelation as *divine dictation*: it is clearly implied in the biblical account of God's dealings with Moses. Yahweh made himself known to the prophets in visions and dreams, but with Moses he spoke "face to face, as one speaks to a friend" (Exod. 33:11; Num. 12:8). Moses heard his voice (Num. 7:89) and was instructed to write down Yahweh's words (Exod. 34:27). In Leviticus each new section is introduced by the formula, "The LORD spoke to Moses, saying, . . ." and in the RSV the metaphor of dictation is heightened by the use of quotation marks around Yahweh's words (cf. Num. 1:1–2, 48–49; 2:1–2; etc.). To modern readers, who see no instance of divine dictation in their own experience, it seems unlikely that all the minute cultic prescriptions in Exodus 25–40, Leviticus, and Numbers were the *ipsissima verba* of Yahweh. Acknowledging that "those former ways of God's revealing his will unto his people [have] now ceased," the Westminster divines inferred the necessity for a written record of what God once said. Holy Scripture is the Word of God written (Westminster Confession 1). The metaphor of dictation is thus extended to the whole of Scripture, not limited to the words God spoke to Moses. Calvin had another metaphor, however, as we have seen, which the present-day theologian can more readily appropriate: he compared the Word of God to *spectacles* for weak vision.

3. The Urim and Thummim were sacred lots held in a pocket (the breastpiece) attached to a priest's apron (ephod). They bore symbolic inscriptions, and in response to an inquiry the priest must have taken them out at random and declared what they "said" (Exod. 28:15–30; cf. Lev. 8:6–9). In the NT, ascertaining God's choice by casting lots was the method by which Matthias was selected to take the place of Judas (Acts 1:15–26).

The dictation metaphor lent itself to what we may call the "classical view" of revelation: revelation as the supernatural communication of truths about divine matters that would otherwise remain hidden, and faith as the belief that assents to them. It is not difficult to find statements in Calvin that share this understanding of revelation. But Calvin could also suggest that the Scriptures are like corrective lenses that clear our misty sight and enable us to perceive the true God clearly (*Institutes*, 1:70). If we borrow Calvin's metaphor of spectacles for weak eyes, we may go a step further and say that revelation is not supernaturally conveyed information but improved vision; accordingly, faith is not so much belief or assent as insight or discernment. Or, as I have put it more formally elsewhere, *"By 'revelation' is meant a moment of disclosure that focuses our perception of our world and of ourselves, and 'faith' is the enduring insight that corresponds to this disclosure."*[4] Less formally: The proper response to revelation, so understood, is not "I believe it" but "Oh, I see!" Consider, for instance, what happens, or may happen, when someone goes to church, hears the sermon, and finds her way of seeing the world and living in the world decisively shaped by the disclosure and insight given through the Word: the pattern of her existence is reconfigured. For Christian faith it is, of course, a God-filled pattern, and we may equally well say that in revelation God discloses *Godself*, not information about God. Hence Calvin defined faith—the correlate of revelation—as "recognition." What Christian faith recognizes in the course of events is a fatherlike goodwill or, more simply, the "face" of God (*Institutes*, 1:560, 562, 573–74). Faith, in this sense, has its evidence, albeit not coercive proof. It is the way Christians construe the call of Israel, the gift of the law, and the manifestation of the gospel in Jesus Christ.

3. Special Revelation

Obviously, we are not talking about "revelation" in its theological sense unless the Christian story is not just a product of the imagination, but the correlate of divine action. In the mid-twentieth century, G. Ernest Wright published the classic of the biblical theology movement, *God Who Acts: Biblical Theology as Recital* (1952). He argued that the distinctively biblical understanding of revelation does not look within, to the inner consciousness of a human, but outward, to the objective acts of God. The Old Testament prophets who proclaimed the "words" of the Lord were interpreting history. God, Wright concluded, is known by what he has done, and the Bible is a recital of God's acts together with the teaching inferred from them.

Wright's argument evoked a host of criticisms. The critics did not deny that he gave a sound reading of biblical theology. They asked how far the theology of the prophets is available for a present-day systematic theology. How can divine action be harmonized with what we now know about natural causality? What does it mean to speak still of an "act of God"? To put it in terms of our previous discussion, the question is whether our exclusion of divine interventionism necessarily excludes also the possibility of what is usually called

4. My formal definition (Gerrish 2010: 42) is intended to be generic, applicable to other religions and worldviews as well as to Christianity.

"special revelation." I think we must agree with Schleiermacher's categorical assertion, "we do not admit the reality of any individual and temporal divine acts" (*CF* 569). The notion of particular *acts* of God in history is improperly anthropomorphic. There is only the continuous divine *activity* that coincides with natural causality.

There is, however, the possibility of affirming special revelation if we think of God's activity not as resembling the interaction between one self and another but as more like the relationship between a single self and its own mental activities or bodily cells—the kind of analogy suggested, with variations, by Schleiermacher and Hartshorne. Still anthropomorphic, no doubt! But more properly so insofar as the comparison avoids misrepresenting God's activity as akin to the activity of one finite agent among others. It requires us not to deny special or historical revelation but to rethink it. For although everything I do is my activity, some of the things I do are better indications than others of my essential and characteristic self and may be said to reveal who I am. Similarly, special divine revelation is not inconsistent with the view that the living God's activity grounds every historical event and cannot properly be construed in terms of particular acts *within* history.

Accordingly, the lead-in to my thesis 9, *no event can be either more or less the effect of divine activity than any other event,* does not exclude the affirmation that *God the Creator is made known in the [particular story of the] covenant of grace.* This yields what we may take as the meaning not only of "special revelation" but also of the expression that summed up the thinking of the biblical theologians: "the mighty acts of God" (Pss. 106:2; 145:12; 150:2). Of course, the Old Testament authors represented the acts of God as mighty because miraculous and interventionist, and in that we will not follow them. We may even admit that, in part, their interpretation of history created the story as it has come down to us. For Christian faith, the question of history and miracles becomes most urgent in the third part of the story: the activity of God in *the manifestation of the gospel in Jesus Christ,* to which we turn next. There we will have to ask about the historical reliability of the sources for the life and teaching of Jesus—for Christian faith, the mightiest of God's mighty acts. As the stately opening of the Letter to the Hebrews declares, "Long ago God spoke to our ancestors in many and various ways by the prophets, but in these last days he has spoken to us by a Son, whom he appointed heir of all things, through whom he also created the worlds" (Heb. 1:1–2). The following two chapters deal with Christology, the work and person of God's Son as the Messiah or Christ.

10. The Work of the Redeemer

Christ's lordship, or "kingly office," is exercised through the word of the gospel, which creates faith in God as "the Father of Jesus Christ" and creates the community of faith as the means by which the contagion of sin is countered and the reign of God extended; so that Christ is said to rule as both "prophet" (revealer of God's goodwill) and "priest" (savior from sin).

The old Reformed divines dealt with Christology under the rubric "The Mediator between God and man," more particularly "The Mediator of the covenant of grace," which binds the Old Testament and the New together (Heppe 1950, chap. 17). Their main biblical warrants were 1 Timothy (2:5–6) and the Letter to the Hebrews (9:15; 12:24; cf. Mark 14:24). Chapter 11, on the person or identity of the Redeemer, will consider their belief that the Mediator was active already during the Old Testament dispensation and, indeed, that he is the Mediator for all humanity in every time. But the theme of the present chapter is the work or activity of Jesus of Nazareth, for which Christian faith acknowledges him as "the Redeemer." The question is: What did Jesus do that mended the broken relationship between God and humanity? He could do what he did only because of who he was, and most treatments of Christology, including Calvin's and Schleiermacher's, discuss the "person" before the "work" of Christ. But it makes good sense to begin with his activity, which first occasioned the question, "Who then is this?" (Mark 4:41), and Jesus' own question, "Who do you say that I am?" (Mark 8:29). From there we can go on to look at so-called atonement theories and, finally, to offer the statement on the redeeming work of Christ summarized in my tenth thesis.

I. The Words and Work of Jesus

Everything Jesus said and did and suffered, according to the Gospels, is pertinent to understanding his "work," as also is all that is said about him in Acts, the New Testament letters, and Revelation. Plainly, my outline has to be selective. I simply rehearse the broad, generally agreed features of what we may call "the gospel story," and I then take a closer look at two Scripture texts, Mark 10:45 and Romans 3:25, that tell us about the Apostolic witness to the meaning of Jesus' death. The historian will ask to what extent the four Gospels yield a single, consistent gospel story and to what extent the story can be authenticated as history. But the dogmatic theologian will point out that it is the gospel story itself, in all its versions and with all its variations, that gives rise to faith, and always has. If the concern of dogmatics is with the Christian way of having faith, detailed reconstruction of what actually happened, even when it is possible, is not directly relevant. More on this in chapter 11.

1. The Gospel Story

Aside from the birth and boyhood stories in Matthew and Luke, the Synoptic Gospels relate no more than two or three years, possibly less, from the life of the young man Jesus: the time from his baptism by John the Baptist to his death and resurrection. Their narrative falls roughly into two parts: his public ministry in Galilee and his last days in Jerusalem. (The Fourth Gospel has no account of the baptism and mentions more than one visit of Jesus to Jerusalem.) The beginning of the Galilean ministry is reported by Mark: "Now after John was arrested, Jesus came to Galilee, proclaiming the good news of God, and saying, 'The time is fulfilled, and the kingdom of God has come near; repent, and believe in the good news'" (Mark 1:14–15). From the first, in Luke's account, Jesus perceived his ministry as the fulfillment of what he read in the book of Isaiah: "The Spirit of the Lord is upon me, because he has anointed me to bring good news to the poor. He has sent me to proclaim release to the captives and recovery of sight to the blind, to let the oppressed go free, to proclaim the year of the Lord's favor" (Luke 4:18–21; Isa. 61:1–2).

At Caesarea Philippi, the turning point in Jesus' short career is reached when Peter confesses, "You are the Messiah [the Christ], the Son of the living God" (Matt. 16:16; cf. Mark 8:29). In response, Jesus begins to teach his disciples "that he must go to Jerusalem and undergo great suffering at the hands of the elders and chief priests and scribes, and be killed, and on the third day be raised" (Matt. 16:21; cf. Mark 8:31; 9:31; 10:33–34). It was probably the book of Isaiah, once more, that formed Jesus' self-understanding—this time the description of Yahweh's Suffering Servant in the fourth Servant Song in Second Isaiah.[1] When Paul recites the primitive Christian tradition that "Christ died for our sins in accordance with the scriptures" (1 Cor. 15:3), it is generally assumed that the Scripture reference is mainly to Isaiah 53. That this identification goes back to the consciousness of Jesus himself has been questioned. Luke represents him as expressly quoting Isaiah 53:12 (Luke 22:37), and this perhaps fits well with Jesus' words at the Last Supper (passed over in silence by John). He is reported to have given his approaching death a sacrificial significance: while presenting the cup, he says, "This is my blood of the covenant, which is poured out for many" (Mark 14:24).

The heart of Jesus' preaching and teaching, according to the Synoptic Gospels, was his eschatological announcement of the kingdom of God. (The Fourth Gospel again differs: John makes no express mention of the kingdom of God except in his account of Jesus' conversation with Nicodemus [John 3:3, 5].) The

1. Most biblical scholars hold that only Isa. 1–39 can be attributed to Isaiah, the son of Amoz; they assign chaps. 40–55 to an anonymous "Second Isaiah," chaps. 56–66 to a "Third Isaiah" or perhaps to several hands. The majority opinion is that there are four so-called Servant Songs (42:1–4, 49:1–6, 50:4–11, 52:13–53:12), but there is no agreement about the identity of the Servant.

Greek word translated "kingdom," *basileia*, may mean the territory ruled over by a king (Matt. 4:8; Mark 6:23; Luke 21:10). But it can also denote royal power or rule (Luke 19:12, 15; 1 Cor. 15:24; Rev. 1:6), and it is mainly in this sense that "the kingdom of God" or "the kingdom of heaven" is to be understood in the proclamation of Jesus. According to Luke, Jesus expressly stated that to proclaim the gospel of the kingdom was the purpose for which he was sent (Luke 4:43), and the sense of a new age is apparent in another Lukan saying: "The law and the prophets were in effect until John came; since then the good news of the kingdom of God is proclaimed, and everyone is pressing into it" (Luke 16:16; see NRSV note; cf. Matt. 11:11–12). Did Jesus' proclamation mean, then, that the new age had already come? Initially, he asserted that the kingdom was "near" (*ēngiken*, Mark 1:15; Matt. 4:17). But other sayings affirm the actual presence of the kingdom in his own activity (Matt. 11:2–6; 12:28; Luke 4:21; 11: 20; 17:20–21); and some of the parables that have traditionally been supposed to speak of a future coming, or second coming, of Jesus and the kingdom may originally have conveyed his rebuke that his hearers failed to recognize the kingdom's arrival *in him* (see Dodd 1936 on "realized eschatology"). His ethical teaching, which went beyond the morality of the Old Testament, characterized the behavior now demanded under the rule of God (Matt. 5:17–43).

The four Gospels all attest that, besides preaching and teaching, Jesus' ministry included acts of healing. Throughout Galilee, "they brought to him all the sick, those who were afflicted with various diseases and pains, demoniacs, epileptics, and paralytics, and he cured them" (Matt. 4:23–24; 11:5; cf. Luke 7:22). The modern historian is naturally at a loss for an explanation of the healing miracles, even more for an explanation of the three recorded instances of raising the dead: Jairus's daughter (Matt. 9:25; Mark 5:41; Luke 8:41), the son of the widow of Nain (only in Luke 7:14–15), and Lazarus (only in John 11:43–44). Many have suggested that, unlike the so-called nature miracles (such as the feeding of the five thousand or Jesus' walking on water), healing stories can be interpreted with our modern medical knowledge. But some take them as legendary; others think they can be read as allegories of Jesus' power to cure "the sin-sick soul," a power known to us from centuries of Christian experience. Amid the rival explanations, the main point must not be overlooked: the gospel story requires us to recognize the twofold work of Jesus as herald of the kingdom *and* healer of the sick.

2. *The Apostolic Witness*

The First Letter of John may speak for every witness to the redemptive work of Christ: "We declare to you what was from the beginning, what we have heard, what we have seen with our eyes, what we have looked at and touched with our hands, concerning the word of life—this life was revealed, and we have seen it and testify to it" (1 John 1:1–2). While John speaks here of testimony to the revelation of life, the death of Christ plainly held a special place in the Apostolic witness—including the witness of John (1 John 1:7; 2:2; 3:16; 4:10).[2]

2. The Apostles were witnesses also of the resurrection (Acts 2:32; 3:15; 10:40–41), taken to be conclusive proof of his identity as Messiah or the Son of God (Rom. 1:4).

Two New Testament passages have always been central to discussion of the place of Jesus' death in the gospel story.

One passage comes from the Gospel of Mark (and the parallel in Matthew), where Jesus himself speaks of his death as *a ransom for many* (Mark 10:45; Matt. 20:28). In response to the request of James and John, the sons of Zebedee, to sit one at his right hand and the other at his left in his glory, Jesus is reported as saying that whoever wished to become great among his disciples would have to be their servant: "For the Son of Man came not to be served but to serve, and to give his life a ransom for many." The second part of the saying has been the subject of debate. Some take it as evidence that Jesus himself understood his coming death as a vicarious sacrifice for sin. Others doubt that "to give his life a ransom for many" can be an authentic saying of Jesus. (1) It uses the word *lytron* ("ransom") that occurs nowhere else in the New Testament (but see *antilytron* in 1 Tim. 2:6). (2) It conveys a thought without parallel in the teaching of Jesus, unless perhaps in the reported saying of Jesus at the Last Supper, "This is my blood of the covenant, which is poured out for many" (Mark 14:24). (3) Within the verse itself the thought of a sacrificial death seems not to fit with the first part of the saying. Jesus is talking about a life of service to others: he came to serve. Even if we could take "to give his life" (*dounai tēn psychēn autou*) in the sense of *devoting* his life to service rather than *surrendering* it to death, the idea of a ransom looks like a notion imported from Christian reflection after his crucifixion. In that case, it belongs under "Apostolic witness" to the meaning of Christ's death. But, unlike Jesus' words at the Last Supper, "ransom" does not evoke the cultic language of vicarious sacrifice for sin. For this we turn to our second passage.

The second passage comes from Paul: explaining redemption, he says that God put Christ Jesus forward as *expiation for sin* (Rom. 3:25; cf. 1 John 4:10). Some scholars maintain that the Greek word *hilastērion* refers to the "mercy seat," the cover on the ark of the covenant, on which blood was sprinkled on the Day of Atonement (Lev. 16:14–15). The NRSV allows for this interpretation by giving "place of atonement" as an alternative translation; but the preferred translation "sacrifice of atonement" is more plausible. What, then, does it mean to call Christ a "sacrifice of atonement"? Many have supposed that the application of Old Testament sacrificial language to the death of Christ is proof of the penal-substitution theory of atonement, according to which the guilt of sinners was transferred to the crucified Christ, who appeased God's anger by dying as substitute in their place. But the Levitical sin offering (*ḥaṭṭa't*) of a slaughtered animal was not intended to *propitiate* an angry God but to *expiate* the defilement of sin, including inadvertent sin. There is no suggestion that the priest transferred the sins of the people to the sacrificial victim. That was the point rather of the scapegoat ritual, which, however, was not a sacrifice: the goat was driven out live into the wilderness (Lev. 16:20–22). The purpose of expiation was to ensure the presence of Yahweh in the holy place by cleansing the altar and the sanctuary. Whereas the object of propitiation is an angry God, the object of expiation is the defilement of sin. God is *the subject* of expiation in that *he* provides it through the hand of the priest, and this is of fundamental importance when the language of sacrifice is applied to the work of Christ. As Paul says, it is *God* who "put [Christ Jesus] forward as an expiation by his blood" (Rom.

3:25 RSV); "in Christ *God* was reconciling the world to himself" (2 Cor. 5:19; my emphasis). Similarly, the Letter to the Hebrews states that Christ was to be "a merciful and faithful high priest in the service of God, to make expiation for the sins of the people" (Heb. 2:17 RSV). Still, it should not be assumed that the meaning of the death of Christ could be simply deduced from the Levitical cult; the earliest Christians were influenced as much, or more, by the portrayal of Yahweh's Suffering Servant in Second Isaiah.

II. Atonement Theories

Attempts to order the various biblical terms in a dogmatic "theory" of atonement have been legion (for a still valuable survey, see Franks 1962). Attempts have also been made to classify the theories into types. Best known is Gustaf Aulén's *Christus Victor: An Historical Study of the Three Main Types of the Idea of the Atonement,* which first appeared in English in 1931. It had become customary to distinguish the objective, *satisfaction* type, in which the atonement is intended to effect a change in the disposition of God, from the subjective, *moral influence* type, in which reconciliation with God is achieved by a change only in the human subject. Aulén pointed out that there is a relatively neglected third type: he called it the *classic* theory of the Fathers, for whom the atoning work of Christ was presented in colorful language as a victorious struggle with the devil. The three kinds of atonement theory are best thought of as ideal types, often mixed in the thinking of individual theologians. Anselm, for example, was author of the best-known statement of the satisfaction theory, but he freely availed himself of language characteristic of Aulén's third type (see LCC 10:139–40, 161). We will keep that in mind as we attempt to illuminate the types by highlighting the main differences between, respectively, Anselm and Abelard, Calvin and Schleiermacher, Hodge and Nevin.

1. Anselm and Abelard

The contrast between the objective and the subjective theories is commonly illustrated from the differences between Anselm of Canterbury (1033–1109) and Peter Abelard. *Anselm's* dialogue with Boso, *Why God Became Man,* ranks as the first monograph ever written on the doctrine of atonement, and it has retained its status as a Christian classic. Anselm does not deny that unbelievers will dismiss picture language about the work of Christ as "painting on a cloud" (LCC 10:105). But he asserts that if we put ourselves in the place of the unbeliever and (for a moment) bracket faith in Christ, rational argument can demonstrate the necessity for God to become man. Sin is the failure to render to God his due. Satisfaction *must* be made to God; but satisfaction *cannot* be made by sinful humans, who would owe everything to God even if they had never sinned. Hence the necessity for a God-Man. It cannot be his *life* that makes satisfaction for the sins of humanity, since as man he will owe obedience for himself. But as God-Man he will not owe his *death,* because death is the penalty for sin and "sin will be impossible for him because he is God" (156). Rational argument thus shows the necessity for what the church believes about Christ: he "paid for sinners what he did not owe for himself" (177). The Father was bound to reward him for laying down his life; but because the Son already possessed everything that belonged to his Father, it was fitting for the reward to be paid instead to "those for whose salvation . . . [the Son] made himself man" (180). Salvation, then, is made possible—indeed, is only possible—by way of the satisfaction the God-Man paid to his Father.

Why God Became Man does not simply offer one atonement theory, to be accepted or rejected. Although its language is largely time-bound, it has always been, and still is, a rich source of theological insight even for those who dissent from Anselm's acute, if somewhat contrived, argument. We must set aside the questions that have been raised about the theological method of the treatise and cannot hope to review all the many criticisms of its substance. Our interest is in the pivotal assumption that the reconciliation of God and humanity demands the payment of satisfaction to God. Perhaps, as is often said, Anselm's notions of sin and satisfaction reflect the feudal concept of the overlord's honor. But sin, for him, was not simply a personal affront to an imperious deity: it was a breach of a just order. "Therefore, if it is not fitting for God to do anything unjustly or without due order, it does not belong to his freedom or kindness or will to forgive unpunished the sinner who does not repay to God what he took away" (LCC 10:121).

In view of its pertinence to our later discussion, I should also note at least one of the criticisms leveled at Anselm's argument. It has been objected that in *Why God Became Man* "the death of Christ is entirely severed from His life-work on earth, and isolated. This God-man need not have preached, and founded a kingdom, and gathered disciples; he only required to die" (Harnack 1976, 6:76). The criticism is well taken, and Anselm's idea of satisfaction is not the only atonement theory that is exposed to it. He paid no attention to the details of the God-Man's life. The best one might say in his defense is that he did represent Christ's death as of one piece with what he assumed to have been a life of obedience. The point is summed up in the words put into the mouth of Boso and buttressed with numerous quotations from the New Testament: "death was inflicted on him because he persevered in obedience, and he endured it" (LCC 10:112). Without Christ's willing *acceptance* of death, it would not have been redemptive (164). Very different was the approach of Anselm's younger contemporary Abelard.

Abelard was not strictly Anselm's adversary, but he is credited with being the champion of the subjective alternative to the satisfaction theory. In his *Exposition of the Epistle to the Romans,* he rejects the idea, common in the early church, that "redemption" through Christ meant paying a price to the devil for releasing sinners from his dominion. Satan had *no* rights or power over sinners except by permission of the Lord. But Abelard's thoughts take a turn more subversive of the prevailing view of Christ's work when he goes on to argue that our true Master, who could claim the right to a price for our forgiveness, does not ask for one. Christ forgave sins quite apart from his passion—that is, without any mention of a price to be paid. "Indeed, how cruel and wicked it seems that anyone should demand the blood of an innocent person as the price for anything, or that it should in any way please him that an innocent man should be slain—still less that God should consider the death of his Son so agreeable that by it he should be reconciled to the whole world!" (LCC 10:283).

What, then, is the true meaning of Christ's death? Abelard answers that the love of God, demonstrated to us when his Son assumed our nature and persevered "in teaching us by word and example even unto death," evokes our answering love; and it is love that justifies us in God's sight (LCC 10:283). Hence Christ says of the woman who was a sinner, "Many sins are forgiven her because she hath loved much" (Luke 7:47, as cited in LCC 10:279). And "everyone becomes more righteous—by which we mean a greater lover of the Lord—after the Passion of Christ than before" (284). Abelard's case is that love does not ask for satisfaction. Anselm, by contrast, held that the measure of God's love was precisely the God-Man's provision of satisfaction for sin (see *Why God Became Man*, chap. 6).

2. *Calvin and Schleiermacher*

Calvin introduces his treatment of Christ's work by distinguishing the duties of prophet, king, and priest (*Institutes*, 1:494–503 [2.15]). Each "office" (*munus*) Christ carries out both *for* us and *in* us. He received his anointing as *prophet* "not only for himself that he might carry out the office of teaching, but for his whole body that the power of the Spirit might be present in the continuing preaching of the gospel." The anointing was "diffused from the Head to the members, as Joel had foretold: 'Your sons shall prophesy and your daughters . . . shall see visions,' etc." (496; Joel 2:28). Similarly, Christ rules as *king* more for our sake than for his. "[H]e shares with us all that he has received from the Father" and equips us with his power, so that "believers stand unconquered through the strength of their king" (499, 500). And, most explicitly, Calvin states the twofold function of Christ's office as *priest:* "Christ plays the priestly role, not only to render the Father favorable and propitious toward us . . . but also to receive us as his companions in this great office" (502). The repeated correlation Calvin makes of a work *for* us and a work *in* us is striking. But he asserts expressly, with a reference to the Letter to the Hebrews, that "the principal point on which . . . our whole salvation turns" is the sacrificial death of Christ for our sins; in this, the "priestly office belongs to Christ alone" (ibid.). And in his next chapter (16) the threefold office fades as Calvin develops the "principal point."

Not that Calvin's thoughts concerning atonement focus exclusively on the death of Christ. After an initial statement on God's *love* as the moving cause of atonement (God's *wrath* is an accommodated expression), he launches into seemingly ambivalent assertions about the relationship between Christ's death and his life (*Institutes*, 1:507–8). Christ removed the separation between God and fallen humanity "by the whole course of his obedience." But "to define the way of salvation more exactly, Scripture ascribes this as peculiar and proper to Christ's death." This is why the Apostles' Creed passes immediately from the birth of Christ to his death and resurrection, "wherein the whole of perfect salvation consists." Yet "the remainder of the obedience that he manifested in his life is not excluded," and "even in death itself his willing obedience is the important thing because a sacrifice not offered voluntarily would not have furthered righteousness." This, obviously, agrees with Anselm, though Calvin does not say so. It is perhaps the language of sacrifice that best holds Calvin's statements together: only a perfect life can be offered as the sacrifice of an unblemished victim. But the key metaphor in his view of atonement is judicial rather than cultic.

In Calvin's mind, of course, sacrificial language and judicial language coincide. He takes sacrifice to be the transference of sin and guilt to the victim (see *Institutes*, 1:510, where he alludes to Isa. 53), and the premise of his entire presentation, stated in legal terms, is that "since [God] is a righteous Judge, he does not allow his law to be broken without punishment" (504). Accordingly, the atonement was a "substitution" (*compensatio*): the punishment due to sinners was transferred to the crucified Christ. He could not suffer just any kind of death but had to die as a criminal—condemned by Pontius Pilate and executed between two thieves (509–10). The price he paid for our redemption was "suffering in his soul the terrible torments of a condemned and forsaken man" (516). In chapter 17 Calvin concludes the discussion of Christ's work by asserting that Christ is properly said to have "merited" God's grace for us by the shedding of his blood. "God's judgment was satisfied by that price" (531). But this is not the satisfaction theory of Anselm, who did not say that Christ bore our punishment in our place. Anselm's formula, "*either* punishment *or* satisfaction," actually excluded any thought of penal substitution. The death of Christ, for him, was a substitute for punishment, not the transference of punishment from guilty sinners to the innocent Christ.

Calvin pieced together his principal chapter on the work of Christ (*Institutes* 2.16) by incorporating fragments from earlier editions and adding to them. In the course of his presentation, he takes up all the pertinent motifs he found in the Old and New Testaments, including—along with propitiation and satisfaction—reconciliation, ransom, redemption, expiation, and triumph over the forces of evil. But his main line of thought is clear—penal substitution: "he appeased God by taking upon him the penalty to which we were subject" (532). It must be admitted that this leads Calvin into problematic tensions in his picture of God: between God the Father and God the Son, between love and wrath. He takes Romans 5:10, for example, to mean that *God was our enemy* until made favorable by the death of Christ, and he marvels that God "loved us even when he hated us" (504–6; see also 557), whereas what Paul actually says is that *we were enemies of God* until God reconciled us by the death of his Son (cf. 2 Cor. 5:18–20). The tensions throughout Calvin's presentation arise, as often happens, from his determination to take account of everything pertinent that he found in Scripture, including the "wrath" of God, which Schleiermacher dismissed as a primitive notion with no place in present-day dogmatics.

Schleiermacher's tightly packed account of the work of Christ defies summary. But while I must leave much unsaid, I think it possible to lift up the two cardinal assertions on which everything turns. He maintains (1) that redemption is Christ's drawing us to himself, as he drew his first disciples, by the power of his person, which was constituted by the unique being of God in him. The difference between the disciples and us is that in our time the activity of Christ is mediated through the picture of him maintained in the community he established. Schleiermacher expects today's believers to recognize that, yes, this is in fact what Christ does for them. "This exposition," he says, "is based entirely on the inner experience of the believer; its only purpose is to describe and elucidate that experience" (*CF* 428). It may be that, more than he realized, his thoughts on Christ mirrored the experience of one particular kind of believers: the Moravian Pietists with their emphasis on conversion and love for the Savior. Be that as it may, this is how Schleiermacher sums up the meaning of redemption: *"The Redeemer assumes believers into the power of His God-consciousness, and this is His redemptive activity"* (*CF* 425; see also 363, 427).[3]

It follows (2) that the personal impact Christ made, and makes, must be seen as community-forming. Schleiermacher anticipated this requirement in his interpretation of sin, which, with an eye to redemption, we can understand only in its social character. The Redeemer instituted *"a new divinely-effected corporate life, which works in opposition to the corporate life of sin"* (*CF* 358). The power of his person gathered around him a band of disciples, and his continuing activity in the proclaimed Word reaches individuals today through the Christian community (477–78). Indeed, he brought into existence not only a new community, but also a new humanity and a new world. Just as the doctrine of creation is about the creation of *the world*, "the activity of the Redeemer too is to be world-forming, and its object is human nature, in the totality of which the powerful God-consciousness is to be implanted as a new vital principle" (427). The expression "implanted as a new vital principle" is critical: it indicates that although Schleiermacher rejected the satisfaction theory of atonement, his own view cannot be reduced to a subjective, moral influence theory but rests on the objective, historical reality of the incarnation—the being of God in Christ.

For the further development of his doctrine of Christ's work, Schleiermacher adopts the inherited scheme of the three offices, and he does so for what is, I think, exactly the right reason: it prevents, or should prevent, one-sidedness in describing the work of Christ. The *kingly* office readily lends itself to Schleiermacher's understanding of Christ's redeeming activity. The kingdom of God is the new corporate life that Christ brought into being and over which he holds sway. The object of his kingly power "cannot be an individual as such, but only a society, and the individual only in so far as he belongs to the society" (466). Similarly, the heart of Christ's *prophetic* office was his proclamation of the kingdom of God, "the new corporate life to be founded by Him" (444). The *priestly* office, too, proves amenable to what Schleiermacher sees as Christ's mission—to bring the new community into existence. Here, however, his exposition leads to revision of his church's teaching on penal substitution.

The church doctrine made a distinction in the priestly office between the active and the passive obedience of the Redeemer. In Schleiermacher's view, the *active obedience* was not, as the official doctrine maintained, Christ's perfect fulfillment of the law, but rather "His perfect fulfilment of the *divine will*" for him (*CF* 456; references to John 4:34; 5:30; and 6:38): he came "to call into being" the new community (453). Clearly, we cannot say that he fulfilled the divine will in our stead, as though we were relieved of the necessity to fulfill the divine will for ourselves. On the contrary, because of our union with him, his "motive principle"—his "will for the Kingdom of God"—becomes ours also (456–57;

3. From this *redemptive* activity Schleiermacher distinguishes the *reconciling* activity of Christ. But it will be convenient to postpone this to our chap. 12.

see further 509, 519–22, 576–77). The will for the kingdom is what holds the church together: "the vital unity" of the entire church, "its common spirit in each individual" (536).

What, then, of Christ's *passive obedience*? The church doctrine was that Christ's death was vicarious satisfaction for the sins of humanity. Schleiermacher has no difficulty with the idea of vicarious suffering: in the corporate life of sin everyone suffers for the sins of others. The suffering can even be considered "punitive" in the general sense that God ordains evil as the punishment for sin, although "each individual does not wholly and exclusively suffer precisely the evil which is connected with his personal sin" (*CF* 457). The point is, however, that for Christ to take us into fellowship with him, he had first to enter *our* company, and his suffering was the consequence. "In His suffering unto death, occasioned by His steadfastness, there is manifested to us an absolutely self-denying love. . . . [T]he conviction both of His holiness and of His blessedness always comes to us primarily as we lose ourselves in the thought of His suffering" (458–59). But his suffering was not, as such, redemptive. It occurred, rather, from his persistence in his redemptive activity. In short, the Redeemer's active obedience was not vicarious (in our stead), and his passive obedience was not satisfaction (460–61).[4]

Denial that Schleiermacher had a doctrine of atonement comes from critics who prejudge the issue by defining "atonement" as "satisfaction" paid to God. But there seems to be no compelling reason for such a narrow equivalence, especially if we bear in mind that the original meaning of the English expression "to atone" was simply "to set at one" persons formerly estranged. The German term for the Redeemer's "redemptive activity" (*erlösende Tätigkeit*) suited Schleiermacher well because, as he pointed out, "redemption" (*Erlösung*) implies release from a condition of restraint or captivity, which can only mean (in the realm of religion) "an obstruction or arrest of the vitality of the higher self-consciousness"—the consciousness of God (*CF* 54). Not as colorful a notion as the patristic talk about emancipation from the devil! But it brings Schleiermacher's thoughts closer to the type of atonement theory that Aulén considered to be the neglected "classic" type of the early church fathers. In John Williamson Nevin (1803–86), who learned from Schleiermacher, the patristic connection is plainer; in Nevin's adversary, Charles Hodge (1797–1878), we find the denial that Schleiermacher and Nevin had a doctrine of atonement at all (Hodge 1857: 381–84). I must be briefer in commenting on Hodge and Nevin, but for further documentation and details I can refer to my essays noted in the bibliography.

3. *Hodge and Nevin*

In his *Systematic Theology*, volume 2, *Hodge* presents a detailed defense of the satisfaction theory of atonement (or one version of it), which he takes to be the orthodox doctrine of all the churches. Like Calvin and Schleiermacher, he starts from the three offices of Christ. The threefold office is not merely an

4. Schleiermacher complicates his presentation when he suggests further that the word "satisfaction" (*Genugtuung*) could be applied to Christ's active obedience, though it was not vicarious, and that Christ may be called "our satisfying representative" (*genugtuender Stellvertreter*) because he is the perfecting of human nature and perfects our consciousness of sin (*CF* §104.4 [461]).

organizational convenience but something that "must be retained in our theology if we would take the truth as it is revealed in the Word of God" (1981, 2:461). What follows, however, is not a balanced treatment of each office. Hodge needs only two pages for the prophetic office, fourteen for the kingly office, but devotes 132 pages to the priestly work of Christ, most of them on the idea of satisfaction for sin. "Satisfaction" may be referred to "all [Christ] has done to satisfy the demands of the law and justice of God, in the place and in behalf of sinners" (470), but it denotes in particular Christ's vicarious suffering and death. Hodge can even say that Christ "became man in order that he might die" (612). In an apparent difference with Calvin, he insists that Christ "did not suffer either in kind or degree what sinners would have suffered" (471).[5] Christ's penal satisfaction was rather a *just equivalent* to the punishment due to the sins of humanity, as agreed upon in eternity by the covenant of redemption between the Father and the Son (357–58). Hodge admits that talk of such an inner-Trinitarian "transaction" (his term) may sound anthropomorphic. "But it must be received as substantial truth" (360–61). "Guilt must, from the nature of God, be visited with punishment. . . . There can be no remission [of sins] without such punishment, vicarious or personal" (478).

As consistently as Hodge took his stand on the centrality of Christ's propitiatory death, *Nevin*, his one-time student, insisted on the centrality of Christ's saving life—that is, on the incarnation, the union of divine and human in his person. Nevin continued to speak of the atoning death of Christ, but he thought that the meaning of Christ's death could not be understood when detached from its context in his life. When rightly seen not as a self-contained event but as a moment in the life of the incarnate Word, Nevin described the crucifixion as—with the resurrection—the decisive victory in the conflict incited by the entrance of the divine life into human history. His thoughts on Christ's person and work echoed the incarnational theology of the ancient Greek fathers; so, in particular, did his understanding of the atonement as a triumph over sin, death, and the powers that once held humanity in bondage. "The mediation of Christ, we say, holds primarily and fundamentally in the constitution of his person. His Incarnation is not to be regarded as a device *in order* to his Mediation . . . it is itself the Mediatorial Fact" (1850: 170). And Nevin tirelessly insisted that the "theanthropic" life of the incarnate Christ continues in the life of the church. The church is not a merely human organization; it is also superhuman "in virtue of its organic outflow from the fountain head of all grace and truth in the world, the union of the divine and human in the Person of our Lord and Saviour Jesus Christ, through the mystery of the Incarnation" (1978: 391).

The affinity between Schleiermacher and Nevin on the work of Christ is unmistakable. But Nevin made the link with the ancient Greek fathers explicit and kept closer to patristic orthodoxy. Although for Schleiermacher Christian faith depended entirely on the union of Deity and humanity in the personality of Christ (*CF* 738), he was critical of the two-natures dogma by which the

5. This does not prevent Hodge from saying that Christ "endured the wrath of God" (1981, 2:614–15). Calvin, for his part, asserted that God could not have been actually angry with his beloved Son (*Institutes*, 1:517). There are some obvious linguistic problems with Hodge's satisfaction theory, not least his free use of the expression "vicarious punishment" for what, in his view, was not strictly punishment at all but a substitute for it.

union was traditionally affirmed. Nevin, by contrast, relished talk about the "hypostatical union" of two natures in Christ's person. And whereas Christ's resurrection was fundamental to Nevin's notion of liberation from death and corruption, Schleiermacher thought that the fact of the resurrection (which he affirmed) could be a matter only of *factual* belief, whereas genuine faith in Christ arises from the impression made by the being of God in him. "The disciples recognized in Him the Son of God without having the faintest premonition of His resurrection and ascension, and we too may say the same of ourselves" (*CF* 418; cf. 416, 420, 530).

III. The Twofold Work of Christ

The three contrasts I have drawn—between Anselm and Abelard, Calvin and Schleiermacher, Hodge and Nevin—may suffice to illustrate the main types of atonement theory. Other voices deserve to be heard, including Luther's, whom Aulén credited with recovering patristic language about Christ's victory over sin, death, and the devil. (Luther added the law and the wrath of God to the "tyrants" vanquished by *Christus Victor*.) But I must move on from historical analysis to the dogmatic task, which calls for noting the limitations of the old theories and proposing a view of atonement, summed up in thesis 10, that learns from them all without simply endorsing any one of them.

1. Critical Review

Satisfaction theories of atonement have always resonated with the Christian's experience of penitence and gratitude before the cross of Christ. But the difficulties with the idea of satisfaction are attested by centuries of criticism that simply will not go away, beginning with Abelard and renewed at the time of the Protestant Reformation by Faustus Socinus (1539–1604). It cannot be shown from Scripture, taken as a whole, that God's justice absolutely demands punishment of the sinner, much less that it could be satisfied by punishing the innocent instead of the guilty. Reconciliation happens by way of forgiveness (2 Cor. 5:19), and in the final analysis forgiveness and retributive justice are mutually exclusive. Where there is forgiveness, the demand for punishment has been transcended, and the glory of the biblical God is that, unlike other gods, "he does not deal with us according to our sins, nor repay us according to our iniquities" (Ps. 103:10; cf. Mic. 7:18). Other passages of Scripture may seem to limit God's free forgiveness—sometimes (as in Exod. 34:6–7) in the same breath as those that affirm it. But it is hardly strict exegesis to argue (e.g., from Rom. 3:25, Heb. 13:8, or Rev. 13:8) that God is able to forgive sins, even when no mention of punishment is made, only because God always has the punitive suffering of his Son in mind.

Talk of the wrath of God has served to accentuate the gravity of sin. But it is a problematic notion: Calvin apologized for it; Schleiermacher rejected it. Even if we take *hilastērion* in the sense of "propitiation," Romans 3:25 does not say that "the effect of the blood is to satisfy the wrath of God against sin" (Marshall 2004: 310). And we must demur when one expositor of Romans describes the death of God's Son as a "full vent" of God's wrath or asserts, "What God did on Calvary was to pour out upon His only begotten and beloved Son His wrath upon sin" (Lloyd-Jones 1970: 78, 104). Of course, the advocates of penal substitution say that it is the angry God who provides the means of propitiation. But the incongruity of supposing that God propitiates himself is one good reason for taking *hilastērion* in the sense of "expiation" rather than "propitiation." And these days, the defense of penal substitution must take account of feminist theologians who have argued for a connection between the image of the patriarchal God who unleashes severe, undeserved punishment on his only Son and the social problem of parental child abuse.

Moral influence theories do not necessarily win by default. Their strength lies not only in their unequivocal affirmation of the primacy of love but also in their recognition that "reconciliation" with God cannot be a work entirely outside the sinner. This is obvious if we use the English word *atonement* in its etymological sense: "being made at one." In the nature of the case, the atoning work of Christ must then be understood as something that happens *to* us, or *in* us—not apart from us, or in our stead. There has to be an altered subjectivity, a conversion of the fallen will. This is what the champions of the subjective theory of atonement have meant by calling it the "moral influence" theory. God's deed in Jesus Christ is not a legal transaction of which we were not even witnesses, but a transformation of our moral selves—our personalities.

For all that we can and should learn from the subjective theories about the personal operation of grace, they too have their faults. The theories cannot all be reduced to a single formula, but the fundamental thought in them all is that the death of Christ so exhibits God's love as to awaken in us an answering love, and in this way reconciliation with God takes place. The echo here of a genuine New Testament theme is unmistakable (John 15:13; Rom. 5:8; 1 John 4:19). But the subjective theories, while they rightly present an atonement in which the human subject is engaged, labor under an obvious weakness: they seem to presume that God saves us by showing us his love, whereas the Christian confession is surely that God shows us God's love by saving us. To the assertion that in the death of Christ God exhibited the divine love, the question must always be: What is it about the death of Christ that makes it an exhibition of love? Any attempt to answer the question can only make a subjective theory dependent on an objective theory. For Abelard, the proof of love was that the Son of God assumed our nature and persevered "in teaching us by word and example even unto death." But to this it must be said that just as the satisfaction theories locate atonement one-sidedly in the priestly office of Christ, Abelard's subjective theory, as stated in his *Exposition of Romans*, does not go beyond the prophetic office of Christ the Teacher.

Some of the difficulties in the satisfaction and moral influence theories of atonement are resolved by what we may agree to call (following Aulén) the *classic theory*, in which the life and death of Christ are portrayed as victory over the devil. In objective, satisfaction theories atonement took place in the past, in the crucifixion interpreted as effecting a change in God; in subjective, moral influence theories the accent falls on a change of mind in the present human subject. The classic theory holds past and present together as moments in the one great struggle of God with evil, a struggle in which the decisive engagement has already been fought and won by God incarnate. The conflict is not over; it continues as a conflict in which humanity is still engaged. But Christ's victory created a new situation, a new age. Moreover, by setting the death of Christ in the context of the incarnation, the classic theory of atonement makes it natural to think of the church as the continuation of the divine life that came into the world in Jesus Christ and defeated the forces of darkness. The idea of penal substitution, by contrast, has lent itself to an individualistic confession of belief in the Christ whose death was "for me." The two ways of thinking are not exclusive. But it is a distinctive contribution of the classic theory to show that atonement and ecclesiology can no more be detached from each other than can the death of Christ from his life. The evil against which Christian faith struggles is a collective, social force. The counterforce, too, must be collective and social. Indeed, it is represented in the New Testament as a *cosmic* struggle (e.g., Gal. 4:3; Eph. 6:12; Col. 2:20).

A weakness of the classic theory of atonement, however, is that when it calls for attention to the "life of Christ," the point sometimes appears to be more metaphysical than historical. It is not inappropriate that the dominant idea of redemption in the Greek fathers is designated the "physical" theory, in which the central idea is the union of the divine *physis* ("nature") with the human *physis*. Nevin accused his theological opponents of neglecting the historical facts and realities of Christ's life, but he leaves himself open to the same charge. For while he never tires of stating that it is the divine-human life of the incarnate Word that restores fallen humanity to God, it is the "hypostatic union" of the two natures that captivates him. He has less to say about the Jesus of the Synoptic Gospels, who announced the reign of God, preached good news to the poor and release to the captives, healed the sick, and was despised as a friend of sinners (Matt. 11:19; Luke 7:34). There, surely, was God in Christ reconciling the world to Godself—the "theanthropic" life that brought about the atonement. The life of Christ, as Calvin says, is to seek and to save the lost (OS 2:42).

2. *Saving Faith and the Community of Faith*

The aim of our dogmatics must be to give unity and direction to the biblical, historical, and critical reflections now before us. To begin with, we must acknowledge that the New Testament presents the meaning of salvation through Christ not in a single, well-honed doctrine but in a wealth of intuitive metaphors that had their linguistic home in the various departments of Jewish and Gentile life in the ancient world: cult, commerce, slavery, law, warfare, and personal relationships. The work of Christ was a sacrifice (Mark 14:24; John 1:29, 36; Acts 8:32–35; Rom. 3:25; 5:9; 1 Cor. 5:7; Eph. 1:7; 2:13; 5:2; Col. 1:20; Heb. 2:17; 9:5, 12, 26; 10:12–14; 1 Pet. 1:2, 19; 1 John 1:7; 2:2; 4:10; Rev. 1:5; 5:6; etc.), a payment (1 Cor. 6:20; 7:23), liberation or emancipation (Mark 10:45; John 8:36; Rom. 6:22–23; 8:2; Gal. 5:1; 1 Tim. 2:6; 1 Pet. 1:18), the cancellation of a debt (Col. 2:13–14), victory over the forces of evil (1 Cor. 15: 24–25; Col. 2:15; 1 Pet. 3:22; cf. Acts 2:34; Phil. 2:10; Heb. 10:13), reconciliation of the parties to a quarrel (Rom. 5:10; 2 Cor. 5:18–20; Col. 1:20). Each of the metaphors makes its point: for example, that Christ's unswerving faithfulness to his mission was a fearful struggle or that our freedom came at a terrible price. But they belong to the primary language of the Christian community, and problems arise when they are taken for dogmatic concepts—as when the fathers of the church debated the question, To whom was the ransom paid? The task of dogmatic theology is not to elaborate any one metaphor, turning it into an exclusive doctrine or theory of atonement, but to ask: What *did* Jesus do that the metaphors point to? And that question must draw in another: What *does* Jesus do for believers today?

To answer the two questions, I avail myself of the traditional scheme of the three offices of Christ—not as sacrosanct dogma, but as a way of ordering the data and avoiding one-sidedness. I depart from the tradition in subsuming the *twofold* activity of Christ as prophet and priest under his kingly office. This provides the systematic link with what has been said already about the two-sidedness of estrangement as both mistrust and the contagion of sin and with what will need to be said later about the two-sided Christian experience of reconciliation and renewal.

To speak of the *kingly office* of Christ may sound antiquated in our more democratic day. But it has played a prominent role in the history of the church and cannot be passed over lightly. It echoes the earliest Christian confession, "Jesus is Lord," and it connects the Apostolic preaching of the atoning work of Christ with Christ's own proclamation of the kingdom of God (often ignored in accounts of the atonement). True, the notion of the kingdom of God has been the subject of exegetical and theological controversy, and to speak of Jesus as the "founder" of the kingdom is open to objection. But it is plain that Jesus did not merely predict the coming of the kingdom. Although he taught his disciples to pray "Your kingdom come" (Matt. 6:10), he spoke of it as already present, or dawning, in his own activity (Matt. 12:28; cf. 11:2–6; Mark 3:23–24; Luke 17:21). And Paul explains that it is Christ who reigns until the end, when he will hand over the kingly office to God the Father (1 Cor. 15:24–25; cf. "my kingdom" in John 18:36).

The Protestant Reformers took up the theme of Christ's reign, which they perceived as compromised by ecclesiastical abuses. Hence Calvin presented his treatise *On the Necessity of Reforming the Church* (1544) "in the name of all who wish Christ to reign" (*TT* 1:121). But, as Luther never tired of saying, Christ's only weapon is the Word. In his admonition *To the Princes of Saxony* (1524) he wrote: "in his realm Christ will 'smite the earth with the rod of his mouth, and with the breath of his lips'" (LW 40:58; Isa. 11:4). With this in mind, I take Christ's kingship, which is "not of this world" (John 18:36), as a symbol for the continuance of his redemptive activity in the word of the gospel. It is a "kingly" activity insofar as it governs the life and witness of the church; and its effects are, first, the creation and nurture of *faith* through the proclamation of the kingdom, which is Christ's prophetic activity; and second, the creation and governance of the *community* of faith as the vehicle of the kingdom, which is Christ's priestly activity.

Faith is taken here in the sense defined: not as belief, but as the insight or discernment evoked by the Christian story, in particular by the manifestation of the gospel in Jesus Christ. In the theory of penal substitution faith is bound to be belief—belief that the transaction between God the Father and God the Son happened and that it happened on my behalf. I have suggested that we understand faith rather as the reconfiguration of our existence brought about by hearing the word of the gospel. This, we can now say, is the meaning of reconciliation with God: it is discerning the "paternal face" in the words and work of Jesus and finding there the clue to the meaning of our existence. That Jesus' story led through suffering and death ensures that Christian faith cannot be a breezy or sentimental optimism but must be a confidence that encompasses tragedy. Not even the terrifying sense of abandonment by God (Mark 15:34) will cancel the final, victorious word of trust: "Father, into your hands I commend my spirit" (Luke 23:46).

"So," as Paul says, "faith comes from what is heard, and what is heard comes through the word of Christ [*dia rhēmatos Christou*]" (Rom. 10:17; cf. Gal. 3:2). Perhaps Paul means "the word *about* Christ" (see NRSV note). But the parallel expression "the word of God " (*rhēma theou*), used elsewhere (Eph. 6:17; Heb. 6:5; 11:3; cf. Heb. 1:3; 1 Pet. 1:25), favors the preferred translation of the NRSV, in which case Paul evidently thinks of the risen Christ himself as speaking through his messengers. This is certainly the way the Protestant Reformers thought of the act of preaching. As Luther wrote, "What [the minister of Word and Sacrament] says or does is not his, but Christ, your Lord, and the Holy Spirit say and do everything, in so far as he adheres to correct doctrine and practice."[6] If we ask, then, what the work of Christ is, the first answer must be: his work is *the gift of faith*. Through the word of the kingdom he creates faith in God, his Father. We may call this his *prophetic activity* if we understand prophecy in its biblical sense, not merely as foretelling the future but as declaring ("forth-telling") the mind of God. And if we think of the Word as conveyed by what Jesus did as well as what he said, we can appropriate the Johannine description of Jesus Christ as the Word become flesh (John 1:14).[7] More will need to be said later of Christ's activity as prophet, viewed from the perspective of the believer's experience of Christ (Chap. 12). But we must turn now to his priestly office.

The work of Christ is not only the gift of faith to the individual but also *the gift of the community of faith*, and this is symbolized as his *priestly activity*. It is true that many discussions of the redemptive work of Christ must be faulted for passing over his activity as prophet or teacher, which is so prominent in the gospel story. He denies that he is the prophet foretold by Moses, but some of those who hear his teaching are convinced that he must be; and that is how Peter identifies him in Acts (Acts 3:22; cf. Deut. 18:15; John 1:21; 7:40). He styles himself "the Teacher" (Mark 14:14), and others call him "Teacher" or "Rabbi" (4:38; 5:35; 9:5, 17, 38; 10:17, 20, 35, 51; 11:21; 12:14, 32; 13:1; 14:45). He taught with authority (1:22), and according to Matthew he did not hesitate to correct the inherited commandments and prohibitions with his declaration, "But I say to you . . ." (Matt. 5:22, 28, 32, 34, 39, 44). Nevertheless, it is plainly inadequate to *reduce* his work to teaching—or, as one fashionable watchword says, to "the

6. Martin Luther, *On the Councils and the Church* (1539), LW 41:156. Calvin thought of the Word as, like a sacrament, the instrument of the Lord's power and presence (*Institutes*, 2:1017, 1286, etc.). But in Rom. 10:17 he followed a variant reading (as does KJV) and read "the word of God" for "the word of Christ" (see Comm. ad loc.).

7. When it refers to the Christian message, "word" (*logos or rhēma*) is variously qualified in the NT as the word of the cross, faith, the gospel, grace, the kingdom, life, promise, reconciliation, righteousness, or salvation. When it stands alone, particularly when the incarnate or preached *logos* is meant (Luke 1:2; Acts 6:4; 11:19; 14:25; 2 Tim. 4:2), it is natural to capitalize it as "the Word."

ethics of the Sermon on the Mount." What would then be missing is all that the cultic metaphor of Christ's priestly sacrifice stands for.

In the Hebrew Scriptures, prophet and priest sometimes appear to be opposed as representatives of two very different kinds of religion. Whereas the priest represents the institutional religion of the temple, the prophet is a charismatic figure, called by Yahweh to speak out against the people's blind trust in priestly ritual. Amos, the herdsman of Tekoa and dresser of sycamore trees, makes a point of denying that he is a professional prophet (Amos 7:10–15). But to protest against the abuse of ritual need not require its abolition. Priestly religion exposes sin's defilement of the community; the priest's duty, in God's name, is to provide expiation or cleansing of the sanctuary, so that the relationship of the people with God will not be broken by their "uncleannesses" (Lev. 16:16, 19). The priestly expiation is, of course, a symbolic act. As C. H. Dodd says, "if we think realistically, there is no way of disinfecting moral corruption except by creating a new centre of healthy life capable of absorbing the diseased tissue" (1954: 22).

If we ask *how* Christ created such a "centre of healthy life," we can borrow Calvin's formula: "by the whole course of his obedience" (*Institutes*, 1:507). And although I do not follow Calvin on the meaning of the death of Christ (as penal substitution), I agree with him when he adds that Scripture ascribes the way of salvation particularly to Christ's death. As Paul says, Christ Jesus "became obedient to the point of death—even death on a cross" (Phil. 2:8; see also Rom. 5:19). His death, willingly accepted, was the culmination of a life totally committed to his mission, which was not to propitiate the anger of God but to extend God's reign in the new age.

It was natural for the earliest Christians, who were steeped in the Levitical law, to make sense of the crucifixion by understanding it as the sacrifice of an innocent victim for the good of the people. But in our time the language of a bloody sacrifice is usually either avoided as repellent or else attenuated as an inoffensive *façon de parler* for giving something up for the sake of something better. Already in the sixteenth century, Calvin thought that animal sacrifices must have been revolting and hideous to behold (Comm. Isa. 34:6; cf. *Institutes*, 1:349). But this did not deter him from accepting the language of sacrifice as a metaphor for the death of Christ (cf. Heb. 10:4–10). And we could do the same if, with Vincent Taylor, we take the underlying idea of sacrifice to be not (as Calvin thought) propitiation but "the conception of sharing in the cleansing power of life which has been released in death, dedicated, and presented to God" (Taylor 1945: 187). But there is another metaphor that may serve us better.

It is interesting to observe how ubiquitous in Christian writers, including Calvin and Schleiermacher (and C. H. Dodd), is a metaphor that transcends the more time-bound symbolism of animal sacrifice but preserves its reference to the community. I have in mind the metaphor of sin as contagious (see my thesis 7), an epidemic that passes from person to person and infects an entire community, initially unnoticed and undiagnosed; salvation, accordingly, is a process of healing or disinfection. Calvin calls original sin a "contagion" and a "pestilence" (*contagio, lues*: *Institutes*, 1:249, 251). Schleiermacher cites with approval the definition of original sin as an "original disease" (*morbus originis*, *CF* 289); and, albeit without continuing the medical metaphor, he describes the redemptive activity of Christ as the founding of a new "corporate life" that works against the "corporate life" of sin. In the second part of my thesis 10, which gives my second answer to the question of Christ's work, I retain the language of "contagion" to state the corporate aspect of his redemptive activity: his work is *the new community*. He *creates the community of faith as the means by which the contagion of sin is countered and the reign of God extended,* which in the traditional language is his priestly activity. Naturally, the immense importance of a "social" understanding of sin and salvation leads us into the doctrine of the church as the vehicle of the kingdom of God. But we must ask next: Who *is* this person who appears so suddenly in the Gospels, "proclaiming the good news of God, and saying, 'The time is fulfilled, and the kingdom of God has come near; repent, and believe in the good news'"?

11. The Person of the Redeemer

The Redeemer is not the so-called Jesus of history (not, that is, a historical reconstruction) but the Christ of faith who is proclaimed in the church as the living Savior; and the content of the proclamation, represented in the dogma of Christ's "two natures," is the disclosure both of authentic humanity and of the design of God the Creator.

Christians believe that in Christ they have God. But how to think of the relationship between God and Christ has been variously answered from the beginning of Christianity. There is an official answer in church dogma. The declaration of the Council of Nicaea (325) that the Son is "of the same substance" (*homoousios*) as God the Father did not at first win universal acceptance, but it was reaffirmed by the Council of Constantinople (381). Seventy years later, the Council of Chalcedon (451) taught that in Jesus Christ are two natures, one divine and the other human, without either confusion or separation. In the one nature he is of the same substance as the Father; in the other, of the same substance as ourselves. The Chalcedonian Definition, summed up in the formula "two natures in one person," set the terms for what is considered the orthodox or catholic understanding of the incarnate Son of God as truly God and truly human. Neither the term *homoousios*, however, nor an explicit two-natures doctrine appears in the New Testament, which contains the seeds of both orthodox and heretical views of Christ. The task for dogmatic theology is to review the New Testament data and to note the main turning points in the history of christological doctrine before making a constructive statement. The cardinal importance assigned to the subject of Christ's person in traditional dogmatics will excuse the length of the present chapter.

I. Jesus Christ in the New Testament

If we venture to make a working distinction between "lower" and "higher" estimates of Christ's person, we may say that the New Testament writers exhibit a variety of christological descriptions that can be represented as points on a scale. At the bottom, Jesus is a man chosen by God; at the top, he is worshipped as divine. In between is the most characteristic New Testament perception of Christ as coming from God but distinct from God.

1. The Acts of the Apostles

The lowest end of the scale is found in the Acts of the Apostles. Peter's sermon on the day of Pentecost (Acts 2:14–36) describes Jesus as "a man attested to you by God with deeds of power, wonders, and signs that God did through him among you, as you yourselves know" (v. 22). He was crucified and killed, but God raised him up and made him "both Lord and Messiah" (v. 36). Similarly, Peter recalls before Cornelius "how God anointed Jesus of Nazareth with the Holy Spirit and with power; how he went about doing good and healing all who were oppressed by the devil, for God was with him" (10:38). God raised him when put to death and instructed certain chosen witnesses "to testify that he is the one ordained by God as judge of the living and the dead" (v. 42). But a *crucified* Messiah was not what the people expected.

In his address at Solomon's Portico (Acts 3:11–26), Peter explains the crucifixion as the fulfillment of "what [God] had foretold through all the prophets, that his Messiah would suffer" (v. 18). He identifies Jesus as God's *pais* (vv. 13, 26), a Greek word that can mean either "child" or "servant." Here the meaning is clearly "servant," since Peter's explanation of the crucifixion must refer mainly, though not solely, to the vicarious suffering of Yahweh's Servant in the fourth Servant Song of Second Isaiah (Isa. 52:13–53:12; see also Acts 3:13, 26; 4:27, 30). To orthodox Jews the idea of a crucified Messiah was anathema (a *skandalon,* 1 Cor. 1:23), and they did not interpret the fourth Servant Song as a messianic prophecy. But it is plain from Acts that the identification of Jesus with Yahweh's Suffering Servant was fundamental to the earliest Christian witness; the connection is explicit in the narrative of Philip's encounter with the Ethiopian eunuch (Acts 8:26–39).

2. The Synoptic Gospels

In general, the Synoptic Gospels stay within the frame of Peter's portrayal of Jesus in the Acts of the Apostles. Each of the evangelists, it is true, highlights distinctive features in his portrait, but in all of them Jesus announces the kingdom of God and is identified as Messiah, Son of Man, and Son of God.[1] Many New Testament scholars doubt that Jesus ever claimed to be *the Messiah* (Greek *ho christos,* "the Christ"), though he is reported to have accepted the title in his response to the high priest (Mark 14:62; cf. Matt. 26:64) and implicitly in his admonition to his disciples, "you have one instructor, the Messiah" (Matt. 23:10). In Acts, Peter seems to say that God made Jesus "Lord and Messiah" after the crucifixion; in the Gospels, by contrast, he already confesses Jesus as the Messiah at Caesarea Philippi, and Jesus admonishes him to keep silent about it (Mark 8:29–30; cf. 1:34, 44; 3:12; 4:11–12; 5:43; 8:30; 9:9, 30–31). The "messianic secret," as it has been called, would have helped the earliest Christians to explain why so many of his own people failed to recognize Jesus as the

1. In the Synoptic Gospels the title "Savior" (*sōtēr*) is applied to Christ only once, in Luke 2:11 (cf. Acts 5:31; 13:23). In the Magnificat (Luke 1:47), and sometimes in the Pastoral Epistles, it is God who is named "Savior" (1 Tim. 1:1; 2:3; 4:10; Titus 1:3; 2:10; 3:4; cf. Jude 24); but Christ is also so named in the Pastorals (2 Tim. 1:10; Titus 1:4; 2:13; 3:6) and in 2 Peter (1:1, 11; 2:20; 3:2, 18). See also John 4:42; Eph. 5:23; Phil. 3:20; 1 John 4:14.

Messiah; if it goes back to Jesus himself, he no doubt intended it to head off misunderstandings of his mission—so different was he from the messianic king expected by his contemporaries.

Jesus' own preferred title for himself, as is evident in his answers to Peter and the high priest (Mark 8:29–31; 14:61–62), was *the Son of Man* (literally "the son of the man"). The title appears so frequently in Mark (fourteen times) and the other Gospels, including John, that it would be implausible to attribute it to the evangelists rather than to Jesus himself. But why he chose it, and what he meant by it, are questions open to debate. In the Old Testament "son of man" (*ben 'ādām*) means simply "mortal" or "human being" (e.g., Num. 23:19; Ps. 8:4); it is the form of address by which Yahweh speaks to the prophet-priest Ezekiel (NRSV "O mortal"; cf. Dan. 8:17). But by the time of Jesus "Son of Man" was being used as a messianic title, not merely as a circumlocution for "man" or "mortal." Throughout Christian history it has been supposed that, as a title of Jesus, "Son of Man" must be intended to stress his genuine humanity in contrast to "Son of God," taken to affirm his divine nature. But Jesus' reported answer to the high priest makes a connection with the prophecy of Daniel about "one like a son of man" coming with the clouds of heaven to receive everlasting dominion from the Ancient of Days (Dan. 7:13–14; Mark 14:62; see also Mark 8:38; 13:26). To be sure, the passage in Daniel means only that the one who is to come will *look like* a man. But what is said of him takes him out of the category of human being. Transformed into a title of Jesus, "Son of Man" hardly stresses his humanity.[2]

Difficulties of interpretation also attend the third title, *the Son of God*, applied occasionally to Jesus by others in the Synoptic Gospels, including the unclean spirits (Mark 3:11; 5:7) and, in Matthew's Gospel, by Peter and the disciples (Matt. 14:33; 16:16). Matthew also gives the high priest's demand to Jesus as: "tell us if you are the Messiah, the Son of God" (Matt. 26:63; cf. Luke 22:70). The voice from heaven at Jesus' baptism and the transfiguration (Mark 1:11; 9:7) sets him apart as God's special Son, and the centurion's testimony at the crucifixion could perhaps be translated: "Truly this man was God's Son" (Mark 15:39).[3] The Synoptic Jesus seems not to have applied the title "Son of God" to himself, but in all the Gospels, including John, he addresses God as "*my* Father"; and in the Markan account of the agony in the garden he uses the Aramaic word *abba* (14:36), originally a child's term of affection for father. The most remarkable Synoptic testimony to Jesus' sense of unique intimacy with his Father is given in his prayer reported in Matthew 11:25–27 (cf. Luke 10:21–22), culminating in the claim: "no one knows the Father except the Son and anyone to whom the Son chooses to reveal him." Some scholars identify this as, with variations, a "migratory" saying, a saying attributed to several religious leaders and found first in the hymn of Pharaoh Ikhnaton, the reformer of Egyptian religion. But if it is not an authentic and unique saying of Jesus, its application to him attests

2. The ambiguity of the expression "son of man" is evident from divergent translations of Rev. 1:13 and 14:14: the Greek lacks the definite article, but the NRSV replaces the RSV's "a son of man" with "*the* Son of Man." As a messianic title, "Son of Man" appears in the pseudepigraphal Similitudes of Enoch (1 Enoch 37–71), roughly contemporary with Jesus. Some scholars suggest that if the strictly apocalyptic Son of Man sayings in the Gospels (e.g., Mark 8:13; 13:26) are authentic sayings of Jesus, he may not be referring to himself at all.

3. Here too (see the previous note) there is no definite article in the Greek, and the centurion's statement could also be translated, "Truly this man was *a* son of God."

his significance to those who believed in him and wished others also to come to him (cf. Matt. 11:28).

3. The Letters of Paul

Paul's sermon in the synagogue at Pamphylian Antioch, as reported in Acts 13:16–41, agrees closely with the "low" Christology in the preaching of Peter. Jesus of Nazareth is the promised Savior of Israel, God's Son whom God raised from the dead. As in the rest of Acts, he is a man chosen by God for a special mission; and the words of Psalm 2:7, "You are my son; today I have begotten you," are connected with the resurrection (Acts 13:33), whereas one reading of Luke 3:22 connects them with Jesus' baptism. Perhaps there is a trace of the primitive Christology in Romans 1:4, where Paul says that Jesus was "designated the Son of God" by the resurrection (RSV). But the Christ who appears in Paul's letters is a heavenly being who enters the world of humanity from another realm. Paul's gospel requires the manifestation of Christ in the likeness of sinful flesh (Rom. 8:3) or in human likeness and form (Phil. 2:7); but it is not the Son of Man and his proclamation of the kingdom of God that stand at the center of Paul's faith in Christ.[4] While he can occasionally recall sayings attributed to Jesus (1 Cor. 7:10; 9:14; 11:23–25; cf. Acts 20:35), he seems indifferent to Jesus' ministry, about which he may have known very little. It was enough for him to assert that the Son of God was descended from David "according to the flesh" (Rom. 1:3) and "born of a woman" (Gal. 4:4); that he was crucified; and that God raised him from the dead. To the Corinthians he says: "we proclaim Christ crucified. . . . I decided to know nothing among you except Jesus Christ, and him crucified" (1 Cor. 1:23; 2:2). When Paul writes of "the life of Jesus" (2 Cor. 4:10–11), he does not mean what a modern quester for the historical Jesus would mean. He no longer knows Christ "according to the flesh" (5:16)—Christ lives *in him* (Gal. 2:20).

Two passages in Paul's letters show clearly that he thought of Christ as existing alongside God before he was sent into the world: he was God's intermediary in the cosmos before he became God's instrument of salvation. (1) In the Letter to the Philippians, apparently citing an early Christian hymn, Paul expresses his belief in Christ as a heavenly being who did not see fit to seize equality with God but took the form of a servant (*doulos*) and by his humility won the name "Lord" (Phil. 2:5–11; see also Rom. 8:3; 2 Cor. 8:9; cf. Mark 10:42–45; John 13:2b–17). The RSV translation of *harpagmon* in Philippians 2:6 as "a thing to be grasped" is linguistically sounder than the NRSV's "something to be exploited." But either way, whether he was unwilling to seize what he did not have or to make the most of what he did have, "equality with God" obviously implies that Christ was *not* God.

The activity of Christ as God's agent in creation, before his work of redemption, is affirmed (2) in the Letter to the Colossians (1:15–20). That he is "the firstborn [*prōtotokos*] of all creation" (v. 15) can hardly mean that he was the first

4. Note, however, that according to Acts the kingdom of God was the theme of Paul's testimony to *the Jews* in Ephesus and Rome (Acts 19:8; 28:23, 31), and in his letters he asserts that with the coming of Christ a new age is dawning (see, e.g., Rom. 13:11–14).

created being if "all things have been created through him and for him" and "he himself is before all things" (vv. 16–17). Yet he is not God but "the image [*eikōn*] of the invisible God" (v. 15), and "in him all the fullness [of God] was pleased to dwell" (v. 19; 2:9 adds "bodily"). The figure of the cosmic Christ, the agent of creation, has sometimes been taken as evidence that Colossians could not have been written by Paul. But the language is required by the deceitful philosophy against which the letter was written (2:8–23). The author asserts the sole mediation of Christ against the heretical teaching that a whole hierarchy of elemental spirits mediates between the supreme God and humans and that they impose on humans a regimen of ritual observances and ascetic practices. Besides, the language about the cosmic Christ, though rare in Paul, is not unique to Colossians. It appears in 1 Corinthians: "for us there is one God, the Father, from whom are all things and for whom [*eis auton*] we exist, and one Lord, Jesus Christ, through whom are all things and through whom we exist" (1 Cor. 8:6). In the same letter Christ is said to belong to God, who is the head of Christ as Christ is the head of every man and a husband is the head of his wife (3:23; 11:3). Christ is also identified as the heavenly man or "man from heaven," the "last Adam" (15:45, 49; cf. Rom. 5:12–21), who serves as God's temporary vicegerent until the end, when he will return the kingdom to God the Father (1 Cor. 15:24–28).

4. *The Fourth Gospel*

All three of the Synoptic christological titles are found in the Fourth Gospel, which was written so that the reader might come to believe "that Jesus is the Messiah, the Son of God" (John 20:31). John's Jesus refers to himself as "Son of Man" but more often as "Son of God" or simply "the Son." He calls God "my Father," and he says: "The Father and I are one. . . . Whoever has seen me has seen the Father" (10:30; 14:9; cf. 12:45). This, of course, does not imply the numerical identity of Jesus and God, since he prays to the Father for his disciples "that they may be one, as we are one" (17:11; cf. v. 21). After the resurrection, he appears to Mary Magdalene and instructs her to tell the disciples (his "brothers"): "I am ascending to my Father and your Father, to my God and your God" (20:17). Yet the uniqueness of Jesus' relation to the Father is expressed by the description "the only [KJV 'only begotten'] Son of God" (1:14, 18; 3:16, 18; cf. 1 John 4:9). He is "in the bosom of the Father" (RSV) or "close to the Father's heart" (NRSV), who loved him before the foundation of the world (John 1:18; 17:24). The Son of God, or Son of Man, belongs to the heavenly realm, from which he descended and to which he returns; and this is the guarantee that he utters the words of God, who sent him (1:18; 3:13, 31–35; 6:62; 8:28–29). But his humanity is real: in him the Word became flesh (1:14). The First Letter of John makes the confession that Jesus Christ has come in the flesh as the test of sound belief (1 John 4:2–3).

In the Gospel of John, early Christian witness to Jesus Christ has moved further than Paul into the world of Hellenistic religious thought. Jewish belief in a better age to come is transformed by the idea of a better world that is eternally present; a dualistic metaphysic modifies eschatological expectations. Jesus descends from the world above, and he tells Nicodemus that "no one can see the kingdom of God without being born from above" (John 3:3). More than one suggestion has been made about the particular affinities of the Fourth Gospel with Hellenistic ideas; the background of the Letter to the Hebrews, by contrast, is certainly the Alexandrian Judaism of Philo, in which Jewish thought had been adapted to the legacy of Platonism.

5. *The Letter to the Hebrews*

The author of Hebrews thinks of Jesus, above all, as "high priest," and the premise of his argument for the superiority of Jesus' priesthood is a dualism of earthly shadow and heavenly reality. Jesus performs his priestly task in the heavenly sanctuary; the Levitical priests serve only "a copy and shadow of the heavenly sanctuary" (i.e., the tabernacle, Heb. 8:5 RSV; see also 9:11–14, 23–24; 10:1). Yet Hebrews presents a very human Jesus, made like his brothers in every respect, able to help those who are tempted because he himself suffered and was tempted, though without sinning; he lived in undeviating faithfulness to him who appointed him (2:17–18; 3:2; 4:15), and he became a priest "through the power of an indestructible life" (7:16). These thoughts are not alien to Paul (see, e.g., Rom. 8:29; Phil. 2:8). But the author of Hebrews seems more interested than Paul in the details of Jesus' life, and there is an unmistakable allusion to Jesus' agony in the garden—the proof that "he learned obedience through what he suffered" (Heb. 5:7–8). Yet these remarkable testimonies to Jesus' humanity are introduced by a prologue (1:1–4) that identifies the Son as God's agent in the creation and preservation of all things, "the reflection of God's glory and the exact imprint of God's very being." He is God's firstborn (*prōtotokos*, 1:6). When his priestly sacrifice had been made, he sat down at the right hand of the heavenly throne of God, the majesty on high (1:3; 8:1; 12:2).

6. *Jesus as God?*

In the Gospels Jesus does not claim to be God, but to be sent by God. "Why do you call me good? No one is good but God alone" (Mark 10:18). "[W]hoever welcomes me welcomes not me but the one who sent me" (9:37). But the question remains whether, at the highest end of the christological scale, other New Testament writings do attribute deity to Jesus. The Revelation to John can be said to end the Bible at the highest point of christological belief. Unlike the angels (Rev. 19:10; 22:9), the Lamb is joined with the Father in receiving adoration (5:13; 7:10); and the words, "I am the Alpha and the Omega," "the beginning and the end," first uttered by the Lord God (1:8; also 21:6), are later applied by Christ to himself (22:13; cf. 1:17). That the Lamb stands *beside* the throne and is distinguished from the enthroned Deity (5:6) may be required by the nature of the metaphor. But John can also speak of "the throne of God and of the Lamb" (22:1, 3); and in his letter to the angel of the church in Laodicea (3:14–22), the exalted Christ pledges to share his throne with the one who conquers, "just as I myself conquered and sat down with my Father on his throne" (v. 21). Still, the distinction between the Lord and his Messiah is plain (11:15; 12:10).[5]

5. Elsewhere in the NT, the "Lord" (*kyrios*) *is* the Messiah. In the Septuagint, *kyrios* denotes Yahweh. But some have argued that early Christian usage reflected the significance of *kyrios* in Hellenistic

There are, however, nine or ten passages in the New Testament that have been adduced as explicit affirmations of Christ's deity: one or two in Paul, three in the Fourth Gospel, one in Hebrews, and the rest in 2 Thessalonians, Titus, 2 Peter, and 1 John. Other passages that some appeal to can safely be left aside (see, e.g., the commentaries on 1 Tim. 3:16). If the NRSV rendering of Colossians 2:2 is correct (Christ not as God, but as God's mystery), there is but one verse in Paul that could be construed as identifying Christ with God: in Romans 9:5 the NRSV has "the Messiah [Christ], who is over all, God blessed forever." But the correct rendering depends on the punctuation. Since there is no other passage in which Paul calls Christ "God," the earlier translation of the RSV is more plausible: it takes the verse to end in a doxology, "God who is over all be blessed forever. Amen." Similarly, the solitary verse in the Letter to the Hebrews (1:8) is grammatically ambiguous, as is the Old Testament verse that it cites (Ps. 45:6). Is the Son addressed as God ("Your throne, O God"), or is the meaning "God is your throne"? The choice must be in line with everything else the author says, which presupposes that Jesus is *not* God. As for the tandem expressions, "our God and the Lord Jesus Christ" (2 Thess. 1:12; cf. 1:1), "the great God and our Savior Jesus Christ" (Titus 2:13), and "our God and the Savior Jesus Christ" (2 Pet. 1:1), it is unlikely that they assign a double description to Christ as both God and Savior (Lord); more likely, they distinguish Christ from God, as in 1 Corinthians 8:6 and John 17:3 (cf. 2 Cor. 1:3; Eph. 1:17; 1 Tim. 2:5; 1 Pet. 1:3).

Most commentators think it improbable that the statement in 1 John, "He is the true God" (1 John 5:20), refers to Christ. The three passages in the Gospel of John, on the other hand, are intriguing. Two appear in the first chapter. (1) The very first verse of the prologue states in the NRSV that "the Word [*logos*] was God." But in the Greek there is no definite article with *theos* ("God"), and some scholars argue that a more correct rendering of *theos ēn ho logos* would be "the Word was divine" (James Moffatt's translation). In any case, the prologue does not say that Jesus is God but that the *logos* became flesh (1:14). (2) One reading of verse 18 has the remarkable expression *monogenēs theos*, the "only begotten God." But once again the verse has generated disagreement, and the RSV followed the alternative reading *monogenēs huios*, "only [or only begotten] *Son*."

This leaves (3) the one remaining Johannine text (20:28) as the sole place in the New Testament where, everyone agrees, Jesus is incontestably called "God": Thomas addresses the risen Jesus as "my Lord and my God." In the ancient world to call someone, or even some *thing*, "god" meant less than it would mean today (see Ps. 82:6, cited by Jesus in John 10:34). It has been suggested that John 20:28 was the Christian retort to the insistence of Emperor Domitian (51–96 CE) that *he* should be addressed as "lord and god" (*dominus et deus*). Whether that is correct or not, the suggestion serves as a reminder that the ancient world applied the word *god* liberally to who or what was held to be of high value and worthy of allegiance (cf. John 10:34–35; 1 Cor. 8:5). And it remained for later theology to ask how Thomas's obeisance is to be harmonized

religious cults. In the Gospels it is sometimes no more than a respectful form of address, like our "sir" (e.g., Matt. 27:63; John 12:21).

with the emphatic subordination of Jesus to the Father that the Fourth Gospel repeatedly underscores (e.g., John 5:19, 30; 8:28).

Four observations may conclude this brief survey of the pertinent New Testament materials. (1) It is the sheer variety of Christologies that must surely strike us first. Eventually, catholic orthodoxy imposed on the diversity a dogmatic unity that was not there to begin with, and the distinct strands came to be viewed as stages in progressive revelation or the development of doctrine. But the variety urges caution in pronouncing the charge of heresy on deviations from catholic dogma. If it is asserted that one cannot be a Christian without saying, "Jesus is God," the basis for the assertion will have to be found somewhere other than in the varied witness to Jesus as Lord and Christ in the New Testament.

To be sure (2), there are some constants. The picture of *the postresurrection Lord* is common to all our sources. The cosmic Christ of Paul, the eternal Word of John, and the priestly Son of God in Hebrews all add the vision of *a preexistent being* subordinate to God. In language that echoes descriptions of the cosmic Wisdom personified in the Old Testament and the Apocrypha, the Son is pictured alongside God in God's creative activity (cf. Prov. 8:30; Wis. 8:3–4). But nowhere does the New Testament incontrovertibly assert that Christians need to speak of "God the Son." The only true God is the Father; Jesus Christ is the Son whom he has sent (John 17:3). The Pauline formula, "for us there is one God, the Father, . . . and one Lord, Jesus Christ" (1 Cor. 8:6), seems as close as we can get to christological harmony in the New Testament (cf. the Apostles' Creed); it forms Paul's favorite greeting, "Grace to you and peace from God our Father and the Lord Jesus Christ," which opens his letters to the Romans, Corinthians (1 and 2), Galatians, Philippians, and Philemon (cf. Eph. 1:2; 2 Thess. 1:2). Similarly, the opening salutation of 1 Timothy names "God the Father and Christ Jesus our Lord" (1 Tim. 1:2; cf. 2 Tim. 1:2; Titus 1:4), and the summary confession in chapter 2 reads: "there is one God; there is also one mediator between God and humankind, Christ Jesus, himself human" (2:5).

Nevertheless (3), there is some foreshadowing of the shift from the primitive Christian confession "Jesus is Lord" (1 Cor. 12:3; 2 Cor. 4:5; cf. Luke 2:11) to the Nicene Creed's "true God from true God." It appears explicitly in Thomas's obeisance before the risen Lord, and it is present in embryo in the broader impulse to pay homage to Christ, along with God the Father, as the one through whom access to the Father has been opened (e.g., John 5:23; 14:1; Rev. 5:13; 7:10).

Finally (4), it is evident that progress in christological construction happens by appropriation of conceptual schemes first from within, then from beyond, the matrix of Jewish religious ideas in which Christianity was born. The borrowing of Hellenistic religious and philosophical ideas provided a bridge between primitive Christianity and the Greco-Roman world. But it was a fertile source of Christologies eventually excluded as heretical, all of which could appeal to biblical texts in their support. Catholic theologians, too, availed themselves of Hellenistic metaphysical speculation in order to *combat* heresy, and the use of alien philosophical concepts proved to be ambivalent even in the service of orthodoxy.

II. The Making of Christological Dogma

Even more has been written about the person of Christ than about his work. I cannot hope to touch on the full story but may defer to the surveys in, among others, H. R. Mackintosh and John Macquarrie.[6] This does not, in my opinion, leave a serious lack in my presentation. Much christological speculation goes far beyond the affirmations of Scripture and Christian experience and runs the risk of turning dogmatic attention from its center, which is the gospel. But something does need to be said about the making of christological dogma, in which the vocabulary of theological reflection on the person of Christ was formed, and about the attempts to revise or replace the dogma in modern times. I can then address my eleventh thesis. Reflections on the Holy Spirit and the full doctrine of the Trinity will be postponed to the chapters on the church (14–19) and chapter 20.

The road to Chalcedon was long, beginning with the intuitive faith of the Apostolic Fathers and ending with the definitive pronouncements of the Fathers assembled in one of the church's most important councils. The journey took more than three hundred years, during which the Godhood-Manhood of Jesus was promoted by diligent biblical exegesis and astute argument but also by imperial politics and by ecclesiastical intrigue, intimidation, and coercion. The presumed "consensus of the undivided church" was made possible only by leaving hundreds of casualties along the way. However, the dogmatic task is only to identify the most important christological *concepts* that emerged, leaving the history proper to the church historians.

1. Ignatius of Antioch

Particularly interesting among the Apostolic Fathers (for our present theme) is Ignatius, bishop of the church in Syrian Antioch, martyred in Rome under the emperor Trajan (ca. 110 CE). He does not hesitate in his letters to name Christ "God," "my God," "*the* God." If this appears surprising so soon after the passing of the Apostles, the explanation may be sought in the move of the gospel from a Jewish to a wider Hellenistic environment. But Ignatius can also call Christ God's "thought," "knowledge," "mouth," or "word"—expressions that seem to imply something other than a simple identification of Christ with God. The language of identity and the language of distinction lie side by side. Expressly excluded, however, are two christological errors: the judaizing error that fails to see the difference of Christ from the Old Testament prophets (ANF 1:84–85) and a hellenizing error for which Christ only *appeared* to be a real man of flesh and blood (69–71). The letters of Ignatius thus document both the deep source of christological affirmations in devotion to the Redeemer and the rise of erroneous views that called for theological correction.

6. H. R. Mackintosh, *The Doctrine of the Person of Jesus Christ* (Edinburgh: T. & T. Clark, 1923); John Macquarrie, *Jesus Christ in Modern Thought* (Philadelphia: Trinity Press International, 1990).

2. *Christological Heresies*

Many accounts of the person of Christ in the second century were eventually judged heretical; some came to be thought of as perennial deviations from catholic orthodoxy that are always with us. A fair account of them is doubly difficult because, despite modern archaeological discoveries, we still know them mainly from their orthodox adversaries and because the types named include both internal variations and mixtures with other types. No more than general descriptions can be attempted here. (See further the general works listed in the bibliography.)

Some heresies are commonly classed as either judaizing or hellenizing. (1) *Ebionism* was of the first type. The name, derived from Hebrew, characterizes its adherents or their doctrine as "poor" or "beggarly." A typical Ebionite Christology made Jesus the son of Joseph and Mary, chosen by God and endowed with the Spirit to be the Messiah—his reward for teaching fidelity to the law.

(2) *Gnosticism* was a heresy of the second, hellenizing type. Fundamental to all the gnostic systems is a dualistic metaphysic of spirit and matter that represents humans as imprisoned in a material world. The origin of the world is not to be attributed to a creative act of the Supreme God, for whom no contact with matter is possible. But from him there proceeded a succession of "aeons" (emanations), and it was the lowest of them, the Craftsman (*dēmiourgos*), who created the world and humans out of matter. In humans, however, there is a divine spark, smuggled in by a higher aeon without the Creator-God's notice. Because of the divine spark, humans are strangers in the world and long for redemption; but because the world is material and evil, it cannot be redeemed. The only hope is to escape, and this is achieved by the descent of a redeemer from a higher aeon who makes humans, or some humans, aware of their heavenly origin and destiny. It is the truth that makes them free (cf. John 8:32), but knowledge (*gnōsis*) is imparted to them not so much by rational argument as by myth, ritual, and the prescription of suitable patterns of behavior.

Obviously, since matter is evil, there could be no real incarnation of the redeemer. Some of the gnostics spoke of a temporary association of Christ and the man Jesus, whom he deserted before the crucifixion; others suggested that he came with a spiritual body or only appeared to have a body. Whereas the Ebionites, then, could not affirm the deity of Christ, the gnostics could not affirm his genuine humanity: they were guilty of *docetism*, the view that the Redeemer only *seemed* to be a human being (Greek *dokeō*, "to seem"). Nowadays, the elaborate mythology of Gnosticism strikes us as fantastic and absurd. But it spoke persuasively to the deep human sense of not being at home in the world, and this is an essential part of the Christian consciousness (Phil. 3:20–21; Heb. 13:14). It is not surprising that, for a time, Gnosticism seemed able to win the church.

A third heretical type, (3) *Marcionism*, had some affinities with Gnosticism, but it arose from a compelling sense of the grace of God. Marcion appeared in Rome around 140 CE and was shocked by the crude legalism of popular Christian piety. He learned from his teacher, the gnostic Cerdo, that there must be two Gods: the vindictive Creator-God of the Old Testament and the benevolent God of the New. Excommunicated for blaspheming the God of law, he established his own church and provided it with a drastic revision of the Bible. His remedy for the deplorable state of religion in Rome was to dissociate Christian belief entirely from the Old Testament and to ply an editorial knife on the New; from the New Testament he kept only an emended version of Luke and the "authentic" letters of Paul, rejecting as spurious the Pastorals and the Letter to the Hebrews. With his truncated Bible in hand, Marcion explained that redemption is simply the self-revelation of the God of love. In Christ the benevolent God, previously unknown, came in person. The distinction between the Father and the Son is in name only: "Son," or "Christ," denotes the one God in the mode of revelation. Marcion could not say that Christ assumed a real human body, and yet he thought that the crucifixion was the means by which humanity was redeemed from bondage to the Creator-God—"a glaring contradiction" perhaps, as Harnack judged, but Marcion held the docetic opinion that Christ suffered and died only in appearance. All in all, we may judge Marcionism a strange mixture, and yet we can hardly deny that Marcion himself showed a deeper insight into the gospel of grace than the orthodox divines who vehemently opposed his Christology.

Neither the Ebionites nor the gnostics succeeded in affirming both the deity and the humanity of Christ. The name "monarchians" was given to others who sought a way to secure the unity of the one sovereign God while giving Christ his due as Redeemer. They made their appearance in the second century, but their foremost champions flourished in the third. They too were eventually judged heretical, and the two kinds of monarchianism reflect, to some extent, the contrast between the Ebionite and the gnostic heresies. According to (4) *dynamic monarchianism*, the divine in Jesus was not deity incarnate but an influence or "power" (*dynamis*) from the one true God, conferred at either his birth or his baptism. He *became* God's Son; hence the dynamic monarchians are sometimes called *adoptionists*. Jesus was not a divine being who descended from above but a man of whom God gradually took complete possession. As Paul of Samosata, bishop of Antioch (deposed in 269), said of him, he was "Christ from below" (*Christos katōthen*).

(5) *Modalistic monarchianism* (or *Sabellianism*) was formulated partly in opposition to dynamic monarchianism, which the modalists rejected as a plain denial of Jesus' deity. Like Marcion, they argued that "Father" and "Son" are simply two names of one God in different modes of being. God in the flesh is called "the Son"; God apart from the flesh is called "the Father." But strictly speaking the Son *is* the Father (cf. John 10:30; 14:9). It was probably Sabellius (fl. ca. 215–220) who furthered earlier modalism by taking the Holy Spirit into account: "Father," "Son," and "Spirit" are three manifestations of the one God, "modes" God assumed in the course of his activity. But there is a good deal of uncertainty about the teaching of Sabellius. Some have held that he illustrated his meaning by a theatrical metaphor, taking the Greek word *prosōpon* in one of its senses: the identifying "mask" worn by an actor on the ancient Greek stage. Revelation is then like a divine drama in three acts: the same God appears successively behind the masks of Creator, Redeemer, and Sanctifier. That Sabellius did use the word *prosōpon* in this way is doubtful, but the metaphor may not be far from his thought.

If this secures the deity of the Son, it is not at all clear that modalism also required his genuine humanity. Perhaps the modalistic monarchians thought of God's second manifestation as only in a human *body*. In any case, if "Father" and "Son" are manifestations of one and the same deity, it is hard to account for the fact that the Gospels present Father and Son as (so to say) partners in dialogue. And the ancient critics of modalism were horrified at the implication that God the Father was born, suffered, and died. The modalists were *patripassians*, according to their adversaries, and orthodox Christianity has always held it to be utterly unthinkable that deity could undergo suffering. This, indeed, was the presupposition of the Logos theology, which set Christian faith on the path to Trinitarian orthodoxy by arguing for distinctions within the being of God rather than transient modes of God's existence. According to the Logos theologians, it was not God the Father who became incarnate but his Son, who is the Reason and Word of the Father.

3. The Logos Christology

For *Justin Martyr*, a pioneer of Logos Christology, the main christological problem was not how to reconcile the deity of Christ with strict monotheism but how to square the ineffability of God, which he learned from Middle Platonism, with the Old Testament stories about God's conspicuous activity in the world. The solution he proposed in his *Dialogue with Trypho* was that besides the ineffable Father, who cannot be seen by mortal eyes, there is his Son, the God of the Old Testament theophanies who walks and talks with humans (ANF 1:263). Christ is properly called "God" because he was not made but "begotten" by the will of the ineffable God before the work of creation (228–29). He is the Logos—the Word of God—as God's Son, not just as a messenger who brings tidings from God (264). The *logos* concept suited Justin's argument well. The Greek word means both "reason" and the spoken "word" that expresses reason. When we utter a word, he points out, we "beget" it, but not by cutting it off (not by "abscission"); though numerically distinct, it remains undiminished (it is still our thought), as a fire is not diminished when used to kindle other fires (227, 264). From the standpoint of later Trinitarianism, however, the difficulty is the apparent subordination of the Son; in his *First Apology* Justin calls him God "in second place" (166–67). And it is incongruous that he identifies the ineffable Deity with the Father of Jesus Christ, transforming the name of affection and intimacy (*abba*, "Father") into an expression of remoteness and unknowing. In this respect, he bequeathed a problem that Trinitarianism was never quite able to resolve.

For the antignostic father *Irenaeus* (ca. 130–ca. 200), as for Justin Martyr, Christ was God's Logos, but his chief point of entry into Christology was not Justin's problem of the ineffability of the Father. In his great treatise *Against Heresies*, known to us mainly in Latin translation, he argues from what Christ *did* to who he must *be*—both God and a real man (not a man in appearance only). In particular, he anticipates the so-called physical theory of atonement of the Alexandrian theologians that salvation is the imparting of divine life to humanity by the incarnation. Christ became what we are "that He might bring us to be even what He is Himself." For "unless man had been joined to God, he could never have become a partaker of incorruptibility." "Or how shall man pass into God, unless God has [first] passed into man?" (ANF 1:448, 507, 526).

But the incarnation was not the moment when the Word first began to be. Irenaeus guards against a possible misuse of the analogy between God's Word and a human word. Human words exist only when they are uttered, but the Logos, as the Father's Son, was with the Father from the beginning. We simply do not know how he was generated (375, 401, 445–46, 487–88). What we do know is that the incarnate Son was the second Adam, who by "recapitulation" reversed the consequences of the old Adam's disobedience (446, 454, 544, 548–49; cf. 391).

Some of Irenaeus's statements sound modalist: he says that the Father is "a simple, uncompounded Being"; that God is "all Logos"; that the Father is "the invisible of the Son," as the Son is "the visible of the Father"; and that God "rendered Himself visible" in the Son (374, 400, 469, 489). On the other hand, a personal distinction is presupposed when Irenaeus speaks of God's addressing the Word (his Son) and Wisdom (the Spirit) in the Genesis account of creation: "Let *us* make," etc. (487–88). In his later work, *Demonstration of the Apostolic Preaching*, he writes: "the Father is God and the Son is God; for that which is begotten of God is God. And so in the substance and power of His being there is shown forth one God; but there is also according to the economy of our redemption both Son and Father."[7] That certainly appears to be a kind of modalism, or at least a merely "economic Trinitarianism," in which it was only the implementation of God's redemptive "plan" (*oikonomia*, Eph. 3:9) that required the differentiation of Father, Son, and Spirit. But in J. N. D. Kelly's opinion Irenaeus recognized "the fact that there are real distinctions in the immanent being of the unique, indivisible Father, and that while these were only fully manifested in the 'economy,' they were actually there from all eternity." Be that as it may, we can agree with Kelly that it was "the great illustrative image . . . of a man with his intellectual and spiritual functions" that opened the path to orthodox Trinitarianism (1977: 108). Quite apart from the apparent ambiguity in Irenaeus's Christology, however, he clearly did not resolve the problem of the subordination of the Son to the Father: "for among men also," he says, "every son is the servant of his father."[8]

The second great antignostic theologian, and the first of the Fathers to write major theological treatises in Latin, *Tertullian* (ca. 160–ca. 220) defended the idea of an economic Trinity against the modalistic monarchians. There is indeed, as they insist, one God, but they wrongly suppose that we can believe in one God and avoid polytheism only if "Father," "Son," and "Spirit" are simply names of the self-same person in different, successive circumstances. The truth is, according to Tertullian, that the work of creation and redemption demanded in the divine being an actual "economy," by which he meant, like Irenaeus, the order, arrangement, or functional distribution required by the divine plan (rather than the plan itself, as in Eph. 3:9). The catholic faith is that the unity of the divine *substance* is distributed into a Trinity of three *persons* as "number without division" (*Against Praxeas*, ANF 3:598). Tertullian gave currency to the word *Trinity*, and his distinction between "substance" and

7. Iain M. MacKenzie, *Irenaeus's Demonstration of the Apostolic Preaching: A Theological Commentary and Translation* (Aldershot: Ashgate, 2002), 15. The translation is by J. Armitage Robinson (1920).
8. *Demonstration*, §51 (MacKenzie, 16).

"person" entered the standard language of orthodox Trinitarianism. *Substantia* (Greek *ousia*) referred to the divine essence; *persona* (Greek *hypostasis*) meant an individual subsistence—not, or not necessarily, an individual consciousness like "person" in our usage.

Tertullian also anticipated the orthodox formula that the incarnate Word was composed of two distinct substances or natures in one person. He was both God and Man, and each nature retained its distinctive properties. The divine nature (the Spirit) worked the miracles; the human nature (the flesh) hungered, suffered, and died (*Against Praxeas,* ANF 3:624). As the divine Reason, the Logos had existed from eternity within God; to bring about the creation, the Logos proceeded from God as his Word, and this is what we are to understand as the "begetting" of the Son (600–602). If we say, "There was a time when the Son was not" (a sentiment that was fiercely contested in the later Arian controversy), we can only mean that the eternal Logos first became also the *Son* of God when he proceeded from the Father (*Against Hermogenes,* ANF 3:478).[9] Like Justin, Tertullian asserted that in the Old Testament it was not the ineffable Father but the Son who "came down to hold converse with men," and he represented the theophanies as rehearsals for the incarnation (*Against Praxeas,* ANF 3:612).

Once again, the mystery of deity is explained partly by analogy with the mind and speech of a human, and Tertullian finds his warrant for the analogy in the creation of humanity in the image and likeness of God (*Against Praxeas,* ANF 3:600–601). The resulting subordination of the Son as "second to God the Father" (602) is accentuated when Tertullian says, "the Father is the entire substance, but the Son is a derivation and portion of the whole" (603–4). He points out, however, that there is no Father without the Son. A father makes a son, but it is equally true that a son makes a father: "A father must needs have a son, in order to be a father" (604). Perhaps, then, it makes better sense when Tertullian suggests that, since God was always God, "God" is more properly "the designation of the substance itself" (*Against Hermogenes*, ANF 3:478). The obvious alternative would be to assert that God *was* always a Father, and this is the alternative stated by Origen of Alexandria. Origen brought the Logos doctrine closer to orthodoxy by maintaining that the distinction between Father and Son denotes a timeless relationship within the being of God (*On First Principles,* ANF 4:246). Yet Origen still judged it acceptable to call the Son a "second God" (*Against Celsus,* ANF 4:561), and he thought it inappropriate to address every kind of prayer to Christ: there is a kind of prayer (*proseuchē*) that should be addressed only to the Father, to whom the Savior himself prayed and teaches us to pray (*On Prayer,* LCC 2:266–71, interpreting 1 Tim. 2:1).

4. From Nicaea (325) to Chalcedon (451)

The christological options that sprang up in the first three centuries of the church were in detail diverse, partly because of the diversity of the New Testament witness to Christ. But they were not chaotic; a pattern is perceptible.

9. Tertullian described the begetting of the Son as "prolation," which effects distinction without division as a root puts forth a tree, a spring a river, and the sun its ray (*Against Praxeas,* ANF 3:602–3, 617; cf. 607). But *prolatio* (Greek *probolē*) was tainted by gnostic usage and did not become a regular part of Trinitarian discourse.

The antithesis of a judaizing and a hellenizing type of heresy in the second century was reflected during the third century in the two varieties of monarchianism. Against them, the Logos theologians insisted that the Son of God was not merely an extraordinary man, chosen and empowered by God (dynamic monarchianism), and that "Son" is not simply another name for one and the same God the Father (modalistic monarchianism). Justin, Irenaeus, and Tertullian related Father and Son by means of a psychological analogy: the two are related as are a human person and the person's thought or speech. The Son is thus other than the Father and yet of the same essence or substance. Looking back from the Council of Nicaea, then, we may conclude that by the beginning of the fourth century the church was moving toward a common mind on the person of Christ, yet without the benefit of a formal dogmatic definition. But the appearance of Arianism on the theological scene around 319 CE threw the church into a protracted and bitter controversy. The Council of Nicaea was called to settle it but had only limited success.

Arius (d. 336) argued that there cannot be divisions within the Godhead and that God cannot communicate his substance to another; such thinking subjects the indivisible God to physical categories. We have to distinguish two *logoi*: the immanent Logos in God is an impersonal function within the being of God, who brought the Son into existence as a second Logos to be his intermediary in the work of creation. Accordingly, there was a "then" when the Son did not exist and God, a pure monad, dwelt alone. Even though the generation of the Son was unique, "begetting" is only a special kind of "making" or "creating"; the Son, begotten by God, is a created being. He is not of the same substance as the Father, and he has only a very limited knowledge of the Father, who is finally ineffable even to the Son. We call him "Logos" as a courtesy—"by grace"—because he participates in his Father's immanent Logos. It is the second Logos that became flesh, that is, who came to occupy a human body, just as the body in an ordinary human is occupied by a soul. He received the title "Lord" (Phil. 2:9–11) and may even be called "God" in recognition of his special status as God's vicegerent.

We know the teaching of Arius chiefly from the refutation of it in the polemical treatises of Athanasius (ca. 296–373), who became bishop of Alexandria (328 CE) after the Council of Nicaea.[10] Given his conception of what it means to be saved by Christ, it is understandable that he became the implacable foe of Arius. In his treatise *On the Incarnation of the Word,* written before the appearance of Arius, Athanasius had spoken for the typically Alexandrian idea of Christ and his mission: "he was made man that we might be made God" (NPNF[2] 4:65). When the controversy began, he had his major weapon already in hand: he confronted Arianism with the physical idea of redemption as the imparting of divine life to humanity—in a word, "deification." Later, in his second discourse *Against the Arians,* he wrote: "man had not been deified if joined to a creature, or unless the Son were very God . . . [and] we had not been delivered from sin

10. The most important work by Arius, his *Thalia,* written in meter, is liberally quoted in Athanasius, *Against the Arians,* Discourse I, 2.5–6 (NPNF[2] 4:308–9), and *Councils of Ariminum and Seleucia,* Part II, §15 (NPNF[2] 4:457–58).

and the curse, unless it had been by nature human flesh which the Word put on" (NPNF² 4:386).

The anti-Arians won the day at the Council of Nicaea. The council declared in its creed that the Son is of one substance with the Father and added express anathemas against the Arian teaching that the Son is a created being who did not always exist.[11] In addition to the five christological heresies already named, the ancient church thus denounced (6) *Arianism* also as heretical: in a word, the belief in a supernatural but not strictly divine being that became incarnate in Jesus Christ. But the Arian controversy continued, and interest was extended from the internal relations within the Godhead to the relationship between the divine and human natures in the incarnate Lord.

The two-natures dogma of the Council of Chalcedon is not a precise explanation of the relation between deity and humanity in Jesus Christ; in the main, it is an explicit exclusion of three explanations found wanting. These too must be added to the list of christological heresies. (7) *Apollinarianism*, named for Apollinarius (the Younger) of Laodicea (ca. 310–390), proposed that in the incarnate Lord the eternal Reason of God (the Logos) took the place of the human spirit or intellect. The obvious flaw in this proposal was that it left Jesus only two-thirds human (see 1 Thess. 5:23). (8) *Nestorianism*, attributed to Nestorius (patriarch of Constantinople, d. ca. 451), preserved the full humanity of Christ by explaining the indwelling of the Logos as a conjunction (*synapheia*) of two wills. Nestorianism represented the christological approach of the school of Antioch through moral categories rather than the metaphysical categories of the rival school of Alexandria. (9) *Eutychianism* (Eutyches, ca. 378–ca. 455), reacting to the apparent dualism of Nestorian Christology, maintained that after the union there was only one nature in the person of Christ. Against these three unacceptable views, the Chalcedonian Definition proclaimed that the true humanity of Christ includes "a rational soul" (against the Apollinarians) and that in the one person of Christ are two natures "without confusion or change" (against the Eutychians) and "without division or separation" (against the Nestorians).

Not even the decisions made at Chalcedon silenced the christological debate: *monophysites* insisted that deity and humanity in the incarnate Lord are fused into one entity (*physis*), and *monothelites* argued that the human and divine wills in Christ are fused into one will (*thelēma*). The anti-Chalcedonian gainsayers were excluded from the mainline churches in both the East and the West. But the Monophysite tradition has been preserved to the present day in the Oriental Orthodox (not Eastern Orthodox) churches, though some deny that it is their official doctrine; and Nestorianism, the polar opposite of Monophysitism, has always had its champions in the Assyrian Church of the East.

From the believing standpoint of "the Great Church," the course of christological doctrine was a providentially governed advance to orthodoxy through the minefields of heresy. But in every later time the point of arrival must be

11. The creed of the Council of Nicaea is not our Nicene Creed, promulgated by the Council of Constantinople (381). The Nicene Creed reaffirms the Council of Nicaea's declaration that the Son is "of one substance with the Father" and adds, albeit without the term *homoousios*, that the Holy Spirit is worshipped and glorified together with the Father and the Son. It should be noted that *homoousios* (of the same substance or essence) was no absolute guarantee of orthodoxy (it had been used by the heretic Paul of Samosata) and that the Council of Nicaea used *ousia* and *hypostasis* synonymously.

open to reassessment by our two main dogmatic criteria: the Apostolic witness to Jesus Christ and contemporary thought and experience. The task requires not only knowledge of the formulas the church arrived at, but also an understanding of the theological motives that led to them and the intellectual conditions that determined them. The *motive* of Athanasius, for example, in his polemic against Arianism, clearly showed what I take to be the logic of a sound christological argument: from the nature of the salvation sought and bestowed (for Athanasius, the "deification" of humanity) to the attributes of the Savior who bestows it. Arthur Cushman McGiffert may illustrate what I have in mind by the prevailing intellectual *conditions* of christological construction: "If the Stoic metaphysic had been dominant instead of the Platonic, and the immanence of God, or the oneness of divine and human nature, had been recognized by the Nicene theologians, the doctrine of the Trinity would have been unnecessary" (1954: 1:275). But now, before shifting to the constructive mode, I must turn, much more briefly, to some of the internal criticisms and revisions of Chalcedon that have emerged within the Western churches in modern times.

III. The Remaking of Christological Dogma

The Chalcedonian Definition ("two natures in one person") was the authorized christological doctrine of the Eastern and Western churches throughout the medieval period, and it still is for the majority of churches in the present. The Protestant Reformation witnessed the emergence of anti-Trinitarian dissent, notably in the theology of the Socinians, named after Laelius Socinus (1525–62) and his nephew Faustus (1539–1604). But the Protestants remained faithful to the ancient creeds. Luther, it is true, could say in one of his sermons, "Christ is not called 'Christ' because he has two natures. What is that to me?" (WA 17/1:255). And in another sermon he said, "To believe in Christ does not mean to believe that Christ is a person who is both God and man. That helps nobody" (WA 16:217). This, of course, is not heresy but the preacher's concern to bring home to his hearers the meaning of Christ's person for their salvation. Melanchthon makes the same point in his *Loci Communes* (1521): "to know Christ is to know his benefits, and not . . . to reflect upon his natures and the modes of his incarnation" (LCC 19:21–22). The Lutherans did suspect the Calvinists of the Nestorian heresy, and the Calvinists retorted that the Lutherans were guilty of Eutychianism; but the reciprocal accusations rested on unquestioning fidelity to Chalcedonian Christology.[12]

12. Other disputed issues between the Lutherans and the Calvinists were certainly christological. The doctrine of the communication of attributes between Christ's two natures (the *communicatio idiomatum*) was essential to Lutheran eucharistic teaching on the ubiquity of Christ's body. Another dispute concerned what the Lutherans called *illud extra calvinisticum*—Calvin's insistence that the Word was not confined in the incarnation but remained active also *extra carnem* ("outside the flesh"): he "continuously filled the world even as he had done from the beginning" (*Institutes*, 1:481). This says no more than Athanasius said in his *On the Incarnation of the Word*, §17 (NPNF^2 4:70). It is not to be identified with the later Reformed watchword *finitum non capax infiniti* (literally, "the finite not capable of the infinite"), which, as far as I know, does not appear in Calvin.

1. Two Developments in Modern Christology

The seventeenth century was the heyday of Protestant orthodoxy. But the eighteenth century witnessed numerous departures from church dogmas—and, indeed, direct and explicit criticisms of them. There is no possibility of reviewing all the new departures here, not even all the new directions in Christology. But I should note at least two developments that, carried over into the nineteenth century, transformed the inherited doctrine of Christ's person in the thinking of many Protestant theologians.

(1) First, *the christological question* changed. In traditional orthodoxy, the cardinal problem was how to think of the relationship between the divine and the human *natures* in the incarnate Christ; the new question was how the religious *ideal* is related to its manifestation in Jesus. It is not so much that God walked the soil of Galilee as that God embodied in one person God's design for all humanity. What was incarnated was not a divine being, but the ideal relationship between God and humans. Of course, the new question was not unprecedented; it was foreshadowed in the second Adam theme of Paul and Irenaeus. If we put it in terms of Logos Christology, we may say that the original linguistic development—from the personification of a divine faculty to the name of a divine person—was reversed. The *logos* that "became flesh" was not a personal being, the supposed subject of the Redeemer's earthly activity, but rather a personification of God's eternal plan for the world and humanity. Christological differences may then be said to lie partly in different interpretations of the ideal, partly in different estimates of the extent to which the ideal was manifested in Jesus. For Kant, the ideal was a person morally well-pleasing to God, of which we may become aware through the example of Jesus, though no example is strictly necessary. For Schleiermacher, it was God-consciousness, the consciousness of absolute dependence, embodied absolutely in Jesus. For Hegel, it was the oneness of deity and humanity, infinite Spirit and finite spirit, brought by Jesus the "God-Man" into the consciousness of humanity.

One effect of the new christological question was to focus attention on the humanity of Jesus as the embodiment of the ideal. Hence (2) *the christological method* turned toward the presumed historical narratives in the Gospels. A conservative approach then explained the evident limitations of the man Jesus (see, e.g., Mark 13:32) by arguing that he must have concealed some of his divine attributes, or even (for a time) divested himself of them. The notion that he "emptied himself" produced a variety of so-called *kenosis* theories, which appealed to Philippians 2:7 (*heauton ekenōsen;* cf. 2 Cor. 8:9). Unfortunately, as interest in the life of Jesus grew, the difficulty of recovering historical knowledge about him became only too clear. One problem was that the Gospels related supernatural events that were beyond the credence of "the modern mind." Perhaps the Gospels were written as deliberate frauds by Jesus' disciples (Reimarus) or as innocent myths generated in the community of devout believers in Christ (Strauss). Or perhaps, as the so-called rationalists thought, it was possible to recover at least a core of credible facts by attributing the miracle stories to prescientific ignorance of natural causes; with the aid of modern science, the historian was at last able to recover fact from fantasy (Paulus). By the end of the nineteenth century, neither kenotic nor rationalist readings of the life of Jesus had escaped trenchant criticism. Ritschl judged that a kenotic Christology was "pure mythology"; A. E. Biedermann (1819–85) remarked that a complete kenosis of the intelligence was required to believe it. Of the *rationalist* reading of the Gospels, Otto Pfleiderer (1839–1908) decided that it "everywhere retains the husk and surrenders the religious kernel." A fresh beginning was called for; I take note of it in my constructive section. But first I should pause long enough to assign Schleiermacher his place in the development of modern Christology.

2. *The Contribution of Schleiermacher*

Schleiermacher offered a double test, experiential and historical, for a sound christological statement: "nothing concerning Him [the Redeemer] can be set up as real doctrine unless it is connected with His redeeming causality [experienced in the Christian community] and can be traced to the original impression made [on the first disciples] by His existence" (*CF* 125). Because his dogmatics was written for the Church of the Union, Schleiermacher also gave due attention to the Lutheran and Reformed confessions, but always critical attention. His critique of Chalcedonian orthodoxy, which the confessions affirmed, has been misunderstood as a total dismissal of the idea of incarnation. Sometimes, indeed, he is represented as inclined to Ebionism, whereas in fact he considered Ebionism to be not merely wrong but heretical (*CF* 99, 396),[13] and it might be better to compare his Christology with the second Adam doctrine of Irenaeus. Like Irenaeus and Athanasius, he rested his conception of the Redeemer partly on the experience of redemption in the Christian community, which meant, for him, the experience of being drawn into the captivating power of Christ's consciousness of God. Christ's person was constituted by the unique awareness of God that made him founder of the new corporate life. In him, and him alone, was realized the possibility of original perfection—a life determined in every moment by consciousness of God, which is what Schleiermacher meant by Christ's "sinless perfection." The Redeemer was not simply an example (*Vorbild*) of God-consciousness, not even an exceptional example, but the ideal (*Urbild*) "become completely historical," and this can only be understood as an actual being of God in him. "[F]or to ascribe to Christ an absolutely powerful God-consciousness, and to attribute to Him an existence [*Sein*] of God in Him, are exactly the same thing" (*CF* 377, 385, 387).

By this route Schleiermacher affirms, with the tradition, the unique union of deity and humanity in Christ, even though he goes on to subject the ecclesiastical *formulas* for Christ's person, including the two-natures dogma, to a searching critique. He states categorically that "unless the being of God in Christ is assumed, the idea of redemption could not be . . . concentrated in His Person" (*CF* 738). However, we should not speak of the divine *nature* uniting with human nature in Christ's person but rather of the *being* of God in Christ. The preferred expression echoes, of course, Paul's statement that "God was in

13. Cf. his critique of "empirical" ideas of redemption and reconciliation as effected merely by teaching and example (*CF* §100.3 [430–31]; §101.3 [434–35]). It is astonishing that some who think they must disapprove of Schleiermacher's Christology can charge him with holding precisely the view of Christ's work and person that he most firmly rejected (see, e.g., McCready 2005: 28–29, 260).

Christ" (2 Cor. 5:19; see *CF* 397, 458). In short, Schleiermacher's understanding of Christ's person as the source of redemption rests on the objective union of the divine being and human nature in the incarnation: it is in the incarnation, together with the union of divine and human in the church, that the uniqueness of Christianity consists. "Otherwise, if in other faiths also we find God becoming Man [*Menschwerdung Gottes*], and a communication of the Divine Spirit [like the communication of the Spirit to the church], what would be the absolutely new thing in Christianity?" (46; cf. 738).[14]

Although in general, as we will see, I affirm the two christological developments I have noted, they cannot be taken for the only, or even the main, direction in the many-sided present-day reflection on the person of Christ, and they are not immune to criticism. Neither is Schleiermacher. Already in his own day he was charged with *imposing* the ideal on the historical Jesus. The very notion of an absolute embodiment of the ideal in a single person (*CF* 377) struck many of his contemporaries as a thoroughly unhistorical notion. For Schleiermacher, the absolute perfection of Christ was a clear implication of the Christian consciousness; he thought it would be all over with Christian faith if we could not rule out the appearance of another, more perfect God-consciousness in the future (378). In his lectures on the life of Jesus, published posthumously (1864), he accepted the challenge to show the harmony between his dogmatic Christ and the historical Jesus. But his *Life of Jesus* was severely criticized (notably by D. F. Strauss), and I will need to avoid what I too must consider the indefensible claim he fell into. It is one thing to say that Christ *disclosed* or *presented* the ideal, quite another to believe he *actualized* it.

IV. God in Christ

The heart of Christian faith is finding God in Jesus Christ. His words and deeds convinced the first disciples that he was the long-awaited Messiah, sent to announce the imminent coming of the reign of God. They recognized in him a singular intimacy with God, whom he called his Father, and an unshakable commitment to his Father's will. Driven at first to despair by the shattering events of his suffering and death, they became convinced that his death was not the end, that he had risen and would come again in glory like Daniel's son of man. The title "Messiah" served to convey the significance of Jesus in the Jewish world into which he was born. But in the wider Gentile world it lost its original meaning and became a proper name, "Christ." Similarly, the title "the Son of Man" was severed from its roots in Jewish apocalyptic and became simply a token of his humanity. Other ways of conveying the experience of finding God in Jesus moved to the center, some taken from the original gospel story, some not.

14. Occasionally, as here, Schleiermacher uses *Menschwerdung Gottes* ("God's becoming man"), the customary German word for "incarnation" (see also *CF* §13.1 [64]; §118.1 [540]). But it does not suit his understanding of Christ's person as well as the language of "union" (*Vereinigung*), which is actually closer to Chalcedonian orthodoxy.

1. Christ as Lord and God Incarnate

Thomas's confession, "My Lord and my God" (John 20:28), is a compelling expression of finding God, or being found by God, in Jesus Christ. We may say the same of the later affirmations "Jesus Christ is God and man" and "God became man." They too can be understood as expressions of the discovery of faith. But they cannot be taken literally as factual assertions. John Hick rightly insists, "to say, without explanation, that the historical Jesus of Nazareth was also God is as devoid of meaning as to say that this circle drawn with a pencil on paper is also a square" (in Hick 1977: 178). And we have to agree with Paul Tillich: "the assertion that 'God has become man' is not a paradoxical but a nonsensical statement. It is a combination of words which makes sense only if it is not meant to mean what the words say" (1951–63, 2:94). The dogmatic theologian, then, is bound to prefer the biblical affirmations "Jesus is *Lord*" and "God was *in* Christ." And even they, appropriate as they are at the primary linguistic level, need historical and theological interpretation if they are to meet the requirements of dogmatic understanding.

We can say that the catholic church was right to reject the Arian view of Christ as a supernatural but not divine being, even though it seems to be a sound reading of the early Christian hymn in Philippians 2:6–11. The reason for rejection is not the one usually given: that only God can reveal God. If strictly applied, that would raise doubts about the prophetic claim, "Thus says the Lord," and even about Jesus' saying, "My teaching is not mine but his who sent me" (John 7:16). The Word of God in Scripture is mediated—spoken in various ways by the prophets and in the last days by a son (Heb. 1:1–2)—but the revealer is invariably God. The Arians could be faulted for attributing to the Logos only a limited knowledge of God but not for assuming that God's revelation can be, and is, mediated. The problem with Arianism, however, is that its second Logos belonged to a mythological world inhabited by supernatural beings whose activity resembled the activity of humans. The ancients believed in such a world; today we don't.

But must we not find equally problematic the orthodox notion of the Lord as a preexistent supernatural being who assumed human form and became incarnate in Jesus of Nazareth? Taken literally, such a notion is incurably docetic, impossible to square with Jesus' real humanity, and it too has every appearance of being mythological. But metaphorically taken, as the poetic style of Philippians 2:6–11 suggests, it attests the appearance of Christ as a cosmic event. It affirms, in its own way, the traditional persuasion that Christ was already present and active in the world before his manifestation and that the efficacy of his once-for-all sacrifice for sin is not time-bound (1 Cor. 10:4; Rev. 13:8, NRSV note). The work and person of Christ were creative events that brought about a new situation in human history; yet Christian faith sees them as woven into the fabric of the creation. The picture of the Lord as the cosmic Christ, God's agent in creation and preservation, though mythological in form, upholds the harmony of creation and redemption against the Marcionite heresy. The coming of Christ is placed in the setting of the Creator's design for humanity; but strictly it is the divine plan, not Christ the divine person, that is preexistent. In the narrative mode, as in Philippians 2, the cosmic Christ serves also as a symbol of the humility of the Son of Man, who might have lived in undisturbed communion with his Father but had nowhere to lay his head (Matt. 8:20; Luke 9:58) and gave his life as a ransom for many (Mark 10:45).

The christological dogma, however, calls the Son of Man not merely "Lord," but "God." If we are to avoid the unacceptable consequences of taking literally the language of identity—"Jesus Christ *is* God"—the Pauline expression "God was *in* Christ" (2 Cor. 5:19) is clearly preferable. It harmonizes well with other christological statements in the New Testament. Paul writes elsewhere that the Son is "the image [*eikōn*] of the invisible God" and that "in him the whole fullness of deity dwells bodily" (Col. 1:15; 2:9; cf. 1:19). The Letter to the Hebrews declares that the Son "is the reflection of God's glory and the exact imprint of God's very being" (Heb. 1:3). In the Fourth Gospel Jesus himself says, "Whoever has seen me has seen the Father" (John 14:9). All of these locutions point to Christ not as God but as the way to God (cf. John 14:6). The Pauline language in 2 Corinthians, however, is particularly apposite because it tells of an *activity* of which God is the subject: "God was in Christ reconciling the world to himself" (or, "in Christ God was reconciling the world to himself"). Paul's language in this passage does not amount to an explanation of how God's activity and Christ's are related, but it points further thought in the right direction. In the words of P. T. Forsyth, God and man "meet in action . . . not as two entities or natures which coexist, but as two movements in mutual interplay, mutual struggle, and reciprocal communion" (1909: 336).[15] What Forsyth called "the moralising of dogma" recalls the christological approach of the school of Antioch, which was intended to affirm the presence of the deity in Christ without compromising the humanity that made him "the firsborn among many brothers" (Rom. 8:29 NRSV note; cf. Heb. 2:11; 1 John 3:2). But what do we really know about the man Jesus?

2. *The Jesus of History*

The story of what is nowadays called "the *first* quest for the historical Jesus" was told in Albert Schweitzer's magisterial study, *The Quest of the Historical Jesus,* first published in 1906. In Schweitzer's view the story ended with his demonstration, in agreement with Reimarus (1694–1768) and Johannes Weiss (1863–1914), that the historical Jesus was a failed eschatological prophet whose prediction of the end proved mistaken; he was a man of his own time and not a teacher with a moral and spiritual message for every time. But the second edition of Schweitzer's book (1913) showed that the quest was not over: he had to take account of new work on the life of Jesus, and he entered into the fierce public debate launched by the "Christ-myth" thesis of Arthur Drews and others that the "historical Jesus" was a pious fiction. In the preface to the sixth edition (1950) Schweitzer stood by his eschatological interpretation of the Synoptic Gospels, but he admitted that it had not succeeded in dominating the latest writing on the life of Jesus, and he left it to others to bring order to the chaos.

15. The language of "mutual interplay" is preferable to saying, as many have said in the recent christological discussion, that Christ's humanity was "transparent to deity." But the notion of interplay between deity and humanity does raise again the questions discussed in chaps. 5–6.

However, he reaffirmed his view that the spiritualizing of the kingdom of God began with Jesus himself and continued under the influence of his Spirit. By his ethical emphasis on love as the condition of belonging to the kingdom, Jesus transformed the Jewish idea of the kingdom into "the spiritual and ethical reality that it is for us." Johannes Weiss had made a similar concession to modernity. After razing the exegetical foundations of the Ritschlian notion of the kingdom of God as an ethical and social ideal, Weiss endorsed its use in systematic theology, and he recognized that Jesus' teaching on the goodness and love of God was independent of his eschatological proclamation (Weiss 1971: 23, 51–53). But neither Weiss nor Schweitzer showed how the eschatological vision might itself be appropriated in the modern world. That was the task that Rudolf Bultmann undertook.

That Jesus never existed was not the opinion of serious New Testament scholars, but in his book *Jesus* (1926) Bultmann appeared to offer little more: "I do indeed think that we can now know almost nothing concerning the life and personality of Jesus, since the early Christian sources show no interest in either." His own interest was in the message of Jesus, of which "we know enough . . . to make for ourselves a consistent picture." Bultmann found the meaning of New Testament eschatology in an existentialist view of the human situation. Jesus' proclamation of the kingdom is not about something to come in the course of time: it compels a person to decision *here and now.* "If men are standing in the crisis of decision, and if precisely this crisis is the essential characteristic of their humanity, then every hour is the last hour, and we can understand that for Jesus the whole contemporary mythology is pressed into the service of this conception of human existence" (Bultmann 1958: 8, 12, 51–52). In other words, eschatology is not dead: it only needs to be demythologized. But Bultmann's former students came to believe there was more to be said about the life and personality of Jesus even if the fragmentary character of the sources, as shown by form criticism, made a continuous biography in the strict sense impossible. The so-called *new* quest was launched.

Before the end of the twentieth century there was also a *third* quest that asked what light could be shed on the historical Jesus from research into his world, particularly the Jewish world. And there was an extraordinary flurry of other proposals about the "real" Jesus, ranging from technical works of esoteric scholarship to racy publications that courted a public sensation. The search for the historical Jesus continues in the twenty-first century. I have offered some further thoughts on the subject in *Saving and Secular Faith.* But it is not the duty of the dogmatic theologian to review what Schweitzer already in 1950 called "the chaos of modern lives of Jesus," only to ask, What is its pertinence to Christian faith? My answer, stated in thesis 11, is of course aligned with my previous conclusions about the nature of faith (in chaps. 1 and 9) and Christ's twofold work as the gift of faith and the creation of the community of faith (chap. 10).

3. *The Christ of Faith*

Throughout the quest for the historical Jesus, a constant theme has been the existence of a troublesome gap between the church's Christ and the "real" Jesus. Indeed, if—with Schweitzer—we take the work of Reimarus as the point of departure, it is evident that the quest was first undertaken to discredit the preaching even of Jesus' original disciples as an attempt to cover up the alleged failure of his mission. Sometimes, however, the intention has been to reassure Christian faith with historically verifiable facts about him; and this, I think, has been misguided. To shift attention from the "power" of the Word (Rom. 1:16; 1 Cor. 1:18) to the historical quest is to risk distracting faith from its actual foundation. Hence my eleventh thesis states that *the Redeemer is not the so-called Jesus of history (not, that is, a historical reconstruction) but the Christ of faith who is proclaimed in the church as the living Savior.*

No one has seen more clearly than Schleiermacher that the *genesis* of Christian faith (perhaps we should say "evangelical faith") is the same in us as in the first disciples: Christ works faith by the irresistible impression of his person. In agreement with the Reformation confessions, Schleiermacher writes: "The constant factor is above all the divine power of the Word—taking the expression in its widest sense—by which conversion is still effected and faith still arises. The difference is simply that the self-revelation of Christ is now mediated by those who preach Him; but they being appropriated by Him as His instruments, the activity really proceeds from Him and is essentially His own" (*CF* 490–91; cf. 477–78).[16] In Schleiermacher's view, the sermon that effects conversion and faith is the presentation of the New Testament "picture" of Christ by one who has experienced its redeeming power and whose preaching is therefore testimony (68–69, 363–64, 587–88, etc.). And he held that the New Testament writings themselves already have the character of a "preaching" from which comes faith—independently of any theory about biblical inspiration (592–93).

Echoes of Schleiermacher's insights on the genesis of Christian faith can be heard in Wilhelm Herrmann (1846–1922) and Martin Kähler (1835–1912). Kähler wrote, "When . . . Christian faith is defined [by Wilhelm Herrmann] as a being 'overpowered' by Christ as he encounters us in the picture the Bible paints of him, that seems to me a fitting definition so far as it refers to the finally decisive and sufficient motivating factor in faith and piety" (1964: 77). The trajectory from Schleiermacher to Kähler is persuasive. The Gospels were not written as historical sources for reconstructing the Jesus of history (though the historian may use them as such) but rather as witnesses: they tell us what Jesus *meant* to the first generation of believers in order to kindle the same faith in others (cf. John 20:30–31; see further Ogden 1982).

But if faith is not produced by the quest for the historical Jesus, could it be either confirmed or shaken by it (depending on its results)? The answer is, I think, that just as the picture of Christ is (as a matter of fact) the *source* of Christian faith, the *confirmation* of faith lies (as a matter of fact) in the transmission of the picture in the corporate life of the Christian community. The security of faith rests not on what historians can reconstruct behind the New Testament picture of Christ but on the picture itself as the sacramental Word by which the historical community is continually recreated. In this sense, the new community of faith is part two of the work of Christ. Strictly, of course, the picture

16. By "the Word in its widest sense" Schleiermacher means "the whole prophetic activity of Christ" (*CF* 490; cf. 444–45). Those who follow Bultmann say (more narrowly) that faith is a response to the kerygma.

of Christ comes to us in several portraits and through several communities of faith. But the variations are not mutually exclusive, and the total picture is consistent enough for the churches to agree in their exclusion of the apocryphal gospels and to be perplexed even at some of the sayings attributed to Jesus in the canonical Gospels (e.g., Mark 7:27; 11:14, 21).

It remains to add (the second part of thesis 11) that the proclamation of the Word is *the disclosure both of authentic humanity and of the design of God the Creator.* By adding that this is *represented in the dogma of Christ's "two natures,"* I would not wish to imply that this is *all* the Chalcedonian formula, "two natures in one person," does and means. The relation of the divine and the human in Jesus of Nazareth remains a legitimate theological question. But the primary interest of dogmatic theology is to understand the meaning and implications of the faith that actually occurs through Jesus Christ. And by "faith" I mean *insight* through Christ, not *beliefs* about him. This must be asserted against two possible distractions.

(1) Faith in Christ has often been commended by pointing to his miracles. It is true that, although Jesus was troubled by the demand for a sign from heaven (Mark 8:11–12), his healing miracles evidently carried conviction, or were expected to carry conviction, with at least some who witnessed them (Matt. 11:4–5; 12:22–28; John 10:38). But for us today, who cannot witness them, the appeal to miracles can only impose on us a demand for *belief;* it is the present encounter with Christ in the Word that creates *faith.* For many, the gift of faith may well incline them to belief in the miracles, but that is quite different from expecting the reported miracles to generate faith: the belief is the implication, not the precondition, of faith.

(2) Admittedly, this is not the "faith" of the so-called Athanasian Creed, a Western creed that cannot be attributed to Athanasius but must have made its appearance sometime during the christological controversies after his death. It warns us (in the standard English translation, *CC* 2:66): "Whosoever will be saved: before all things it is necessary that he hold the Catholic Faith, which Faith except everyone do keep whole and undefiled: without doubt he shall perish everlastingly." It then proceeds—in abstract, metaphysical terms—to state the orthodox doctrines of the Trinity and the incarnation. On Christ's person the creed declares: "the right Faith is, that we believe and confess that our Lord Jesus Christ, the Son of God, is God and Man; God, of the Substance of the Father, begotten before the worlds, and Man, of the Substance of his Mother, born in the world" (68), and so on. We must resist this equation of "right faith" with authorized belief. Whatever one may make of the Athanasian Creed as a statement of Trinitarian and christological orthodoxy, the saving faith that the Christ of faith creates is clearly something else: a transformed perception of the meaning of one's life rather than assent to objective metaphysical propositions. (Recall Luther's admonition, "To believe in Christ does not mean to believe that Christ is a person who is both God and man. That helps nobody.") The following two chapters will look more closely at the *experience* of faith through the two traditional doctrines of justification and sanctification, or, as I prefer to say, reconciliation and renewal.

12. Living by Faith (I): Reconciliation

The confidence of faith, as restoration of the elemental trust that estrangement erodes, is reconciliation to God and God's purposes; and since faith is created through the proclamation of God's "paternal" goodwill in Christ (Christ's prophetic activity), reconciliation by the free forgiveness of sins is called "adoption into the household of God" or being "born again."'

Luther singled out *justification* (or some equivalent expression) as "the chief article" and "the sum of the gospel." In his *Lectures on Galatians* (1535) he declared: "As I often warn, therefore, the doctrine of justification must be learned diligently. For in it are included all the other doctrines of our faith; and if it is sound, all the others are sound as well" (LW 26:283). The charter document of the Lutheran reformation, the Augsburg Confession (1530), showed that for the Lutherans the doctrine of justification not only regulated other doctrines but also provided a critical standard by which (in the second part of the confession) abuses in the life of the church were to be identified and censured: "Moreover it is taught [by the Lutherans] that all ordinances and traditions instituted by men for the purpose of propitiating God and earning grace are contrary to the Gospel and the teaching about faith in Christ" (*BC* 36–37). The "teaching about faith in Christ" means justification by faith, which the Lutherans held to be the main point of the gospel. In his defense of the confession (the *Apology*), Melanchthon expressly equated the gospel with justification by faith in Christ, or the free forgiveness of sins (110, 113, 123, 124, 132, 148).

Despite these remarkable claims for the dogmatic and practical importance of justification, it is one of the ironies of the history of Christian thought that what Luther meant by it has been a matter of disagreement. The chief article became not only a bone of contention with the Roman Catholics but also the cause of debates among Lutheran theologians and Luther scholars down to the present time. And whatever Luther meant, recent New Testament scholarship has cast doubt on his interpretation of Paul, since he imposed the Reformation context on Paul instead of reading him in the context of first-century Palestinian Judaism. The concerns of scholars and theologians may not percolate down to ordinary believers; indeed, it must surely be said that the one-time "chief article" no longer belongs in the everyday conversation of most Christians, and it should not be forgotten that it has never been a major theme in Eastern Orthodox thinking. Nevertheless, eminent Lutheran theologians continue to see in "the article of a standing and falling church" the center of the Christian faith (e.g., Jüngel 2001), and it retains its cardinal role in arcane ecumenical discussions.

This is not the place to enter into specialized Luther research. My present intention is to provide a note on the biblical sources for the doctrine of justification before offering a necessarily brief and selective account of the doctrine in the Western theological tradition. My concluding dogmatic reflections will show that I am not finally persuaded that "justification" is the only or the best rubric under which to interpret and communicate the gospel today; better, I think, is to speak rather of "reconciliation." But I do take it that the theme of the present chapter is precisely the nature of the gospel.

I. Justification in Scripture

Strictly speaking, a biblical doctrine of justification appears only in two of Paul's letters, but to understand his teaching requires a wider look at the vocabulary of salvation in the Old and New Testaments. In the letters to the Romans and the Galatians, as in Judaism, the condition for salvation is *dikaiosynē*, usually translated "righteousness." Sometimes Paul uses *dikaiosynē* in its ethical sense as the opposite of "impurity" or "iniquity" (e.g., Rom. 6:19). But in the context of justification the Greek noun carries over from its use in the Septuagint the *forensic* or *judicial* connotation of the Hebrew *ṣedeq* or *ṣĕdāqâ*: it refers not to a moral quality but to a person's standing in the verdict of a judge or court of law. When the reference is to the righteousness of God, not the righteousness required of humans, it sometimes means the activity by which God delivers his people rather than a moral attribute of God—in a word, "salvation" (see, e.g., the KJV of Isa. 46:13 and 51:5; Rom. 1:16–17). The cognate Greek verb *dikaioō*, translated "to justify,"[1] bears the same forensic connotation as *dikaiosynē*: the justified person is acquitted, vindicated, declared innocent or in the right, and the contrary of "justified" is "condemned" (Rom. 8:33–34; cf. 2 Cor. 3:9). The forensic sense of "to justify" is confirmed by its use outside the context of salvation. We read in the Gospel of Luke that all the people who heard Jesus "justified" God (7:29 RSV; cf. Ps. 51:4, cited in Rom. 3:4); that "wisdom is justified by all her children" (7:35 RSV); and that the lawyer who asked Jesus, "What must I do to inherit eternal life?" wanted to justify himself (10:29), as did the Pharisees (16:15). Closer to Pauline usage is the verdict that the tax collector in Jesus' parable went home justified rather than the Pharisee (18:14).

In common with Judaism, Paul understood justification not only as a forensic concept but also as *eschatological* (cf. Matt. 12:36–37). It used to be supposed that he differed from his contemporaries in that for him the new age had already dawned and forensic-eschatological righteousness was a present reality, anticipating the final judgment to come (Rom. 5:1; Gal. 5:5; cf. Phil. 1:9–11). But since the discovery of the Dead Sea Scrolls, scholars recognize that the eschatological presence of the divine verdict was not uniquely Pauline. His

1. Because the use of two English words, "righteousness" and "justify," obscures the common *dik-* root of the Greek *dikaiosynē* and *dikaioō*, it has been suggested that for "justify" we might substitute the obsolete Middle English verb "rightwise." But the suggestion has not caught on.

essential difference from the Judaizers was that whereas they insisted on retaining the prescriptions of the law, Paul taught righteousness not through the law, but through faith in Christ (Rom. 3:21–22; 9:30–31; 10:4–6). "For we hold that a person is justified by faith apart from works prescribed by the law" (Rom. 3:28; cf. Gal. 2:16; 3:11). Justification, accordingly, is a gift of grace, a righteousness that is not the Christian's own but comes from God (Rom. 3:24; 10:3; 11:6; Gal. 5:4; cf. Phil. 3:9). Paul can say both that it comes through *faith* in Jesus Christ (Rom. 3:22), so that we are "justified by faith" (3:28; 5:1), and that it comes through the *redemption* that is in Christ Jesus (3:24), so that we are "justified by his blood" (5:9). The connection is given in the description of atonement by Christ's blood as "effective through faith" (3:25; but see KJV).

In his interpretation of the Lord's covenant with Abraham (Rom. 4; Gal. 3), Paul may seem to assign an intrinsic value to faith because it is counted or reckoned as righteousness (Gen. 15:6). But he sets the righteousness of faith over against any supposed righteousness of works, and, obviously, he does not understand faith to be righteous apart from faith's object: Abraham's faith was in God's promise that he would become the father of many nations (Rom. 4:13, 16–18), and the faith of his spiritual descendants is trust in "him who justifies the ungodly" (4:5).

Paul's expression *pistis Christou* is ambiguous. Where our English versions take *Christou* for an objective genitive (Rom. 3:22, 26; Gal. 2:16; 3:22) and assume Paul is speaking of righteousness through faith *in* Christ, some have suggested that he intended a subjective genitive and meant righteousness through the faith *of* Christ. But Paul nowhere makes Christ the subject of the verb *pisteuō*, "to believe" or "to have faith," and the suggestion has not won over the majority of New Testament scholars.

Apart from Romans and Galatians, the term *to justify* seldom appears in the Letters of Paul (1 Cor. 4:4; 6:11) or, in something like Paul's sense, elsewhere in the New Testament (Acts 13:39 KJV; Titus 3:7). In the Letter of James the Pauline terms are used in a different sense and for a different purpose: to deny that a Christian may rest content with mere intellectual *belief* (Jas. 2:14–26). Whether justification is the heart of the gospel, then, or only a polemical form of it in the context of Paul's controversy with the Judaizers is open to disagreement. Arguably, it did not become a central dogmatic concept until Augustine's polemic against the Pelagians.

II. Justification in the Western Theological Tradition

It will be convenient, for the sake of order, to consider justification in the Western theological tradition under the separate headings "Roman Catholic Interpretations" and "Protestant Interpretations." This may seem to be a self-evident decision, but the separation should not be taken too rigidly. At the time of the Reformation, Catholics and Protestants alike often claimed Augustine for their cause even on the divisive issues of justification and the sacraments. It is hardly too much to say that the Western tradition, for all its diversity, is the tradition of Augustine. Historical analysis shows, and present-day ecumenical conversations confirm, that the two subtraditions are not wholly exclusive. But in each of them there are internal strains and ambiguities that defy consistent, straightforward description.

1. Roman Catholic Interpretations

The spirit of Paul's teaching shines through the passionate assaults of Augustine on pride or boasting, but it is mixed with some un-Pauline elements. Augustine takes the meaning of the verb "to justify" from the etymology of the Latin *iustificare*, "to make just" (*iusti-ficare*), which is not an exact equivalent to the forensic Greek term *dikaioō* ("to declare just"), though always so used in the Latin version of the Pauline Epistles. In *The Spirit and the Letter* (412), for example, Augustine notes that "justified" *can* mean "deemed, or reckoned as just," but he describes justification as a *making* righteous (NPNF[1] 5:102). Here, as elsewhere, he interprets "the love of God" in Romans 5:5 not as "*God's* love for us," but as "*our* love for God." Justification is a healing activity in which, by pouring love for God into our hearts through the Holy Spirit, God redirects our desires from earthly things to himself as our highest good (84–85, 86, 98, 100–101). The infusion of love, which coincides with the concept of grace, enables us to make progress in righteousness, and what is still lacking God overlooks. In *The City of God* (413–27) Augustine says, "Our very righteousness, though genuine because of the genuine good at which it aims, is nevertheless of such measure in this life that it consists more in the remission of sins than in the perfection of virtues" (NPNF[1] 2:419, alt.).

Much the same view, translated into Aristotelian categories, prevailed in Thomas Aquinas, who thought of justification as the effect of an infusion of grace that imparts the "habit" of love for God to the soul (*ST* 1133, 1151). Thomas extolls the gift of grace by declaring, in agreement with Augustine, that the justification of the ungodly, which ends with the eternal good of participation in God, is a greater work of God than the creation of heaven and earth, which will pass away (1152). The later, nominalist schoolmen could also sing the praises of divine grace. But they compromised the Augustinian scheme by teaching that justifying grace must be earned—even if only by the deficient ("congruous") merit of doing the best one can without it.[2] Thomas, by contrast, followed Augustine in holding that no merit can precede justifying grace: it is "first grace" that makes merit possible (1156–57; cf. NPNF[1] 5:102). On this the authoritative Council of Trent (1545–63) seems to have endorsed Thomas's view—though not, perhaps, closing the door against the nominalists (sess. 6, chap. 5).

2. Protestant Interpretations

Luther's doctrine of justification has been understood as strictly *forensic*: justification, in this view, is not the transformation of sinners by the gift of infused

2. Translation of a representative nominalist text from Gabriel Biel (ca. 1420–95) will be found in Heiko Augustinus Oberman, *Forerunners of the Reformation: The Shape of Late Medieval Thought Illustrated by Key Documents* (New York: Holt, Rineheart & Winston, 1966), 165–74. The theme of winning God's help by doing the best one can is at least as old as Origen, *Against Celsus* (ANF 4:628), and as new as the Protestant hymn "On Our Way Rejoicing," which says: "If with honest-hearted love for God and man,/ Day by day Thou find us doing all we can/ Thou who giv'st the seed-time/ Wilt give large increase."

love for God but a declarative act by which God acquits sinners despite their sinfulness, imputing to them the righteousness of Christ. Second thoughts about Luther's teaching were occasioned by the surprising discovery of the handwritten manuscripts for his *Lectures on Romans*, delivered in 1515–16 and first published in 1908. The eminent Luther scholar Karl Holl (1866–1926) showed that in these lectures Luther understood justification in the Augustinian manner as a process of healing, that is, as an actual but incomplete *making* righteous. The divine verdict is proleptic: Luther can say that the Christian *is* righteous—in hope or in promise (cf. Rom. 8:24)! His view of justification in the *Lectures on Romans*, then, was not forensic but *sanative*. Holl's critics replied that this proves only that in 1515–16 the young Luther was not yet a Lutheran. But my own early work on the mature Luther's *Lectures on Galatians* convinced me that he never did hold an exclusively forensic doctrine of justification, and confirmation has recently come from the new Finnish Luther research. Moreover, after he had made his decisive theological breakthrough, Luther acknowledged (with one reservation) that what he had discovered was the understanding of the righteousness of God in Augustine's *The Spirit and the Letter*: not, that is, the righteousness by which God punishes sinners, but the righteousness by which God justifies us or makes us righteous (LW 25:151–52; 34:327–28; cf. Augustine, NPNF[1] 5:89, 90, 96).

In the *Lectures on Galatians* Luther has several explanations for why justification can only be by faith; they correspond to the several facets of his idea of faith. He certainly does not have in mind a merely external arrangement by which Christ's righteousness is credited to the account of believers but leaves their sinful persons unchanged. Rather, it is the presence of Christ within them that justifies. "Therefore the Christ who is grasped by faith and who lives in the heart is the true Christian righteousness, on account of which God counts us righteous and grants us eternal life" (LW 26:130; cf. 132). Whereas the medieval schoolmen said that faith is formed by love, Luther says that faith is formed by the living presence of Christ within—a real and efficacious presence—and he therefore considers the righteousness of faith to be a real ("formal") righteousness (129, 167, 357).

Luther's comments on Galatians 3:6 explain that Abraham's faith was counted, or imputed, as righteousness because that is what faith really is. But it is only an incipient or inchoate righteousness, and the divine imputation overlooks what is still lacking (LW 26:229–30). "Imputation" here does not mean a reckoning of Christ's righteousness to us such that we are not really righteous at all. It means that there are two parts to Christian righteousness: the gift of faith, which is indeed a formal righteousness, and the divine imputation that, for Christ's sake, disregards the fact that faith is only a small beginning. The Christian is at once righteous and a sinner (229–32). Luther can speak of imputation both positively, as God's taking faith for righteousness, and negatively, as God's not counting the sin that remains. But in the entire passage on Galatians 3:6 he does not speak of an imputation of Christ's righteousness to us any more than Paul does.[3] It follows that when he says our righteousness is

3. Surprisingly, the notion of an "imputation of Christ's righteousness" did appear in the supposedly "pre-Reformation" *Lectures on Romans* (LW 25:336). When Luther states there that the Christian

"outside us" (e.g., 234), he can only mean that it is not generated within by our own efforts but always *comes from* outside.

In Luther's eyes, the nominalists made a fatal mistake in teaching that the order of salvation must begin with doing one's best. The mystical treatise he discovered and published as *A German Theology* (2nd ed. 1518) confirmed for him the Augustinian image of the sinner as turned in upon himself. If sin is self-will, then any exhortation to the sinner to *do* something can only, in the nature of the case, rouse him to more sinning. Luther knew from his own experience that it is a poor counselor who tells the sinner to do what he can. It is as if one beggar should come to another to make him rich: as the proverb says, the one is milking a billy goat, and the other holds out a sieve (LW 26:403–4). Better to reassure the sinner that salvation begins and ends with grace and that even the faith that responds to the Word of grace is *God's* work, not ours. "The truth of the Gospel is this, that our righteousness comes by faith alone, without the works of the Law. . . . [B]ut faith itself is a gift of God, a work of God in our hearts, which justifies us because it takes hold of Christ as the Savior" (88). "By faith in the Word of grace, therefore, the Christian should conquer fear, turn his eyes away from the time of Law, and gaze at Christ Himself and at the faith to come" (343).

Although he cites Augustine on justification (as on practically everything else), *Calvin* seems further removed than Luther from the Augustinian scheme because he distinguishes more sharply and consistently between justification and sanctification (that is, the practice of purity of life; *Institutes*, 1:725, 776), which we will need to take up in chapter 13. To be sure, Calvin knows of a divinely imparted love, but he assigns it to sanctification, not to justification. Though there is indeed a "partial righteousness in works," so far from contradicting justification by faith alone it too stands in need of justification by faith. "Accordingly, we can deservedly say that by faith alone not only we ourselves but our works as well are justified" (747, 813; cf. 352, 820). Calvin finds support in Augustine, but with the gentle reservation that Augustine's way of putting it "still subsumes grace under sanctification" (746, 752). Rightly understood, justification is not a quality but a relation, not a magnitude subject to growth but a divine verdict that is total and instantaneous (727, 739).[4] It is simply a way of speaking about the forgiveness of sins (728; cf. 811, where Calvin finally arrives at his formal definition of justification). In short, God "justifies by pardoning" (738).

Like Luther, Calvin thinks of the righteousness of the justified as "outside" them. "We are reckoned righteous before God in Christ and outside ourselves [*extra nos*]" (*Institutes*, 1:729; cf. 741). "[W]e see that every particle of our salvation stands thus outside us" (784). Yet, like Luther, he insists that reconciliation or justification is the gift of *participation* in Christ. He began the third book of the *Institutes* by laying down the principle that "as long as Christ remains *extra nos* . . .

---

is a sinner in fact (*re vera*) but righteous by imputation (260), he comes close to the dubious notion of a "legal fiction" in later Protestant theology.

4. Luther, too, could speak of acceptance by *grace* as total in contrast to the *gift* of healing, which is partial and "works so as to purge away the sin for which a person has already been forgiven" (*Against Latomus* [1521], LW 32:208, 226–30; quotation on 229). But in the 1535 *Lectures on Galatians* he reverses the order of the two benefits of the gospel: there it is the righteousness of faith that is partial, requiring the nonimputation of the sin that remains, and this moves him closer to Augustine than to Calvin.

all that he has suffered and done for the salvation of the human race remains useless and of no value for us" (537). What is offered through the gospel is an actual imparting of Christ (*communicatio Christi*) by the Holy Spirit (537–38; see also 541, 570–71). In his chapter on justification (chap. 11) Calvin then calls this joining of Head and members "mystical union" with Christ, and says, "We do not, therefore, contemplate him *extra nos* from afar in order that his righteousness may be imputed to us but because we put on Christ and are engrafted into his body—in short, because he deigns to make us one with him" (737). Once again, as with Luther, it would clearly be a mistake to imagine that imputation, in the teaching of the Reformers, is an event entirely outside the believer, though it does rest on a work of Christ outside us. Paradoxically, then, "You see that our righteousness is not in us but in Christ, that we possess it only because we are partakers in Christ" (753).

It is presumably the ambiguity in Pauline usage—*dikaiosynē* as both an ethical and a forensic term—that led Calvin to such confusing statements as that by imputation we who are "not righteous in ourselves" are "reckoned as such in Christ" (*Institutes*, 1:728), or that the person whom God forgives is "righteous not in fact [*re ipsa*] but by imputation" (739; cf. 740, 753). Criticism of such language came not only from the Roman Catholics but also from the renegade Lutheran Andreas Osiander (1498–1552): it seems to assert that the divine Judge takes us to be what we are not, thereby acquitting the guilty—the so-called legal fiction. Perhaps the criticism can be answered satisfactorily without abandoning the forensic idiom. But we may be left wondering how helpful the language of justification has become. For what is really being affirmed is that the gift of reconciliation with God turns neither on being righteous nor on being reckoned as righteous when we really are not, but simply on faith in Christ. As one nineteenth-century admirer of Luther concluded, "Faith is the right attitude of the human spirit towards God—the due response to His revelation of Himself to us, in rendering which our hearts are right towards God" (Campbell 1869: 390).

As a matter of fact, while Calvin can thread his way through some subtle theological differences with his adversaries, he can also sum up the meaning of justification by faith with practical simplicity—and without the forensic metaphor. Throughout the chapters on justification, he speaks of "reconciliation," "forgiveness," "acceptance," being "received into friendship" with God. Above all, he invokes his favorite metaphor and equates justification with "the grace of adoption" (*Institutes*, 1:807; cf. 768, 794). We might say that at his hands the language of justification self-destructs: it means that we "have in heaven instead of a Judge a gracious Father" (725). Calvin contrasts the nervousness of slaves or servants, who constantly worry whether they have done enough to satisfy their master, and the assurance of children, who do not hesitate to show father projects they have only half finished or even spoiled a little, confident he will be happy with their efforts. "And we need this assurance in no slight degree, for without it we attempt everything in vain. . . . But how can this be done amidst all this dread, where one doubts whether God is offended or honored by all our works?" (837).

It is the same familial metaphor that, in Calvin's view, excludes all talk of "merit." He knew that the "sounder Schoolmen" only introduced merit *after* the reception of justifying grace (*Institutes,* 1:778), but he held that the grace of adoption precludes merit altogether. It is true that Scripture speaks of "reward," and his adversaries held that this warrants their belief that, finally, eternal life itself is merited as a reward. But the reward is not servants' pay: it is the inheritance of God's children, promised to counterbalance the troubles they must bear in the present life (794, 822, 828–29).

Schleiermacher's treatment of justification is among the most intriguing sections of *The Christian Faith* and deserves to be compared, step by step, with Calvin's, which he often seems to be following. But we cannot trace his intricate and highly schematic discussion as a whole; we will note only one fundamental respect in which he agrees with Calvin, and one in which he departs from him. Detailed comparison, were we to attempt it, would be complicated by their divergent use of terms: it can be hard to decide whether, or how far, terminological differences betray differences of substance. Suffice it to say that whereas Calvin assigns regeneration and repentance to sanctification, Schleiermacher brackets them both with justification as descriptions of the *beginning* of life in union with Christ. Sanctification is about the *growth* of the new life begun in regeneration.

Schleiermacher rules out the alleged Roman Catholic confusion of justification with sanctification (*CF* 497, 503), but we would not expect him to describe justification as a divine act outside us. Like Calvin, he represents both justification and sanctification as effects of living union with Christ. The turning point from the old, sinful life to the new he calls "regeneration" (*Wiedergeburt,* the "new birth"), which consists in conversion and justification. *"Assumption into living fellowship with Christ, regarded as a man's changed relation to God, is his Justification; regarded as a man's changed form of life, it is his Conversion"* (478). *Justification* includes both forgiveness and adoption; *conversion* consists in faith and repentance. The two are simultaneous, and we cannot have either one without the other (479). Particularly interesting is Schleiermacher's dissatisfaction with the Lutheran and Reformed confessions because they do not speak of "adoption" as the positive counterpart to the negative expression "remission of sins" (497). For the idea of being adopted as children of God he could appeal to the dogmatic theologians, but not, he thought, to the confessions. (He forgot the Westminster Confession, which, immediately after justification, devotes an entire chapter to the grace of adoption.) He must have recognized that in seeing adoption as a cardinal metaphor he was in agreement with Calvin. His conception of God, on the other hand, inevitably set him at odds with the individualistic treatment of justification in Calvin and the entire dogmatic tradition.

In the language of Christian devotion, the individual sinner is traditionally pictured standing alone before the judgment seat of God and awaiting the Judge's verdict of acquittal or condemnation. But because dogmatics, in Schleiermacher's view, must move beyond picture language as far as possible, the dogmatic theologian should not think of God's activity as though it consisted in individual acts in time: there can only be an individual and particular *effect* of divine activity. The moment of a person's justification is strictly the breakthrough of God's eternal decree for *humanity* into the consciousness of the individual: the forgiveness of sins is the cessation of a guilty conscience (*CF* 501–2; cf. 515). It is understandable that a theologian with a traditional conception of God would protest: "For Schleiermacher . . . justification meant little more than the sinner's becoming conscious of his mistake in thinking that God was angry with him" (Berkhof 1949: 513). True, Schleiermacher did maintain that the picture of an angry deity belonged to a superseded stage of religious development (*CF* 350), but his understanding of justification by faith should not be trivialized. Justification, for him, was a new relation of the individual to God brought about by union with Christ (479). He was at pains to insist that it must be seen as *Christ's* work;[5] he therefore repudiated the misunderstanding that "each man justifies himself" (499). And we must return later (in chap. 14) to his crucial grounding of justification in the divine decree for *humanity*; typical of Schleiermacher's consistent focus on the corporate rather than the individual aspect of redemption, it reflects a new stage in the doctrine of election and predestination.

Conclusion

Clearly, there are differences in the way justification is treated in the Western theological tradition. Yet we might well conclude that they are variations on the two-sidedness of the Augustinian correlation of healing and forgiveness, and the differences might appear less divisive if we would acknowledge the *intention* of the scholastic terms *gratia operans* and *gratia acceptans* that Calvin censures (see *Institutes*, 1:263, 779, 820; cf. Thomas, *ST* 1136–37). I don't mean to say that the differences are unimportant. But when Calvin states that what is *most* important in the doctrine of justification is to secure the glory of God's free kindness, along with peace of conscience (*Institutes*, 1:763, 784), we should recognize the same *intention* in the teaching of his adversaries. It does not follow, of course, that the various attempts to carry out this intention are equally successful or that it is never diluted by other objectives, and we will have to consider the relation of justification and sanctification more closely in the next chapter. But first I must turn from historical review to explanation of my twelfth thesis.

III. Faith and Reconciliation

The saving work of Christ is the gift of faith and the creation of the community of faith. What, then, does it mean to *live* by this faith? No categorical separation is imagined when attention moves from the activity of the Redeemer to the life of the redeemed, since Christian faith takes the activity of the Redeemer as a work in, not only for, the redeemed. Under the headings of "reconciliation" and "renewal" belong further reflections on the work of Christ, but from the perspective of the believer. They reach back to the twofold nature of estrangement from the Creator as both mistrust and defiance, which, I have said, cannot be separated from the anxiety and abuse that subvert the relation of humanity to the created order. And my corresponding distinction between faith as

5. He held that one cannot speak of the moment of conversion as a cooperative activity. Christ alone communicates the "higher form of life"; on the side of the convert there is only "receptivity" or "susceptibility" (*Empfänglichkeit*), a "capacity" (*Fähigkeit*) that belongs to human nature as such (*CF* 283–84, 492–95).

confidence and faith as obedience determines the division between the present chapter, on faith as *confidence* (cf. Eph. 3:12), and the next, on faith as *obedience* (cf. Rom. 1:5; 16:26).

1. Reconciliation and Adoption

In Protestant interpretations, the forensic metaphor of justification has given rise to the problematic appearance that in justifying the ungodly (Rom. 4:5) God, so far from proving God's justice (3:26), violates it. The Judge seems to pronounce innocent those who are not innocent—to take the unrighteous for righteous, or to treat them *as if* righteous while leaving them in their sin. But this was not at all what Luther and Calvin meant, or implied, by justification. Their meaning—and Paul's—is conveyed better if we drop the legal metaphor and say, quite simply, it is faith in Jesus Christ that puts the ungodly *right* with God; and this is best described as "reconciliation." The question, *Why* does faith put one right with God? is answered in all we have said about the prophetic and priestly work of Christ, to which faith (in John McLeod Campbell's phrase) "responds in Amen." We are not talking here about a merely abstract, notional faith but about the faith in Christ, or in God "the Father of Jesus Christ," that Christ himself gives—*saving* faith. More than belief, saving faith is "accepting, receiving, and resting upon Christ alone for justification, sanctification, and eternal life" (Westminster Confession 14.2). And faith, in this sense, is not a human work: it is the work of Christ, *"created through the proclamation of God's 'paternal' good will in Christ (Christ's prophetic activity)."*

Everyone agrees that reconciliation is, or includes, forgiveness: God reconciles the world, puts sinners right with Godself, "not counting their trespasses against them" (2 Cor. 5:19). Accordingly, my thesis 12 describes reconciliation as *by the free forgiveness of sins.* But any suggestion that the gift of saving faith does nothing to transform the sinner would be absurd. No such absurdity is implied in calling God "him who justifies the ungodly." The testimony of the Fourth Gospel is that to all who received the incarnate Word by faith "he gave power [or 'right,' *exousian*] to become children of God" (John 1:12). To be made right with God by faith is to begin living confidently as sons and daughters of God, no longer as defendants in a court of law or as slaves. To be sure, the change in the dominant picture of God, from Judge to Father, is a change of relation. But it hardly leaves the ungodly unchanged in themselves: it makes them children of God. In this sense, justification or reconciliation begins a new form of life.

The connection Calvin and Schleiermacher drew between justification and the grace of adoption was firmly grounded in the New Testament. It is striking, for example, how closely justification and adoption are intertwined in Romans 8. Those who receive the spirit not of servitude but of adoption do not succumb to fear: called and justified, they are convinced that in everything God works for good (Rom. 8:14–15, 28–30). Hence *the confidence of faith . . . is reconciliation to God and God's purposes . . . and is called "adoption" into the household of God* [Eph. 2:19; cf. Gal. 6:10; 1 Tim. 3:15], *or being "born again."* We must comment next on the actual transition from servant to child of God, that is, on regeneration or the new birth.

2. Reconciliation and the New Birth

Origen of Alexandria may speak for the Eastern Orthodox tradition when he urges, "Let us . . . take up eternal life. Let us take up that which depends upon our decision. God does not give it to us. He sets it before us. 'Behold, I have set life before thy face' [Deut. 30:15]. It is in our power to stretch out our hand" (*Dialogue with Heraclides* [ca. 244], LCC 2:454). Very different was the Western tradition shaped—not without dissenters—by Augustine, who finally concluded in his anti-Pelagian treatise *On the Predestination of the Saints* (428 or 429) that even the faith that assents to the gospel must be God's work, not ours; otherwise, it would not be true that we have nothing we did not receive as a free gift (1 Cor. 4:7). The ability to have faith (*fidem posse habere*) is a natural human capacity, but actually to have faith (*fidem habere*) is a special gift of God. If a person comes to faith, it is because "in the elect the will is prepared by the Lord." For "between grace and predestination there is only this difference, that predestination is the preparation for grace, while grace is the donation itself" (Eph. 2:8–10; NPNF[1] 5:503, 507). In opposition to the nominalists, Luther reaffirmed Augustine's case against the Pelagians, which he took to require a flat denial of free will, and he sought to clinch it with John Wycliffe's thesis that "everything happens by absolute necessity."[6]

The Lutheran Formula of Concord (1577) claimed Luther's authority for the comparison of a sinner to a pillar of salt, a log, a stone, a lifeless statue. Indeed, sinners are worse than a lifeless block, according to the formula, because they *resist* the will of God. They cannot believe the gospel, assent to it, or accept it as true. The testimony of Scripture (Eph. 2:5; Col. 2:13) is that a person in sin is not weak, but dead. Conversion is wholly a creative work of the Spirit (*BC* 522–26, 532–33, 536). Calvin tried to be more cautious: "in man's conversion what belongs to his primal nature remains entire" (*Institutes*, 1:297). And in an acerbic retort to a Roman Catholic critic of Protestant teaching on the bondage of the will, he protests: "who is such a fool as to assert that God moves man just as we throw a stone? And nothing like this follows from our teaching" (334).

I will have more to say later about election and predestination as the sole preparation for grace. On the actual reception of the gospel we do well to exercise reserve. Why grace succeeds in one and not in another was hotly debated in both the Catholic and the Protestant churches after the Reformation. Jesus' parable of the Sower points to some of the possibilities (Mark 4:3–20), but they are not the whole story and their application in particular cases eludes us. The arguments in favor of irresistible or efficacious grace are often a priori: they tell us what befits the glory of God or the gratitude owed to God by the redeemed. We certainly do not exclude such considerations, but an irreducible element of mystery will always remain when the preaching of the gospel meets either with assent or with refusal. The church is not asked to clear up the mystery but

6. As early as his *Disputation against Scholastic Theology* (1517), Luther stated that "the sole means of obtaining grace is the eternal election and predestination of God" (thesis 29, LW 31:11). In his *Assertion of All the Articles Condemned by the Latest Bull of Leo X* (1520), he enlisted Wycliffe's necessitarian thesis in support of his argument that free will is a fiction (WA 7:146), and this became the central issue in his controversy (1524–27) with Erasmus.

commissioned to sow the seed and to be persistent in proclaiming the Word (2 Tim. 4:2).

In his conversation with Nicodemus (John 3:1–21) Jesus describes the new birth, or birth "from above" (*anōthen*), precisely as a mystery: "The wind [*pneuma*] blows where it chooses, and you hear the sound of it, but you do not know where it comes from or where it goes. So it is with everyone who is born of the Spirit [*ek tou pneumatos*]" (v. 8).[7] William James made us familiar with the contrast between the once-born and the twice-born varieties of religious experience. The contrast has its uses, but Jesus knows only of the twice-born: no one can see the kingdom of God, or enter it, without being born again, or born from above (vv. 3, 5). It could not be said more forcefully that the transition from flesh to spirit (v. 6) goes against the grain of sinful human nature as we have described it: no mere effort of the human will can bring it about, which is what we mean, in part, by calling it a work of grace. In Paul's words, "if anyone is in Christ, there is a new creation" (2 Cor. 5:17). It is unfortunate, however, that being born again is so often equated with a dramatic emotional crisis. Although the moment of birth *is* an amazing drama—it seems right to call it "the miracle of birth"—it is not only a new beginning but also the culmination of an invisible growth, and we will need to take this into account when we speak of baptism, which is surely what Jesus refers to when he says that one must be born of *water* and the Spirit (John 3:5). We cannot presume to point to the beginning of anyone's new life, not even our own. As Schleiermacher says, "just as in the natural life birth is not the absolute beginning, so here a period of hidden life precedes it, and at first even the newly-born life remains unconscious" (*CF* 486–87).

3. Reconciliation and the Gospel of Grace

Even if we admit, in agreement with the New Testament scholars, that in some respects Luther's "justification by faith alone" does not come up to the standards of historical-critical exegesis, we can still say that what he made of the Pauline doctrine was a powerful witness to the gospel for his time. The Augsburg Confession states that the Lutheran teaching about faith cannot be understood apart from the conflict of the terrified conscience (*BC* 43). Luther himself certainly spoke from his own experience of doubt and despair—resolved only when it dawned on him that the anguish created by a false religiousness is the first step in God's redemptive design, which is to slay the old self and to create the new. "Thus when God makes alive he does it by killing" (*Bondage of the Will* [1525], LW 33:62). The crucial question Luther posed for his time can be put like this: Who *are* they who are touched by grace? Is it those who can climb no higher because their resources are finite but who take help for granted because they have done all they can, or is it those who can slip no lower because they have hit the bottom of despair and expect nothing but judgment? Is grace aid for the weak, or is it the promise of new life for the

7. The ambiguity of the two Greek words *anōthen* and *pneuma* can be indicated in an English translation only by parentheses or footnotes. To be born *anōthen* may mean either "born again" or "born from above," and *to pneuma* means both "the wind" and "the Spirit."

dead? The continued pertinence of Luther's answer may be illustrated if we recall that in the 1920s his theology of the cross inspired the theology of crisis. The early Barth wrote: "The thoughts of the Bible touch just those points where the negative factors in life preponderate, casting doubt over life's possibilities. . . . The Bible, with uncanny singleness of interest, omits all the stages of human life where this crisis is not yet acute . . . but it does become concerned with [a person], and with weird intensity, at the stage—shall we call it the highest or the lowest?—where doubt has seized him" (Barth 1957:116–17). But dare we conclude that grace reaches a person *only* at the nadir of the terrified conscience?

Even in Luther's own day the bitter sense of failure and guilt was not everyone's problem. While Luther agonized over his doubt whether he had really done all he could to merit God's grace, Ulrich Zwingli scoffed that the nominalist formula, "God does not refuse grace to those who do their best," made justification by works all too easy: everyone always does what he can, however trifling it may be (*LWZ* 3:103). The church's sale of indulgences may have stirred for a moment the popular fear of God's wrath, but only to provide a quick cash remedy for it. Part of Luther's protest in the Ninety-five Theses was that the offer of indulgences for money obscured the need for true contrition (thesis 39). Perhaps it will be said that if the gospel does not find terrors of conscience, the preacher must cause them by announcing the threats and curses of God's law. But it is, I think, a matter of plain experience that the awareness of sin grows in Christ's company. Is it not possible that his *first* word may be directed to other human needs besides calming terrors of conscience?

Some of the profoundest thoughts on justification by faith have come from theologians who have understood Luther's doctrine well enough to adapt it for another day. My quotation from Barth already generalizes the Lutheran principle beyond the sphere of the terrified conscience. One thinks, too, of Reinhold Niebuhr's astute claim that justification by faith may have relevance to public life, or even international affairs, once it is seen to voice the ambiguity of all human achievements and our willingness nonetheless to risk relative judgments (Niebuhr 1950). Or one thinks of Paul Tillich's declaration that the Protestant principle of justification by faith alone "means that no individual and no human group can claim a divine dignity for its moral achievements, for its sacramental power, for its sanctity, or for its doctrine" (Tillich 1951: 226). In *The Courage to Be*, as we have noted, Tillich also described the change of the dominant religious question from one historical period to the next—in which case we may say that sometimes the point is not to *adapt* the message of justification by faith but to *replace* it as the chief article.

In our modern world, Tillich suggested, the medieval anxiety of guilt and condemnation is overshadowed by the anxiety of emptiness and meaninglessness. This was the theme of the remarkable declaration made at the meeting of the Lutheran World Federation in Helsinki in 1963: The person of today "no longer suffers under the wrath of God, but under the impression of God's absence; he no longer suffers under his sin, but under the meaninglessness of his existence; he no longer asks about the graciousness of God, but about the reality of God." Perhaps that puts the contrast too sharply: the alternatives are not exclusive, even if one rather than the other becomes dominant. Tillich was careful to assert that the three forms of anxiety he distinguished, though normally under the dominance of one of them, are immanent in one another.[8]

To what then, shall we conclude, is the gospel addressed? The traditional Protestant answer has always been that the Christian proclamation speaks to human sin and guilt, so that where guilt is not present it must be induced: the bad news of the law must precede the good news of the gospel. The forensic language of justification—of condemnation or acquittal by the divine Judge—lends itself to such an *ordo salutis*, but it is more context-bound than Protestant evangelists have been ready to admit. A message of guilt and pardon suited the Reformation struggle with the terrified conscience, and I do not doubt that it will always have its place in "the gospel of the glory and grace of God." But in all I have said about elemental faith, estrangement, and the work of Christ I have opened the possibility of identifying another point of contact that lies deeper and may come to expression in more ways than one: the loss of confidence in a reliable environment, a coherent world *order* in which it makes sense to ask for the meaning of our existence—our place in the whole. I have argued that this confidence has the logical status of an "inevitable belief," not open to proof but tacitly presupposed by our theology, our science, and—quite simply—our daily existence as human beings; in this lies its rational justification.

In everyday experience, however, an appeal to rational justification cannot be counted on to ward off the intrusion of the sense of emptiness or meaninglessness that theologians, philosophers, and psychologists have identified as a characteristic sickness of our time. But the gospel is addressed precisely to the predicament of elemental faith under siege: it comes with the reassurance that this faith is not, after all, a delusion. Reconciliation with God "the Father of Jesus Christ" is *restoration of the elemental trust that estrangement erodes.* And there is another side of Christian faith—faith as obedience—that resonates with the other side of elemental faith, which construes our daily existence as laying obligations on us, that is, our sense of *moral* order. This too is threatened by estrangement from God the Creator and provides a point of contact for the gospel. To it we turn next.

8. So formulated, the contrast between the Reformation question and the religious quest of modern humans is less vulnerable to Barth's indignant outburst in *CD* IV/1:530 (§61.2).

13. Living by Faith (II): Renewal

The obedience of faith, as restoration of the elemental sense of moral demand that estrangement blunts or rejects, is the "growth in grace" of those to whom God's commandments are no longer burdensome; and since to the new perception of God's "paternal" will is added the efficacy of Christ's work in the Christian community (Christ's priestly activity), the new obedience is described as life together "in the Father's household."

In the dogmatic systems of the old Reformed divines, justification was followed by "sanctification" (Heppe 1950, chap. 22). The Lutherans generally preferred to speak of "renewal" (*renovatio*), though they recognized "sanctification" as a synonym (Schmid 1961: §48), and in our day "renewal" sounds less esoteric to most of us. Whichever term is used, the subject in traditional Protestant dogmatics, past or present, is the gradual transformation of believers, who have been *declared* righteous, by the bestowal of an *inherent* righteousness or holiness. As a favorite watchword puts it: The righteousness of Christ is imputed to sinners by justification; by sanctification it is imparted to them. The Holy Spirit is identified as the agent of renewal, and the instrumental cause of renewal is the Word of God. Various biblical expressions are employed to describe the process: it is restoration of the divine image, imitation of Christ, the fruit of the Spirit, mortification of the old self and quickening of the new, the struggle of the spirit against the flesh. In addition, scholastic concepts excluded from justification reappear in the context of Protestant accounts of sanctification: we read of supernatural gifts, the infusion of a habit, cooperation with grace, and the need for the help of grace even for those who have been sanctified by grace.

Much of what was included in the traditional doctrine of sanctification may be reassigned to the fields, or subfields, of Christian ethics and the practice of piety (spirituality). But the fundamental principle of sanctification is that the renewal of the Christian is an activity of God through Jesus Christ (see 1 Thess. 5:23; Heb. 13:20–21); moral duties and spiritual exercises—even when intended to be Christian—are not, or not necessarily, viewed from this perspective. Accordingly, the subject raises once more dogmatic questions already touched on concerning grace, law and gospel, works approved by God, and the relationship between justification and sanctification. We must now consider these questions further.

More perhaps than any other dogmatic locus, the doctrine of sanctification yields an empirical picture of the person of faith—or pictures (plural), since there are clearly more than one in the various Christian communities (see Dieter 1987; Alexander 1988). Jesus' rule for distinguishing true from false prophets was: "You will know them by their fruits" (Matt. 7:15–20). According to the Fourth Gospel, he applied a similar test to his disciples: "By this everyone will know that you are my disciples, if you have love for one another" (John 13:35). Elsewhere, Jesus' test for separating those who will inherit the kingdom from those who won't is what they have done for the hungry, the thirsty, the stranger, the unclothed, the sick, and the prisoner (Matt. 25:31–46). To those who are content simply to believe, James says, "What good is it, my brothers and sisters, if you say you have faith but do not have works? . . . Show me your faith apart from your works, and I by my works will show you my faith" (Jas. 2:14, 18). Insofar, then, as sanctification is about the test of authentic Christian faith—and about the very purpose of salvation through faith—it is a subject of pivotal importance for dogmatics. "For we are what [God] has made us, created in Christ Jesus for good works, which God prepared beforehand to be our way of life" (Eph. 2:10; see also Rom. 8:4).

I. Sanctification in Scripture

The Christian idea of sanctification (from the Latin *sancti-ficare*, "to make holy") may be said to have had its origin in the injunction of the God of Israel, "sanctify yourselves . . . and be holy, for I am holy" (Lev. 11:44; see also 11:45; 19:2; 20:7). The root meaning of the Hebrew word for "holy" (*qādôš*; LXX *hagios*) is brought out in Leviticus 20:26: "You shall be holy to me; for I the LORD am holy, and I have *separated* you from the other peoples to be mine" (my emphasis). The holiness of Yahweh is his otherness, especially in comparison with the gods of the heathen (Exod. 15:11), and he has set apart for himself a holy people: "you shall be for me a priestly kingdom and a holy nation" (Exod. 19:6). The idea of a holy, separate people is carried over into the New Testament, most explicitly in 1 Peter, where the Levitical injunction is quoted, along with Exodus 19:6, and applied to the new people of God. Christians are a holy priesthood, called to be holy (*hagioi*) in all their conduct, to offer spiritual sacrifices acceptable to God through Jesus Christ, and to proclaim the mighty acts of God (1 Pet. 1:15–16; 2:5, 9–10). "Saints" (*hagioi*) is Paul's collective style of address to the Christians in Rome, Corinth, Philippi, and Colossae (cf. Eph. 1:1).

It would of course be anachronistic to look in the Synoptic Gospels for a doctrine of sanctification (as the Protestant schoolmen understood it). But what we do see in the words of Jesus is a portrayal of those who will enter the kingdom of God. We must confine our attention to one major source: the Sermon on the Mount.[1] Only a very superficial reading can account for the common assumption that a simple ethic—as distinct from theological niceties—is to be found in the sermon. Beginning with his blessing of the meek and the poor in spirit (Luke has simply "you who are poor," Luke 6:20), Jesus reassesses the piety

1. Most NT scholars maintain that Matt. 5–7, commonly referred to as "the Sermon on the Mount" (cf. the so-called Sermon on the Plain in Luke 6:20–29), represents the evangelist's editing of several existing traditions. But there is no serious doubt that the fragments go back to Jesus and in the main are reliable sources for his teaching.

of his day and its preeminent interpreters. It is not surprising that very different readings of the Sermon have appeared throughout the church's history, always hung up on the troublesome question whether Jesus' most stringent imperatives (Matt. 5:21–48) can possibly be taken as still binding on everyone, or even on every Christian. "For I tell you, unless your righteousness exceeds that of the scribes and Pharisees, you will never enter the kingdom of heaven" (5:20). "Be perfect, therefore, as your heavenly Father is perfect" (5:48). Jesus' portrayal of the poor in spirit who are to "strive first for the kingdom of God and his righteousness" (6:33) is set against images of the unloving and unforgiving (5:43–48; 6:14–15); the hypocrites who want their godliness to be noticed and think it entitles them to be censorious of others (6:1–18; 7:1–5); and those who are distracted from the heavenly kingdom by preoccupation with earthly goods and wealth (6:19–20, 24). "Not everyone who says to me, 'Lord, Lord,' will enter the kingdom of heaven, but only the one who does the will of my Father in heaven" (7:21).

In the New Testament letters the focus shifts to the figure of Christ himself, and those whom God calls are "predestined to be conformed to the image [*eikōn*] of his Son" (Rom. 8:29; in Col. 3:10 the pattern of renewal is the image of the Creator). The letters pay scant attention to the words of Jesus—although he said at the conclusion of his Sermon on the Mount, "Everyone then who hears these words of mine and acts on them will be like a wise man who built his house on rock. . . . And everyone who hears these words of mine and does not act on them will be like a foolish man who built his house on sand" (Matt. 7:24, 26; cf. Col. 3:16). Moreover, the figure of Christ is not the figure of the Teacher but of the dying and rising Lord, and the summons is to die to one's old self and rise with Christ to the new. Indeed, Paul finds the meaning of sanctification (*hagiasmos*) in the fact that believers *have* died and been raised with Christ.[2] But that does not cancel the imperative to live accordingly (Rom. 6:1–14, 22; Col. 3:1–5, 9–10; cf. Eph. 4:22–24); for "what the flesh desires is opposed to the Spirit, and what the Spirit desires is opposed to the flesh" (Gal. 5:17; cf. Rom. 7:14–23). It is in the context of the opposition between flesh and spirit that Paul gives his portrayal of those who will, and those who won't, inherit the kingdom. The works of the flesh are not only sensual sins but also "strife, jealousy, anger, quarrels, dissensions, factions." "By contrast, the fruit of the Spirit is love, joy, peace, patience, kindness, generosity, faithfulness, gentleness, and self-control" (Gal. 5:19–23). A similar profile of Christians appears in the Letter to the Colossians: "As God's chosen ones, holy and beloved, clothe yourselves with compassion, kindness, humility, meekness, and patience. Bear with one another and, if anyone has a complaint against another, forgive each other; just as the Lord has forgiven you, so you also must forgive. Above all, clothe yourselves with love, which binds everything together in perfect harmony" (Col. 3:12–14). It is impossible to doubt that the image of Jesus himself, as preserved in the memory of the church (Matt. 12:15–21; Luke 4:16–21), lies behind these profiles of the Christian.

2. In the NT "death" is used as a metaphor in more ways than one: for being dead in trespasses *before* salvation by Christ (Eph. 2:5), for dying to the law *through* Christ (Rom. 7:4), and for dying *with* Christ to one's old self (Rom. 6:5–6).

II. Sanctification in Protestant Dogmatics

Roman Catholic critics of the Protestant Reformation objected that *sola fide* (justification "by faith alone") undermined the necessity for good works. *Luther's* untiring retort, many times repeated, was that although faith alone justifies—without works (Rom. 3:28)—it does not remain alone: it works through love.[3] In a famous preface to Paul's Letter to the Romans (1522/1546), he wrote: "O it is a living, busy, active, mighty thing, this faith. It is impossible for it not to be doing good works incessantly" (LW 35:370). To be justified by faith alone, crucial though it is, was not Luther's last word about being a Christian. In his *Disputation concerning Justification* (1536), for example, he portrayed Christians as travelers on the way or as sick persons undergoing healing (LW 34:152, 182). Those who are justified are not yet righteous (that is, not righteous in themselves) but moving toward righteousness. They are still sinners, yet God forgives them and considers them righteous because the righteousness of Christ is like an umbrella against the heat of God's wrath. Christians live continually by the remission of sin, justified daily until the day they die (152–53, 164, 167, 190). Works, then, are not necessary for justification by faith, but they do serve as evidence that faith is genuine (161, 176, 190–92). Faith itself is not a work—unless we call it a work of *God* (159–60, 189). For it is God who first pronounces us clean by imputation, then gives us the Holy Spirit to cleanse us "in reality" or "in substance" (168, 191).

What, according to Luther, makes good works "good"? For whose benefit are they to be done? Although they are useful in reassuring the Christian of the genuineness of his faith, they are not needed for his salvation. "Therefore he should be guided in all his works by this thought and contemplate this one thing alone, that he may serve and benefit others in all that he does, considering nothing except the need and the advantage of his neighbor." Good works are works done for others; hence Paul says of the Christian life that inwardly it is faith toward God, and outwardly it is love or works toward one's neighbor. God has no need of our works; it is our neighbor who needs them, and the man who knows that God is not angry with him is free to turn to his neighbors and do the best he can for them. However, it goes against nature to put love for others before self-love; the power of the Word is the only spring from which love for the neighbor flows. Luther denies that the commandment to love your neighbor as yourself (Lev. 19:18; Mark 12:31) is an endorsement of a proper self-love. He knows that some say you must love yourself first, then you will have the model for loving your neighbor. But the Lord said, "Whoever would love his life, will lose it, and he who hates his life will find it" (not quite what Mark 8:35 says, but see the preceding verse!). Luther can assert, then, that to love God is to love one's neighbor, and to love one's neighbor is to hate oneself.[4] Presum-

3. In harmony with their view of "faith formed by love," Luther's adversaries interpreted *pistis di' agapēs energoumenē* in Gal. 5:6 to mean "faith made effective by love," so that love appears to be what actually justifies. For his rejection of this interpretation see his *Lectures on Galatians* (1535), LW 27:28–31.

4. My sources for this paragraph were (in chronological order): *Lectures on Romans* (1515–16), LW 25:512–13; *The Freedom of a Christian* (1520), LW 31:365; *Sermon on the Sum of the Christian Life* (1532), LW 51:269–72, 283; *Lectures on Galatians* (1535), LW 27:30; WA *Tischreden* (Table Talk), 5:397. Other sources could equally well be cited for these recurring features of Luther's thought.

ably, we should take that as a rhetorical hyperbole for Jesus' admonition that to follow him calls for *denying* oneself (Mark 8:34)—that is, for the radical change of mind that the New Testament calls "repentance" (*metanoia*).

The first of Luther's Ninety-five Theses (1517) stated that when Jesus said, "Repent," he meant the entire life of believers to be a life of repentance (LW 31:25). Calvin agreed, and he took "repentance" as his regulative term for the renewal of the Christian, which he also called "regeneration," "sanctification," and "newness of life." But unlike Luther, he set his thoughts on repentance in a systematic context. In the third book of his 1559 *Institutes*, after he has given an account of how faith possesses Christ (chaps. 1–2), Calvin turns to explication of the two main effects the Christian experiences as the result of faith-union with Christ: newness of life and free reconciliation (*Institutes*, 1:592). Since both effects spring simultaneously from the same source, there is no compelling reason to begin with one rather than the other. But to emphasize that holy living cannot be separated from the free imputation of righteousness, Calvin decides to deal first with newness of life (593): in the more usual terms in later Reformed theology, he puts sanctification before justification. His systematic order has been found surprising, even questionable, and some interpreters have hastened to insist that of course he does not really mean to jeopardize the centrality of justification in Reformation theology. But his point is that the absolute center is *Christ*. As he says later, "Do you wish, then, to attain righteousness [i.e., justification] in Christ? You must first possess Christ; but you cannot possess him without being made partaker in his sanctification, because he cannot be divided into pieces" (798; cf. 1 Cor. 1:30).

We can still ask how these two benefits, each related to Christ, are related to each other. The answer is, I think (*pace* many of his interpreters), that Calvin subordinates justification to sanctification as *means* to end. Again, he sees justification as the permanent *foundation* of sanctification. In yet another metaphor, he makes justification by faith the main *hinge* on which religion turns. This agrees well with the overall design of the *Institutes* as a *pietatis summa* (a "summary of piety"): its subject is the right attitude to God, which is *pietas*, and the pure religion that flows from it. And "unless you first of all grasp what your relationship to God is, and the nature of his judgment concerning you, you have neither a foundation on which to establish your salvation nor one on which to build piety toward God" (*Institutes*, 1:613, 726; but see also 624–25, 650, 788, 794).

A further mark of Calvin's dogmatic order is that, as he sees it, "repentance not only constantly follows faith [i.e., faith-union with Christ], but is also born of faith" (*Institutes*, 1:593). He gives a reason that is psychologically astute. True repentance, which Luther usually attributed to the law of God (e.g., *Freedom*, LW 31:364), springs, in Calvin's view, from recognition of God's fatherly favor, which is to say, from faith. It is certainly possible to be overwhelmed by terrors of conscience before one is imbued with knowledge of grace. But such "initial fear" would be only the *beginning* of repentance, which is a *lifelong* turning of the heart to God. "No one will gird himself willingly to observe the law but him who will be persuaded that God is pleased by his obedience. This tenderness in overlooking and tolerating vices is a sign of God's fatherly favor" (*Institutes*, 1:594). (Recall Calvin's contrast between the obedience of slaves or servants and the obedience of children.) Luther, too, could speak of taking pleasure in God's commandments (e.g., LW 35:371), and Calvin, for his part, can go on to say more about repentance induced by fear of divine judgment than his preamble on repentance as the effect of faith leads us to expect (*Institutes*, 1:599). The distinction between the two sides of repentance, mortification and vivification, may explain the apparent shift in his argument: mortification corresponds to the initial fear of which he has already written. But repentance is not a transient crisis: it is the entire life of Christians, in which initial fear passes over into continually saying no to their inborn disposition (595, 599–600).

An interesting clue to what sixteenth-century English readers especially valued and looked for in Calvin's *Institutes* is that the first part to appear in English was his sketch of the Christian life (Thomas Broke, 1549); even after the first complete translation of the 1559 edition (Thomas Norton, 1561), in which it became chapters 6–10 of book 3, it continued to be published separately as *The Golden Booklet of the Christian Life*. There Calvin declines to deal exhaustively with individual virtues or to get carried away with exhortations. He offers only a general rule or pattern by which devout persons can frame their lives and determine their responsibilities; in this sense "doctrine" comes first (*Institutes*, 1:685, 688). His design, we may say, is to set out the dogmatic principles that shape, or should shape, the life of Christians. His very first sentence is this: "The object of regeneration . . . is to manifest in the life of believers a harmony and agreement between God's righteousness and their obedience, and thus to confirm the adoption that they have received as sons" (684). The filial metaphor is pervasive: Christians are God's adopted children and owe a debt of gratitude to their heavenly Father (*Institutes*, 1:686–87).

God's children are not their own but the Lord's; they do not so much live as heed Christ living and reigning within them (*Institutes*, 1:690; 1 Cor. 6:19; Gal. 2:20). "Show me a man, if you can, who, unless he has according to the commandment of the Lord renounced himself [Mark 8:34], would freely exercise goodness among men" (691; see also 693). Calvin goes on to deal with the necessity to "get out of yourself" as the condition for a right attitude to both God and one's fellows (chap. 7) and with the role of self-denial in bearing the cross of pain and suffering (chap. 8). Adversities turn our thoughts to the afterlife (chap. 9), but even as pilgrims we should use the gifts of the present life gratefully—with moderation and yet for delight and good cheer in proportion to our God-given station, not out of bare necessity (chap. 10). Throughout, Calvin presents his understanding of self-denial in express opposition to the philosophers, who imagine that the good life is living according to nature and who commend virtue because it ministers to one's self-respect (686–87, 691). He also rebukes them for their cold and unfeeling ethics (688, 709). Evidently, he has chiefly Stoicism in mind, from which he is anxious to distinguish his "Christian philosophy" (690). His pastoral insight is engaging and often eloquently expressed (see, e.g., 693–94); we can understand its appeal to Calvin's English disciples. But we cannot delay over the details.

Like Luther, Calvin held that Christians are travelers who may make progress but in this life never reach their destination: entire sanctification eludes them until the day of their death (*Institutes*, 1:601–2, 689, 739; 2:1161). But there were "perfectionists" among the Anabaptists of the Reformation era, and in eighteenth-century England the Methodists taught Christian perfection as a possibility for the living. Entire sanctification became a controversial issue both within and beyond Methodism. But I must confine my attention here to John Wesley (1703–91). In *A Plain Account of Christian Perfection*, published in 1767, he reviewed and defended his statements on the subject. But his clearest statement, presented in question-and-answer form, was *Thoughts on Christian Perfection*.[5] There he begins with a definition of Christian perfection as "loving God with all our heart, mind, soul, and strength," and adds: "This implies that no wrong temper, none contrary to love, remains in the soul and that all the thoughts, words and actions are governed by pure love" (284; cf. 288, 293). Of course, everyone makes *mistakes* in judgment and practice that deviate from what the perfect law requires, and everyone therefore needs to ask for forgiveness through the merits of Christ. But such defects, according to Wesley, are not *sins* if love is the principle of the action; as Paul says, love is the fulfilling of the law (Rom. 13:10). For example, the man who wore an iron girdle for the sake of mortification made a mistake out of ignorance, but he made it out of love for God. It was not a sin because sin, properly so called, is a voluntary transgression of a known law.

The critics were not mistaken in attributing a doctrine of sinless perfection to Wesley. In his sermon on Christian perfection he stated his conclusion unmistakably in italics: "In conformity, therefore, both to the doctrine of St. John, and to the whole tenor of the New Testament, we fix this conclusion: *a Christian is so far perfect, as not to commit sin*" ("Christian Perfection," 267). But the critics did not do justice to the foundation on which his conclusion rested: the idea of a love for God that fills the heart and crowds out the false temper from which deliberate sins come. And they wrongly inferred that for him Christian perfection meant a state of total freedom from any defect whatever—a faultless condition that would leave the atoning work of Christ behind. Because the critics thus failed to acknowledge his distinction between voluntary sins and involuntary mistakes, Wesley thought it best not to speak of *sinless* perfection at all (*Thoughts*, 287). Moreover, he never intended Christian perfection to be taken as a static plateau—the final stage of arrival and permanent rest. He did think of it as an instantaneous change, received by faith. But it must be awaited with disciplined obedience and prayer; lack of diligent preparation explains "why so few have received the blessing" (294). And after it is given, the Christian should continue to progress. "There is no 'perfection of degrees,' as it is termed; none which does not admit of a continual increase. So that how much soever any man has attained, or in how high a degree soever he is perfect, he hath still need to 'grow in grace' [2 Pet. 3:18] and daily to advance in the knowledge and love of God his Saviour" ("Christian Perfection," 258; cf. *Thoughts*, 294).

Wesley was wrestling with some challenging New Testament texts: not only express commands to be "perfect" (*teleios*, Matt. 5:48; 19:21), or statements that in the KJV appear to entail the possibility of perfection (1 Cor. 2:6; Eph. 4:13;

5. It appeared first in vol. 4 of *Sermons on Several Occasions* (1760). An abridged version is given in the *Plain Account*, but my page references are to the full reprint in Outler 1964 (283–98), who also includes three other writings of Wesley that I cite by his pagination: "Christian Perfection" (sermon, 1741; Outler, 252–71), *Cautions and Directions Given to the Greatest Professors in the Methodist Societies* (pamphlet, 1762; Outler, 298–305), and "The Scripture Way of Salvation" (sermon, 1765; Outler, 271–82).

Phil. 3:15; Col. 1:28; 4:12; Jas. 1:4; 3:2),[6] but also the seeming contradiction in 1 John between a denial and an affirmation of sinlessness (1 John 1:8–10; 3:9; cf. 2:1–2). Wesley was troubled when some who understood Scripture to teach the possibility of perfection announced that they had attained it. He warned against pride and a divisive spirit, and he thought it might be best to avoid describing particular changes wrought by God—victory over pride, or anger, or unbelief, for example—with such general names as "perfection," "sanctification," "the second blessing," or "the having attained" (*Cautions and Directions,* 299, 304). The editor of Wesley's *Standard Sermons*, Edward Sugden, writes that "he came more and more to see that [Christian perfection is] an ideal, to which the believer approximates ever more closely, though it may be impossible to say that he has absolutely attained it" (Wesley 1921, 2:150).

The experience of entire sanctification as a transient but repeatable "second blessing" or "baptism with the Spirit"—after justification by faith—continues to occupy many Christian groups and denominations, especially the Holiness churches. Wesley never settled the matter to everyone's satisfaction, but his insistence that salvation by faith includes sanctification as well as justification has remained influential in and beyond Methodism; many have said that this is his most important theological legacy. In "The Scripture Way of Salvation" he wrote: "Hence may appear the extreme mischievousness of that seemingly innocent opinion that there is no sin in a believer . . . the moment a man is justified" ("The Scripture Way of Salvation," 280). It remains to add that while Wesley spoke of perfect love more often as love for God, he certainly did not neglect love for neighbor. Perhaps, as some have argued, his social activity was condescending and short-lived, but he addressed the desperate needs of the day out of a passionately held faith. He was an ardent abolitionist, and his organization of care for the sick and the poor, many of them victims of the Industrial Revolution, was one of the most remarkable features of the Methodist movement.[7]

Schleiermacher's thoughts on sanctification keep close (as usual) to the treatment of it in the dogmatic tradition he inherited, and (as usual) he has some modifications to propose. He justifies retention of the term *sanctification* as scriptural, and in the light of Scripture and tradition he analyzes the pertinent features of "the evangelical Christian self-consciousness" (*CF* 505, 514–15). Like Calvin, he views sanctification as the effect of union with Christ. He finds that the Old Testament notion of a holy *people* called to be separate fits well with his understanding of Christ's work as the creation of a new *corporate* life. But holiness is progressive: it is becoming, not being, holy (506; cf. 512–13). The habitual power of the old life, though in the regenerate it loses its dominance (cf. Rom. 6:14), is not simply extinguished; the new strength of the Christian's consciousness of God "is a gift which becomes ours only after sin has developed

6. Much depends on how *teleios* is translated. In all these texts from the epistles except the last the NRSV has "mature" or, in one instance, "maturity": in Eph. 4:13 *eis andra teleion* (KJV "unto a perfect man") is rendered "to maturity." The KJV similarly translates *teleioi* simply as "men" in 1 Cor. 14:20 (NRSV "adults") and "them that are of full age" in Heb. 5:14.

7. See the letter to William Wilberforce written just days before Wesley's death (Outler, 85–86) and *A Plain Account of the People Called Methodists* (1749), for which I use Herbert Welch, ed., *Selections from the Writings of the Rev. John Wesley, M.A.*, rev. ed. (New York: Abingdon, 1918), 171–98; see esp. 190–97. Reappraisals of Wesleyan sanctification and social change from the perspectives of black, liberation, and feminist theologies will be found in Runyon 1981.

its power; and what has emerged in time can be removed in time only by its opposite" (507), which is the perfect God-consciousness of Christ working in us. Still, although there is a continual struggle of the new self against the old, Schleiermacher's Calvinism is showing when he sides with those confessions and doctors that deny the possibility of ever losing the grace of regeneration (513). But he does not always reaffirm Calvinist teaching. It will suffice to note just two important respects in which he departs from the teaching of his Reformed predecessors on sanctification.

First, throughout his discussion he takes a pivotal concept from the Synoptic Gospels and maintains that to be conformed to the likeness of Christ must mean receiving from Christ *the will for the kingdom of God*—the will "on which every single act and resolve of Christ was based" (*CF* 509). "Fellowship with Him is always a fellowship with His mission to the world" (517). The good works of the Christian, approved by God, are not motivated by the idea of reward, nor do they aim at enhancing the Christian's own spiritual progress; they must be understood strictly as activity in the kingdom of God in faithful pursuit of one's vocation (521–22). In the age of Protestant orthodoxy, the doctrine of sanctification had not been shaped by the idea of the kingdom of God; after Schleiermacher, the place of the kingdom in Protestant views of Christian renewal took on cardinal significance, from Albrecht Ritschl to the advocates of the social gospel. Since the studies by Johannes Weiss and Albert Schweitzer, New Testament scholars have generally agreed that Jesus' proclamation of the kingdom was apocalyptic: its imminent coming would be entirely an act of God breaking into human history. Believers could pray for it, prepare for it, and "enter" it, but not make it happen. The idea of *working* for the kingdom, however, was not simply a modern invention; it seems to have been an early revision required by the unexpected postponement of the kingdom's arrival. Hence, in the Letter to the Colossians, Paul could speak of his "co-workers [*synergoi*] for the kingdom of God" (Col. 4:11; cf. 1 Cor. 3:9).

Second, whereas Calvin taught that *the principal use of the law* is its use in the regenerate, Schleiermacher allows no value whatever to law in the sphere of sanctification. Even the Decalogue has no place in Christian instruction. Love does much more than law can do, and in our vision of the perfection of Christ we have a far more perfect means even for recognizing sin (*CF* 484, 523).[8] Schleiermacher insists that neither Christ's endorsement of the two great commandments (Mark 12:28–31) nor his new commandment to love one another as he has loved (John 15:12) can strictly be taken for legal prescriptions. He ends by recommending a Christian ethic that drops the imperative mood altogether and simply describes how Christians live within the kingdom of God (524). That is perhaps a salutary reminder that Christian behavior flows from the transforming influence of the Redeemer; as Schleiermacher claims, a descriptive ethic answers to the proper relationship between Christian ethics and dogmatics. How well it works as ethics we can leave to the ethicists; we must turn to the dogmatic task of critically appropriating the biblical and historical material on sanctification now before us.

8. Nothing in the German original calls for the misleading expression "the law of Christian morality" in the English translation of *CG* §111.4 (*CF* 516).

III. Faith and Renewal

To live by faith is to live confidently as children of God. It is also to live *obediently*. In the traditional terms, not only justification but sanctification also is by faith (cf. Acts 26:18). My thesis 13 is intended to show the systematic connection of sanctification or renewal with two of our previous themes: the elemental sense of moral demand and Christ's work in the Christian community, "the household of God" (Eph. 2:19). The obedience of faith is *restoration of the elemental sense of moral demand that estrangement blunts or rejects,* and it *is described as life together in "the Father's household."* In this way, we can keep in mind the point of contact for the gospel, which speaks to defiance as well as mistrust—not only to those who have lost the sense of life's meaning, but also to those who (as we say) have lost their moral compass. And we can preserve the familial metaphor that we have maintained throughout. It will be clear once more that our subject, from first to last, is Christian faith—*the distinctively Christian way of having faith, in which elemental faith . . . is confirmed, specified, and represented as filial trust in God "the Father of Jesus Christ"* (thesis 1).

1. The Obedience of Faith

The gospel of salvation by grace may seem to invite the objection that it subverts morals. It was so from the beginning. Paul's controversy was with those who thought it possible to justify themselves by obedience to God's law, as he himself once sought from the law a righteousness of his own (Rom. 10:3; Phil. 3:9; cf. Rom. 10:3). He opposed them with a righteousness of God "apart from law"—through faith in Jesus Christ, who is the end of the law (Rom. 3:21–25; 10:4). But he recognized the possible retort, "Should we continue in sin in order that grace may abound? . . . Should we sin because we are not under law but under grace?" (Rom. 6:1, 14–15; cf. Gal. 5:18).

Paul's negative answer presupposes that even those who boast of the law have not been good at keeping it (Rom. 2:17–3:20): "just as you once presented your members as slaves to impurity and to greater and greater iniquity, so now present your members as slaves to righteousness for sanctification [*eis hagiasmon*]" (6:19). He admits the harshness of the expression "slaves to righteousness" and gives a more appropriate metaphor later when he writes, "you did not receive a spirit of slavery to fall back into fear, but you have received a spirit of adoption" (8:15; cf. Gal. 4:3–7). However, good behavior is required even of children, and God's call to holiness goes with the promise, "you shall be my sons and daughters" (2 Cor. 6:14–7:1). Paul can therefore speak of a coming judgment according to works: "For all of us must appear before the judgment seat of Christ, so that each may receive recompense for what has been done in the body, whether good or evil" (2 Cor. 5:10; cf. 4:5; Rom. 14:10–12). He does not mean the judgment to determine who is to be saved (as in Rom. 2:5–11) but a judgment to assess the *deeds* of the saved—God's children—and to reward them accordingly (cf. 1 Cor. 3:10–15; 9:27).

Salvation by grace, as Paul explains it, does not subvert morals; on the contrary, grace provides the stimulus for a distinctively evangelical morality in which the strongest motive for "good works" comes from the gospel of grace itself. Not to recognize the *demand* of the gospel would be to accept the grace of God in vain (cf. 2 Cor. 6:1). Hence Paul's *therefore* when he turns from his message of justification and election to the behavior expected of the justified: "I appeal to you therefore, brothers and sisters, by the mercies of God, to present your bodies as a living sacrifice, holy and acceptable to God, which is your spiritual worship [*logikēn latreian*, perhaps 'reasonable worship']. Do not be conformed to this world [*aiōni*, this 'age'], but be transformed by the renewing of your minds, so that you may discern what is the will of God—what is good and acceptable and perfect" (Rom. 12:1–2). The Heidelberg Catechism follows the same logic: in part 3, instruction in the Decalogue is placed under the heading "Thankfulness," gratitude for redemption by grace. Indeed, a similar sequence from gift to demand appears already in the preamble to the Ten Commandments themselves (Exod. 20:2). For the children of God, gratitude and the obedience of faith go together.

2. *The Profile of a Saint*

In the New Testament, Christians are saints (*hagioi*), that is, "set apart" or "consecrated." The cognate Greek words for "sanctify" (*hagiazō*) and "sanctification" (*hagiasmos*) are used both for the initial act of God by which Christians are consecrated and for the holy living for which they are set apart: they have been sanctified (Acts 20:32; Rom. 15:16; 1 Cor. 1:2; Heb. 10:10, 29; cf. 1 Tim. 4:5; 2:21), and they are to be sanctified (1 Thess. 4:3–8). The two uses are not sharply differentiated, and "sanctification" in its second use also, as in the first, is understood to refer to a work of God, Christ, or the Holy Spirit; it *happens* to believers in their union with Christ, who *is* their sanctification (1 Cor. 1:30; 6:9–11; 1 Thess. 5:23; 2 Thess. 2:13; Heb. 2:11; 12:10; 1 Pet. 1:2). But sanctification is also a work of believers; they are summoned to *strive for* sanctification, without which no one will see the Lord (Heb. 12:14; cf. 1 Thess. 4:3).[9] Hence Paul's paradoxical injunction to the Philippians: "[W]ork out your own salvation with fear and trembling; for it is God who is at work in you, enabling you both to will and to work for his good pleasure" (Phil. 2:12–13).

The goal of sanctification is cleansing, obedience to Jesus Christ, eternal life, or, quite simply, salvation (Rom. 6:22; Eph. 5:26; 1 Pet. 1:2; 2 Thess. 2:13). Some interpreters take Paul to say in Romans 8:3–4 that God sent his Son so that the requirement of the law, once out of reach, might be fulfilled in the lives of those who are empowered by the Spirit. As Augustine explained in *The Spirit and the Letter*, "The law was therefore given, in order that grace might be sought; grace was given, in order that the law might be fulfilled" (NPNF[1] 5:97). Others think this would bring back a legalistic piety alien to Paul's gospel of grace. Luther and Schleiermacher insisted that the Christian needs no law. But Luther admitted that there are not many real Christians (*Temporal Authority* [1523], LW

9. In Heb. 12:14 (as in 1 Thess. 4:4, 7, and 1 Tim. 2:15) the NRSV translates *hagiasmos* with "holiness," elsewhere translated "sanctification." The English word "holiness" is the usual translation of other substantives from the same root (*hagiotēs* in Heb. 12:10; *hagiōsynē* in Rom. 1:4; 2 Cor. 7:1; 1 Thess. 3:13) and of the etymologically distinct *hosiotēs* (Eph. 4:24). All these passages would be pertinent to further discussion of the present theme, as would numerous passages in which the theme is addressed without the actual words *sanctification* or *holiness*.

45:91)—an important qualification of his idealistic picture of saints without law. The *ought* of the law cannot be eliminated from sanctification. But the *perception* of law changes for those who are born again: for them, "*God's commandments are no longer burdensome*" (1 John 5:3). Paul says, "neither circumcision counts for anything nor uncircumcision, but keeping the commandments of God" (1 Cor. 7:19 RSV). We must add, though, that whereas laws (plural) command this and that, *love* is the fulfilling of the law, as Paul also says (Rom. 13:8–10; Gal. 5:14); it is the Christian's due response to the divine love (1 John 4:19), which, as a favorite hymn puts it, "demands my soul, my life, my all."

On one thing all the writers we have called to witness agree: sanctification, in a sense, goes against nature—against the inborn self-interest at the heart of sin. Sanctification calls for putting the old nature to death; it is not about self-acceptance. But so insidious is the power of the old Adam that sanctification may itself be pressed into the service of self-interest if it entails an obsessive preoccupation with one's own salvation and with measuring one's daily progress in holiness. For Luther, "progress" meant ever to begin anew (*Lectures on Romans,* LW 25:478); he was suspicious of the yearning to be holy and asserted that "God wants plain sinners . . . God has nothing to do with saints. The word 'saint' [*sanctus homo*] is a fiction" (*Ennaratio Psalmi LI* [1532/38], WA 40^2:327, 347, my trans.; cf. WA 12:325). In much the same way, a present-day Lutheran, Gerhard Forde, finds talk about sanctification to be dangerous. He argues that free grace and the idea of progressive sanctification simply cannot be put together; sanctification can only be the art of getting used to justification (in Alexander 1988, 13, 120–21).[10] I grant the danger but not the remedy: Forde's solution would seriously curtail the New Testament's idea of sanctification, which with its imperatives entails the struggle for progress.

To be sure, progress means growth *in* grace, not growth *out of* grace: it neither implies meritorious attainment nor excludes the possibility of relapse. In the thinking of the Reformers, the danger of a holy narcissism was countered by maintaining an exclusive focus on Christ. This accords with the oft-quoted Scripture, which does not just say, "Grow in grace" (so KJV) but "grow in the grace and knowledge of our Lord and Savior Jesus Christ" (2 Pet. 3:18 NRSV). Luther understood the gospel to deliver Christians from the monster of uncertainty precisely by commanding them to look only at Christ; he believed his theology was sure because, in this way, it took believers out of themselves (*Lectures on Galatians,* LW 26:387). Similarly, Calvin thought that the only way to benefit your neighbor is to "give up all thought of self and, so to speak, get out of yourself" (*Institutes,* 1:695; cf. 417–18). It is hardly too much to say that the heart of the Reformation gospel was conveyed in the conception of faith as *intuitus Christi,* undivided attention to the Christ who is presented in the Word. In this faith Luther and Calvin discovered the source of the love for God and neighbor in which sanctification essentially consists: it sets the believer free from anxiety toward God and free for attention to others.

10. A similar concern underlies Karl Barth's critique of the Roman Catholic doctrine of grace: God's grace never becomes also *our* grace but is always "His sovereign act which is everywhere new and strange and free" (*CD* IV/1:84 [§58.1]). Cf. Schleiermacher's statement that "all divine grace is always prevenient" (*CG* §108.2 [*CF* 485 n. 2]); see also §110.2 (*CF* 506).

What are we to say, then, is the profile of a saint? It will represent the profiles we have found in the teaching of Jesus and Paul—profiles that reflect the image of Jesus himself in the memory of the church. As such, we can now say, it will not be the profile of an individual wholly immersed in cultivation of his piety. One critic of Christian spirituality has described it as "manicuring one's soul." Up to a point the taunt may be well taken, but it does not fit the idea of sanctification by faith in Christ. The view of Luther and Calvin was that faith gets the believer out of herself; hence they had much to say about good works for the benefit of the neighbor. And we can appropriate Schleiermacher's insight that union with Christ must mean receiving from him the will for the kingdom of God. It is being turned by Christ from self to others that identifies the saint. But our historical review has shown the need to allow for variants in our profile of the saint. One example suggests itself from the sources I have quoted. The ideal Lutheran lives in the liberating joy of unconditional forgiveness and is ever watchful for the least trace of a resurgent works righteousness, although eagerness for neighborly good works is not thereby diminished but inspired. The ideal Calvinist is a dutiful son or daughter pledged to willing obedience and always on guard against a complacent faith without works, although it is not filial obedience but fatherly indulgence alone that secures their confidence in God. Because even saints are sinners, in both ideals the saint is viewed through what we may call the "dialectic" of healing and forgiveness; but in each ideal there is a distinctive emphasis. There will always be such modifications in the profile of a saint. They are not exclusive. They need one another to describe the fullness of Christian faith.

IV. Ecumenical Postscript

In the last two chapters, I have avoided undue narrowing of "the manifold grace of God" (1 Pet. 4:10; cf. Eph. 3:10). I have argued that the preaching of the gospel addresses mistrust and anxiety as well as defiance and abuse of the creation and that the gift of Christ is at once the confidence and the obedience of faith. To speak of the gospel in this way is an adjustment to the inherited language, but continuity is evident in that it led us into reflection on the dogmatic differences concerning justification and sanctification, reconciliation and renewal, in the Western theological tradition. I suggested that the differences could be viewed as variations on the two-sidedness of the Augustinian correlation of forgiveness and healing (cf. 1 John 1:9). To put it in my own terms, healing is "incremental" and forgiveness is "iterative"; the two belong inseparably together, and together determine the life of faith. Justification is not a once-for-all divine act at the beginning of the Christian life; never contingent on the patient's improvement but needed by the patient's lack of improvement, it happens again and again until the cure is complete. This, certainly, was Calvin's view: he believed that although by the grace of God Christians make steady, if painfully slow progress in the Christian life, they need God's mercy, which "by continual forgiveness of sins repeatedly acquits us" (*Institutes*, 1:689, 739, 777).

When so stated, such an understanding of the shape of Christian existence would likely meet with wide agreement. But ever since the time of the

Reformation, difficulties have arisen over the definition of terms, in particular the cardinal terms *grace* and *justify*. Recent ecumenical conversations have reconsidered the old divisions in a more amicable spirit. I will offer one or two concluding afterthoughts to place further discussion, which I cannot pursue here, in the new ecumenical context. I should record in advance my persuasion that whenever the accusations made by one party against the other party's language are hotly repudiated, a tacit material agreement is being presupposed and should be made explicit, if possible in less controversial terms.

1. Grace

In everyday language, according to the linguistic analysis of Thomas Aquinas, the Latin word for "grace" (*gratia*) has three uses: it means someone's love or favor, a gift freely given, and gratitude for benefits received (as when we "say grace" at table). The gift comes from the favor, and gratitude from the gift. In the context of theology, the second sense of "grace" denotes a gift imparted to the soul by the gratuitous love of God: the infused habit by which the soul is disposed toward the highest good (*ST* 2–1, q. 110, aa. 1–2 [1:1132–34]). Roman Catholic discussions of grace usually have most to say about grace in this sense, though understood as the effect of grace in the first sense.

Protestant theologians, by contrast, have commonly explained grace as nothing but the unmerited favor of God (Thomas's first sense). Luther rejected the scholastic view of grace as an infused habit, and his adversaries saw this as evidence of Protestant indifference to spiritual and moral transformation. Luther's reply in his treatise *Against Latomus* was that while grace is nothing other than the favor or goodwill of God, Scripture does speak also of "the free gift" (Rom. 5:15) that works to purge away the sin of one whom grace has forgiven. "Everything is forgiven through grace, but as yet not everything is healed through the gift" (LW 32:226–30). And Luther does not hesitate to apply the language of "infusion" to the gift, though not to grace. We have to distinguish the two benefits of the gospel. Why? Because otherwise, he thinks, we risk implying that forgiveness is not free but dependent on our moral and spiritual improvement (LW 32:226–30). Calvin agreed, but he subsumed both benefits under the one term *grace*, which he characterized as "double" or "twofold," and more attention should be given to this obvious opening for comparison with Thomas's threefold grace. "By partaking of [Christ]," Calvin says, "we principally receive a double grace [*duplicem gratiam*]: namely, that being reconciled to God through Christ's blamelessness, we may have in heaven instead of a Judge a gracious Father; and secondly, that sanctified by Christ's spirit we may cultivate blamelessness and purity of life" (*Institutes*, 1:725).[11]

Biblical exegesis provides warrants for both Catholic and Protestant understandings of grace. In the New Testament, *charis* may mean *favor*. But frequently it means something given, a *gift* (Rom. 1:5; 12:3, 6; 15:15; 1 Cor. 1:4; 3:10; 16:3; 2 Cor. 8:1, 4, 6, 19; 9:8, 14–15; Gal. 2:9; Eph. 3:7; 4:7; Jas. 4:6), and sometimes it

11. Cf. the first and second meanings of *gratia* in Thomas Aquinas. The word *gratia* in Calvin's *duplex gratia* is not necessarily to be taken as a technical theological term; it could be translated simply as "benefit" or "gift." But we can certainly take it as a contribution to the theology of grace. See also *Institutes* 2.16.7 (1:511–12); 3.11.6 (1:732), 11.15 (1:745–46).

means transforming *power* (Acts 4:33; 1 Cor. 15:10; 2 Tim. 2:1; Heb. 13:9). When the risen Lord admonishes Paul, "My grace is sufficient for you, for [my] power is made perfect in weakness," grace is identified with the indwelling "power of Christ" (2 Cor. 12:9). The question for ecumenical discussion is how far the opposition between traditional Catholic and traditional Protestant statements about grace, occasioned in part by the multiple meanings of *charis* in Scripture, may conceal an underlying agreement. One must also ask how far the contrary practical concerns—for the *transformation* wrought by grace and for the utter, unconditional *freedom* of grace—may be taken as complementary. There *are* differences that are more than merely semantic. The most important of them will have to be taken up later when we speak of the sacraments. But there, too, when the heat of mutual recrimination dies down, more agreement is possible than has traditionally been supposed.

2. *Justify*

Similar dogmatic issues underlie the differences over the meaning of "justify." Protestants have insisted that "to justify" (*dikaioō*) means "to declare righteous," not "to make righteous." Catholic theologian Hans Küng does not disagree but comments that when God declares a man just, he effects a transformation of the man's very being: he is simultaneously *made* just. "[J]ustification includes in itself all the effects which touch the very being of the man who is justified . . . and thus also includes a positive sanctification effected by God" (in Callahan et al. 1961: 315–16). Küng admits that this is not what Scripture explicitly says. We may prefer to stay with what Scripture does say. But his point is close to what I myself said about the effect of justification. We may agree that justification effects, in *some* sense, a transformation of the one justified.

The so-called new Finnish Luther research argues that even for Luther the transformation is nothing less than the "deification" (*theōsis*) of which the Eastern Orthodox theologians speak, and that this opens up new possibilities for ecumenical conversations. Particular emphasis is placed on Luther's assertion in his *Commentary on Galatians* that Christ is not just the object of faith but "present in faith" (LW 26:129). This has always been a favorite Luther quotation; what is new is inquiry into the ontological status of the existence of Christ (or God) in faith—and the possibilities the inquiry opens up for ecumenical theology (see, e.g., Mannermaa 1995). The inquiry is inspired by 2 Peter 1:4 (that "you may escape from the corruption that is in the world because of lust, and may become participants of the divine nature") and by the aphorism of Athanasius, "He was made man that we might be made God."

Calvin is seldom recruited for this discussion, though the idea of mystical union with Christ was fundamental to his understanding of salvation, and occasionally he used the language of deification (mainly as the eschatological goal of union with Christ). His long refutation of Andreas Osiander, added in the 1559 edition of the *Institutes* (*Institutes*, 1:729–43), might lead us to expect that he would initially be suspicious of talk about the deification of humanity. Osiander deplored the belief that justification was a purely forensic act of God by which sinners were only declared righteous, not made righteous in reality. He spoke rather of an "essential righteousness," imparted by the transfusion of Christ's divine *nature* into humanity. To Calvin's thinking, this bordered on Manicheism. The proper belief, in his view, is that although Christ could not have redeemed humanity if he were not God, he won righteousness for us by his *work* in his human nature—his obedience and sacrificial death. "[A]lthough righteousness comes forth to us from the secret wellspring of his divinity, it does not follow that Christ, who in the flesh sanctified himself for our sake [John 17:19], is righteousness for us according to his divine nature" (742). The Lutherans made a similar case against Osiander (though not by name) in their Formula of Concord (art. 3).

In ecumenical conversation, however, it is crucial to note the distinction Orthodox theology has always drawn between the divine "essence" and the divine "energies." This is how one spokesman for Orthodoxy sums up the Orthodox position: "*Theosis* speaks only of what man can become by faith and grace, that is, a *participant* in the divine life. Sharing in the life and love of the Holy Trinity in His uncreated energies is possible for created nature, but to become of one essence with the uncreated essence of God is not possible!" (Robert Stephanopoulos in Meyendorff and McLelland 1973: 152). "Participation in the divine *life*" is perhaps a less provocative expression than "deification." It underlies Orthodox understanding of atonement and the Eucharist.

This brings to a close not only the theme of "Living by Faith" but also the entire first division of part II of our outline, "Christ and the Christian." From analysis of estrangement the outline has moved to redemption and the way the work of Christ manifests itself in the experience of the individual believer. Since Christ's work includes the creation of the community of faith, the social aspect of redemption has by no means been ignored. But the transition to the second division of part II, "The Spirit and the Church," is directly and explicitly a transition to ecclesiology. One could argue that because in Christian experience the church comes before the believer, dogmatics should follow the same sequence—doing Calvin's *Institutes* backward, so to say, starting with book 4. Calvin was preeminently a churchman; so was Schleiermacher, who sprinkled *The Christian Faith* with reminders of the priority of the community over the individual long before he reached his chapters on the church. But in the order of their presentations neither Calvin nor Schleiermacher put the community in first place; Schleiermacher's argument for dealing first with the individual believer is particularly interesting, as we will see. Calvin, I think, simply followed tradition. For us, too, it will be convenient to follow the traditional dogmatic sequence (soteriology before ecclesiology), as did our two main guides.

Division 2: The Spirit and the Church

14. The Covenant (II): Election

The church, as a servant people of God, does not consist of a few who are the exclusive objects of divine care but of those who, hearing the call of the gospel to be conformed to the image of God's Son and chosen servant, Jesus Christ, bear witness to the care of God for humanity; so that the church, as God's elect, is said to be a "creation of the gospel"—brought into being by the Spirit through the word about Jesus Christ.

Our first look at the concept of covenant ended with some comments on special revelation. The problem addressed was that special revelation, if it is thought of as mediated through "mighty acts of God," appears to require the possibility of supernatural intervention in the regular course of nature and history, and the modern scientific concept of nature has cast doubt on interventionism. At least since Schleiermacher, many Christian theologians have abandoned belief in God's ability (or desire) to interrupt the natural web of events that God has ordained. However, I suggested that the problem can be resolved if we think of God's historical deeds not as resembling the interaction of one finite self with other finite selves but as more like the relation of a single self to the diversity of its own activity. For while everything a person does is her activity, some of the things she does may provide better clues than others to her true character. It is possible to maintain, then, that special revelation does not require a suspension of the natural passage of events; it requires only the recognition that while all events are effects of the divine causality, some are better indications than others of God's character.

If we accept this analogy, however, it still leaves us with another problem: the inescapable particularity of the sequence of events that Christian faith perceives as the history of salvation and therefore as the revelation of the one true God—the unique biblical story that runs from the call of Israel to the manifestation of the gospel in Jesus Christ. Any case for special revelation presupposes that the revelation is given only to one portion of humanity. Accordingly, our second look at the idea of the covenant of grace requires us to move on from revelation to *election*: the favoring of selected individuals and a select people to be the recipients of special revelation.

In the Western theological tradition, thanks mainly to Augustine, the problem of particularity became inextricably entangled with *predestination*. According to the classical doctrine of double predestination, the singling out of some and not others as the recipients of revelation is God's foreordained choice. Few doctrines have been as hotly disputed. It is hard to combine belief in a God of love with the implication that God willfully excludes the vast majority of humankind from revelation and the possibility of redemption. The dispute may be said to have suffered neglect in most Christian communities since the eighteenth century. But election took on a fresh urgency in the twentieth century as the question of Christianity and other religions moved to the center of theological interest, and some of the issues that used to be discussed under "predestination" have been taken up again. Together with the concept of covenant, election and predestination have remained a particular interest of the Reformed or Calvinist churches. But we must start from the fact that election is a biblical doctrine.

I. The Biblical Doctrine of Election

1. Election in the Old Testament

The Old Testament tells of many individuals who were chosen to further Yahweh's designs: patriarchs, judges, kings, priests, and prophets—even rulers of other nations.[1] But election is mainly about Yahweh's choice of a people; it is bound up with the covenant of grace and the revelation of the divine name.[2] Of particular importance for the idea of election is the book of Deuteronomy, where both the foundation and the purpose of election are made clear. The *foundation* of Yahweh's choice was his unmerited love. He gave his chosen people cities they did not build and vineyards they did not plant (Deut. 6:10–12; cf. Josh. 24:13). They were not chosen because they were a great or righteous nation; they were few in number—and stubborn (Deut. 7:7; 9:4–7). "It was because the LORD loved you and kept the oath that he swore to your ancestors, that the LORD has brought you out with a mighty hand, and redeemed you from the house of slavery, from the land of Pharaoh king of Egypt" (7:8). But does continuation of the covenant, once graciously bestowed, depend on the obedience of the chosen people? Is the covenant conditional? The answer is that Yahweh is forever bound by his oath, but that does not guarantee that things will always go well with his people (5:29–33). He warns them not to suppose, when they hear the words of the covenant, "We are safe even though we go our own stubborn ways" (29:19; cf. Amos 3:2). The curses that fall on a disobedient people are horrifying (Deut. 28:15–68). Yet there is always the possibility of repentance, and Yahweh will not forget the covenant but will restore the fortunes of his people when they return to him (4:23–31; 30:1–10; 32:36). We are told elsewhere that Yahweh forgives and restores his penitent people "for his name's sake" or "for his own sake" (1 Sam. 12:22; Neh. 1:5–11; Ps. 79:9; Isa. 43:25; 48:9, 11; Dan. 9:17, 19; etc.). Obviously, however, the restoration of the people leaves numerous casualties along the way.

1. In our English versions "choose" and "chosen" translate the Hebrew *bāḥar, bāḥîr*. The KJV sometimes has "mine elect" where the NRSV has "my chosen" (Isa. 42:1; 45:4; 65:9, 22). The verb *yāda'*, "to know," may also carry the sense of "choose" (Jer. 1:5; Amos 3:2).

2. Hence the ambivalence about *when* Israel was chosen (Deut. 5:2–3; Ps. 105:4–11, 43; Isa. 41:8–9; Ezek. 20:5).

The *purpose* of election is that Yahweh shall have a people who serve him—"joyfully and with gladness of heart"—and keep his commandments, summed up in the duty of love for God (Deut. 5:9–10; 6:5; 11:1, 13; 28:47; cf. Exod. 20:6). They are created for Yahweh's glory (Isa. 43:7). And because Yahweh is uniquely a God of justice and mercy, love for God requires the moral duty of love for neighbors, resident aliens, and strangers (Lev. 19:18, 34; Deut. 10:17–18). The inclusion of others besides the covenant people is striking. But election is by definition exclusive. "Although heaven and the heaven of heavens belong to the LORD your God, the earth with all that is in it, yet the LORD set his heart in love on your ancestors alone and chose you, their descendants after them, out of all the peoples, as it is today" (Deut. 10:14–15).

Nonetheless, the prophecies collected in Isaiah assert, or imply, that Yahweh's goodness will be shared with other peoples—even, perhaps, that Yahweh assigns to his chosen people a mission to bring his goodness to others. The sharing of Yahweh's blessings is made possible both by the dispersion of Israel and by the return to Palestine. Isaiah 19:18–25 suggests that the dispersion could create new centers for the worship of Yahweh beyond Jerusalem. There will be an altar to Yahweh in the land of Egypt, where Jewish refugees fled after the fall of Jerusalem to the Babylonians (587 BCE), and there the Egyptians will come to know Yahweh and will worship him. Israel will then be "the third with Egypt and Assyria." In Isaiah 2:2–4 (// Mic. 4:1–4), by contrast, the movement flows in the other direction: the prophet dreams of a time to come when Yahweh's blessing will reach other nations as they stream to Zion. "For out of Zion shall go forth instruction, and the word of the LORD from Jerusalem." In the chapters commonly assigned to Second and Third Isaiah, the focus shifts decisively from the dispersion to the return, made possible by the fall of Babylon to the armies of Cyrus (539 BCE). But renewed confidence in Jerusalem as the only center for the worship of Yahweh proves ambivalent. That the house of Yahweh is to be a house of prayer for all peoples (Isa. 56:7) is as much a token of particularism as of universalism.

The nations are depicted running to Zion, coming to Zion's light, and the Israelites will be to them the priests and ministers of Yahweh (Isa. 55:5; 60:3; 61:6). The glory of Yahweh thus coincides with the glorification of Zion, and nations that refuse to bow down and serve the city of Yahweh will perish (55:5; 60:9, 12). The Servant Songs are often said to move beyond particularism by depicting Yahweh's Servant as "a light to the nations," so that Yahweh's "salvation may reach to the end of the earth" (49:6; cf. 42:6). The Servant may not be an individual with a mission to the Gentiles as well as to his own people. Perhaps he is Israel itself (see 49:3; cf. 41:8; 44:1; 45:4). But since in one place he is distinguished from Israel (49:6), he would have to be an idealized Israel or the personification of a faithful remnant.[3] In any case, even the Servant Songs do not quite resolve the tension between particularism and universalism, and after the return from captivity Zion-centered piety was bound to be enlivened. Zechariah depicts Yahweh as "jealous for Zion with great jealousy" (Zech. 1:14;

3. The idea of the "remnant" is not explicit in the Servant Songs, but it was important for Isaiah, who named his son *Shear-jashub*, meaning "a remnant shall return" (Isa. 7:3, where the reference is not to the future captivity and return from exile, but simply to the turning back of a penitent people to Yahweh). See further 10:20–22; 11:11, 16; cf. Jer. 23:3; Amos 5:15; Zeph. 3:11–13.

8:2). Yahweh will come and dwell in Zion, and many nations will join themselves to him (2:10–11). "In those days ten men from nations of every language shall take hold of a Jew, grasping his garment and saying, 'Let us go with you, for we have heard that God is with you'" (8:23; cf. 14:16–19; Pss. 22:27; 67:4). The divine benevolence is extended *beyond* Israel only *through* Israel, and a proselyte is likely seen as a second-class citizen of Zion.

It is perhaps too much to speak (as is usually done) of the "mission" of Israel, since the chosen people are passive objects of the nations' admiration and homage. The vision of Israel's calling as a light to the Gentiles had to struggle against the exclusiveness voiced by Zechariah and parodied in the story of Jonah. (The story of Ruth, on the other hand, served to show how important the role of a foreigner could be in the designs of Yahweh.) Some interpreters think that two verses in Malachi affirm an unqualified universalism. Malachi 1:11 reads: "from the rising of the sun to its setting my name is great among the nations, and in every place incense is offered to my name, and a pure offering; for my name is great among the nations, says the Lord of hosts." Malachi 2:10 asks: "Have we not all one father? Has not one God created us? Why then are we faithless to one another, profaning the covenant of our ancestors?" But the first quotation probably intends not the worship of Yahweh by the heathen but the faithfulness of Jews scattered by conquering foreign armies; and the appeal to the covenant in the second quotation surely limits the word "all" to all *Jewish* people.

2. Election in the New Testament

The question of particularism and universalism was bequeathed to the Christians, who came to understand themselves as the new Israel (Rom. 9:23–26; Gal. 6:16; 1 Pet. 2:9; cf. Jas. 1:1; 1 Pet. 1:1). What does that imply for the *old* Israel? The Gospel of Matthew shows a special interest in the question, and for Paul it became paramount in his controversy with the Judaizers. At first glance, the pertinent utterances attributed to Jesus himself in Matthew may appear ambivalent. There are plain assertions, on the one hand, that his mission was only to Israel. He instructs his twelve Apostles: "Go nowhere among the Gentiles, and enter no town of the Samaritans, but go rather to the lost sheep of the house of Israel" (Matt. 10:5–6). In his initial reaction to the plea of the Canaanite woman, he says: "I was sent only to the lost sheep of the house of Israel" (15:24). And he adds the harsh words: "It is not fair to take the children's food and throw it to the dogs" (v. 26). On the other hand, there are sayings of Jesus in Matthew that seem to announce, or at least to threaten, the disinheriting of Israel. For example, "I tell you, many will come from east and west and will eat with Abraham and Isaac and Jacob, while the heirs of the kingdom will be thrown into the outer darkness, where there will be weeping and gnashing of teeth" (8:11–12). Again: "I tell you, the kingdom of God will be taken away from you and given to a people that produces the fruits of the kingdom" (21:43). In Matthew, the parable of the Wedding Banquet ends with the words, "For many are called, but few are chosen" (21:14); in Luke it ends with the stern admonition, "For I tell you, none of those who were invited will taste my dinner" (Luke 14:24).

Matthew, however, identifies those who are rejected as the chief priests, the elders of the people, and the Pharisees (Matt. 21:23, 45). Those to whom Jesus turns with his proclamation of the kingdom are the *lost sheep* of Israel (21:45). And Matthew follows the parable of the Two Sons with Jesus' blunt assertion: "Truly I tell you, the tax collectors and the prostitutes are going into the kingdom of God ahead of you" (21:31). Judgment falls, then, not on all Israel, but on Israel's leaders. It is also noteworthy that, for Jesus' response to the Canaanite (Syrophoenician) woman, Mark has: "Let the children be fed *first*" (Mark 7:27; emphasis mine). The Roman centurion and the Canaanite woman obtained their requests because of their faith—before their time, so to say (Matt. 8:13; 15:28). Of the centurion's plea Jesus says: "Truly I tell you, in no one in Israel have I found such faith" (Matt. 8:10). A Christian reader of the Gospel will naturally hold that, in so saying, he implicitly pointed toward the church as the new chosen people, constituted not by heredity but by faith. Calvin observes that, although the calling of the Gentiles was a notable mark of the New Testament in contrast to the Old, "even Christ at the beginning of his preaching made no immediate progress toward it" (*Institutes*, 1:461). The longer ending of Mark's Gospel arrives at the goal, we may say, when it finally reports that the risen Lord appeared to the Eleven and enjoined them: "Go into all the world and proclaim the good news to the whole creation. The one who believes and is baptized will be saved; but the one who does not believe will be condemned" (Mark 16:15–16; see also Matt. 28:19; Luke 24:47; cf. Acts 1:8).

In the letters of Paul, "the election of grace" (*eklogē charitos,* Rom. 11:5) was bound up with the struggle against the Judaizers, who insisted that Gentile converts to Christianity had to add to their faith in Christ submission to the law of Moses. In his impassioned Letter to the Galatians, Paul asserts that this would substitute another gospel for the gospel of Christ (Gal. 1:6–7), and he argues from Scripture that *those who believe* are the descendants of Abraham, whose faith was counted as righteousness (3:6–7). In Christ the blessing of Abraham comes to the Gentiles, and there is no longer Jew or Greek, slave or free, male or female, but all are one in Christ Jesus (3:14, 28). "And if you belong to Christ, then you are Abraham's offspring, heirs according to the promise" (v. 29). What, then, of Israel "according to the flesh" (*kata sarka*)?

Paul answers in the long excursus, peppered with quotations from Scripture, in Romans 9–11. It calls for a closer exegesis than I can offer here. Briefly: He starts in chapter 9 by affirming that covenant privileges do belong to his "kindred according to the flesh." But he promptly adds that "not all Israelites truly belong to Israel, and not all of Abraham's children are his true descendants." He traces the division between the children of the flesh and the children of the promise to God's plan of election. The Lord says, "I have loved Jacob, but I have hated Esau" (Mal. 1:2–3). That the plan was formed before the twin brothers were born demonstrates for Paul that election has no regard for works: it depends entirely on the mercy of God, who says, "I will have mercy on whom I have mercy, and I will have compassion on whom I have compassion" (Exod. 33:19; cf. Rom. 11:6). No mere mortal can protest, any more than the pot can demand of the potter, "Why have you made me like this?" For what if God has made both vessels of wrath and vessels of mercy? As Isaiah predicted, only a remnant of the children of Israel will be saved (Isa. 10:22; cf. Rom. 11:5).

In the tenth chapter Paul discourses on the word of faith, which has been made accessible to all and makes no distinction between Jew and Greek. In chapter 11 he returns to the question, "[H]as God rejected his people?" and unfolds the view of history that he has hinted at already (in Rom. 9:22–24). Those Israelites who did not believe stumbled because they were "hardened"; but in the divine plan "their rejection is the reconciliation of the world." The Gentile believers have been grafted in to replace the natural branches that were broken off. And if they do not persist in unbelief, God has the power to graft the fallen Israelites back in again. "And so all Israel will be saved . . . for the gifts and the calling of God are irrevocable" (11:26). Perhaps, as some have argued, Paul's conclusion is that not just all Israel, but all humanity will ultimately be saved. "For God," he says, "has imprisoned all in disobedience so that he may be merciful to all. . . . For from him and through him and to him are all things. To him be the glory forever" (11:32, 36).

II. Election and Predestination

1. The Augustinian Tradition

A connection between election and predestination was by no means absent from Paul's excursus on the problem of God's apparent rejection of Israel. (Note the expression "God's plan of election" [*kat' eklogēn prothesis*] in Rom. 9:11.) But in Augustine the question of particularism and universalism was not confined to the Pauline problem: it became the question of divine predestination and human freedom that arises whenever anyone hears the gospel. In his treatise *On the Spirit and the Letter* (412), Augustine repeats like a refrain his favorite Pauline text (1 Cor. 4:7), "What do you have that you did not receive? And if you received it, why do you boast as if it were not a gift?" The capacity to respond to the gospel in faith is a gift of God. Yet the choice to believe or not to believe is the act of a person's own will in response to the preaching of the gospel and God's inward persuasion. To the question *why* one yields to the divine persuasion and another does not, Augustine can only reply with Paul, "O the depth of the riches and wisdom and knowledge of God! How unsearchable are his judgments," and, "Is there injustice on God's part?" (Rom. 11:33; 9:14; NPNF[1] 5:110–11). But later he had second thoughts on the subject.

In one of his last treatises, *On the Predestination of the Saints* (428 or 429), Augustine recalls his change of mind. He had once imagined that to consent to the gospel, when preached to us, is our own doing. The source of his error, he says, was this: "I had not yet very carefully sought, nor had I as yet found, what is the nature of the election of grace, of which the apostle says, 'A remnant are saved according to the election of grace.'" Not only the capacity to have faith, but faith itself is the gift of God, who prepares the will of his elect. Whereas the Pelagians imagined that God elected those he foreknew would have faith, the truth is that God chose his elect not because they would believe but that they might believe. He chose them in Christ——himself the most illustrious instance of predestination—before the foundation of the world (NPNF[1] 5:500–501, 503, 512, 516–17). The question is then, of course, why God chooses to give the gift of faith only to some, not to all; and that, Augustine thinks, is God's secret (506).

Augustine's doctrine of election and predestination remained controversial in the Western church after his death, and it underwent a vigorous renewal on the eve of the Reformation. I cannot trace the story here, but I should at least note that Thomas kept close to the Augustinian doctrine. Like Augustine, whom he cites often, Thomas speaks of the predestination of Christ and says that "by the same eternal act God predestinated us and Christ" (*ST* 2:2152).[4] The number of the predestined is fixed, since they take the place of the fallen angels (1:130): they will *necessarily* be saved by grace, and the reprobates *cannot* obtain grace, but no violence is done to the freedom of either (127).[5] Predestination does not depend on God's foreknowledge of how a person will make use of grace (129). His choice of some displays his mercy, and his rejection of others displays his justice in punishing them; yet we cannot say why one is chosen, another rejected (130; citation from Rom. 9:22–23).

Controversy over predestination and free will continued in the Roman Catholic Church after the Protestant Reformation. It was variously argued (1) that the efficacious grace given to the predestined is intrinsically different from the sufficient grace given indiscriminately to all (the Thomist or Dominican view); (2) that God predestines those who, he foresees, will consent to sufficient grace (the Molinist view); or (3) that God gives his grace to the predestined under such circumstances as he foresees will guarantee their consent (the congruist view). The second and third views were widely held among the Jesuits. (Eventually, in 1613, congruism became the required Jesuit teaching.) A papal commission to study the matter was appointed by Clement VIII (*Congregatio de auxiliis,* 1597), and in 1607 his successor, Paul V, granted interim permission to both Dominicans and Jesuits to teach their respective opinions—provided they did so without bitterness (DS 314). But conflict was sparked anew by the reform movement of the Jansenists, named for Dutch theologian Cornelius Jansen (1585–1638), whose book *Augustinus* was published posthumously in 1640. The long Jansenist controversy, centered in France, became entangled in ecclesiastical politics and dragged on intermittently until the French Revolution. The Jansenists claimed to be simply loyal "Augustinian Thomists": they denied being tainted with Calvinism and protested that their condemnation by Clement XI (in the bull *Unigenitus,* 1713) actually condemned Saints Augustine and Thomas as well (DS 317 n. 1, 347–54).

2. *Development in the Reformed Church*

In what is still one of the most careful studies of the Augustinian doctrine of predestination, J. B. Mozley concluded: "I see no substantial difference between

4. Augustine (NPNF[1] 5:512–13) and Thomas (*ST* 3, q. 24, art. 1 [2:2150]) found the biblical basis for the idea of the elect or predestined Christ in the Latin version of Rom. 1:4, where our English versions have "designated Son of God" (RSV) or "declared to be Son of God" (KJV and NRSV), not "predestined." The Greek *horisthentos* comes from the verb *horizō*, "delimit," "determine," etc.; the idea of "*pre*destine" is conveyed (e.g., in Rom. 8:29–30) by the compound *proorizō*. A different verb (*proginōskō*) lies behind the phrase in 1 Pet. 1:20, "destined [KJV 'foreordained'] before the foundation of the world," which might have served Augustine and Thomas better.

5. For Thomas this means simply that God operates in each thing according to its nature. As First Cause, he moves both natural and voluntary causes; in moving humans he does not deprive their actions of being voluntary, that is, of being caused by their own wills as secondary or mediate causes (*ST* 1, q. 83, art. 1, ad 3 [1:418]).

the Augustinian and Thomist, and the Calvinist doctrine of predestination. S. Augustine and Calvin alike hold an eternal Divine decree, which, antecedently to all action, separates one portion of mankind from another, and ordains one to everlasting life and the other to everlasting punishment" (1878: 393). The qualifying word *substantial* must be duly noted: there are differences that do not affect the definition of the "substance" implied in Mozley's statement (278–93). There are also merely linguistic differences, such as those that lay behind Pascal's attempt in his *Provincial Letters* to dissociate Jansenism from Calvin's view that predestination entails the denial of free choice. Mozley rightly comments: "all that the Augustinian and Jansenist admission with respect to free-will amounts to, is admission of a *will* in man; and this admission Calvin is equally ready to make" (409). That is, grace does not treat humans as inanimate objects—it works in the predestined by moving their wills, so that their response is not coerced but voluntary (cf. n. 5 above).

Mozley could have added Luther to his list of predestinarians. In his book against Erasmus, *The Bondage of the Will* (1525), Luther argued that freedom to *choose* is an illusion; and he added his own special reason, borrowed from Wycliffe, that everything happens by necessity. If a person is saved, it can only be because God has irresistibly directed the human will, which is utterly incapable of turning itself toward salvation (LW 33:37, 116, 160, etc.). Why, then, doesn't God change *everyone's* will if, as the prophet says, he does not desire the death of a sinner (Ezek. 18:23)? Luther replies that the prophet "is here speaking of the preached and offered mercy of God, not of that hidden and awful will of God whereby he ordains by his own counsel which and what sort of persons he wills to be recipients of his preached and offered mercy" (LW 33:139). Erasmus goes wrong, Luther thinks, because he fails to distinguish between the revealed and the hidden God—the Word of God and God himself (140; see also 108). Lutheranism shied away from Luther's determinism in *The Bondage of the Will*, as perhaps did Luther himself, although he considered *Bondage* one of his best books. But the Calvinists continued to worry about predestination, and out of their preoccupation came some alternatives for revising the inherited doctrine.

The definition *Calvin* himself gives is clear enough: "We call predestination God's eternal decree, by which he determined with himself what he willed to become of each man. For all are not created in equal condition; rather, eternal life is foreordained for some, eternal damnation for others" (*Institutes*, 2:926). The definition is nothing new; it sets Calvin in the Augustinian succession. But four features of his discussion of predestination should be noted.

(1) To begin with, in the 1559 *Institutes* he places election and calling in his third book, chapters 21–24, where they serve as appendages to the themes of reconciliation and renewal in Christ—not unlike his discussions of Christian freedom (chap. 19) and prayer (chap. 20), which are also treated as vital postscripts to the twofold grace of God in Christ presented in the preceding chapters of book 3 (833, 850). In its new location, election is the final proof that God's grace in Christ is *free*, totally unconditioned by anything outside the will of God, who "gives to some what he denies to others" (921). "The very inequality of his grace proves that it is free" (929). Eternal life, when given, is *God's* free choice, not a free *human* choice.

(2) In the 1541 French edition of the *Institutes*, predestination went with providence, as it did in Thomas (*ST* 1:26). By separating the two in the 1559 edition (providence is placed in 1.16–18), Calvin gave added emphasis to what was already his starting point in the earlier version: he begins (chap. 21) with the observed fact that the covenant of life is not preached to all, and among those to whom it is preached it does not meet with the same reception (2:920). The inequality of election is interwoven with the observed inequality that runs through all human existence: "We teach nothing not borne out by experience" (932). Those who protest against the supposed unfairness of election should tell us why they were born men—not oxen, asses, or dogs. Will they allow the animals to argue with God (933; cf. 1:200–201)? The fact of election is attested by experience, but *why* God chooses one and not another is hidden from us in his secret will (1:212–13, 233–34; 2:906, 946–47).[6]

(3) Although observation confirms that inequality is a fact of life, in chapter 22 Calvin rests his case for election in Christ entirely on his reading of Scripture, fortified with quotations from Augustine. Many have said that his understanding of election and predestination was governed by an abstract notion of divine omnipotence. In fact, it was governed by what he found in the Word of God (chiefly the Gospel of John, Rom. 9–11, and Eph. 1:3–5). Hence, as a preface to his exegesis, he lays down (in chap. 21) the principle that neither more nor less may be said of predestination than Scripture prescribes (*Institutes*, 2:922–26).

(4) In chapters 23–24 Calvin undertakes a defense of election and calling—again largely with quotes from Scripture and Augustine. This invites a final comment: unlike those of his zealous followers who could sound as if they relished the condemnation of the reprobate, Calvin found the decree horrifying (*Institutes*, 2:955); and he agreed with Augustine that predestination must be preached circumspectly, not turned into cursing the hearers rather than teaching them (963). This leads Calvin to two practical consequences—for us and for our dealing with others. For *ourselves*: "If we seek God's fatherly mercy and kindly heart, we should turn our eyes to Christ, on whom alone God's Spirit rests." Our assurance is not to be found "even in God the Father, if we conceive him as severed from his Son," who is the mirror in which we must and may contemplate our election (970). And for our attitude toward *others*: Calvin has already admonished the Christian (in the chapter on prayer) to "embrace all who are his brothers in Christ, not only those whom he at present sees and recognizes as such but all men who dwell on earth. For what God has determined concerning them is beyond our knowing except that it is no less godly than humane to wish and hope the best for them" (901).

Between Calvin and Schleiermacher, at least three attempts were made to modify the orthodox Reformed understanding of predestination (see Gerrish 2007, chap. 4). Dutch theologian Jacobus *Arminius* (1560–1609) suggested that God's decree was to save those who, he foreknew, would persevere in

6. Cf. J. S. Whale's observation: "The modern mind which is revolted by this doctrine of Election cheerfully accepts the modern doctrine of Selection, and is not appalled by the thought: 'The warm-blooded mammals have I loved, but the Ichthyosauri have I hated'" (*The Protestant Tradition: An Essay in Interpretation* [Cambridge: Cambridge University Press, 1955], 143).

repentance and faith.[7] The orthodox retort was that this got things upside down: election does not rest on foreseen faith but is the cause of faith in those who have it. According to Moses *Amyraut* (1596–1664), theologian at the Huguenot Academy in Saumur, God sincerely offers salvation to all but withholds from most the only condition on which they *could* be saved, which is the gift of faith. A well-meant nod to the universal goodwill of God, Amyraut's theory solved nothing, as his critics recognized; it was condemned in the Helvetic Consensus Formula (1675). Claude *Pajon* (1626–85), last of the Saumur theologians, proposed the most interesting solution to the problem of double predestination. He rejected the belief, shared by the orthodox and dissenters alike, that unequal responses to the gospel must be due to the immediate operation of the Spirit only in the elect. In Pajon's view, it should be explained rather by the unequal circumstances in which the gospel is heard, including the unequal dispositions of the hearers. But he thought he could still maintain that acceptance of the gospel by the elect is foreordained, because the circumstances are foreordained—not just foreseen, but ordered and decreed by divine providence. For Pajon grace works naturally, through the regular course of natural events. And the same "naturalism" was fundamental to Schleiermacher's revisionary view of election and predestination.

The contribution of *Schleiermacher* to the doctrine of election first appeared in 1819 as the lead article in a new theological journal. He notes that he is reputed to be "a bold and determined disciple of Calvin." Although uncertain whether the reputation fits him, in response to a Lutheran critic he steps forward as champion of Calvin's unconditional divine decree. But he proposes an amendment. As usual, he starts from the perspective of the whole, not of the particular, and maintains that we should speak of a single divine decree for *humanity*, not of special decrees for each *individual* (Schleiermacher 2012: 65, 73). But the way in which "the human race is to be transformed into the spiritual body of Christ" is entirely natural, and therefore gradual. For the gospel, by which the decree for humanity is implemented, arose in a particular historical context, and its further progress is still subject to the natural limits of history. This means that only a few can be gathered to the new life at one time, and only by ceaseless preaching of the Word can "the new and living whole gradually increase." There *is* a division between those who are effectively called and those who are passed by; but there is only one decree, and Christians can glimpse "that final instant beyond the unknown and unpredictable apportionments of progress, when all the dead will be made alive and every resistance taken up into the oneness of the whole." The only thorn that Schleiermacher finds in Calvin's double predestination is the assumption that those who are passed by at any one time must be damned for all eternity (44, 75–76). Hardly a *little* thorn! But Schleiermacher's objection misses the mark (as I have shown), and his own solution to the problem of predestination is not likely to satisfy everyone. Critics on the left will take issue with an argument that depends on belief in an afterlife, and critics on the right will question his hope for universal salvation.

7. After his death, the views of Arminius were taken into the "Remonstrance" of his followers (1610) and were rejected by the Synod of Dort (1618–19), the source of the so-called five points of Calvinism familiarly known by the acronym TULIP: total depravity, unconditional election, limited atonement, irresistible grace, and perseverance.

The conclusions of the article were carried over into *The Christian Faith*, where they acquired a systematic location: the doctrine of election is about "The Origin of the Church." Schleiermacher admonishes us to avoid an atomistic view of redemption, as though it were about the choice of one individual and the damnation of another. The incarnation of Christ was the beginning of the regeneration of the human race (*CF* 501, 528, 535, 554). But what God decrees is worked out in accord with the laws of the divine governance of the world. "One such law obviously is, that what proceeds from a single point spreads only gradually over the whole area." All we are entitled to say about those who do not hear the gospel, or who hearing resist it, is that they are *not yet* regenerated: we can never say that they are foreordained to damnation. And in the passage of time the distinction between the regenerate and the nonregenerate is a *vanishing* antithesis (536, 537–38, 540, 547–48). If we ask why it is that a person is drawn from the outer circle to the inner circle of fellowship with Christ (cf. Matt. 22:14), Schleiermacher gives Pajon's answer. It must be attributed not to the arbitrary choice of a capricious deity but to the foreordained circumstances that make this moment *his* time (531, 534–35, 538–39, 543, 546–47, 555–56). "It could not be otherwise if the supernatural in Christ is to become natural, and the Church to take shape as a natural historical phenomenon" (537).

With the idea of a single divine decree, Schleiermacher made a momentous advance in the inherited doctrine of election. But he did not speak the last word on the subject. Major contributions came, in particular, from Schweizer in the nineteenth century and in the twentieth century from Barth. The historian of Reformed theology, Alexander Schweizer (1808–88), commonly dubbed "Schleiermacher's most faithful pupil," believed that the problem with the Calvinist doctrine of predestination was not its determinism but its "dualistic particularism." He thought that determinism, when appropriately defined, is simply consistent theism. His teacher's achievement was to have freed determinism from dualism: the calling of some and the passing over of others is the inevitable form of the divine activity in history and, as such, only temporary—until time moves on and gives the rejected another chance. But the lesson to be learned from the struggle with predestination in the Reformed church, Schweizer concluded, is that it would be best to give it up and reassign its essential content to the doctrine of grace. There it can be treated as an expression of the Christian consciousness that salvation is absolutely dependent on God and wholly unmerited—without tracing it back to antemundane decisions of God. "In short, the inner contradictions in the doctrine of decrees are so glaring and commonly acknowledged that theology [*Glaubenslehre*] will finally drop such an anthropomorphic representation, provided only that the concerns which the devout consciousness meant to satisfy with it are not overlooked but find their fuller satisfaction in a purer doctrinal form" (trans. in Gerrish 2007: 139).

In his *Church Dogmatics* (II/2:3–506) Karl Barth gave extended attention (more than five hundred pages) to the election of grace as "the sum of the Gospel." (In the preface he wonders, "May it not be that I have been too short and not too long at some important points?") I cannot pretend to do justice either to Barth's exegetical and historical reflections or to his constructive argument. But a few observations may go toward locating his presentation in my historical sketch. (1) Barth's familiar christological approach required him to make

Jesus Christ the source and foundation of the doctrine of election. Not that the theological tradition neglected Christ. But especially when predestination was treated as a part of the doctrine of providence, there was always the risk of beginning with an abstract concept of God as omnipotent will, not the electing God in Jesus Christ. (2) The Scriptures witness to Jesus Christ as God and man. This meant, for Barth, that Christ was both the electing God and the elected man. The proper placement for the doctrine of election is under the doctrine of God, before speaking of the creation of the world and man. Accordingly, there can be no suggestion that behind the incarnate God there is a secret or hidden decree. (3) Barth also held that Jesus Christ is both the elect man and the rejected man. Election is the election of all humanity in Christ, and "[w]e are not called upon to bear the suffering of rejection because God has taken this suffering upon Himself" (168).

Barth thus repudiated the notion of a double predestination (as traditionally understood), in which the election of some and the rejection of others are treated as distinct and parallel divine decisions. "[T]he eternal divine decision has as its object and content the execution of the divine covenant with man, the salvation of all men" (*CD* II/2:116; cf. 195, 310, 313, 450). What, then, becomes of those who are said to be "passed by"? Barth answers: "Not every one who is elected lives as an elect man" (321). The circle of those who do affirm their election in Jesus Christ is constantly being enlarged. To assert that the circle "must and will finally be coincident with the world of man as such" would be to impose a limit on the freedom of divine grace. But recognition of the freedom of grace also means that "we cannot venture the opposite statement that there cannot and will not be this final opening up and enlargement of the circle of election and calling" (417–18). Barth was very much aware of his departure from the thinking of his predecessors. He could speak appreciatively of Calvin, but his final judgment on Calvin was severe. The electing God of Calvin, he says, is not the revealed God but a *Deus nudus absconditus*—a hidden God, not God clothed in his revelation. "All the dubious features of Calvin's doctrine result from the basic failing that in the last analysis he separates God and Jesus Christ, thinking that what was in the beginning with God must be sought elsewhere than in Jesus Christ. Thus with all his forceful and impressive acknowledgment of the divine election of grace, ultimately he still passes by the grace of God as it has appeared in Jesus Christ" (*CD* II/2:111). But, we may well ask, isn't Calvin's warning against thinking of God the Father "severed from his Son" precisely Barth's point?

Schleiermacher, as we have seen, had already taken the decisive step of affirming a single divine decree for the regeneration of humanity in Christ. He also had an explanation for the distinction between the elect and the reprobates—a distinction not in the decree itself, but in its historical outworking in the formation and growth of the church. Barth took no account of Schleiermacher's argument. In his list of six alternatives to his own placement of the doctrine of election in dogmatics, he finds no place for Schleiermacher's treatment of election as an ecclesiological doctrine. The third alternative (*CD* II/2:81–84) does connect predestination with the church, but the church as the total company of the elect in every time and place, who are known only to God, not the visible church, in which a portion of the elect at one time is mixed with those who are passed by. To begin with the visible church would violate Barth's determination to speak first of the *Deus elector* (the electing God) before the *populus electus* (the elect people). That may well make sense in the context of Barth's dogmatic scheme, but in the biblical witness the accent falls on the historical formation of a people of God. Election, accordingly, is the first chapter in our doctrine of the church.

III. Election and Church

The New Testament portrays the rise of Christianity as the fulfillment of a divine plan. God sent his Son "when the fullness of time had come" (Gal. 4:4); even the Son's betrayal and crucifixion were "according to the definite plan and foreknowledge of God" (Acts 2:23; cf. 4:28). The earliest Christians understood themselves as included in the "plan for the fullness of time" (Eph. 1:10). "[T]he God and Father of our Lord Jesus Christ . . . chose us in Christ before the foundation of the world to be holy and blameless before him in love. He destined us for adoption as his children through Jesus Christ, according to the good pleasure of his will" (vv. 3–5). Though probably not from Paul, these words in the first chapter of Ephesians echo Romans 8:29: "For those whom [God] foreknew he also predestined to be conformed to the image of his Son, in order that he might be the firstborn within a large family [among many brothers]."[8] Predestination—the anthropomorphic image of God making an antemundane decision in eternity—sustains confidence in the meaning of events set in motion by the appearance of Jesus. They were brought about by God's will to form adopted sons and daughters in the likeness of his one true Son, Jesus of Nazareth.

1. A Chosen People

Predestination is mainly about God's choice of a *people*. Understanding the doctrine is hampered if we define it as Calvin does. Many criticisms of him fail to do him justice, but he does tilt the doctrine the wrong way with his definition, which connects predestination with what God willed to become of each individual (*de unoquoque homine*). Scripture does, of course, tell of the choice (or rejection) of individuals, and Calvin does take account of the Old Testament belief in Israel as God's chosen people. But his definition of predestination mentions only individuals, whereas I take predestination or election to be first and foremost a collective notion. This is what it was in the covenant Yahweh made with Israel, and this it remained in the call of the new Israel. God's choice of the individual is relative to God's choice of the church. As the Acts of the Apostles puts it, "the Lord added to the church daily such as should be saved" (Acts 2:47 KJV).

Not that Calvin's Christianity was *essentially* individualistic. He has been called "the Protestant Cyprian"—the quintessential Protestant churchman. To

8. The Greek word translated "predestined" in Rom. 8:29–30 is from the same verb (*proorizō*) for which the NRSV has "destined" in Eph. 1:5. Several Greek words convey the sense of a "plan": *prothesis*, *boulē*, and in Eph. 1:10 and 3:9, *oikonomia*.

the question whether it is necessary to move on from the benefits of Christ to the holy catholic church, Calvin's *Geneva Catechism* (1545) requires the child to answer: "Yes, of course, unless we want to make Christ's death ineffective [*ociosam*] and count as nothing all that has been related so far. For the one effect of it all is that there should be a church" (q. 94, my trans.; cf. *TT* 2:50). Calvin appropriates Cyprian's (ca. 200–258) metaphor: to have God for Father you must have the church for mother.[9] "For," Calvin says, "there is no other way to enter into life unless this mother conceive us in her womb, give us birth, nourish us at her breast, and lastly, unless she keep us under her care and guidance until, putting off mortal flesh, we become like the angels" (*Institutes*, 2:1012, 1016). It could not be said more plainly that to be born again is to be born a child of Mother Church. Yet, even here, one notes a tinge of individualism in the assumption that the function of the church is nurture, perhaps because Calvin thought the reformation of Geneva had to be entrusted to the civil authorities.

Schleiermacher was even more emphatic in binding faith to community. In *The Christian Faith* he locates the heart of Christ's work in the establishment of a new common life that works against the common life of sin, and he insists that there is no such thing as a solitary Christian. When he moves on from the person and work of the Redeemer, he wonders (*CF* 477–78) whether he should turn next to the community of the redeemed or to the redeemed individual. He thinks that either arrangement would work, but everything he has said so far leads us to expect that he will put the community before the individual, the church before the Christian. In fact, he decides to follow the reverse sequence and gives an interesting reason for his decision (not well conveyed in the English version). It is true that the call to fellowship with Christ comes only from the new community. Still, Schleiermacher points out, just as in the days of his earthly ministry the call of Christ ("Follow me!") laid hold of individuals, so today it is by an act of Christ himself, mediated through his presence in the Word, that the individual is taken up into the fellowship of the new life. The Word of Christ, though proclaimed in and by the community, singles out the individual. Nevertheless, the paramount importance of the community leads Schleiermacher to see the meaning of election in the origin and expansion of the church. The focus shifts from the irrevocable fixing of each person's individual destiny before time began to the historical progress of God's covenant and call in the life of the church. The shift of focus is, I think, a clear gain. It counters the all-too-common reduction of the theme of election to indignant protests about determinism and the injustice of an arbitrary, tyrannical God. As Calvin remarks, when election is mentioned it is as though the bugler had sounded a charge (*Institutes*, 2:947). There is much more to it, especially if we agree with Schleiermacher that it is about the rise of Christianity.

2. Other Peoples of God

The idea of "God's chosen people" invites the presumption of exclusiveness, reflected in the call to be separate. But it is also the testimony of Scripture that the God of the covenant is sovereign over all the peoples of the world: the Lord

9. Cyprian, *The Unity of the Catholic Church*, §6; ANF 5:423. Cf. Luther, *Large Catechism* (1529); *BC* 416.

is *their* God, too, and they will all bow down to him and glorify his name (Ps. 86:9). The tension between particularism and universalism cannot be resolved unless two postulates are affirmed, both of which have their source in Scripture: the calling of a covenant people is for the good of all peoples, and God may have other chosen peoples besides the church.

(1) The original covenant of Yahweh with Abram already implied that particularism actually serves the purpose of God for all humanity: "I will make of you a great nation . . . and in you all the families of the earth shall be blessed," or, "by you all the families of the earth shall bless themselves" (Gen. 12:2–3; cf. 18:18; 22:17–18). How will that happen? "[Y]ou shall spread abroad to the west and to the east and to the north and to the south" (28:14). Israel's awareness of receiving special blessings not for their good only, but also for the blessing of other peoples, is most eloquently declared in the second Servant Song in Isaiah. The servant is Yahweh's "elect" (Isa. 42:1 KJV; cf. 49:1) for a worldwide purpose. Yahweh says to him: "It is too light a thing that you should be my servant to raise up the tribes of Jacob and to restore the survivors of Israel; I will give you as a light to the nations, that my salvation may reach to the end of the earth" (49:6; cf. 42:6). In the Old Testament, then, election is not merely a privilege but a call to service, which includes the commission to bring Yahweh's salvation to the attention of the entire world. And this understanding of election shapes the Christian view of the church as an elect people of God, chosen to "proclaim the mighty acts of him who called you out of darkness into his marvelous light" (1 Pet. 2:9). The first generation of Christians had Jesus as the model Servant of God, and they applied to him the image of the Servant as "a light to the Gentiles" (Luke 2:29–32; Acts 13:47; cf. 26:23).[10] Here, at least in embryo, is a doctrine of the church as a servant people in whom Christ continues his prophetic and priestly work.

Second, in Isaiah and Jeremiah, the sovereignty of Yahweh over all the earth gives rise to the persuasion that Yahweh chooses non-Jewish leaders and nations—even the enemies of Israel—to serve his plans. Nebuchadnezzar is his servant (Jer. 27:6). Cyrus is his anointed (Isa. 45:1): "He is my shepherd, and he shall carry out all my purpose" (44:28). To call Cyrus Yahweh's "anointed" (his "messiah") is remarkable; equally remarkable is Isaiah's foreseeing a time when "Israel will be the third with Egypt and Assyria." Then Yahweh will say: "Blessed be Egypt my people, and Assyria the work of my hands, and Israel my heritage" (19:24–25). Of course, this cannot be taken for the opinion that there are many religions, all equally able to lead to the true God. The miracle the prophet anticipates is rather that Yahweh will turn the brutal dispersion of Israel into the conversion of the Egyptians and the Assyrians to Israel's God (cf. Zech. 2:11). But the question for theology today is whether that goes far enough as the pattern for conversation between Christianity and other religions.

In the current interfaith dialogue three distinct positions have emerged. *Exclusivism* is the view that the only way to salvation is by explicit faith in Christ—that is, faith openly confessed. Its advocates claim that Scripture is on

10. In Luke 3:6 the words "and all flesh shall see the salvation of God" (echoing Isa. 40:5, which falls outside the Servant Songs) are included in John the Baptist's announcement of the coming of Christ.

their side, in particular Acts 4:12: "there is no other name [than Jesus Christ] by which we must be saved." Exclusivism has unquestionably been the official Christian view, supported by Cyprian's aphorism, "No salvation outside the church."[11] In its original context the aphorism was not about other religions; to Cyprian "the church" meant the Roman Church, and those he excluded were not pagans but Christians he deemed heretical. When applied to the relation of Christianity to other religions, "No salvation outside the church" consigns the greater part of humanity to damnation, including millions upon millions who never hear the good news of Jesus Christ.

Inclusivism seeks to avoid the terrible consequence of exclusivism by arguing that some will be saved through Christ without explicit faith in him. From time to time, advocates of inclusivism have made their voices heard in Christian theology. Among the Fathers of the ancient church, for instance, Justin Martyr maintained that before the coming of Christ, who was Reason (*Logos*) incarnate, all who lived in accord with reason were Christians: they possessed fragments of the truth that came whole with Jesus Christ (ANF 1:178, 191). In the age of the Renaissance and the Reformation, more than one theological party argued that there must be places in heaven for some who never hear of Christ. Humanists could not believe that the virtuous heroes of antiquity were all damned. The Calvinists softened exclusivism by pointing out that God, if he chooses, is able to save elect individuals without the normal channels of grace, including elect infants dying unbaptized (see, e.g., Westminster Confession 10.3). In seventeenth-century England, Puritan Richard Baxter (1615–91) agreed that God could, if he pleased, pardon and save humans because of Christ's satisfaction "without letting them once know that Christ satisfied for them." True, Baxter did not venture to infer that all would actually be pardoned, since actual pardon is conditional on its acceptance. "We are conditionally pardoned whether we believe it or not. But we shall not be actually pardoned till we believe." However, the weight of his argument in his striking treatise on universal redemption, published after his death, was to persuade the reader that "the Kingdom of Christ as Redeemer is larger than the Church." Even persons who have no knowledge of the Redeemer are nonetheless his redeemed.[12] In the twentieth century, Jesuit theologian Karl Rahner (1904–84) held that there are "anonymous Christians" in the world who stand outside the social unity of the church (or churches) but nevertheless are living in the state of grace and are saved through an act of faith in the true sense: faith as response to revelation. "The doctrine of the anonymous Christian . . . does not involve the belief that anyone can attain to justification and final salvation even without faith in a strictly theological sense merely because he does not act against his own moral conscience." He is saved by an act of faith that corresponds to "primordial" revelation.[13]

11. "Salus extra ecclesiam non est." Cyprian, Letter 73, §21; ANF 5:384.

12. Richard Baxter, *Universal Redemption of Mankind by the Lord Jesus Christ* (London, 1694); quotations from 477–78, 40, 46. Though generally aligned with the Calvinists, Baxter was correcting the belief that Christ died for the elect only ("limited atonement").

13. Rahner 1976: 280–94; quotation on 285. Rahner found confirmation of his theory in declarations of Vatican II, especially *Lumen gentium*, art. 16 (DV 35); *Gaudium et spes*, art. 22 (DV 220–21); *Ad Gentes*, art. 7 (DV 593).

Critics have countered that inclusivism is presumptuous and no basis for a genuine dialogue with the adherent of another religion. They advocate a third option: *pluralism,* the view that there are many paths to salvation, not only one. Pluralism does not just modify the old maxim "No salvation outside the church" to allow for a few exceptions, or even a multitude of exceptions; it sets it aside as no longer workable in the present-day context, in which Christians daily encounter, or at least learn about, the great religions of humankind. The pluralist points out that there have been several major turning points in the history of religion, each with its charismatic founder, so that the natural starting point for interfaith dialogue is de facto pluralism, or a hypothetical pluralism that is at least willing to say, Let's see if there may be other ways to salvation. The agenda must include rethinking the traditional attitude of the church to Judaism: Christians have been more willing to affirm that *their* salvation is from the Jews (John 4:22) than to consider Jewish faith as itself a way of salvation.

Naturally, I cannot pursue the interfaith dialogue here. But progress along the line of a hypothetical pluralism, which I affirm as the basis for genuine dialogue, requires me to align my understanding of election and the church with what I have already argued in previous chapters about faith, sin, the work of Christ, and salvation. *Faith,* I have argued, is not acceptance of information supernaturally communicated to the church but discernment of an orderly pattern in events that both sustains human existence and makes moral demands on us. Christian faith spells out the nature of the perceived order in ways that go beyond the common faith of humanity and may conflict with alternative accounts of our natural and moral environment. But to say that the Christian receives faith as the gift of Jesus Christ does not imply that the common faith of humanity cannot be had in any other way. Moreover, *salvation* is the promise not simply of a future heaven but of a present life transformed by communion with Christ, who saves the Christian from the anxiety and the moral indifference of estrangement from God. I can now add that the *church* is not just a refuge from the rain of God's wrath, like Noah's ark, while everyone outside perishes.[14] Thesis 14 describes the church, rather, as *a* (not *the*) chosen people of God and defines its main purpose in the biblical terms of the elect Servant of the Lord and conformity to the image of Christ. It can then be affirmed that the church *does not consist of a few who are the exclusive objects of divine care but of those who hearing the call of the gospel to be conformed to the image of God's Son and chosen Servant, Jesus Christ, bear witness to the care of God for humanity.*

3. A Creation of the Gospel

We will need to ask further in the next chapter, What kind of community are the Christian people of God? But from the foregoing we can already state what it is that constitutes the church: the call of Christ, continually renewed in the proclamation of the gospel. The English word *church* goes back to the Greek *kyriakos,* which means "belonging to the Lord," as in the phrase *kyriakon dōma,* "house of the Lord." The adjectives *ecclesial* and *ecclesiastical* come from the Greek *ekklēsia.* One of the words used in the Septuagint for Hebrew *qāhāl, ekklēsia* means

14. Cyprian, Letter 74; ANF 5:394.

"assembly." In the New Testament it does not always refer to the church; in the Acts of the Apostles it is used for the congregation of the Israelites (Acts 7:38; cf. Heb. 2:12), an informal gathering or mob (Acts 19:32), and a regularly convened civic meeting (19:39, 41). But it is often said that the essence of the church fits particularly well with the etymology of the Greek *ekklēsia* (from *ek*, "out," + *kaleō*, "call"): the church is called out—called into existence by the gospel. As Luther argued in his treatise *On the Councils and the Church* (1539), "Now, wherever you hear or see this word preached, believed, professed, and lived, do not doubt that the true *ecclesia sancta catholica*, 'a Christian, holy people' must be there, even though their number is very small. . . . And even if there were no other sign than this alone, it would still suffice to prove that a Christian holy people must exist there, for God's word cannot be without God's people, and conversely, God's people cannot be without God's word" (LW 41:150).

Luther actually listed (in this treatise) seven chief marks or signs by which the presence of the church can be recognized: the Word, baptism, the sacrament of the altar, the keys, the ministry, prayer, and bearing the cross. But the preached Word came first and retained its preeminent place in his thinking. He found support, and perhaps his initial inspiration, in a statement he attributed to Augustine, "The church is begotten, cared for, nourished, and strengthened by the word of God" (LW 41:151; cf. 1 Pet. 1:23);[15] and his teaching on the marks of the church, usually reduced to two, exercised in turn a decisive influence on the churches of the Reformation. Calvin, for example, writes: "Wherever we see the Word of God purely preached and heard, and the sacraments administered according to Christ's institution, there, it is not to be doubted, a church of God exists" (*Institutes*, 2:1023).[16] It is often said that the church is people, not a building. But it was a fundamental principle of the Reformation that there is no people without the proclamation of the gospel; it follows that where the gospel is not proclaimed, even a packed sanctuary is not a church. The principle, I think, is sound. It could be affirmed simply as a *historical* observation about how the church began: with Jesus' announcement of the good news of the kingdom. But it serves also as a *dogmatic* principle. My first chapter on ecclesiology states accordingly that *"the church, as God's elect, is said to be a 'creation of the gospel'— brought into being by the Spirit through the word about Jesus Christ."* But that is certainly not the last chapter: some of what is still missing is best conveyed by the traditional image of the church as the body of Christ, animated by his Spirit.

15. The LW editor, Eric W. Gritsch, notes: "The saying could not be located in Augustine's writings" (LW 41:151 n. 393). Besides *On the Councils and the Church*, my account of what constitutes the church for Luther—making it a creation of the gospel—rests also on his *Babylonian Captivity* (1520), LW 36:107; and *Reply to Ambrosius Catharinus* (1521), WA 7:721.

16. Other Reformed theologians added discipline as a third mark of the church, and in the period of Reformed orthodoxy the preaching of the gospel came to be confused with maintaining correct doctrine (see Heppe 1950: 669–70).

15. The Spirit and the Body of Christ

The church, as the "body" of Christ "animated" by his Spirit, is neither a commonplace association nor a clerical domain, but the organ of Christ's continuing activity as prophet and priest; and because he receives his people as companions in his priestly activity, the church is also said to be a "royal priesthood," in which there is no division between priests and people.

The church is called into being by the Word of the gospel. But this says little about the kind of social entity that results. Throughout Christian history various ideas of the church have appeared, and the dogmatic perspective can make good use of a sociological typology. Ernst Troeltsch's well-known distinction between "church" and "sect" has proved especially fruitful in theology (and church history): "For the church, the individual was the product of the miraculous power of grace in the institution founded by Christ. For the sect, the community was the product of individuals who assemble voluntarily together and are approved by their active holiness" (Troeltsch 1910: 29; trans. mine). More or less in agreement with Troeltsch's definitions, we will look at *community* and *institution* as two ways of understanding the social character of the Christian people of God. Troeltsch further argued that Schleiermacher was the pioneer of a third ecclesiological type that overcomes the opposition between the other two: the church as a historical *organism* (29–32). This will be taken up in the third section. As a fourth ecclesiological concept, I am adding the idea of the church as a "priesthood of all believers" or *royal priesthood.* A dogmatic rather than a sociological concept, it is fundamental to Luther's and Calvin's views of the church—with interesting differences between them—and will provide the bridge to our next chapter, on the apostolic ministry.

There was no straightforward historical development from the church as community to the church as institution and organism, and in any case these three categories are to be taken for ideal types rather than historical descriptions. In actuality the types coexist, overlap, and mingle. Hence the present chapter departs from the chronological sequence followed more closely in the previous chapters. True, Troeltsch read the Reformation story as, among other things, the collapse of the old church concept. In *Protestantism and Progress* he remarked caustically: "Three infallible 'Churches' [Roman Catholic, Lutheran, and Reformed], unchurching and anathematising one another, discredited the idea of the Church, for which there is no plural" (Troeltsch 1986: 54). However, there are still today churches that claim to possess full or maximal truth, denied to others; each understands itself as the one true church. The "old" idea of the church cannot be confined to the Middle Ages. And the pioneers of what we think of as the distinctively modern "free" church, independent of the state, were the Anabaptists of the sixteenth century, persecuted by Catholics and Protestants alike and long neglected by church historians. Other examples of chronological displacement could be mentioned. But the two examples offered should be enough to explain why our inquiry is conceptually, not chronologically, ordered. I must admit that a conceptual order has its own difficulty in the fact that the sociological terms are more fluid and controversial than we might wish. Agreed definitions are hard to come by. But the main lines of the distinctions Troeltsch proposed between three ecclesial types—community, institution, and organism—will suffice for our purposes.

I. The Church as Community

The basic meaning of *ekklēsia* is "assembly." When used of the Christian church, the word most often refers in the New Testament not to the catholic church but to the gathering of a local company of Christians. James uses *synagōgē* ("synagogue") in the same sense (Jas. 2:2).[1] *Ekklēsia* can also refer to the congregation itself: the church in Jerusalem, Antioch, Corinth, and so on. In 1 Corinthians Paul uses the expression *en ekklēsią* ("in church") four times, when he clearly intends "in a *meeting* of the church" (1 Cor. 11:18; 14:19, 28, 35; cf. 6:4). Sometimes the reference is to a house church, and sometimes, in the plural, it denotes several congregations in a wider area: Syria, Galatia, Judea, and so on. But in the authentic letters of Paul the only undisputed instances of *ekklēsia* in the sense of "the catholic church" appear in Colossians, where it is described as the body of Christ, and Christ is identified as its head (Col. 1:18, 24). The two other mentions of *ekklēsia* in Colossians refer to the church in Nympha's house and the church in Laodicea (4:15–16). Outside Paul's letters, there are possible references to the catholic church in Acts 9:31 ("the church throughout Judea, Galilee, and Samaria") and 1 Timothy 3:15 ("the household of God, which is the church of the living God"). In striking contrast to the weight of the New Testament usage everywhere else, the nine references to the *ekklēsia* in the Letter to the Ephesians are all to the catholic church, identified as the body of which Christ is the head (Eph. 1:22–23; 4:15–16; 5:23, 30). This is one reason for doubting that Paul wrote it.[2]

1. For particulars on *ekklēsia* in the NT, see K. L. Schmidt, "*kaleō ktl.: ekklēsia*," *Theological Dictionary of the New Testament*, vol. 3, ed. Gerhard Kittel, trans. Geoffrey W. Bromiley (Grand Rapids: Eerdmans, 1963), 501–36; and Campbell 1965. There are only two places where the word appears in the Gospels, both in Matthew. In Matt. 18:17, where it occurs twice, it denotes a meeting of the local congregation: "tell it to the church," etc. In 16:18, "you are Peter, and on this rock I will build my church," the catholic church must be intended. Note that "catholic church" with a lower-case initial *c* designates what is variously called the "universal," "worldwide," "Great," or simply "Christian" church. With a capital C, "Catholic" refers to the particular communion that the Council of Trent styled both "the Catholic Church" and "the (Holy) Roman Church."

2. That the image of Christ as *head* of the body also appears in Colossians, but not in Rom. 12:4–5 or 1 Cor. 12:14–27, perhaps justifies doubt concerning the authorship of Colossians as well. On the other hand, some interpreters hold that the expression "the church of God," used six times by Paul,

With the spread of Christianity, it was natural that attention should move from the local congregation to the churches in a wider area, and finally to the worldwide church. The question is whether something was lost along the way. In *The Misunderstanding of the Church* (1951), Emil Brunner argued that what we today call "the church" is so far removed from the primitive Christian *ekklēsia* that it is best to leave the Greek word untranslated; and he stood by his argument in the third volume of his *Dogmatics.* The *ekklēsia,* he explained, is a fellowship of persons, "bound to each other through their common sharing in Christ and in the Holy Ghost." This, in fact, is the meaning of the word *koinōnia,* which "signifies a common participation, a togetherness, a community life." The essence of the *ekklēsia* is "communion with God through Jesus Christ, and rooted in this and springing from it, communion or brotherhood with man"; as such, "it has an articulate living order without being legally ordered" (3:10, 51, 107–8). In the course of time, this purely personal understanding of the New Testament brotherhood was buried under a host of binding prescriptions: a community of persons came to be replaced by an administrative institution. Still, the institution can serve as the shell in which the precious kernel is contained, and the shell can take more than one form. The church is a historically evolved "vessel" of the *ekklēsia* (16–17, 112, 116–17).

Brunner recognized that already in the New Testament there are variations in the shape of the first Christian communities. His argument rested mainly on Paul's doctrine of the *ekklēsia,* and he saw the spirit of the ecclesial "brotherhood" exemplified in the primitive Christian communism of Acts (Acts 2:42–45; 4:32). He found an ally in Martin Luther. In his translation of the New Testament (1522), Luther preferred *Gemeine*[3] to *Kirche* ("community" to "church") as the German equivalent of *ekklēsia,* and in his *German Mass* (1526) he looked forward to a time when serious Christians would simply register their names and gather for worship in a house, as the first Christians did (LW 53:63–64). The decisive act of Luther's reformation, Brunner believed, was not the posting of the Ninety-five Theses, but the burning of the canon law (December 10, 1520); his protest was against the institution of the papacy (Brunner 1962: 15, 97).

Many questions remain about community as an ecclesial type. Three concluding observations must suffice. (1) While taking account of Troeltsch's contrast between church and sect, I avoid the word *sect* because it has acquired derogatory connotations and, *pace* Brunner, I use *church* indifferently for every kind of Christian social entity, including the New Testament *ekklēsia.* Qualifiers and context will indicate which kind of church, or church concept, is under discussion.

(2) Present-day eagerness for community sometimes obscures the point of describing the fellowship of the church as *koinōnia.* As J. Y. Campbell put it in a definitive article, "the primary idea expressed by κοινωνός [*koinōnos*] and its cognates is not that of association with another person or other persons, but that of participation in something in which others also participate" (1965: 2). Sometimes the thing participated in is stated expressly, as when Paul says that it is

---

must refer to the catholic church; and some argue that the formula "the church *in* [a particular place]" means a local manifestation of the catholic church.

3. *Gemeinde* in modern German.

participation (*koinōnia*) in the blood and body of Christ that makes the church in Corinth one body (1 Cor. 10:16–17). At other times, there is no express mention of participation, as, apparently, in Acts 2:42, where all our main English versions translate *koinōnia* as "fellowship" (NRSV: "They [the new converts] devoted themselves to the apostles' teaching and fellowship," etc.; cf. perhaps "the communion of the Holy Spirit" in 2 Cor. 13:13). But the primary meaning of *koinōnia* must not be disregarded even if it can be used (as the grammarians say) absolutely.

(3) Although the sociological idea of community may serve our understanding of the social character of the church as a fellowship of persons, my use of it will agree with the conclusion already reached that the church, from the dogmatic perspective, is a creation of the gospel. When the church is understood as a community, belonging to it implies association by a free decision; but the decision itself is a response to the creative, community-forming word of the gospel. It would be misleading to define the church, without qualification, as a voluntary association. We will need to come back to this point when we turn to the sacraments, particularly to the diverse views of baptism in the Christian churches. For now, we need to ask next whether my third observation on the community type of ecclesiology may amount to a word in favor of the institutional type, in which, as Troeltsch says, the individual is the product of the power of grace.

II. The Church as Institution

Roman Catholicism may be taken to exemplify the institutional idea of the church, and in modern times the First Vatican Council (1869–70) was one of its most forthright expressions. The council's Dogmatic Constitution on the Catholic Faith presents the faith in terms of revealed truths that must be believed. Accordingly, it is of the utmost importance that an authoritative structure should be in place to define and prescribe them. "[I]n order that we may satisfactorily perform the duty of embracing the true faith and of continuously persevering in it, God, through His only-begotten Son, has instituted the Church, and provided it with clear signs of His institution, so that it can be recognized by all as the guardian and teacher of the revealed word" (DS 446). The Dogmatic Constitution on the Church of Christ, *Pastor aeternus* (451–57), goes on to state the form of church government instituted by Christ: it is a hierarchy, with the pope of Rome as its pinnacle.

The primacy of Peter and his successors belongs to the essence of the Roman Catholic understanding of the church. But the idea of the church as an institution exists elsewhere without it; and quite apart from the Petrine office (postponed to chap. 17), the First Vatican Council used the typically institutional language of jurisdiction, supreme power, and government—together with the corresponding terms "subordination" and "obedience." It warned: "This is the doctrine of Catholic truth from which no one can deviate and keep his faith and salvation" (DS 454). Like a secular state, the church has a legally binding constitution, which distinguishes sharply between the priestly guardians of truth and the people who passively receive it from them. The first draft of the Constitution on the Church described the church as an unequal society, in which some possess an exclusive power of jurisdiction "that is absolute and perfectly complete, legislative, judicial, and coercive." The pastors and teachers "rule the Church of God with laws that are necessary and binding in conscience, with judicial decrees, and, finally, with salutary punishments" (*CT* 93–94).

There is much more to Roman Catholic teaching on the church. The First Vatican Council's Dogmatic Constitution on the Church was not completed—the Franco-Prussian War intervened. The Second Vatican Council (1962–65) produced a Dogmatic Constitution on the Church, *Lumen gentium,* which describes the church, first of all, as a sacrament—a sign and instrument of union with God and of the unity of all humankind. *Lumen gentium* reviews the biblical story of redemption and the various biblical images of the church. It describes the church as "the community of faith, hope, and charity" and compares it to the mystery of the incarnation: just as human nature served the divine Word as a living instrument of salvation, the church serves Christ's Spirit, who vivifies it (*DV* 22; cf. 26). An entire chapter is devoted to the church as the new people of God, and another to the laity. All of which provides some balance to the institutional and hierarchical language of Vatican I, but in express continuation of the interrupted work of the previous council. The chapter on the church as the people of God is followed by a chapter titled "The Hierarchical Structure of the Church, with Special Reference to the Episcopate." The Catholic intention, plainly, is to hold community and institution together. Can the same be said of mainline Protestant ecclesiological intentions?

Among the first generation of Protestant Reformers, it was Calvin who developed the most systematic ecclesiology. Book 4, by far the longest book of the 1559 *Institutes,* is given entirely to the doctrine of the church. After summary statements on the church as mother and the ministry and marks of the true church, Calvin deals in turn with the church's government, orders, and power—power in doctrine, legislation, and jurisdiction. The remainder of book 4 moves on to the sacraments and, finally, the church's relation to the state (see Calvin's outlines: *Institutes,* 2:1012, 1149). It is on the government, orders, and threefold power of the church that Calvin has most to say, closely followed by his extensive discussion of the sacraments. It is curious that he is often said to belittle the visible church because he speaks of the church as the number of the elect. He does so speak, but only in passing: to make the Augustinian point that the visible church contains many reprobates and does not contain all of God's elect. (He cites Augustine's aphorism that "many sheep are without and many wolves are within.") We *believe* the church (not *in* the church) but leave to God the *knowledge* of who are his (1013; cf. 2 Tim. 2:19). Calvin twice says expressly—as if it were not sufficiently obvious—that his business is with the visible church (1013, 1016; cf. 1021–23). I cannot review his discussion in detail, though I will refer to some of its main features as we go along. But just from his principal headings it is easy to see how much at home he was in medieval ecclesiology and in the institutional view of the church (even though he criticizes what the Roman Church made of it). He can even begin his treatment of church discipline with the suggestion: "To understand it better, let us divide the church into two chief orders: clergy and people" (1229).

Despite his special interest in the institutional church and its government, Calvin elsewhere grants that there is no scriptural basis for the distinction traditionally made between the "clergy" and the church as a whole, "since Peter calls the whole church 'the clergy,' that is, the inheritance of the Lord" (*Institutes*, 2:1076–77; 1 Pet. 5:3). Still, it hardly needs to be said that his thoughts on the church have a different feel from the way Luther liked to speak of the Christian community. Luther's vision of house churches as models of ecclesial fellowship, however, remained unfulfilled. The Lutheran church in Germany developed its own institution, separate from Rome, and by the end of the seventeenth century there were those who found its rigidity unproductive of true godliness. The Pietists complained that the Lutheran church had become a pale reflection of the Catholic Church. Under the leadership of Philip Jacob Spener (1635–1705), they began to form *collegia pietatis,* private gatherings for spiritual reading and discussion. Their meetings were not initially intended as alternatives to the established Lutheran church; they were miniature churches within the big church (*ecclesiolae in ecclesia*). But as such they could easily be substitutes for the church. A few Pietist cells did become separatist, and Lutheran churchmen naturally found this regrettable. Still, it is also regrettable when institutional management becomes oppressive and "the church" signifies, to all intents and purposes, the clergy who control the means of salvation. If the church is not exactly a voluntary association just like any other, neither is it properly a clerical domain; to treat it as such invites precisely the reaction on behalf of the *ekklēsia* that we have noted in Luther, Spener, and Brunner and will find again in Schleiermacher. I will have more to say about church order in due course. But I need to ask next what insight may be gained from the idea of the church as more like a biological organism than either an association or an institution.

III. The Church as Historical Organism

Ernst Troeltsch credited the later Schleiermacher, the "church theologian," with an innovative view of the church as an organism. We will turn to this in a moment. But the earlier Schleiermacher, the apologist, had commended a very different view to the cultured despisers, whose opposition to the church and its clergy was even more vehement than their opposition to religion. His defense of association in religion in the fourth of his *Speeches on Religion,* like his defense of religion itself, took its start from human nature. "If there is religion at all, it must be social, for that is the nature of man, and it is quite peculiarly the nature of religion" (1994: 148). But the ideal religious association—the true church—is nothing like the empirical church: its purpose is mutual communication of the religious affections. When a devout impulse stirs the soul, there is an urge to share it with others and to listen in turn to what *they* have to say. It follows that religion, so understood, "withdraws itself from too wide circles to the more familiar conversation of friendship or the dialogue of love, where glance and action are clearer than words, and where a solemn silence also is understood" (150). If a person stands up to speak in the assembly, he does it not by reason of any "office" but simply to share his religious affections; and when he has spoken, others will take their turn. "Each in turn is leader and people" (153). The empirical church, by contrast, is made up not of those who have religion to share but of those who are searching for religion. Instead of mutual communication, they all want to receive; only one is supposed to give. And what they expect to receive is not the higher and freer inspiration that is proper to religion, but the results of reflection on religion, delivered in a school-mastering, mechanical way (158, 161). "Thus in point of fact the church, as it exists among us, becomes of less consequence to men the more they increase in religion, and the most pious sever themselves coldly and proudly" (160). "[W]e expect a time when no other society preparatory for religion except the pious family life will be required" (178). Of course the fourth speech, "Association in Religion, or Church and Priesthood," was shrewd apologetics, not dogmatics. To the cultured despisers Schleiermacher said in effect: Think again about religion; what you do not like about it I do not like either; as the cultivators of humanity, you are more religious than you suppose.

In his influential *Social Teaching of the Christian Churches* (German 1912), Troeltsch's three types of religious organization were church, sect, and mysticism. He assigned the true church of Schleiermacher's *Speeches* to the third type, in which individuals, with no thought of the outward trappings of religion, get together to share their immediate religious experience (Troeltsch 1992, 2:793–99). "Mysticism" is not perhaps an adequate term. Schleiermacher's true church reflected the Pietism in which he had been nurtured from his boyhood. He was commending something like the *collegia pietatis*, and, in common with most of the leading Pietists, he saw the *collegia* as forces for good within the big church. There had to be a bond of union with those who were still searching for religion; consequently, a standing distinction between priests and laity was inevitable. His hope was that the visible church would take its priests from the true church (Schleiermacher 1994: 161); and in 1821 he added a further thought: "By observation and joyful experience I have reached the conviction that truly believing and pious persons exist in adequate number in our congregations, and that it is good to strengthen as much as possible their influence on the rest" (206).

In an important but neglected essay on "Schleiermacher and the Church" (1910), Troeltsch described a different third ecclesial type to go with his distinction between church and sect, institution and community, and he saw the later Schleiermacher as its creator. The Protestant Reformation, Troeltsch maintained, never rejected the medieval view of the church as a supernatural *institution*, founded by Christ to dispense the truth and grace that confer salvation; it only modified the institutional view by elevating the Word above the sacraments as the actual means of grace. The sixteenth-century sects, on the other hand, thought of their religious *community* as the outcome of a voluntary union between professing believers. The Enlightenment of the eighteenth century then erased the distinction between church and sect by thinking of *all* communities as associations of like-minded individuals. Such broad generalizations, intriguing though they are, are certainly open to criticism. But I am interested here in Troeltsch's further argument that the nineteenth century witnessed the emergence of a third alternative, which did not erase the contrast between church and sect but rather transcended it. And here the later Schleiermacher appears not as representative of the mystical type but as maker of the new: the church as a social *organism* (cf. Schleiermacher, *CF* 560–65). In the sociological theory that influenced him, according to Troeltsch, every community included the idea of an "organic radiation from some strong nodal point in the development of life." Schleiermacher could then distinguish the Christian church by the connection of the particular religious content of Christianity with the figure of Christ, continually re-presented as the Christian archetype. If such a conception differs from the old church concept, which could not see the church as structurally comparable with other social and religious groups, it differs sharply, Troeltsch points out, from the atomistic idea of an "association." The primacy belongs not to the activity of individuals who get together but to the generative power of the whole. Yet Schleiermacher's Christian church included elements of the sect type insofar as he replaced purely passive reception of the means of grace with the individual's active life in the life of the historical organism (Troeltsch 1910: 29–32).

Schleiermacher's originality need not be questioned. But one can surely argue that his notion of the church as an organism was foreshadowed in the way the theological tradition had developed the scriptural analogy of the church as the body of Christ. In the New Testament the analogy comes in two forms that serve, in part, to make different points. In one form, the saints at Corinth and Rome *are* the body of Christ. "Now you are the body of Christ and individually members of it" (1 Cor. 12:27; cf. 6:15; 10:16–17; 11:29; 12:12). "[W]e, who are many, are one body in Christ, and individually we are members one of another" (Rom. 12:5). The lesson to be learned is that the gifts of grace (*charismata*) or of the Spirit (*pneumatika*) vary, but those to whom they are given are like the members of a single body, functioning together for the good of the whole, "that there may be no dissension within the body, but the members may have the same care for one another" (1 Cor. 12:7, 25).

In the other form, Christ is *head* of the body, the church (Col. 1:18), which is still described—a little incongruously—as his body (1:24; see also 2:9–10, 19; 3:15).[4] Head language in Colossians contributes to the overall purpose that the Son of God "might come to have first place in everything" (1:18; RSV "might be preeminent"). In particular, the church's very life comes from the head, "from whom the whole body, nourished and held together by its ligaments and sinews, grows with a growth that is from God" (2:19). The Letter to the Ephesians, very likely dependent on Colossians, similarly speaks of Christ as head and the church as his body (Eph. 1:22–23; 4:12, 15; 5:23, 32) and similarly exploits the analogical language of bodily parts, ligaments, and growth (4:15–16, 25; 5:30). The one body is a symbol of unity: it unites Jews with Gentiles (2:16; 3:6; 4:4).[5] And the headship of Christ over the church is also a symbol of authority—the model for a wife's subjection to her husband (5:22–24).

4. Possibly the "hymn" in Col. 1:15–20 is an adaptation of Hellenistic-Jewish speculation that everything was brought into existence, and is sustained in existence, through the divine Wisdom, a heavenly being whose body is *the world*. Verse 18 may then be understood as a correction: "He is the head of the body, *the church*" (cf. v. 24). See E. Schweizer 1964: 64–66; for the more recent discussion, Marshall 2004: 369.

5. The inclusion of "Greek and Jew, circumcised and uncircumcised, barbarian, Scythian, slave and free" in the church appears in Col. 3:11 without use of the analogy of the body. Cf. 1 Cor. 12:13.

The biological analogy of the ecclesial body has only a limited use in the New Testament, but it has been taken up and extended in the theological tradition. Augustine set the pattern of identifying the "soul" of Christ's body with the Spirit: "What the soul is in our body, that is the Holy Spirit in Christ's body, the church" (Serm. 267; MPL 38:1231). Two modern encyclicals of the Roman Catholic Church, one on the Holy Spirit and one on the Mystical Body, exemplify the Augustinian extension of the biblical analogy. The encyclical *Divinum illud* of Leo XIII (1897) cites Augustine in confirmation of its conclusion, "Let it suffice to state that, as Christ is the Head of the Church, so is the Holy Spirit its soul." This is cited in turn in the encyclical *Mystici corporis* of Pius XII (1943), which explains that while the church rests on juridical principles, "what lifts the society of Christians far, far above the whole natural order is the Spirit of the Redeemer, who until the end of time penetrates every part of the Church's being and is active within it" (*CT* 115, 116).

My thesis 15 adopts the metaphor of *the church as the "body" of Christ, "animated" by his Spirit.* The New Testament is not so explicit. But in 1 Corinthians 12 it is the Spirit who distributes the gifts of grace and "activates" or "energizes" them (*energei*, v. 11; cf. v. 6); their distribution is a manifestation of the Spirit (v. 7); and the Spirit is throughout so closely united with Christ (vv. 4–5, 11–12, etc.) that we may fairly say the body is *animated by his Spirit* (cf. Acts 16:7; Rom. 8:9–10; 2 Cor. 3:17; 1 Pet. 1:11). The association of church and Spirit supplies a link with the belief that the existence of the church had its origin in Jesus' promise of "another Advocate" (John 14:16, 26; 15:26; 16:7) and the outpouring of the Spirit on the day of Pentecost (Acts 2:1–47); and that leaves us with Trinitarian questions for chapter 20. For now, our conclusion is that the organic analogy provides imagery appropriate to the Christian sense of total dependence on a grace that is nothing other than the presence of Christ in the Christian church—like the branches of a vine (John 15:5) or the limbs of a body. As Luther observes, the eye does not earn a place in the body because it can see: only because it belongs to the body is it an eye and can see at all (WA 17/2:33–34). The church, in short, is *the organ of Christ's continuing activity as prophet and priest.*

This is not to exclude the language of "community" and "institution," but it should count against any reduction of the community to a commonplace association or of the institution to a clerical domain. It may also serve as a counterweight against any tendency to turn the *creatura evangelii* motif (the church as creation of the gospel) into the radical occasionalism of Karl Barth's insistence that the congregation is always an event: the church is "gathered" again and again, not constituted once and for all (1948: 68–69). The objection to this view is that it seems to dissolve the continuity of the church into "a series of totally disconnected events," leaving no room for a continuing historical institution (Newbigin 1953: 48–49). I would rather say that it is difficult to harmonize with the New Testament image of the body that "grows with a growth that is from God" (Col. 2:19; but see Barth, *CD* IV/2:641–60). Moreover, I need (as usual) to align the present chapter with my previous conclusions, and here a problem, or potential problem, with the analogy of the body must be noted.

Paul thought of the body of Christ as a self-contained entity: it looks inward, to the interaction of the individual members or the growth of the whole. And in the theological tradition the body is identified as Holy Mother Church, nurturing her children. True enough! But the body should also look outward, to the mission of the servant people of God. It is called to be the body of Christ *in the world*. Each of the ecclesiological terms we have looked at discloses an indispensable facet of the church; together, they supplement one another and guard against one-sidedness. The systematic drive of dogmatic theology seeks harmony, not uniformity. Metaphors, in particular, do not have to be reduced to a single dogma: they can be mutually corrective. This holds good not only for the organic language of "the body of Christ," but also for our final ecclesiological metaphor: the church as a "royal priesthood" (1 Pet. 2:9; Rev. 1:6).

IV. The Church as a Royal Priesthood

The common priesthood, or priesthood of all believers, came to be regarded as one of the three pillars of Protestant theology, along with biblical authority (*sola scriptura*) and salvation by faith (*sola fide*). In the beginning, this was not so. At the Diet of Augsburg (1530) Melanchthon advised against discussion of the priesthood of all believers on the grounds that it was a contentious but unessential doctrine. Subsequently, it moved into its privileged place among the *most* essential of Protestant doctrines. It has even been ranked, in effect, above the other two. Understood as every believer's free, direct admission to the presence of God, it ensured "the right of private judgment" in the reading of Scripture (without an authoritative interpreter) and faith's "immediate access to God" (without priestly mediation). If that were what the doctrine really meant, it would have no pertinence to ecclesiology but would represent the triumph of a radical individualism. Not only the medieval priesthood but the evangelical ministry, too, would seem to be superfluous. It would mean that every man is his own priest, and every man his own church. But is that what Luther and Calvin meant by the common priesthood or (in Calvin's preferred expression) the royal priesthood?

Luther had more than one use for the idea of the common priesthood, as he returned to it in various situations. (1) He does say in one place that in matters of faith every Christian is his own pope and church (WA 5:407). (2) In his appeal *To the Christian Nobility of the German Nation* (1520), however, the common priesthood was largely a weapon against papal obstruction of church reform by the secular authorities: those who wield the temporal sword are also priests with responsibilities for the well-being of the church (LW 44:126–27, 131–33). (3) A different problem was how a congregation could acquire ministers when the papal incumbent had been driven out and there was no bishop to perform ordinations. In this context Luther argues that the use of "the keys" (the power of absolution) is given to the whole church and to every Christian by virtue of being a member of the body. We must come back to that in our next chapter, on the ministry. (4) Most important for our present theme, and already implicit in points 2 and 3, is Luther's insistence that the Christian is priest not for himself but *for others*. The duties of a priest are to intercede for others and to teach them. Strictly, there is but one priest of the new covenant, Christ; but all who are united with him by baptism are his *consacerdotes* ("fellow priests"), who participate in his double office of intercession and instruction. To be sure, Christians are kings as well as priests (Rev. 1:6, as in the KJV). But to be priests is far more excellent: as priests with Christ we are worthy to appear before God to pray for others, and to teach one another in turn (*invicem*) the things of God (*The Freedom of a Christian* [1520], LW 31:353–55). Here, we might say, the priesthood of all believers is a fifth means of grace. It is, I think, quintessential Luther when he adds to the Word, baptism, the Eucharist, and the keys "the mutual conversation and consolation of brethren" (Smalcald Articles [1537], part 3, art. 4; *BC* 310).

Calvin agrees that Christians participate in the priestly office of Christ (Comm. 1 Pet. 2:9). The priestly office of making sacrifice for sin is Christ's alone. But he receives us as companions in his priestly office in that, although defiled in ourselves, we can offer ourselves to God in him and he makes our sacrifice of *praise* "acceptable and sweet-smelling before God" (*Institutes*, 1:502). There is not very much in Calvin about fraternal conversation and consolation, and what there is he does not connect with the priesthood of all believers; he says that, although we should all console and encourage one another (Jas. 5:16), it is preferable to unburden ourselves to an ordained minister (636–37). To Calvin the royal priesthood is a collective, not a reciprocal idea; that is, it is not about the interaction of one believer with another, but about the priestly sacrifice of praise owed by the church in the sanctuary (2:1473, 1476).

Clearly, Calvin's thoughts on the royal priesthood are doubly controlled by 1 Peter 2:9: the language is *liturgical* and it concerns the *people* of God. He does not derive the pastoral office from the common priesthood, as Luther sometimes did (see Gerrish 2004), but connects it with the Eucharist (*Institutes*, 2:1445). This is not only closer to Scripture than Luther's idea of the common priesthood but also agrees with the understanding of the royal priesthood in Catholic theology, which never neglected it.[6] The profound insight of Luther's talk of a mutual priesthood, even if it is not strict exegesis of 1 Peter, is not to be denied. With good reason, it has often reappeared in Christian thinking about the church. Spener, for example, made use of the common priesthood, in Luther's sense, to justify the gatherings of the Pietists (Spener 1964: 92–95). To Schleiermacher, the priesthood of all believers meant a kind of interim state pending arrival of the day when even *mutual* instruction will no longer be needed: "No longer shall they teach one another, or say to each other, 'Know the LORD,' for they shall all know me, from the least of them to the greatest,' says the LORD" (Schleiermacher 1994: 152–53, 185–86; Jer. 31:34; cf. Isa. 54:13; John 6:45; Heb. 8:11). But one thing is clear: whether the priesthood of all believers is taken for a mutual priesthood *within* the church or for a priestly duty *of* the church, it has nothing to do with individualism and excludes the temptation to clericalism: *because [Christ] receives his people as companions in his priestly office, the church is . . . said to be a "royal priesthood," in which there is no division between priests and people.*

6. See my references to the studies by John H. Elliott and Paul Dabin in Gerrish 2004: 320 n. 65 and 315 n. 1, respectively; cf. Vatican II's *Lumen gentium* (DV 26–27). Calvin thinks of Christ's *prophetic* office also as continued in "his whole body," in the preaching of the gospel (*Institutes* 2.15.2 [1:496]); but this is not expressly included in his text from 1 Peter.

16. The Church's Minister

The apostolic ministry of witness and healing is committed to the whole church as a servant people of God and the body of Christ "sent out" into the world; and the pastoral office is not the apostolic ministry, but the means by which Christ, through the gifts of the Spirit, equips the church for its task of ministry.

The images of the church as "a servant people of God" and "the body of Christ" come together in the Christian belief that a mission has been assigned to the church. The mission must be defined, at least initially, by the ministry of Jesus reported in the Gospels. But there are obstacles in the way of building a dogmatic account of the church's mission on this foundation alone. To begin with, it is unlikely that Jesus envisioned a Christian church, or churches, spanning many centuries of history. He reportedly spoke of the Son of Man coming in glory in the lifetime of his hearers (Mark 9:1; 13:30; 14:62; Matt. 10:23). The future church was beyond Jesus' horizon (cf. Mark 13:32; Acts 1:6–7). In the Gospels the word *ekklēsia* is unique to two places in Matthew, and because there are no parallels in Mark, Luke, or John, many scholars doubt that they represent authentic words of Jesus. As Alfred Loisy observed, "Jesus foretold the kingdom, and it was the Church that came" (1976: 166). What the church is commissioned to do in the changing circumstances of some two millennia is bound to vary with the needs and the opportunities of the day, even if it is conformed to the activity of the Redeemer.

Further, although there is a near consensus of present-day Christians about the kinds of responsibility entrusted to the church, differences arise not only because responsibility must be translated into policies and actions for the day, but also because the responsibility has to be divided among the church's membership. Dogmatics defers to Christian ethics and practical theology on the details of what ought to be done and how it should be done. On the division of responsibility there is a measure of agreement—more, though, from the church's leadership than from Christians generally, who are inclined to ask on occasion when some task is urged on them, "Isn't that what the clergy are supposed to do?" The Faith and Order Paper of the World Council of Churches, *Baptism, Eucharist and Ministry* (*BEM* 1982) rightly states: "The word *ministry* in its broadest sense denotes the service to which the whole people of God is called, whether as individuals, as a local community, or as the universal Church." I take it that, in this context, "ministry" and "mission" are virtual synonyms: ministry is the service for which the church is called and *sent*. This then poses the question how ministry in its broadest sense, which I am calling "the apostolic ministry" of *the church*, is related to what *BEM* calls "ordained ministry": the office or offices for which certain individuals in the church are set aside. Answers commonly given to the question expose the diversity of terms in which the churches speak of ministry, not always in harmony with New Testament usage.

The first task, then (section I), is to comment on some pertinent New Testament terms and to describe the foundations of the church's ministry in the ministry of Jesus and the mission of his disciples. Next (section II), we need to look at some of the ways in which the apostolic ministry of the people of God (*BEM*'s ministry in its broadest sense) has been understood. A detailed historical review is out of the question. The point, rather, is to arrive at an idea of the church's mission pertinent to the task of dogmatics. Account must be taken of one of the last century's most important documents on the subject, the decree of the Second Vatican Council (1962–65) on the apostolate of the laity. A provisional conclusion can then be drawn (section III)—pending a broader discussion of church order, or polity, in chapter 17—on the apostolic ministry today and its relation to the pastoral office (*BEM*'s ordained ministry, or one kind of it).

I. Ministry in the New Testament

1. Ministry and the Servant People of God

In the KJV, "minister," "to minister," and "ministry" were used regularly, though not invariably, for the Greek words *diakonos, diakoneō,* and *diakonia*. Hence Mark 10:45 is translated: "For even the Son of man came not to be ministered unto, but to minister" (see also Rom. 15:8). This made it easier for English readers to note some connections that are obscured by the translators of the NRSV, who generally prefer "servant," "serve," and "service" (as in Mark 10:45) but retain "minister" and "ministry" where ordained or official ministry is presumably meant (Acts 1:17, 25; 21:19; Rom. 12:7; 15:25; 2 Cor. 3:4–11; 4:1; 5:18; 6:3; 8:4; 9:1, 13; Eph. 4:12; 6:21). Ministry, however, is service. Something of the range of meanings that the verb *diakoneō* may have is indicated by the way the NRSV translates it when *not* taken for official ministry: "wait on," "provide for," "take care of" (Mark 1:13; 15:41; Matt. 25:44; Luke 8:3). Similarly, in Acts 11:29 the noun *diakonia* is translated as "relief."[1] In the expression "the apostolic ministry" I take the qualifier "apostolic" to mean, in harmony with the root sense of the Greek *apostellō*, "sent out" in continuity with the sending out of Jesus' first disciples. It is the *church* that our Nicene Creed describes as "apostolic," and I take the apostolic ministry to mean service *committed to the whole church as a servant people of God and the body of Christ "sent out" into the world.*

Thesis 16 speaks also of *the pastoral office*. It is surprising, in a way, that "pastor" (*poimēn*, as in Eph. 4:11) appears to be generally acceptable to Christians

1. The NRSV does not always use "ministry" for *diakonia* even when official ministry could be understood: Acts 6:4 (where NRSV has "serving"); 12:25 ("mission"); Col. 4:17 ("task"); 1 Tim. 1:12 ("service"); 2 Tim. 4:5 ("work"). Likewise, in 1 Cor. 3:5 *diakonoi* is translated "servants," and in Col. 1:23 the singular (*diakonos*) becomes "servant."

(the sheep!); but their favorite psalm has always been Psalm 23, and in John 10 Jesus is the good shepherd (cf. Heb. 13:20; 1 Pet. 2:25; 5:4). In this context, the word "office" (rather than "ministry") is meant to suggest a duly appointed function *within* the church's ministry, like the function of one member of a body (cf. Rom. 12:4). My intention is to avoid using the terms *clergy* and *priesthood* to describe *BEM*'s ordained ministry, for two reasons. (1) The distinction commonly made between laity and clergy finds no support in the New Testament, where both *laos* and *klēros* refer to the church, or *a* church. Though the English *laity* is derived from *laos,* the Greek word denotes the people as a whole, not people contrasted with professional clergy. Our word *clergy* does come from *klēros.* But the Greek means "lot," or "something assigned by lot," and in 1 Peter 5:3 *tōn klērōn* refers not to clergy but to a congregation or congregations. To be sure, they are "the flock of God" (v. 2) allotted to the elders' care, so that a distinction is implied between sheep and shepherds; but it is *not* a distinction between laity and clergy. (2) The shepherds of the flock, the elders ("presbyters"), are nowhere called *priests* in the New Testament, and here again etymology can mislead. The English word *priest* comes (by contraction) from "presbyter." Hence John Milton's angry rebuke to domineering Presbyterians, "New *presbyter* is but old *priest* writ large." But the Greek for "priest" is *hiereus,* not *presbyteros.* Christ is the only priest of the new covenant (Heb. 7:20–22); into his priestly office he draws *all* his people, not one class only, to make their sacrifice of self-offering and praise.[2]

2. *The Ministry and Mission of Jesus*

The idea of an apostolic ministry ("sent out") is rooted in Jesus' own awareness of being sent. The Gospel of John depicts him praying to the Father on behalf of those the Father has given him: "As you have sent me into the world, so I have sent them into the world" (John 17:18). To his disciples he says: "As the Father has sent me, so I send you" (20:21). Jesus' references in the Fourth Gospel to being sent by God, his Father, are too numerous for exhaustive listing.[3] The reason for his emphatic claim to have been sent is clear: he wants it to be understood that he speaks and acts with divine authority. "[T]he word that you hear is not mine, but is from the Father who sent me" (14:24; cf. 7:29). "[T]he works that the Father has given me . . . testify on my behalf that the Father has sent me" (5:36). Hence, although the Father is greater than the Son (14:28), Jesus warns: "Anyone who does not honor the Son does not honor the Father who sent him" (5:23).

New Testament scholars agree that the author of the Fourth Gospel, to make a point, takes liberties with the sayings he attributes to Jesus. But Jesus'

2. With 1 Pet. 2:9–10 cf. the metaphor of sacrifice in Rom. 12:1 and Phil. 2:17. In Rom. 15:16 Paul calls himself "a *leitourgos* [servant] of Christ Jesus to the Gentiles," and he describes his service to the gospel as sacred or priestly (*hierourgounta to euangelion*) because it aims at an acceptable self-offering by the Gentiles. This is the only occurrence of the Greek word *hierourgeō* in the NT. Paul thinks of himself as the "priestly" agent of the "sacrifice" he has urged on the Roman Christians in Rom. 12:1; both words are metaphorical.

3. There are more than forty such references. In just over half of them, John uses the Greek word *pempō* for "send." In the rest, he uses *apostellō,* which suggests "send out" or "send off" (*apo* + *stellō*); from it come our English words *apostle* and *apostolic.* In Heb. 3:1 the word *apostolos* is used of Jesus. See also 1 John 4:9, 10, 14.

consciousness of being sent is by no means absent from the Synoptic Gospels. It is implicit in his claim to intimacy with the Father (notably, Matt. 11:27) and explicit when he says, "whoever welcomes me welcomes the one who sent me" (Matt. 10:40; Mark 9:37; Luke 9:48; cf. John 13:20), and, "whoever rejects me rejects the one who sent me" (Luke 10:16). The parable of the Vineyard, or the Wicked Husbandmen (Mark 12:1–12), may be cited here, although its received form may reflect a time after Jesus' death. Partly echoing Isaiah 5:1–7, it tells how the vineyard's owner, in another country, sends a succession of slaves to collect his share of the produce, and all of them are abused, beaten, or killed. The owner decides to send his beloved son, thinking his tenants will surely respect him. But they seize him, too, and kill him. Jesus ends with a quotation from Psalm 118:22–23, and the chief priests, scribes, and Pharisees realize that they are his intended targets. The parable corresponds to sayings in which Jesus expressed his persuasion that he had been sent—and rejected (cf. Matt. 23:37 // Luke 13:34–35; Acts 7:51–53).

Why, then, was Jesus sent? The answer is given in all that we said about the activity of the Redeemer: his proclaiming the kingdom, healing the sick, and welcoming sinners; his creation of faith and a community of faith. It is summed up in the saying already quoted from the Gospel of Mark: "For the Son of Man came not to be served [ministered unto] but to serve [minister], and to give his life a ransom for many" (Mark 10:45 // Matt. 20:28; cf. Phil. 2:7). In Luke and Matthew his service is interpreted in the language of Isaiah. According to Luke, the nature of his ministry came to Jesus, at the outset, in his awareness that with him the words of Isaiah 61:1–2 were fulfilled: "The Spirit of the Lord is upon me, because he has anointed me to bring good news to the poor. He has sent me to proclaim release to the captives and recovery of sight to the blind, to let the oppressed go free, to proclaim the year of the Lord's favor" (Luke 4:16–21; cf. v. 43). And according to Matthew, Jesus' healing ministry fulfilled the description of Yahweh's Servant in the first Servant Song (Isa. 42:1–4): "Here is my servant, whom I have chosen. . . . He will not break a bruised reed or quench a smoldering wick until he brings justice to victory" (Matt. 12:15–21).

Jesus' critics were offended that he ate and drank with tax collectors and sinners. In derision, they gave Jesus his noblest christological title: he was the "friend of sinners," even tax collectors (Matt. 11:19). That, in a word, was the heart of his *ministry*, and Luke follows the critics' unintended compliment with the story of the woman who was a sinner, despised by the Pharisee but forgiven by the Savior. "[H]er sins, which were many, have been forgiven; hence she has shown great love. But the one to whom little is forgiven, loves little" (Luke 7:34, 47). In another setting in Luke, the encounter with the chief tax collector Zacchaeus, Jesus sums up the good news: "For the Son of Man came to seek out and to save the lost" (19:10; see also Matt. 15:24; 18:11 [NRSV note]; Luke 15:2–7; John 10:11; cf. Ezek. 34:1–24).

3. The Mission of the Apostles

It was an extension of his own ministry that Jesus passed on to the Twelve and the Seventy. He was moved with compassion for the crowds who surrounded him, likening them to helpless sheep without a shepherd, and he called laborers to share his work (Matt. 9:35–10:1; Luke 10:2). Textual variants and the differences between the three versions of the sending of the Twelve (Mark 6:7–13; Matt. 10:1–42; Luke 9:1–6) should not unduly detain us. At the hands of Matthew, the sending seems to become a general guide for future missionaries of the church (cf. Luke 10:3–12). But the original commission to the Twelve is clear: to proclaim the good news of the kingdom (and with it the necessity for repentance: Mark 6:12; cf. 1:14–15), to cast out demons, and to heal the sick. Matthew adds that they were to raise the dead and cleanse the lepers (Matt. 10:8). The account of the sending of the Seventy (in some manuscripts, seventy-two) is peculiar to Luke 10:1–17, though parts of it (vv. 3–12), presumably from Q (see n. 4 in chap. 7 above), are attached by Matthew to the sending of the Twelve, and verses 13–15 appear elsewhere in Matthew (Matt. 11:21–23). The Seventy, like the Twelve, are commissioned to cure the sick, announce the kingdom, and cast out demons; but nothing is said of raising the dead or (specifically) of cleansing the lepers (Luke 10:9, 11, 17). The accounts of the sending of the Twelve and the Seventy warn of rejection and persecution, since the servant is not above his master (Matt. 10:24–25; cf. John 13:16; 15:20); and the identity of the disciples' mission with the mission of Jesus is stressed further in the affirmation that whoever listens to them is listening to him (Matt. 10:40; Luke 10:16; cf. Matt. 18:5; Mark 9:37; Luke 9:48; John 13:20).

Matthew calls the Twelve *Apostles* (Matt. 10:2), and in some ancient manuscripts of Mark it is Jesus himself who gives them this title (Mark 3:14). Why twelve? No doubt because their mission was not to the Gentiles or the Samaritans but to the lost sheep of the house of Israel (Matt. 10:5–6), which agrees with Jesus' reported pledge that those who had followed him would "sit on twelve thrones, judging the twelve tribes of Israel" (Matt. 19:28 // Luke 22:30).[4] The Twelve had a place of unique importance in the primitive church (see, e.g., Acts 6:2). Even when the mission had been extended to "all nations," the Great Commission at the end of Matthew's Gospel was apparently addressed to the Eleven (Matt. 28:16–20), and it was considered necessary to restore their full number after the defection of Judas (Acts 1:21–26). But the apostolic title was not reserved for them alone, and Luke testifies that Jesus sent others out, the Seventy, with the selfsame commission as the Twelve.

Paul considered himself to be an Apostle, sent to the Gentiles, as Peter was "an apostle to the circumcised" (Gal. 1:1; 2:8). He defended his apostolic claim on the grounds that he had seen the Lord and that his work had manifestly been blessed in the conversion of the saints at Corinth (1 Cor. 9:1–2). "Last of all, as to one untimely born, [Christ] appeared also to me. For I am the least of the apostles, unfit to be called an apostle, because I persecuted the church of God" (15:8–9). In Acts the dual qualification of Matthias for being counted an Apostle (see chap. 3, n. 2) is that he not only witnessed the resurrection but also

4. The pledge is presumably, though not expressly, addressed to the Twelve. The context in Luke connects it with the dispute between James and John, the sons of Zebedee, about which of them was the greatest. Jesus' answer is that to lead is to serve, as he himself is "among [them] as one who serves" (Luke 22:24–27). It is difficult to harmonize this with sitting on thrones, etc. (v. 30). An eschatological reversal seems to promise that the disciples will, after all, be like "the kings of the Gentiles"—only not now. In Mark and Matthew the incident ends not with the pledge of grandeur to come, but with the saying, "the Son of Man came . . . to serve [minister]," etc. The sending of the Seventy was also rooted in the OT (see Num. 11:16).

accompanied the original Twelve "during all the time that the Lord Jesus went in and out among [them]" (Acts 1:21–22, 26; cf. John 15:27). The Twelve were witnesses of Jesus' life as well as his resurrection. Confirmation of their special place in the earliest church came in the attribution to them of miraculous powers (Acts 2:43). Evidently, however, the Apostolic title was not restricted to them, nor was it extended only to include Paul ("last of all"!). Acts names Barnabas and Paul together as "apostles" (14:14). Paul could speak of "the other apostles," among whom he included James the Lord's brother, who was not one of the Twelve (1 Cor. 9:5; Gal. 1:19; cf. Mark 6:3). He speaks of apostles of the churches, including Epaphroditus (2 Cor. 8:23; Phil. 2:25), and he describes Andronicus and Junia as "prominent among the apostles" (Rom. 16:7). That mission belongs to the very definition of the church is a dogmatic principle with a long and checkered history. The details must be left to the church historians, but one or two highlights will serve dogmatic understanding.

II. The Apostolic Ministry AND the Concept of the Church

In the Acts of the Apostles, Barnabas and Paul are missionaries called by the Holy Spirit, set apart by the church, and sent on their way by the laying on of hands; their mission is to proclaim the Word of God (the good news) in places where there are as yet no Christian congregations (Acts 13:2–3, 5, 32, etc.). The pattern must have been repeated many times over in the early centuries of the church. But as Kenneth Scott Latourette wrote in the first volume of his monumental *History of the Expansion of Christianity* (on the first five centuries), "The chief agents in the expansion of Christianity appear not to have been those who made it a profession or a major part of their occupation, but men and women who earned their livelihood in some purely secular manner and spoke of their faith to those whom they met in this natural fashion" (1937, 1:116). Latourette also notes that the church attracted converts partly by its humanitarian activity, building hospitals, hospices for strangers, and houses for orphans, widows, and the indigent (186). Plainly, the church's mission is misconceived if it is assumed to have been exclusively the task of "professionals" who only preach. Furthermore, mission is always shaped, in part, by circumstances. The so-called Constantinian shift provides a case in point.

1. Constantine and the Mission of the Church

Before Constantine I (ca. 274–337), the Roman state regarded Christianity as a minority religion, generally to be tolerated but subject to surveillance and sporadic persecution. Compromise with the state religion was one option for the Christian: it required only a willingness to offer incense to the Roman divinities, which included the emperor, or even (during the persecution under Decius) to buy a certificate of compliance when the buyer had not in fact complied. For those who refused to conform in times of persecution, the possibilities included anonymous Christianity, an underground existence, torture, or martyrdom. Persecution did not halt the growth of the church, but the world surrounded the Christians less as a potential harvest than as a menace to be evaded or endured. There could be little thought of changing their world; their ministry was to one another in secret communities, to which the trickle of converts was added. But Constantine's conversion (312) and eventual victory as sole ruler of the Roman Empire (324) brought about the transformation of the minority sect into the empire's dominant religion. Under his lavish patronage, the church steadily grew in wealth and political influence; after his death, Theodosius I (ca. 346–395) declared Catholic (that is, Nicene) Christianity to be the state religion of Rome (380). Dissent was suppressed, and the now "orthodox" church had new opportunities for unimpeded mission.

The transformation looked like a remarkable triumph for the once beleaguered church, which now flourished under state protection, and missionaries carried the faith beyond the borders of the empire. But while the church transformed the world, engagement with the world transformed the church. Monks, the pioneers of the church's missionary expansion, became wealthy landowners; their abbots, notably Bernard of Clairvaux, enjoyed spiritual and worldly authority beyond their cloisters. The power acquired by the bishops of the church drew them into cooperation—or conflict—with the temporal authorities, and it became hard to distinguish princes of the church from earthly princes. Demands for reform were intermittently put forward long before the Protestant Reformation. The concluding article of the Lutheran Augsburg Confession (1530) on the power of bishops made no claim to novelty in protesting against the confusion of episcopal and temporal power, by which the bishops not only coerced consciences but also occasioned wars and turmoil. "These wrongs have long since been rebuked in the church by devout and learned men." The Lutheran remedy was to teach the difference between the power of the church and the power of the sword. Both "are to be held in reverence and honor as the chief gifts of God on earth," but the power of bishops is nothing other than "a power or command of God to preach the Gospel, to remit and retain sins, and to administer the sacraments" (*BC* 81). The Anabaptist remedy, roundly condemned in article 16 of the Augsburg Confession, was more radical.[5]

To the Anabaptists, the Constantinian shift meant the fall, not the triumph, of the church, and they sought to restore the true church of the Apostolic age. Everyone is *born* into the state church whereas the demand of the gospel, the Anabaptists pointed out, is to repent and make the *decision* of discipleship. The true church is a fellowship of brothers and sisters who have pledged to follow Christ. The outward splendor of the establishment, its formalism, and its coercion of dissent all betray a decline from the church of the New Testament. But the Anabaptists saw the clearest token of the difference between the established church and the true church in baptismal practice: in the one, infants were routinely baptized; in the other, believer baptism was administered only after a credible profession of faith. The baptism of infants was "the highest and chief abomination of the pope" (Schleitheim Confession [1527], art. 1). Utterly different rules of behavior distinguish the Christian fellowship from civil society. The Anabaptists did not deny that the civil authorities are ordained by God

5. In the sixteenth century, Protestants and Catholics alike used the name "Anabaptists" indiscriminately for several groups of Radical Reformers and took them all to be seditious. In present-day American historiography, the name is restricted, as a rule, to the Swiss Brethren, the Hutterites, and the Mennonites, and I use it in this sense. German historians prefer simply *Täufer* ("Baptists").

(Rom. 13:1). But "the sword is ordained of God outside the perfection of Christ" (Schleitheim, art. 6).[6] To *distinguish* between the power of the church and the power of the sword is not enough: the Christian *withdraws* from civic life, refusing to bear arms or to assume public office. Separation from the world is not only from worldly wickedness but also from the civil government's methods of restraining it. The Lord's command is plain: "Do not resist an evildoer" (Matt. 5:39). Yet in the Anabaptist communities separation went hand in hand with evangelistic zeal.

2. The Reformation and the Great Commission

Loyalty to Scripture generated a missionary zeal among the Anabaptists unrivalled by the Protestant Reformers. The Lutherans and Calvinists pointed out that the Great Commission to make disciples of all nations was addressed to the Apostles (Matt. 28:16–20); it bestowed on them their special "office," which in fact they carried out.[7] For the Anabaptists, by contrast, the commission laid a missionary obligation on the true church of every time—the church they were trying to bring back—and it applied to every Christian. As one historian writes, "The missionary mandate was no longer the prerogative of special orders [the monks and friars] or selected individuals. . . . In Anabaptist opinion, the craftsman might make a better missioner than the cultured man. Jesus himself preached to men in terms of their trade, not with many books" (Littell 1958: 113). Ironically, persecution and forced migration contributed to the spread of Anabaptist missionaries. When they arrived in Lutheran territory, Luther wrote his letter *Infiltrating and Clandestine Preachers* (1527; a less sanitized translation of the German title would be "On the Creeps and Corner Preachers"). He identifies them as emissaries of the devil who want to infect "our people" with their poison. The remedy is to ask them to show certification of their call. They cannot. They have no proper ministerial *office* and so are guilty of nullifying the divinely ordained parish system (LW 40:383–86).

Calvin, too, entered the lists against the Anabaptists. He had even less respect for the missionaries of the Church of Rome, who followed Spanish, Portuguese, and French colonists into the New World—and sometimes went before them. When he read Jesus' curse of the scribes and Pharisees who crossed sea and land to make a single convert and made the new convert twice as much a child of hell as they were, it was the Catholic missionaries who came to Calvin's mind (Comm. Matt. 23:15). But a plea for help arrived from the tiny French enclave in the Guanabara Bay of Rio de Janeiro, and Reformed Geneva seized

6. The Mennonite Dordrecht Confession (1632) affirms prayer for the civil government, even payment of taxes, "so that we may live under its protection" (arts. 13–14).

7. See Warneck 1906, chap. 1. Warneck names Adrian Saravia (1532–1612), the Flemish Reformed pastor who settled in England and defended Anglican episcopacy, as the sole Protestant theologian who rejected the prevailing interpretation of the Great Commission (20–22). Critics of Warneck's classic study have shown that there is much more to be said about the missionary zeal of the Reformers if "mission" does not refer only to organized foreign missions. And Luther, at least, did not think of the Great Commission as carried out completely by the Apostles; they threw the stone into the water, but ever since, in the preaching of the Word after them, the waves roll on (Serm. Mark 16:14–20; WA 10/3:140).

the opportunity, no doubt with Calvin's approval (1556).[8] The hope was that the island (which still bears the name of the French governor Villegaignon) would serve as a haven for Huguenot refugees and a base for missions to the Tupí Indians. Geneva contributed both pastors and craftsmen to the Huguenot reinforcements, and the mission to the Indians began. As so often, circumstances dictated theological adjustment. But this solitary Reformed venture in foreign missions failed when the governor turned against the Calvinists; eventually the Portuguese took over the settlement.

Throughout the age of Lutheran and Reformed orthodoxy (the seventeenth century), the belief that the Great Commission was addressed only to the Apostles continued to stand in the way of Protestant missionary activity; it was overcome not by the occasional protests but by the opening up of colonies by the Protestant nations: Holland, England, and Denmark. Once again opportunity overcame dogma, and the idea of the church changed. The flowering of Protestant missions had to wait for what Latourette fitly called "the great century, AD 1800–1914," and then the inspiration came less from the Reformation than from Pietism and the evangelical revival of the previous century—the same source from which came the ardent evangelism and compassionate social activism of the "home" mission. Missionary boards and societies, both denominational and interdenominational, set the Great Commission on an organized platform; and where new churches were built, schools and hospitals followed. At the beginning of the great century, Schleiermacher suggested the possible inclusion of "the theory of missions" in the theological curriculum as a part of practical theology.[9] At the end of the century, Lutheran theologian Gustav Warneck (1834–1910) became the founder of "missiology" as an academic discipline. His "epoch-making achievement" was acknowledged by Josef Schmidlin (1876–1944), who became the leading exponent of Roman Catholic mission theory, and once more the definition of the church was at stake.

2. *Vatican II and the Lay Apostolate*

Schmidlin states the traditional Roman Catholic view of missions as *planting the* (*Catholic*) *Church*: "we include among the tasks of the missions, not merely extension of Christianity, but also incorporation in the true Church, and we further claim for the Catholic Church the right to convert, not alone pagans, but also non-Catholics, and lead them all into the one true fold" (1931: 35; cf. 41). The venerable *Catholic Dictionary* of Addis and Arnold begins its entry on "Missions" with the blunt assertion: "Mission is inseparably connected with jurisdiction, so that he who is validly 'sent' exercises a lawful jurisdiction in the place to which, and over the persons to whom, he is sent." That, no doubt,

8. A useful essay by R. Pierce Beaver on the Genevan mission to Brazil (1967), based mainly on the fascinating journal of Jean de Léry, is reprinted in John H. Bratt, ed., *The Heritage of John Calvin: Heritage Hall Lectures, 1960–1970* (Grand Rapids: Eerdmans, 1973), 55–73.

9. Schleiermacher 1966: 102. He himself actually addressed the subject of missions in his posthumously edited and published lectures on Christian ethics, never translated in their entirety into English: *Die christliche Sitte*, ed. L. Jonas, 2nd ed., Friedrich Schleiermacher's sämmtliche Werke (Berlin: Reimer, 1884), I/12:378–83; supplement, 176–83.

is a top-heavy judgment that hardly conveys the motives of missionaries in the field (see the subsequent entry on "Missions, Popular"!). In any case, the pronouncements of the Second Vatican Council (1962–65) seem to move us into another world—both by what they say about mission and by what they don't say. For the most part, the language is not juridical; the accent is on dialogue and cooperation, not management of indigenous peoples or competition with non-Catholic missionaries. Scripture is liberally cited not to prove a point but to elicit a point. As John O'Malley says, Vatican II "moved from the dialectic of winning an argument to the dialogue of finding common ground" (O'Malley 2008: 46; cf. 307–8). Important for our present theme is the repeated emphasis on the place of "the laity" in the church's mission.

By "the laity" the Dogmatic Constitution on the Church (*Lumen gentium*) does not mean the New Testament *laos*, the entire people of God, but "all the faithful except those in holy orders and those in a religious state sanctioned by the Church." This, however, does not prevent a sustained effort to counter the tendency to think of the laity merely as passive subjects of the hierarchy. They have their own active part to play in the mission of the whole Christian people. Precisely because they have secular callings and live in the world, they are able to work for the sanctification of the world like leaven—from within. "[T]he laity are called in a special way to make the Church present and operative in those places and circumstances where only through them can she become the salt of the earth." In this way, the lay apostolate participates in the saving mission of the church (*DV* 57–59). These thoughts are developed at length in the decrees on the Apostolate of the Laity (*Apostolicam actuositatem*) and the Church's Missionary Activity (*Ad Gentes*). I can mention only one or two additional points made in these two decrees.

The purpose of *the apostolate of the laity* is twofold: to make the gospel known and to penetrate the temporal sphere through the spirit of the gospel. "Christ's redemptive work, while of itself directed toward the salvation of men, involves also the renewal of the whole temporal order" (*DV* 495). The apostolate of the laity consists not only in the witness of their lives, but also in looking for opportunities to announce Christ to their neighbors through the spoken word. "For there are many persons who can hear the gospel and recognize Christ only through the laity who live near them" (505). Further, the laity, both individually and in various groups and associations, are bound by Christian charity to seek out those who lack food, clothing, housing, medicine, employment, education—in short, those who "lack the facilities necessary for living a truly human life" (499). The duty of Christian witness requires the cooperation of Catholics with other Christians; the duty of social action calls for cooperation with all men of goodwill. And the penetration of the temporal sphere with the gospel reaches out to family life, culture, economic and political affairs, the arts and professions, and even international relations.

The decree on *the church's missionary activity* may be said to extend the reach of lay apostles to the ends of the earth. God's plan is to make one people of the human race, and carrying out the plan requires marshaling the forces of all the faithful. The purpose of missionary activity is "evangelization and planting the Church among those peoples and groups where she has not yet taken root." But the manner in which missions are to be carried out is described less as extending the jurisdiction of the Catholic Church than as adaptation to the local cultural and social life; the goal is to establish particular indigenous churches that "can make their contribution to the good of the Church universal." Since the life of the church is apostolic, the new catechumens will learn "to cooperate actively, by the witness of their lives and by the profession of their faith, in the spread of the gospel and in the upbuilding of the Church." The faithful will draw their clergy from their own number: "ministers of salvation," all versed in the culture of their people and some undertaking missionary work beyond their own territory (*DV* 591, 601, 604, 609–10). In the attainment of the church's missionary goals, however, the laity have an especially important role. Their duty is to bear witness to Christ "by their life and works in the home, in their social group, and in their own professional circle"; and they must do so "in the social and cultural framework of their own homeland, according to their own national traditions." "For the lay faithful fully belong at one and the same time both to the People of God and to civil society. They belong to the nation in which they were born" (603, 611; cf. 628–29).

In sum, the Second Vatican Council made a strong case for understanding the church as missionary by its very nature, because its source is the mission of the Son and the mission of the Spirit (*DV* 585). "[T]he whole Church is missionary, and the work of evangelization is a basic duty of the People of God" (623). In general, if we make allowances for terminological differences, the missionary principles of Vatican II may speak for Protestant, as well as for Catholic, understanding of Christian faith and its nisus to mission and ministry.

III. The Apostolic Ministry and the Pastoral Office

It used to be taken for granted (and by some it still is) that "ministry" is what ordained clergy do; and whenever it was reported that "the church" had said this or done that, the leadership of the institution was invariably meant. But in the second half of the twentieth century attention turned to the ministry of "the people of God." Although differences over the forms of professional ministry continued to divide the churches, the people's ministry was increasingly understood to define the essence of the universal church. Moreover, ecumenical theology moved closer to agreement on what belongs in the church's ministry, which is more than the means to institutional advancement, more even than the means to individual salvation. At the same time, it is not evident that the fresh perspective has been translated into successful action. The churches in Europe and North America are mostly in retrenchment. The demise of colonialism has called for rethinking missionary activity without the old assumption that the Europeans are the guardians of Christianity. Angry protests have been leveled against the perceived complacency of "North Atlantic" Christians—or even their complicity—in the face of Third World poverty and suffering. As always, ministry must adapt to the situation. For their agenda, the churches look to Christian ethics and practical theology; the task of dogmatics is to develop a workable idea of the church's ministry that will inform and guide the agenda.

1. A Ministry of Witness and Healing

If the ministry of the entire church is to reflect the activity of the Redeemer reported in the Gospels, it will be a ministry of witness and healing. It is "apostolic" in the sense that Christians, individually and collectively, are sent out into the world by the Redeemer as he was sent by his Father. Jesus announced the coming of the kingdom; the *witness* of the first disciples was to the presence of the kingdom and to Jesus himself as the Messiah with whom the kingdom came. Thus we are told in the Acts of the Apostles that Philip the deacon proclaimed the good news about the kingdom of God and the name of Jesus Christ (Acts 8:12). The same double message of Christ and the kingdom is ascribed to Paul. He bore witness to the kingdom of God and tried to convince his hearers about Jesus (28:23); he proclaimed the kingdom and taught about the Lord Jesus Christ (28:31). Like Jesus' own preaching, the message of the disciples was proclamation—good news of things that had happened—and a call to repent.[10] The witness of the church, when faithful to the original message, has always retained at its center this special character of an announcement that summons hearers to change the way they think. Witness includes the entire behavior of the penitent in the daily pursuit of their various callings, but readiness to speak the apostolic Word is not left to the professionals. "Mission" has, indeed, often been equated with overseas missions: programs and organizations for sending trained personnel to foreign parts. But there is, in principle, no difference between foreign and home missions or between the work of professionals and the witness of each and every Christian. All are instances of the "evangelism" that defines the church. As testimony to an event, or a series of events, Christian witness spreads from its point of origin to cover the globe. The Lord's commission, as it appears in the Acts of the Apostles, was: "you will be my witnesses in Jerusalem, in all Judea and Samaria, and to the ends of the earth" (Acts 1:8).

The dissemination of Christian faith includes all that flows from the gospel center. Much has been said and written about the cultural impact of Christianity, and it may be asked whether this, too, belongs to the church's mission or is better understood as a byproduct of it. Jesus and the first disciples lived under an alien imperial power, and they could have had no thought of making an impact on Roman civilization. "Render to Caesar the things that are Caesar's, and to God the things that are God's" (Mark 12:17 RSV). The words imply separation, not an invitation to cultural influence. But postcanonical changes in the church and its environment have opened up opportunities and responsibilities that were not within the horizon of the primitive church. The idea of Christian witness will take account of them. The opportunities will not be equally available in every type of relationship between church and culture. (H. Richard Niebuhr's classic study *Christ and Culture* [1951] added two more types to Troeltsch's three.) In a democratic society, with present-day means of communication, Christians have the possibility of influencing public opinion and offering a

10. The Greek for "good news" (*euangelion*) is the source of the archaic English "evangel" and its living cognates "evangelical," "evangelism," and "evangelist." "Proclamation" (*kēryssō*) is what a herald (*kēryx*) does. According to 1 and 2 Timothy, Paul claimed he was appointed "herald and apostle" (1 Tim. 2:7), or "herald, apostle, and teacher" (2 Tim. 1:11). "Repentance" (*metanoia*) is literally "change of mind."

Christian perspective on the various forms of cultural expression: family relationships, economic activity, party platforms, education, the arts, literature, and so on. There is no reason not to count this conscious influence among the tasks of Christian witness.

The activity of Jesus was not only proclamation but also *healing*, and this too belongs to the ministry of his people. It is surprising that such a vital part of his ministry, as reported in the Gospels, is not reflected in the Great Commission. In Matthew, the commission is to go and "make disciples of all nations, baptizing them in the name of the Father and of the Son and of the Holy Spirit, and teaching them to obey everything that I have commanded you" (Matt. 28:19–20). In Luke, the risen Lord appears to the Eleven and their companions and describes the Apostolic witness (in fulfillment of Scripture) as a worldwide proclamation of repentance and forgiveness in his name (Luke 24:45–48). In some manuscripts, the shorter ending of Mark mentions "the sacred and imperishable proclamation of eternal salvation" (Mark 16:8b). Only the longer ending of Mark connects the commission to proclaim the good news with casting out demons, healing the sick, and other signs (16:15–17). The origin of the longer ending is unknown, but in itself the correlation of preaching and healing is faithful to the Synoptic account of Jesus' ministry and his instructions for the Twelve and the Seventy. The other signs mentioned—speaking in tongues, snake handling, drinking poison (see NOAB note)—can perhaps be described as occasional wonders not so indelibly written into the record. (Speaking with tongues assumes importance later in the history of the church.) But, of course, the stories of healing raise questions in the mind of the modern reader. Each of the healing narratives in the Gospels needs to be considered individually. I cannot even begin to attempt that here. One or two more general observations must suffice for our purposes.

Most devout Christians take the narratives to be accounts of miraculous deeds, and they think it frivolous either to offer natural explanations of Jesus' healing activity or to allegorize it. But the risk is then that his healing activity will be treated as evidence of his divinity rather than as part of his ministry. A common view among Protestants has been that the miracles of the Apostolic age were a temporary expedient needed to launch and authorize the church; their miraculous character must accordingly be affirmed, but not their continuance in the life of the church. But it seems to me unwise to make a literal reading of the miracle stories a required item of Christian *belief*; better to admit that we do not really know what bare facts may lie behind reports couched in the language of another time (e.g., in terms of the malevolent activity of demons). What Christian *faith* discerns in the stories is a form of ministry that includes healing. We may take "healing," in its broadest sense, to mean restoring the wholeness of humanity wherever it has been frustrated or injured. I naturally think first of remedying the sin and estrangement outlined in previous chapters. But bodily healing is not excluded. It will be undertaken with all the proven means, physical and nonphysical, available in our day.[11] Christians are

11. Though dated in detail, Weatherhead 1952 retains its value as a comprehensive "critical study of all the non-physical methods of healing." He rightly acknowledged the need for "further investigation and action in this field."

not so presumptuous as to undertake such healing without acknowledging that the work is still Christ's work. Even the Christian physician who heals with the resources of modern medicine may see her work as a vocation, undertaken in Christ's name and moved by the eschatological vision of health and wholeness that so obviously impelled *him* (cf. Isa. 35:5–6).

2. *The Pastoral Office*

How, then, is the ministry of the people related to ministry in what is still perhaps the more usual sense: the *office* of pastor? Here, too, the last century saw a theological convergence. A clue was found in Ephesians 4:11–12. In the original Greek verse 12 is ambiguous, and our English versions offer two different interpretations. (1) The KJV reads: "[v. 11] And he [Christ] gave some, apostles; and some, prophets; and some, evangelists; and some, pastors and teachers; [v. 12] For the perfecting of the saints, for the work of the ministry, for the edifying of the body of Christ." In this interpretation, verse 11 lists the titles of those who, by the gift of Christ, hold what we are accustomed to call "ordained offices," and verse 12 lists three purposes for which the offices exist. The second purpose, "for the work of the ministry," clearly assigns the ministry to officebearers. (2) The NRSV reads: "[v. 11] The gifts he [Christ] gave were that some would be apostles, some prophets, some evangelists, some pastors and teachers, [v. 12] *to equip the saints for the work of ministry*, for building up the body of Christ" (italics mine). Here it is the saints, the people of God, who are entrusted with the work of ministry; the responsibility of the pastors and teachers (or perhaps of all those who hold ordained offices) is to enable them for their task.[12]

The grammatical difference between the two interpretations is very slight: it amounts to the question whether to supply a comma after "the saints." (New Testament Greek texts lacked punctuation.) Theologically, however, the difference is immense, and it has occasioned controversy among theologians and New Testament scholars. The first reading of Ephesians 4:12 (as in the KJV) may claim to be the traditional reading. Calvin, for example, took the entire passage to be about the external ministry of the Word, and he inferred that we must let go our pride and "allow ourselves to be ruled and taught by men" (Comm. Eph. 4:11–14). The second reading (as in the NRSV) became the dominant one in the last century, and it invited fresh thought on the role of the "laity" in the church. Not without dissenters, however! Catholic biblical scholar John Collins, for example, answered the question of his trenchant study *Are All Christians Ministers?* with an emphatic no. Though he was able to cite Calvin on his side (Collins 1992: 24–25), he saw the new consensus, reflected in the responses to *BEM*, as "a truly representative *Protestant* point of view for our time" (2; emphasis mine). He faults the NRSV translation of Ephesians 4:12, anticipated in the second edition of the RSV (1971), because it "switches the role of ministry from pastors to saints" (20). I don't myself see it quite that way.

12. Note that instead of KJV's "the work of *the* ministry" NRSV has "the work of ministry," which is more faithful to the Greek (*ergon diakonias*) and a useful reminder that the NT speaks of more than one ministry or service. It is a *particular* ministry that is assigned to the Twelve (Acts 1:17) or to Paul (20:24; 21:19).

The pastors do not surrender ministry to the saints. The ministry of witness and healing committed to the whole church includes the pastors: their pastoral responsibility is a function *within* the apostolic ministry of the church. This, too, is ministry (service), and there should be no objection to the contrast *BEM* draws between two ministries: ministry in its broadest sense and ordained ministry. But I hope it is an aid to clarity if I prefer to make it a contrast between apostolic *ministry* and the pastoral *office*. Hence, although my case does not rest on a particular interpretation of a single text, I am adapting the language of the second reading of Ephesians 4:12 when I say that *the pastoral office is not the apostolic ministry, but the means by which Christ, through the gifts of the Spirit, equips the church for its task of ministry.* Pius XI spoke of "the participation of the laity in the apostolate of the hierarchy" (his definition of Catholic Action). If we use *laos* in its biblical sense, we might better say that the pastors participate in the apostolate of the laity. And this leads us to the further question we have postponed to the next chapter: What does our conclusion about the proper distinction between ministry and office imply for the various forms of so-called ecclesiastical order that continue to divide the churches from one another?

17. Faith and Order

Christ's headship over the church (his kingly office), exercised through the Word and not delegated to any group or individual, has assumed various forms of church order, none of which exists by exclusive divine right; and the promise of Christ's presence through the Spirit does not guarantee the infallibility of any person, institution, or gathering of the church, but rather confirms Christian faith in the indefectibility of the Word.

The last chapter drew a distinction between the church's ministry and the pastoral office and showed how the two are related. But it was not my intention to reduce so-called ordained ministry to the pastoral office; I described the conclusion to chapter 16 as provisional, pending a broader discussion of church order or polity. Ecumenical dialogue has demonstrated again and again that here lies the most intractable issue that separates the churches, dividing Orthodox from Catholics, Catholics from Protestants, and Protestants among themselves. The problem is not only that denominational interests are at stake; indeed, ecumenical dialogue also demonstrates that commitment to rigorous standards of historical inquiry *can* hold party bias in abeyance. But, for all the industrious research into the canonical and postcanonical sources, the evidence for the origin and development of what is variously called "official," "ordained," or "institutional" ministry (as distinct from the ministry of the entire people of God) leaves us with gaps and ambiguities that defy a scholarly consensus.

Does it really matter? There is no agreement even on that. Some say that ecclesiastical polity should be classed with *adiaphora*, things indifferent, and has no place in dogmatic theology. Others insist that polity belongs to the essence of the church, either because Scripture is the sole norm for church order (as of everything else) or because a particular form of church government (the historic episcopate) has served the church for two millennia as the bond of unity with the church of the Apostles. Obviously a third, mediating course is possible: to agree that polity does matter but to argue that our dogmatic norms do not exclude organizational diversity but *require* it. This, in general, is the course I follow. In the present chapter I document the diversity that is already apparent in the New Testament before attempting a brief critical review of the principal types of polity that have emerged in the history of the church. In the third section I draw some constructive conclusions and note the crucial importance of faith in Christ's headship and ecclesial presence for understanding the authority of the church.

I. Gift and Office in the New Testament

The New Testament attests the independent emergence of two kinds of church order, commonly distinguished as "charismatic" and "official." Whereas charismatic order (from the Greek *charismata*, spiritual "gifts") stresses the variety of *functions* in the body of Christ, official order has more to say about the status of *persons* who hold office in the church. For the former kind, Paul's First Letter to the Corinthians is our main source; for the latter, Acts and the Pastoral Letters. The two kinds of order must not be too sharply drawn. Paul traces spiritual gifts to the divine appointment of Apostles, prophets, teachers, and others (1 Cor. 12:28; cf. v. 18), and the Letter to the Ephesians attributes the existence of officials in the church to the gifts of Christ (Eph. 4:8–11). Gift and office are not necessarily exclusive, and Paul moves easily from talk about gifts to talk about the persons who have them (1 Cor. 12:7, 28).[1] But a difference between two kinds of order, however blurred, is unmistakable: order determined by spiritual gifts, or order determined by ecclesiastical office. The difference reflects the contrast between the church as community and the church as institution.

1. Charismatic Order

Paul's First Letter to the Corinthians was written (in 54 or 55 CE) to a Gentile church established by his own missionary activity (Acts 18:1–11). It is impossible to say how representative the Corinthian church was of first-generation Gentile congregations, but in chapters 12 and 14—on the gifts of the Spirit (*pneumatika, charismata*)—we have our earliest picture of a living Christian community. The two chapters call for much more careful study than can be attempted here. Suffice it to say, for our purpose, that the letter gives a vivid portrayal of a community in which every member plays an active part for the common good (1 Cor. 12:7). True, some of the Spirit's gifts are more to be desired than others (12:31), yet there is no hint of hierarchy—if hierarchy means a chain of officials, or of ranks, each compliant to the official or rank above it. Paul's analogy of the body suggests not subordination but interaction: the cooperation of limbs or functions for the benefit of the whole (12:12–26; cf. Rom. 12:3–8). He does not hesitate to say that some members are weaker or less respectable than others. But if one is tempted to feel superior, another to feel unwanted, he admonishes them both that the body functions only because all are indispensable and must work together. "God has so arranged the body, giving the greater honor to the inferior member, that there may be no dissension within the body, but the members may have the same care for one another" (1 Cor. 12:24–25).

Paul's instructions concerning prophecy show that he does not assign every gift to a particular class within the congregation: he writes of prophets but does not think of what they do as their exclusive privilege. Special importance belongs to prophecy as a counterbalance to speaking in tongues. "I would like

1. Indeed, 1 Cor. 12 can be taken to be about either "spiritual gifts" or "spiritual persons": in v. 1 the Greek *peri de tōn pneumatikōn* is ambiguous, and in v. 28 Paul switches from titling persons (Apostles, prophets, and teachers) to naming functions (healing, speaking in tongues, etc.). Note that in vv. 4–6 he moves from "varieties of gifts" to "varieties of services" (or "ministries": *diakoniōn*) and "varieties of activity."

all of you to speak in tongues, but even more to prophesy" (1 Cor. 14:5; cf. vv. 1, 39). Speaking in tongues is a gift of the Spirit, but it benefits the church only when someone interprets it.[2] Paul depicts a free and spontaneous gathering (vv. 26–33) in which each contributes a hymn, a lesson, a revelation, a "tongue," or an interpretation. Those who speak in tongues should take turns (not all speaking at once). There should be no more than two or at most three of them; and if there is no one to interpret, they should not speak in church at all. Two or three prophets may likewise speak in turn; and "if a revelation is made to someone else sitting nearby, let the first person be silent." Paul states expressly that all can prophesy one by one (v. 31). But everything must be done in an orderly manner for the sake of edification; "for God is a God not of disorder but of peace" (vv. 26, 33). In the conclusion to his discussion of spiritual gifts (vv. 37–40), Paul claims to speak with the Lord's authority and gives a summary statement on balancing free participation with proper order. "So, my friends [Greek *brothers*], be eager to prophesy, and do not forbid speaking in tongues; but all things should be done decently and in order." The intervening verses (vv. 33b–36) expressly decline to extend to women the right for "all" to speak in church. But since Paul has already stated that a woman who prays or prophesies must have her head covered (11:5),[3] it seems likely that those verses were an editorial insertion by a scribe whose sense of social propriety, for which he claimed the authority of all the churches, was even more restrictive than Paul's (cf. 1 Tim. 2:12–15). The likelihood is strengthened by the fact that some ancient authorities give verses 34–35 a different location, after verse 40.

Charismatic church order risked confusion. Perhaps one is tempted to say that the assemblies of the church in Corinth *lacked* order. But it would be more correct to say that Paul spoke of an order of the Spirit (capital S) without a hierarchy. His observations on Christian assemblies are not to be taken merely as commonsense rules of thumb: they arise out of the understanding of spiritual gifts that is conveyed in his analogy of the body. In his study of ecclesiastical office and spiritual power in the first three centuries, Hans von Campenhausen concluded: "In Paul's thought, therefore, the congregation is not just another constitutional organisation with grades and classes, but a unitary, living cosmos of free, spiritual gifts, which serve and complement one another" (1969, 63–64).

2. *Official Order*

A different picture of congregational order appears in the Acts of the Apostles, written later than 1 Corinthians (perhaps ca. 80 CE) but purporting to tell the story of the church from its beginning. It is evident from Acts that the first Christians found a model for church order in the Jewish synagogues, which were the initial bases for Christian missions. The synagogues had no priests: the priesthood

2. The ecstatic phenomenon of unintelligible glossolalia is different from the Pentecostal speaking in foreign languages reported in Acts 2:1–13. It has been argued from 1 Cor. 13:8 that although Paul himself claimed to "speak in tongues" (14:18), he expected glossolalia to be a transient phenomenon in the life of the church. But he is speaking there of the end, not the next stage, of church history. He would probably judge that the later neglect or suppression of ecstatic utterance quenched the Spirit (1 Thess. 5:19).

3. Cf. Acts 21:9, where the four daughters of Philip the evangelist are said to have the gift of prophecy. See also n. 5 below.

was connected exclusively with the temple, and the sacrificial cult was considered by the Christians to have been superseded by the priestly work of Christ. Supervision of the synagogues was entrusted to a body of *elders* (*presbyteroi*).[4] They were not ordained ministers in our sense—not, that is, a special group set aside to preach and perform the sacraments. Any adult male could be invited to read and interpret the Law and the Prophets in the synagogues, as were Jesus and Paul (Luke 4:16–21; Acts 13:14–16). But the judicial and administrative business of the Jewish community was in the hands of the elders. Luke's picture in Acts shows the first Christian congregations brought into being by the Apostolic preaching as communities independent of the parent religion but setting aside elders from their own number on the Jewish pattern. The story of the Jerusalem Council (Acts 15:1–29) depicts a body composed of the Apostles and the elders, apparently presided over by James the Lord's brother. The phrase "the apostles and the elders" is used repeatedly (vv. 2, 4, 6, 22, 23; cf. 21:18); verse 22 has "the apostles and the elders, with the consent of the whole church" (cf. v. 4); and verse 23 has "the brothers, both the apostles and the elders." Clearly, we have here not charismatic but official order, that is, church order constituted by office.

The choosing of the Seven in Acts 6:1–6 has traditionally been held to mark the institution of a second office, the office of *deacons.* The reason for appointing the Seven was to spare the Apostles the distraction of taking care of widows, some of whom were being neglected: it was not right to neglect the Word of God in order to wait on tables. The Seven were chosen by the community and brought to the Apostles, who prayed and laid hands on them. But they are not called "deacons." The word for *deacon* (Greek *diakonos*) does not appear in the account, but *diakonia* does. If we translate *diakonia* consistently as "ministry," the account contrasts the everyday ministry of waiting on tables with the ministry of the Word (see the KJV for vv. 1 and 4). Preaching appears to be the distinctive task of the Apostles. In fact, however, the Seven did not all confine themselves to waiting on tables but also engaged in the ministry of the Word. One of their number, Stephen, disputed and preached openly and became the first Christian martyr (6:8–7:60); another, Philip, carried the good news beyond Jerusalem, baptized the Ethiopian eunuch, and came to be known as "Philip the evangelist" (8:4–13, 26–40).

Paul mentions deacons,[5] but he says nothing about elders. He addresses one of his letters, perhaps written during his imprisonment in Rome (ca. 61–63 CE), "to all the saints in Christ Jesus who are in Philippi, with the bishops [*episkopois*] and deacons" (Phil. 1:1). Were there, then, no elders in the Philippian church? And who were the bishops or overseers?[6] The usual answer is that

4. The literal meaning of *presbyteroi* is "old (or older) men," and it is sometimes so used in the NT (e.g., Acts 2:17). When it has an official connotation, "elders" is the usual translation, but it is often transliterated as "presbyters." Calvin seems occasionally to make a distinction between *presbyteri* and *seniores.*

5. He describes himself as a *diakonos,* but not in the ecclesiastical sense of a "deacon": he is minister or servant of a new covenant, of God, of the gospel, of the church (2 Cor. 3:6; 6:4; Col. 1: 23, 25; cf. 1 Cor. 3:5). He calls "our sister Phoebe" a *diakonos* ("minister"?) in Rom. 16:1. Perhaps even the author of 1 Timothy, who desired women to keep silent (1 Tim. 2:12), had no problem with women as deacons; and he seems to recognize the possibility that some of the widows could be officially recognized as church workers (3:11; 5:9).

6. In the NT *episkopos* does not have the technical sense that the later term "bishop" would acquire. Sometimes the NRSV translates it as "bishop" but sometimes as "overseer"; in Phil. 1:1 both options are indicated. In 1 Pet. 2:25 Jesus is called "the shepherd and guardian [*episkopon*] of your souls."

in the New Testament elders and bishops must have been one and the same: when described in terms of their general function, the elders were "overseers." Accordingly, in Acts 20 Paul addresses the elders of the church in Ephesus collectively as "bishops" (NRSV "overseers"). The Ephesian elders are considered to be also "pastors," since they are exhorted "to shepherd [*poimainein*] the church of God that he obtained with the blood of his own Son" (Acts 20:17, 28). The elders' oversight is described in terms of pastoral care rather than government (but see 1 Thess. 5:12–13). In sum, the principal settled office in the church (in contrast to the Apostolate, which was not tied to any particular place) was that of the presbyter-pastor-bishop in continuity with the eldership in the Jewish synagogues (cf. 1 Pet. 5:1–2).

The identity of bishop and presbyter continued to be presupposed in the deutero-Pauline Pastoral Letters, which must date from the beginning or middle of the second century. The First Letter to Timothy mentions elders (5:17–19); but when describing the qualifications for office bearers, it refers only to bishops and deacons (3:2–13). The omission of the elders would be inexplicable if they constituted a third group—not, however, if they are the bishops. In the Letter to Titus the directive to appoint elders in every town is followed immediately by a list of qualifications for an *episkopos:* "For an overseer, as God's steward, must be blameless," etc. (Titus 1:5–9; cf. Acts 14:23; 1 Pet. 5:1–2). Apparently, *episkopos* is simply a description of an elder.

From 1 Timothy 5:17 some have inferred that there must have been two orders of presbyter: preaching elders and ruling elders. The text reads: "Let the elders who rule well be considered worthy of double honor, especially those who labor in preaching and teaching." The more natural conclusion is simply that only some of the elders in fact preached; there is no reason to suppose that they must have constituted a separate order. It seems likely enough that in time preaching and teaching did become the special concern of the presbyterial office, and this is presumably the implication of the tandem expression in Ephesians 4:11, "pastors and teachers." Even in the relatively late time of the Pastorals there is no hint of the belief that the office of presbyter-bishop was sacerdotal. They were not priests, ordained to procure atonement by means of propitiatory sacrifices; they were ordained to be teachers of sound doctrine, guardians of received truth (2 Tim. 1:13–14; 3:14; Titus 1:9). On the other hand, the Pauline notion of a *charisma* freely given by the Spirit has become a *charisma* of office, imparted by the laying on of hands—either by the presbytery (1 Tim. 4:14) or by "Paul," the simulated author of the Pastorals (2 Tim. 1:6). The suggestion that these passages may refer to the *charisma* not of ordination but of baptism has not won much support from New Testament scholars.

II. The Types of Church Polity

The organization of the earliest Christian churches did not conform to a single pattern—or even two patterns, the charismatic and the institutional. Institutional order itself took more than one form. Three perennial types are usually distinguished, each of which has been defended as biblical: congregationalism, presbyterianism, and episcopacy. Variations within each type have occurred throughout church history, but it is the broad contrast between them that chiefly interests the dogmatic theologian. We may treat Roman Catholic polity as, in effect, a distinctive type because of the Catholic claim that the episcopal hierarchy culminates in the person of the pope as the successor of Peter. This claim, too, is defended as biblical.

1. The Three Main Types

The English separatist Robert Browne (1550–1633) is often singled out as the father of *congregationalism*. The Congregationalists who came after him were not wedded to the separatist part of his program, but he gave them a pioneering account of the true church as a fellowship of believers under the government of Christ. He spoke his mind in three contentious treatises published in the Netherlands (Middelburg, 1582).[7] In *Reformation without Tarrying for Any*, he rejects control of the church by the civil authorities. Reform cannot wait for an act of parliament, and faithful preachers will not let themselves be silenced by the magistrates. Nothing can be achieved by force. The Lord's people are "of the willing sort": "For it is the conscience and not the power of man that will drive us to seek the Lord's kingdom" (162). In *A Treatise on Matthew 23* Browne pours scorn on the pretentiousness of the establishment clergy, and he accuses the English bishops of blocking thorough reform by refusing to license reform-minded preachers. His remedy is an appeal to the priesthood (and kingship) of all believers, who have no need of an episcopal certificate: "[I]s not every Christian a king and a priest to rule with Christ?" (214–15). Browne formulates his understanding of the true church more fully in the third and longest treatise, *A Book Which Shows the Life and Manners of All True Christians*. It deserves to be regarded as the charter of congregationalism, although the term *congregationalism* came later. That Browne finally conformed to the established church takes nothing away from the force of this notable document.

As the title of the book implies, it is a comprehensive review of Christian faith and practice. Only Browne's idea of the church interests us here. His answer to the first of his 185 questions states his understanding of the church as constituted by a voluntary agreement. "Why are we called the people of God and Christians?" Answer: "Christians are a company or number of believers, which by a willing covenant made with their God are under the government of God and Christ, and keep his laws in one holy communion because they are redeemed by Christ unto holiness and happiness forever, from which they were fallen by the sin of Adam" (227). Later, Browne describes this as the church "planted or gathered" (cf. Matt. 18:20), in which the government is "the Lordship of Christ in the communion of his offices, whereby his people obey his will and have mutual use of their graces and callings, to further their godliness and welfare" (253). That is to say, the lordship of Christ is exercised as he communicates his threefold office to the company of believers and as they share his

7. Reprints of the three treatises are in Peel and Carlson 1953, to which my citations refer; when quoting, I modernize Browne's sixteenth-century English. The affinity of his case with the Anabaptist understanding of the church is plain. Whether it proves dependence is debated. In any case, the idea of the church as a voluntary fellowship did not lead him to repudiate infant baptism (Peel and Carlson, 258–59).

graces and employ his offices toward one another. Under Christ, they are kings, who watch over one another; priests, who pray for one another; prophets, who teach one another (276–78). When Browne speaks of "the body, which is the church of Christ," he is echoing Paul's language in 1 Corinthians 12; in his own terms, "The communion of graces is a mutual using of friendship and callings" (262–63). He does affirm the need, with the consent of the people, for particular office bearers in the church (his list of offices follows Calvin's); and he allows for "synods" between one church and another, meetings for the weaker to seek the help of the stronger and for deciding "matters which cannot well be otherwise taken up." But he stresses *every man's* "gift, in talk, reasoning, exhortation, or doctrine," and states that "church meetings are the due resorting and coming together of Christians for mutual comfort by their presence and communion of graces, to further all godliness" (270, 271, 327, 341). In the Lord's Supper he finds a seal of this growing together in one body (279).

Browne points the way to a polity in which the congregation is the heart of the church, and the relationship between believer and believer, and between one congregation and another, is not hierarchical but complementary. As a modern Congregationalist puts it, the true ecclesiastical succession lies in "the links of recognition between church and church," that is, "the recognition of sister churches without subservience or conformity" (Horton 1952: 10, 62). Congregationalism, we might say, is a reminder that when the life of the congregation is dictated from the outside, the church as fellowship is at risk. Fellowship requires independence.

While congregationalism recaptured the Pauline image of the church (in 1 Cor. 12), *presbyterianism* has always been more interested in the other strand in New Testament ecclesiology, which grew out of the office of elder in the Jewish synagogues. John Calvin is often named as the architect of presbyterian polity by reason of his fourfold scheme of church governance by pastors, teachers, elders, and deacons. In actual fact, the full development of presbyterianism came only as Calvinism spread beyond Geneva, and Calvin seems to have learned his fourfold scheme, during his sojourn in Strasbourg, from Martin Bucer (1491–1551). After his return to Geneva, he incorporated it in the *Ecclesiastical Ordinances* (1541; LCC 22:58–66) and in the 1543 edition of his *Institutes*, whence it was carried over into the 1559 edition (*Institutes*, 2:1056–62).

Starting with the five classes of official mentioned in Ephesians 4:11, Calvin drew a distinction between temporary and permanent offices. The Lord raised up Apostles, prophets, and evangelists to usher in his kingdom; occasionally he raises up evangelists again, in place of the Apostles, as the times demand. But at no time can the church be without *pastors* and *teachers*. In a way (*quodammodo*), teachers correspond to the prophets, and pastors to the Apostles. The teachers (or doctors) came to play a prominent part in the educational program of reformed Geneva (cf. LCC 22:62–63), but in the *Institutes* Calvin had more to say about the pastors as successors of the Apostles (*qui in Apostolorum locum succedunt, Institutes*, 2:1058). Strictly, the title of "Apostle" belongs only to the Twelve, to whose number Paul was later added. But "by the meaning and derivation of the word all ministers of the church can properly be called 'apostles,' because all are sent by the Lord and are his messengers." Jesus commissioned the Twelve to preach the gospel and to perform baptisms and the Lord's Supper

(Matt. 28:19; Luke 22:19; 1 Cor. 11:24–25). The pastors, then, as successors of the Apostles, are commissioned for the same ministry of Word and Sacrament; like Paul, they are "ministers of Christ and stewards of the mysteries of God" (1 Cor. 4:1). But "what the Apostles performed for the whole world, each pastor ought to perform for his own flock, to which he is assigned" (1059). In addition, the pastors are "to keep and exercise upright discipline" (ibid.).

Calvin notes that Scripture uses the terms "bishops," "presbyters," "pastors," and "ministers" interchangeably. But his text (Eph. 4:11) does not name the third or fourth class of official. He thinks that the third class, the *elders*, are intended when Paul speaks of church "government" in Romans 12:8 and 1 Corinthians 12:28.[8] Calvin comments: "Governors were, I believe, elders [*seniores*] chosen from the people, who were charged with the censure of morals and the exercise of discipline along with the bishops" (*Institutes*, 2:1061). He thinks that from the beginning each congregation had its "senate" of elders. If we look back, then, over the first three offices in Calvin's church order, we see that while the pastors had three functions—to preach or teach, to administer the sacraments, and to exercise discipline—the teachers were only to teach, and the elders were only to assist in the exercise of discipline (1057–58). Hence, in Calvin's so-called fourfold ministry only the bishop-presbyter-pastor, not the teacher or the elder, was properly a "minister." Sometimes Calvin argues from 1 Timothy 5:17 that Paul distinguished two kinds of presbyter: those who labor in the Word and those who do not and yet who rule well (1211–12; cf. Comm. ad loc.). Presbyterians have inferred that there are two orders or classes of elder, teaching elders and ruling elders, and that the teaching elders are the same as the ministers of Word and Sacrament. But, as I have already said, I doubt that the passage in 1 Timothy requires such a distinction. It may mean only that, like some of the deacons, some elders engaged in a preaching of the Word that was not in their job description. Finally, Calvin takes the traditional view that Acts 6 tells of the institution of the fourth office, the office of the *deacons*, but he does not comment on the apparent anomaly that two of them immediately undertook the task they were supposed to enable the Apostles to perform. In a far-fetched piece of exegesis, he finds an allusion to two kinds of deacon in Romans 12:8: those who distribute alms ("the givers") and those who care for the poor and the sick ("the compassionate").

Variations of Calvin's fourfold governance of the church have appeared from time to time, making generalizations hazardous. But it is commonly said that his enduring legacy was his insistence on "the parity of presbyters" in the church instituted by Christ, that is, on the identity of bishops and presbyters. The other side of presbyterianism, developed in lands beyond Geneva, is the extension of the idea of a local senate of presbyters (the session or consistory) to higher "courts" or "judicatories" that link the congregations together in widening circles (regional presbyteries, provincial synods, and a nationwide

8. He is referring to the words translated by the NRSV as "the leader" in Rom. 12:8 (*ho proistamenos*) and "forms of leadership" in 1 Cor. 12:28 (*kybernēseis*). The KJV has "he that ruleth" and "governments"—which may come closer to Calvin but not to Paul. Note the occasional expressions of (uncharacteristic!) tentativeness in Calvin's description of the four permanent ministerial offices: "I believe" (*puto, existemo*), "unless my judgment deceive me" (*Institutes*, 2:1057, 1061).

general assembly).[9] Each is presided over by a "moderator," whether pastor or "lay" elder elected by the members to serve as primus inter pares for a limited term. The higher judicatories have carefully circumscribed powers, less than hierarchical but more than the congregational system allows to its synods. The presence of so-called lay elders with the ministers at every level of ecclesiastical government is sometimes held to be a second fundamental principle of presbyterianism (along with the parity of presbyters).

The advocates of *episcopacy* point out that by the end of the second century a threefold order of bishops, presbyters, and deacons had become the regular pattern throughout the churches: by then, "bishop" and "presbyter" were not interchangeable. But whether a distinction between bishops and presbyters can be traced back to the New Testament is a matter of dispute. James, the brother of the Lord, exercised something like a presidential function without the title of bishop (Acts 15:13, 19), and the advice given to Timothy and Titus in the Pastoral Letters presupposes that they had a special administrative authority to implement it (see, e.g., Titus 1:5). Some argue that the Pastorals imply a distinction between presbyters and bishops by using "presbyters" in the plural and "the bishop" always in the singular. In any case, it is said, the advocates of congregationalism and presbyterianism are guilty of reconstructing the Apostolic age without the Apostles: the bishops are the Apostles' successors. But not all defenders of monarchical episcopacy consider it necessary to find explicit evidence for it in the New Testament. In his classic essay "The Christian Ministry," J. B. Lightfoot (1828–89), himself a bishop in the Church of England, concluded that "the episcopate was formed not out of the apostolic order by localization but out of the presbyteral by elevation; and the title, which originally was common to all, came at length to be appropriated to the chief among them" (1983: 46; cf. 75). In this view, the postcanonical emergence of an episcopal presidency within each Christian community and in a wider group of Christian communities (diocesan episcopacy) resulted from the need to maintain the unity of the catholic church and to guarantee continuity with the Apostolic tradition against the gnostic heretics. Irenaeus initiated the practice of seeking to verify the Apostolic succession, so understood, by compiling consecutive lists of bishops in some of the principal churches.

The episcopal form of church government has been preserved in Eastern Orthodoxy and Roman Catholicism, but at the time of the Reformation it became controversial. Some of the Protestant churches abandoned it, and even in the churches that retained it different views were held of its status and importance. In some regions the resistance of Catholic bishops to the cause of reform led to the appointment of evangelical bishops, sometimes—when certain of the old bishops were won for the Reformation—without breaking the chain of episcopal consecrations. During the bitter controversies between conformists and nonconformists in sixteenth- and seventeenth-century England, the rival polities of episcopacy and presbyterianism were each defended as the exclusive divine institution (*de jure divino*). But Anglicans subsequently divided over

9. In *The Form of Presbyterial Church-Government* (1645), one of the charter documents of Presbyterianism, the Westminster divines wrote: "Synodical assemblies may lawfully be of several sorts, as provincial, national, *and oecumenical*" (emphasis mine). But an ecumenical council remained only a dream.

the question whether episcopacy belongs to the essence (*esse*) of the church, to its well being (*bene esse*), or to its fullness (*plene esse*). Their adversaries could hardly appeal to Calvin for support. While he called for the establishment in Geneva of the order instituted by Christ, Calvin found tolerable the postcanonical development in the organization of the ancient church (*Institutes*, 2:1068–84), and his letters to Archbishop Cranmer (April 1522) and the king of Poland (December 1554) show that he raised no objection to the retention of episcopacy in Protestant England and elsewhere (*SWC* 5:345–48; 6:99–109). He recognized that a hierarchical ordering of bishops, priests, and deacons need not lead to the presumptuous arrogation of power that he perceived in the medieval papacy (*Institutes*, 2:1121–24, 1217–25, etc.).[10] Wholly abhorrent to him, however, was the notion of a sacerdotal priesthood ordained to offer sacrifices to propitiate God (1089, 1193).

Lightfoot, too, was critical of the postcanonical rise of a sacerdotal understanding of ordained ministry. He believed that an exclusive sacerdotalism (in contrast to the common priesthood of all believers) contradicts "the general tenor of the Gospel," and he was uneasy with the related, postcanonical meanings assigned to the words *clergy* and *priesthood*. He concluded that there is no place for a priestly ministry in the New Testament, and "it might have been better if the later Christian vocabulary had conformed to the silence of the apostolic writers." The word *priest* is justifiable only if used in the broader sense of one who represents God to humans and humans to God (1983: 93, 111–14).

2. The Primacy of Rome

In response to Protestant censure, the Roman Catholic Church reaffirmed the sacrificial priesthood and the hierarchy of bishops, priests, and deacons and rejected the claim of evangelical bishops to stand in the Apostolic succession.[11] In the Catholic judgment, the defect in every form of Protestant church order is not simply abandonment of the *sacerdotium* but severance of communion with the Church of Rome, whose pope, as the successor of Peter, is held to be the universal bishop of the entire church. The claim to papal primacy rests heavily on the words attributed to Jesus in Matthew 16:18, "You are Peter, and on this rock [*petra*] I will build my church." The interpretation of this saying has been the subject of continuing argument. There is good reason to doubt that it can be an authentic saying of Jesus: it is without parallel anywhere else in the Gospels, and the notion of building the *ekklēsia* is not easily harmonized with the eschatological kingdom Jesus proclaimed, as the Synoptic Gospels unanimously attest.[12] Whether authentic or not, what does it say? It does not tell us

10. He writes: "[W]e know that church organization admits, nay requires, according to the varying condition of the times, various changes" (*Institutes*, 2:1134; cf. 1109, 1205, 1208). I think it unlikely that he would ever have agreed to recent ecumenical proposals for introduction of monarchical episcopacy into churches that had established a biblical polity without it, but I am not persuaded by the suggestion that he tolerated Protestant episcopacy only as a temporary concession, pending further reform (Ainslie 1940: 93).

11. See the Council of Trent, sess. 23, on the sacrament of order; DS 292–95. Leo XIII later summed up the Catholic view of Anglican ordinations: they were, and are, "invalid and entirely void" (*Apostolicae curae* [1896]; DS 496–97).

12. Oscar Cullmann argued, against Bultmann, that the unparalleled attribution to Jesus of the word *ekklēsia* in Matt. 16:18 and 18:17 does not conclusively disprove the genuineness of the saying (1962:

that Peter became the first bishop of Rome (many historians have doubted that he was ever in Rome at all), and it says nothing about future bishops of Rome being Peter's successors. The play on the word *Peter* is in any case not about his person in abstraction from his confession to Jesus, "You are the Messiah, the Son of the living God" (v. 16).[13] The image of the *man* Peter in the New Testament is complex. He is not always the rock: even his confession of Jesus as the Messiah falls short, and he earns the rebuke, "You are a stumbling block [*skandalon*] to me" (v. 23). Later, he denies Jesus (26:69–75). Still, it may be possible, as some have argued, to discern in the various New Testament images of Peter a "Petrine trajectory" and to view the postcanonical traditions about him as further protraction of it (see Brown et al. 1973: 167).

The prominence of Simon Peter in the New Testament is not in question; his name, appropriately, is first in the list of Jesus' Apostles (Mark 3:16). But others, too, have prominent roles in the Gospels and Acts, and we need to ask *what kind* of prominence Peter has in relation to them. In the Gospels there is an inner circle of three among the twelve Apostles: Peter (always named first), James, and John are with Jesus when he raises Jairus's daughter, when he is transfigured, and when he prays in the Garden of Gethsemane (Mark 5:37; 9:2; 14:33). The Gospels may be said to attest the preeminence of Peter even among the select group. But there is no suggestion that he officially outranks them. He is simply charged to strengthen his brothers and to feed the Lord's sheep (Luke 22:32; John 21:15–17).[14] The keys of the kingdom are indeed given to Peter, so that whatever he binds on earth will be bound in heaven, and whatever he looses on earth will be loosed in heaven (Matt. 16:19). But the same power is given to all the disciples (Matt. 18:1, 18; cf. John 20:23).[15]

According to Acts, Peter comes forward as leader and spokesman of the Twelve after Jesus' ascension (Acts 1:15; 2:14, 37; 3:12; 4:8; 5:3; etc.), sometimes in association with others (e.g., John in chaps. 3–8). But Paul openly rebukes Peter for his hypocrisy in avoiding table fellowship with the Gentiles in Antioch. Apparently, Peter is intimidated by a deputation from James, the Lord's brother, who assumes the leadership in the Jerusalem church (Gal. 2:11–14; Acts 15:6–21; 21:17–18).[16] Cullmann's conclusion is that Peter was indeed the rock on which Jesus built his church: in fulfillment of the Lord's promise, he led the original church in Jerusalem. But only for a time! Another, James, took over the leadership (Cullmann 1962: 229–31). In any case, the architectural metaphor in the New Testament is sometimes applied more *inclusively* to others

172, 197–98). Perhaps not, but the idea of "building the *ekklēsia* on Peter" does sound utterly alien to the proclamation of Jesus.

13. Against the view of the Protestant Reformers that the rock is Peter's *faith*, Cullmann insists that Jesus "really means the *person* of Simon" (1962: 213; emphasis mine). But this seems to me an unhelpful contrast, as my formula "not his person *in abstraction from* his confession" tries to convey.

14. From the two letters attributed to Peter in the NT it has been inferred that he was also chosen to teach. But many scholars, probably most, consider the first letter to be pseudonymous (it is not the work of an untutored fisherman; see Acts 4:13), and very few attribute the second letter to him.

15. "The keys of the kingdom" is a symbol for the power of binding and loosing as a matter either of discipline (Matt. 18:15–18) or of absolution (John 20:19–23). Calvin speaks for the Reformation view of the keys when he says: "[W]e must always beware lest we dream up some power separate from the preaching of the gospel." The right of binding or loosing is "bound to the Word" (*Institutes* 3.14.14 [1:639]).

16. Gal. 1:18–19 seems to indicate that at one time Paul recognized the priority of Peter over James. Later, he mentions James first, then Peter (Cephas), and then John (Gal. 2:9).

besides Peter: the "acknowledged pillars," James, Peter, and John (Gal. 2:9), or the "twelve foundations" of all the Apostles (Rev. 21:14). And sometimes it is applied *exclusively* to Jesus Christ as the sole foundation (1 Cor. 3:10). Combining both perspectives, the Letter to the Ephesians says that the household of God is "built upon the foundation of the apostles and prophets, with Christ Jesus himself as the cornerstone" (Eph. 2:20; cf. Matt. 21:42; Acts 4:11; 1 Pet. 2:6). To rest the papal primacy on the supposedly unique status accorded to Peter in the New Testament is a fragile argument, hard to sustain by strict exegesis; it seems to read back into Scripture the later traditions that it is intended to authenticate. Still, the notion of a Petrine *trajectory* is a possible alternative to the purely exegetical argument for a Petrine *office.*

The claim to the primacy of the papal see has had a long history, which we must leave to the church historians. Our interest is in the primacy as a distinctive type of church polity and its place in present-day ecumenical theology. The Second Vatican Council, even while giving fresh recognition to the "college" of bishops, stated that the bishops have no authority apart from the head, the Roman pontiff, who—as Peter's successor and the Vicar of Christ—has "primacy over all, pastors as well as the general faithful." The episcopal order has full power over the universal church by reason of consecration and office, but the power can be exercised only with the consent of the Roman pontiff (*DV* 43, 49–50; cf. 38, 40, 98–101, 344). Christian communions divided from the Apostolic See of Rome are either "separated churches" or "ecclesial communities" (361–66). In Vatican II the point was made delicately—and without naming the ecclesial communities—in the interests of ecumenical dialogue and cooperation. But it was reiterated more forthrightly in the declaration *Dominus Jesus* (2000), signed by Joseph Ratzinger (then the prefect of the Congregation for the Doctrine of the Faith) and ratified by Pope John Paul II. The declaration states that the salvific *action* of Jesus Christ "extends beyond the visible boundaries of the Church to all humanity" (art. 12); but it rejects the misunderstanding that his *church* "could subsist also in non–Catholic Churches and ecclesial communities" (art. 16, n. 56).[17] "Separated churches" are those that have the Apostolic succession and a valid Eucharist but lack full communion with the Catholic Church because they do not accept the primacy of Rome. "Ecclesial communities" (not identified) are Christian bodies that have neither the valid episcopate nor the genuine Eucharist and therefore are not churches at all "in the proper sense" (art. 17).

The publication of *Dominus Jesus* stirred up a storm of controversy, although it purported to be no more than an explication of Vatican II. Spokespersons for the "ecclesial communities" were dismayed. They saw the declaration as a setback to ecumenical relations, and some of them warned that their "communities" would take no part in future dialogue unless they were recognized as delegates from sister churches. This, I think, was a mistake. The resentment was understandable, but beliefs that the Catholic Church may require of the

17. This is said in reply to readers who found significant a change in the wording of Vatican II: whereas earlier drafts of *Lumen gentium*, art. 8 (*DV* 23), asserted that the church of Christ *is* the Catholic Church, the final version said that the church of Christ *subsists in* the Catholic Church—and so, it was inferred, could also subsist elsewhere (see, e.g., Dulles 1978: 126, 139). Rejection of this "misunderstanding" presupposes the Catholic conception of the church as a visible society.

Catholic faithful can only have, in the context of ecumenical conversations, the status of claims to be tested. If a Protestant participant is willing to hear the Catholic claim that her faith community is not a proper church, the Catholic will be willing to hear that in the view of many Protestants, myself included, the story of Peter and his successors is best understood as the founding myth of the Church of Rome.

But it would be another mistake to let ecumenical dialogue become obsessed with the details of ecclesiastical polity—if the price paid were to be neglect of the mission of the church. The wisdom of Vatican II was its emphasis on cooperation between the churches in a shared task rather than negotiation of the intractable differences that divide them. I would not wish old-style ecumenical discussion to be abandoned but rather to be viewed in perspective. A better model is the growth of interfaith faculties of divinity in which Catholic and Protestant theologians bring their respective resources to bear on a common agenda, determined by the gospel and the needs of the day. This surely agrees well with the original program of Protestantism, which began not as a revolt against the papacy but as *witness for* the gospel (Latin *pro-testari*). Melanchthon wrote, when signing Luther's Smalcald Articles (1537): "I, Philip Melanchthon, regard the above articles as right and Christian. However, concerning the pope I hold that if he would allow the Gospel, we, too, may concede to him that superiority over the bishops which he possesses by human right, making this concession for the sake of peace and general unity among the Christians who are now under him and who may be in the future" (*BC* 316–17). The Catholic Reformation (or "Counter-Reformation") of the sixteenth century and the ecumenical movement of the twentieth century have brought Protestants and Catholics closer together on the nature of the gospel. The institutional division that remains should not be allowed to inhibit *the apostolic ministry of witness and healing . . . committed to the whole church as a servant people of God and the body of Christ "sent out" into the world.*

III. Church Order and the Headship of Christ

The existence of a multitude of Christian denominations may seem of minor importance, or no importance at all, at the local level in countries like the United States, where priests and pastors mingle in ministerial associations and churchgoers move freely from one congregation to another with hardly a thought about denominational affiliation. But the divisions have always seemed scandalous to the theological and administrative leadership of the churches, and in some contexts they have proved to be an obstacle to the church's mission. Competition rather than cooperation is a prodigal misuse of limited resources, and it appears to contradict the message of peace and reconciliation.

The watchword "Faith and Order," which in 1948 became the title of a World Council of Churches commission, may seem to make belief and polity two separate issues. The preoccupation with polity in churches of British origin was sometimes defended on the grounds that there was no fundamental disagreement on beliefs. But polity itself becomes an item of belief when one form of order is thought to be the special, or even the exclusive, channel of divine grace.

The famous bull *Unam sanctam* (1302) of Pope Boniface VIII, for example, made belief in the primacy of Rome a condition of salvation. An extreme case perhaps, but the bitter invective once exchanged between Protestant and Catholic, and between Presbyterian and Episcopalian, sometimes left them all in peril of the unforgivable sin, which is attributing the work of the Spirit to Satan (Mark 3:22–30). Ecumenical conversation flourishes only when the faithful work and witness of other communions are thankfully acknowledged, and that does relativize the differences in polity. It does not follow, however, that polity is entirely a matter of indifference. The claims of every church order can be, and should be, tested. But by what criteria? For dogmatic theology, the same norms are valid by which everything else is tested.

1. The Types of Ecclesiastical Polity Tested

The first dogmatic norm is formulated to allow for the *development* of church doctrine beyond what is explicitly taught in Scripture. But it also insists that Scripture has a unique place in a church's tradition: it is always possible to judge that a tradition professing to interpret and develop the Apostolic witness in fact falsifies it (cf. Mark 7:13). The second norm allows for *adaptation* to prevailing conditions that have their origin outside the church's immediate orbit: more particularly, adaptation to present-day thought and experience insofar as they call for reinterpretation of the tradition. Application of the two norms to ecclesiastical polity is bound to leave room for disagreement, since Scripture is not a uniform blueprint for the constitution of the church and the prevailing conditions change. But we may draw a few conclusions from my sketch of the two strands in New Testament ecclesiology and from my critical review of the three main historical types of polity (together with the Catholic modification of the third type).

Congregationalism does well when tested by Scripture—that is, by the charismatic or community strand of New Testament ecclesiology—and it is by no means the ideal of just one denomination. On the contrary, every system of ecclesiastical government will somehow make room for a polity that reflects the lively Christian community in Corinth, a communion of saints who were also sinners. Time and again reformers have recognized the need for recapturing the New Testament vision of the church as a visible fellowship of the redeemed, not to renounce the institutional church but to enliven it. In Protestantism, Pietism was the most notable of such reform movements, but the vision was already there in Luther's thoughts on the mutual priesthood of all the baptized and Robert Bowne's gathered company of believers. It appeared again in Schleiermacher's ideal of religious association as the sharing of religious affections and in Brunner's *ekklēsia* as a spiritual brotherhood that is not, as such, an institution. But the congregational ideal has its place also in Orthodoxy, Catholicism, and Anglicanism. Douglas Horton thinks we might consider monasticism "a wry expression of the latent hunger for Congregationalism" (1952: 9). We may say much the same thing (without the "wry") concerning the myriad groups, associations, unions, societies, clubs, and fellowships that spring up in every denomination. Insofar as they nurture Christian witness to Christ, they are images of the New Testament *ekklēsia*.

The fundamental principle of congregational polity is the autonomy of the individual congregation under the immediate headship of Christ, though links with other congregations are certainly fostered. *Presbyterianism*, which takes up the official or institutional strand in New Testament ecclesiology, advocates a more formal bond between congregations, and its ecclesiological center is the presbytery. In actual practice, the difference may appear to be slight: delegation of responsibilities happens among Congregationalists, and Presbyterians can, and sometimes do, emulate the lively congregational meetings of the Congregationalists. The two traditions share a Calvinist heritage that many historians think influenced the development of democratic ideals and institutions in the United States. At the very least, the affinity between Calvinist polity and democratic order satisfies the adaptation prescribed by our second dogmatic criterion. Congregationalism has been described as participatory democracy, Presbyterianism as representative democracy.

Calvin did not oppose *episcopacy* as such—government of the church by diocesan bishops—although he thought it to be a postcanonical development. And in fact presbyterian polity has sometimes made room for officials who in some measure resemble bishops. Before the organization of the presbyteries, the reformed Church of Scotland, for example, provided for regional "superintendents" (1560), and in our time a presbytery may have a "general" or "executive" presbyter. The reasons are mostly pragmatic. (One distinguished scholar, when chosen to be moderator of the Presbyterian Church of England, thanked the fathers and brethren for the honor but remarked memorably that what presbyterianism really needs is not a moderator but an accelerator.) However, the defense of episcopacy is not usually pragmatic. Presbyterians (and I must own up to being one of them) oppose the idea that bishops stand at a hierarchical rank above presbyters; and they hold that to defend the tactual succession of bishops as the guarantee of possessing the Apostolic faith inverts the proper order, in which fidelity to the Apostolic gospel is the test of an authentic bishop. Every presbyter is successor of the Apostles insofar as he or she proclaims the gospel of the grace and glory of God.

Ecumenical discussions have weighed the proposal that nonepiscopal churches might take the historic episcopate into their system of church government by a mutual laying on of hands, in which each party would be free to interpret the act according to its own principles. But the Presbyterians were unwilling to accept the inevitable, if unspoken, assumption that this would make up for a defect in the ministry of the nonepiscopal churches. The ingenious compromise of the Church of South India (formed in 1947) seems not to have established itself as the dominant model. It was made possible by mutual recognition of the ministers of all the uniting traditions (Anglican, Congregational-Presbyterian, and Methodist) and agreement that all *future* ordinations would be by episcopal laying on of hands. The church is governed by a biennial synod, which includes lay as well as clerical delegates and is presided over by one of the bishops elected as moderator. In this way two traditions were happily married.

The difficulties in fraternal relations between episcopal and nonepiscopal churches are compounded when the primacy of the bishop of Rome is brought into the discussion. Catholic historians and theologians are well aware that modern historical-critical approaches to Scripture and tradition raise questions about the Petrine primacy, and they recognize that a monarchical, authoritarian institution is out of step with the democratic aspirations of the modern world. Adaptation is called for. Walter Kasper speaks for the Catholic viewpoint when he says: "The Catholic Church can and will not give up the dogmas of the First Vatican Council. It regards the Petrine ministry as having been founded by Jesus Christ and as the Lord's gift to his church." But Kasper insists that no "explicit, historically obtainable saying of Jesus" is needed. The way forward is through a rereading of Vatican I in the wider context of Catholic history and teaching. "The *communio* ecclesiology of the first millennium, brought out and recognized anew by Vatican II, therefore sets the hermeneutical framework for Vatican I." The way is then clear for fellowship among the churches in the third millennium (in Puglisi 2010: 216–19, 222 n. 33).

Lutherans have been particularly willing to discuss with Catholics the possibility of defining the Petrine ministry (note the word *ministry*!) in a manner acceptable to Catholics and non-Catholics alike. The discussion continues. I cannot pursue it further here but may refer to the reports and arguments in the volumes edited by Paul Empie and T. Austin Murphy (1974) and James Puglisi (2010), as well as the long encyclical of John Paul II *Ut unum sint* (1995) that has spurred the discussion. I hope I have said enough in this chapter to justify my assertion in thesis 17 that *Christ's headship over the church . . . has assumed various forms of church order, none of which exists by exclusive divine right.* I must add a final word about the headship of Christ.

2. *Ecclesiastical Authority and the Headship of Christ*

No Christian, of whatever theological or confessional persuasion, is likely to deny that the church is *the organ of Christ's continuing activity as prophet and priest* (thesis 15). But it is easy to forget it in the endless arguments about the preferred shape of ecclesiastical polity. If we grant the Reformers' description of Christian faith as focusing one's attention on Christ (*intuitus Christi*),[18] we will have to admit that the discussion of polity often gets out of focus. It surely misses the mark to speak of anyone but Christ as "head" of the church or to speak of the "vicar" of Christ as though Christ were absent.[19] In a controverted section of *The Christian Faith* (§24), Schleiermacher suggests that the actual difference between Protestantism and Catholicism might provisionally be conceived like this: whereas Protestantism makes the individual's relation to the church dependent on his relation to Christ, Catholicism makes the individual's relation to Christ dependent on his relation to the church (*CF* 103). Easily misunderstood, the formula is not an affirmation of so-called Protestant individualism, which was totally foreign to Schleiermacher's thinking; he says here, as so often elsewhere, that Christian piety arises only in community. He means rather, as he goes on to say, that two different views of the church lie behind

18. As Calvin puts it in his commentary on Acts 20:21, Scripture makes Christ the mark at which our faith must aim; faith should be completely fixed in looking to Christ (*fidem debere in Christi intuitu prorsus esse defixam*).

19. According to Vatican I, *Peter* lives, presides, and exercises judgment in the church—that is, in the bishops of the Holy See of Rome, founded by him and consecrated by his blood (DS 453).

the antithesis of Protestant and Catholic: whereas in the one view the church is the instrument of Christ's efficacy, in the other Christ's efficacy is transferred to the church (106–7). Similarly, Barth insisted that the Word of God in Scripture never becomes the possession of its interpreters, whether popes or professors, but addresses even the church's teaching office as authority and judge (see, e.g., *CD* I/1:256–67). In christological terms, Jesus Christ is the Word of God and "speaks for Himself whenever He is spoken of" (IV/1:227–28). Hence my thesis 17: *Christ's headship over the church (his kingly office) [is] exercised through the Word and not delegated to any group or individual.* The crown rights of the Redeemer, as the Congregationalists like to declare, are not transferable.

Naturally, this leaves us with the question of ecclesiastical authority, which, we might say, is precisely the question how a church's dogmas (its authorized doctrines) are related to the crown rights of the Redeemer. In the Catholic understanding, revealed truth is a "deposit" entrusted to the church; the gift of divine revelation would have been fruitless if God had not added the gift of an infallible teaching authority to preserve and propagate it. The decrees of bishops in an ecumenical council are said to be free from error; and, according to the First Vatican Council, when the pope speaks *ex cathedra*—with the intention to define a doctrine on faith or morals—he is endowed with an infallibility that makes his definitions irreformable by nature (*ex sese*) and not by reason of the consensus of the church (cf. DS 457).[20] In this way, the certainty and uniformity of belief are supposedly guaranteed—in contrast to the alleged confusion generated by the Protestant sects and their enshrinement of the right of private judgment.

Calvin, for one, was not greatly impressed with the right of private judgment. He held that in the event of doctrinal disagreement "the best and surest remedy is for a synod of true bishops to be convened." A definition on which the pastors agree, invoking the Spirit of Christ, will have much more weight than whatever any individual may think up at home (*Institutes*, 2:1176; cf. 1159–60). If the Spirit is not separated from the Word, we may even say that "the church cannot err in matters necessary to salvation" (1162; cf. 1:95–96). Of course, not every purported interpretation of Scripture is true and certain. Even a *council* may err. Yet the truth does not die in the *church* but will triumph in its time (2:1177). It follows that any particular definition proposed by a council has the status of a "provisional judgment" (*instar praeiudicii*, 1171).[21] Besides the test of fidelity to Christ or the Word, Calvin insisted on a properly historical reading of a council's decree: we are "diligently to ponder at what time it was held, on what issue, and with what intention, what sort of men were present." Even in the ancient and purer councils, learned and wise men missed a lot because

20. Catholic canon law makes the authority of the twenty-one ecumenical councils in effect dependent on papal control (canon 222; cf. *DV* 44). In actual fact, Byzantine emperors convoked the first four, in which the bishop of Rome was not present. The Eastern Orthodox recognize three additional councils, also convoked by imperial authority, and consider the remaining fourteen, which were called or confirmed by popes, to be merely Western synods.

21. Cf. Barth's statement that, for the Reformed, a confession of faith (the principal embodiment of Reformed dogmas) holds good "for the time being" (*bis auf weiteres*, 1962: 114–15). Barth maintained that if ecclesiastical dogmas are taken to be irreformable, they hinder the authority of the free Word of God. In his distinctive sense, dogma is "the agreement of Church proclamation with the revelation attested in Holy Scripture"; as such, it is what the church's dogmas (plural) *aim at* (*CD* I/1:265, 267). See also Schleiermacher, *CF* 690; Westminster Confession 31.

they were preoccupied with more serious matters; and sometimes lack of skill or too much passion deceived them (1171; cf. 1173). But Calvin's main concern was that a council must speak only in conscious and openly acknowledged subordination to Christ and the Word.

John T. McNeill argued in an important book, *Unitive Protestantism* (1964), that the Protestants inherited the reform program of the fourteenth- and fifteenth-century conciliarists, who asserted the superiority of ecumenical councils to the pope but (usually) without claiming infallibility for them. Luther appealed for a free general council, that is, a council not under papal control but representing the entire catholic church. And "the polity developed by Calvin and his associates is purely conciliar" (1964: 109). McNeill quotes from Calvin's reply to Sadoleto (1539): "For, although . . . fathers and councils are of authority only in so far as they accord with the rule of the Word, we still give to councils and fathers such honor and rank as it is meet for them to hold, under Christ" (110; *TT* 1:66; cf. *Institutes*, 2:1166).

The second part of my thesis is intended to draw together these reflections on the contrast between Catholic and Reformed perceptions of dogma. There is, of course, so much more to be said—on both sides. But for now my conclusion is that, whereas Catholics speak (quite rightly: Matt. 16:18!) of the indefectibility of the church, we might better speak of the indefectibility of the Word. The church cannot fail, not because it has the gift of infallibility but because it is a creation of the Word, which cannot fail: *the promise of Christ's presence through the Spirit does not guarantee the infallibility of any person, institution, or gathering of the church, but rather confirms Christian faith in the indefectibility of the Word* (cf. Isa. 55:10–11). The task of dogmatics is accordingly critical, as I have said: it is not merely propagation of dogmas but critical testing of them in the light of the dual criteria of fidelity to the Word and pertinence to the ever-changing situation of the church. This has been my approach in previous chapters, and it will guide our thoughts in the chapters that follow on baptism and the Lord's Supper.

18. Baptism: Sign of New Birth

Baptism, as "the washing of regeneration," represents the new birth in Christ that is offered and given by the Spirit in the word of reconciliation; and since the new birth is mediated through the Christian community, whose faith is a condition but not the guarantee of faith in the one baptized, baptism is also called "adoption into the family of faith" or "reception into the covenant people."

Reconciliation and renewal in Christ, proclaimed in the preached Word, are pictured in the Christian rites of baptism and the Eucharist. Ritual washings are not peculiar to Christianity; they are a common feature in the history of religions. In the Gospels, John the Baptist already practices a baptism of repentance to prepare for the coming of the kingdom and the one who will baptize with the Spirit, and Jesus presents himself for baptism by John. But Christian baptism, supposedly instituted by Jesus,[1] has its distinctive nature as baptism into Christ (Rom. 6:3; Gal. 3:27), or into the name of the Father, the Son, and the Holy Spirit (Matt. 28:19), or into the name of Jesus Christ or the Lord Jesus (Acts 2:38; 8:16; 10:48; 19:5). As the use of the preposition "into" (*eis*) implies—better than "in"—baptism is understood as a rite of initiation. On this defining characteristic there is general agreement. Yet the meaning, efficacy, and necessity of the initiatory rite have been matters of theological controversy, and the discord is reflected in the practical questions: Who are the proper recipients of baptism, adults only or also children and infants? Who may legitimately administer it? And what is the proper mode of administration, by sprinkling, pouring, or immersion? Other questions arise from the customary treatment of baptism and the Eucharist as instances of a generic class of "sacraments," visible signs of an invisible grace. For what does a visible sign effect? How is it related to what it signifies? Details must await treatment of the individual rites, but I may offer a preliminary statement on sacraments in general.

I. Sacraments in General

In most dogmatic works, both Roman Catholic and Protestant, a chapter on sacraments in general precedes chapters on baptism and the Eucharist. For the

1. See Mark 16:16 and Matt. 28:19. But the longer ending of Mark is a later addition to the Gospel, and the Great Commission in Matthew does not harmonize with the evidence of Acts that the primitive church in fact baptized in the name of Jesus Christ or the Lord Jesus, not in the Trinitarian name.

ancient Latin-speaking churches, the association of baptism with initiation into the Christian community made it natural to describe the baptismal ritual, as Tertullian did, by the word *sacramentum*, which in military parlance meant the oath of allegiance required for enlistment into the army. This was the meaning of *sacramentum* exploited by Zwingli at the time of the Protestant Reformation: a sacrament, for him, was a profession of loyalty that identified a person with the Christian community. Without ruling out a secondary function of a sacrament as a mark of identity and commitment, Calvin took the primary meaning from the use of *sacramentum* as the Latin translation of *mystērion* in the Greek New Testament (he cites Eph. 1:9; 3:2–3; Col. 1:26–27; 1 Tim. 3:16). The word *mystērion* invited comparison with the rituals of the Hellenistic mystery religions, but Calvin rejected the comparison (*Institutes*, 2:1295). It is clear, then, that sharply contrasting views of the rite are latent in the meanings ascribed to the word *sacrament*.

Just which rituals should be termed "sacraments" was subject to variation. Augustine's definition of a sacrament as "a visible sign of a sacred thing," or "a visible form of an invisible grace," allowed in principle for a generous number of possibilities. But in the Middle Ages a distinction was drawn between sacraments in the strict sense and "sacramentals," sacred signs (such as making the sign of the cross or wearing vestments) that may accompany a sacrament but do not, by themselves, mediate the redeeming action of Christ. In the twelfth century, Peter Lombard set the rule of limiting the number of sacraments to seven: besides baptism and the Eucharist, he included confirmation, penance, ordination, marriage, and extreme unction.

Calvin followed medieval precedent by devoting a chapter of his *Institutes* to sacraments in general (book 4, chap. 14) before he turned to baptism; and after his treatment of baptism and the Lord's Supper he added a chapter rejecting the "five other ceremonies falsely called sacraments" (chap. 19). Naturally, the definition of a sacrament determines their number. Calvin's definition was twofold. He followed Luther in defining a sacrament as a sign by which the Lord, to strengthen and increase our faith, "seals" the promise of his goodwill,[2] and he amicably added Zwingli's definition of sacraments as "marks of profession" by which we swear allegiance to the Lord in the presence of fellow believers. The Lutheran part of the definition left some uncertainty about the Protestant reduction of the sacraments to two. Luther began his *Babylonian Captivity* (1520) with three sacraments, including penance along with baptism and the Sacrament of the Bread; but by the time he ended the treatise, he had decided to drop penance. Calvin, like Melanchthon, was tempted to include ordination as a third sacrament. However, because ordination is not given to everyone in the church, he too decided to admit only baptism and the Lord's Supper as "ordinary sacraments," while granting that the term "sacrament" could be taken more broadly to include "all those signs which God has ever

2. The analogy of a seal that validates a document was suggested by Rom. 4:11, where the seal is the sign of circumcision. There may also be indirect allusions to the seal of baptism in 2 Cor. 1:22 and Eph. 4:30. For Luther's use of the seal analogy in his *Babylonian Captivity*, see LW 36:47, 66. Note that, in effect, Luther requires three things for a genuine sacrament, since the promise and the seal must be traceable to an explicit dominical institution (92, 107, 118, 121). Usually, Luther specifies the promise as the promise of forgiveness.

enjoined upon men to render them more certain and confident of the truth of his promises" (*Institutes*, 2:1294).

Calvin's chapter on the sacraments in general included principles that were fundamental to his teaching on baptism and the Lord's Supper: in particular, that the visible signs strengthen the faith of sense-bound humans by picturing what is promised by the Word; that their efficacy, as "visible words," is no different in kind from the efficacy of the spoken Word; that they achieve their purpose only as the means by which the Holy Spirit acts; that Christ is their matter or substance, since they do not promise anything apart from him; and that God truly performs what he promises and represents in the signs. In sum, "let it be regarded as a settled principle that the sacraments have the same office as the Word of God: to offer and set forth Christ to us, and in him the treasures of heavenly grace" (*Institutes*, 2:1292). The chapter ends with a detailed argument for the fundamental identity of the Old Testament "sacraments," especially circumcision, with those of the New (§§20–26), so that what is presented to Christians in sacraments today the Hebrews received in their day: Christ with his spiritual riches. I will take up Calvin's sacramental principles in my individual treatment of baptism and the Lord's Supper.

The objection to prefacing the doctrines of baptism and the Lord's Supper with a chapter on sacraments in general is that it risks imposing on them ideas that have no basis in the New Testament, which has no explicit doctrine of sacraments. It is true enough that the Latin *sacramentum* is used to translate the Greek *mystērion,* but the New Testament does not call baptism and the Lord's Supper "mysteries,"[3] and sacramental theology in the Western church has read more into the word "mystery" than the biblical usage warrants. The fountainhead of Western sacramental theology was Augustine's theory of signs; medieval and Reformation debates about the sacraments invariably reach back to his reflections on the relation of a sign to what it signifies. Schleiermacher, however, dispensed with the traditional chapter on sacraments in general; it became, for him, a postscript on the *name* "sacraments," appended to his doctrines of baptism and the Lord's Supper. He urges caution, pending the time when the word "sacrament" will (so he thinks) be given up. But although he questions the inclusion of baptism and the Lord's Supper under the generic term "sacrament," he does find that the two rites have something in common: by means of them Christ continues his priestly activity.

II. Baptism in the New Testament

All the diverse accounts of baptism in the history of the Western church appeal to the authority of Scripture. In the New Testament, baptism is associated with a number of key ideas: admission to the Christian community; dying and rising with Christ; faith, repentance, and forgiveness; rebirth or newness of life; and

3. The union of a man and his wife is called a *mystērion* in Eph. 5:32 as an analogy for Christ's relation to the church, and Catholics sometimes cite this as the ground for classing marriage as a sacrament. In 1 Tim. 3:16 the incarnation is "the *mystērion* of our religion," and this has been interpreted to mean that Christ himself is the principal Christian sacrament. I retain the traditional term "sacrament," and by "the two evangelical sacraments" I mean baptism and the Lord's Supper as signs of the gospel.

the gift of the Holy Spirit. The basic meaning of the Greek words *baptō* or *baptizō* is "dip." It is sometimes used figuratively. Jesus asks his disciples whether they can be baptized with the baptism he is baptized with (Mark 10:38–39; cf. Luke 12:50). Paul speaks of the Israelites as "baptized into Moses in the cloud and in the sea" (1 Cor. 10:2). In John the Baptist's testimony to the one who was to come there is an explicit contrast between his literal "baptizing with water" and the coming one's "baptizing with the Holy Spirit" (Mark 1:8). Baptism with the Spirit does not imply dipping, not even when the preposition *en* is added (Matt. 3:11; Luke 3:16; John 1:33); it suggests pouring. In Matthew's and Luke's versions of John's testimony, the one who is to come will baptize with the Holy Spirit and fire, and in Acts baptism with the Spirit is identified with Pentecost (Acts 1:5). The bestowal of the Spirit on the day of Pentecost is likened to tongues of fire settling on each of the disciples in fulfillment of the prophecy of Joel: "In the last days it will be, God declares, that I will pour out my Spirit upon all flesh" (Acts 1:5; 2:3–4, 16–18, 33).

When used for the actual rite of Christian baptism, there are two different understandings of the water symbolism: it suggests either washing or immersion. Ananias bids Paul, "Get up, be baptized, and have your sins washed away" (Acts 22:16), and most commentators assume that in the Letter to Titus "the washing of regeneration" is an allusion to baptism (Titus 3:5 RSV; cf. John 3:5; 1 Cor. 6:11; Eph. 5:26). But in the authentic letters Paul takes baptism as a figure for dying with Christ, which implies immersion: "Therefore we have been buried with him by baptism into death, so that, just as Christ was raised from the dead by the glory of the Father, so we too might walk in newness of life" (Rom. 6:4; cf. Col. 2:12). The baptism of the Ethiopian eunuch by Philip perhaps implies a similar mode of baptism, though without express mention of dying and rising with Christ: "both of them, Philip and the eunuch, went down into the water, and Philip baptized him" (Acts 8:38). But this could mean (as in some pictures of the baptismal rite) that both stood in the water and Philip baptized the eunuch by pouring water on him (affusion).

Paul states the fundamental meaning of the rite of baptism as the sign of initiation: it is incorporation by the one Spirit into the body of Christ (1 Cor. 12:13; cf. Acts 2:41). The association with repentance, forgiveness, and receiving the Holy Spirit is clear from the narrative of Pentecost. To the crowd who hear his sermon and ask what they must do, Peter replies: "Repent, and be baptized every one of you in the name of Jesus Christ so that your sins may be forgiven; and you will receive the gift of the Holy Spirit" (Acts 2:38). The relationship of baptism to reception of the Spirit varies. Converts in Samaria accepted the Word and were baptized, but only later were Peter and John sent to confer the Spirit on them by the laying on of hands (8:14–17). The disciples in Ephesus, who had been baptized with John's baptism but had never even heard of the Holy Spirit, were baptized in the name of the Lord Jesus; the Holy Spirit came upon them when Paul laid his hands on them, "and they spoke in tongues and prophesied" (19:1–7). On the other hand, Peter ordered the baptism of the centurion Cornelius, with his assembled family and friends, in recognition that the Holy Spirit had already fallen on them and had imparted the gift of tongues as Peter preached the Word (10:44–48). In these passages baptism with the Spirit is a distinct event: the laying on of hands may confer it, and it may precede or follow water baptism. The story of Cornelius raises a number of questions, two in particular. Were children present and included in the baptizing of the assembled company? And since the Spirit had already fallen on those who heard the Word (v. 44), before they were baptized, what does that say about the relationship between baptism and the Word?

The earliest reference to *the baptism of minors* is in Tertullian's treatise *On Baptism* (ca. 200), and he mentions it only to urge postponement of the rite until they are growing up (ANF 3:678). No actual case of infant or child baptism is recorded in Scripture or anywhere else in Christian literature of the first two centuries. Whether the household baptisms reported in the New Testament may have included children and infants is disputed (see Acts 10:47; 16:15, 33; 18:8; 1 Cor. 1:16). Some argue that since baptism is associated with the call for faith (Acts 8:12; 16:31–33), the baptism of an infant would have been ruled out by the very meaning of the rite as a profession of faith. Others counter that the exclusion of infants and children would have been incompatible with the biblical understanding of the covenant people of God; a similar exclusion of infants would have precluded circumcision as the sign of the Abrahamic covenant. And while there is no direct evidence of infant baptism in the primitive Christian churches, Jewish proselyte baptism included the entire family and may have influenced the Christian rite. However, since Christian baptism in Acts is baptism of *converts*, neither side of the debate tells us what we chiefly want to know: whether the early church baptized children *born* into a Christian family. The origin of infant baptism as an essential rite of the church remains controversial. The pertinent evidence and the diverse interpretations of it are exhaustively reviewed in Everett Ferguson's massive (953-page) volume. Ferguson's own conclusion is that infant baptism arose from the occasional emergency baptism of a gravely sick child but only began to become the normal Christian practice in the late fourth century (2009: 378–79). Be that as it may, the dogmatic theologian is obliged to conclude that although the practical and theological questions cannot be wholly severed from the historical problems, she cannot wait for the historians to reach a consensus.

The relationship between *baptism and the Word* in the New Testament is complicated by the fact that what is attributed to the one is elsewhere attributed to the other, and the two sometimes appear to be in competition. Two passages appear to link regeneration with baptism. In John 3:5 Jesus says to Nicodemus: "Very truly, I tell you, no one can enter the kingdom of God without being born of water and Spirit." Titus 3:5 reads (in the RSV): "He [God our Savior] saved us . . . through the washing of regeneration [*dia loutrou palingenesias*] and renewal by the Holy Spirit." Yet 1 Peter attributes regeneration to the Word: "You have been born anew, not of perishable but of imperishable seed, through the living and enduring word of God" (1 Pet. 1:23). Further, Paul said he was glad that he baptized no one at Corinth, as far as he remembered, except Crispus and Gaius and the household of Stephanas: "For Christ did not send me to baptize but to proclaim the gospel" (1 Cor. 1:17).[4] The point of Paul's disavowal must of course be understood in context, but it is hard to disagree with Bultmann's

4. Cf. the testimony of the Fourth Gospel that it was not Jesus himself but his disciples who baptized (John 4:2).

inference that in 1 Corinthians 1:17 "baptism obviously plays a subordinate role to the word" (1951–55, 1:312). This is not to say that the New Testament writers themselves consciously opposed Word and sacrament. But some historians conclude that the biblical data do in fact confront us with a mingling of two types of religion, even in the selfsame author (Paul): a sacramental "mystery" religion and an "ethical" religion of the Word. In the one type, regeneration is a mysterious, impersonal operation of the Spirit; in the other, regeneration is a metaphor for a new pattern of life. The same antithesis meets us in the biblical accounts of the Lord's Supper and in postcanonical Christian theology— especially since the Age of the Reformation, when Word and sacrament threatened to fall apart in two different ways of being religious.[5]

II. Baptism in Theological Controversy

Major turning points in postcanonical theology of baptism were occasioned by Augustine's controversy with the Donatists and the controversy of the Protestant Reformers with both Rome and the Anabaptists. The divisions opened up in the sixteenth century continue to this day. But they no longer follow strictly denominational lines. Misgivings about the baptism of infants are voiced within the Reformed churches; and there are Baptists who, while advocating believer baptism, recognize the legitimacy of baptizing infants. Ecumenical dialogue helps by seeking the common ground occupied by all the churches, not focusing obsessively on the differences that divide them.

1. Augustine and the Donatists

The Donatist churches of North Africa (named after their leader Donatus) grew up in the aftermath of the persecutions under Diocletian (303 CE), during which many Christian leaders obtained immunity by surrendering the Scriptures to the Roman authorities. They were branded as *traditores*, traitors who had "handed over" the sacred writings. Rigorists rejected the consecration of Caecilian to the see of Carthage on the ground that the presiding bishop had been a *traditor,* and they chose their own candidate to be their bishop instead (312). They wanted a pure church and held that sacraments performed by impure clergy were ineffectual. For a long time, they flourished. But to the Roman Church they were schismatics. As such they were opposed by Optatus of Milevis, whose arguments Augustine developed (nearly a century after the first appearance of the schismatic church) in his polemic *On Baptism, Against the Donatists* (ca. 400).

Augustine could not doubt that the sacrament of baptism obtained salvation only in the Catholic Church. Neither, however, could he bring himself to suppose that baptism, duly administered in the name of the Trinity, was an empty

5. Two further NT passages whose interpretation is difficult should at least be mentioned. In 1 Cor. 15:29 Paul alludes to the practice of baptism for the dead, which seems to rest on belief in the absolute necessity of the rite—even for those who had died without it. In 1 Pet 3:21, where baptism is said to save as an *eperōtēma,* the meaning could be either "as an *appeal* to God for a good conscience" or (better, I think) "as a *pledge* to God from a good conscience." Either way, baptism *saves.*

rite even when practiced by schismatics. The solution lay in his distinction between the gift given by baptism and its effect or use. The inherent sanctity of what the sacrament conveys is not corrupted, however unclean its ministers may be: "the baptism of Christ cannot be rendered void by any perversity on the part of man, whether in administering or receiving it" (NPNF[1] 4:439–40, 479). Something sacred is conferred and cannot be lost or revoked. It is like the tattoo on the hand of a Roman soldier: it does not need to be repeated when an enlisted man returns to service (414, 423).[6] "But it is one thing not to have, another so to have as not to be of use" (458). "So, therefore, the baptism of the Church may exist outside, but the gift of the life of happiness is found alone within the Church" (447). For those who have received it among heretics and schismatics, baptism is of no use until or unless they return to the unity of the Catholic Church. The medieval formula *ex opere operato* encapsulates Augustine's stand against the Donatists: the sacraments are effective by being duly performed, not by reason of anything in the one who performs or receives them (not *ex opere operantis*). The Protestant Reformers agreed with the repudiation of Donatism, but they rejected *ex opere operato* as an impersonal and mechanical perversion of sacramental working.

2. *Reformation, Anabaptism, and Counter-Reformation*

Luther's first thoughts on baptism, in a treatise of 1519, were free of polemic. But the following year, in his *Babylonian Captivity,* he launched a radical critique of Roman Catholic teaching on the sacraments. He agreed that the efficacy of a sacrament is not hindered by the unworthiness of the priest who administers it. But his understanding of a sacrament as a sign added by the Lord to the promise of forgiveness left no room for the Catholic view that a sacrament confers grace simply by being performed—provided only that no obstacle is placed in the way. For Luther, everything turned around the word of promise, and a promise is effective only when it is understood and answered by faith. It would be a mistake to infer that in this way he subordinated the gift of God to a human work. Faith is "a work of God, not of man," created through God's word of promise, sometimes during the actual administration of the sacrament. "For unless faith is present or is conferred in baptism, baptism will profit us nothing" (LW 36:62, 59). The efficacy of baptism is precisely the creation or awakening of faith. Luther drew the plain inference that "a man can have and use the word . . . apart from the sign or sacrament" (44). It does not follow that the sign of baptism is superfluous: it remains throughout life as an unsinkable ship. Unbelief may cause one to jump overboard, but there is no need for Jerome's view of penance as "the second plank after shipwreck" (61).

Luther's cardinal emphasis on baptismal faith required him later to open a second polemical front: against the Anabaptists, who rejected infant baptism and administered the "ordinance" only to those who made a profession of faith. Baptism, for them, was "the first proof of obedience" on the part of one who

6. On the notion of a permanent "character" see further Augustine, *Letters* 173, 185 (FC 30:75, 164). The Greek word *charaktēr* originally denoted an instrument for engraving; by derivation it meant an engraved or impressed mark, such as the stamp on coins or seals. Augustine likens the *dominicus character* of baptism (and ordination) not only to a military tattoo, but also to the mark branded on a sheep.

had entered into covenant with Christ. Luther wrote the *Babylonian Captivity* before his encounter with the Anabaptists, but the seeds of conflict are already there. He took it for granted that baptism strictly means immersion, during which the infant is purely passive: "The minister's immersing the child in the water signifies death; his drawing it forth again signifies life" (LW 36:64, 67–68). Yet he made the effectiveness of a sacrament turn on the explicit faith of the recipient: "Therefore, let this irrefutable truth stand fast: Where there is a divine promise, there every one must stand on his own feet, his own personal faith is demanded" (49). What, then, of infants, who cannot even grasp the promise? Is faith, after all, not always necessary, or is infant baptism without effect? Luther fell back on the medieval view that infants are helped by the faith of those who present them for baptism (*fides aliena*), and "through the prayer of the believing church the infant . . . is changed, cleansed, and renewed by inpoured faith [*fides infusa*]" (73).

In his letter *Concerning Rebaptism* (1528), Luther turned directly to the Anabaptist refusal to baptize infants. The letter is virtually a compendium of the arguments commonly made in defense of infant baptism: the practice is very ancient, going back to Apostolic times; Christ commands us to let the little children come to him; circumcision, the sign of the old covenant, included children in the promise, and so must the sign of the new; admittedly there is no specific command in Scripture to baptize infants, but neither is there a specific command to baptize women; the household baptisms reported in Acts must have included children; and so on. As for the Anabaptist question, "How do you know you have been baptized?" Luther replies that a person is certain of his baptism through the witness of others. What you never really know is whether someone has faith. "So whoever bases baptism on the faith of the one to be baptized can never baptize anyone" (LW 40:239–40). Besides, how do the Anabaptists know that children cannot have faith? The unborn John the Baptist leaped in his mother's womb at the approach of the unborn child of the Virgin Mary (Luke 1:41)—evidence that infant faith (*fides infantilis*) is possible. Still, Luther's main point is that even if *not* received in faith when rightly administered, baptism is God's work and can nurture faith in due course. Once again, as in his argument with Rome, it is the absolute priority of the Word that determines Luther's stand: "When faith comes, baptism is complete. A second baptism is not necessary" (246).

Before Luther's letter on rebaptism, Zwingli wrote his treatise *Of Baptism* (1525) in the midst of controversy with the Swiss Brethren, the pioneer Anabaptists. He begins by telling us—regretfully, he says—that since the time of the Apostles all the doctors have been wrong about baptism: they have ascribed to water a power it does not have, for no external thing can make us pure or righteous. God alone can give the baptism of the Spirit; properly understood, baptism in water is "a covenant sign which indicates that all those who receive it are willing to amend their lives and to follow Christ" (LCC 24:141). Zwingli sees no intrinsic connection between inward and outward baptism: you can have either one without the other. External baptism is simply an "illustration" to provide instruction about internal baptism. Water baptism is indeed a pledge, but it is a pledge made not by God, to confirm our faith, but by the one being baptized, to declare his faith before the company of believers. "For baptism is given and received for the sake of fellow-believers, not for a supposed effect in those who receive it" (136). In short, "we see that baptism is an initiatory sign or pledge with which we bind ourselves to God, testifying the same to our neighbour" (148). All of which was very close to the thought—and language—of Zwingli's Anabaptist adversaries.[7] So how did he justify the practice of infant baptism? Zwingli did not have recourse to the traditional belief that infants need baptism to cleanse them of original sin. (The Anabaptists agreed with him about that.) He argued that baptism, as a covenant sign, signifies belonging to the people of God and does not exclude infants any more than circumcision did; and this became the cornerstone of the Reformed case for baptizing infants. But it is generally agreed that, in the final analysis, what he was fighting for was the idea of an inclusive state church, and he warned that the Anabaptist call for separation could only result in a "sect" (148).

Calvin, as I have noted, adds Zwingli's understanding of a sacrament to Luther's. Accordingly, his definition has two parts: a sacrament is "an outward sign [*symbolum*] by which the Lord seals on our consciences the promises of his good will toward us in order to sustain the weakness of our faith; and we in turn attest our piety toward him in the presence of the Lord and of his angels and before men" (*Institutes*, 2:1277; cf. 1296). However, God's confirmation of faith and our confession of faith are not of equal importance, and Calvin is sharply critical of those who make what is secondary "the first and even the only point" (1289; cf. 1304). But his willingness to include the Zwinglian idea of a sacrament naturally heightens the difficulty Luther had in making an evangelical case for infant baptism, to which Calvin devotes an entire chapter in the 1559 *Institutes* (book 4, chap. 16). His case is complex, perhaps confused, and I can only sketch what I take to be the main steps in his argument from chapter 14 to chapter 16. I think we can say that the argument turns around the three tenses in which he speaks of infant baptism: future, past, and present.

Calvin's debt to Luther is evident in his description of a sacrament as added to the divine promise like the seal that ratifies an official document. "[S]acraments are truly named the testimonies of God's grace and are like seals of the good will that he feels toward us, which by attesting that good will to us, sustain, nourish, confirm, and increase our faith" (*Institutes*, 2:1282; see also 1280). It is therefore mere superstition to imagine that the sacraments work *ex opere operato* by "some sort of secret powers" (1289, 1303) or that, in the absence of a minister, a layman or laywoman must administer emergency baptism to those in danger of dying unbaptized (1320–23). Sacraments simply picture the content of the promise, and they achieve nothing if not received by faith (1280, 1289–90, 1292, 1315). Yet repentance and faith may not come until years after baptism has been administered; then the power of baptism extends throughout life (1306–7, 1317). As an adjunct of the Word, baptism points to *the future*: "infants are baptized into future repentance and faith" (1343; cf. 1344).

7. This can be verified from the selections in Klaassen 1981: 162–89, e.g., the statement from Hubmaier (167). For Zwingli's development of the case against the Anabaptists, see his *Refutation of the Tricks of the Catabaptists* (1527); *SWZ* 123–258, summarized in his conclusion on pp. 235–37.

The main line of Calvin's reply to the Anabaptists echoes Zwingli's: baptism replaces circumcision as the sign of the covenant.[8] As such, it does not make infants into children of God but testifies that they already belong to God's covenant people. "[T]he children of believers are baptized not in order that they who were previously strangers to the church may then for the first time become children of God, but rather that, because by the blessing of the promise they already belonged to the body of Christ, they are received into the church with this solemn sign" (1323). As the sign of the covenant, baptism points to *the past*: it assures the parents of what the infant already has and is. "God declares that he adopts our babies as his own before they are born, when he promises that he will be our God and the God of our descendants after us" (1321). Hence baptism is "a solemn symbol of adoption" (1332; cf. 1360). Calvin concludes: "in infant baptism nothing more of present effectiveness must be required than to confirm and ratify the covenant made with them by the Lord. The remaining significance of this sacrament will afterward follow at such time as God himself foresees" (1345).

Difficulties arise chiefly when Calvin turns from the future and the past and tries, after all, to say something more about what happens to a baptized infant in *the present*. The symbolism of the rite pictures both cleansing from sin (or forgiveness) by the death of Christ and regeneration (or mortification) in union with him (1325–26). Calvin could perhaps have assigned regeneration to the past or the future of the one baptized. But the medieval view of baptism as the sacrament of regeneration (cf. Titus 3:5) seduces him into thinking further about what happens in the actual moment of administration, and he establishes (to his own satisfaction) what he calls "the dogma" of infant regeneration (1349). As the sign of regeneration, baptism points to the present. Calvin asks, "why may the Lord not shine with a tiny spark at the present time on those whom he will illumine in the future with the full splendor of his light?" (1342). So what *is* this "tiny spark" with which the Lord shines on infants? Calvin describes it in cognitive terms: it is a tiny spark of "the knowledge of faith." But quite what that might mean eludes him. "I would not rashly affirm that they are endowed with the same faith as we experience in ourselves, or have entirely the same knowledge of faith—this I prefer to leave undetermined" (1342). Would Calvin's case have been stronger if he had left out his entire discussion of infant regeneration? We will need to return to that possibility.

In the sacramental theology of the Protestant Reformers the Catholics could see nothing but the dissolution of sacramental objectivity. The Council of *Trent* follows its doctrine of justification with canons on the sacraments, since it is through the sacraments that "all true justice either begins, or being begun is increased, or being lost is restored." The sacraments were not instituted merely to nurture faith or to serve as tokens of Christian profession. They contain the grace they signify and confer it *ex opere operato* on those who place no obstacle

8. Calvin cites the texts regularly put forward in support of infant baptism: Acts 2:39 (RSV: "the promise is to you and to your children"), 1 Cor. 7:14 (the children of believing parents are "holy"), and Col. 2:11–12 (baptism is "the circumcision of Christ"). See his commentaries on these texts. Cf. his *Brief Instruction for Arming All the Good Faithful against the Errors of the Common Sect of the Anabaptists* (1544), in Calvin, *Treatises against the Anabaptists and against the Libertines*, ed. and trans. Benjamin Wirt Farley (Grand Rapids: Baker, 1982), 44–55.

in the way. Accordingly, "If anyone shall say that . . . faith alone in the divine promise suffices to obtain grace, let him be anathema" (DS 261–63). For the Tridentine fathers, the instrumental *cause* of justification is the sacrament of baptism; what they say about the Word (the "call" of God) belongs to the *preparation* for justification. Adults "are disposed to that justice when, aroused and assisted by divine grace, receiving faith 'by hearing' [Rom. 10:17], they are freely moved toward God, believing that to be true which has been divinely revealed and promised, and this especially, that the sinner is justified by God through his grace." The preparation for justification is then followed by justification itself (DS 250–51). The contrast with Luther, or with some of Luther's more exuberant utterances, is remarkable. In his 1519 *Lectures on Galatians*, for example, he says: "If you want to obtain grace, then see to it that you hear the Word of God attentively or meditate on it diligently. The Word, I say, and only the Word is the vehicle of God's grace" (LW 27:249).

It may seem that we have here two very different varieties of religion. Some of the mutual anathemas can be overcome, or at least minimized, by noting the different meanings given by Catholics and Protestants to the key terms we have previously looked at: "faith," "grace," and "justification." For now, I want only to underscore that Luther and Calvin, unlike Zwingli, never abandoned the sacramental principle that material things can serve as the instruments or vehicles of the Holy Spirit—a principle rightly held to be "an immediate corollary of the Incarnation wherein the 'Word became flesh'" (Palmer 1957: vi). Luther's most forceful statement on the sacramental principle was made in his treatise *Against the Heavenly Prophets* (1525), in which he insisted that God deals with us in a twofold manner: outwardly through the spoken word of the gospel and the material signs of baptism and the sacrament of the altar, inwardly through the Holy Spirit and faith. "God has determined to give the inward to no one except through the outward" (LW 40:146). If Luther is to be faulted for a momentary lapse in speaking of the Word *alone* (in the 1519 *Lectures on Galatians*), it is worth noting Calvin's antidote to the Council of Trent's description of baptism *alone* as the instrumental cause of justification: "What then will become of the gospel?" (*Acts of the Council of Trent with the Antidote* [1547], *TT* 3:116). Luther and Calvin included the proclamation of the gospel among the Spirit's instruments; the idea of instruments of grace did not trouble them as it did Zwingli. To Zwingli's disciple Bullinger, Calvin even wrote that the sacraments *do* "contain and confer grace," as the medieval schoolmen affirmed: they contain grace as the gospel contains Christ, and they confer grace by exercising faith (CO 12:484; cf. *Institutes*, 2:1284, 1293). Instead of rejecting Trent's reaffirmation of the old scholastic formula, as Bullinger wished, Calvin gave it an evangelical interpretation.

3. *Reappraisal in the Reformed Tradition*

Reformed teaching on baptism did not stand still after the Protestant Reformation and the age of Protestant orthodoxy. I can mention only the contributions of Schleiermacher and Barth, both of whom had doubts about infant baptism. *Schleiermacher* was sharply critical of the historical assumptions and exegetical fantasies in the inherited case for baptizing infants—a practice in which he saw the main reason why "some people attribute magical powers to baptism" (*CF* 636). He could view with equanimity the possible abolition of infant baptism—but not the condemnation of it as absolutely invalid. Parents should decide for themselves whether to present their children for baptism, and church fellowship with the Baptists should be possible on the basis of mutual recognition of the practices of the two communions (637–38). True, "baptism is received wrongly if it be received without faith," but Schleiermacher endorsed Calvin's view that in the case of infants baptism points to *future* repentance and faith: "personal confession of faith is the *goal* of infant baptism" (630, 635–36, my emphasis; cf. 490). Hence "it is only as combined with confirmation that infant baptism answers to Christ's institution" (637). If we ask what, then, baptism meant for Schleiermacher, his answer is clear: Although baptism of itself produces no inward result, as the sign of entrance into the church it attests the influence of the community as the means through which regeneration takes place (624). A defensible position, I think, but it might have been stronger if Schleiermacher had made more of his usual distinction between the outer and the inner circles of the church (635–36; cf. 525–26). We will need to come back to that possibility also.

Barth's lecture on baptism, published in 1947 as *The Teaching of the Church regarding Baptism,* met with dismay from many of his Reformed brethren. "From the standpoint of a doctrine of baptism," he said, "infant-baptism can hardly be preserved without exegetical and practical artifices and sophisms—the proof to the contrary has yet to be supplied!" (1948: 49) In Barth's opinion, the real motive for infant baptism came not from exegesis, but from allegiance to the idea of a state church. (He spoke from a European context.) He anticipated that the flaws in the church's baptismal practice would have to be endured for a long time but called for reinstatement of baptism as (from the standpoint of the baptized) "a responsible act" (54). Nevertheless, even for those who had no recollection of their baptism but only a certificate of baptism, the sign was an actual occurrence—"a representation that took place"—so that we can say, like Luther when he was confused about everything else, *Baptizatus sum,* "I have been baptized" (61–62). For Zwingli, on the other hand, Barth had no good word in the lecture; he judged Zwingli's teaching on baptism and the Lord's Supper "strangely flat and cold" (28).

Further reflection brought Barth closer to Zwingli. In the fragment on baptism in the *Church Dogmatics,* he rejected the sacramental understanding of baptism as a means of grace and distinguished sharply between baptism with the Spirit and baptism with water. Baptism with water is an act of free obedience in response to the work of the Holy Spirit: it is a true and genuine *human* action that responds to the *divine* action and word. The meaning of baptism, in a word, is "conversion," the determination to leave the old way and enter on the new (see *CD* IV/4:27, 101–2, 128, 138, etc.). And this, Barth admits, brings him close to Zwingli, even though Zwingli's theology of baptism remained "sterile," lacking a "true elucidation of what takes place" in baptism. "[W]e can raise little objection if it occurs to someone that the doctrine presented here should be labelled (either approvingly or critically) Neo-Zwinglian, even though its development does not in fact owe anything to Zwingli's influence" (129–30). And, of course, Zwingli cannot escape Barth's detailed critique of the case made by the Protestant Reformers for baptizing infants, who are incapable of a responsible act of obedience (165–94).

III. The Grace of Baptism

Baptism is practiced as the rite of initiation in nearly all Christian churches, and many a catechism or liturgy shows that baptismal *symbolism* is readily understood. In Calvin's Geneva Catechism, for example, the pastor asks what resemblance water has to the forgiveness of sins and spiritual regeneration; the pupil answers that forgiveness of sins is like washing away stains from the body, and a momentary immersion in water is a figure of dying and rising to new life. Insofar as the symbolism is interpreted in much the same way in all the churches, baptism is a bond of union between them, and this agrees with explicit Scripture references: there is only "one Lord, one faith, one baptism" (Eph. 4:5), and to those who have been baptized Paul writes, "There is no longer Jew or Greek, there is no longer slave or free, there is no longer male or female; for all of you are one in Christ Jesus" (Gal. 3:27–28; cf. 1 Cor. 12:13). Nevertheless, an eminent theologian of the last cenury felt bound to remark that the *doctrine* of baptism is "like a jungle" (Brunner). Our review of the history of the doctrine, selective though it had to be, sufficiently documents the remark.

There is no need to deny the legitimacy of multivalence in a religious ritual. However, a dogmatic statement on the meaning of Christian baptism must attempt to strike a path through the "jungle," taking account of diversity in the biblical data and conflict in the theological controversies of the Reformation era. Biblical figures and metaphors vary, sometimes clash—cleansing is not drowning, adoption is not rebirth—but they are mutually exclusive only when they are promoted too quickly into fixed concepts and dogmas. Harder to deal with are the dogmatic definitions that set church against church in the sixteenth century. They run all the way from Trent's reaffirmation of the medieval doctrine of baptismal regeneration to the Zwinglian and Anabaptist contention that baptism is not a means of grace. And it must be admitted that there *seem* to be not one but two baptisms, one for adults and another for infants.

Baptism is still a bone of contention at the present day. As one of the most frequent occasional services of the churches, its meaning can hardly be dismissed as a merely academic question. It is a constant pastoral challenge for the minster who must interpret it—sometimes to candidates or parents whose thoughts on the subject have little or nothing to do with the official teaching of the minister's church. And as a theological problem, baptism, like everything else in dogmatic theology, draws in other fundamental questions. If the rite is in fact a means of grace, what is the nature of the grace imparted? And what does it mean to be received into the church? I cannot hope to cover all the pertinent issues exposed in our look at the biblical and controversial resources, but my thesis 18 addresses these two questions by drawing some conclusions on the relation of baptism first to the Word, then to the Christian fellowship.

1. Baptismal Grace and the Word of Faith

My statements on baptism and the Lord's Supper reach back to the statements on reconciliation (chap. 12) and renewal (chap. 13) as the two main strands in the life of faith. There are differences in the way these and other terms descriptive of the Christian life have been used throughout the history of Christian thought. In my usage, "reconciliation" with God denotes the *beginning* of the life of faith, "renewal" its *continuance*; and because the continuance is interrupted by repeated failure, new beginnings are needed again and again. In the familial metaphors I have used throughout, reconciliation is adoption into the family of faith, or being born again; renewal, or growth in grace, is life together in the Father's household. Correspondingly, baptism pictures new birth; the Lord's Supper pictures nurture and growth. "Adoption" and "new birth," though not synonymous, both point—as metaphors for the beginning of the new life—to the moment of conversion, which is sometimes felt to call for giving the new person a new name.

How, then, does reconciliation happen? It happens through the Word, the proclamation of the gospel of God's "paternal" goodwill in Christ (thesis 12). This fits our quotation from 1 Peter: "You have been born anew . . . through the living and enduring word of God." The New Testament can also attribute the new birth to baptism. But if we accept Augustine's description of a sacrament as a visible word, any thought of an actual competition or conflict between Word and sacrament is in principle ruled out. Indeed, the two forms of word are mutually supportive: the spoken word determines the meaning of the visible word, and the visible word confirms the spoken word by lively depiction of its content. This is not, as such, a novel idea of the Protestant Reformers; it is rooted in the sacramental theology of Augustine. But whereas the medieval schoolmen generally thought of the sacramental word as the formula of consecration, I follow the Reformers and take it to mean the preached Word, "the word of faith" (Rom. 10:8). It is a mistake to charge Luther and Calvin with depreciating the sacraments by their stress on the Word and faith; we should rather say that while verbalizing a sacrament, they sacramentalized the Word. They held that material things may become vehicles of the divine promises, and they assigned to the Word a power and efficacy that the medieval church credited to the sacraments. Not, to be sure, the Word as mere instruction or a consecrating formula muttered in Latin, but the Word proclaimed to the congregation.[9] It follows, however, that the meaning of sacramental grace is thereby transformed from what it meant to the schoolmen, and it is here that Calvin fell into difficulties.

Calvin believed that his argument against the Anabaptists had established the dogma of infant regeneration. This was not the only part of his threefold case for infant baptism. But it was the weakest. To the objection that infants are incapable of knowing God, he replied that God sometimes gives knowledge of himself by the inward illumination of the Spirit—without the medium of preaching. And he asks "what the danger is if infants be said to receive now some part of that grace which in a little while they shall enjoy to the full" (*Institutes*, 2:1342). The danger, I should think, is that Calvin risks moving grace out

9. See Calvin, *Institutes* 4.14.3–5 (2:1278–80). When Thomas Aquinas says that words are required to establish the signification of the sacrament, he means the formula of administration or consecration: in baptism, *Ego te baptizo* (*ST* 3, q. 60, art. 6 [2:2348–49]). Both Thomas and Calvin appeal to Augustine's dicta: "The word is added to the element and there results the Sacrament, as if itself also a kind of visible word," and the word itself is effective "not because it is uttered, but because it is believed" (*Tractates on John* 80.3 [NPNF[1] 7:344]).

of the personal and cognitive domain, where he has placed it, into an impersonal discourse better suited to the scholastic language of infused grace. How can even a portion of grace, if grace is knowledge of God, be "poured in" an infant? It does not help when Calvin speaks also of the "seed" of repentance and faith hidden in baptized infants by a secret operation of the Spirit (1343). The possibility of future repentance and faith lies not so much in a seed miraculously implanted in the infants as in the infants' circumstances—that is, their reception into the covenant people of God, *whose faith is a condition but not the guarantee of faith in the one baptized.* It is certainly true that the influence of the covenant people on a child cannot be reduced to the transfer of a conscious knowledge of God: over time it operates, at least in part, at subconscious levels and works for an eventual affirmation of the community's knowledge of God.

2. *Baptismal Grace and the Covenant People*

From the Acts of the Apostles we learn about the baptism of converts, who voiced their repentance and faith as conditions of their acceptance into the Christian community; and wherever the missionary situation is repeated today—whether in foreign missions or at home—the same conditions will apply. But in the overwhelming majority of today's churches baptism is mostly administered to infants, who cannot make a personal response to the gospel. It need not follow that we have to speak of "the sacrament of infant baptism" as though it were a special rite, distinct from the baptism of adult converts. My thesis 18 is intended to be simply about *baptism*—baptism as symbol of the new birth in Christ that is offered and given by the Spirit in the word of reconciliation.

Baptism cannot guarantee that the new birth has happened, or will happen, in the life of a particular individual—any more than the proclaimed Word can. What it does is set her in the sphere in which the new birth has always happened and still does, sometimes after many years of belonging to the Christian community. More precisely, we may say, "belonging to the outer circle of the community," which I take to be the meaning of *reception into the covenant people.* When—or whether—the transition is made to the "inner circle" of the regenerate (cf. Rom. 9:6), no one can say. The church can only ask the *adult* candidate for a profession of faith and pray that a baptized *infant* will in time be brought to profession of faith. Baptismal grace is not a secret operation of the Spirit in the individual. It is "the grace of the Lord Jesus Christ" (2 Cor. 13:14) mediated through the life and witness of the Christian community. It includes preaching, but it is more: we might call it the total ambience in which an individual may come to faith and the new birth.

This, to be sure, is a necessarily brief attempt to describe the faith of those (myself among them) who are not persuaded by the case against pedobaptism. In the New Testament there is neither a command to baptize infants nor a prohibition of it, and the historical evidence for and against the baptism of infants in the Apostolic church remains inconclusive. The dogmatic task for the theologians on each side of the debate is to form a doctrine of baptism in the setting of the distinctive theological witness of their church. I think we may say that the divergence in Christendom with respect to baptism has its roots in two equally valid theologies: a corporate theology of covenant and a theology of individual commitment. Of course, neither side neglects what serves as the focus of the other. But advocates of the baptism of infants have usually seen it as the point in the life of the church at which the primacy of grace over conversion, Word over faith, God's decision over human decisions, and the community over the individual is most strongly affirmed. The advocates of believer baptism, on the other hand, warn that baptizing infants tends to become a routine affair that obscures the call for personal decision; like Zwingli and Barth, they identify true baptism with the human *response* to the grace of God.[10]

Choices have to be made and defended, but they do not have to be accompanied by anathemas against anyone who chooses otherwise. Ecumenical openness enables a fresh look at baptism that crosses denominational and party lines without erasing every theological difference. There are Reformed theologians who, like Schleiermacher, unreservedly—and contritely—"cancel the sentence of condemnation passed on the Anabaptists"; and there are Baptists who acknowledge two legitimate modes of initiation. Baptist theologian Arthur Crabtree asked hopefully: "Can there be a mutual recognition of the validity of two modes of initiation into Christ and the church: infant baptism followed by confirmation, or the blessing of infants followed by believers' baptism?"[11] There we must leave the first evangelical sacrament and turn to discussion of the second, which will provide the opportunity for a closer look at the language of "signs," "symbols," and "sacraments."

10. For further reflections on what I take to be the strength of Calvin's case for infant baptism, despite my criticism of him, see Gerrish 2001: 119–23. Beasley-Murray (1962) concludes with a strong case for the other side. Representatives of the rival positions have their say in Wright 2009.

11. Crabtree 1980: 75. This possibility, suggested also in the ecumenical document *Baptism, Eucharist and Ministry*, has not won universal acceptance among Baptists. On the other hand, the *method* of baptism—by affusion or by immersion—has been a less intractable issue: it is commonly taken to be contingent on such practical conditions as the climate and the availability of water.

19. The Lord's Supper: Sign of New Life

The Lord's Supper, as the effectual sign of new life in the household of God, represents Christ himself as "the Bread of Life" proffered and given by the Spirit in the word of renewal; and in partaking of the one bread and the one cup the family of faith is renewed as a covenant people and the body of the crucified and living Lord.

The second of the two evangelical sacraments goes by many names. Even after he had launched his assault on the Roman Catholic sacramental system, Luther retained the medieval term "Mass" and could still speak of "the Sacrament of the Altar." "Mass" had no intrinsic sacramental meaning; it was derived from the words of dismissal when the liturgy was ending (*Ite, missa est*). But "Sacrament of the Altar" carried with it the understanding of the Mass as a propitiatory sacrifice—the chief target of Luther's assault. Other names came to be preferred among the Protestants: "Lord's Supper," "Eucharist," "Communion," "Breaking of Bread," all of which they found used or implied in Scripture. In 1 Corinthians, Paul spoke of "the Lord's Supper" (*kyriakon deipnon*, 1 Cor. 11:20; cf. Rev. 19:9) and asked, "The bread which we break, is it not a participation [or communion, *koinōnia*] in the body of Christ?" (1 Cor. 10:16 RSV). The notion of a Eucharist, or giving of thanks, appears in the reported words and actions of Jesus at the Last Supper: he took a loaf of bread, and "when he had given thanks [*eucharistēsas*], he broke it" (11:23–24; cf. Mark 14:23; Matt. 26:27; Luke 22:17, 19; Acts 20:7). "Eucharist" has become the most common name for the Sacrament in ecumenical conversations—though not to the exclusion of other names, each of which tends to carry somewhat different semantic freight.

It has traditionally been supposed that the meaning of the Sacrament can be, and should be, taken chiefly from the New Testament accounts of Jesus' last meal with his Apostles (1 Cor. 11:23–25; Mark 14:22–25; Matt. 26:26–29; Luke 22:14–23; cf. John 13–17). His reported words on that occasion have been read as the institution of the Sacrament, and they are recited whenever the Sacrament is celebrated. There are, to be sure, difficulties with harmonizing the several reports of the Last Supper, and in recent times fresh textual and historical inquiries have figured prominently in the discussions of it by New Testament specialists. Historical-critical proposals about the origin of the Eucharist—its relation to the early Christian love feast[1] and the banquets of other Mediterranean communities—should not be ignored. Sometimes they may strike a

1. The love feast (Agape) is mentioned by name in the NT only in Jude 12 and perhaps 2 Pet. 2:13. But see Acts 2:43–47.

believer as subversive, but sometimes they contribute to a fuller understanding of the Eucharist.[2] However, they have not been allowed to govern the work of liturgical scholars and dogmatic theologians, who do not move far from the pertinent New Testament texts themselves in their received, canonical form.

The task for dogmatic theology is not to discover the sources, or possible sources, of the central Christian rite, but to state its meaning for the church. This calls, first of all, for determining its meaning in the normative witness of the New Testament—not only in the accounts of the Last Supper but also in Paul's admonitions to the Corinthians (1 Cor. 10:14–22; 11:17–33) and the discourse on the bread of life in the Fourth Gospel (John 6:25–59). It does not follow that the task *ends* there. The plea one occasionally hears to rely only on biblical exegesis, setting aside all the theological controversy that has dogged the history of eucharistic thought, allows too little to the theological and exegetical insights of so-called precritical exegesis. But I begin, as usual, by deferring consideration of the postcanonical developments and bracketing the conclusions to come.

I. The Lord's Supper in the New Testament

1. The Lord's Supper and the Last Supper

New Testament scholars distinguish two traditions behind the accounts of the Last Supper in the Synoptics and Paul, pairing Mark's version with Matthew's and Paul's with Luke's; and there are differences of detail within each pair. Luke's account expressly identifies the Last Supper as a Passover meal (Luke 22:15); implicitly, Mark and Matthew agree. But the actual narratives in the Synoptic versions do not suggest the Passover ritual; and Paul does not mention the Passover at all, although elsewhere he can identify Christ as "our paschal lamb" (1 Cor. 5:7). John's version places the Last Supper *before* the Passover festival (John 13:1) and does not represent it as the setting for the institution of the Lord's Supper. Some suggest that John's dating of events was influenced by a desire to make Christ's crucifixion coincide with the slaying of the paschal lambs. But there are many who think that John's chronology was right, and whether Jesus' last meal with the Twelve was a Passover celebration remains disputed. On the other hand, two pivotal motifs in the accounts of the Last Supper are well attested: the covenant in Jesus' blood and the eschatological banquet.

The *covenant* motif appears in all four main accounts, including the longer version of Luke,[3] and is associated with the giving of the cup. (The account in John is so different that one can only speak of it separately.) We are told that

2. One influential tendency has been to reverse the traditional view of the Last Supper as the institution of the Lord's Supper and to argue that the church's eucharistic practice may actually have shaped the accounts of Jesus' last meal with his Apostles. On the other hand, Jesus' frequent sharing of meals with a variety of companions, which is well attested and left him open to scorn (Matt. 11:19 // Luke 7:34; cf. Mark 2:15), may have provided both a kind of dominical warrant for the Sacrament and also the interpretation of it as essentially table fellowship with the Lord.

3. The covenant appears in Luke 22:19b–20, missing (in whole or part) from some manuscripts and perhaps interpolated in others from the tradition recited by Paul (1 Cor. 11:24b–25). The Lukan version reports that Jesus took the cup twice: once before and once after taking the bread. The second occasion was "after supper" (*meta to deipnēsai*). Paul says nothing of the first occasion, but he too reports

Jesus took a loaf of bread, blessed it (or gave thanks: Paul/Luke), broke it, and gave it to his disciples, saying: "This is my body."[4] Then (after supper, according to Paul and Luke), he took a cup, gave thanks (Paul says simply "in the same way") and declared, "This cup is the new covenant in my blood" (Paul) or "This is my blood of the [new] covenant, which is poured out for many" (Mark; also Matthew, who adds "for the forgiveness of sins"). Simply put, Jesus foresees his coming death but assures the Apostles that it is to be the means for establishing a new relationship between God and God's people. There is an apparent allusion to Exodus 24:8, and the word "new" in some ancient manuscripts links Jesus' death with Jeremiah 31:31–34. How much of this goes back to Jesus' self-testimony and how much attests the meaning of Jesus to his first disciples is impossible to say. Dogmatic theology asks for the meaning of Jesus to faith, and faith has two millennia of evidence that his death did indeed establish a new relationship with God. Further reflection on the "blood of the covenant" belongs under atonement (see chap. 10 above).

The *banquet* motif appears in all the Synoptic accounts; it is most prominent in the shorter version of Luke, which says nothing about a new covenant. (Paul, by contrast, says nothing of the eschatological banquet.) Jesus' first words in Luke's account are these: "I have eagerly desired to eat this Passover with you before I suffer, for I tell you, I will not eat it [again] until it is fulfilled in the kingdom of God" (Luke 22:15–16). Taking a cup, he adds: "I tell you that from now on I will not drink of the fruit of the vine until the kingdom of God comes" (v. 18; cf. Mark 14:25).[5] Luke follows his account of the Last Supper with Jesus' words (probably on another occasion): "I confer on you, just as my Father has conferred on me, a kingdom, so that you may eat and drink at my table in my kingdom" (Luke 22:29–30). The words echo Jesus' image of the banquet for the consummation of the kingdom (Matt. 8:11 // Luke 13:29; Matt. 22:2 // Luke 14:16). When will that be? In view of our earlier conclusions about the eschatological message of Jesus, it is unlikely that he would have foreseen a long interval between his death and the consummation of the kingdom, in which case the notion that he inaugurated a permanent Christian ritual may be a retrospective view on the Last Supper from later Christian experience. That Jesus' actions did inaugurate the Lord's Supper is not in question; that he was fully conscious of where his actions would lead seems unlikely (cf. Mark 13:32).

2. *The Witness of Paul and John*

It is Paul whose account of the Last Supper expressly treats it as the institution of the Lord's Supper. After giving the bread, Jesus says in Paul's version: "Do this in remembrance of me." After giving the cup, he says: "Do this, as often as you drink it, in remembrance of me." The formula "in remembrance

---

that Jesus took the cup after supper (1 Cor. 11:25). There is a hint here of the time when the sacrament would be detached from the meal (cf. v. 34).

4. Before "This is my body" Mark has the invitation, "Take"; Matthew has, "Take, eat." Paul adds that the body is "for you" or, in some manuscripts, "broken for you." Luke has "given for you."

5. Mark has: "Truly I tell you, I will never again drink of the fruit of the vine until that day when I drink it new in the kingdom of God." Matthew has: "until that day when I drink it new *with you*," making it more explicit that table fellowship—an eschatological feast—is intended (Matt. 26:29; my emphasis).

of me" (*eis tēn emēn anamnēsin*) appears nowhere else in the accounts of the Last Supper except once in the longer version of Luke (Luke 22:19b), where it is likely an interpolation. "Remembrance" implies a lapse of time, and Paul comments: "For as often as you eat this bread and drink the cup, you proclaim the Lord's death *until he comes*" (1 Cor. 11:26; emphasis mine). But many scholars have argued that, in this setting, *anamnēsis* does not mean merely a reminder. Anderson Scott maintained that the natural Greek word for "in memory of" is not *anamnēsis* but *mnēmē*, and Old Testament scholars have held that we should look behind Paul's Greek for such Hebrew words as *zikkārôn*, which suggests "making present." Liturgical scholars have made a similar case.[6] In the only other appearance of *anamnēsis* in the New Testament, it does mean "a reminder" (Heb. 10:3). But Paul's understanding of the term must be aligned with what he has said previously about the Lord's Supper. In 1 Corinthians 10:16 he says: "The cup of blessing which we bless, is it not a participation [*koinōnia*] in the blood of Christ? The bread which we break, is it not a participation [*koinōnia*] in the body of Christ?" (RSV). Paul intends something more than a reminder of an absent Christ. Whether or not the Last Supper was a Passover meal, it took place when the Passover celebration was in everyone's thoughts. It was a time when the people looked back to the exodus as their founding event and in so doing brought it into the present as the determinant of their existence. Similarly, Paul could say, "our paschal lamb, Christ, has been sacrificed. Therefore, let us celebrate the festival" (1 Cor. 5:7–8).

There has been much discussion about the meaning of Christ's "body" in 1 Corinthians 10 and 11. Since Paul also speaks of participation in Christ's "blood," it may appear that he intends the crucified, *natural* body. But he immediately follows his statement on participation in Christ's blood and body by saying, "Because there is one bread, we who are many are one body, for we all partake of the one bread" (10:17). A long exegetical tradition takes "body" in 11:29 to mean the *ecclesial* body of Christ—the church.[7] Accordingly, when Paul says, "all who eat and drink [in an unworthy manner] without discerning the body, eat and drink judgment against themselves," he is reproaching the Corinthians who carry their partisan spirit with them even into the Lord's Supper: they form cliques that disregard the nature of the church as the body of Christ. Paul's description of the Lord's Supper is his answer to the divisiveness of the Christians in Corinth. His expression "without discerning the body" (11:29) is exactly parallel to "showing contempt for the church of God" (11:22).

There are obstacles that frustrate any attempt to reconstruct exactly what was said and done at Jesus' last meal with his disciples. But Christian faith, if it takes the several accounts as facets of the Apostolic witness to Christ, will find that the church's proclamation is not impeded by the variations but enlarged. And Paul also touches on another cherished eucharistic motif that entirely governs the witness of the Fourth Gospel: he says that our ancestors "all ate the

6. See Charles A. Anderson Scott, *Christianity according to St Paul* (Cambridge: Cambridge University Press, 1932), 191; Douglas Jones, "Αναμνησις in the LXX and the Interpretation of 1 Cor. xi.25," *Journal of Theological Studies*, n.s. 6 (1955): 183–91; Gregory Dix, *The Shape of the Liturgy*, reprinted with additional notes by Paul V. Marshall (San Francisco: Harper & Row, 1982), 161.

7. See James Moffatt, "Discerning the Body," *Expository Times*, n.s. 30 (1918): 19–23.

same spiritual food, and all drank the same spiritual drink. For they drank from the spiritual rock that followed them, and the rock was Christ" (1 Cor. 10:3–4).

Although *John* has a long account of the Last Supper, he says nothing about the institution of the Lord's Supper. (We are indebted to him instead for the report of Jesus' washing the disciples' feet [John 13:2b–11].) But it is generally agreed that Jesus' discourse on the bread of life (6:25–59) is to be understood as a tacit eucharistic statement, at least in part.[8] John places it after the feeding of the five thousand (vv. 1–14). The crowd pursues him, and Jesus rebukes them: "you are looking for me . . . because you ate your fill of the loaves. Do not work for the food that perishes, but for the food that endures for eternal life. . . . For the bread of God is that which comes down from heaven and gives life to the world. . . . I am the bread of life" (vv. 26–27, 33, 35). To receive eternal life, one need only believe in him whom God has sent (vv. 29, 47). But as the discourse continues (vv. 51b–58), the language changes from eating the living bread to eating Jesus' flesh and drinking his blood. Those who eat his flesh and drink his blood have eternal life—plainly an allusion to the Eucharist. When he says, "the bread that I will give for the life of the world is my flesh" (v. 51b), he is anticipating his death. But after the discourse is ended, he says in response to the perplexity of his disciples: "It is the spirit that gives life; the flesh is useless. The words that I have spoken to you are spirit and life. But among you there are some who do not believe" (vv. 63–64). The apparent contradictions in chapter 6 are probably traceable to redaction; in any case, it was the received text that occasioned fierce eucharistic controversies at the time of the Reformation.

II. The Eucharist in Theological Controversy

1. *Realism and Symbolism*

The Eucharist was not a matter of theological controversy until the ninth century, when two Benedictine monks from the same monastery wrote significantly different treatises on the subject. But the Fathers of the ancient church bequeathed a legacy of liturgical and theological expressions to which the later disputes appealed. Particularly important was the patristic evidence on three related issues that were to become controversial: the bodily presence of Christ in the Eucharist, the sacrificial nature of the Sacrament, and the transformation of the consecrated elements. I cannot review the patristic evidence here but can recommend the two collections of pertinent sources by Paul Palmer and Maxwell Johnson (see in particular Palmer 1957: 195–221). A large part of the eucharistic controversies turned, of course, on the question how far the Fathers preserved the witness of the Apostles. There was certainly development. Most critical was the fact that the Eucharist lost its connection with table fellowship. As one scholar characterizes the change, it was "the evolution of the ritual from the dining table to the altar and from the social world of the banquet to that

8. Bultmann plausibly argued that in vv. 51b–58 an editor inserted an interpretation of the bread of life as the sacrament of the Lord's Supper; no sacramental act is implied in the preceding discourse. See Rudolf Bultmann, *The Gospel of John: A Commentary*, trans. G. R. Beasley-Murray, ed. R. W. N. Hoare and J. K. Riches (Philadelphia: Westminster, 1971), 234–37; cf. 219.

of church order" (Smith 2003: 287). Whether this was a salutary development has been the most intractable question in ecumenical conversations on the Eucharist.

The very first monograph to be written on the Eucharist came from Paschasius Radbertus (d. ca. 860), abbot of Corbie. Titled *On the Body and Blood of the Lord,* it was composed about 831 CE and revised about 844 as a Christmas present for the Frankish king, Charles the Bald, later to become Holy Roman emperor. Soon after, at the king's request, a monk of the same monastery, Ratramnus (d. ca. 868), wrote another treatise on the subject; usually cited by the same title, it is assumed to be a rejoinder to Radbertus (not mentioned by name). Understanding the points at issue between Radbertus and Ratramnus is hampered by the state of the texts, ambiguity in the employment of terms, and the polemical use of the two treatises in later controversies. Printed versions first appeared in the sixteenth century, when they were taken up as weapons for rival parties in the Reformation debates on the Eucharist.

The eucharistic theory of Radbertus reflects the so-called *conversionist* strand in the thinking of the Fathers, notably (in the Western Church) Ambrose of Milan (340–397), and it points toward the scholastic doctrine of transubstantiation. According to Radbertus, "the bread and wine must be believed to be fully, after the consecration, nothing but Christ's flesh and blood . . . nothing different . . . from what was born of Mary, suffered on the cross, and rose again from the tomb." The miraculous change must be *believed* because it is not visible (LCC 9:94–95). Oddly, however, the treatise of Radbertus contains stories about communicants who *saw* fragments of the Lord's body: a bloody finger, a piece of bloody flesh, and so on (MPL 120:1318–19). Perhaps the stories were interpolated. They represent a crude, as distinct from a more refined, realism. For Radbertus, the Sacrament is both figure and truth: what the priest does outwardly is a figure of the truth that "the Lamb is daily sacrificed as he was once for all" and that his flesh is truly our spiritual food. But Radbertus rejects any suggestion that the body of the Lord is devoured with the teeth (101–4). At first glance, that seems to be precisely the view of his supposed adversary, Ratramnus.

Ratramnus cites several of the early church fathers, but his eucharistic doctrine has the strongest affinities with the *symbolist* strand in patristic thought, particularly in Augustine's theory of signs. In the mystery of the Eucharist, therefore, the body and blood of the Lord are present not "with a naked manifestation of truth" but under a figure or symbol (LCC 9:118). Radbertus would agree. But Ratramnus draws a crucial inference that sets his theory apart. If the body and blood are present in a symbol, there is no need to speak of the elements undergoing a change. Radbertus had said that the bread and wine, after the consecration, are nothing but Christ's flesh and blood. Ratramnus says: "With respect to the substance of things created, what [the elements] had been before consecration, that they afterward are." Apparently, he does not wish to exclude entirely Ambrose's language of change, since he immediately adds that what feeds the soul "has been changed inwardly by the mighty power of the Holy Spirit." He means, I take it, that the food of the soul, which was not received before the consecration, can now be received by faith because the consecrating word makes the bread and wine into something they were not before: *symbols* of the body and blood of the Lord (133; cf. 122–23). And the body and blood in the Eucharist cannot be simply identified (as Radbertus supposed) with the body that was born of Mary, suffered, and rose again; the ascended body of the Lord is spiritual (136–43).[9]

The eucharistic theory of Ratramnus has always been suspect in the Roman Catholic Church. Indeed, scholars have debated what exactly his theory was, and it is hard to deny that there are inconsistences and ambiguity in his treatise. In his study of Ratramnus, John Fahey argued that he must be understood as faithful to Augustine's teaching that sacramental signs participate in the reality they signify; hence the language of figures or symbols was not, for him, antirealistic.[10] Though admittedly controversial, Fahey's argument is, I think, successful. Accordingly, we have to distinguish two varieties of eucharistic *realism*: conversionist and symbolist. If we speak of "the real presence" in the Sacrament, we should include Ratramnus among its advocates—precisely as an Augustinian symbolist. But little attention was paid to his treatise throughout the Middle Ages. When Berengarius of Tours (d. 1088) read it and commended its thesis, the book (wrongly attributed to John Scotus Erigena) was ordered destroyed, and Berengarius was obliged to confess that the real body and blood of Christ on the altar "are held and broken by the hands of the priests and are crushed by the teeth of the faithful." The adoption of Aristotelian categories made possible the more sophisticated conversionism that affirms a change of substance but not of accidents—not, that is, a change of form, color, taste, and so on. In 1215 "transubstantiation" became an official Roman Catholic dogma at the Fourth Lateran Council (DS 169), and it was explained in detail by, among others, Thomas Aquinas (*ST* 2:2445–71). In the later Middle Ages a few theologians (such as Wycliffe) defended *remanence:* the belief that in the Eucharist the substances of the bread and the wine, not the accidents only, remain unchanged. But not until the Reformation—aided by the printing press—did the symbolist theory come into its own.

2. *The Eucharist and the Reformation*

Luther's understanding of the Sacrament of the Altar evolved during his twofold campaign against "papists" and "fanatics." His earliest statement on the subject, *The Blessed Sacrament of the Holy and True Body of Christ* (1519), contained some hints of the conflict to come, but it was not directed against the papists. It was a pastoral admonition to the lay fraternities about the meaning of the Sacrament as *incorporation:* their exclusiveness and self-indulgence tacitly denied the true brotherhood, the fellowship of saints, in which everything is shared in mutual love. "To receive this sacrament in bread and wine, then, is nothing else than to receive a sure sign of this fellowship and incorporation with Christ and all saints" (LW 35:51). Luther ignores the sacrificial understanding of the Mass, and he mentions transubstantiation only to say that the conversion of the

9. In one place Ratramnus describes the Eucharist as a twofold symbol: "in that which is enacted through the mystery there is a figure not only of Christ's own body, but also of the people who believe in Christ, for it bears a figure of both bodies, that is, the one which suffered and rose again, and the body of the people reborn in Christ" (146–47).

10. John F. Fahey, *The Eucharistic Teaching of Ratramn of Corbie* (Mundelein, IL: Saint Mary of the Lake Seminary, 1951), 54–55, 85, 154–56.

elements into Christ's natural body and blood is an analogue to the conversion of the congregation into his spiritual body, the church. And he says: "It is more needful that you discern the spiritual than the natural body of Christ" (62).

The next year (1520), in Luther's *Treatise on the New Testament*, the accent shifts from incorporation to *testament*, and the target now is the papists; for to say that the sacrament is Christ's testament is to deny that it is a priestly sacrifice. By "testament" Luther means, following Hebrews 9:16–17, a promise made by someone who is about to die. God's approach to humans is in the form of a promise that evokes the response of faith, and he usually adds a sign as a kind of seal to produce greater confidence in his promise, as, for instance, he gave Noah the rainbow. At the first Mass, shortly before his death, Christ promised forgiveness to his disciples (Matt. 26:28), and as a sign he added his own true body and blood under the bread and wine (LW 35:79–111). The same year, Luther carried these thoughts over into his *Prelude on the Babylonian Captivity of the Church,* in which he assailed the three captivities to which the Sacrament of the Bread had been subjected: the withholding of the cup from the laity, transubstantiation, and the interpretation of the Mass as a good work and a sacrifice. He treats transubstantiation as a matter of opinion, and he thinks that Pierre D'Ailly (d. 1425) came up with a better opinion: that the bread and the wine, not just their accidents, could remain on the altar (had the church not decreed otherwise). But the sacrifice of the Mass is not a matter of opinion; it is the worst of abuses. For a testament is something we receive and a sacrifice is something we give. The Roman Mass turns God's gift into a human work (LW 36:52).

Luther's polemic against the assortment of adversaries he calls "fanatics" (*Schwärmer*) was even more impassioned than his critique of the papists. He accused his colleague Carlstadt of turning a means of grace into a devotional exercise; for "remembrance" in the Eucharist is in truth a public celebration, not private meditation (LW 40:205–8). But Luther observed that Carlstadt's poison crawled far, and in his *Sacrament of the Body and Blood of Christ, against the Fanatics* (1526), he turned his attention to Zwingli and the Swiss Reformed. His charge, in brief, is that whereas the papists fail to grasp the eucharistic gift, despite their belief in the presence of Christ's body, the worse error of the fanatics is denial of the presence: they come together to commemorate Christ's death (LW 36:346–54). In his treatise on *The Words of Christ* (1527), Luther traces their error to their insistence that "This is my body" must be taken figuratively. The fanatics appeal to Augustine, but they fail to perceive that a sacrament, for Augustine, was a sign of something invisibly present, not a sign of something absent (LW 37:104–5). Finally, in his *Confession concerning Christ's Supper* (1528), Luther states that a single new entity comes into existence out of the eucharistic bread and the body of Christ. If we want to say that there is a figure of speech in "This is my body," it can only be synecdoche—naming the part (i.e., either the bread or the body) for the whole, which has become "fleshbread" (LW 37:262–68, 301–3). The gulf between this and the sacramental theology of Zwingli is formidable.

Zwingli's Augsburg confession (presented to the emperor at the Diet of Augsburg, 1530) rejects the concept of a means of grace. His fundamental principle is that the Holy Spirit acts directly, without means. A sacrament, therefore, can only picture what the Spirit has done: it is *factae gratiae signum*, a sign of what grace has already accomplished. We may say that in the Eucharist Christ's body is *as if* present in the contemplation of faith but not that it is *really* present (*LWZ* 2:46, 48, 49). Zwingli explains in his *Commentary on True and False Religion* (1525) that to eat Christ's flesh and drink his blood is to proclaim his saving deed on the cross (1 Cor. 11:26). Eating is believing, and to believe is to be thankful. "We therefore now understand from the very name what the Eucharist, that is, the Lord's Supper, is: namely, the thanksgiving and rejoicing of those who declare the death of Christ" (*LWZ* 3:200). Zwingli goes further in his *Exposition of the Faith*, written in the year of his death and published posthumously (1536), and suggests that the outward eating and drinking of the elements signals the parallel occurrence of an inward feeding on Christ by faith, who is present in the soul's embrace (LCC 24:258–59, 263). But his theory of signs does not permit him to grant that the outward event causes, or gives rise to, the inward. In the three terms I coined in an old article (1966), he moves from "symbolic memorialism" to "symbolic parallelism," and this falls short of the "symbolic instrumentalism" of Calvin.

Zwingli believed that in his view of the Eucharist he was simply expounding Scripture. But he also gave theological reasons for rejecting the rival views of the papists and the Lutherans. If the giving of grace were bound to the sacraments, priests would have God at their disposal and could grant or withhold salvation at will. But even Luther's sacramental ideas failed, in Zwingli's judgment, to carry through Reformation principles consistently. The very notion of sacramental grace implies another way of salvation, in competition with *sola fide* ("by faith alone"). To eat Christ's flesh, if it saves, cannot mean anything more than to believe in him (*LWZ* 2:113, 118; LCC 24:205). Echoes of Zwingli's critique can be heard in twentieth-century and present-day theology, especially where Karl Barth's influence has been strong.

The fiasco of the Marburg Colloquy (1529) appeared to leave no bridge between two irreconcilable concepts in the eucharistic doctrines of the Protestants. But a third, mediating party emerged, of which Calvin became the foremost spokesman. The mediating theologians, as we may name them, called for a sounder interpretation of Augustine than Luther had found in Zwingli. They argued that although a sign is not itself the signified reality, it nonetheless attests and *proffers* a present reality: communion with Christ or participation in his body. "For," says Calvin, "why should the Lord put in your hand the symbol of his body, except to assure you of a true participation in it?" (*Institutes*, 2:1371). He agreed with Zwingli that Christ's ascension marked a decisive break with the manner of his presence during his earthly ministry, but he held that it was the work of the Holy Spirit to bridge the distance between heaven and earth (1370, 1373, 1405). The sacraments were for him precisely what Zwingli said they were not: the Spirit's instruments (1284–87, 1293). Calvin did not profess to understand *how* the Spirit achieved the miracle of Christ's sacramental presence: "I rather experience than understand it. . . . In his Sacred Supper [Christ] bids me take, eat, and drink his body and blood under the symbols of bread and wine. I do not doubt that he himself truly presents them [*vere porrigat*], and that I receive them" (1403–4).

On the two main points at issue in the controversy with Rome—transubstantiation and the sacrifice of the Mass—Calvin calls for some distinctions.

(1) It is true that the Fathers sometimes spoke of a *conversion* of the elements in the Eucharist, and Calvin agrees. For the bread becomes something far different from common bread: it does not cease to be bread, but it becomes a sign of the spiritual food of the soul. A change of signification and use is not a change of material substance; if the accidents only were left after the consecration, the analogy between food for the stomach and food for the soul would be canceled (*Institutes*, 2:1374–76; cf. 1378). (2) It is also true that the Fathers sometimes spoke of the Eucharist as a *sacrifice*. But Calvin insists on a distinction between the propitiatory sacrifice Christ made once and for all on the cross and the sacrifice of praise and thanksgiving (*eucharistikon*) that the church makes whenever his death is remembered in the Lord's Supper. The sacrifice of thanksgiving is essential to the Sacrament but not confined to it: it includes all the duties of brotherly love that honor the Lord in his members. The twofold symbolism of the Sacrament thus points both to Christ as the bread of life and to the church as a brotherhood of mutual love and a royal priesthood with its sacrifice of praise (1414–16, 1438–45). In *Concerning the Order of Worship in the Church* (1523), Luther had declared that a Christian congregation should never gather without the preaching of God's Word; Calvin upheld the ancient rule that there should be no meeting of the church without partaking of the Lord's Supper (1422–23).

Rome ceded little to the "heretics." The Council of *Trent* rejected Protestant insistence that the eucharistic wine must always be administered to the laity and the Sacrament always celebrated in the vernacular (DS 287, 291–92; see O'Malley 2013: 190, 194–95). It did express its wish for more frequent reception of Communion by the faithful. But it approved Masses in which the priest alone communicates (DS 290–92). And the requirement that the faithful should communicate every year, "at least at Easter," would hardly have discouraged the popular belief that, essentially, the Mass was between the priest and God (271). Moreover, the council upheld the established doctrines of the Eucharist (sess. 13) and the Sacrifice of the Mass (sess. 22) and pronounced anathemas on dissenters.

Transubstantiation was declared to be the appropriate and proper term for the conversion of the whole substance of bread into the substance of the body of Christ and of the whole substance of the wine into the substance of his blood, only the species (accidents) of bread and wine remaining (DS 267–68, 270). For the Catholics, the conversion of the elements was not, as Luther thought, a theological opinion; the issue had already been settled by the Fourth Lateran Council, which expressly sanctioned the term *transubstantiation*. In the twentieth century, a view of the eucharistic conversion akin to Calvin's appeared in the ideas of transignification and transfinalization proposed by a few eminent Catholic theologians, particularly in the Netherlands. But the encyclical *Mysterium fidei* of Pope Paul VI (1965) admonished them that it is not permissible to modify the language of dogma, which is not tied to a particular time but "adapted to men of all times and all places": transubstantiation is forever the teaching of the Catholic Church. Nevertheless, some Catholic theologians do not see this as excluding a "re-reception" of an old dogma by paying closer attention to the historical circumstances of its original production and to the ecumenical situation of the present.

Trent was adamant that the Mass is a truly *propitiatory sacrifice*, by which the Lord is appeased, not merely a sacrifice of praise and thanksgiving (DS 292). The Christ who once offered himself in a bloody sacrifice is immolated bloodlessly in the Mass. Strictly speaking, the agent of the bloodless sacrifice is Christ himself, "the same one now offering by the ministry of the priests as He who then offered Himself on the Cross, the manner of offering alone being different" (289). In answer to the Protestant misunderstanding that Catholic Masses detract from Christ's once-for-all sacrifice, the council declared that through the Mass the fruits of Christ's oblation on the cross are received (289–90); he left to the church a visible sacrifice by which his sacrifice on the cross might be represented (*repraesentaretur*) and the memory of it remain (288). "Represented" could perhaps be taken as "made present" (cf. the Greek word *anamnēsis*). The catechism of the Council of Trent (1566) uses a different verb, *instaurare*, which suggests "to renew"; it insists, however, that the sacrifice of the Mass is not another sacrifice, but one and the same with the sacrifice of the cross.

III. The Grace of Holy Communion

The Eucharist is commonly identified as the central rite of Christianity. But in fact its place in the life and worship of the churches varies; even within the selfsame church there are often surprising differences of opinion about the importance (or unimportance) of the Sacrament, and the patterns of worship vary accordingly. Generalizations are hazardous. However, an observer in, say, mid-twentieth-century England would notice that for the majority of Anglican churchgoers the standard form of Sunday worship was not the Sacrament, but Morning Prayer with Sermon. If the observer ventured into a Presbyterian church, she would discover that quarterly Communion was deemed sufficient by Calvin's offspring, and that even on Communion Sundays some members of the congregation would hurry to the exits when the sacramental part of the service was about to begin—often sent on their way by a misplaced benediction from the minister. In the Roman Catholic churches, if Mass was being celebrated in the presence of a congregation, our observer might suppose that the people in the pews were silent spectators of a strange priestly drama. (I recall a popular guide, available in the narthex of a Catholic church in England, titled *What's He Doing at the Altar?*) And, of course, there were churches that had dispensed with sacraments as merely temporary aids to Christian devotion, no longer needed.

Today's observer would notice some changes. During the second half of the twentieth century, ecumenical encounters spawned a widespread concern, both in and between the churches, for liturgical renewal and sacramental theology. The liturgical movement, with roots as far back as the nineteenth century, had been making progress in the Roman Catholic Church, and a fresh impetus came from the Second Vatican Council. The council's Constitution on the Sacred Liturgy stressed the importance of the sermon—understood as proclamation, not just instruction—and called for active participation of the faithful, not least in receiving the consecrated elements. Wherever possible, communal celebration was to be preferred to individual or quasi-private celebration. Communion under both kinds and the use of the vernacular were (within limits) encouraged. Protestants may applaud these reforms as delayed endorsement of some of Luther's proposals, and they may be surprised that the frequent Communion Calvin desired is more likely to be had these days in a Catholic congregation than in a Presbyterian one. It would be a mistake to suppose that the battle lines of the Reformation era are intact. But it would also be a mistake to imagine that no differences remain. The nature of the real presence and the sacrificial character of the Eucharist are still debated, though with more willingness to listen than seemed possible in the sixteenth century.

1. The Sacramental Presence and the Eucharistic Sacrifice

Luther thought (in 1520) that explanations of *the real presence* were matters of opinion; but he made no impression on the Council of Trent, which anathematized anyone who failed to affirm transubstantiation. The Lutherans responded in kind by condemning "papistic transubstantiation" in the Formula of Concord. Their alternative was to say that the body and blood of Christ are present to the communicant "in, with, and under" the bread and wine, which do not undergo physical change. (Lutherans reject "consubstantiation" because it is a philosophical, not a biblical, term and could be taken to imply that the body and blood are coextensive with the bread and wine in a *local* union.) The Reformed were not all of one opinion. An appeal to Christian experience is always open to question (*Whose* experience? *Which* Christians?). But there is abundant testimony that, for many of the Reformed, the eucharistic celebration does not merely *remind* the congregation of something that has happened, or *signal* something that is happening independently, but *brings about* the reality it symbolizes. Together with the preached word, the visible word is the means by which the Spirit *presents* Christ to the congregation. But why Christ's body and blood? What, after all, *is* the body that is present in the Sacrament?

In the sixteenth century, the Lutherans and the Reformed argued endlessly about the eucharistic body of Christ. The Reformed pointed to the statement in the Apostles' Creed that Christ "ascended into heaven and sits on the right hand of God the Father Almighty"; and this, they inferred, is where his body must be. The Lutherans replied that the right hand of God is everywhere, so Christ's body is everywhere—in the Sacrament the body is there *for me.* The Reformed pronounced a ubiquitous body to be a contradiction in terms; it is Christ's *rule* that cannot be spatially circumscribed. Calvin sometimes spoke of the eucharistic gift as a life-giving "virtue" from Christ's body, and at other times he seemed to have in mind a kind of "operative" or "dynamic" presence, according to which the substance of Christ's body is present in its effects.[11] "For if we see that the sun, shedding its beams upon the earth, in a way casts its substance upon it in order to beget, nourish, and give growth to its offspring—why should the radiance of Christ's Spirit be less able to impart to us the communion

11. What Calvin meant by *virtus* in this connection can be judged from his alternative expressions. Perhaps "vigor" or "energy" comes close, and it is no accident that a Lutheran adversary called Calvinists "Energists" (further details and documentation in Gerrish 2001). A similar problem appears in Schleiermacher's term, the *Wirkung* of Christ, for which the usual translation "influence" seems too weak.

of his flesh and blood?" (*Institutes*, 2:1373, alt.; cf. Comm. 1 Cor. 11:24). I would only wish to say (without Calvin's endorsement) that the point from which the "virtue" radiates is the *historical* Christ, the Word made flesh, and it comes to us through the historical community he established. The eucharistic presence is an ecclesial presence, intensified in the Sacrament. I remain agnostic about the *glorified* body of the ascended Christ.

Lutherans and Calvinists never arrived at a consensus on the real presence, but they did agree in their thoughts on *the eucharistic sacrifice*: there is a sacrifice of praise in the sacrament, but no propitiation. Catholics refuted some of the Protestant accusations. The fathers at the Council of Trent denied that in the Mass the priest sacrificed Christ as a kind of supplement to Christ's offering of himself on the cross; on the contrary, they affirmed that through the priest Christ himself offers the sacrifice of the Mass, by which he makes available the benefits of his oblation on the cross. And the Second Vatican Council denied that the Mass is solely a priestly act; even when performed privately, the priest acts as representative of the faithful. It is true, on the other side, that Calvin could use the language of "offering Christ to God" (Comm. Num. 19:2–3). But that is not how he understood the Lord's Supper. Christ, he says, has "given us a Table at which to feast, not an altar upon which to offer a victim; he has not consecrated priests to offer sacrifice, but ministers to distribute the sacred banquet" (*Institutes*, 2:1440). Protestants are glad to have their misconceptions corrected, and today the gap between the Protestant Lord's Supper and the Catholic Mass is narrower. But it is not entirely bridged. Indeed, the gap has widened for those of us who have concluded that Christ's self-offering on the cross was not propitiation of an angry God. The words of institution of the Lord's Supper certainly include "the blood of the covenant." But our interpretation of the words must be in line with our doctrine of the atonement. If we have reason to doubt propitiatory theories of atonement, we will not look for a propitiatory sacrifice in the Lord's Supper.

2. *The Banquet and Holy Communion*

The debates over the real presence carry us a long way from the plain analogy that likens dependence on Christ to food for the body and sees the heart of the Eucharist in the simple invitation, "Take, eat." Calvin's profession of faith in the mystery ("I rather experience than understand it") may do more for our account of Christian faith than his increasingly complex analysis of the nature of Christ's bodily presence. But he managed a less complicated statement of what was, for him, the essence of the matter in his interpretation of Jesus' discourse on the bread of life (John 6:25–59). It is a statement that, in essence, I consider sound—with one qualification.

There are some, Calvin admits, who say that eating Christ's flesh and drinking his blood are nothing more than to believe in him. But Christ meant to teach something more sublime, which is rather the *effect* of faith than faith itself. The life we receive from him is not received by mere cognition: it is by a real imparting of himself (*vera sui communicatione*) that his life passes into us, just as bread imparts vigor to the body (*Institutes*, 2:1365). Christ is speaking of a vital union with him that is more than beliefs about him, more than calling to mind the benefits he has won for us. Because the union is mysterious, it can only be represented by images and metaphors; one such image is eating in order to live, and this is the subject of Christ's discourse. The union of which he speaks does not take place only when the Lord's Supper is celebrated: it is continuous in the life of the believer. "And yet, at the same time," Calvin adds, "I acknowledge that there is nothing said here that is not figuratively represented, and actually bestowed on believers, in the Lord's Supper" (Comm. John 6:54). We may accept Schleiermacher's comment that in the Calvinist view of the Lord's Supper there is "a real presence of [Christ's] body and blood not to be had anywhere else" (*CF* 649) only if we recognize that for the Calvinist the Sacrament does what the Word does but does it more vividly and compellingly. As Calvin sees it, the Lord's Supper makes more evident than the gospel (that is, more evident than preaching) what is happening in the life of believers all the time (*Institutes*, 2:1364; cf. 1280). By way of qualification, however, I take his understanding of the real, bodily presence of Christ in conjunction with my proposal that we should be thinking of the *historical,* rather than the *glorified,* body of Christ as the point from which his "virtue" radiates.

Thesis 19 not only epitomizes what I take to be the meaning of the Lord's Supper; it also ends part II of my outline and reflects its overall shape. It echoes the distinction between reconciliation and renewal in division 1 (chaps. 12 and 13) and the ecclesiological definitions in division 2 (chaps. 14 and 15). And to display the systematic connection between the two chapters on the sacraments, I have recourse, once again, to familial metaphors: as baptism is the sign of new birth, the Lord's Supper is the sign of continuing life in "the household of God" (Eph. 2:19), "the family of faith" (Gal. 6:10). In the present chapter I have explored many more eucharistic themes than could be included in a single sentence. But to sum up what I take to be the indispensable essence of the Sacrament, the two members of my thesis affirm the dominant motifs of both John and Paul: Jesus Christ is the bread of life, and partaking of him constitutes the church. The grace of the Lord's Supper is the gift of this twofold communion with the Lord and with fellow believers. As such, it sums up the two divisions of part II: on Christ and the Christian, and on the Spirit and the Church.

CONCLUSION

20. The Trinity

For Christian faith, God "the Father Almighty" is "the Father of Jesus Christ," who brings wayward children home by reconciliation through the one true Son and cares for them through the Spirit in the church; Christian faith accordingly bears witness to Father, Son, and Holy Spirit and declares that God's nature is love.

The account of creation (in part I) and of the two divisions of redemption (in part II) has brought forward the three names of the Christian God, who is Father, Son, and Holy Spirit. To conclude, we must ask about the relationship between them. The subject is particularly difficult. On the one hand, the importance of the doctrine of the Trinity lies partly in that it distinguishes Christianity from other monotheistic faiths; in bygone times, it even served as the justification for Christian persecution of Jews and Muslims. Further, it is one belief on which all the separated churches—Orthodox, Catholic, and Protestant—are officially agreed. At the time of the Reformation, the Protestants defended their catholicity by professing loyalty to the ecumenical creeds. The Apostles', the Nicene, and the Athanasian Creeds were all expressly endorsed, for example, in the Lutheran *Book of Concord* (1580), the Reformed French Confession (1559), and the Anglican Thirty-nine Articles (1571).

On the other hand, Trinitarian speculation has always seemed remote from the faith and life of believers innocent of theology and philosophy, and Adolf von Harnack (1851–1930) proposed the famous thesis that the Trinitarian and christological dogmas, however justified in defense against heresy, marked the fateful hellenization of Christianity. "Dogma in its conception and development is a work of the Greek spirit on the soil of the Gospel" (1976, 1:17). But Harnack's thesis has gone out of style, and a fresh preoccupation with the dogma of the Trinity and its pertinence to Christian faith and life is characteristic of both Catholic and Protestant theology today. Our threefold agenda will be to trace the emergence of the dogma in the ancient church, to see what Calvin and Schleiermacher made of it, and to comment on the renewed interest in it at the present time.

I. The Dogma of the Holy Trinity

Neither the term "Trinity" nor a doctrine of the Trinity appears in the New Testament. The three names are formally correlated only once: in the commission of the risen Jesus to the eleven disciples they are treated as together a single name.[1] According to Matthew, the disciples were instructed to baptize "in the name [*eis to onoma*] of the Father and of the Son and of the Holy Spirit" (Matt. 28:19). But since the first Christian communities, as reported in Acts, did not baptize in the threefold name, Matthew's wording of the commission was presumably influenced by later practice. Paul's threefold blessing at the end of 2 Corinthians is also pertinent despite lacking the actual names "Father" and "Son": "The grace of the Lord Jesus Christ, the love of God, and the communion of the Holy Spirit be with all of you" (2 Cor. 13:14). This, of course, is not a *doctrine* of the Trinity, and in Scripture the identity of the Christian God is more often reflected in the formula "[God] the Father of Jesus Christ." But we can say that Paul's threefold benediction pointed forward to the ecclesiastical dogma, and it is true that the framers of the dogma believed they were simply putting together the individual pieces of biblical testimony to Father, Son, and Spirit. However, the Pauline benediction implicitly raises one of the first questions to engage the theologians of the early church: What is the relationship between Christ and God, here so plainly distinguished? In due course, the further question had to be addressed: What is the relationship between Christ's activity and the activity of the Spirit? This is the question we must turn to next.

1. Christ and the Spirit

The postcanonical progress of christological doctrine from the Apostolic Fathers to the Council of Chalcedon (451) has been traced already (in chap. 11). But it would oversimplify the development of Trinitarian thinking to assume that it was only, or even mainly, about the divinity of Christ. Justin Martyr made clear that for him, as we have seen, the question was not how to reconcile the church's adoration of the Redeemer with Jewish monotheism but how to reconcile the Old Testament manifestations of God with the transcendent deity of Middle Platonism. His solution was to argue that besides the ineffable Father there is his Son, the divine Logos, and it was he who walked the earth and talked with humans. A similar argument appears in Tertullian, and the philosophical idea of the ineffable Absolute continued to influence patristic thinking about God. Cyril Richardson argued in an acute study (1958) that the doctrine of the Trinity was developed in answer to the problem of God Absolute and God Related and that it failed because Father-Son language is not well suited to describe either the Absolute God or the equal deity of the Son.

Whichever way the beginning of Trinitarian thinking is framed—as a question about the deity of the Son or a question about the relation of the Absolute God to the world and humanity—the place of the Holy Spirit was not at first a focus of discussion. The creed promulgated by the Council of Nicaea (325) followed its detailed affirmation of belief in the Lord Jesus Christ with the laconic afterthought: "And in the Holy Spirit." No elaboration was added. Our

1. Sometimes the Father is less formally linked with Christ/the Lord and the Spirit (Acts 2:33; Eph. 2:18; 4:4–6; 1 Pet. 1:2; cf. Rom. 1:1–4); and sometimes the triad is *God*—Christ/Lord—Spirit (Rom. 15:15–16; 1 Cor. 12:4–6; Jude 20–21). See also Eph. 1:17, where the Father is "the God of our Lord Jesus Christ" and spirit is "a spirit of wisdom and revelation." The Trinitarian formula in 1 John 5:7 may be set aside because it lacks strong manuscript support (see NRSV).

Nicene Creed, adopted by the Council of Constantinople (381), went further: it identified the Holy Spirit as "the Lord and giver of life, who proceeds from the Father"[2] and is worshipped and glorified with the Father and the Son. As the Council of Nicaea's formula "of the same substance [*homoousios*] with the Father" excluded Arian denial of the equal deity of the Son, so the fathers at the Council of Constantinople excluded the so-called Macedonian denial of the deity of the Holy Spirit. But their creed did not extend the *homoousios* formula to the Spirit; they added only that the Spirit spoke through the prophets. And there lay an obvious problem: when the Holy Spirit moved toward the center of Trinitarian thinking, it was difficult to distinguish what the Spirit did from the activity of the Logos or Word, God's Son.

The root meaning of the biblical words translated "spirit" (Hebrew *rûaḥ*; Greek *pneuma*) is "breath" or "(strong) wind," and it is not always possible to tell whether they are being used literally or metaphorically (Gen. 1:2; Ezek. 1:12; 37:5–9, 14). The ambiguity is the basis of the wordplay in Jesus' conversation with Nicodemus (John 3:8). "The wind [*pneuma*] blows where it chooses. . . . So it is with everyone who is born of the Spirit [*pneumatos*]." "Spirit" is contrasted with "flesh" (*sarx*): "What is born of the flesh is flesh, and what is born of the Spirit is spirit" (v. 6). In John's restrictive usage, "spirit" differentiates the supernatural domain, the heavenly realm above, from the merely natural, earthly realm of the flesh (vv. 3, 6–7, 12–13; 8:23; cf. Rom. 8:5; 1 Cor. 2:9–16). Elsewhere, it refers to an aspect of common human nature—the breath of life, which humans share with animals (Gen. 6:17; Ps. 104:29; etc.). When it refers to God and God's activity in the Hebrew Scriptures, "spirit" suggests divine energy, a supernatural force: creating, inspiring, empowering (Gen. 1:2; Num. 11:25; Judg. 14:6; Ps. 104:30); sometimes driving to frenzy, sometimes imparting the calmer gifts of wisdom and knowledge (1 Sam. 19:20–24; Isa. 11:2).

Crucial for our present theme are the New Testament testimonies to the bond of the Spirit with Christ. In the Gospel of Luke, the story of Jesus, at each step on the way, is told as a work of the Holy Spirit: Jesus' conception, baptism, temptation, mission, teaching, praying, and working miracles are all traced to the agency of the Spirit (Luke 1:35; 3:21–22; 4:1, 14–19; 10:21; 12:10 [with Mark 3:22–30]). John the Baptist foretells that the coming one will baptize with the Holy Spirit (Luke 3:16). Jesus promises his disciples that the Holy Spirit will teach them what to say when they have to defend themselves against those who afflict them (12:11–12). And it is the exalted Jesus, according to Luke's report in his sequel, the Acts of the Apostles, who pours out the Holy Spirit on the day of Pentecost (Acts 2:33).

In the Gospel of John, the notion of the Spirit as spokesperson on behalf of the disciples is developed in the sayings about "another advocate," "intercessor," or "helper" (*allos paraklētos*). To the four explicit Paraclete sayings (John

2. The addition "and from the Son" (one word in Latin: *filioque*) was inserted into the Western version of the Nicene Creed, perhaps in the sixth or the seventh century; it was made a matter of controversy by Charlemagne (742–814 CE), who accused the Eastern Orthodox of *removing* it. The *filioque* remains a divisive issue between East and West. The NT sometimes refers to the Spirit of God (Matt. 3:16; 12:28; Rom. 8:9, 14; 1 Cor. 2:11, 14; 3:16; 6:11; 7:40; 12:3; 2 Cor. 3:3; Eph. 4:30; 1 Thess. 4:8; 1 John 4:13) or of the Father (Matt. 10:20; Luke 11:13); sometimes to the Spirit of Christ (Gal. 4:6; 2 Cor. 3:17; Phil. 1:19; 1 Pet. 1:11); and sometimes a reference to God's spirit, or Jesus' spirit, does not intend the Holy Spirit at all (e.g., when Jesus is said to have "sighed deeply in his spirit" [Mark 8:12]).

14:15–17; 14:25–26; 15:26–27; 16:5–11) we may add 16:12–15, where the title of the Paraclete "Spirit of truth" appears without the name. The general sense of these passages is clear: Jesus is returning to the Father, from whom he came, and the Father, or Jesus himself, will send another Advocate to be with the disciples. The role of the Paraclete is to remind them of all Jesus has said to them: he will take what is his and declare it to them. The Paraclete will be Jesus' witness (15:26). Jesus even tells the disciples: "it is to your advantage that I go away, for if I do not go away, the Advocate will not come to you; but if I go, I will send him to you" (16:7). In view of the great "I am" sayings in the Fourth Gospel, it would be absurd to infer that henceforth Jesus will be strictly *absent.* His injunction to abide in him as the True Vine (15:1–6), for instance, could hardly have been superseded with his departure to the Father. It is precisely the role of the Paraclete to make Jesus present, but *in another mode.* That the true Spirit "abides with you, and he will be in [or among] you" means: "I will not leave you orphaned; I am coming to you" (14:17–18; cf. v. 23). Why, then, is it an advantage for him to go away? Christian interpreters have commonly argued that Christ's presence in the Holy Spirit liberates him from the temporal and spatial limits of individual bodily existence: in the Spirit he reaches out, beyond first-century Palestine, to people of every place and time. This is not explicit in the texts, but perhaps there is at least a hint of it in Jesus' words, "I will ask the Father, and he will give you another Advocate, to be with you *forever*" (14:16; my emphasis). Toward the end of the Gospel (20:22), we are told that it was the risen Lord in person who bestowed the Spirit on the disciples: "he breathed on them and said to them, 'Receive the Holy Spirit.'"

In 1 John the advocate (*paraklētos*) is Jesus Christ himself on the strength of his expiation of sins (1 John 2:1–2). To call him advocate *with the Father* is different from the idea of the Paraclete in John's Gospel, whose case is *against the world* (John 16:8–11); it belongs rather to the priestly work of Christ as intercessor (cf. Heb. 7:25).

In Paul both the Spirit and Christ are said to intercede for us (Rom. 8:26–27, 34), and in one and the same verse (v. 9) we find "the Spirit of God" and "the Spirit of Christ" used (it seems) interchangeably. We may well wonder how, then, Paul understands the relationship between God, Christ, and the Spirit in this passage. But he is not doing systematic theology or offering dogmatic definitions, and it is more important to note the progress of his argument. *Pneuma,* which seldom appears in chapters 1–7, appears more than twenty times in chapter 8. The previous chapters have been concerned mainly with the righteousness of God through faith in Jesus Christ (3:22) and what it means to be no longer under law but under grace (6:15). In chapter 8 the perspective shifts from Christ *for* us to Christ *in* us, and Christ in us is the indwelling of the Spirit (8:9–11). In other places, too, Paul conveys the intimate relationship between Christ and the Spirit. "God has sent the Spirit of his Son into our hearts, crying, 'Abba! Father!'" (Gal. 4:6; cf. Rom. 8:14–17). "[N]o one can say 'Jesus is Lord' except by the Holy Spirit" (1 Cor. 12:3). It is one and the same Spirit that activates the many gifts bestowed on the body of Christ (1 Cor. 12:11). The virtues of those who belong to Christ are fruits of the Spirit (Gal. 5:22–26). In one place, Paul seems to *identify* Christ with the

Spirit: "Now the Lord is the Spirit, and where the Spirit of the Lord is, there is freedom" (2 Cor. 3:17; cf. v. 18).[3]

The original sense of the biblical words *rûaḥ* and *pneuma* invites the perception of the Holy Spirit as a divine function or an impersonal force, represented in Christian art as a dove or a flame rather than a person. But to speak of another Advocate, and of the Spirit's interceding with the Father, points to something more: a "he" rather than an "it." The Holy Spirit is other than Jesus, who sends the Advocate in his place, and other than the Father, with whom the Spirit intercedes. The impetus is clearly toward thinking of the Holy Spirit as a person, although the intercession of which Paul speaks is nonverbal ("with sighs too deep for words," Rom. 8:26). Once theological interest shifts to the neglected Spirit, the challenge is to show how—if faith acknowledges God not only in the Father, but also in the Son and the Spirit—the three are somehow one. "One substance [*ousia*], three persons [*hypostaseis*]," became the orthodox formula. The terms and the relations between them, however, were not always taken in the same sense, and it is usually said that Trinitarian thinking developed in two directions.

2. *Two Kinds of Trinity*

Athanasius, the great adversary of Arian Christology, led the way by convincing the Council of Alexandria (362) that the Holy Spirit, too, is of the same substance as the Father, not a "creature." But peace among the dissenting parties was mainly the achievement of the Cappadocian Fathers: Basil and the two Gregories (Gregory of Nyssa and Gregory Nazianzus). The creed of the Council of Nicaea had used the two Greek words *ousia* and *hypostasis* interchangeably, condemning those who asserted that the Son of God is "of a different *hypostasis* or *ousia*" than the Father. Basil of Caesarea (d. 379) wrote, possibly to his younger brother, Gregory of Nyssa (d. ca. 395),[4] that the two terms were better distinguished, and he recommended as analogy the distinction between man in general and a particular man. In the former use we employ the noun to indicate the common nature of humanity; but to refer to any one man, such as Peter or John, requires some note of distinction. Those who share a common nature or essence are *homoousioi*; what distinguishes them individually is indicated by the term *hypostasis* (Letter 38, NPNF^2 8:137; cf. Letter 214, NPNF^2 8:254). Basil tried to specify what belongs to the shared nature of Father, Son, and Spirit and what distinguishes them. He admitted that his talk of "conjoined separation and separated conjunction" had its limits. "Yet receive what I say as at best a token and reflection of the truth; not as the actual truth itself" (139).

The risk of the human analogy is that it may be taken to imply that there are three gods, just as Peter, James, and John are three men. Father, Son, and Spirit would then be instances of a class, and that would be polytheism. In

3. Some interpreters maintain that because 2 Cor. 3:16 echoes Exod. 34:34, "the Lord" in v. 17 must refer to God, not Christ; and "the glory of the Lord" in v. 18 (cf. 4:6) is likely suggested by the same passage in Exodus. However, Paul says in 2 Cor. 3:14–15 that "only in Christ is [the veil] set aside" and that "when one turns to the Lord, the veil is removed." There, at least, "the Lord" surely means Christ.

4. The attribution of Letter 38 to Basil is disputed; it is possible that Gregory of Nyssa was the author, not the recipient. Either way, it speaks for the Cappadocian approach to the Trinity.

Not Three Gods (ca. 375), his reply to Ablabius, Gregory of Nyssa argues that "deity" (*theotēs*) does not refer to God's nature, which is ineffable, but to God's operation; and that when we speak of God as overseer of the universe, the operation of oversight is not assigned to any one person of the Trinity. "Rather does every operation which extends from God to creation . . . have its origin in the Father, proceed through the Son, and reach its completion by the Holy Spirit. . . . No activity is distinguished among the Persons, as if it were brought to completion individually by each of them or separately apart from their joint supervision." Thus there are not three gods: the unity of operation forbids the plural (LCC 3:261–64; cf. NPNF[2] 5:334–35).[5] Gregory's notion of the "joint supervision" of Father, Son, and Spirit anticipated the later term *perichōrēsis,* the mutual indwelling of the persons, which better preserved Trinitarian activity from being construed as the cooperation of three individuals, each of whom does part of an operation.

In his great work *On the Trinity,* Augustine wrote the classic treatise on the subject in the Latin West. Begun around 399 CE and not finished until some two decades later, it is a challenging work of intricate theological reasoning; Augustine feared that few would be able to understand it. His achievement was to transplant the Trinitarian thinking of the Greeks further into Latin and to develop a distinctive alternative to the Cappadocian Trinity. In terminology that owed its currency to Tertullian, the Greek words *ousia* and *hypostasis* had been put into Latin as *substantia* and *persona* (anglicized as "substance" and "person"). Augustine was not happy with either term.[6] He preferred "essence" to "substance" and professed himself unable to understand the distinction the Greeks drew between *ousia* and *hypostasis.* Translated into Latin, "one *ousia,* three *hypostaseis,*" would be "one *essentia,* three *substantiae,*" two words that mean the same. Augustine reluctantly acquiesced in what had become, by his time, the standard use of *persona* for whatever it is that distinguishes Father, Son, and Spirit. But he acquiesced not so much to say something as not to say nothing (NPNF[1] 3:92). The point was to rule out heretical alternatives. To the modalists, for instance, Father, Son, and Spirit were simply attributes of one and the same God. Orthodoxy needed a term to indicate that, although the three are equally God, the Father is not the Son and the Spirit is neither the Son nor the Father. Moreover, "God" is not to be taken generically, as though Father, Son, and Spirit were instances of a class: the essence is identical in them all "as if according to a matter that is common and the same," like the gold in statues (NPNF[1] 3:109, 112).

Augustine's divergence from the Cappadocians appears in the analogies by which he attempts to shed light on the mystery of the three in one. He thinks

5. To his opponents' insistence that "deity" must refer to God's nature, not God's operation, and that Father, Son, and Spirit are *not* of the same nature, Gregory replies that the sole way of distinguishing the persons from one another is by the concept of causation, which refers not to nature but to "mode of existence." The Father is uncaused, while the Son and the Spirit are dependent on the Father as cause. "The principle of causality distinguishes, then, the Persons of the Holy Trinity" (LCC 3:267).

6. NT usage does not help. *Ousia* appears only twice, both times in the parable of the Prodigal Son, where it means "wealth" or "property" (Luke 15:12–13; in v. 13 KJV has "wasted his substance"). The slippery term *hypostasis* occurs five times. NRSV translates it three times as "confidence" (2 Cor. 11:17; Heb. 3:14) or "assurance" (Heb. 11:1), once as an "undertaking" (2 Cor. 9:4). The pertinent use for the doctrine of God is in Heb. 1:3: the Son is called "the exact imprint of God's very being [*hypostasis*]." That, however, is what the Greek Fathers meant by the *other* term: God's *ousia.*

of the three *personae* in terms of relations, not substances. (It is the entire Trinity that is one *substantia*.) We speak of Father, Son, and Spirit relatively to one another: the Father as begetting the Son, the Son as begotten by the Father, and the Spirit as proceeding from both (NPNF[1] 3:93, 225–26). Although there are vestiges of the Trinity everywhere in creation, the best analogies are to be found in humanity, for a man is made in the image of God. Augustine considers first the nature of human love, in which he distinguishes a trinity of the one that loves, who (or what) is loved, and the love that unites them (123–24). But he finds the analogy of love inadequate—as well he might, seeing that love for brother or neighbor is love between individual persons in *our* sense. He moves on to analysis of the inner consciousness of a single man and comes up with three analogies that he finds, as far as they go, more satisfactory: the mind, its knowledge of itself, and its love of itself; memory, understanding, and will; remembering, knowing, and loving God (127–29, 142–43, 191–94; cf. the recapitulation on 201–2).

The long history of the Augustinian tradition in the Trinitarian reflections of the West cannot be reviewed here. It must suffice to have shown that in the ancient church two types of Trinitarianism developed within the limits of the orthodox formula, "One substance, three persons." In the standard reading of the story, one party started from the three and arrived at the one by means of a *social* analogy; the other started from the one and arrived at the three by means of *psychological* analogies. In fact, both parties used both kinds of analogy, but the emphasis was different, and it warrants talk of two types of Trinity. Each pushes close to heresy, only at opposite ends of the Trinitarian spectrum: the Cappadocians had to insist that the social analogy did not mean tritheism, and the Augustinians denied that the psychological analogies meant modalism. The tension between the two continues in present-day attempts to formulate a viable doctrine of the Trinity. But we will look first at what Calvin and Schleiermacher made of it.

II. The Trinity in Calvin and Schleiermacher

Calvin's placement of the Trinity in the first book of the 1559 *Institutes* (chap. 13), under the Knowledge of God the *Creator*, is open to criticism. He reminds us several times that he is not yet speaking of redemption or the person of the Mediator. He believes that Christ, as the Word of God, was active already in the Old Testament (*Institutes*, 1:133, 156). But his concern is to defend the deity of Christ against the rise of anti-Trinitarianism (122 n. 5), and it makes little sense to exclude the knowledge of God the *Redeemer* from his defense. The problem is mitigated if we note that, despite the overall rubric of book 1, Calvin does not deal with creation until *after* the chapter on the Trinity, and most of what comes *before* his doctrine of the Trinity could be called "introduction." But the difficulty is not entirely resolved. Despite his announced postponement of redemption, Calvin finds it impossible not to introduce New Testament proofs of Christ's divinity (134–38). Moreover, his arrangement fosters the common misconception that his doctrine of God is completed in the chapters on providence in book 1—supplemented (of course!) by just the chapters on predestination pulled out from book 3. There is much more to the knowledge of God the Redeemer in Christ than the doctrine of predestination, and it must inform any doctrine of the Trinity.

Calvin takes his stand on the traditional dogma that God is a single, undivided essence subsisting in three persons. He generally prefers *essentia* to *substantia* and recommends *subsistentia*, rather than *persona*, as the Latin for the Greek word *hypostasis*. "'Person,' therefore, I call a 'subsistence' in God's essence, which, while related to the others, is distinguished by an incommunicable quality [*proprietate*]. . . . Nor am I displeased with Tertullian's definition, provided it be taken in the right sense, that there is a kind of distribution or economy in God which has no effect on the unity of essence" (*Institutes*, 1:128). What, then, *are* the distinguishing properties of Father, Son, and Spirit? Calvin answers: "to the Father is attributed the beginning of activity [*principium agendi*], and the fountain and wellspring of all things; to the Son, wisdom, counsel, and the ordered disposition of all things [*in rebus agendis*]; but to the Spirit is assigned the power and efficacy of that activity [*virtus et efficacia actionis*]" (142–43). It is then Calvin's delicate task to insist that although the Father is rightly deemed "the beginning and fountainhead of the whole of divinity [*divinitatis*]"—we can even say that the name "God" applies peculiarly to him—Christ does not receive his deity (*deitas*) from the Father but has it in his own right. Not the *deity* but the *person* of the Son is from the Father (152–54).

The accusation of Pierre Caroli that Calvin's refusal to subscribe to the ecumenical creeds betrayed a closet Arianism was mistaken. But Calvin was never at ease with the language of the inherited Trinitarian dogma. He wished that such unbiblical terms as *persona, trinitas,* and *homoousios* could all be buried. True, they say no more than Scripture attests, and they are justified by the need to unmask heretics. But Calvin's chapter on the Trinity is suffused with a characteristic reserve, lest practical knowledge of God be overshadowed by "any idle speculation." "There, indeed, does the pious mind perceive the very presence of God, and almost touches him, when it feels itself quickened, illumined, preserved, justified, and sanctified" (*Institutes*, 1:138). This is followed by a brief but strikingly experiential demonstration of the deity of the Spirit (138–40; cf. 537–42). For Calvin, what the Christian knows of God is rooted in experience and normed by Scripture; he is reluctant to move beyond experience and Scripture into speculation. The attempt to find analogies of the Trinity in humanity he considers fruitless. In his commentary on Genesis 1:26, he singles out Augustine's analogical speculations as particularly overdone (though he grudgingly allows anyone who has the time to look into some of his favorite Father's book *On the Trinity*). We should play the philosopher "soberly and with great moderation," remembering that "men's minds, when they indulge their curiosity, enter into a labyrinth." Following Hilary's advice, we must be willing to leave to God the knowledge of himself (*Institutes*, 1:146; cf. 164).

Schleiermacher rejects the usual arrangement, in which a finished locus on God appears early in a theological system, before all the fundamental facts of Christian faith have been laid out: "the doctrine of God, as set forth in the totality of the divine attributes, can only be completed simultaneously with the whole system" (*CF* 128; cf. 749–50). His own procedure, accordingly, is to include in each of the three main themes of *The Christian Faith*—the religious consciousness of world, sin, and grace—a statement on its meaning for the doctrine of God. The third and final section on the Christian consciousness of grace ends with the divine attributes that relate to redemption: love and wisdom. Recognition of God's love comes only with redemption, and wisdom is the principle that orders the world for love, which is God's self-imparting (728–29, 732; cf. 741). But why add the conclusion on the Trinity (738–51)?

Something like Calvin's reserve with respect to the doctrine of the Trinity reappears in Schleiermacher as a methodological principle that distinguishes dogmatics from philosophy. The problem is that the orthodox doctrine of the Trinity loses the anchorage of dogmatics in Christian experience, and we must oppose real Christian dogmatics to the scholastic confusion of it with speculative philosophy (*CF* 122). Not that speculation is presumptuous and unedifying, as Calvin could say; but it follows a different methodological procedure than dogmatics. Dogmatic propositions arise out of reflection on Christian faith—the Christian religious consciousness (82). And "the assumption of an eternal distinction in the Supreme Being [*im höchsten Wesen*] is not an utterance concerning the religious consciousness, for there it never could emerge" (739; cf. 144, 748–50).

It is a mistake, frequently made, to dismiss Schleiermacher's conclusion on the Trinity as a feeble afterthought that only proves he attached no importance to the doctrine. On the contrary, his conclusion treats the Trinity as the "keystone" of Christian doctrine (*Schlußstein:* Eng. trans. "coping-stone"). As a keystone is set in place to finish an arch and lock the whole together, *what is essential* in the doctrine of the Trinity draws together everything he has been saying about redemption, which presupposes the union of the divine essence with human nature in both the personality of Christ and the common Spirit of the church.[7] But there Schleiermacher calls a halt because, given his dogmatic method, he sees no way to trace the twofold union back to a distinction within the divine essence itself. In any case, our living fellowship with Christ needs no knowledge of any such transcendent fact (*CF* 738–39, 741).

When the first edition of *The Christian Faith* (1821–22) appeared, Schleiermacher published as a supplement a long article contrasting the Sabellian and the Athanasian doctrines of the Trinity (1822). In fact, it is mostly about Sabellius and the modalists, and it continues to be the best place for understanding Schleiermacher's brief allusion to "the Sabellian view" in the second edition of *The Christian Faith* (*CF* 750). The article is not simply an endorsement of Sabellius, as is sometimes supposed, but an erudite effort to determine from the ambiguous sources what his view was; to untangle it from other modalist views; and to urge that the church, which never examined Sabellianism as thoroughly as Arianism, should take it into account in future reconstruction of the doctrine of the Trinity.

7. Schleiermacher did not attempt to unify everything Scripture says about God's Spirit (*CF* §123.1 [570]). By the Holy Spirit in the church he meant the "common Spirit" (*Gemeingeist*) of the new corporate life, which, though unique as established by Christ, can be compared with the common spirit generated in other enduring, as distinct from transient, human associations, e.g., a nation that has a distinctive national character (§121 [560–65]). This it is that presupposes a second union of the divine essence with human nature "in so far as in its operations it meets us within our Christian self-consciousness" (§123.1 [569]).

The prevailing view was (and still is) that for the modalist monarchians "Father," "Son," and "Spirit" were not distinct hypostases but attributes or names of the one God who reveals himself in creation, the incarnation, and the church. The orthodox objection was twofold: that modalism "crucifies the Father" and turns the Son and the Spirit into transient moments in the life of the one God. Schleiermacher argues that Sabellius at least, properly understood, was not exposed to the two standard criticisms but should be hailed as the one who could save the orthodox doctrine of the Trinity from its ineradicable subordination of the Son to the Father. Sabellius held that the Son is not derived from the Father: all three persons of the Trinity proceed from the One, and as such they are equal (1835, 6:48). The divine One is the hidden God; the Trinity is God revealed. The Father is God continually revealed in the works of creation; the Son is God revealed in human flesh; and the Spirit is God revealed in the church. But what first comes to be in the Son and the Spirit is not transient but enduring (53, 59). Father, Son, and Spirit, though not eternal hypostases, are not mere names or attributes of the One; they are particular modes of revelation (61). In Sabellius's term they are *prosōpa*, and Schleiermacher takes a *prosōpon* to be, for Sabellius, a figure of speech signifying a countenance or visage presented to our apprehension (66)—meaning, I take it (in Schleiermacher's language), the way we perceive and represent the twofold union of the divine essence with human nature.

There are many historical and dogmatic questions one might wish to put to these reflections, briefly rehearsed in the second edition of *The Christian Faith* (*CF* 742–51). Schleiermacher offers them only as a first step toward a reconstruction of a doctrine of the Trinity that looks back to its beginnings. His fundamental principle is that dogmatics "has only to do with the God-consciousness given in our self-consciousness along with our consciousness of the world" (748). Dogmatics is about God in relation, not the being of God in himself. But is it possible that Schleiermacher transgresses his own dogmatic boundaries? Perhaps he could justify the identification of God's essence with love, since love is simply "the inclination [*Richtung*] to unite oneself with an other and to will to be in an other" (726, alt.)—a clear implication of redemption as the twofold union of the divine essence with human nature in Christ and the Spirit. We may see no violation of his fundamental dogmatic principle even when Schleiermacher suggests that it might be better not to refer the term "Father" to a distinction in the divine essence (as in the ecclesiastical dogma) but "rather to the unity of the of the Divine Essence as such" (751). But how can Schleiermacher know the simplicity of God—that is, the inappropriateness of positing distinctions within the divine essence—except by importing a speculative idea?[8] He is right in granting that more remains to be done (749).

III. Trinitarian Theology Today

1. *Fresh Approaches*

The alleged neglect of the doctrine of the Trinity in the nineteenth century has been exaggerated, but in the twentieth century it did become a subject of more

8. "Simplicity" does not mean only the absence of parts. "For the relative separation of function itself conflicts with simplicity" (*CF* §56 [231]).

intense theological interest, and the flow of books and articles on the Trinity continues.[9] The influence of two of the most eminent theologians of the time, Protestant Karl Barth and Catholic Karl Rahner, was pivotal. The special place of the Trinity in Barth's *Church Dogmatics* is credited with quickening a constructive reassessment of the doctrine in Protestant theology, which had often been critical, sometimes even dismissive, of it.

The old systems of Reformed dogmatics began by establishing the authority of Scripture as the sole dogmatic norm (Heppe 1950: 12). *Barth's* prolegomena to his *Church Dogmatics* work with a more complex concept of the revealed, written, and proclaimed Word as *Dei loquentis persona,* God speaking in person (*CD* I/1:136). No doctrine of the Trinity as such is to be found in Scripture, but in Scripture, Barth says, God reveals himself as the Lord (especially in the proclamation of the kingdom), and God's self-unveiling as Lord is the root of the doctrine of the Trinity. "We arrive at the doctrine of the Trinity by no other way than that of an analysis of the concept of revelation." In this sense, "the doctrine of the Trinity is a work of the Church" (312, 308; cf. 333). God the Lord reveals himself three times: in his inscrutability apart from his own free act, in his self-impartation to humanity, and in his coming to individual persons (325–26, 331). There is a "threeness" of revealer, revelation, and revealedness (295).[10]

Rather than talking of three "persons," which risks obscuring the unity of God, Barth proposes "modes [or ways] of being" (*Seinsweisen*). Father, Son, and Spirit are "three modes of being of the one God subsisting in their relationships with one another" (348, 359–60). The interrelationship of the three rules out the heresy of modalism, and Barth presents God the Father first as Creator, then as the *eternal* Father; God the Son first as Reconciler, then as the *eternal* Son; God the Holy Spirit first as Redeemer, then as the *eternal* Spirit (§§10–12). This requires him to borrow extensively from themes only to be developed later in the *Church Dogmatics.* The economic Trinity of God in his works is the sole route to knowledge of the immanent Trinity of God in himself, and it is the self-*distinction* in God himself that makes his self-*disclosure* as Father, Son, and Spirit possible (318; cf. 382). God can reveal himself as Father and can *be* our Father because he is eternally Father of the Son: "fatherhood is an eternal mode of being of the divine essence" (390).

What, then, is the point of placing the doctrine of the Trinity in prolegomena? "In giving this doctrine a place of prominence," Barth says, "our concern cannot be merely that it have this place externally but rather that its content be decisive and controlling for the whole of dogmatics" (*CD* I/1:303). More precisely it is the revelation of God in Jesus Christ, the second of the Trinitarian modes of being, that must control everything else (314–15). Barth's repudiation of natural theology applies even to the use of worldly analogies for the relations

9. In the final chapter of his important study *Nicaea and Its Legacy,* Lewis Ayres argues that the Trinitarian "revival" actually fails to engage the Nicene legacy, when correctly understood. But I cannot go into his arguments here.

10. The German word *Offenbarungsein,* here translated "revealedness," is difficult to put into ordinary English; elsewhere it is translated "revealing" or "being revealed" (e.g., *CD* I/1:314 [§8.2]). This, the third concept in Barth's threefold analysis, highlights the unpredictable *event* of revelation (in the Spirit) as distinct from *who* reveals (the Father) and *what* is revealed (through the Son). "We had Pentecost in view when we called revelation an event that from man's standpoint has dropped down vertically from heaven" (331). While there is a givenness or objectivity of the Father's revelation in the Son, "[t]he Spirit guarantees man . . . his personal [subjective] participation in revelation" (449, 453 [§12.1]).

among the three persons of the Trinity. "Is not even the desire to illustrate revelation . . . already to be regarded as tantamount to a desertion of revelation?" (345, 347). The same christocentric principle leads Barth to insist that the *Deus absconditus* and the *Deus revelatus* (the hidden God and the revealed God) are one and the same God, who hides himself in his self-revelation. "As a matter of fact even Jesus did not become revelation to all who met Him but only to a few" (321–23, 330). Luther rightly spoke of God veiled in his revelation; but he also spoke, in *The Bondage of the Will*, of God apart from his revelation in Christ,[11] and this Barth firmly repudiates. There is no decision of God apart from Christ, though God remains mystery even in his free decision to reveal himself (II/1:541–42; II/2:65–66).

Rahner's contribution is presented in his seminal essay *The Trinity*, which first appeared in German in 1967. The neoscholastic textbooks had treated the doctrine of the Trinity as an isolated locus unconnected with the theme of salvation. Rahner protests: "we can really grasp the content of the doctrine of the Trinity only by going back to the history of salvation and of grace, to our experience of Jesus and of the Spirit of God, who operates in us, because in them we really already possess the Trinity itself as such" (1997: 40). Hence, what has become known as "Rahner's Rule" states (in his own italicized words): *"The 'economic' Trinity is the 'immanent' Trinity and the 'immanent' Trinity is the 'economic' Trinity"* (22). He can say this because God's revelation, as he understands it, is the actual self-imparting of the Trinity—not just the information that God is three in one. It follows that the God who is revealed to us as Father, Son, and Spirit (the economic Trinity) is God as he is in himself (the immanent Trinity). Without the actual presence of the Trinity in revelation, there could be no true self-communication of God (38, 55, 100).

The distinctions between the three persons, however, are not just nominal. "[E]ach one of the three divine persons," Rahner says, "communicates himself to man in gratuitous grace in his own personal particularity and diversity" (1997: 34–35). Thus, for example, only the second person of the Trinity could become incarnate (23). What, then, *is* a "person" in its Trinitarian sense? Rahner proposes "distinct mode of subsisting" (*Subsistenzweise*) as a modification of Barth's "mode of being" (*Seinsweise*), not to replace "person," which is sanctioned by the Catholic Church, but to explain it (44, 74, 110). But because the history of salvation is twofold—it is about the activity of Christ and the Holy Spirit—there is an important difference between the person of the Father and the other two persons of the Trinity. In Scripture "God" (without qualification) refers to the Father, and the theologians of the ancient church spoke of the Father as the unoriginate origin of the Son and the Spirit (18, 78). He is already Father before he is revealed as such, and we are not to conceive of a divine essence, or God in himself, *behind* the person of the Father (17, 60, 112).

Although Barth and Rahner expressly warned against taking "person" in its presumed modern sense—as an individual center of consciousness—Barth used language that, taken at face value, could imply that Father, Son, and Spirit

11. That God does not desire the death of a sinner (Ezek. 18:23) refers, in Luther's view, not to his revealed will but to his dread, hidden will that foreordains some to accept the gospel and others to reject it.

are three individual *subjects.*[12] But advocates of a "social Trinity" have charged Barth and Rahner with the opposite error: employing language that could be taken for modalist. Jürgen Moltmann, for example, in *The Trinity and the Kingdom of God* (German 1980), argues that the three persons of the Trinity are one, not as a single divine subject existing in three modes, but as a unity of *perichōrēsis* or coinherence, that is, a union *in,* not only *with,* each other (cf. John 17:21). They are not individuals who enter into relationship; they actually exist through one another, and this is the real modern sense of the word *person* (1981: 145, 150, 174–76, 201–2). Moltmann finds the practical importance of this conception in its use as a critique of inappropriate political and ecclesiastical structures: "So the Trinity corresponds to a community in which people are defined through their relations with one another and in their significance for one another, not in opposition to one another, in terms of power and possession" (198).

The idea of a social Trinity is well adapted to the liberation and political theologies of Latin America. The fundamental principle was summed up in the aphorism of Brazilian theologian Leonardo Boff: "human society is a pointer on the road to the mystery of the Trinity, while the mystery of the Trinity, as we know it from revelation, is a pointer toward social life and its archetype" (1988: 119). By invoking the concept of *perichōrēsis,* the advocates of a social Trinity may have successfully defended themselves against the charge of imagining three gods (tritheism). But it is hard not to suspect that they are framing a theological construct to suit a form of human community they would believe in without it, and that invites a Feuerbachian reduction of theological language to anthropological language about human ideals.

2. *The Trinity and Christian Dogmatics*

The Athanasian Creed identified the Catholic faith with the dogma of the Trinity and warned that anyone who failed to keep it whole would perish everlastingly. But, as the old saw has it, while a man may imperil his soul by not believing it, he imperils his wits if he tries to understand it. Renewed interest in the Trinity has stressed its connection with Christian faith and life but has not made it any more accessible to ordinary Christian believers; it remains largely the province of philosophically minded theologians, and it might be better to delegate it to philosophical rather than dogmatic theology. Insofar as doctrines of the Trinity arise out of reflection on the history and experience of redemption, a connection with dogmatics is self-evident. But if the proper task of dogmatic theologians is to give an account of the distinctive way a Christian has faith, normed by Scripture, they must preserve the focus of their discipline on actual Christian experience. Dogmatics, as I understand it, is not the whole of Christian theology but "theology within the limits of piety alone."

There will always be differences of opinion about the biblical norm—about what is "either expressly set down in Scripture, or by good and necessary

12. See, e.g., Barth, *CD* I/1:139–40 (§5.2). The intention of such language is not to imagine the Trinitarian *personae* as three "Thous" in commerce with one another but to maintain that "the being of God is being-in-relation" (Robinson 2006: 333). Barth had no difficulty with the concept of the *one God* as a self-conscious Thou (cf. Rahner 1997, 75–76, 107), but the difficulty then is how to preserve the notion that the relationships among the three *personae* are relationships of mutual love.

consequence may be deduced from Scripture" (Westminster Confession 1.6). It is especially difficult to adjudicate between interpretations when the testimony of Scripture is diverse. However, I venture to offer some brief observations in line with my conclusions in previous chapters, my review of some types of Trinitarian thinking in the present chapter, and my understanding of the limits of dogmatic theology.

(1) The Trinity is not a revealed doctrine but the product of reflection on revelation, by which I mean reflection on *a particular story that includes the call of Israel, the gift of the law, and the manifestation of the gospel in Jesus Christ* (thesis 9). While the assumed priority of the "triune" God in the order of *being* may recommend discussion of the doctrine at the beginning of dogmatics, the priority of revelation in the order of *knowing* justifies placement at the end, when the history of redemption and its sequel in the beginnings of the church have been told. Ruled out is treatment of the Trinity in a self-contained locus that follows a general *locus de Deo* and precedes even a brief, proleptic account of redemption. But it remains a difficulty that the idea of a triune God, wherever placed in a dogmatic system, arises from a variety of scriptural testimonies that are not easily put together, and the church's dogma by no means excludes variety.

(2) The ecclesiastical dogma of the Trinity is summed up in the formula, "One substance, three persons," intended to fence the Christian doctrine of God against both polytheism and modalism. However, no authoritative definitions of the terms "substance" and "person" accompany the formula. Even the expression "of the same substance" (*homoousios*) proved to be ambiguous in the controversy over Arianism: it could be taken for either generic or numerical identity. To give a standard if crude illustration: Two wooden platters are of the same substance because each is made of wood, but they need not have been made from the same piece of wood. What, then, can dogmatics say about the three "persons" in the one divine "substance"?

(3) God is *the Father* preeminently as "the God and Father of Jesus Christ." But Christian faith does not restrict the metaphor of "Father" to God's relationship with Jesus Christ; the christological reference determines, rather, how Christians *perceive* divine fatherhood. A Father-God appears in other religions (Dyaus-pitar, Zeus Pater, Jupiter, etc.); Hebrew religion, which provides the particular form of theism presupposed by Christian faith, likens God to a father as both procreator and provider. In the New Testament "God" evidently refers to the Father-God, and postcanonical theologians gave precedence to the Father as the "unoriginate origin" of all—even though this made it a challenge to explain the assumed equality of Father, Son, and Holy Spirit. The Apostles' Creed begins with "God the Father Almighty, Maker of Heaven and Earth," then moves on to "Jesus Christ his only Son."

(4) The three "persons" of the Trinity have to do with God's threefold relation to the world, in general and in two particular histories. The dogma exists to affirm the redemptive activity of the Father Almighty in the history of a singular human being, his Son, and in the history of the singular human community the Son brought into existence. Nicene orthodoxy states that *the Son* is *homoousios* with the Father and projects the historical relationship between Father and Son into eternity. Further Trinitarian reflection tries to show why this "pretemporal" relationship is necessary and how it is possible. Initially, however, we

will not say that the Son is *homoousios* with the Father but rather that God in Christ *is* the Father and that Jesus Christ was a *real* human being. The humanity of Christ is endangered in many Christologies, not all of them considered heretical,[13] and metaphor is being strained, to say the least, when one speaks of the Son being "eternally begotten," or of "God begetting himself."

(5) The Father-Son relationship is so fundamental to the God of Christian faith that theological accounts of the Christian doctrine of God sometimes appear to be binitarian rather than Trinitarian. But if, as I have shown, redemption through Jesus Christ cannot be isolated from the preceding history of the covenant of grace, neither can it be separated from the sequel in the life of the church. There are scriptural warrants for assigning the sequel to the work of *the Spirit* (as in part II, division 2, of the outline). It remains ambiguous whether the Spirit of the Father is meant, or the Spirit of Christ. Perhaps we may say *both*. In general the Spirit is a symbol of the divine energy, and in the ecclesiological context it may be taken as symbol of the divine energy mediated through Christ and continuing to create a new humanity in the church. Even the Johannine expression "another Advocate," which appears to make the Spirit numerically other than Christ, is intended to affirm the presence of Christ in another manner. Without entering into the intricacies of Trinitarian speculation, Christian faith recognizes what we may call "the dual incarnation" of God the Father Almighty, Maker of Heaven and Earth, both in the words and works of Jesus Christ and also in the community of the Spirit, which is the ecclesial body of Christ.

(6) Mainline Trinitarian theology insists that the presence of God in Jesus Christ and the church requires us to think of two further eternal hypostases in addition to the Father. There are ways of interpreting the New Testament in support of this view, including the Pauline testimony to the preexistence of the Son and the Johannine notion of another Paraclete. But orthodox Trinitarianism must be understood contextually, as refutation of particular ancient "heresies," and is not immune to critical questions in another day. To begin with, there are questions about a too literal reading of symbolic and analogical language. Further, although the possibility of distinctions within the Godhead (*Deus in se*) need not be ruled out, the supposed logical inference from what the New Testament says of Father, Son, and Holy Spirit to what "must" be affirmed about an immanent Trinity is not self-evidently convincing. Finally, debate continues about the three eternal hypostases and their interrelationships, especially when they are enlisted for ethical causes (the commandment to love or an egalitarian social order).

Thesis 20 leaves further discussion open. It does not so much present a finished doctrine of the Trinity as rehearse the point of departure for a doctrine of the Trinity. It is simply an epitome of my outline. Christian dogmatics, as I understand it, is most faithful to its task when it does not let the presumed eternal background of redemption overshadow the historical and experiential foreground. However, theologians of every sort agree that there is at least one

13. Orthodoxy rejects Docetism and Apollinarianism. But although considered orthodox, the technical Trinitarian terms *anhypostasia* and *enhypostasia*, which mean that the personal subsistence of Christ's human nature was the personal subsistence of the Logos, are also difficult to harmonize with his genuine humanity.

thing that can be said of God in Godself (*in se*). The Johannine confession "God is love," twice affirmed (1 John 4:8, 16), is the high point of Christian faith and refers to God's *nature,* not just to one divine attribute among many. "Love" has many meanings. Schleiermacher's definition—"the inclination to unite oneself with an other and the will to be in an other"—fits John's twofold evidence for the love of God: the sending of the Son and the gift of the Spirit (vv. 9, 13). That "God is love" is thus the final affirmation of my twentieth thesis: it is *both* "expressly set down in Scripture" *and* a "good and necessary consequence" of the scriptural narrative of redemption.

21. The End

Christian language about "the end" does not merely predict the temporal goal of the individual, the human race, or the world, but represents the eternal meaning of temporal existence (that is, its significance in every present moment); and this meaning is relative to the manifestation of God's glory as Creator and Redeemer, in which the final meaning of the cosmos consists.

In addressing the doctrine of the Trinity, the previous chapter offered a *retrospective* conclusion to the entire theme of Christian faith in God the Creator and God the Redeemer in Christ. The present chapter offers a *prospective* conclusion: I ask about the meaning of Christian faith for the future. In conventional Christian piety, the question is mainly about an individual afterlife or the immortality of the soul. But that imposes an unwarranted limit on the biblical witness, and these days advances in our understanding of the human species and its place in the cosmos increase the complexity of the biblical witness. Only a small fragment of the pertinent data, canonical and extracanonical, can be considered here as we pose the question more broadly: What does Christian faith *hope* for?

The biblical data show that, for Christian faith, the destiny of the individual is inseparable from the prospect for the people of God and that the believer must die and rise to newness of life even before the dissolution of the body (section I). A gap between traditional and modern ways of thinking about death and dying begins to appear in the transition from Calvin to Schleiermacher; it widens with increasing acceptance of human finitude (section II). The hope for eternal life must mediate between the old and the new, and this may be achieved by rethinking biblical eschatology and retrieving the neglected theological watchword *Soli Deo gloria*, "Glory to God alone" (section III).

I. The People, the Believer, and the New Age

The Scriptures of the Old and New Testaments are full of references to the goal toward which God is guiding history, but the end envisioned is not always the same. It is impossible to derive a single, uniform doctrine of the end from the Bible, and on the death of the individual there is a difference between the Old Testament and the New.

Hebrew faith was trust in Yahweh's promise to the chosen people. The hope of the individual was to be blessed with length of days and, when his sojourn was over, to be gathered to his people, buried with his ancestors.[1] The psalmist spoke of the "sleep" of death (Ps. 13:3), and the story of the medium of Endor rested on the belief that a spirit could be awakened and "brought up" again (1 Sam. 28:7–15). A major strand in Hebrew thought on death attests the belief, common in antiquity, of an underworld (Sheol, the Pit; Greek Hades) to which the dead are consigned. There they exist like shadows of their former selves; it is the land of forgetfulness, in which God is no longer praised (Pss. 6:5; 30:9; 88:5, 10–12; 115:17; but see 139:8). Ezekiel pictured a separate region of Sheol, "the uttermost parts of the Pit," reserved for the uncircumcised and those who had been "killed by the sword" (Ezek. 32:18–32). Of two exceptional Israelites, however, it is reported that they never died: God took Enoch and took Elijah up to heaven (Gen. 5:24; 2 Kgs. 2:1). It has been suggested that God's taking Enoch and Elijah explains two passages in the Psalter (Pss. 49:15; 73:24) that have been taken for evidence of a heavenly afterlife. But their meaning is unclear, and in any case neither of them demonstrates a general belief in individual immortality. Nor does the ending of Psalm 23: Where the KJV had, "I will dwell in the house of the LORD for ever," the NRSV reads, "I shall dwell in the house of the LORD my whole life long [for length of days]" (v. 6). What, then, is the prospect for the chosen people as a whole?

The vision of the prophets foresees the blessing of a new age to come, a time of justice, peace, and plenty (Isa. 2:4 [// Mic. 4:3–4]; 32:15–18; 60:1–22; etc.) ruled by a messianic king whose kingdom will fulfill the covenant with David and will never end (Isa. 9:6–7; 11:1–9; Jer. 23:5–6; 30:1–8; 33:14–26; Ezek. 34:23–24; 37:24–25). But the blessed time to come will be preceded by the terrifying Day of the Lord. Before the exile, Amos predicted that the Day of the Lord would be darkness, "gloom with no brightness in it" (Amos 5:18–20); it would mean the punishment of Israel for its transgressions, perhaps even Israel's total destruction.[2] During and after the exile, although the chastisement of Israel is not neglected, the accent falls on the destruction of Israel's enemies and the restoration of the chosen people (e.g., in the prophecies of Joel and Obadiah). Of increasing importance to Israel's faith was the later idea of a resurrection of the dead, by which the dead might share in the new age of God's people. In Ezekiel, the opening of the graves is a metaphor for the restoration of Israel after the exile (Ezek. 37:11–14; cf. Isa. 26:19); in Daniel (164 BCE in its present form), the resurrection of many to everlasting life or everlasting contempt is apparently meant literally as part of an apocalyptic vision (Dan. 12:1–2). But the reference in Daniel is without parallel in the Old Testament and may indicate Zoroastrian influence on second-century BCE Judaism. If there is a belief in "survival" in the Hebrew Scriptures, it cannot be taken for a general endorsement of individual immortality but rather for confidence in the permanent future of God's people. Job wished there were a way out of Sheol, but he admitted there was

1. See, e.g., the course of Jacob's life as narrated in Gen. 46:1–4; 47:9; 49:28–35.

2. The possibility that Yahweh might yet be gracious to a remnant makes the prophecy of Amos, as we have it, a call to repentance (Amos 5:4–5, 14–15); but the possibility is so discordant with his message of doom that many scholars suspect the intrusion of later additions, especially in 9:8–15. Zephaniah echoes Amos, and there too an editorial hand may have added the message of hope for a remnant and even for the nations. In chap. 1, however, the Day of the Lord—the *dies irae*—is not a cataclysmic event in history preceding the new age; it is the *end* of history, the *last* day, which will not inaugurate a time of blessing but will "cut off humanity from the face of the earth" (Zeph. 1:2–3, 14–18).

none (Job 7:6, 9, 21; 10:21–22; 14:10–14; 16:22). Reluctant acceptance of mortality lent a note of melancholy to Hebrew poetry, as it did to Classical Greek poetry. "As for mortals, their days are like grass; they flourish like a flower of the field, for the wind passes over it, and it is gone." All that endures is Yahweh's faithfulness to his covenant people (Ps. 103:15–18; cf. Isa. 40:6–8).

By the time of Jesus, the resurrection of the dead had become a controversial issue that divided the Pharisees, who believed in it, from the Sadducees, who denied it (cf. Acts 23:6–8). To show the problematic consequences of belief in the resurrection, the Sadducees put a test question to Jesus (Mark 12:18–27). The Mosaic law required a man to marry the childless widow of his deceased brother, but what if there were seven brothers, each of whom in succession married the woman and died? In the resurrection of the dead whose wife would she be? Jesus' answer appears to side with the Pharisees, but with a qualification: "When they rise from the dead, they neither marry nor are given in marriage, but are like angels in heaven" (v. 25). And he adds that the God of Abraham, Isaac, and Jacob is "God not of the dead, but of the living" (v. 27). The anecdote is intriguing, if not transparently clear, and it is usually assumed to report authentic words of Jesus.

In the "Little Apocalypse" of Mark 13 (cf. Matt. 24:1–44; Luke 21:1–36), sayings of Jesus were seemingly mixed with apocalyptic material from other sources as the Romans laid siege to Jerusalem (70 CE). However, the Markan apocalypse reflects, in general, the dual pattern of prophetic forecasts in the Old Testament. During the lifetime of the present generation (cf. Mark 9:1; 13:30) there will be fearful turmoil and suffering followed by the gathering of God's elect. But even Jesus cannot say when. The allusion to "the Son of Man coming in clouds" predicts what came to be called *the second coming* of Jesus "with great power and glory" (v. 26; cf. 14:61–62). The themes of *the last judgment* and *eternal blessedness,* which along with *the resurrection of the dead* and *the second coming* of Christ make up the four so-called last things, are powerfully represented by the discourse in Matthew 25:31–46. The sharp point of the discourse—that whatever is done to the weak and needy is done to Jesus himself (vv. 40, 45)—echoes sayings of Jesus reported elsewhere (10:40–42; Mark 9:37). When the Son of Man comes in glory, he will separate the sheep from the goats and judge them by how they treated those in need, just as if they did it, or failed to do it, to him. "And these will go away into eternal punishment, but the righteous into eternal life" (v. 46).[3]

Paul writes of "the day of . . . Christ" (1 Cor. 1:8; Phil. 1:6, 10; 2:16), meaning the day when Christ will return. He provides eschatological details in 1 Thessalonians 4:13–18 and more fully in 1 Corinthians 15:12–58. His argument in both letters bases the resurrection of the dead on the dying and rising of Jesus. "For since death came through a human being [Adam], the resurrection of the dead has also come through a human being" (1 Cor. 15:21; cf. 1 Thess. 4:14). Some of what he says is presumably metaphorical—the sound of the trumpet, being taken up into the clouds, and so on—as is appropriate

3. When Jesus is reported speaking of hades (hell), the word may stand simply for death (Matt. 11:23 // Luke 10:15; Matt. 16:18), but in the parable of Dives and Lazarus it denotes a place of torment (Luke 16:23). As a symbol of hell he also employs the word *geenna* (Gehenna), which alludes to the rubbish dump outside Jerusalem in the Valley of Hinnom (e.g., Mark 9:43–47).

to a mystery (1 Thess. 4:16–17; 1 Cor. 15:51–52; cf. Isa. 27:13). To the Thessalonians, Paul writes as one who expects to be still alive when the Lord comes, but he assures the Thessalonians that those who have fallen asleep will be raised and, together with the living, will meet the Lord in the air. To the Corinthians, he explains the nature of the resurrection body. Not all bodies are alike, and it is true that "flesh and blood cannot inherit the kingdom of God" (1 Cor. 15:50). But the mortal body is like a seed that comes to life only when it has died. "It is sown a physical body [*sōma psychikon*], it is raised a spiritual body [*sōma pneumatikon*]" (v. 44; cf. Phil. 3:10–11, 21). Paul describes Christ—the second Adam, the man from heaven—as "a life-giving spirit," so that the mortal body of those who bear Christ's image will put on immortality. But the coming of Christ and the resurrection of those who belong to him are not, for Paul, the final chapter: the end will come when Christ has vanquished all his enemies and hands the kingdom over to God the Father, "so that God may be all in all" (1 Cor. 15: 23–28).

If Paul's notion of resurrection as transformation, not mere continuance, echoes Jesus' answer to the Sadducees, his notion of an orderly sequence of eschatological events may be said to point toward more elaborate visions of the end, such as the Revelation to John (cf. 2 Thess. 2:1–12; 1 John 2:18–24; 4:1–3; 2 John 7). It must not be overlooked, however, that much of what Paul says about death and resurrection is not directly about the last day: to die then appears not in the future tense but in the past (you *have* died) and the imperative (you *must* die). Dying and rising with Christ is what it means to be a Christian (cf. Luke 15:24, 32). "Do you not know that all of us who have been baptized into Christ Jesus were baptized into his death? Therefore we have been buried with him by baptism into death, so that, just as Christ was raised from the dead by the glory of the Father, so we too might walk in newness of life. . . . So you also must consider yourselves dead to sin and alive to God in Christ Jesus" (Rom. 6:3–4, 11; cf. Col. 3:1–10). Besides dying to sin, Paul thinks of suffering as dying; there is a link in his mind between metaphorical and literal death in that he sees the one as preparation for the other, so that he can say in the midst of his eschatological teaching in 1 Corinthian 15, "I die every day!" (v. 31; cf. 2 Cor. 4:7–12; 5:14–15).

In the Gospel of John a comparable drawing of the future into the present appears in the description of judgment, eternal life, and resurrection as present experiences (contrast the saying of Jesus in Mark 10:30). The eschatological message of the imminent coming of the kingdom is overshadowed by the idea of an otherworldly realm above, from which Jesus has been sent (John 3:1–16; cf. 18:36). God did not send his Son to condemn the world; but the *judgment* is that when light came into the world, there were those who loved darkness rather than light, and they are condemned already (3:17–21). *Eternal life* is the present possession of whoever believes in the Son (v. 36); anyone who hears Jesus' word and believes "has passed from death to life" (5:24; cf. 1 John 3:14). For eternal life is to know the only true God and Jesus Christ, whom God has sent (John 17:3). The raising of Lazarus demonstrates that *resurrection* is not postponed to the last day. Jesus says: "I am the resurrection and the life. Those who believe in me, even though they die, will live, and everyone who lives and believes in me will never die" (11:25–26; cf. 14:6). Not that John, any more than

Paul, denies a future judgment on the last day (see 12:48),[4] but what will happen then is the consummation of what is happening now.

II. Tradition, Modernity, and the Future

Even before he reaches his chapter on "The Final Resurrection" (*Institutes* 2:987–1008), *Calvin* has considered self-denial, bearing the cross, and meditation on the future life as the heart of the Christian life (chaps. 7–9). The ambiguity of the present life is that it is at once full of misery and a foretaste of the blessed life to come. Heaven is our homeland, earth our place of exile; the world is a tomb, the body a prison. The final day of resurrection will be release from the emptiness of earthly existence (1:714–17). When he turns directly to the final resurrection, Calvin takes from Scripture the image of the body as a tent (2 Pet. 1:14; 2 Cor. 5:1). From it the soul departs at death; this, he assumes, is how we are to understand Jesus' words to the thief on the cross, "Today you will be with me in Paradise" (2:997; Luke 23:43). The resurrection of the flesh will not provide the soul with a new body but with a changed body.[5] The godly will then receive everlasting life, and the ungodly will be condemned. But "Christ came properly not for the destruction of the world but for its salvation. Hence in the creed also there is mention solely of the blessed life" (2:1004). Calvin believed in the condemnation of the wicked to eternal misery, but he insisted that to talk of their torments is to use inadequate physical metaphors for the ultimate misery of being "cut off from all fellowship with God" (1008). Talk of hell is not edifying to the pious. In the Geneva Catechism the minister asks why the Apostles' Creed mentions only eternal life, not hell. The student replies: "Because nothing is introduced here that does not tend to the consolation of pious minds" (*TT* 2:53).

Calvin admits it is difficult to believe that bodies eaten up with decay will be resurrected (*Institutes*, 2:990). But Schleiermacher felt the difficulties of traditional Christian eschatology more deeply than Calvin, and others such as the young Feuerbach, under the influence of Hegel, dealt more radically with eschatological imagery than Schleiermacher. The first thoughts of Schleiermacher on the subject are presented in the *Speeches on Religion* and the *Soliloquies*. He takes issue with the desire for immortality as the persistence of the self beyond the present life. In truth, religion is the sense of oneness with the Infinite, and facing death is an invitation to self-transcendence. In our relation to God everything individual and fleeting disappears. Aversion to the very aim of religion is therefore the source of the immortality most people long for; while

4. According to some commentators, John means judgment, eternal life, and resurrection to refer *wholly* to the present, so that the allusion to the last day in 12:48b must be an editor's accommodation to the futuristic eschatology of the early church. Even if that is not a sound conjecture, there cannot be any doubt that John's *main* concern is to bring eschatology into the present. Still, the future tense in 11:25–26 perhaps indicates a final resurrection; and in 5:28–29 the final judgment is apparently to come soon, in the near future ("the hour is coming").

5. Since the transformed body is strictly for the saved (as in Paul), it is not clear how Calvin envisions the resurrected body of the damned. It is also noteworthy that he stresses the metaphorical character of biblical language about damnation but not about salvation. However, he finds the hope of an afterlife in the OT by treating the "land" as a symbol of our heavenly heritage (*Institutes* 2.11.1–2 [1:450–51]).

agonizing over future immortality, they forfeit the immortality they could always have now. For whoever would find his life must lose it (1994: 99–101). And what of the bereaved? Schleiermacher points out that true friendship is not lost by separation, and what is death but a greater distance? "I can assert that to me my friends do not die, for I take up their lives in mine, and their influence upon me never ceases" (1957: 23–25). Language is being stretched in both these meditations—on "immortality" as present union with the Infinite and as the indestructible influence of friends who have died. But Schleiermacher insisted that in the *Speeches* he was only concerned to expose unworthy views in which the desire for immortality springs from self-love. For the Christian view of immortality he refers us to *The Christian Faith.*

There, characteristically, he takes a corporate view of eschatology: the subject is subsumed under "The Consummation of the Church" (*CF* 696–722). The essential content of Christian belief in personal survival is the reunion of believers with Christ, but fellowship of believers with Christ cannot be separated from their communal life with one another (708, 718). However, Schleiermacher finds himself in a methodological bind, for the future cannot be an element in the present Christian consciousness, which dogmatics seeks to describe. The consummation of the *church*—that is, the state in which nothing of the world stands any longer over against the church—lies beyond history: representation of it is directly useful only as "a pattern [*Vorbild*] to which we have to approximate" (696). Similarly problematic is the urge to form a conception of the state of the *individual* after death. Indeed, faith in the Savior would lack nothing essential if we spoke only of the communication of his blessedness in each moment of life, including the last (698). Schleiermacher concludes that he cannot ascribe to the church's doctrines of the last things the same value as he ascribed to the doctrines previously set out. "[S]omething is being attempted here," he admits, "which cannot be secured by doctrines proper [*Glaubenssätze*] in our sense of the word" (703). But to deal faithfully with Christian tradition (*mit guter Treue*), dogmatics cannot surrender belief in personal survival (700–701). Hence Schleiermacher reviews the last things as doctrines of a lower rank, "prophetic doctrines" (*prophetische Lehrstücke*), which are "the efforts of an insufficiently equipped faculty of presentiment" (706, alt.).[6] Christ's return, the resurrection of the flesh, the last judgment, and eternal blessedness are *images*, and Schleiermacher prefaces his treatment of them with the preliminary remark that his main task will be critical: to rule out prevailing misconceptions of the future life (703). I cannot trace the details of his critique. But I should at least note his brief appendix on eternal damnation. Whereas there have been Christian theologians who have included among the joys of heaven a clear view of hell, Schleiermacher thinks there can be no eternal bliss for Christians as long as others are consigned to eternal damnation (721).

The indispensable content of the church's eschatology, then, according to Schleiermacher, consists in the two "presentiments" of personal survival and the consummation of the church. Although we cannot form clear conceptions of them, we cannot dispense with them: we receive them in images that dogmatics

6. "Presentiment" is better for the German *Ahnung* than "premonition" (Eng. trans.) because it does not necessarily imply (etymologically at least) a forewarning.

submits to criticism. And this, in the opinion of many of Hegel's disciples, was mere timidity in the face of naive popular longings. To their way of thinking, eschatological language was not figurative talk about another, future world but figurative talk about *this* world and its possibilities. For some, such as A. E. Biedermann, philosophical theologian and Swiss Reformed pastor, the point of unrelenting criticism was to purify Christian faith. For others, such as Ludwig *Feuerbach*, it called for ruthless eradication of Christian illusions. In his early work, *Thoughts on Death and Immortality*, first published anonymously (1830), Feuerbach identified Christianity as the religion of individualism, especially in its most virulent, Protestant variety. A new life—and true religion, which is total surrender to God—will be possible only when an individual recognizes that death is *really* death. Human existence is finite, bodied existence. The soul is not like a bird in a cage, ready to fly out. It is more like the burning of a fire: when its fuel, the body, is consumed, the fire goes out (Feuerbach 1980: 10–11, 17, 99–100). Belief in immortality is *true* belief only if it is belief in the infinity of Spirit and the unfading youth of humanity. While finite spirits come and go, the Infinite Spirit is immortal and continually unfolds itself in new individuals out of the womb of its plenitude (137). The immortality of the individual, as the ancients realized, is in the memory of the people—whether a judgmental or a thankful memory. Heaven and hell exist only in history (134).

The thoughts of the process theologians on immortality might be described as a modification of Feuerbach's view in the light of the post-Hegelian metaphysic of Whitehead, who argued that every actual occasion in the temporal world is received into God's "consequent" nature.[7] This is the "objective" immortality of finite entities, including humans, in God. In a seminal essay on "Time, Death, and Eternal Life," Charles *Hartshorne* compares a human life to a book. Death is the last page of the last chapter but not the annihilation of the book. "It is the setting of a definite limit, not the obliteration of what is limited" (1962: 260). Who, then, are the potential readers of the book? The obvious answer is future human beings, and this has been termed "social immortality." But no human being can ever "read" another's book of life adequately. Only God can. "In short, our adequate immortality can only be God's omniscience of us" (250–52). A difficulty with this view, from the standpoint of theological orthodoxy, is that God must take into himself our ugliness as well as our goodness. For Hartshorne, heaven and hell are the conceptions God forms of our actual living, synthesized with God's responses to our life experiences. While a conservative theologian will have no objection to the thought that much in our experience must be traced to our perversity, she may not be reassured by Hartshorne's remark that the divine synthesis cannot remove it but only make the best of it, "bringing out of it whatever good is possible" (258). Process thinkers have continued to wrestle with traditional Christian beliefs in life after death and the eventual triumph of good over evil. The influential contribution of Marjorie Hewitt Suchocki, *The End of Evil* (1988), was taken up in the symposium *World without End: Christian Eschatology from a Process Perspective* (edited

7. In Whitehead's dipolar theism the "consequent" nature of God is so called as consequent upon the formative influence of *actual* occasions on God; the "primordial" nature is God's vision of all that is *possible*.

by Joseph Bracken, 2005), together with her response to her critics. But now I must draw my own conclusions on the often discordant biblical and theological utterances concerning eternal life and the final consummation.

III. Christian Faith and Hope

There are a few who give little thought to death, and some who are driven by pain and suffering to plead, "Come, sweet death." But in most the fear of dying is persistent or breaks through in moments of crisis. Remedies vary. Some turn to religion for reassurance that death is not the end; others insist that *really* to live is to face the inescapable fact that death is *really* death. In times past, the church has fostered the dread of death as an inducement for sinners to repent before they meet the heavenly judge. The Letter to the Hebrews says, "it is appointed for mortals to die once, and after that the judgment" (Heb. 9:27). Artists have depicted in vivid detail the division of the world to come into heaven for the just and hell for the wicked. But today it is more likely the prospect of annihilation that people dread; and even when one is able to reflect dispassionately about annihilation, it appears to rob human life of ultimate meaning.

The difficulty with determining "the Christian answer" to the problem is manifold: there are more Christian answers than one; they are wrapped in apocalyptic imagery; and they need to be qualified by scientific views of the end of humanity. There are certainly present-day theologians who discover insight and vitality in apocalyptic imagery. There is no denying, for instance, the powerful vision of the new Jerusalem in the Revelation to John (Rev. 21:1–8). It moves the heart. But the dogmatic theologian will not leave it at that; it begs for critical interpretation. Other aspects of John the Divine's apocalyptic vision (20:1–6), taken literally, have led to fruitless arguments about the millennium: whether the second coming of Christ will precede or follow an earthly golden age—or neither (amillennialism). Outside fundamentalism, probably few Christians today regard such language as other than symbolic, and scholars look first of all for its meaning in its original time. There is, besides, a notable caution—one might say agnosticism—in John's admission, "we are God's children now; what we will be has not yet been revealed." We only know we shall be like him (1 John 3:2). Still, Peter enjoins: "Always be ready to make your defense to anyone who demands from you an accounting for the hope that is in you" (1 Pet. 3:15). The Letter to the Hebrews calls faith "the assurance of things hoped for, the conviction of things not seen" (Heb. 11:1). What, then, does Christian faith hope for? Our discussion so far suggests three answers that need not be viewed as mutually exclusive.

(1) If we take account of the transformation of eschatology in one strand of the New Testament witness, most strikingly in the Fourth Gospel, we may say, to begin with, that Christians hope for *the presence of eternity* throughout their earthly existence. John transforms the Hebrew idea of a succession of ages into a Hellenic idea of two coexisting levels of reality: the better world is above rather than yet to come. Jesus has descended from the heavenly realm, and his gift of eternal life is *now,* not something promised for when he returns. Those who hear his word and believe have passed from death to life; they enjoy the

eternal life they already have (cf. John 15:11). Paul admonishes the Colossians to set their minds on things above (Col. 3:1–3). Yet he immediately adds: "When Christ who is your life is revealed, then you also will be revealed with him in glory" (v. 4). It is possible to read John's language about eternal life as excluding any future reference. Paul's statements, on the other hand, oscillate between present and future: he can say, for example, that we *are* God's adopted children and yet we *await* adoption (Rom. 8:15, 23). The Letter to the Hebrews similarly combines the two-story worldview with the expectation of Christ's second coming (Heb. 9:23–28; cf. 10:25). Although the author writes that believers *have come* to the heavenly Jerusalem, he also says that here they have no lasting city but look for the city that is *to come* (12:22; 13:14).[8]

If we set aside for a moment the prediction of an afterlife, Christian hope, like the hope of the Old Testament saints, will be for length of days to live among the covenant people: to be thankful for the blessings and to meet the demands of the present life—to see the salvation of the Lord and depart in peace (Luke 2:29–30). In that case, the heavenly Jerusalem may be understood as neither a literal prediction nor an empty fantasy but a powerful symbol of an ever-present ideal; to borrow Schleiermacher's description of the consummation of the church, the Jerusalem above is "a pattern to which we have to approximate." That, to be sure, does not state explicitly the crucial point that the prophetic visions of justice, peace, health, and truth rest on faith in the sovereignty of God, not on human effort. However, they call not for passive contemplation but for obedience to the heavenly vision, as Paul says of his vision of the Lord on the road to Damascus (Acts 26:19). Should we conclude that the presence of eternity requires no additional belief in a heavenly world to come or an afterlife for those who have lived well in the earthly world?

(2) There can be no doubt that, to many believers, the hope for *personal survival* of death is the heart of religion. Occasional rebukes from Christian theologians expose the risk that individual salvation, in this sense, may become a self-centered preoccupation, which the Christian religion contests rather than satisfies. When Calvin was dismissed from his first term in Geneva, Cardinal Sadoleto urged the people to return to the Church of Rome, where their prospect for salvation was brighter. Calvin rebuked him: "[I]t is not very sound theology to confine a man's thoughts so much to himself. . . . [I]t certainly is the part of a Christian man to ascend higher than merely to seek and secure the salvation of his own soul" (*TT* 1:33–34). True enough. But belief in survival is not always about getting a passport to paradise: it may arise from desire for further spiritual growth than this brief life affords; from grief at the death of an intimate friend or lifelong companion; or from hope that the appalling inequities of earthly existence will one day be put right. And the hope for an afterlife can hardly be eliminated from the New Testament, even if there are those who wish to *reinterpret* the afterlife as a symbol for the enduring worth of the present life. Paul writes: "If for this life only we have hoped in Christ, we are of all people most to be pitied" (1 Cor. 15:19). We may well ask how this agrees with

8. Paul, too, mixes local with temporal language when he contrasts "the Jerusalem above" with "the present Jerusalem" (Gal. 4:25–26). He speaks of "being saved" in both the present (1 Cor. 1:18; 15:2; 2 Cor. 2:15) and the future (Rom. 5: 9–10; 11:26; 13:11; 1 Cor. 5:5; 1 Thess. 2:16); and in one place he says we have been "saved in hope" (Rom. 8:24).

Paul's belief that we *have been* raised with Christ and what difference, if any, it will make to the Christian's resurrected body that the ascended body of Christ is said to have undergone a further metamorphosis after his resurrection. But it is not open to question that Paul did anticipate a future resurrection of the dead, whatever difficulties he leaves unanswered. He thought of personal survival as a radical transformation.

The woman of Tekoa did not speak the last biblical word on death when she said: "We must all die; we are like water spilled on the ground, which cannot be gathered up" (2 Sam. 14:14). But the supposition that the soul is immortal because it is by nature a substance separable from the body is impossible to justify on biblical, any more than scientific, grounds. Paul states that by the resurrection of the dead we will be *changed*, not freed from bodily existence but equipped with *spiritual* bodies (1 Cor. 15:51, 52). The idea of a spiritual body may have been suggested to him by Stoic philosophy, but it sounds to us like a self-contradiction, and to Paul it was a mystery. In our time some have held that spiritualism—belief in our ability to make contact with the spirits of the departed—strengthens the case for an afterlife. Ever since the founding of the Society for Psychical Research (1882) and its American counterpart (1885), spiritualism has been a subject of rigorous academic inquiry. Though frauds have been uncovered, theories have become necessary to account for certified phenomena. Still discussed is C. D. Broad's suggestion in *The Mind and Its Place in Nature* (1925) that a "psychic factor" does seem to survive death and may enter the consciousness of a medium. But Broad's "psychic factor" is not the continuing mind or consciousness of the deceased, and there is no reason to suppose it is immortal: it is more likely a bundle of mental elements—perceptions, feelings, memories, and the like—that soon disintegrates. As Broad remarks in a later essay, introducing psychical research to support belief in personal survival may be opening the gates to a Trojan horse (1953: 236). The survival may be neither conscious nor permanent. For myself, I think the weight of tradition advises Christians, despite modern skepticism, not to surrender the belief in personal survival too quickly and yet to remain frankly agnostic about its nature and, more important, not to make it the whole of Christian hope for the future.

(3) Some of the difficulties with the idea of personal survival are met by theories of *objective immortality,* that is, theories that understand individual immortality as the continued existence not of the individual subject but of its objective effects that continue after the subject's demise. For the *humanists* this means effects on *humanity*. George Eliot longed to join the "immortal dead who live again / In minds made better by their presence." Thus Moses is not really dead but "lives as Law."[9] A problem with this view is exposed in the noble passage from Ecclesiasticus often read at memorial services ("Let us now sing the praises of famous men," Sir. 44:1–15). Besides the famous, there are countless others of whom there is no memory, who "have perished as though they had never existed" (v. 9). Ecclesiasticus declares that these, too, were godly persons

9. George Eliot, "The Choir Invisible" and "The Death of Moses." Cf. Sydney Carter's hymn "I Danced in the Morning," in which the Lord of the Dance says, "They buried my body and they thought I'd gone, / But I am the dance and I still go on."

and appears to include them in the congregation's praise (v. 15). Many a devout Christian will say the dead live on in their continuing influence on family and friends—children, grandchildren, pupils, and others who were once touched by their presence. Eliot, however, took a more melancholy view, recognizing that even humanity itself is not immortal: eventually, the scroll will lie unopened in the tomb. The *process theologians,* by contrast, argue that the dead are retained forever in the memory of *God,* as we have seen.

The two versions of objective immortality, humanist and process, certainly give the believer something to hope for after physical death, but neither holds out the expectation of personal survival. Believers may protest that unless individual immortality is the conscious survival of the person, it is nothing. But the protest overlooks the long-term prospect opened up by the unimaginable extension of time and space in today's scientific cosmology. In the popular imagination, survival is like stepping through an open doorway into a neighboring room; it is simply a prolonging of mundane existence. But if the prospect is for billions and billions of years to come, such an afterlife is anything but comforting. Ernst Troeltsch held that belief in the value of personality marked the superiority of Christianity to Buddhism, and that this required an eschatology of continued moral growth beyond the grave. Yet the thought that it might go on *forever* horrified him, and he could only hope that the end would be the dissolution of his individual consciousness as it sinks into the divine life (see Gerrish 2004: 218–20). In other words, the survival of the individual person, if it happens, may be an interim state between death and the end, when God will be "all in all" (1 Cor. 15:28). To be sure, even foursquare Christian mystics vacillate between the end as surrender of selfhood and the end as purgation of the self from improper self-love.[10] I am bound to say that I think the eventual cessation of selfhood is the more likely outcome. It does not exclude hope for objective immortality—nor, indeed, for an extension of *finite* personal existence beyond death. However, what matters most, in my judgment, are the possession of eternal life now and the willingness to let God be God both now and hereafter.

My last thesis accordingly moves the twofold focus of eschatology, first, from a remote, unknown future to the eternal life Christians experience here and now; second, from the ultimate end of humanity to God as the end of all things. Some think the transformation of the finite self, as in the resurrection foreseen by Paul, opens the possibility of individual survival under different, as yet unknown conditions. But Christians, like everyone else, must face the likelihood that the end of humanity will coincide with the end of our world, or its inability to sustain human life any longer. When or how exactly that will happen is a matter of scientific debate. To predict the final stage in the story of humankind, there is probably no need to inquire further than the death of the

10. Augustine pictured the eternal rest of the soul as the moment of mystical insight prolonged forever (*Confessions* 9.25). The "beatific vision" could perhaps be thought of as the last moment in the life of the finite person, but it is not usually taken to mean the end of selfhood; indeed, it is said to be immediate *knowledge* of God. Selfhood is created in community, and John Hick argues for *corporate* blessedness by applying "the trinitarian conception of the one-in-many and many-in-one to the eschatological community of perfected human persons" (1994: 461). But he recognizes that this is highly speculative—at best "a possible eschatology"—and I remain uncommitted. Pertinent to last things are the problems of the persistence of evil and the particularity of divine election. But I cannot pursue them any further here (see chaps. 8 and 14).

solar system; the end of the *universe* is another question. Even if we allow for speculation on the possibility of life on other planets or the availability of other planets for human colonization, for all practical purposes the story of humankind is the story of life on this tiny speck we call earth.

True, it has traditionally been a part of Christian eschatology to expect a renewal of the whole creation, believed to have been subjected to suffering, futility, and decay because of the fall of humanity (Rom. 8:18–25; Gen. 3:17–19). The notion of a *cosmic* change due to Adam's sin is mythological; in view of the immeasurable vastness of the cosmos disclosed by modern science, to take it literally would be absurd. Still, the disastrous effect of human sin on what we may properly call *our world* is a present reality, only to be overcome by redemption; and experience shows that the vision of a redeemed creation functions as an energizing ideal, whether or not one wishes to understand it as also a prediction (Rom. 8:21; Eph. 1:10; Col. 1:20). The first part of thesis 21, then, to borrow an expression from the biblical theologians, proposes a "realized eschatology." By saying that language about the end does not *merely* predict the temporal goal of the individual, the human race, or the world, I leave the door open to what we may call an "inaugurated eschatology." But, like John the Evangelist, I mean to focus first on the present experience of those who have passed from death to life.

The second part of thesis 21 moves the eschatological focus from human felicity to the glory of God. Preoccupation with the well-being of humanity may be altruistic and admirable, the heart of the love for neighbor that is inseparable from love for God and is the gift of the Spirit (Gal. 5:22). But it may also become turned in upon itself in the self-love that Christian theologians have identified with sin. The message of redemption, which comes as a call to transcend self-interest, can then be twisted into a gospel of success in this life and everlasting happiness in the next. The idea of a "crown of glory" for the faithful, when Christ appears, is not absent from Scripture (1 Pet. 5:1, 4; cf. Rom. 8:21; 9:23; 1 Cor. 2:7), and it has had its place in conventional Christian piety.[11] But the overwhelming weight of scriptural testimony is summed up in the words of the psalmist: "Not to us, O LORD, not to us, but to your name give glory, for the sake of your steadfast love and your faithfulness" (Ps. 115:1; cf. 79:9; 96:8). The Lord chose Israel and Judah to be for him "a people, a name, a praise, and a glory" (Jer. 13:11). The vision of the prophet Habakkuk was for the day when "the earth will be filled with the knowledge of the glory of the LORD, as the waters cover the sea" (Heb. 2:14). Paul echoes Jeremiah's admonition that one who "glories" (*ho kauchōmenos*) should "glory" in the Lord (1 Cor. 1:31 KJV; Jer. 9:24; cf. 2 Cor. 10:17), and he testifies: "We do not proclaim ourselves; we proclaim Jesus Christ as Lord. . . . For it is the God who said, 'Let shine out of darkness,' who has shone in our hearts to give the light of the knowledge of the glory [*doxēs*] of God in the face of Jesus Christ" (2 Cor. 4:5–6).[12]

In his provocative essay "A Free Man's Worship," Bertrand Russell concluded from our modern understanding of the cosmos that "we must learn,

11. Over the top perhaps, though it admits of a sympathetic understanding, is the well-known refrain, "Oh, that will be glory for me, / Glory for me, glory for me."

12. The NRSV translates *ho kauchōmenos* as "one who boasts." But the point is the same: to establish a sharp antithesis between a self-centered piety and a theocentric (or christocentric) piety.

each one of us, that the world was not made for us."[13] According to Calvin, the world *was* made for humanity, but humanity was made for *God*. His rebuke to Sadoleto, that it is not sound theology to confine a man's thoughts to himself, is followed by the admonition to "set before him, as the prime motive of his existence, zeal to illustrate the glory of God. For we are born first of all for God, and not for ourselves." Calvin's vision of the primacy of God's glory is an austere version of Christian faith. It is not peculiar to him; James Gustafson writes: "The only good reason for claiming to be Christian is that we continue to be empowered, sustained, renewed, informed, and judged by Jesus' incarnation of theocentric piety and fidelity" (1981: 277). But a theocentric piety goes against the grain of humankind's natural self-estimate and aspirations, and it is not likely to be as popular as some other gospels that Gustafson excoriates. Still, in its own way, the worldview opened up by modern science urges us not to think of ourselves more highly than we ought to think (Rom. 12:3). The old motto *Soli Deo gloria* gives the Christian a better reason "to think with sober judgment," and it determines the second part of my eschatological thesis. For Christian faith, the meaning of the epic of humanity can only be understood as *relative to the manifestation of God's glory as Creator and Redeemer, in which the final meaning of the cosmos consists.*

13. Bertrand Russell, *Why I Am Not a Christian and Other Essays on Religion and Related Subjects* (New York: Simon & Schuster, 1957), 111.

Appendix: Dogmatic Theses

Introduction: Dogmatics as a Field of Inquiry

1. **Subject Matter of Dogmatics.** *Christian dogmatics, as a part of Christian theology, has for its subject matter the distinctively Christian way of having faith, in which elemental faith is confirmed, specified, and represented as filial trust in God "the Father of Jesus Christ."*

2. **Definition of Dogmatics.** *Christian dogmatics is distinguished from every other part of Christian theology as the theoretical, critical, and systematic discipline that seeks to establish the unity, and to test the adequacy, of the beliefs and dogmas in which Christian faith is expressed.*

3. **Method of Dogmatics.** *Christian dogmatics tests the "proper doctrine of faith" (redemption) and the theistic doctrine of faith presupposed therein (creation) both by Christian tradition, which interprets the Apostolic witness to Jesus Christ, and by present-day thought and experience, insofar as they call for reinterpreting the tradition.*

Part 1—Creation: Theism as the Presupposition of Christian Faith

4. **The World as Creation.** *Faith in God "the Father of Jesus Christ" presupposes that the world is neither an accident nor a mechanism, but a moral order experienced as both support and demand; and this is what is meant by representing the world as "creation."*

5. **God as Creator.** *Faith in God "the Father of Jesus Christ" presupposes that the creative principle of cosmic order is not only inconceivably powerful and mysterious, but also the source of goodness and justice, like authentic parental care; and this is what is meant by representing the creative principle as "Creator" and "Father Almighty."*

6. **Humanity as Created.** *Faith in God "the Father of Jesus Christ" presupposes that humanity is uniquely endowed with the capacity to respond freely to the Creator not only with awe or dread, but also with thankful confidence and willing obedience; and this is what is meant by representing humans as God's "children," created in the image and likeness of God.*

Part II—Redemption: The Distinctive Affirmations of Christian Faith

Division 1: Christ and the Christian

7. **Estrangement.** *Estrangement from the Creator may, as mistrust, be guiltless, but as defiance to the Creator it is sin, which arises from inborn egocentrism and the collective pressures of society, infects a person's entire existence with self-interest, and makes the self powerless to achieve the purpose of its creation without redemption.*

8. **God and Evil.** *Estrangement from the Creator cannot be separated from the way in which the creation is perceived but is precisely being at odds with the world order, either through anxiety about the course of the world (in particular, about natural evil) or through abuse of its resources and inhabitants for self-centered ends (which is social evil); and the magnitude of evil in the world raises the question of theodicy, which faith answers with commitment to the healing work of God in Jesus Christ.*

9. **The Covenant (I): Revelation.** *Although no event can be either more or less the effect of divine activity than any other event, God the Creator, the Father Almighty, is made known in the covenant of grace, that is, in a particular story that includes the call of Israel, the gift of the law, and the manifestation of the gospel in Jesus Christ; and this is what is meant by "special revelation" and "the mighty acts of God."*

10. **The Work of the Redeemer.** *Christ's lordship, or "kingly office," is exercised through the word of the gospel, which creates faith in God as "the Father of Jesus Christ" and creates the community of faith as the instrument by which the contagion of sin is countered and the reign of God extended; so that Christ is said to rule as both "prophet" (revealer of God's goodwill) and "priest" (savior from sin).*

11. **The Person of the Redeemer.** *The Redeemer is not the so-called Jesus of history (not, that is, a historical reconstruction) but the Christ of faith who is proclaimed in the church as the living Savior; and the content of the proclamation, represented in the dogma of Christ's "two natures," is the disclosure both of authentic humanity and of the design of God the Creator.*

12. **Living by Faith (I): Reconciliation.** *The confidence of faith, as restoration of the elemental trust that estrangement erodes, is reconciliation to God and God's purposes; and since faith is created through the proclamation of God's "paternal" goodwill in Christ (Christ's prophetic activity), reconciliation by the free forgiveness of sins is called "adoption into the household of God," or being "born again."*

13. **Living by Faith (II): Renewal.** *The obedience of faith, as restoration of the elemental sense of moral demand that estrangement blunts or rejects, is the "growth in grace" of those to whom God's commandments are no longer burdensome; and since to the new perception of God's "paternal" goodwill is added the creative efficacy of Christ's work in the Christian community (Christ's priestly activity), the new obedience is described as life together "in the Father's household."*

Division 2: The Spirit and the Church

14. **The Covenant (II): Election.** *The church, as a servant people of God, does not consist of a few who are the exclusive objects of divine care but of those who, hearing the call of the gospel to be conformed to the image of God's Son and chosen Servant, Jesus Christ, bear witness to the care of God for humanity; so that the church, as God's elect, is said to be a "creation of the gospel"—brought into being by the Spirit through the word about Jesus Christ.*

15. **The Spirit and the Body of Christ.** *The church as the "body" of Christ, "animated" by his Spirit, is neither a commonplace association nor a clerical domain, but the organ of Christ's continuing activity as prophet and priest; and because he receives his people as companions in his priestly activity, the church is also said to be a "royal priesthood," in which there is no division between priests and people.*

16. **The Church's Ministry.** *The apostolic ministry of witness and healing is committed to the whole church as a servant people of God and the body of Christ "sent out" into the world; and the pastoral office is not the apostolic ministry, but the means by which Christ, through the gifts of the Spirit, equips the church for its task of ministry*

17. **Faith and Order.** *Christ's headship over the church (his kingly office), exercised through the Word and not delegated to any group or individual, has assumed various forms of church order, none of which exists by exclusive divine right; and the promise of Christ's presence through the Spirit does not guarantee the infallibility of any person, institution, or gathering of the church, but rather confirms Christian faith in the indefectibility of the Word.*

18. **Baptism: Sign of New Birth.** *Baptism, as "the washing of regeneration," represents the new birth in Christ that is offered and given by the Spirit in the word of reconciliation; and since the new birth is mediated through the Christian community, whose faith is a condition but not the guarantee of faith in the one baptized, baptism is also called "adoption into the family of faith" or "reception into the covenant people."*

19. **The Lord's Supper: Sign of New Life.** *The Lord's Supper, as the effectual sign of new life in the household of God, represents Christ himself as "the bread of life" proffered and given by the Spirit in the word of renewal; and in partaking of the one bread and the one cup the family of faith is renewed as a covenant people and the body of the crucified and living Lord.*

Conclusion

20. **The Trinity.** *For Christian faith, God "the Father Almighty" is "the Father of Jesus Christ," who brings wayward children home by reconciliation through the one true Son and cares for them through the Spirit in the church; Christian faith accordingly bears witness to Father, Son, and Holy Spirit and declares that God's nature is love.*

21. **The End.** *Christian language about "the end" does not merely predict the temporal goal of the individual, the human race, or the world, but represents the eternal meaning of temporal existence (that is, its significance in every present moment); and this meaning is relative to the manifestation of God's glory as Creator and Redeemer, in which the final meaning of the cosmos consists.*

Selected Bibliography

After providing data for general works cited (besides the works listed in the abbreviations), the bibliography selects only a few (around ten) of the many pertinent titles in English for each chapter. I have had to exclude entirely the enormous secondary literature on Calvin, Schleiermacher, and other individual theologians. But I have dealt more fully elsewhere with many of the themes presented here; to maintain the brevity of the present outline, I have added in the bibliography for several chapters references to publications in which I discuss a theme further and take note of pertinent secondary literature.

General Works Cited in Historical and Constructive Theology

Berkhof, Louis. *Systematic Theology* [1941]. 4th ed. Grand Rapids: Eerdmans, 1949.

Brueggemann, Walter. *Theology of the Old Testament: Testimony, Dispute, Advocacy.* Minneapolis: Fortress, 1997.

Brunner, Emil. *Dogmatics* [German 1946–60]. 3 vols. Vols. 1–2 trans. Olive Wyon. Vol. 3 trans. David Cairns and T. H. L. Parker. London: Lutterworth, 1949–62.

Bultmann, Rudolf. *Theology of the New Testament* [German 1948–53]. Trans. Kendrick Grobel. 2 vols. New York: Scribner, 1951–55.

Harnack, Adolph (Adolf von). *History of Dogma* [German 1886–90]. Trans. of the 3rd German ed. by Neil Buchanan (1896–99). 7 vols. reprinted in 4. Gloucester, MA: Peter Smith, 1976.

Heppe, Heinrich. *Reformed Dogmatics Set Out and Illustrated from the Sources* [German 1861]. Rev. and ed. Ernst Bizer (1935). Trans. G. T. Thomson (1950). Reprint, Grand Rapids: Baker, 1978.

Hodge, Charles. *Systematic Theology* [1871–72]. 3 vols. Reprint, Grand Rapids: Eerdmans, 1981.

Kelly, J. N. D. *Early Christian Doctrines* [1958]. 5th ed. London: Continuum, 1977.

Klaassen, Walter, ed. *Anabaptism in Outline: Selected Primary Sources.* Classics of the Radical Reformation 3. Scottdale, PA: Herald, 1981.

Marshall, I. Howard. *New Testament Theology: Many Witnesses, One Gospel.* Downers Grove, IL: InterVarsity Press, 2004.

McGiffert, Arthur Cushman. *A History of Christian Thought* [1932–33]. 2 vols. Reprint, New York: Scribner's Sons, 1954.

Schmid, Heinrich. *The Doctrinal Theology of the Evangelical Lutheran Church* [German 1843, 7th ed. 1893]. Trans. Charles A. Hay and Henry E. Jacobs (1875, 1899). Reprint, Minneapolis: Augsburg, 1961.

Tillich, Paul. *Systematic Theology.* 3 vols. Chicago: University of Chicago Press, 1951–63.

Troeltsch, Ernst. *The Christian Faith* [German 1925]. Fortress Texts in Modern Theology. Trans. Garret E. Paul. Minneapolis: Fortress, 1991.
Wollebius, Johannes. *Compendium of Christian Theology* [Latin 1626]. Trans. in John W. Beardslee III, ed. and trans., *Reformed Dogmatics: J. Wollebius, G. Voetius, F. Turretin.* Library of Protestant Thought. New York: Oxford University Press, 1965.

Chapter 1: Subject Matter of Dogmatics

Calvin, *Institutes,* prefaces (1:3–31); 1.1–6 (1:35–74).
Schleiermacher, *CF* preface (vii–viii); §§1–16 (1–83).

Balfour, Arthur James. *Theism and Humanism.* New York: Doran, 1915.
———. *Theism and Thought: A Study in Familiar Beliefs.* New York: Doran, 1924.
Brunner, Emil. *Revelation and Reason: The Christian Doctrine of Faith and Knowledge* [German 1941]. Trans. Olive Wyon. Philadelphia: Westminster, 1946.
Daly, Mary. *Beyond God the Father: Toward a Philosophy of Women's Liberation.* Boston: Beacon, 1973.
Frankl, Viktor E. *The Will to Meaning: Foundations and Applications of Logotherapy* [German 1946]. 1st Eng. ed. 1959. Expanded ed. New York: Meridian, 1988.
Gerrish, B. A. *Saving and Secular Faith: An Invitation to Systematic Theology.* Minneapolis: Fortress, 1999.
Gilkey, Langdon. *Naming the Whirlwind: The Renewal of God-Language.* Indianapolis: Bobbs-Merrill, 1969.
Ogden, Schubert M. *The Reality of God and Other Essays* [1966]. Paperbound ed. with a new preface. New York: Harper & Row, 1977.
Soskice, Janet Martin. *Metaphor and Religious Language.* Oxford: Clarendon, 1985.
Stiver, Dan R. *The Philosophy of Religious Language: Sign, Symbol & Story.* Oxford: Blackwell, 1996.

Chapter 2: Definition of Dogmatics

Crooks, George R., and John F. Hurst. *Theological Encyclopædia and Methodology: On the Basis of Hagenbach* [1884]. Rev. ed. Library of Biblical and Theological Literature 3. New York: Eaton & Mains, 1894.
Ebeling, Gerhard. *The Study of Theology* [German 1975]. Trans. Duane A. Priebe. Philadelphia: Fortress, 1978.
Farley, Edward. *Theologia: The Fragmentation and Unity of Theological Education* [1983]. Reprint. Eugene, OR: Wipf & Stock, 2001.
Gerrish, B. A. "From *Dogmatik* to *Glaubenslehre*: A Paradigm Change in Modern Theology?" [1989]; "*Ubi theologia, ibi ecclesia?* Schleiermacher, Troeltsch, and the Prospect for an Academic Theology" [1992]. Chapters 11–12 in *Continuing the Reformation: Essays on Modern Religious Thought.* Chicago: University of Chicago Press, 1993.
Kirk, Kenneth E., ed. *The Study of Theology.* London: Hodder & Stoughton, 1939.
Ogden, Schubert M. *On Theology.* San Francisco: Harper & Row, 1986.
Schleiermacher, Friedrich. *Brief Outline on the Study of Theology* [German 1811, 2nd ed. 1830]. Trans.Terrence N. Tice. Richmond, VA: John Knox, 1966.
Troeltsch, Ernst. "Half a Century of Theology: A Review" [German 1908]. Pages 53–81 in *Writings on Theology and Religion.* Trans. and ed. Robert Morgan and Michael Pye. Atlanta: John Knox, 1977.

Chapter 3: Method of Dogmatics

Calvin, *Institutes* 1.6–9 (1:69–96); 4.8–9 (2:1149–79).
Schleiermacher, *CF* §§17–31 (83–128); §§127–32 (586–611).

Achtemeier, Paul J. *Inspiration and Authority: Nature and Function of Christian Scripture.* Peabody, MA: Hendrickson, 1999. Rev. ed. of *The Inspiration of Scripture:Problems and Proposals.* Philadelphia: Westminster, 1980.

Barr, James. *The Bible in the Modern World.* [1973]. Reprint, London: SCM, 1990.

Barth, Karl. "Concluding Unscientific Postscript on Schleiermacher" [German 1968]. Trans. George Hunsinger (1978). Reprinted as an appendix, pp. 261–79. In Barth, *The Theology of Schleiermacher: Lectures at Göttingen, Winter Semester of 1923/24.* Ed. Dietrich Ritschl. Trans. Geoffrey W. Bromiley. Grand Rapids: Eerdmans, 1982.

———. "The Word in Theology from Schleiermacher to Ritschl" [German 1927]. Pages 200–217 in *Theology and Church: Shorter Writings 1920–1928.* Trans. Louise Pettibone Smith. London: SCM, 1962.

Calvin, John. *The Bondage and Liberation of the Will: A Defence of the Orthodox Doctrine of Human Choice against Pighius* [Latin 1543]. Ed. A. N. S. Lane. Trans. G. I. Davies. Texts and Studies in Reformation and Post-Reformation Thought 2. Grand Rapids: Baker, 1996.

———. *Sermons on the Epistle to the Ephesians.* Trans. Arthur Golding [1577]. Rev. ed. Edinburgh: Banner of Truth Trust, 1973.

Engel, Mary Potter, and Walter E. Wyman, Jr., eds. *Revisioning the Past: Prospects in Historical Theology.* Minneapolis: Fortress, 1992.

Fretheim, Terence E., and Karlfried Froelich. *The Bible as Word of God in a Postmodern Age.* Minneapolis: Fortress, 1998.

Gerrish, B. A. "Continuity and Change: Friedrich Schleiermacher on the Task of Theology." Pages 13–48 in *Tradition and the Modern World: Reformed Theology in the Nineteenth Century* [1978]. Reprint, Eugene, OR: Wipf & Stock, 2007.

———. "From Calvin to Schleiermacher: The Theme and the Shape of Christian Dogmatics" [1985]. Chapter 8 in *Continuing the Reformation: Essays on Modern Religious Thought.* Chicago: University of Chicago Press, 1993.

———. "The Nature of Doctrine." *JR* 68 (1988): 187–92.

———. "The Word of God and the Words of Scripture: Luther and Calvin on Biblical Authority" [1957]. Chapter 3 in *The Old Protestantism and the New: Essays on the Reformation Heritage* (1982). Reprint, London: T. & T. Clark, 2004.

O'Malley, John W. *Trent: What Happened at the Council.* Cambridge: Belknap Press of Harvard Univeristy Press, 2013.

Schleiermacher, Friedrich D. E. *On the Glaubenslehre: Two Letters to Dr. Lücke* [German 1829]. Trans. James Duke and Francis Fiorenza. AAR Texts and Translation Series 3. Chico, CA: Scholars Press, 1981.

Tracy, David. *Blessed Rage for Order: The New Pluralism in Theology* [1975]. Paperback ed. Chicago: University of Chicago Press, 1996.

Viviano, Benedict Thomas. "The Normativity of Scripture and Tradition in Recent Catholic Theology." Pages 125–40 in *Scripture's Doctrine and Theology's Bible: How the New Testament Shapes Christian Dogmatics.* Ed. Markus Bockmuehl and Alan J. Torrance. Grand Rapids: Baker Academic, 2008.

Warfield, Benjamin Breckinridge. *The Inspiration and Authority of the Bible.* Ed. Samuel G. Craig. London: Marshall, Morgan & Scott, 1951.

Chapter 4: The World as Creation

Calvin, *Institutes* 1.14, 16–18 (1:159–82, 197–237).
Schleiermacher, *CF* §§32–49 (131–93); §§57–59 (233–44).

Barbour, Ian G. *Myths, Models, and Paradigms: A Comparative Study in Science and Religion.* New York: Harper & Row, 1974.
Behe, Michael J. *The Edge of Evolution: The Search for the Limits of Darwinism.* New York: Free Press, 2007.
Davies, Paul. *The Mind of God: The Scientific Basis for a Rational World.* New York: Simon & Schuster, 1992.
Einstein, Albert. *Ideas and Opinions.* Based on *Mein Weltbild,* ed. Carl Seelig, and other sources. New translations and revisions by Sonja Bargmann. New York: Crown, 1954.
Gerrish, B. A. "Nature and the Theater of Redemption: Schleiermacher on Christian Dogmatics and the Creation Story" [1987]. Chapter 9 in *Continuing the Reformation: Essays on Modern Religious Thought.* Chicago: University of Chicago Press, 1993.
———. "The Reformation and the Rise of Modern Science: Luther, Calvin, and Copernicus" [1968]. Chapter 10 in *The Old Protestantism and the New: Essays on the Reformation Heritage* (1982). Reprint, London: T. & T. Clark, 2004.
Gilkey, Langdon B. *Creationism on Trial: Evolution and God at Little Rock.* Minneapolis: Winston, 1985.
Gunton, Colin, ed. *The Doctrine of Creation.* Edinburgh: T. & T. Clark, 1997.
Harrison, Peter. *The Bible, Protestantism, and the Rise of Natural Science.* Cambridge: Cambridge University Press, 1998.
———, ed. *The Cambridge Companion to Science and Religion.* Cambridge: Cambridge University Press, 2010.
Peacocke, A. R. *Creation and the World of Science.* Bampton Lectures 1978. Oxford: Clarendon, 1979.
Peters, Ted, ed. *Cosmos as Creation: Theology and Science in Consonance.* Nashville: Abingdon, 1989.
Polkinghorne, John. *Science and Theology: An Introduction.* London: SPCK, 1998.
Stewart, Robert B., ed. *Intelligent Design: William A. Dembski and Michael Ruse in Dialogue.* Minneapolis: Fortress, 2007.

Chapter 5: God as Creator

Calvin, *Institutes* 1.10–13 (1:96–159).
Schleiermacher, *CF* §§50–56 (194–232).

Brooke, John Hedley. *Science and Religion: Some Historical Perspectives.* Cambridge History of Science. Cambridge: Cambridge University Press, 1991.
Davies, Paul. *God and the New Physics.* New York: Simon & Schuster, 1983.
Einstein, Albert. *Ideas and Opinions.* Based on *Mein Weltbild,* ed. Carl Seelig, and other sources. New translations and revisions by Sonja Bargmann. New York: Crown, 1954.
Frankenberry, Nancy K., ed. *The Faith of Scientists: In Their Own Words.* Princeton: Princeton University Press, 2008.
Gilkey, Langdon B. *Maker of Heaven and Earth: The Christian Doctrine of Creation in the Light of Modern Knowledge* [1959]. Reprint, Lanham, MD: University Press of America, 1985.

Hartshorne, Charles. "The New Pantheism." *Christian Register* 115 (1936): 119–20, 141–43.
Haught, John F. *God and the New Atheism: A Critical Response to Dawkins, Harris, and Hitchens.* Louisville: Westminster John Knox Press, 2008.
Hick, John. *An Interpretation of Religion: Human Responses to the Transcendent.* New Haven: Yale University Press, 1989.
Kaufman, Gordon D. *In the Beginning . . . Creativity.* Minneapolis: Fortress, 2004.
Phipps, William E. *Darwin's Religious Odyssey.* Harrisburg: Trinity Press International, 2002.
Polkinghorne, John. *Science and Theology: An Introduction.* Minneapolis: Fortress, 1998.
Schleiermacher, Friedrich D. E. *On the Glaubenslehre: Two Letters to Dr. Lücke* [German 1829]. Trans. James Duke and Francis Fiorenza. AAR Texts and Translation Series 3. Chico, CA: Scholars Press, 1981.
Wieman, Henry N. *The Source of Human Good* [1946]. Reprint, with an introduction by Marvin C. Shaw. American Academy of Religion Texts and Translations Series 8. Atlanta: Scholars Press, 1995.

Chapter 6: Humanity as Created

Calvin, *Institutes* 1.15 (1:183–96).
Schleiermacher, *CF* §§60–61 (244–56).

Barbour, Ian G. *Nature, Human Nature, and God.* Theology and the Sciences. Minneapolis: Fortress, 2002.
Brunner, Emil. "The New Barth." *Scottish Journal of Theology* 4 (1951): 123–35.
———, and Karl Barth. *Natural Theology.* Trans. Peter Fraenkel. London: Geoffrey Bles, Centenary Press, 1946. Eng. trans. of Brunner's *Natur und Gnade* (1934) and Barth's reply, *Nein* (1934).
Corey, M. A. *God and the New Cosmology: The Anthropic Design Argument.* Lanham, MD: Rowman & Littlefield, 1993.
Davies, Paul. *God and the New Physics.* New York: Simon & Schuster, 1983.
Gerrish, B. A. "The Mirror of God's Goodness: Man in the Theology of Calvin" [1981]. Chapter 9 in *The Old Protestantism and the New: Essays on the Reformation Heritage* (1982). Reprint, London: T. & T. Clark, 2004.
Gleick, James. *Chaos: Making a New Science.* New York: Viking Penguin, 1987.
Goetz, Stewart, and Charles Taliaferro. *A Brief History of the Soul.* Oxford: Wiley-Blackwell, 2011.
Hartshorne, Charles. *Omnipotence and Other Theological Mistakes.* Albany: State University of New York, 1984.
Pinnock, Clark, ed. *The Openness of God: A Biblical Challenge to the Traditional Understanding of God.* Downers Grove, IL: InterVarsity Press, 1994.
Polkinghorne, John. *Science and Theology: An Introduction.* Minneapolis: Fortress, 1998.
VanHuyssteen, J. Wentzel. *Alone in the World? Human Uniqueness in Science and Theology.* Grand Rapids: Eerdmans, 2006.
Whitehead, Alfred North. *Modes of Thought.* New York: Capricorn, 1938.
———. *Process and Reality: An Essay in Cosmology* [1929]. Corrected ed. (keyed to the pagination in the original). Ed. David Ray Griffin and Donald W. Sherburne. New York: Free Press, 1978.

Chapter 7: Estrangement

Calvin, *Institutes* 2.1–3 (1:241–309).
Schleiermacher, *CF* §§62–74 (259–314).

Bernard of Clairvaux. "On Grace and Free Choice." Trans. Daniel O'Donovan. In Bernard, *Treatises III*. Cistercian Fathers Series 19. Kalamazoo: Cistercian Publications, 1977.

Brunner, Emil. *Man in Revolt: Christian Anthropology* [German 1937]. Trans. Olive Wyon. London: Lutterworth, 1939.

Kierkegaard, Søren (Vigilius Haufniensis). *The Concept of Anxiety: A Simple Psychologically Orienting Deliberation on the Dogmatic Issue of Hereditary Sin* [Danish 1844]. Ed. and trans. Reidar Thomte in collaboration with Albert B. Anderson. Princeton: Princeton University Press, 1980.

——— (Anti-Climacus). *The Sickness unto Death: A Christian Psychological Exposition for Upbuilding and Awakening* [Danish 1849]. Ed. and trans. Howard V. Hong and Edna H. Hong. Princeton: Princeton University Press, 1980.

Müller, Julius. *The Christian Doctrine of Sin* [German 1839]. Trans. from the 5th German ed. by William Urwick. 2 vols. Edinburgh: T. & T. Clark, 1885.

Niebuhr, Reinhold. *The Nature and Destiny of Man: A Christian Interpretation*. Gifford Lectures 1939. 2 vols. London: Nisbet, 1941–43.

Plaskow, Judith. *Sex, Sin and Grace: Women's Experience and the Theologies of Reinhold Niebuhr and Paul Tillich*. Lanham, MD: University Press of America, 1980.

Ricoeur, Paul. *The Symbolism of Evil* [French 1960]. Trans. Emerson Buchanan (1967). Reprint, Boston: Beacon, 1969.

Saiving (Goldstein), Valerie. "The Human Situation: A Feminist View." *JR* 40 (1960): 100–112.

Tillich, Paul. *The Courage to Be*. Terry Lectures 1952. London: Nisbet, 1952.

Chapter 8: God and Evil

Calvin, *Institutes* 2.4–5 (1:309–40).
Schleiermacher, *CF* §§75–85 (315–54).

Barbour, Ian G., ed. *Western Man and Environmental Ethics: Attitudes Toward Nature and Technology*. Addison-Wesley Series in History. Reading, MA: Addison-Wesley, 1973.

Braithwaite, R. B. *An Empiricist's View of the Nature of Religious Belief*. Eddington Lecture 9. Cambridge: University of Cambridge Press, 1955.

Davis, Stephen, ed. *Encountering Evil: Live Options in Theodicy* [1981]. Rev. ed. Louisville: Westminster John Knox, 2001.

Flew, Antony, and Alasdair MacIntyre, eds. *New Essays in Philosophical Theology*. London: SCM, 1955.

Griffin, David Ray. *Evil Revisited: Responses and Considerations*. Albany: State University of New York Press, 1991.

———. *God, Power, and Evil: A Process Theodicy* [1976]. Reprint, with a revised version of the preface to the 2nd ed. (1991). Louisville: Westminster John Knox, 2004.

Hick, John. *Evil and the God of Love* [1966]. 2nd ed. 1976. Reprint, Houndmills, Basingstoke: Palgrave Macmillan, 2010.

Leibniz, G. W. *Theodicy: Essays on the Goodness of God, the Freedom of Man and the Origin of Evil* [French 1710]. Ed. Austin Farrer. Trans. E. M. Haggard (1951). Reprint, La Salle, IL: Open Court, 1985.

Linzey, Andrew. *Animal Theology*. London: SCM, 1994; Urbana: University of Illinois Press, 1995.
Plantinga, Alvin. *God, Freedom, and Evil* [1974]. Reprint, Grand Rapids: Eerdmans, 1977.
Ritschl, Albrecht. *The Christian Doctrine of Justification and Reconciliation: The Positive Development of the Doctrine* [German 1874, 2nd ed. 1883, 3rd ed. 1888]. Eng. trans. ed. H. R. Mackintosh and A. B. Macaulay (1900). Reprint, Clifton, NJ: Reference Book Publishers, 1966.
Rubenstein, Richard L. *After Auschwitz: Radical Theology and Contemporary Judaism*. Indianapolis: Bobbs-Merrill, 1966.
White, Lynn. "The Historical Roots of Our Ecologic Crisis" [1967]. Reprint, pages 18–30 in *Western Man and Environmental Ethics: Attitudes Toward Nature and Technology*. Ed. Ian G. Barbour. Addison-Wesley Series in History. Reading, MA: Addison-Wesley, 1973.

Chapter 9: The Covenant (I): Revelation

Calvin, *Institutes* 2.6–11 (1:340–464).

Avis, Paul, ed. *Divine Revelation*. Grand Rapids: Eerdmans, 1997.
Baillie, John. *The Idea of Revelation in Recent Thought*. New York: Columbia University Press, 1956.
Barr, James. *Biblical Faith and Natural Theology*. Gifford Lectures 1991. Oxford: Clarendon, 1993.
Brunner, Emil. *Revelation and Reason: The Christian Doctrine of Faith and Knowledge* [German 1941]. Trans. Olive Wyon. Philadelphia: Westminster, 1946.
Fackre, Gabriel. *The Doctrine of Revelation: A Narrative Interpretation*. Grand Rapids: Eerdmans, 1997.
Gerrish, B. A. "Errors and Insights in the Understanding of Revelation" [1998]. Chapter 2 in *Thinking with the Church: Essays in Historical Theology*. Grand Rapids: Eerdmans, 2010.
Harvey, Van A. *The Historian and the Believer: The Morality of Historical Knowledge and Christian Belief* [1966]. Reprint, with a new introduction. Urbana: University of Illinois Press, 1996.
Niebuhr, H. Richard. *The Meaning of Revelation* [1941]. Reprint, with introduction by Douglas F. Ottati. Louisville: Westminster John Knox Press, 2006.
Pannenberg, Wolfhart, et al., eds. *Revelation as History* [German 1961]. Trans. David Granskou. New York: Macmillan, 1968.
Robinson, James M., and John B. Cobb, Jr., eds. *Theology as History*. New Frontiers in Theology 3. New York: Harper & Row, 1967.
Ward, Keith. *Religion and Revelation: A Theology of Revelation in the World's Religions*. Oxford: Clarendon, 1994.
Wright, G. Ernest. *God Who Acts: Biblical Theology as Recital*. Studies in Biblical Theology 1/8. London: SCM, 1952.

Chapter 10: The Work of the Redeemer

Calvin, *Institutes* 2.15–17 (1:494–534).
Schleiermacher, *CF* §§100–105 (425–75).

Abailard (Abelard), Peter. *Exposition of the Epistle to the Romans: An Excerpt from the Second Book.* Trans. Gerald E. Moffatt. Pages 276–87 in *A Scholastic Miscellany: Anselm to Ockham.* Trans. and ed. Eugene R. Fairweather. LCC 10. Philadelphia: Westminster, 1956.

Anselm. *Why God Became Man.* Pages 100–183 in *A Scholastic Miscellany: Anselm to Ockham.* Trans. and ed. Eugene R. Fairweather. LCC 10. Philadelphia: Westminster, 1956.

Aulén, Gustaf. *Christus Victor: An Historical Study of the Three Main Types of the Idea of the Atonement* [Swedish 1930]. Trans. A. G. Hebert (1931). Paperback ed. New York: Macmillan, 1969.

Brown, Joanne Carlson, and Carole R. Bohn, eds. *Christianity, Patriarchy, and Abuse: A Feminist Critique.* New York: Pilgrim, 1989.

Campbell, John McCleod. *The Nature of the Atonement and Its Relation to the Remission of Sins and Eternal Life* [1856]. 3rd ed. London: Macmillan, 1869.

Dodd, C. H. *The Bible and the Greeks.* London: Hodder & Stoughton, 1935.

———. *Three Sermons.* London: SCM, 1954.

Franks, Robert S. *A History of the Doctrine of the Work of Christ* [1918]. 2 vols. Reprint, London: Nelson, 1962.

Gerrish, B. A. "Charles Hodge on the Death of Christ" and "John Williamson Nevin on the Life of Christ." Chapters 9 and 10 in *Thinking with the Church: Essays in Historical Theology.* Grand Rapids: Eerdmans, 2010.

Godbey, John Charles. "A Study of Faustus Socinus' *De Jesu Christo Servatore.*" Ph.D. diss. 2 vols. University of Chicago, 1968.

Hodge, Charles. *Essays and Reviews.* New York: Carter, 1957.

Lloyd-Jones, D. M. *Romans: An Exposition of Chapters 3.20–4.25: Atonement and Justification.* Grand Rapids: Zondervan, 1970.

Nevin, John Williamson. *Vindication of the Revised Liturgy, Historical and Theological* [1867]. Reprinted in *Catholic and Reformed: Selected Theological Writings of John Williamson Nevin.* Ed. Charles Yrigoyen, Jr., and George H. Bricker. Pittsburgh Original Texts and Translations 3. Pittsburgh: Pickwick, 1978.

———. "Wilberforce on the Incarnation." *Mercersburg Review* 2 (1850): 164–96.

Ritschl, Albrecht. *A Critical History of the Christian Doctrine of Justification and Reconciliation* [German 1870]. Trans. John S. Black. Edinburgh: Edmonston & Douglas, 1872.

Taylor, Vincent. *The Atonement in New Testament Teaching* [1941]. 2nd ed. London: Epworth, 1945.

Chapter 11: The Person of the Redeemer

Calvin, *Institutes* 2.12–14 (1:464–93).

Schleiermacher, *CF* §§86–99 (355–424).

Bultmann, Rudolf. *Jesus and the Word* [German 1926]. Trans. Louise Pettibone Smith and Erminie Huntress Lantero. New York: Scribner, 1958.

Forsyth, P. T. *The Person and Place of Jesus Christ.* London: Hodder & Stoughton, 1909.

Gerrish, B. A. "Jesus, Myth, and History: Troeltsch's Stand in the 'Christ-Myth' Debate" [1975]. Chapter 14 in *The Old Protestantism and the New: Essays on the Reformation Heritage* (1982). Reprint, London: T. & T. Clark, 2004.

Hick, John, ed. *The Myth of God Incarnate.* Philadelphia: Westminster, 1977.

Kähler, Martin. *The So-Called Historical Jesus and the Historic Biblical Christ* [German 1892]. Trans. and ed. from the 2nd German ed. (1896) by Carl E. Braaten. Philadelphia: Fortress, 1964.

McCready, Douglas. *He Came Down from Heaven: The Preexistence of Christ and the Christian Faith.* Downers Grove, IL: InterVarsity Press, 2005.
Ogden, Schubert M. *The Point of Christology.* San Francisco: Harper & Row, 1982.
Schleiermacher, Friedrich. *The Life of Jesus* [German 1864]. Ed. Jack C. Verheyden. Trans. S. Maclean Gilmour. Mifflintown: Sigler, 1997.
Schweitzer, Albert. *The Quest of the Historical Jesus* [German *Von Reimarus zu Wrede,* 1906; 2nd ed., *Geschichte der Leben-Jesu-Forschung,* 1913]. First complete ed., trans. from the 9th German ed. (1984, virtually identical with the 2nd), with Schweitzer's preface to the 6th ed. (1950). Ed. John Bowden. Trans. W. Montgomery et al. London: SCM, 2000.
Strauss, David Friedrich. *The Christ of Faith and the Jesus of History: A Critique of Schleiermacher's Life of Jesus* [German 1865]. Trans. and ed. Leander E. Keck. Philadelphia: Fortress, 1977.
———. *The Life of Jesus Critically Examined* [German 1835–36]. Trans. from the 4th German ed. (1840) by George Eliot. Reproduced from the 2nd English ed. (1892). Philadelphia: Fortress, 1972.
Weiss, Johannes. *Jesus' Proclamation of the Kingdom of God* [German 1892, 2nd ed. 1900, 3rd ed. 1964]. Trans. of the 1st German ed. Trans. and ed. Richard Hyde Hiers and David Larrimore Holland. Philadelphia: Fortress, 1971.

Chapter 12: Living by Faith (I): Reconciliation

Calvin, *Institutes* 3.1–2, 11–19 (1:537–92, 725–849).
Schleiermacher, *CF* §§106–12 (476–524).

Aune, David E., ed. *Rereading Paul Together: Protestant and Catholic Perspectives on Justification.* Grand Rapids: Baker Academic, 2006.
Barth, Karl. *The Word of God and the Word of Man.* Trans. Douglas Horton [1928]. Reprint, New York: Harper, 1957.
Gerrish, B. A. "The Chief Article—Then and Now" [1983]. Chapter 1 in *Continuing the Reformation: Essays on Modern Religious Thought.* Chicago: University of Chicago Press, 1993.
———. "Luther's Conception of Justifying Faith and Its Significance for Theology Today." S.T.M. thesis, Union Theological Seminary, New York, 1956.
———. "New Light on Luther's Rediscovery of the Gospel" [1963]. Revised as "By Faith Alone: Medium and Message in Luther's Gospel." Chapter 4 in *The Old Protestantism and the New: Essays on the Reformation Heritage* (1982). Reprint, London: T. & T. Clark, 2004.
Husbands, Mark, and Daniel J. Treier, eds. *Justification: What's at Stake in the Current Debates.* Downers Grove, IL: InterVarsity Press, 2004.
Jüngel, Eberhard. *Justification, the Heart of the Christian Faith: A Theological Study with an Ecumenical Purpose.* Trans. of the 3rd German ed. (1999) by Jeffrey F. Cayzer. Edinburgh: T. & T. Clark, 2001.
Küng, Hans. *Justification: The Doctrine of Karl Barth and a Catholic Reflection* [German 1957]. Trans. Thomas Collins et al. (1964). 40th anniversary ed. Louisville: Westminster John Knox Press, 2004.
Lane, Anthony N. S. *Justification by Faith in Catholic-Protestant Dialogue: An Evangelical Assessment.* London: T. & T. Clark, 2002.
Lutheran World Federation, The, and The Roman Catholic Church. *Joint Declaration on the Doctrine of Justification.* Grand Rapids: Eerdmans, 2000.

Niebuhr, Reinhold. "The Relevance of Reformation Doctrine in Our Day." Pages 249–64. In *The Heritage of the Reformation: Essays Commemorating the Centennial of Eden Theological Seminary*. Ed. Elmer J. F. Arndt. New York: Richard J. Smith, 1950.

Schleiermacher, Friedrich. "Necessity of the New Birth." Pages 83–102 in *Selected Sermons of Schleiermacher*. Trans. Mary F. Wilson. London: Hodder & Stoughton, 1890.

Tillich, Paul. *The Courage to Be*. London: Nisbet, 1952.

———. *The Protestant Era*. Trans. and ed. James Luther Adams. London: Nisbet, 1951.

Watts, Fraser, and Liz Gulliford, eds. *Forgiveness in Context: Theology and Psychology in Creative Dialogue*. London: T. & T. Clark, 2004.

Chapter 13: Living by Faith (II): Renewal

Calvin, *Institutes* 3.3–10, 20 (1:592–725; 2:850–920).

Schleiermacher, *CF* §§106–12 (476–524).

Alexander, Donald L., ed. *Spirituality: Five Views of Sanctification*. Downers Grove, IL: InterVarsity Press, 1988.

Callahan, Daniel J., Heiko A. Oberman, and Daniel J. O'Hanlon, eds. *Christianity Divided: Protestant and Roman Catholic Theological Issues*. New York: Sheed & Ward, 1961.

Dieter, Melvin E., et al. *Five Views on Sanctification*. Grand Rapids: Zondervan Academic, 1987.

Mannermaa, Tuomo. "Theosis as a Subject of Finnish Luther Research." *Pro Ecclesia* 4 (1995): 37–48.

Meyendorff, John, and Joseph McLelland, eds. *The New Man: An Orthodox and Reformed Dialogue*. New Brunswick, NJ: Agora, 1973.

Outler, Albert C., ed. *John Wesley*. Library of Protestant Thought. Oxford: Oxford University Press, 1964.

Runyon, Theodore, ed. *Sanctification and Liberation: Liberation Theologies in Light of the Wesleyan Tradition*. Nashville: Abingdon, 1981.

Wesley, John. *A Plain Account of Christian Perfection* [1767]. Reprint, London: Epworth, 1952.

———. *Wesley's Standard Sermons*. Ed. Edward H. Sugden. 2 vols. London: Epworth, 1921.

Chapter 14: The Covenant (II): Election

Calvin, *Institutes* 3.21–24 (2:920–87).

Schleiermacher, *CF* §§113–20 (525–60).

Berkouwer, G. C. *Divine Election*. Trans. Hugo Bekker. Grand Rapids: Eerdmans, 1960.

Boettner, Loraine. *The Reformed Doctrine of Predestination*. Grand Rapids: Eerdmans, 1932.

Calvin, John. *Concerning the Eternal Predestination of God* [Latin 1552]. Trans. and ed. J. K. S. Reid (1961). Paperback ed. Louisville: Westminster John Knox Press, 1997.

Campbell, J. Y. "The Origin and Meaning of the Christian Use of the Word ΕΚΚΛΗΣΙΑ" [1948]. Reprint, pages 41–54 in *Three New Testament Studies*. Leiden: Brill, 1965.

Gerrish, B. A. "Grace and the Limits of History: Alexander Schweizer on Predestination." Chapter 4 in *Tradition and the Modern World: Reformed Theology in the Nineteenth Century.* (1978). Reprint, Eugene, OR: Wipf & Stock, 2007.
Mozley, J. B. *A Treatise on the Augustinian Doctrine of Predestination.* 2nd ed. New York: Dutton, 1878.
Ogden, Schubert M. *Is There Only One True Religion or Are There Many?* Dallas: Southern Methodist University Press, 1992.
Rahner, Karl. *Theological Investigations.* Vol. 14: *Eclesiology, Questions in the Church, the Church in the World.* Trans. David Bourke. London: Darton, Longman & Todd, 1976.
Rowley, H. H. *The Biblical Doctrine of Election.* London: Lutterworth, 1950.
Schleiermacher, Friedrich. *On the Doctrine of Election: With Special Reference to the Aphorisms of Dr. Bretschneider* [German 1819]. Trans. and ed. Iain G. Nichol and Allen G. Jorgenson. Columbia Series in Reformed Theology. Louisville: Westminster John Knox Press, 2012.
Sullivan, Francis A. *Salvation Outside the Church? Tracing the History of the Catholic Response.* New York: Paulist, 1992.

Chapter 15: The Spirit and the Body of Christ

Calvin, *Institutes* 4.1 (2:1011–41).
Schleiermacher, *CF* §§121–25 (560–91).

Barth, Karl. "The Church—The Living Congregation of the Living Lord Jesus Christ." Pages 67–76 in *The Universal Church in God's Design: An Ecumenical Study Prepared under the Auspices of the World Council of Churches.* Amsterdam Assembly Series 1. London: SCM, 1948.
Brunner, Emil. *The Misunderstanding of the Church* [German 1951]. Trans. Harold Knight. London: Lutterworth, 1952.
Campbell, J. Y. "KOINΩNIA and Its Cognates in the New Testament" [1932] and "The Origin and Meaning of the Christian Use of the Word EKKΛHΣIA" [1948]. Reprint, pages 1–28 and 41–54, respectively, in *Three New Testament Studies.* Leiden: Brill, 1965.
Gerrish, B. A. "Priesthood and Ministry in the Theology of Luther" [1965]. Chapter 5 in *The Old Protestantism and the New: Essays on the Reformation Heritage* (1982). Reprint, London: T. & T. Clark, 2004.
Newbigin, Lesslie. *The Household of God: Lectures on the Nature of the Church.* New York: Friendship, 1954.
Schleiermacher, Friedrich. *On Religion: Speeches to Its Cultured Despisers* [German 1799]. Trans. from the 3rd German ed. (1821) by John Oman (1894). Reprint, Louisville: Westminster John Knox Press, 1994.
Schweizer, Eduard. *The Church as the Body of Christ.* Richmond: John Knox, 1964.
Spener, Philip Jacob. *Pia Desideria* [German 1675]. Trans. and ed. Theodore G. Tappert. Seminar Editions. Philadelphia: Fortress, 1964.
Troeltsch, Ernst. *Protestantism and Progress: The Significance of Protestantism for the Rise of the Modern World* [German 1906]. Trans. from the 2nd German ed. (1911) by W. Montgomery (1912). Reprint, Fortress Texts in Modern Theology. Philadelphia: Fortress, 1986.
———. "Schleiermacher und die Kirche." In *Schleiermacher der Philosoph des Glaubens.* [Essays by Troeltsch and others.] Moderne Philosophie 6. Berlin-Schöneberg: Buchverlag der "Hilfe," 1910.

———. *The Social Teaching of the Christian Churches* [German 1912]. Trans. Olive Wyon. 2 vols. (1931). Reprint, Library of Theological Ethics. Louisville: Westminster John Knox Press, 1992.

Chapter 16: The Church's Ministry

Calvin, *Institutes* 4.2, 20 (2:1041–53, 1485–1521).
Schleiermacher, *CF* §§133–35 (611–19).

Baptism, Eucharist and Ministry. Faith and Order Paper no. 111. Geneva: World Council of Churches, 1982.
Collins, John N. *Are All Christians Ministers?* Collegeville, MN: Liturgical Press, 1992.
Latourette, Kenneth Scott. *A History of the Expansion of Christianity.* 7 vols. New York: Harper & Brothers, 1937–45.
Littell, Franklin Hamlin. *The Anabaptist View of the Church: A Study in the Origins of Sectarian Protestantism.* 2nd ed. Boston: Starr King, 1958.
Loisy, Alfred. *The Gospel and the Church* [French 1903]. Trans. Christopher Home (1903). Reprint. Philadelphia: Fortress, 1976.
O'Malley, John W. *What Happened at Vatican II.* Cambridge: Belknap Press of Harvard University Press, 2008.
Schmidlin, Joseph (Josef). *Catholic Mission Theory* [German 1919, 2nd ed. 1923]. Trans. and ed. Matthias Braun. Techny, IL: Mission, 1931.
Warneck, Gustav. *Outline of a History of Protestant Missions from the Reformation to the Present Time* [German 1882]. Trans. of the 8th German ed. (1904). Ed. George Robson. New York: Revell, 1906.
Weatherhead, Leslie D. *Psychology, Religion and Healing* [1951]. 2nd, enlarged ed. London: Hodder & Stoughton, 1952.

Chapter 17: Faith and Order

Calvin, *Institutes* 4.3–13, esp. 3, 6, 8–9 (2:1053–1276, esp. 1053–68, 1102–18, 1149–79).
Schleiermacher, *CF* §§144–56 (660–95).

Ainslie, James L. *The Doctrines of Ministerial Order in the Reformed Churches of the Sixteenth and Seventeenth Centuries.* Edinburgh: T. & T. Clark, 1940.
Barth, Karl. "The Desirability and Possibility of a Universal Reformed Creed" [German 1925]. Pages 112–35 in *Theology and Church: Shorter Writings 1920–1928.* Trans. Louise Pettibone Smith. London: SCM, 1962.
Brown, Raymond E., Karl P. Donfried, and John Reumann, eds. *Peter in the New Testament: A Collaborative Assessment by Protestant and Roman Catholic Scholars.* Minneapolis: Augsburg; New York: Paulist, 1973.
Campenhausen, Hans von. *Ecclesiastical Authority and Spiritual Power in the Church of the First Three Centuries* [German 1953]. Trans. J. A. Baker. London: Black, 1969.
Carey, Kenneth M., ed. *The Historic Episcopate in the Fullness of the Church: Six Essays by Priests of the Church of England* [1954]. 2nd ed. London: Dacre, 1960.
Cullmann, Oscar. *Peter—Disciple, Apostle, Martyr: A Historical and Theological Study* [German 1952]. Trans. of the 2nd ed. (1960) by Floyd V. Filson. London: SCM, 1962.
Dulles, Avery. *Models of the Church* [1974]. Expanded ed. New York: Doubleday, 1987.
Empie, Paul C., and T. Austin Murphy, eds. *Papal Primacy and the Universal Church.* Lutherans and Catholics in Dialogue 5. Minneapolis: Augsburg, 1974.

Horton, Douglas. *Congregationalism: A Study in Church Polity.* London: Independent, 1952.
Lightfoot, J. B. *The Christian Ministry* [1868]. Reprint, ed. Philip Edgcumbe Hughes, Wilton, CT: Morehouse-Barlow, 1983.
McNeill, John T. *Unitive Protestantism: The Ecumenical Spirit and Its Persistent Expression.* Richmond: John Knox, 1964.
Peel, Albert, and Leland H. Carlson, eds. *The Writings of Robert Harrison and Robert Browne.* Elizabethan Nonconformist Texts 2. London: Allen & Unwin, 1953.
Puglisi, James F., ed. *How Can the Petrine Ministry Be a Service to the Unity of the Universal Church?* Grand Rapids: Eerdmans, 2010.

Chapter 18: Baptism: Sign of New Birth

Calvin, *Institutes* 4.14–16, 18 (2:1276–1359, 1448–84).
Schleiermacher, *CF* §§136–38, 143 (619–38, 657–60).

Barth, Karl. *The Teaching of the Church regarding Baptism* [German 1947]. Trans. Ernest A. Payne. London: SCM, 1948.
Beasley-Murray, G. R. *Baptism in the New Testament.* Grand Rapids: Eerdmans, 1962.
Byars, Ronald P. *The Sacraments in Biblical Perspective.* Interpretation: Resources for the Use of Scripture in the Church. Louisville: Westminster John Knox Press, 2011.
Crabtree, Arthur B. "The Augsburg Confession in Baptist Ecumenical Perspective." Pages 61–81 in *The Augsburg Confession in Ecumenical Perspective.* Ed. Harding Meyer. LWF Report 6/7. Geneva: Kreuz Verlag Erich Breitsohl, 1980.
Ferguson, Everett. *Baptism in the Early Church: History, Theology, and Liturgy in the First Five Centuries.* Grand Rapids: Eerdmans, 2009.
Gerrish, B. A. *Grace and Gratitude: The Eucharistic Theology of John Calvin* [1993]. Reprint, Eugene, OR: Wipf & Stock, 2001.
Jeremias, Joachim. *Infant Baptism in the First Four Centuries* [German 1958]. Trans. David Cairns. London: SCM, 1960.
Johnson, Maxwell E., ed. *Sacraments and Worship.* Sources of Christian Theology. Louisville, KY: Westminster John Knox, 2012.
Palmer, Paul F., ed. *Sacraments and Worship: Liturgy and Doctrinal Development of Baptism, Confirmation, and the Eucharist.* Sources of Christian Theology 1. London: Longmans, Green, 1957.
Riggs, John W. *Baptism in the Reformed Tradition: A Historical and Practical Theology.* Columbia Series in Reformed Theology. Louisville: Westminster John Knox, 2002.
Wright, David F., ed. *Baptism: Three Views.* Downers Grove, IL: IVP Academic, 2009.

Chapter 19: The Lord's Supper: Sign of New Life

Calvin, *Institutes* 4.17–18 (2:1359–1448).
Schleiermacher, *CF* §§139–42 (638–57).

Bradshaw, Paul F. *Eucharistic Origins.* Oxford: Oxford University Press, 2004.
Byars, Ronald P. *The Sacraments in Biblical Perspective.* Interpretation: Resources for the Use of Scripture in the Church. Louisville: Westminster John Knox Press, 2011.
Clark, Francis. *Eucharistic Sacrifice and the Reformation.* Westminster, MD: Newman, 1960.

Davis, Thomas J. *This Is My Body: The Presence of Christ in Reformation Thought*. Grand Rapids: Baker Academic, 2008.

Gerrish, B. A. *Grace and Gratitude: The Eucharistic Theology of John Calvin* [1993]. Reprint, Eugene, OR: Wipf & Stock, 2001.

———. "Sign and Reality: The Lord's Supper in the Reformed Confessions" [1966]. Chapter 7 in *The Old Protestantism and the New: Essays on the Reformation Heritage* [1982]. Reprint, London: T. & T. Clark, 2004.

Johnson, Maxwell E. *Sacraments and Worship*. Sources of Christian Theology. Louisville: Westminster John Knox Press, 2012.

Palmer, Paul F., ed. *Sacraments and Worship: Liturgy and Doctrinal Development of Baptism, Confirmation, and the Eucharist*. Sources of Christian Theology 1. London: Longmans, Green, 1957.

Power, David N. *The Sacrifice We Offer: The Tridentine Dogma and Its Reinterpretation*. New York: Crossroad, 1987.

Smith, Dennis E. *From Symposium to Eucharist: The Banquet in the Early Christian World*. Minneapolis: Fortress, 2003.

Chapter 20: The Trinity

Calvin, *Institutes* 1.13 (1:120–59).
Schleiermacher, *CF* §§164–72 (723–51).

Ayres, Lewis. *Nicaea and Its Legacy: An Approach to Fourth-Century Trinitarian Theology*. Oxford: Oxford University Press, 2004.

Boff, Leonardo. *Trinity and Society* [Portuguese 1986]. Trans. Paul Burns. Maryknoll, NY: Orbis, 1988.

Davis, Stephen T., Daniel Kendall, and Gerard O'Collins, eds. *The Trinity: An Interdisciplinary Symposium on the Trinity*. Oxford: Oxford University Press, 1999.

Emery, Gilles, and Matthew Levering, eds. *The Oxford Handbook of the Trinity*. Oxford: Oxford University Press, 2011.

Gerrish, B. A. "Theology within the Limits of Piety Alone: Schleiermacher and Calvin's Notion of God" [1981]. Chapter 12 in *The Old Protestantism and the New: Essays on the Reformation Heritage* (1982). Reprint, London: T. & T. Clark, 2004.

———. "'To the Unknown God': Luther and Calvin on the Hiddenness of God" [1973]. Chapter 8 in *The Old Protestantism and the New: Essays on the Reformation Heritage* (1982). Reprint, London: T. & T. Clark, 2004.

Moltmann, Jürgen. *The Trinity and the Kingdom: The Doctrine of God* [German 1980]. Trans. Margaret Kohl. New York: Harper & Row, 1981.

Phan, Peter C., ed. *The Cambridge Companion to the Trinity*. Cambridge: Cambridge University Press, 2011.

Rahner, Karl. *The Trinity* [German 1967]. Trans. Joseph Donceel (1970). Reprint, with an introduction by Catherine Mowry LaCugna. New York: Crossroad, 1997.

Richardson, Cyril C. *The Doctrine of the Trinity*. New York: Abingdon, 1958.

Robinson, John A. T. *Thou Who Art: The Concept of the Personality of God*. New York: Continuum, 2006.

Schleiermacher, F. D. E. "On the Discrepancy between the Sabellian and Athanasian Methods of Representing the Doctrine of the Trinity" [German 1822]. Trans. and ed. Moses Stuart. *The Biblical Repository and Quarterly Observer* 5 (1835): 34–353; 6 (1835): 1–116.

Chapter 21: The End

Calvin, *Institutes* 3.25 (2:987–1008).
Schleiermacher, *CF* §§157–63 (696–722).

Bracken, Joseph A., ed. *World without End: Christian Eschatology from a Process Perspective.* Grand Rapids: Eerdmans, 2005.

Broad, C. D. *Religion, Philosophy and Psychical Research: Selected Essays.* London: Routledge & Kegan Paul, 1953.

Feuerbach, Ludwig. *Thoughts on Death and Immortality from the Papers of a Thinker, along with an Appendix of Theological-Satirical Epigrams.* [German 1830]. Trans. and ed. James A. Massey. Berkeley and Los Angeles: University of California Press, 1980.

Gerrish, B. A. "Image and Truth: A. E. Biedermann on the Life Everlasting." Chapter 5 in *Tradition and the Modern World: Reformed Theology in the Nineteenth Century* (1978). Eugene, OR: Wipf & Stock, 2007.

———. "The Possibility of a Historical Theology: An Appraisal of Troeltsch's Dogmatics" [1976]. Chapter 13 in *The Old Protestantism and the New: Essays on the Reformation Heritage* (1982). Reprint, London: T. & T. Clark, 2004.

Gustafson, James M. *Ethics from a Theocentric Perspective.* Vol. 1: *Theology and Ethics.* Chicago: University of Chicago Press, 1981.

Hartshorne, Charles. "Time, Death, and Everlasting Life" [1952]. Chapter 10 in *The Logic of Perfection and Other Essays in Neoclassical Metaphysics.* LaSalle, IL: Open Court, 1962.

Hick, John. *Death and Eternal Life.*[1976]. Reprint, with a new preface, Louisville, KY: Westminster John Knox Press, 1994.

Kübler-Ross, Elisabeth. *On Death and Dying* [1969]. Reprint, in one volume with *Questions and Answers on Death and Dying* [1974] and *On Life After Death* [1991]. New York: Quality Paperback Book Club, 2002.

Moltmann, Jürgen. *The Coming of God: Christian Eschatology* [German 1995]. Trans. Margaret Kohl. Minneapolis: Fortress, 1996.

Schleiermacher, Friedrich. *On Religion: Speeches to Its Cultured Despisers* [German 1799]. Trans. from the 3rd German ed. (1821) by John Oman (1894). Reprint, Louisville, KY: Westminster John Knox Press, 1994.

———. *Schleiermacher's Soliloquies* [German 1800]. Trans. Horace Leland Friess (1926). Reprint, Chicago: Open Court, 1957.

Index of Ancient Sources

Index of Subjects

CPSIA information can be obtained
at www.ICGtesting.com
Printed in the USA
FFOW04n2041090815
15672FF